Using I 3

Walter R. Bruce III
E. David Kramer

que®
CORPORATION
LEADING COMPUTER KNOWLEDGE

Using Paradox® 3

Library of Congress Catalog No.: 88-63222
ISBN 0-88022-362-6

92 91 90 89 8 7 6 5 4 3 2 1

Interpretation of the printing code: the rightmost double-digit number is the year of the book's printing; the rightmost single-digit number, the number of the book's printing. For example, a printing code of 89-1 shows that the first printing of the book occurred in 1989.

Using Paradox 3 is based on Versions 3.0 and 2.0.

Dedication

To Richey, Robby, and Heather

Publishing Manager

Lloyd J. Short

Product Director

David Maguiness

Production Editor

Gregory Robertson

Editors

Kelly Currie
Kelly D. Dobbs
Alice Martina Smith

Technical Editor

Randy Cali

Indexed by

Brown Editorial Service

Book Design and Production

Dan Armstrong
Brad Chinn
Cheryl English
David Kline
Jennifer Matthews
Cindy L. Phipps
Dennis Sheehan
Mae Louise Shinault
Peter Tocco

Composed in Helvetica and Excellent No. 47
by Que Corporation

About the Authors

Walter R. Bruce III

Walter R. Bruce III lives in the Washington, D.C., suburb of Springfield, Virginia, with his wife, two sons, and infant daughter. He is a free-lance writer and microcomputer consultant. He is the author of Que's *Using Enable/OA* and has written several instructional texts for use in intermediate and advanced workshops on using popular microcomputer software packages. He has also led workshops for government and private industry clients from coast to coast.

Mr. Bruce is a licensed attorney who practiced for three years in North Carolina and six years in the United States Air Force. For three years his duties included acting as an advisor on computer and office automation-related issues to The Judge Advocate General of the Air Force, the chief military attorney in the Air Force.

E. David Kramer

E. David Kramer, a microcomputer consultant, wrote Chapters 14 and 15. He lives in Reading, Pennsylvania, with his wife and son and is managing partner of Mount Penn Associates, a microcomputer consulting firm specializing in Novell Networks, Paradox-based systems, and microcomputer software training seminars. He has designed both mainframe and microcomputer-based information systems. Mr. Kramer holds a bachelor's degree in Management Information Systems, as well as an MBA.

Contents at a Glance

Table of Contents

II Tapping the Power of Paradox

III Developing Menu-Driven Applications with Paradox

Trademark Acknowledgments

Que Corporation has made every effort to supply trademark information about company names, products, and services mentioned in this book. Trademarks indicated below were derived from various sources. Que Corporation cannot attest to the accuracy of this information.

1-2-3, Lotus, VisiCalc, and Symphony are registered trademarks of Lotus Development Corporation.

3Com is a registered trademark of 3Com Corporation.

CompuServe is a registered trademark of H&R Block.

dBASE III Plus and dBASE IV are trademarks of Ashton-Tate Corporation.

IBM and Filing Assistant are registered trademarks and OS/2 and PS/2 are trademarks of International Business Machines, Inc.

Novell and NetWare are registered trademarks of Novell, Inc.

Paradox, Turbo C, Turbo Pascal, Quattro, and Paradox Application Language are registered trademarks and Reflex is a trademark of Ansa-Borland.

PFS is a registered trademark of Software Publishing Corporation.

PostScript is a registered trademark of Adobe Systems, Inc.

Conventions Used in This Book

The conventions used in this book have been established to help you learn to use the program quickly and easily. As much as possible, the conventions correspond with those used in the Paradox documentation.

To help you learn Paradox's commands, this book shows complete words for single-key commands. In commands and menu options, the letter or number you press to choose a command is printed in boldface type. For example,

Setting **F**ormat **G**roupOfTables

means to press S F G.

Sometimes a command consisting of two or more words does not have a space between the words, as in GroupOfTables in the preceding example.

Words you type are in *italic type* or on a line by themselves. Screen messages are in a `special typeface`.

Keys are written as they appear on the IBM keyboard (Ins, Del, Alt, and so on). Key combinations are connected by a hyphen. For example, Alt-J means to press the Alt key and hold it down while you press the J key.

Introduction

Welcome to *Using Paradox 3*. With this book as your guide, you are about to become a Paradox® pro!

The program's authors christened their creation Paradox because they believed it to represent what others thought a contradiction—a full-featured database program that is easy to learn and use. Although the concepts of "ease of use" and "ease of learning" are relative to your previous experience, once you try Paradox you will agree that the name fits the program's capabilities well.

If the program is so easy to learn and use, then why do you need a book to help you? Traveling even a well-marked road for the first time is always easier if you follow someone who has been down that road before. As you journey through Paradox, this book points out the most direct route while showing you how to avoid hidden potholes and unnecessary tolls. With this book, you're ready to buckle up and hit the Paradox road.

What Is Paradox 3.0?

Paradox, a relational database management system first released in 1985 by Ansa Software (since purchased by Borland International), is a PC-based program that enables you to collect, sort, and retrieve information on a computer and then generate reports that consolidate or summarize any or all of this information in nearly any order or format that you choose. You can even create representations of your numeric data by using color graphics.

The program is designed to allow you to work with your data in ways that seem natural and familiar and yet achieve quite sophisticated results. You probably already know how to select choices from Paradox menus. They are similar in style to those found in Lotus® 1-2-3®. By reading these menus and using the on-line help documentation, you could learn how to use the basic features of Paradox without ever opening a book. But don't be content with just the basics. This book shows you how to use Paradox to converse with your data as if you were old friends, create reports from your data as if you were a seasoned mainframe programmer, and create graphic representations of your data that show relationships you didn't even realize existed.

The Heart of Paradox: Query By Example

The heart of Paradox is the method it uses to ask questions of your data, called Query By Example (QBE). You first type into a list, referred to as a *table*, the information you want to save. Then you use QBE to get at your data whenever you need it. Query By Example doesn't require you to memorize any syntax, and is so forgiving that you don't even have to know exactly how to spell the information you are trying to retrieve. QBE is the key to the simplicity and power of Paradox.

For example, you can use QBE to find the phone number of Joanne Smythe from a table of thousands of phone numbers, even if you think her name might be Joan Smith.

Of course, Paradox has been designed to handle database problems much more complicated than retrieving a telephone number. Because of the program's *relational* design, you are able to work with more than one database table at a time just as easily as with one. By using the QBE methodology, you can create queries that generate answers from your data in seconds—answers that would take hours or even days to generate by hand. Turning these answers into hard copy is also a snap, using the *Instant Report* feature. Or, as easily as you can type a simple letter, you can design a custom report around your data that meets the most demanding requirements of your chief executive officer.

Features for the Power User and Application Developer

For the power user or programmer, Paradox 3.0 also includes comprehensive form design capabilities, and a full procedural database application development environment called the *Paradox Application Language* or *PAL*. A module called the *Personal Programmer* allows even nonprogrammers to generate turnkey menu-driven systems customized to solve unique database management problems. A special *Data Entry Toolkit* is also included to give you greater control over data entry through custom forms.

At the time of this writing, Borland International has announced its intention to implement a Structured Query Language (SQL) interface for Paradox in the first half of 1989. Paradox will act as an SQL front end that will allow use of Paradox queries against an SQL server engine (for example, IBM® OS/2® Extended Edition). PAL programs also will be able to use SQL queries to be passed directly to an SQL server. In addition, Borland will soon release a special version of Paradox, called Paradox Engine, intended for use by Turbo C® and Turbo Pascal® programmers.

What's New?

Since the program's introduction, Ansa-Borland has progressively enhanced Paradox while remaining true to the program's original design concepts. Paradox 3.0, released in 1989, includes a number of significant enhancements not found in earlier versions of the program. In fact, you would be hard pressed to find another PC-based relational database program with more impressive features. These features are summarized in table I.1.

Paradox 3.0 is compatible with Paradox 2.0. Paradox 2.0 database files and applications will work as before, without modification. Borland has announced that it still plans to sell Paradox 2.0. Paradox 2.0 can be used on dual floppy PCs, unlike Paradox 3.0, which requires a hard disk.

Both Paradox 2.0 and 3.0 are network ready and are available licensed for use by a single user or in a six-user network pack.

Borland has also released Paradox OS/2 and Paradox 386. At the time of this writing, both products are versions of Paradox 2.0, designed to take full advantage of the OS/2 operating system and the Intel 80386-based PCs, respectively. Borland has announced its intention to release OS/2 and 386 versions of Paradox 3.0 in the near future.

Table I.1
New Features in Paradox 3.0

Category	*Enhancement*
Query By Example	Inclusion operator Set operations Or operator As operator Controlled sort ordering of answer tables
Relational Enhancements	Multitable forms Multirecord forms and scrolling regions Linked tables in forms Referential integrity Multitable reports
Presentation Enhancements	Graphics Crosstabs Full color customization Color forms Negative numbers displayed in red
PAL/Script Enhancements	Greater screen and canvas control Control over the Edit transaction log Memory management tools RepeatPlay New PAL commands/functions to support new interactive features
Miscellaneous Enhancements	Multiuser enhancements to support Paradox 3.0 features Support for LIM 4.0 Import and export of Quattro® and Reflex™ files Copy individual forms and reports between tables

What Should Your System Have?

To run Paradox 2.0 or Paradox 3.0 as a single-user program, your system must have at least 512K of system memory (RAM), and DOS 2.0 or higher. Paradox 2.0 runs on either two floppy disk drives or one floppy drive and a hard disk, but a hard disk is required for Paradox 3.0.

For network use, Paradox 2.0 and 3.0 both require a PC workstation with 640K RAM and DOS 3.1 or higher, connected to a network running one of the following network operating systems:

Novell® Advanced Netware®, Version 2.0A or higher 3Com® 3+, Version 1.0 or higher
IBM PC Local Area Network Program, Version 1.12 or higher
Torus Tapestry Network, Version 1.45 or higher
AT&T STARLAN Network, Version 1.1 or higher
Banyan Vines or Vines/286 Network, Version 2.10 or higher

Performance and capacity are improved in either stand-alone systems or network workstations if your system includes expanded memory (LIM/EMS or EEMS).

To take advantage of all the capabilities of Paradox, you also should have a graphics capable monitor and a graphics printer or plotter.

Who Should Read This Book?

Using Paradox 3 is for you if you are a new Paradox 2.0 or Paradox 3.0 user who wants to get the most from this fantastic product. Experienced users also will find the book helpful in gaining a clear understanding of the 3.0 enhancements and may even learn a few new tricks along the way.

The approach of this book mirrors that of the software it describes. You don't have to be a programmer to learn and use Paradox. This book likewise makes no assumptions about your background or experience in the use of PCs or database management systems. If you are a new database user, start at the beginning of the book and move through it at a comfortable pace. More experienced users can skim Part I, "Paradox Fundamentals," and study the text more closely beginning in Part II, "Tapping the Power of Paradox." Power Paradox users may want to breeze through Parts I and II and concentrate on Part III, "Developing Menu-Driven Applications with Paradox."

Because both Paradox 2.0 and 3.0 are current versions at the time of this writing, the book generally assumes that you are using one or the other. Discussions involving features new in Paradox 3.0 are marked with an icon (3) in the margin. Paradox 2.0 owners who have not yet chosen to upgrade to 3.0 should simply skip these sections. Special considerations of interest to network users are also addressed.

What Is Covered in This Book?

This book is divided into three major parts: Part I, "Paradox Fundamentals"; Part II, "Tapping the Power of Paradox"; and Part III, "Developing Menu-Driven Applications with Paradox." Parts I and II begin with a Quick Start lesson that previews the topics to be discussed. Use the Quick Start lessons to get your feet wet, and then examine the chapters that follow for detailed explanations.

Paradox Fundamentals

The first part of the book covers the most elementary aspects of creating a database with Paradox: entering data, editing data, asking questions of the data, and printing simple reports.

Quick Start 1, "Your First Paradox Session," tells you how to start Paradox and takes you through the creation of a simple database table. You then ask a few questions of the table, and print two sorted lists derived from the table you created.

Chapter 1, "Navigating Paradox," explains how to use the keyboard, menus, screens, views, and prompts in Paradox.

Chapter 2, "Creating Database Tables," describes how to define and modify the structure of a Paradox database.

Chapter 3, "Using Paradox To Enter, Edit, and View Data," discusses the basics of entering new data into a database table, as well as how to edit and sort the data after you have entered it.

Chapter 4, "Getting Started with Query By Example," takes a first look at the feature that makes Paradox both powerful and easy to use: Query By Example (QBE).

Chapter 5, "Paradox Reporting Fundamentals," covers how to create relatively simple tabular reports, as well as mailing labels.

Chapter 6, "Recording Paradox Scripts and Keyboard Macros," describes how you can easily automate frequently used Paradox operations by recording your keystrokes. This chapter describes how to record scripts, play them, and make changes by using the Script Editor.

Tapping the Power of Paradox

Once you have an understanding of Paradox fundamentals, you are ready to tap the power of Paradox. The seven chapters in this part of the book discuss in detail all the capabilities of Paradox used interactively (without programming).

Quick Start 2, "Experimenting with More Advanced Paradox Features," shows you how to perform multitable queries, design a data-entry form and add validity checking, design custom reports, and create graphs.

Chapter 7, "Asking Complex Questions with Query By Example," gets to the heart of Paradox. Although the basics of QBE are discussed in Chapter 4, this chapter explores queries that use multiple tables, group operations, set queries, and inclusive links. Master this chapter, and you are well on your way to mastering Paradox.

Chapter 8, "Designing and Using Paradox Forms," explains how to create custom forms for entering, editing, and viewing Paradox data. In addition to discussing single-table forms with calculated numeric fields, word-wrap text fields, and multiple pages, the chapter describes how and why to create multitable and multirecord forms.

Chapter 9, "Using Paradox Power Entry and Editing Features," shows you how you can increase the ease and accuracy of your data entry by creating validation criteria. The chapter also discusses the nuances of editing data in multitable forms and on a network.

Chapter 10, "Creating Tabular Reports," picks up where Chapter 5 leaves off. This chapter goes into detail about the use of the *table band* concept to customize tabular reports. The chapter covers summary fields, calculated fields, sorting, grouping, headings, report summaries, multifield columns, word wrap, and multitable reports.

Chapter 11, "Creating Free-Form Reports," goes a step further and shows you how to design on-screen custom reports in which the fields can be placed anywhere on the form rather than in tabular fashion. Examples of this type of report are form letters, mailing labels, and invoices.

Chapter 12, "Creating Paradox Graphics," discusses the new business graphics module of Paradox 3.0. The chapter demonstrates how to create sophisticated graphs from your data with just a few keystrokes. The discussion includes the *crosstab* feature; graph types; graph elements; customizing color, grid, titles, labels, legends, fonts, and other graph settings; exploding pie slices; using scripts; and printing.

Chapter 13, "Using Paradox Tools," shows you how to rename Paradox tables; speed up queries; export data to formats compatible with other programs; import data from other program formats; copy tables, forms, reports, and scripts; delete tables, forms, reports, scripts, and graphs; choose image settings and use validity checks; display information about Paradox objects and network information; set and remove network locks and privileges; and set the autorefresh interval. A number of other Paradox tools are also discussed, such as password protection and temporary suspension of Paradox to go to DOS.

Developing Menu-Driven Applications with Paradox

The final section of this book describes two of the most advanced and powerful parts of Paradox: the Personal Programmer and the Paradox Application Language (PAL).

Chapter 14, "Using the Personal Programmer," takes you through a Personal Programmer session resulting in a complete menu-driven application. The chapter demonstrates menu building; selecting actions; specifying tables, records, fields, forms, and reports for use in the application; creating multitable views; and the use of *tilde variables*; as well as explains how to run and modify the completed application.

Chapter 15, "An Overview of the Paradox Application Language," discusses the fundamentals of PAL, the application development environment and programming language. This chapter also provides an overview of the programming capabilities of PAL. An in-depth discussion of all the PAL commands and capabilities is beyond the scope of this book.

Using the Appendixes and the Command Chart

For those of you who have not yet installed Paradox, Appendix A describes the necessary steps to install and start Paradox 3.0. Appendix B briefly discusses use of the Custom Configuration Program (CCP) to modify the video configuration, report settings, default working directory, international features, network features, and other settings.

Finally, at the back of the book, you can find a pull-out card showing a complete chart of the Paradox menu commands.

Now that you know what to expect, you're ready to get to the business at hand: learning Paradox. Let this book be your guide, and let Paradox be your friend. Get to know it well, and it will give you everything you could possibly want from a database management system.

I

Paradox Fundamentals

Includes

Quick Start 1: Your First Paradox Session

Navigating Paradox

Creating Database Tables

Using Paradox To Enter, Edit, and View Data

Getting Started with Query By Example

Paradox Reporting Fundamentals

Recording Paradox Scripts and Keyboard Macros

Quick Start 1

Your First Paradox Session

This lesson is the first of two Quick Starts presented in this book. Each lesson is designed to help you get a running start with Paradox. Both Quick Starts take you step-by-step through simple examples of techniques and concepts that are discussed in the chapters that follow the Quick Start. This format gives you a preview of what is to come, and allows you to begin using Paradox without much reading. The Quick Starts also may encourage you to experiment as you continue through the book.

Quick Start 1 walks you through Paradox start-up. You create a simple database table consisting of a list of company employees, and enter several records. You then ask a few questions of the data. Finally, you print the list of employees, sorted first by employee number and then by name.

Before you can begin, you must install Paradox. First, refer to Appendix A for information on how to ready the program for use on your system. Next, locate the appropriate keyboard template for your keyboard (enclosed in the box with the diskettes) and place the template on your keyboard. Finally, you're ready to begin the lesson.

Starting Paradox on a Hard Disk System

Version 3

Paradox 3.0 is designed to work from a hard disk, but you can use Paradox 2.0 on dual floppy systems. The appropriate start-up steps for hard disk systems and floppy disk systems are therefore presented separately. If you are using Paradox from a hard disk, take the following steps:

1. Start your system, and access the root directory on the hard disk that contains Paradox. From the DOS prompt (probably `C>`), make a directory to hold your Paradox files. For example, to create a directory with the name PDATA, at the DOS prompt type *md \pdata* and press Enter. Change to the new directory by typing *cd \pdata* and pressing Enter. Starting Paradox from this directory causes new database files to be stored here.

2. In order for DOS to find the Paradox program files, draw the system a "map" by defining the *path* to the Paradox directory with the DOS command PATH. If you're using Paradox 2.0, type (at the DOS prompt) *path c:\;c:\dos;c:\paradox2* and press Enter.

   If you're using Paradox 3.0, type *path c:\;c:\dos;c:\paradox3* and press Enter.

   Both of these PATH statements assume that your DOS files are in the directory C:\DOS. Insert the appropriate directory name into the PATH statement for your system.

3. To start Paradox 2.0, type *paradox2* and press Enter.

   To start Paradox 3.0, type *paradox3* and press Enter.

As Paradox loads, you see a title screen similar to figure QS1.1, showing the "signature" information you supplied during the installation process. This screen is immediately followed by the screen in figure QS1.2, the Main menu.

Starting Paradox 2.0 on a Floppy Disk System

To start Paradox 2.0 from a dual floppy disk system, take the following steps:

1. Boot your system with the DOS disk that was modified by the Paradox installation procedure. Replace the DOS disk with the Paradox System I disk (System I/II disk on 3 1/2-inch drive systems), and place a formatted disk in your second floppy disk drive. This second disk will hold the files created by Paradox.

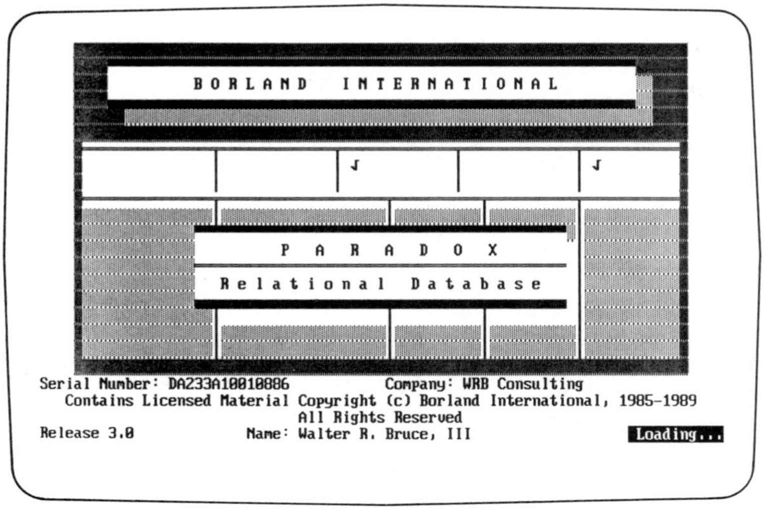

Fig. QS1.1.

The Paradox 3.0 start-up screen.

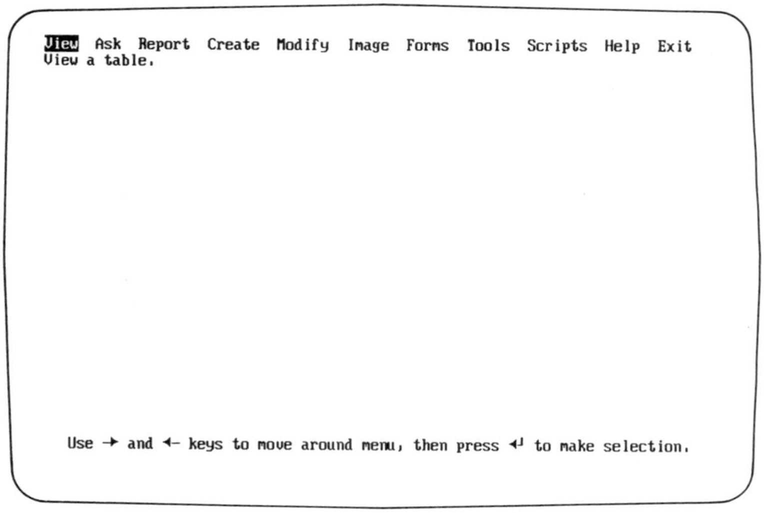

Fig. QS1.2.

The Paradox Main menu.

2. At the DOS prompt (probably A>), type *paradox2* and press Enter. Paradox displays the title screen and your "signature" information (see fig. QS1.1).

3. When prompted at the bottom of the screen, remove the System I disk, replace it with the System II disk, and press Enter. (This step is not applicable to 3 1/2-inch drive users.) Paradox displays its Main menu (see fig. QS1.2).

Never remove the System II disk while you're using Paradox, unless prompted to do so.

Creating the Employee Database

In some ways, entering information in a Paradox table is similar to typing the same data in columns with a typewriter, word processor, or spreadsheet. But unlike those other methods, before you can begin entering information into a database table, you must first describe to Paradox the general nature of the data. Will the data be alphanumeric (text), numbers, currency, or dates? How long will the longest name be? How many characters are in the largest address? This description of the table is called its *structure* or *definition*. Follow these steps to define the Employee table:

1. First select the **C**reate command from the Main menu. (Press the letter C.) Then type the table name, *Employee*, and press Enter. Paradox displays an image or table (a series of columns) entitled Struct (see fig. QS1.3). In this image, you define the structure of the Employee table.

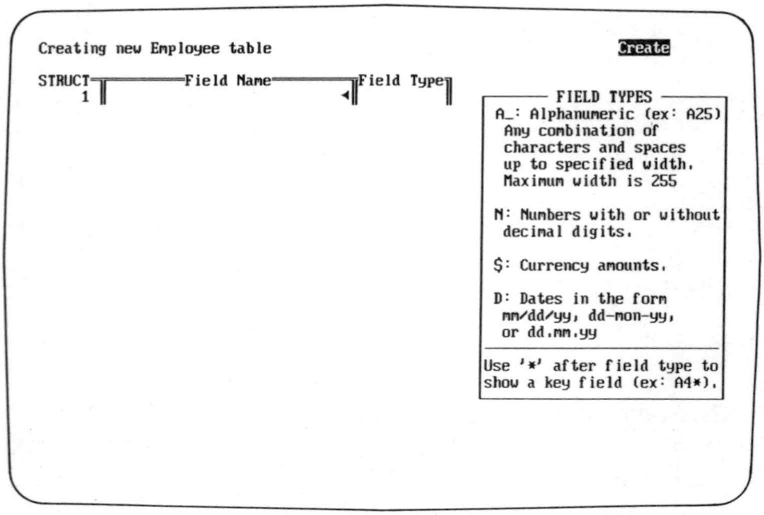
Creating new Employee table
Create
STRUCT
Field Name
Field Type
1
FIELD TYPES
A_: Alphanumeric (ex: A25)
Any combination of
characters and spaces
up to specified width.
Maximum width is 255
N: Numbers with or without
decimal digits.
$: Currency amounts.
D: Dates in the form
mm/dd/yy, dd-mon-yy,
or dd.mm.yy
Use '*' after field type to
show a key field (ex: A4*).

Fig. QS1.3.

The Struct table.

2. Each row in this image defines a column, also called a field, that should appear in the Employee table. You must give each field a name. To name the first field in Employee, type

Emp ID # beneath the Field Name heading and press Enter. The blinking cursor moves to the Field Type column.

3. The choices for field type are explained on the right side of your screen. To define the Emp ID # field as alphanumeric with a maximum length of 11, type *A11* and press Enter. Your screen should then look like figure QS1.4.

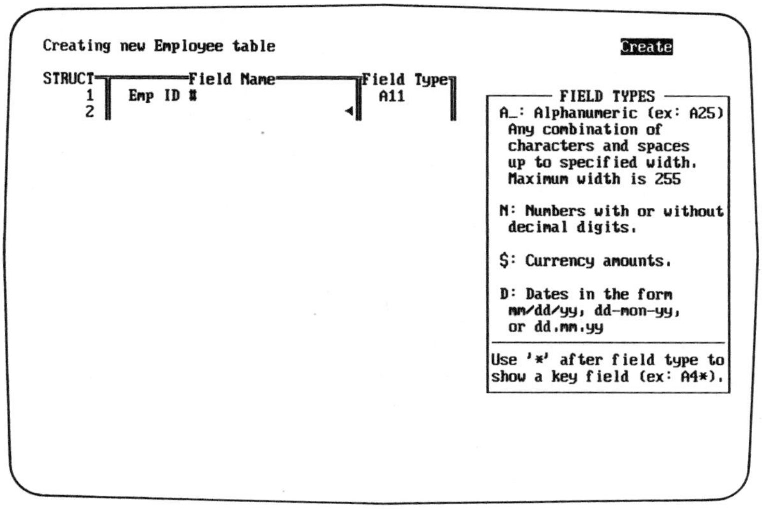
Creating new Employee table
Create
STRUCT Field Name Field Type
1 Emp ID # A11
2
FIELD TYPES
A_: Alphanumeric (ex: A25)
Any combination of
characters and spaces
up to specified width.
Maximum width is 255
N: Numbers with or without
decimal digits.
$: Currency amounts.
D: Dates in the form
mm/dd/yy, dd-mon-yy,
or dd.mm.yy
Use '*' after field type to
show a key field (ex: A4*).

Fig. QS1.4.

The Emp ID # field definition.

4. Following the same procedure, define the rest of the fields as indicated in figure QS1.5. To correct typing mistakes, erase the error with the Backspace key and retype the appropriate entry. You can also use the arrow keys to move in the screen.

5. Once you have completed the definition, tell Paradox you are finished by pressing F2 (DO-IT!). Paradox returns to the Main menu, and you are ready to begin entering data.

Entering Employee Data

Now that you have built a structure for your Employee table, you can enter data. If you have ever typed information in columns, you already know how to complete the next series of steps.

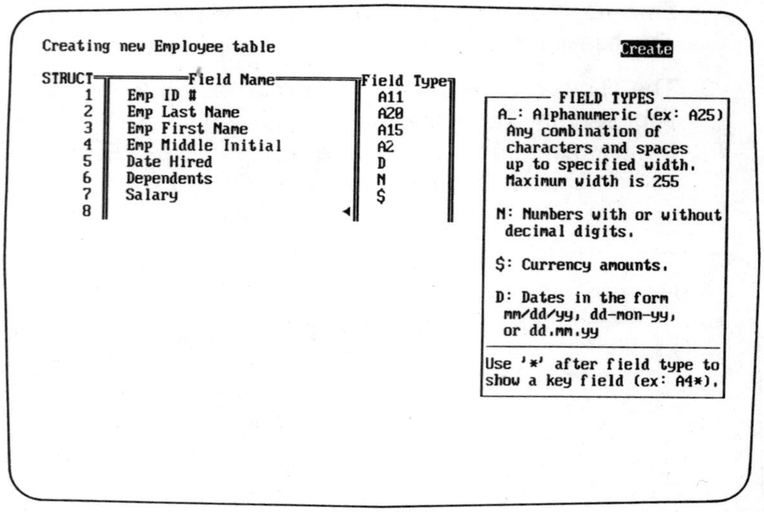

Fig. QS1.5.

The completed Employee table definition.

1. From the Main menu, select **M**odify **D**ataEntry. (Press M and then D.) Type the name of your table, *Employee*, and press Enter. Paradox displays the DataEntry image for the Employee table (see fig. QS1.6).

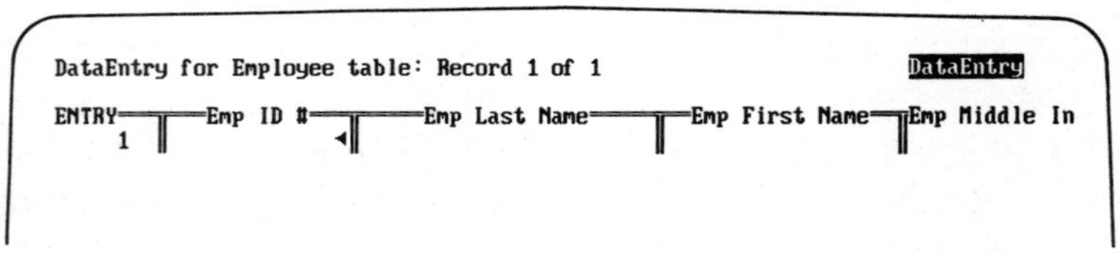

Fig. QS1.6.

The DataEntry image.

2. Type the first employee ID number in the Emp ID # field:

   921-65-1234

   Then press Enter. The cursor moves to the Emp Last Name field. Next, type the following data in the appropriate fields, pressing Enter at the end of each entry:

Emp Last Name	English
Emp First Name	Gertrude
Emp Middle Initial	M.
Date Hired	1/04/71
Dependents	2
Salary	36,750

As in the definition image, use the Backspace key to erase errors. After you press Enter at the Salary entry, Paradox starts a second row, and your screen should look like figure QS1.7.

```
DataEntry for Employee table: Record 2 of 2                   DataEntry

ENTRY══╤══Emp ID #══╤═══════Emp Last Name═══════╤═Emp First Name══╤═Emp Middle In
    1  ║ 921-65-1234║ English                   ║ Gertrude        ║  M.
    2  ║           ◄║                           ║                 ║
```

Fig. QS1.7.

Beginning the second record.

3. Type the following data, using the same procedure:

ID #	*Last*	*First*	*MI*	*Hire Date*	*Dep*	*Salary*
541-67-5555	Kellogs	Emily	Q.	06/10/75	0	23,875.00
230-76-2376	Bronson	Tim	C.	11/23/69	3	41,400.00
111-33-8491	Jones	Harry	H.	06/07/78	2	32,250.00
329-76-2219	Albertson	Sharon	B.	03/04/81	1	21,870.00

4. Toggle on the built-in data-entry form by pressing F7. Use the form to enter the last three records, pressing Enter after every field. Pressing Enter at the last field on the form takes you to the next blank form. Use the PgUp and PgDn keys to move between forms if you need to make corrections.

ID #	*Last*	*First*	*MI*	*Hire Date*	*Dep*	*Salary*
448-09-6721	Green	George	H.	08/15/79	4	49,339.00
129-08-4562	Jones	Samantha	T.	10/02/65	1	75,900.00
987-31-9873	Quick	Joseph	L.	05/21/83	3	53,000.00

Press F7 again to return to the table view.

5. When finished, press F2 (DO-IT!). Paradox saves the new data to disk but does not remove it from the screen. Your screen should look similar to figure QS1.8. To clear the image from the screen, press F8 (Clear Image). The Main menu returns to the screen.

Asking Questions of the Data

Imagine for a moment that you had entered data for 800 employees, or even 8,000 employees, rather than only 8. With Paradox you can easily

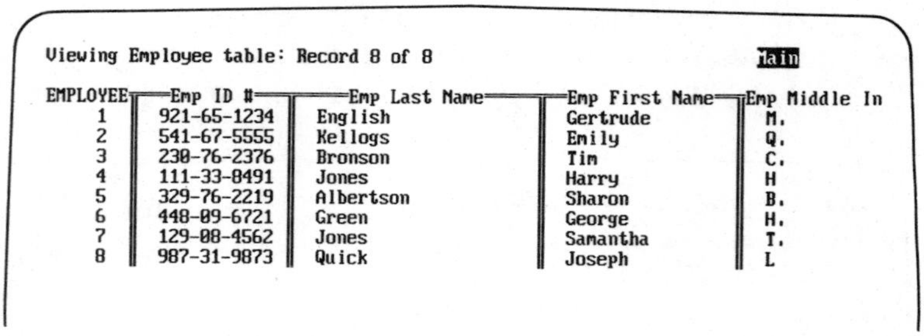
Viewing Employee table: Record 8 of 8
Main
EMPLOYEE Emp ID # Emp Last Name Emp First Name Emp Middle In
1 921-65-1234 English Gertrude M.
2 541-67-5555 Kellogs Emily Q.
3 230-76-2376 Bronson Tim C.
4 111-33-8491 Jones Harry H
5 329-76-2219 Albertson Sharon B.
6 448-09-6721 Green George H.
7 129-08-4562 Jones Samantha T.
8 987-31-9873 Quick Joseph L

Fig. QS1.8.

The Employee table.

search for one of those employees, regardless of how many you have, using a method referred to as Query By Example (QBE). The next several procedures in this Quick Start demonstrate a number of simple queries for your Employee table.

To find the name of the employee whose ID number is 111-33-8491, do the following:

1. From the Main menu, select **A**sk.
2. Type the table name, *employee*, and press Enter. Paradox displays the Employee table again, but this time it is empty. This screen is the query form (see fig. QS1.9).

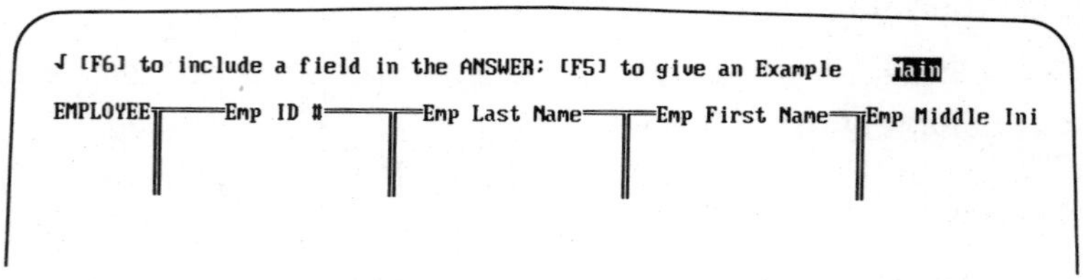
√ [F6] to include a field in the ANSWER; [F5] to give an Example
Main
EMPLOYEE Emp ID # Emp Last Name Emp First Name Emp Middle Ini

Fig. QS1.9.

The query form.

3. As indicated in the message at the top of the screen, you use the F6 key to check off the columns you want to see in the Answer table that will result from your question. Use the right-arrow key to move to the Emp ID # column, and press the F6 key. Paradox places a check mark (the ASCII square root symbol) in the column. Do the same thing in the Emp Last Name and Emp First Name columns.
4. Move the cursor back to the Emp ID # column and type the number that you want Paradox to match, *111-33-8491*. Then press Enter and F2 (DO-IT!). Paradox displays the Answer table just below the query form, as shown in figure QS1.10. Harry Jones is your man. Press Alt-F8 (Clear All) to clear the images.

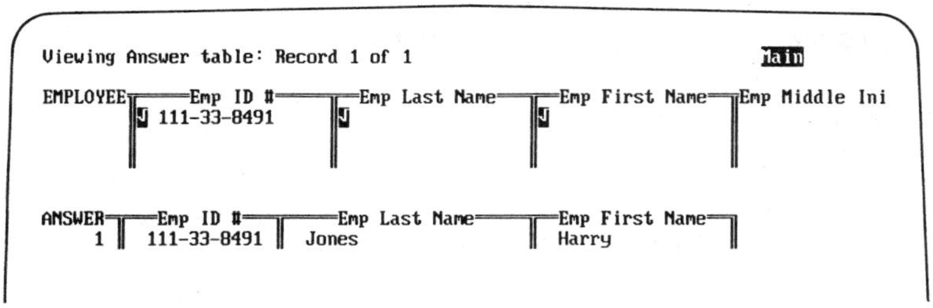

Fig. QS1.10.

Finding Harry Jones.

Suppose that you need to find the salary for Tim Bronson, but you can't remember whether the name is spelled Bronson or Brinson. Paradox allows you to look for text that is *like* the text you provide. Here's how:

1. From the Main menu, select **A**sk, type *employee*, and press Enter. Use F6 to place check marks in the Emp Last Name, Emp First Name, and Salary columns.

2. Move the cursor to the Emp Last Name column, type *like Brinson*, and press Enter. Paradox displays the name and salary for Tim Bronson in the Answer table.

Now suppose that you want to see the salary of Samantha Jones. Because more than one employee is named Jones, you must specify more than just the last name.

1. Press F8 (Clear Image) to clear the Answer table but not the query form.

2. Backspace over the entry in the Emp Last Name column and type *Jones*. Press Enter to move to the Emp First Name column, and type *Samantha*. Press F2 (DO-IT!). Paradox displays Ms. Jones's salary.

You can also use comparison operators in QBE. Assume that you want to see a list of all employees hired before January 1, 1980.

1. Clear all images with Alt-F8, and choose **A**sk from the Main menu. Type *employee* and then press Enter.

2. Use F6 to place a check mark in Emp Last Name, Emp First Name, and Date Hired.

3. Type *<1/1/80* in the Date Hired field, and press Enter. Then press F2 (DO-IT!). The names and hire dates of the six employees hired before January 1, 1980, are displayed.

Sorting and Printing Your Data

Typically, you do not enter rows into a database table in any particular order—which is certainly the case in this example. Paradox can retrieve any information from the table through the QBE process, regardless of the order of the rows in the table. When you display data on the screen, however, or send data to the printer, you often want to see the information in order alphabetically, by date, by ID number, or in some other order. Follow these steps to sort the Employee table by ID number:

1. Start from a blank work area (press Alt-F8 to clear all images) and select **M**odify **S**ort. This time, rather than type *employee*, press Enter to see a list of available tables. Move the highlighted bar to `Employee` and press Enter.

2. To indicate that the results of the sort should replace the current contents of Employee, choose **S**ame. Paradox displays the form shown in figure QS1.11.

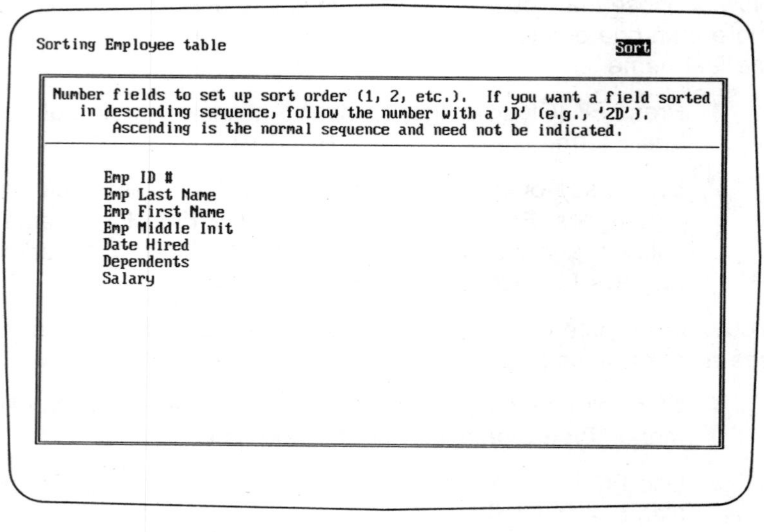
Sorting Employee table
Sort
Number fields to set up sort order (1, 2, etc.). If you want a field sorted
in descending sequence, follow the number with a 'D' (e.g., '2D').
Ascending is the normal sequence and need not be indicated.
Emp ID #
Emp Last Name
Emp First Name
Emp Middle Init
Date Hired
Dependents
Salary

Fig. QS1.11.

The sort form.

3. Paradox displays a cursor to the left of the Emp ID # field name. Type the number *1* to indicate that you want the table rows sorted by that field. Press F2 (DO-IT!). Paradox sorts the data by ID number, as shown in figure QS1.12.

Viewing Employee table: Record 1 of 8 Main

EMPLOYEE	Emp ID #	Emp Last Name	Emp First Name	Emp Middle In
1	111-33-8491	Jones	Harry	H
2	129-08-4562	Jones	Samantha	T.
3	230-76-2376	Bronson	Tim	C.
4	329-76-2219	Albertson	Sharon	B.
5	448-09-6721	Green	George	H.
6	541-67-5555	Kellogs	Emily	Q.
7	921-65-1234	English	Gertrude	M.
8	987-31-9873	Quick	Joseph	L

Fig. QS1.12.

The Employee table viewedd in order by Emp ID #.

Paradox has an *Instant Report* feature that immediately sends the currently viewed table to your printer. As your Employee table is currently displayed, however, it will not fit on normal 8 1/2-inch-wide paper. You therefore need to create an Answer table containing only each employee's ID number, name, and salary.

1. Clear the current image with F8, and then press F10 (Menu).
2. From the Main menu, select **A**sk. Type the table name *employee* (or press Enter and select the name).
3. Use F6 (Check Mark) to tell Paradox to display only the Emp ID #, Emp Last Name, Emp First Name, and Salary fields. Then press F2 (DO-IT!). Paradox displays the Answer table.
4. Make sure that your printer is on and loaded with paper; then press Alt-F7 (Instant Report).

Suppose that you now decide that you would rather see the list of employees in alphabetical order by name.

1. Display the menu by pressing F10 (Menu).
2. From the Main menu, select **M**odify **S**ort. This time, indicate that you want to sort the Answer table (not Employee) by typing *answer* (or pressing Enter and selecting Answer from the list).
3. Select **S**ame. Only the field names from the Answer table display.
4. Move the cursor to the Emp Last Name field and type the number *1*. Press Enter or the down-arrow key and type *2* next to Emp First Name. This setup causes the rows to be sorted in alphabetical order by last name and then by first name. (For example, "Harry Jones" comes before "Samantha Jones.")
5. Press F2 (DO-IT!).
6. Finally, press Alt-F7 (Instant Print). Your report should look similar to figure QS1.13.

Fig. QS1.13.

The Employee table printed in alphabetical order by name.

1/05/89 Standard Report Page 1

Emp ID #	Emp Last Name	Emp First Name	Salary
329-76-2219	Albertson	Sharon	21,870.00
230-76-2376	Bronson	Tim	41,400.00
921-65-1234	English	Gertrude	36,750.00
448-09-6721	Green	George	49,339.00
111-33-8491	Jones	Harry	32,250.00
129-08-4562	Jones	Samantha	75,900.00
541-67-5555	Kellogs	Emily	23,875.00
987-31-9873	Quick	Joseph	53,000.00

Quitting Paradox

You have almost completed your first Paradox session. Clear any remaining image on the screen by pressing Alt-F8 (Clear All). To quit Paradox, select **E**xit **Y**es. Paradox displays the message `Leaving Paradox` in the bottom right corner of the screen, and you are returned to DOS.

Quick Start Summary

This first lesson gets you off to a flying start with Paradox. You practiced starting the program, creating a simple database table, querying, sorting the table, and quitting Paradox. Now you're ready to explore these topics in more detail. Chapter 1 begins the discussion by explaining how to find your way around Paradox.

1

Navigating Paradox

This chapter helps you take an excellent first step in learning Paradox. You examine what computerists call the program's *user interface*—how Paradox looks on-screen and how it requests and responds to your actions. This chapter explains the Paradox screen, keyboard, menus, prompts, online help, and how you should use these features to find your way around the program. Start with this chapter if you are new to Paradox, even if you are an experienced PC user. Seasoned Paradox users may want to at least glance at the tables in this chapter, because several function key and special key commands have been added in Paradox 3.0.

If you have used other database programs, Paradox will probably have a familiar feel to you. But Paradox is also unique in many ways when compared to other popular database programs. This chapter begins introducing you to the fundamental concepts of Paradox. You're ready to proceed with this chapter if you have started Paradox and displayed the Main menu on your screen. Refer to Appendix A if you need instructions for installing and running Paradox.

Becoming Familiar with the Paradox Screen

The first Paradox screen displayed when you start Paradox is the Title screen. The Paradox logo and your signature information are shown as the program is loaded into the computer's memory. Once the program is loaded, Paradox displays a screen like that shown in figure 1.1. This screen, referred to as the Main menu, is the "home base" from which you begin many tasks in Paradox. The following paragraphs describe the parts of the Paradox screen.

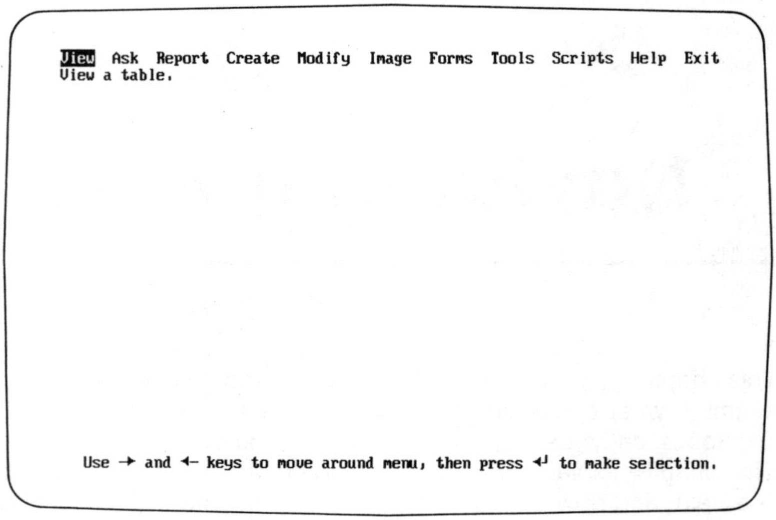
View Ask Report Create Modify Image Forms Tools Scripts Help Exit
View a table.
Use → and ← keys to move around menu, then press ↵ to make selection.

Fig. 1.1.

The Paradox Main menu.

The Menu Area

Paradox makes heavy use of menus. The top line of the screen is the *menu line*, which displays the options of the Main menu. The second line displays a description of each menu option as it is highlighted. Note that in figure 1.1 the **V**iew option is highlighted, and the second line reads `View a table`. Sometimes Paradox does not continuously show the menu. When you are entering data, for example, Paradox does not display a menu, but pressing F10 (Menu) pops a menu to the top of the screen. Refer to this chapter's section on "Using Paradox Menus and Prompts" for a discussion of how best to select menu choices.

The Mode Indicator

The major functions of Paradox are divided into 12 modes—the Main mode and 11 subordinate modes, including the following:

Report
Create
Sort
Edit

CoEdit
DataEntry
Restructure
Forms
Password
Script
Graph

Paradox always displays the current mode in the top right corner of the screen in inverse video. This message is called the *mode indicator*. For example, figure 1.2 shows that Paradox is in the Main mode. Paradox does not display a mode indicator at the Main menu (see fig. 1.1), but if you can display the Main menu by pressing **M**enu (F10), you're in the main mode.

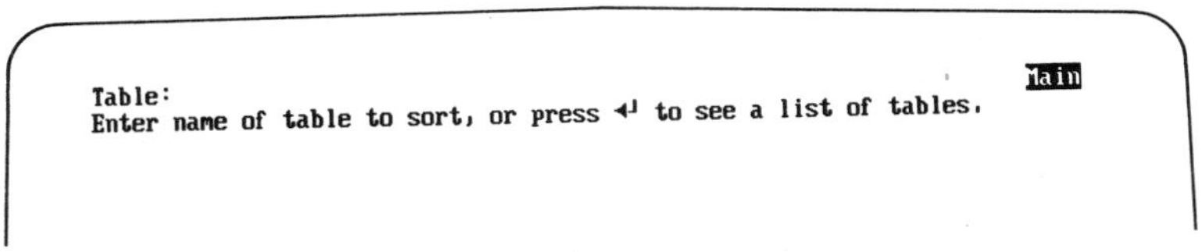
Table:
Enter name of table to sort, or press ↵ to see a list of tables.
Main

Fig. 1.2.

The mode indicator.

Each Paradox mode has its own set of menus and prompts. (The pull-out menu map at the back of this book groups the menus according to mode.) For example, Paradox moves from Main mode to Sort mode whenever you decide to sort your data into an order different from the order in which the information was entered. To accomplish a sort, you first select **M**odify **S**ort from the Main menu (press M and then S). Paradox displays the screen depicted in figure 1.2. Once you enter the name of the table to be sorted and indicate whether the sorted data should be placed in the original table or in a new table, Paradox displays a screen like figure 1.3. Paradox is now in the Sort mode, as indicated by the word `Sort` in the mode indicator.

Database terminology can be a bit confusing, and the purpose of these various modes may not at first be clear. One of the reasons for the mode concept and the mode indicator, however, is to help prevent possible confusion without sacrificing a consistent user interface. In other words, Paradox is designed so that you can enter, view, and edit data from nearly identical screens but still tell one screen from another. This design makes learning Paradox easier. Compare figures 1.4, 1.5, and 1.6. Moving between columns (fields) or rows (records), for example, is the same in any of the three contexts, so you have less to learn. Even so, you should keep in mind that these database management functions are distinct and should not be confused.

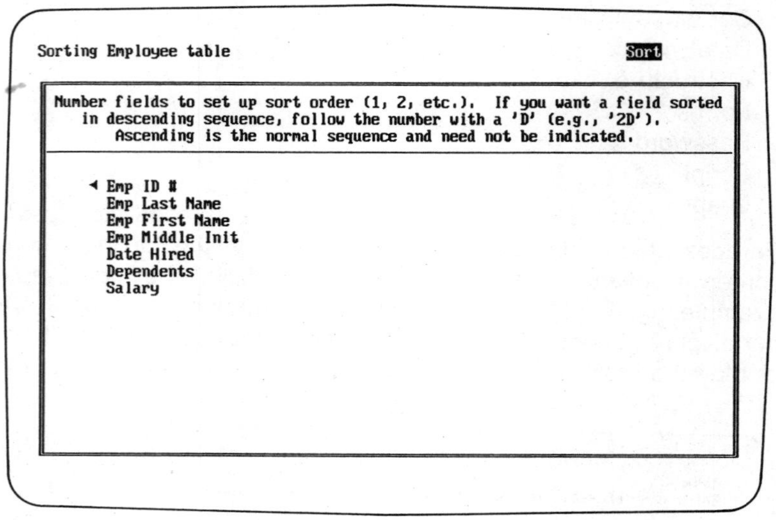

Sorting Employee table
Sort
Number fields to set up sort order (1, 2, etc.). If you want a field sorted in descending sequence, follow the number with a 'D' (e.g., '2D'). Ascending is the normal sequence and need not be indicated.
Emp ID #
Emp Last Name
Emp First Name
Emp Middle Init
Date Hired
Dependents
Salary

Fig. 1.3.

The Sort mode.

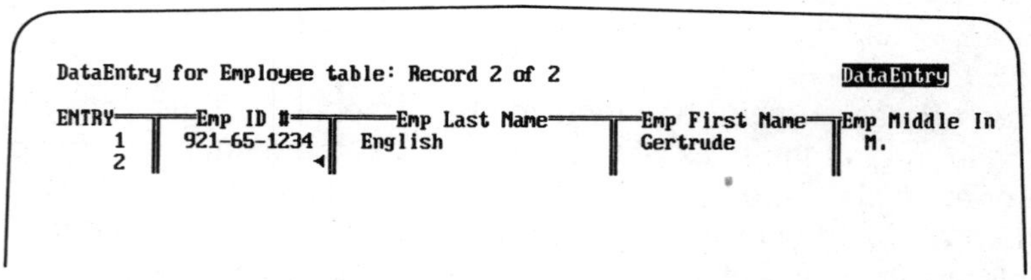

DataEntry for Employee table: Record 2 of 2
DataEntry
ENTRY
Emp ID #
Emp Last Name
Emp First Name
Emp Middle In
1
921-65-1234
English
Gertrude
M.
2

Fig. 1.4.

The DataEntry mode.

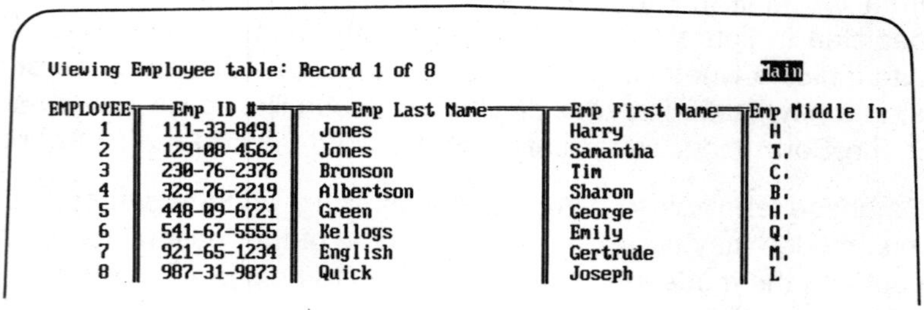

Fig. 1.5.

The Main mode.

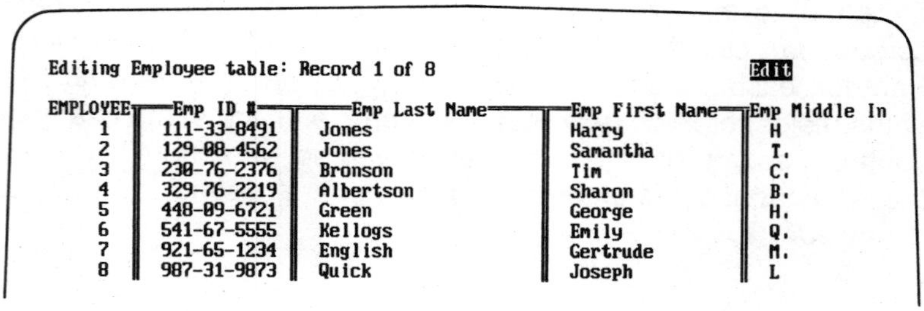

Fig. 1.6.

The Edit mode.

The following rules apply to Paradox modes:

- ❑ Paradox is in only one mode at a time.
- ❑ All modes, except the Main mode, are subordinate to the Main mode.
- ❑ You can access subordinate modes only through the Main mode. For example, you cannot go from the Edit mode directly to the Sort mode.
- ❑ To leave a subordinate mode, you must execute either the Do-It! command (F2) or select the Cancel option from the menu.

The Message Areas

You may have noticed already that the bottom line of the Main menu screen displays a message. This message informs you that you can use the arrow keys to move around the menu and use the Enter key to make a menu selection. At various times, Paradox also displays messages in two other locations.

Information and error messages often appear in inverse video in the lower right corner of the screen. For example, pressing the F6 key while at the Main menu results in the error message shown in figure 1.7. Keep an eye on this corner of the screen for messages from Paradox.

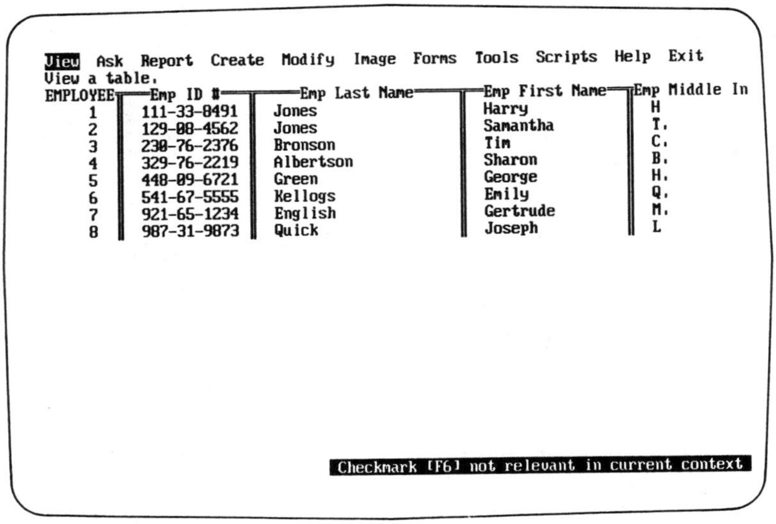
View Ask Report Create Modify Image Forms Tools Scripts Help Exit
View a table.
EMPLOYEE Emp ID # Emp Last Name Emp First Name Emp Middle In
1 111-33-8491 Jones Harry H
2 129-08-4562 Jones Samantha T.
3 230-76-2376 Bronson Tim C.
4 329-76-2219 Albertson Sharon B.
5 448-09-6721 Green George H.
6 541-67-5555 Kellogs Emily Q.
7 921-65-1234 English Gertrude M.
8 987-31-9873 Quick Joseph L
Checkmark [F6] not relevant in current context

Fig. 1.7.

An error message in the message area.

The second message area is in the top left corner of the screen. Figure 1.3, for example, shows the message `Sorting Employee table`; and figure 1.5, the message `Viewing Employee table: Record 1 of 8`. These messages are typical of the information normally displayed here. Generically they are referred to as *status messages*.

The Work Space

The largest portion of the initial Main menu screen is blank and is referred to as the *work space*. This part of the screen is the area in which you enter, display, and edit your data. The Paradox work space is similar in concept to the work area of a spreadsheet, and at times looks almost identical to a spreadsheet. Paradox, however, adds another dimension to the spreadsheet, called the *image*.

Multiple images are allowed in the work space at one time, and each on-screen image can display a different view of a particular table of data, or even a view of another table (see fig. 1.8). This capability is analogous to having more than one spreadsheet displayed on your screen at once (possible with several of the newest spreadsheet packages).

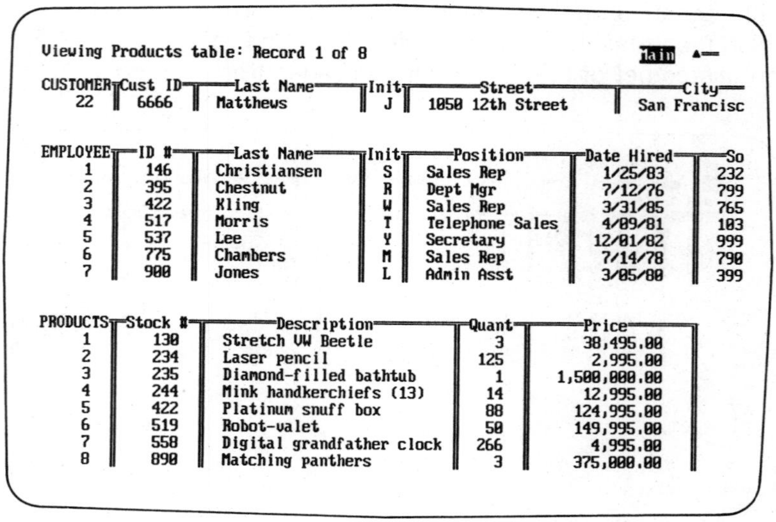

Fig. 1.8.

The work space with multiple images.

The image concept is discussed more fully in a subsequent section of this chapter (see "Understanding the Image Concept"). For now, just think of the work space as a window into your data. Unless you have only a small amount of data in your table, you will not be able to place all the data in the work space at once. At most, you can see only a screenful in the work space at a time, but the actual data in your table is limited in size only by the capacity of your disk drive.

Using the Keyboard

Paradox works with any PC, AT, or PS/2™ style keyboard or equivalent. The program uses practically every key on the keyboard in one way or another, so you need to be familiar with your keyboard (see fig. 1.9). This book uses the labels found on the IBM Enhanced Keyboard to describe the keys you should press.

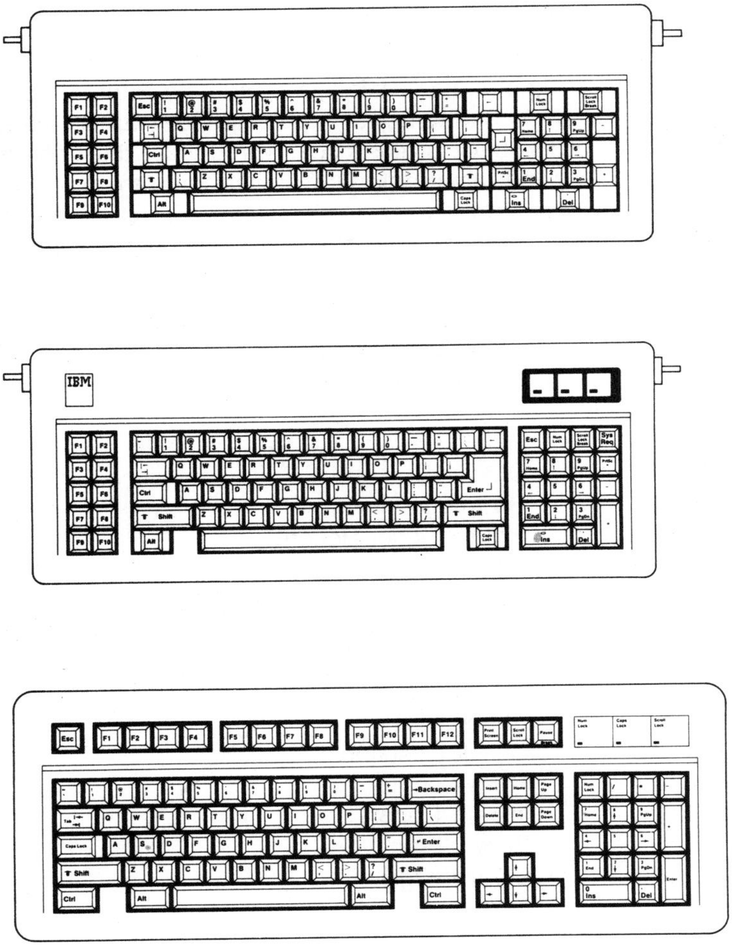

Fig. 1.9.

The IBM PC keyboard (top), the IBM Personal Computer AT keyboard (center), and the IBM Enhanced Keyboard (bottom).

Paradox Function Key Commands

As with many other popular programs, Paradox makes heavy use of the function keys F1 through F10. A keyboard template for each of the two most popular function key layouts (vertical and horizontal) is provided with the program. If you haven't already done so, locate the template and place it on your keyboard so that it can help you learn Paradox. Soon you will have the key commands committed to memory.

Eight of the ten function keys are used with the Alt key as well, and two with the Ctrl key. In some cases a function key command has an equivalent menu command that you can execute through the Paradox menus. Using menus, however, always requires more keystrokes, so you should use the function key method whenever one is available.

Table 1.1 includes a complete list of the function keys and function key combinations along with the names assigned to them by Paradox. Several were used in Quick Start 1. The same list is provided for your convenience on the pull-out card at the back of this book. Throughout the book these keys are referenced by the labels you find on the keys themselves, followed by the Paradox key name in parentheses, as in F2 (DO-IT!) and Alt-F7 (Instant Report). (Note that Alt-F7 means that you should hold down the Alt key while you press the F7 key.)

Table 1.1
Paradox Function Key Names

Function Key	*Name*
F1	Help
F2	DO-IT!
F3	Up Image
Alt-F3	Instant Script Record
F4	Down Image
Alt-F4	Instant Script Play
F5	Example
Alt-F5	Field View
F6	Check Mark
Alt-F6	Check Plus
Ctrl-F6	*Check Descending
F7	Form Toggle
Alt-F7	Instant Report
Ctrl-F7	*View Graph
F8	Clear Image

Table 1.1—*Continued*

Function Key	*Name*
Alt-F8	Clear All
F9	Edit
Alt-F9	Coedit
F10	Menu

*Paradox 3.0 only

The various uses for these keys are explained in subsequent chapters.

Special Key Commands in Paradox

In addition to the function keys, Paradox uses several other keys in combination with either the Ctrl or Alt key for special quick commands. The key combinations and corresponding command names are listed in table 1.2.

Table 1.2
Paradox Special Keys

Key	*Name*
Alt-C	*Color Palette
Ctrl-D	Ditto
Ctrl-F	Field View (same as Alt-F5)
Alt-K	View existing keyed record in CoEdit mode
Alt-L	Lock toggle
Ctrl-O	Suspend Paradox, go to DOS
Alt-O	Suspend Paradox, go to DOS with maximum available RAM
Ctrl-R	Rotate fields in table
Alt-R	Refresh image
Ctrl-U	Undo the last change
Ctrl-V	Show vertical ruler
Alt-X	*Crosstab
Ctrl-Y	Delete line
Ctrl-Z	Zoom (go to) search for value entered at prompt
Alt-Z	Search for next occurrence of value
Ctrl-Backspace	Erase current field

*Paradox 3.0 only

These special keystroke commands are fully explained and demonstrated in subsequent chapters. Like the function key commands, they represent the quickest way to accomplish results. (Note that Ctrl-F, however, is equivalent to Alt-F5; both require the same number of keystrokes.)

Using Paradox Menus and Prompts

Most PC-based programs are command driven, menu driven, or sometimes both. Paradox tends toward the menu-driven side, with the notable exception of the keyboard commands listed in tables 1.1 and 1.2.

Using the "Point-and-Shoot" Selection Method

Paradox menus are in the style of Lotus 1-2-3. You can choose menu options by moving the inverse video bar (the highlight) to the appropriate choice and then pressing the Enter key. This menu selection method is sometimes called the "point-and-shoot" method. While a choice is highlighted (and before you press Enter) Paradox displays a message on the line below the menu. This message briefly describes the effect of selecting the highlighted option. For example, moving the highlight to the **A**sk option on the Main menu displays this message:

```
Get a query form to ask questions about a table
```

Often the effect of choosing a menu option is to display another menu—a submenu—that may contain options that in turn display still other submenus. For example, choosing **T**ools from the Main menu displays a submenu listing these options:

Rename
QuerySpeedup
ExportImport
Copy
Delete
Info
Net
More

Then, selecting **M**ore results in another submenu, which includes these options:

Add
MultiAdd
FormAdd
Subtract
Empty
Protect
Directory
ToDOS

(FormAdd is available only with Paradox 3.0.) You can think of the hierarchical structure of these menus as a tree, with each menu selection moving you out branches or subbranches of the tree. Refer to the pull-out menu map at the back of this book.

If you ever get too far "out on a limb," you can back down by using the Esc key. It uniformly reverses your steps, moving you back to your beginning point, one level at a time. To return to the first level, no matter how deep you are in the menu tree, press F10.

Probably the most common mistake made by a new user of any software package is failing to read the prompts and messages that are provided on-screen. Get in the habit of reading thoroughly all screen messages, especially when you are working with a feature for the first time. Take it slow and be observant. This practice can prevent needless errors, and the screen prompts will help you learn Paradox faster and with less frustration.

Using the First-Letter Selection Method

Once you are more familiar with the choices in the various Paradox menus, you should begin to use the alternative method of selecting menu options. With the appropriate menu displayed, you simply press the first letter of your choice, regardless of the position of the highlight. This first-letter method is quicker and more accurate than the point-and-shoot method. In this book, the first letter of each menu command is in boldface type, as in **A**sk, which indicates that you should press A to select the command.

Many operations require a sequence of menu selections. This book lists the options you should select side-by-side in the appropriate order. For example,

Modify **R**estructure

means that you should press the M and R keys, one after the other.

Every effort has been made to present menu options in this book exactly as they appear on-screen. To be consistent with Paradox menus, no spaces are shown between words of multiword commands if they appear with no spaces on your screen. But if the menu choice separates words with spaces, this book connects the words with underscores. For example,

Tools **E**xportImport **I**mport **1**-2-3 **1**)_1-2-3_Release_1A

means to type *tei11*. Most multiword commands in Paradox appear in the menus without spaces, as in ExportImport.

Responding to Paradox Screen Prompts

As you use Paradox, you are often presented with a prompt, rather than a menu or message, at the top of the screen. A *prompt* is different from a message in that a prompt requests your response. A message is informative only.

Many times, the prompt asks you to enter a name or number of a Paradox object (table, form, report, and so on). For example, to view the Employee table, select **V**iew from the Main menu. Paradox displays the message shown in a screen like figure 1.10, which asks you to enter the name of the table to view. You can always type the name if you want, but, as this prompt suggests, you have the option of pressing the Enter key to see a list of available tables.

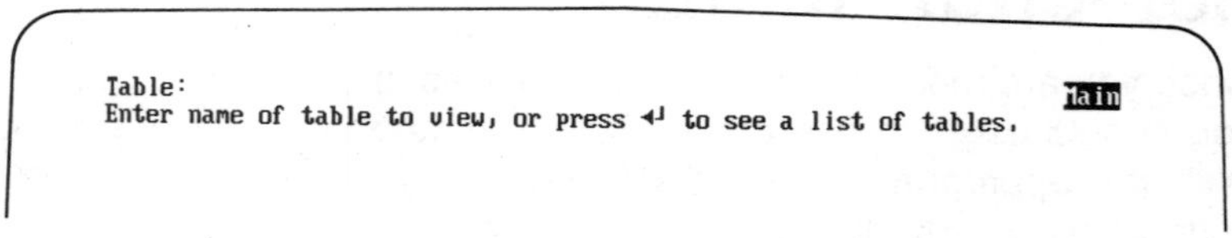
Table:
Enter name of table to view, or press ↵ to see a list of tables.
Main

Fig. 1.10.

A screen prompt asking for the table name.

Once a list is displayed, such as the sample list of tables shown in figure 1.11, you can select from the list just as you select a menu option. Either use the arrow keys to move the highlight to the name of the item you want to view and then press Enter, or press the first letter of the item's name.

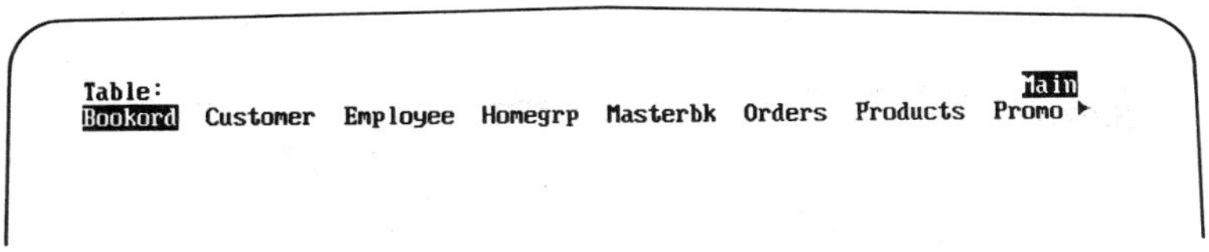

Fig. 1.11.

A list of available tables.

Occasionally, more than one item name begins with the same letter, as do the Products and Promo tables in figure 1.11. In that case, pressing the first letter causes Paradox to narrow your choices a bit by displaying only those that begin with the pressed letter (see fig. 1.12). You then *must* use the point-and-shoot method to complete the selection.

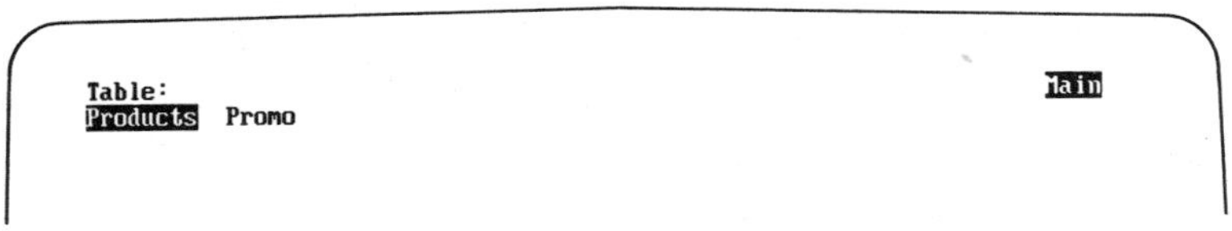

Fig. 1.12.

Two tables starting with the same letter.

Whenever Paradox asks for the name of an existing Paradox table or graph, or the number of a form or report, you can press Enter to display a list of available objects. Then use the first-letter and point-and-shoot methods to choose which object Paradox should use.

Understanding Paradox Views and Images

One of the most important benefits of using a relational database is that you do not have to worry about how data is stored. You do, on the other hand, have to understand how to interpret what is displayed on-screen.

Working in the Table View

Paradox normally displays data in the work area of the screen in a tabular fashion (see fig. 1.13). This look at your data is called the *table view*. It shows as many rows and columns as will fit on the screen—up to 22 rows by 80 characters. Only one row or record is active at a time. The active record is indicated by the position of the blinking cursor. A status message at the top of the screen keeps you informed of the current record (row) number, as well as the total number of available records. Whenever the screen is not wide enough to display all field data, the last column is abbreviated and appears filled with asterisks.

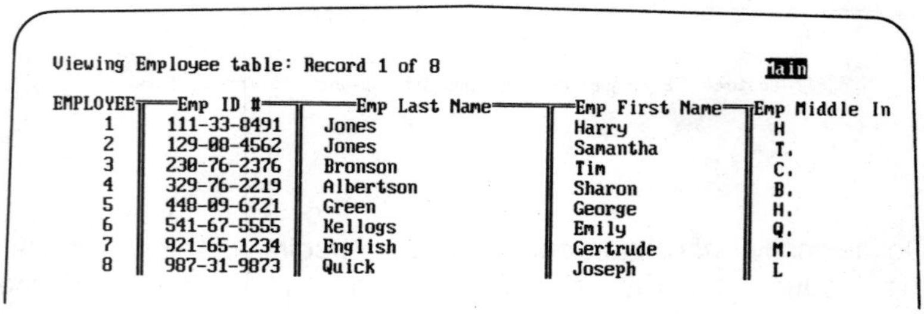

Viewing Employee table: Record 1 of 8
Main
EMPLOYEE Emp ID # Emp Last Name Emp First Name Emp Middle In
1 111-33-8491 Jones Harry H
2 129-88-4562 Jones Samantha T.
3 230-76-2376 Bronson Tim C.
4 329-76-2219 Albertson Sharon B.
5 448-89-6721 Green George H.
6 541-67-5555 Kellogs Emily Q.
7 921-65-1234 English Gertrude M.
8 987-31-9873 Quick Joseph L

Fig. 1.13.

The table view.

Moving the cursor in the table view is easy. Simply use the arrow keys to go from column to column and row to row. You can use all the usual cursor-movement keys—arrow keys, Home, PgUp, End, and PgDn, alone and with the Ctrl key—to move around the table (see table 1.3).

Table 1.3
Using Cursor-Movement Keys in the Table View

Key	*Moves Cursor*
Home	To first record of table
Ctrl-Home	To first field of record
End	To last record of table
Ctrl-End	To last field of record
PgUp	Up one screen
PgDn	Down one screen
Left arrow	Left one field
Ctrl-left arrow	Left one screen
Right arrow	Right one field
Ctrl-right arrow	Right one screen
Up arrow	Up one record
Down arrow	Down one record
Enter	Right one field

Working in the Form View

Sometimes you may prefer to work with only one record on-screen at a time. With Paradox, this feat is as simple as pressing F7 (Form Toggle). Figure 1.14 shows the first record in the table in figure 1.13, but in the *form view*.

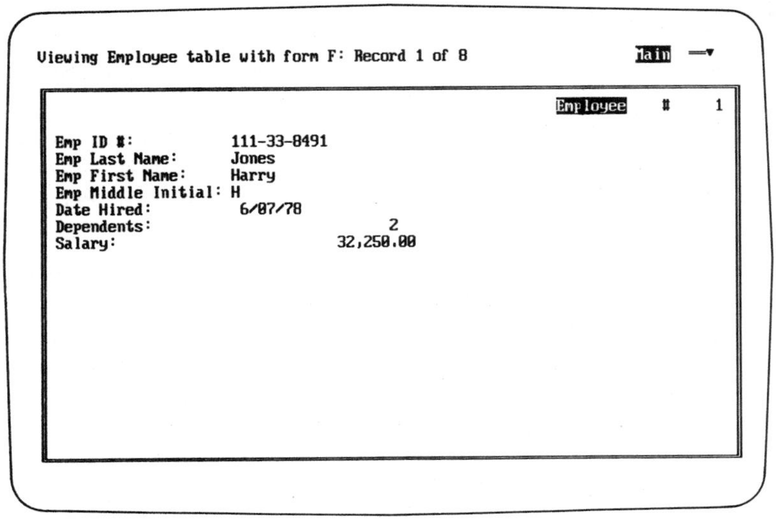

Fig. 1.14.

The form view.

Paradox automatically builds a form for use in form view. This standard form is named *form F*. Paradox permits you to create up to 14 additional forms for use with each table. Chapter 8 covers in detail the many powerful form-design features available in Paradox. Paradox 3.0 even has the capability to create forms for use with more than one table at a time.

As in the table view, you can easily move around the screen by using the cursor-movement keys (see table 1.4).

Table 1.4
Using Cursor-Movement Keys in the Form View

Key	*Moves Cursor*
Home	To first record of table
Ctrl-Home	To first field of record
End	To last record of table
Ctrl-End	To last field of record
PgUp	To previous page or record
Ctrl-PgUp	To same field of previous record
PgDn	To next page or record
Ctrl-PgDn	To same field of next record
Left arrow	To previous field
Right arrow	To next field
Up arrow	Up one field
Down arrow	Down one field
Enter	Next field

Working in the Field View

Two basic tasks in database management are data entry and data editing. Chapter 3 completely explains the basics of both tasks. In either case, you are always entering or editing one field at a time. Paradox normally allows you to change an entry only from the end of the field. To correct a mistake, you back up to the point where the error was made, using the Backspace key, and type the correct data.

As an alternative to having to retype erroneous entries, Paradox provides the *field view* for editing data. To activate this view, place the cursor in the field to be changed and press Alt-F5 (Field View). The cursor becomes an inverse video block to remind you that you are using the field view. Otherwise, the screen looks exactly as it did before you pressed Alt-F5 (Field View). You can use field view while entering and editing data within table view or form view. The cursor keys (listed in table 1.5) are then available for moving within the field without erasing the existing data. You also can use the Ins and Del keys to add or subtract characters or digits from the field.

Table 1.5
Using Cursor-Movement Keys in the Field View

Key	*Moves Cursor*
Home	To first character of field
End	To last character of field
Left arrow	One character left
Ctrl-left arrow	One word left
Right arrow	One character right
Ctrl-right arrow	One word right
Up arrow	Up one line (in wrapped fields)
Down arrow	Down one line (in wrapped fields)

When you have finished correcting an entry, press Enter once to return to the normal table or form view. You need to press Enter again if you want to move to the next field (or next record, if you're editing the last field of a record). Refer to Chapter 3 for a more complete discussion of entering and editing data with Paradox.

Understanding the Image Concept

Understanding the image concept is fundamental to learning Paradox. An *image* is a segment of the work space containing data from one table.

While in table view, Paradox can display multiple images on-screen (see fig. 1.8). Images have the following characteristics:

- ❑ No images are on the opening Paradox screen.
- ❑ Multiple images are allowed in the work space.
- ❑ Paradox adds images to the work space vertically from the top down. (The exception to this rule is when you use a query form. For example, if you have a table in view in the work space and then you bring up a query form, Paradox puts the query form *above* the table image. All subsequent queries will display below the first query, and all subsequent tables will display below the first table.)
- ❑ You can display multiple images on the same screen only in the Table View of the Main and Edit modes. Form view always requires the full screen.
- ❑ The current image is the one containing the cursor.
- ❑ The current image uses no more of the screen (vertically) than is necessary to display all the image's records, up to the maximum of 22 records on-screen at once.
- ❑ You can edit data only in the current image.
- ❑ You can customize field size and the format and number of records displayed in any image.
- ❑ All images on the screen are affected by the current mode. For example, you cannot have one image in Main mode and another image in Edit mode on-screen at the same time.

Because the work space is larger than just one screen, sometimes an image (or more than one image) is in the work space but not fully displayed on-screen. This situation is always the case when you are working in the form view.

In the table view, whenever any portion of an inactive image (not the current one) is hidden, Paradox reminds you by placing a special symbol to the right of the mode indicator. A triangle pointing up means that at least one record is hidden above the current image. A downward-pointing triangle denotes hidden data below the current image. Both triangles together mean that records from inactive images are hidden in both directions (see the upper right corner of fig. 1.15).

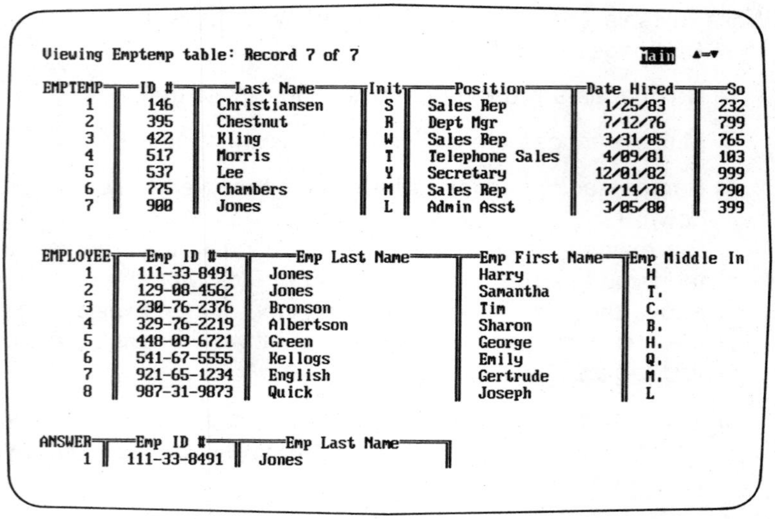

Viewing Emptemp table: Record 7 of 7
Main
EMPTEMP ID # Last Name Init Position Date Hired So
1 146 Christiansen S Sales Rep 1/25/83 232
2 395 Chestnut R Dept Mgr 7/12/76 799
3 422 Kling W Sales Rep 3/31/85 765
4 517 Morris T Telephone Sales 4/09/81 103
5 537 Lee Y Secretary 12/01/82 999
6 775 Chambers M Sales Rep 7/14/78 790
7 900 Jones L Admin Asst 3/05/80 399
EMPLOYEE Emp ID # Emp Last Name Emp First Name Emp Middle In
1 111-33-8491 Jones Harry H
2 129-08-4562 Jones Samantha T.
3 230-76-2376 Bronson Tim C.
4 329-76-2219 Albertson Sharon B.
5 448-09-6721 Green George H.
6 541-67-5555 Kellogs Emily Q.
7 921-65-1234 English Gertrude M.
8 987-31-9873 Quick Joseph L
ANSWER Emp ID # Emp Last Name
1 111-33-8491 Jones

Fig. 1.15.

Triangular symbols indicating hidden images.

The same triangular symbols have a slightly different meaning in the form view. The up-triangle means that more records are above the one currently displayed, and the down-triangle indicates more records below the current record. Notice that figure 1.14 shows only the down-triangle because the first record in the Employee table is current.

Paradox allows you to customize the image at several stages in the database management process. The new graphics capability is accessed through the Image option on the Main menu. These techniques and other aspects of Paradox images are discussed in more detail in later chapters as you learn about using Paradox for entering and editing data.

Version 3

Getting Help from Paradox

Even though Paradox is an easy program to learn and use, at times you may not be sure of exactly what you should do next. Whenever you are looking for a brief explanation or a memory jogger, use the context-sensitive Paradox help system. It is available at the touch of a key. To access on-line help from any screen, press F1 (Help). Paradox displays a screen of information specific to the task at hand.

Using the Help Screen

The Paradox help screen is divided into four areas: the menu area, the screen title, the message area, and the help information itself. The Help menu works in the same manner as all other Paradox menus. Use either the point-and-shoot method or the first-letter method to make your choices. The Esc key retraces your steps and takes you to the previous help screen or the screen at which you started. Because the help system is context-sensitive, the choices on the menu depend on what you are doing when you ask for help. Press F1 (Help) at the Main menu to see the screen shown in figure 1.16.

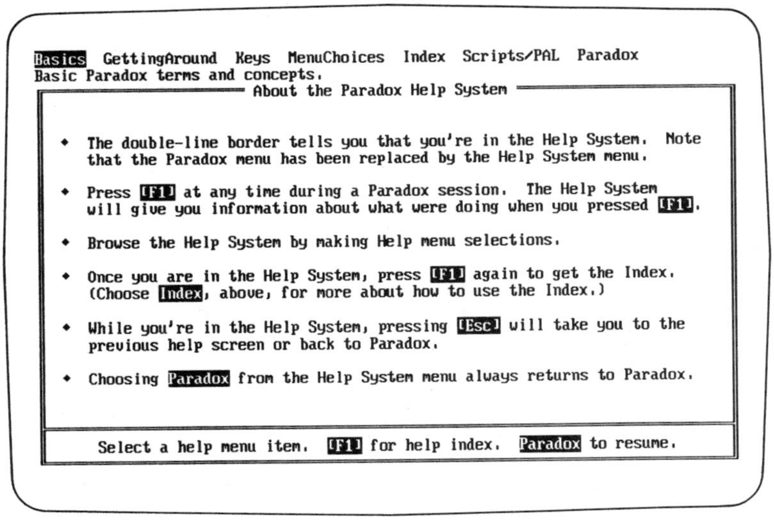

Fig. 1.16.

Help screen describing the Paradox help system.

When you select one of the options listed in the menu area, Paradox displays a help screen about the chosen topic, and another menu appears at the top of the screen, often presenting related topics of a more specific nature. For example, choosing **K**eys from the Help menu in figure 1.16 displays the Paradox Keyboard screen shown in figure 1.17. The information in this screen discusses generally how Paradox uses function keys, control keys, and arrow keys. For more detailed information about one of these groups of keys, you select one of the options from the menu at the top of the screen. Selecting **P**aradox exits the help system.

As you climb through this tree-like menu system, you often can find relevant information quickly. The information supplied by the help system is seldom as detailed, however, as that provided in the Paradox documentation or in this book.

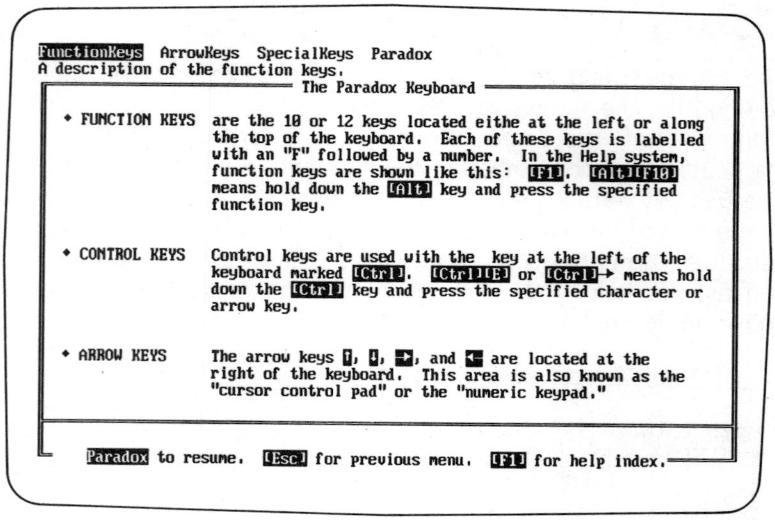

Fig. 1.17.
Help screen describing the Paradox keyboard.

Using the Help Index

An alternative way of finding a help screen about a specific topic is called the *help index*. You first have to access the help system by pressing F1 (Help). A message at the bottom of the screen (the message line) informs you that you should press F1 again for the help index. Do so, and Paradox displays an alphabetically arranged index of the help screens available in the help system.

For example, suppose that you are editing the Employee table and have forgotten how to use the field view. First, from the Edit mode, press F1 (Help). Paradox displays the Editing a Table screen shown in figure 1.18. Press F1 again to access the help index (see fig. 1.19).

You can now use the *zoom search* feature to find quickly any entries about the field view. Press Ctrl-Z (Zoom), and Paradox displays a prompt at the top of the screen, asking you to `Enter value or pattern to search for.` Type *field view* and press Enter. Paradox searches the index and stops on the matching entry (see fig. 1.20).

This entry happens to be a *general topic* and not an *active entry*. Active entries are preceded by a dot and have a corresponding help screen. General topics have no help screen and are simply used in the index to group the entries. Move the highlight to the active entry *arrow keys* and press Enter. Paradox displays the help screen shown in figure 1.21. Press F1 to return to the help index. To return to your work, either press Esc or choose **P**aradox from the menu.

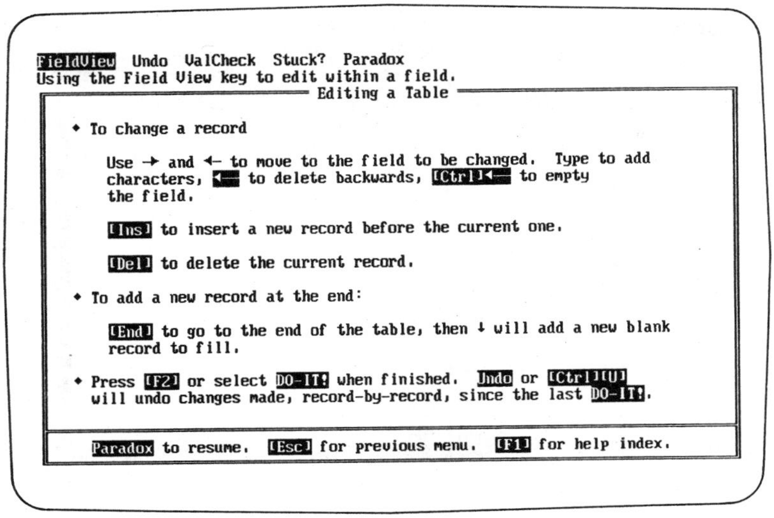
FieldView Undo ValCheck Stuck? Paradox
Using the Field View key to edit within a field.
Editing a Table
• To change a record
Use → and ← to move to the field to be changed. Type to add characters, ← to delete backwards, [Ctrl]← to empty the field.
[Ins] to insert a new record before the current one.
[Del] to delete the current record.
• To add a new record at the end:
[End] to go to the end of the table, then ↓ will add a new blank record to fill.
• Press [F2] or select DO-IT! when finished. Undo or [Ctrl][U] will undo changes made, record-by-record, since the last DO-IT!.
Paradox to resume. [Esc] for previous menu. [F1] for help index.

Fig. 1.18.

Help screen describing how to edit a table.

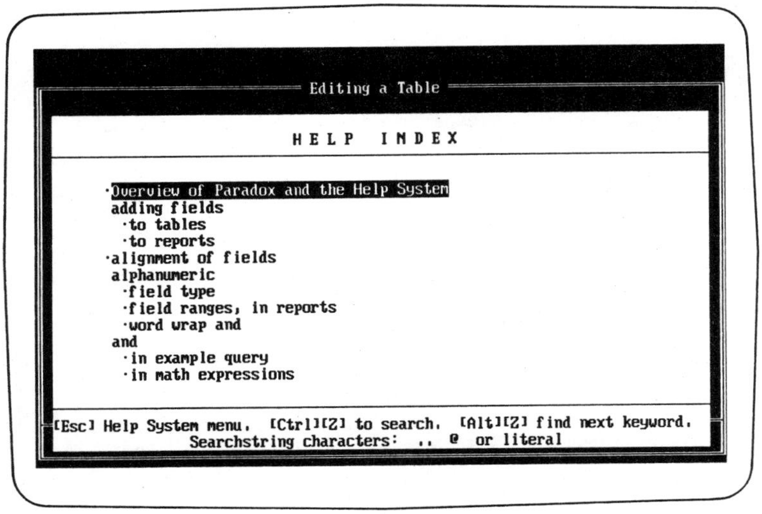

Fig. 1.19.

The help index.

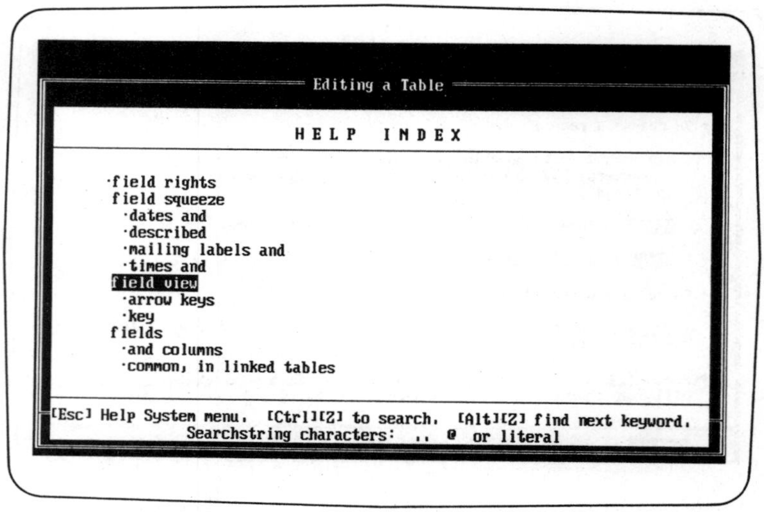

Fig. 1.20.

Finding a field view entry.

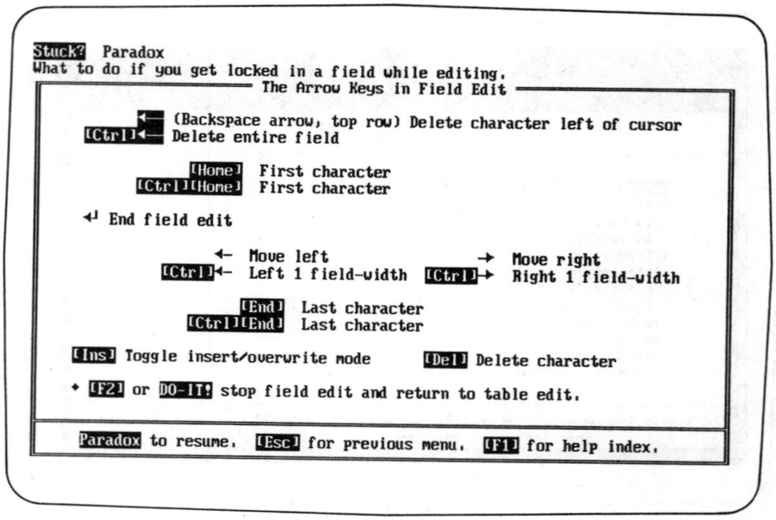

Fig. 1.21.

Help screen describing use of the arrow keys in field view.

The two methods of locating help—by menu and by index—are not exactly equivalent, because only the menu method is context sensitive. Using each method for the same topic may even give you different screens. For example, the screen in figure 1.18, which you accessed by pressing F1 in Edit mode, includes a menu choice called **F**ieldView. Selecting that option displays the screen shown in figure 1.22. This screen is different from the one in figure 1.21, which you accessed through the help index. Experiment with both Paradox help system methods to see which one you prefer. You will soon learn to locate assistance quickly and certainly learn many valuable tidbits about Paradox along the way.

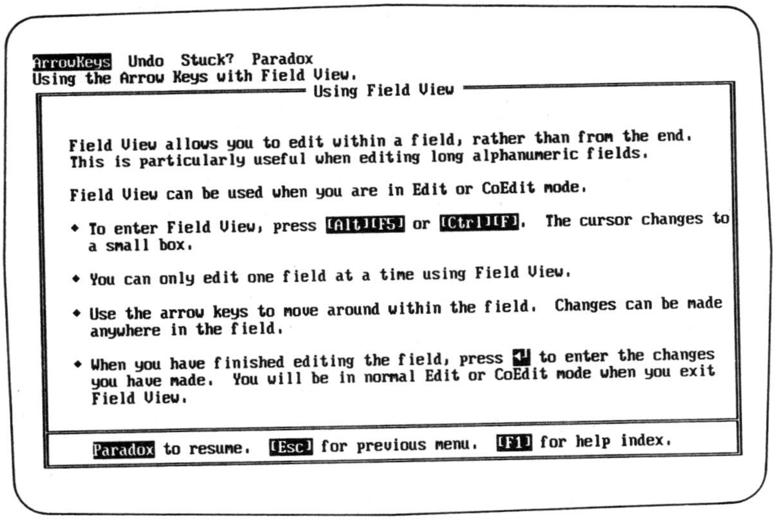
ArrowKeys Undo Stuck? Paradox
Using the Arrow Keys with Field View.
Using Field View
Field View allows you to edit within a field, rather than from the end.
This is particularly useful when editing long alphanumeric fields.
Field View can be used when you are in Edit or CoEdit mode.
◆ To enter Field View, press [Alt][F5] or [Ctrl][F]. The cursor changes to a small box.
◆ You can only edit one field at a time using Field View.
◆ Use the arrow keys to move around within the field. Changes can be made anywhere in the field.
◆ When you have finished editing the field, press ↵ to enter the changes you have made. You will be in normal Edit or CoEdit mode when you exit Field View.
Paradox to resume. [Esc] for previous menu. [F1] for help index.

Fig. 1.22.

Help screen describing the field view.

Chapter Summary

After completing this chapter you probably have a better idea of how Paradox will present itself to you and how you should respond. You are now familiar with the areas of the Paradox screen; have a general understanding of how to begin tasks with Paradox, both through menu commands and keyboard commands; have been introduced to the fundamental concepts of Paradox modes and images; and understand how to access the Paradox help system. As you continue through the book, keep these basic navigational aids in mind, and you will never get lost. The next chapter builds on this foundation and discusses the procedure for designing a new database with Paradox.

2

Creating Database Tables

Now that you are familiar with how to get around in Paradox, you can read this chapter to help you develop a good theoretical and practical understanding of Paradox. If you're a new Paradox user, you should find this chapter especially helpful.

The first portion of the chapter briefly explains what is meant by the term *relational database*. The chapter then goes on to introduce several important Paradox concepts, such as *table*, *object*, *family*, *structure*, and *network locking*.

After this important but mostly theoretical discussion, the chapter turns to the more practical topic of how to create a Paradox database table. The text describes how to define the structure of a Paradox table, define fields and keys, borrow structure, modify the structure of an existing table, and change a table's name.

Understanding Database Terminology

Because of the great speed and storage capacity of computers, they have always been good candidates for storing large amounts of information. With microcomputer technology racing ahead at breakneck speed, and the incredible popularity of PCs in business, the capability to store thousands of pages of information literally on your desktop is the norm. The practical problem with storing that much information lies in developing a system to retrieve the data in some orderly fashion. Relational database programs are designed to solve this problem.

Although you may or may not be aware of the fact, you have built and used databases all your life. You just didn't call them that. Whenever you collect information in some organized fashion so that you can access the data randomly, you are creating a database. Typical databases include the following:

Telephone books
Card catalogs
Recipe cards
Rolodex files
Mailing lists

Computers enable you to store data electronically rather than on cards, in file cabinets, or in books. From this electronic storage, well-designed database programs are then able to retrieve the data almost instantaneously.

What Is a Relational Database?

A *relational database* consists of a collection of related tables made up of rows of data arranged in named columns. Two tables are related when they have columns with the same names. A relational database management system such as Paradox enables you to use data from any number of related tables at once. This structure is an oversimplified distillation of the relational model, originally suggested in 1970 by Dr. Edgar F. Codd—then an IBM scientist, now the president of the Relational Institute and chief scientist of Codd and Date International. Suffice it to say that as PC implementations of the relational model go, Paradox is closer than most.

Paradox database terminology and the program's overall design are more faithful to the Codd/relational model than such popular programs as dBASE III Plus™ (and dBASE IV™). For that reason, experienced dBASE users may find some aspects of Paradox a bit unfamiliar. Although understanding the relative merits of the various database models is not crucial, you do need to understand the terminology adopted by Paradox.

Knowing the Paradox Objects

The term *object* in Paradox is broad in nature and refers to any one of a number of database building blocks. The following are all Paradox objects:

The table *Employee*
The field *Emp ID #*
The form *F*
The report *R*
The script *Instant*

All data in Paradox is stored in *tables* made up of columns (*fields*) and rows (*records*), as shown in figure 2.1. A Paradox database, then, consists of a collection of tables that are *related* or *linked* by common columns.

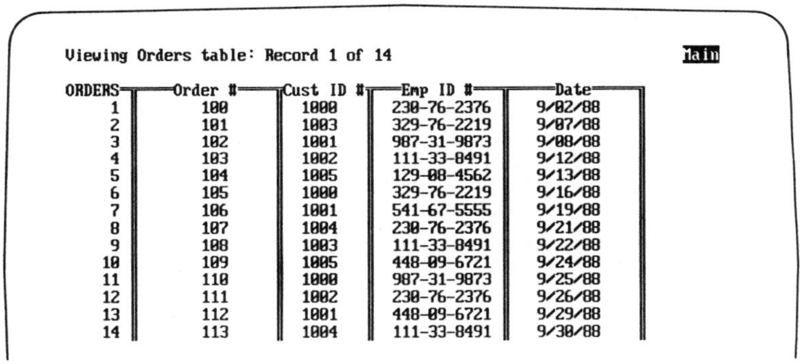
Viewing Orders table: Record 1 of 14 Main

ORDERS	Order #	Cust ID #	Emp ID #	Date
1	100	1000	230-76-2376	9/02/88
2	101	1003	329-76-2219	9/07/88
3	102	1001	987-31-9873	9/08/88
4	103	1002	111-33-8491	9/12/88
5	104	1005	129-08-4562	9/13/88
6	105	1000	329-76-2219	9/16/88
7	106	1001	541-67-5555	9/19/88
8	107	1004	230-76-2376	9/21/88
9	108	1003	111-33-8491	9/22/88
10	109	1005	448-09-6721	9/24/88
11	110	1000	987-31-9873	9/25/88
12	111	1002	230-76-2376	9/26/88
13	112	1001	448-09-6721	9/29/88
14	113	1004	111-33-8491	9/30/88

Fig. 2.1.
A Paradox table.

The table is to Paradox what the worksheet is to Lotus 1-2-3. Once you create a table, even the table definition itself is temporarily stored in a table (see fig. 2.2). Although you have the option of entering and editing data in forms (*form view*), the majority of database tasks in Paradox are performed in a tabular format (*table view*). And, as in the Codd/relational model, any query or other operation performed on a table returns an answer in the form of a table (see fig. 2.3), which in turn can then be the object of further database operations.

Caution: A collection of tables make up a database, but Paradox does not provide an internal way to group tables. Instead, you should reserve a separate directory on your hard disk (or a separate floppy disk) for each database. Place tables from one—and only one—database in each directory. Otherwise, your working directory will quickly become cluttered with unrelated tables, diluting the benefits of a relational database. Refer to Appendix A or Quick Start 1 for information on starting Paradox from the working directory.

Most objects are associated with a particular table. For example, you can design input forms and custom reports for each Paradox table. All the objects associated with a given table are called a *family* of objects. Objects

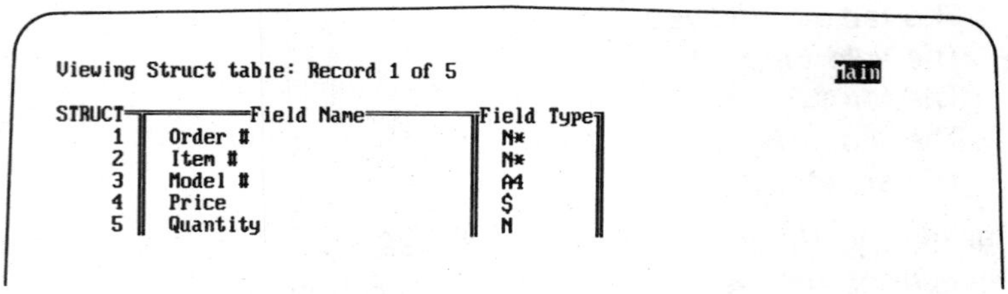

Fig. 2.2.

The temporary table Struct.

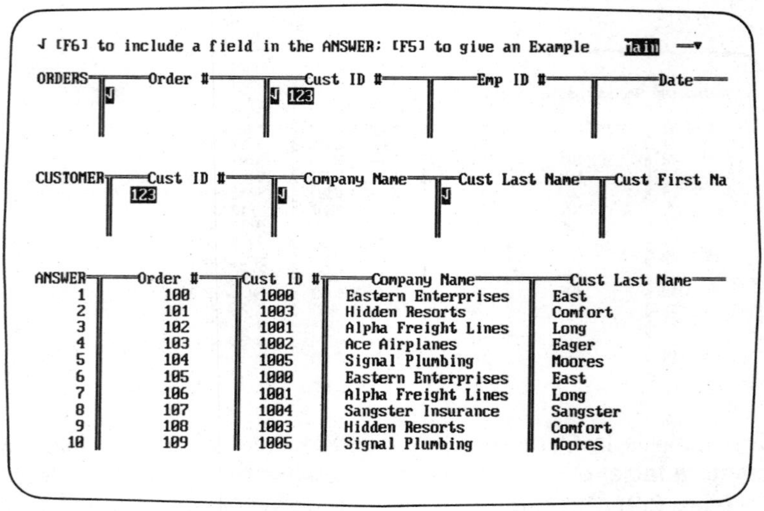

[F6] to include a field in the ANSWER; [F5] to give an Example
Main
ORDERS Order # Cust ID # Emp ID # Date
123
CUSTOMER Cust ID # Company Name Cust Last Name Cust First Na
123
ANSWER Order # Cust ID # Company Name Cust Last Name
1 100 1000 Eastern Enterprises East
2 101 1003 Hidden Resorts Comfort
3 102 1001 Alpha Freight Lines Long
4 103 1002 Ace Airplanes Eager
5 104 1005 Signal Plumbing Moores
6 105 1000 Eastern Enterprises East
7 106 1001 Alpha Freight Lines Long
8 107 1004 Sangster Insurance Sangster
9 108 1003 Hidden Resorts Comfort
10 109 1005 Signal Plumbing Moores

Fig. 2.3.

The result of a query of two tables: the temporary table Answer.

such as forms and reports are stored as separate files on the disk. Paradox automatically saves them for you and uses the table name as the *base name* of these files, distinguishing between family members through file name extensions. The exceptions to this rule are *scripts*, discussed in Chapter 6, which are not part of a family of objects and do not necessarily have the same name as a table. The file name extensions assigned by Paradox are listed in table 2.1. This chapter discusses how to create a Paradox table. Creating and using these objects are discussed in later chapters of this book.

Table 2.1
Paradox Object File Name Extensions

Object Type	*File Name Extension*
Table	.DB
Form	.F or .F*n*
Report	.R or .R*n*
Image settings	.SET

Table 2.1—*Continued*

Object Type	*File Name Extension*
Validity checks	.VAL
Primary index	.PX
Query-speedup (secondary index)	.X*m*
Query-speedup (secondary index)	.Y*m*
Script	.SC

Note: The letter *n* in the file name extensions is replaced by an integer from 1 to 14 representing the name of the form or report. The letter *m* is replaced by two digits, automatically assigned by Paradox.

Designing a Database

As you design your database, you should keep each table small, resisting the temptation to put everything but the kitchen sink into one giant table. The strength of relational database technology is the capability to access easily and simultaneously data in multiple tables. You should almost never create a database consisting of only one Paradox table. Create multiple tables, and use common columns to tie related information together.

Planning the Fields

Keep four goals in mind as you decide on the fields to include in each table:

1. Collect all the information necessary for the reports that must be generated.
2. Do not collect any information that will never be needed for a report.
3. Divide the data into logical and manageable categories.
4. Never enter the same information more than once.

You can meet the first two goals through thoughtful analysis of the real-life data you are now collecting and the reports you currently generate or plan to generate. Careful attention to detail at this early stage of database design can save you countless hours of redesigning later.

You can accomplish goal 4 only if you do a good job at goal 3. In the example shown in figure 2.4, by comparing the Cust ID # columns in the two tables, you can see that customers often place more than one order. Recording Company Name, Cust Last Name, Cust Address, and so forth in the Orders table would require continual reentry of the same information. On the other hand, dividing the data into two tables—Orders and Customer—enables you to enter the Customer information one time only. Figure 2.3 shows an example of how Paradox can pull together the information for these two tables, using the Cust ID # column as a *link*.

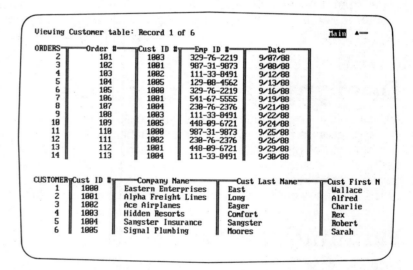

Fig. 2.4.

The related Orders and Customer tables.

Viewing Customer table: Record 1 of 6 Main

ORDERS	Order #	Cust ID #	Emp ID #	Date
2	101	1003	329-76-2219	9/07/88
3	102	1001	987-31-9873	9/08/88
4	103	1002	111-33-8491	9/12/88
5	104	1005	129-08-4562	9/13/88
6	105	1000	329-76-2219	9/16/88
7	106	1001	541-67-5555	9/19/88
8	107	1004	230-76-2376	9/21/88
9	108	1003	111-33-8491	9/22/88
10	109	1005	448-09-6721	9/24/88
11	110	1000	987-31-9873	9/25/88
12	111	1002	230-76-2376	9/26/88
13	112	1001	448-09-6721	9/29/88
14	113	1004	111-33-8491	9/30/88

CUSTOMER	Cust ID #	Company Name	Cust Last Name	Cust First N
1	1000	Eastern Enterprises	East	Wallace
2	1001	Alpha Freight Lines	Long	Alfred
3	1002	Ace Airplanes	Eager	Charlie
4	1003	Hidden Resorts	Comfort	Rex
5	1004	Sangster Insurance	Sangster	Robert
6	1005	Signal Plumbing	Moores	Sarah

This design process is sometimes called *normalization*. The Paradox documentation uses that term. A *normalized* table is as small as possible, is easy to understand and change, contains no duplicate records, and contains little (if any) information already entered in another table.

Design your database on paper first. Write down the table names, and list the field names below them. This "bird's eye view" of your database will be invaluable as you begin to define the structure of the tables and later build forms and reports. Keep the layout next to your keyboard as you work, and file the paperwork away for later reference when you are finished. A worksheet for the two tables shown in figure 2.4 would look like this:

Orders	*Customer*
Order #	Cust ID #
Cust ID #	Company Name
Emp ID #	Cust Last Name
Date	Cust First Name
	Cust Middle Initial
	Cust Address
	Cust City
	Cust State
	Cust ZIP
	Cust Phone

Understanding How Tables Are Related

An important step toward getting the most from any relational database management system like Paradox is to develop an understanding of how the many tables in a database are related to each other.

Two tables are related if they have common field names. An example of related tables is shown in figure 2.4. The Orders table contains the field Cust ID #; so does the Customer table. This common field is often referred to as the *link* between the tables.

The link between tables can be used to define more precisely the relationship between two tables. If the linking column contains unique data—as does the Cust ID # in the Customer table—the column is said to be on the *one-side* of the relationship. When the data in a linking column is not necessarily unique—as in the Cust ID # field in the Orders table—the column is on the *many-side* of the relationship. Therefore, a *one-to-many* relationship exists between Customer and Orders. In other words, you can enter data about a customer only once and then use it many times in processing orders.

Typically, one table in a relationship is referred to as the *master* table. The other table is called the *detail* table. Chapters 8 and 10, in the context of designing forms and reports, discusses how you decide which table is the *master* and which is the *detail*. In an order-placing system, such as the Customer/Orders example in figures 2.3 and 2.4, you might refer to Orders as the master table and Customer as the detail table. Usually the link type is expressed from the point of view of the master table, so the relationship between Orders and Customer is described as a *many-to-one* relationship. Four types of relationships are possible:

- *One-to-one:* A unique field in the master table is linked to a unique field in the detail table. One row in the master table corresponds to one and only one row in the detail table.
- *One-to-many:* A unique field in the master table is linked to a non-unique field in the detail table. One row in the master table links to a group of rows in the detail table.
- *Many-to-one:* A non-unique field in the master table is linked to a unique field in the detail table. A group of rows in the master table corresponds to only one row in the detail table.
- *Many-to-many:* A non-unique field in the master table is linked to a non-unique field in the detail table. A group of rows in the master table corresponds to a group of rows in the detail table.

Relational database systems in general and Paradox in particular can be used most effectively if you avoid *many-to-many* relationships. Paradox 3.0 has a new capability to display data from both tables of one-to-one or one-to-many relationships on one screen, but the program cannot handle many-to-many relationships. Chapter 8 discusses what to do if you need to redesign a database to eliminate many-to-many relationships.

Version 3

You can add links to your database worksheet (see the preceding tip on designing a database) by using lines and arrowheads. Draw lines on the worksheet between common field names. Place a single arrowhead on the *one-side* and a double arrowhead on the *many-side*. The worksheet for the Orders/Customer example, with lines and arrowheads, would look like this:

<u>Orders</u>	<u>Customer</u>
Order #	Cust ID #
Cust ID #	Company Name
Emp ID #	Cust Last Name
Date	Cust First Name
	Cust Middle Initial
	Cust Address
	Cust City
	Cust State
	Cust ZIP
	Cust Phone

Defining Table Structure

Once you have designed your database, the first step at implementation is to create or define the *structure* of each table. Table definition is a task started from the Paradox Main menu. To begin defining a Paradox table, select **C**reate from the Main menu. Then type the table's name and press Enter. Follow these rules when naming the table:

1. You can use up to 8 characters (with no file name extensions).
2. You can use letters, numbers, and these special characters:

   $ # & @ ! ÷ ( ) – _ { } ' ^

3. You cannot include spaces.
4. You cannot use duplicate names.

Paradox displays an image showing a temporary table named Struct (see fig. 2.5). Each row in this table represents the definition of a field in the table you are creating. The first column in Struct displays numbers assigned in the order that you define the fields. The second column holds the name of each field, and the third column contains field types. The next several sections discuss how to assign field names and field types.

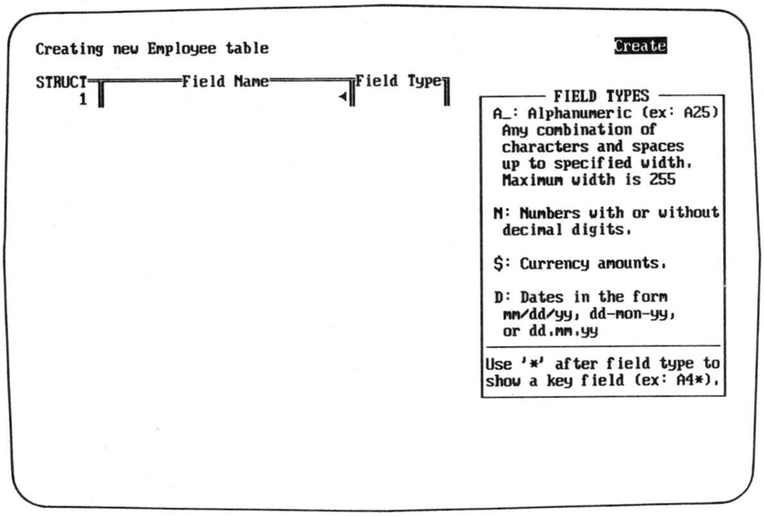
Creating new Employee table
Create
STRUCT
Field Name
Field Type
1
FIELD TYPES
A_: Alphanumeric (ex: A25)
Any combination of characters and spaces up to specified width. Maximum width is 255
N: Numbers with or without decimal digits.
$: Currency amounts.
D: Dates in the form mm/dd/yy, dd-mon-yy, or dd.mm.yy
Use '*' after field type to show a key field (ex: A4*).

Fig. 2.5.

The empty Struct table in Create mode.

Assigning Field Names

One of the more subtle aspects of database table definition is the assignment of field names. Planning is important in almost every step of database design, and the naming of fields is no exception. Follow these rules when you are deciding on field names:

1. You can use up to 25 characters.
2. You can use any printable character except the following:

   " [ ] { } ( )
   # (by itself)
   the combination ->

3. You can include spaces, but not as the first character in a field name.
4. You cannot use duplicate names in the same table.

Also consider the following guidelines:

1. Field names should describe field contents.
2. Always use the same field name for fields that will be used to link tables.
3. If a field's contents will be looked up from another table, use the same field name as the field name in the other table.
4. Don't use a field name in more than one table of a database unless the field is intended to link tables or to be looked up from a linked table. (Refer to this chapter's section on "Borrowing Structure" for a naming shortcut for this type of field.)

When you have decided on a field name, type it in the Field Name column in the Struct table. You can correct mistakes by using the Backspace key to erase the incorrect entry and then retyping it. Alternatively, you can use the field view described in Chapter 1 (press Alt-F5 or Ctrl-F) to edit an errant field name.

Press Enter after the field name is as you want it. Paradox then moves the cursor to the column labeled `Field Type` (see fig. 2.6).

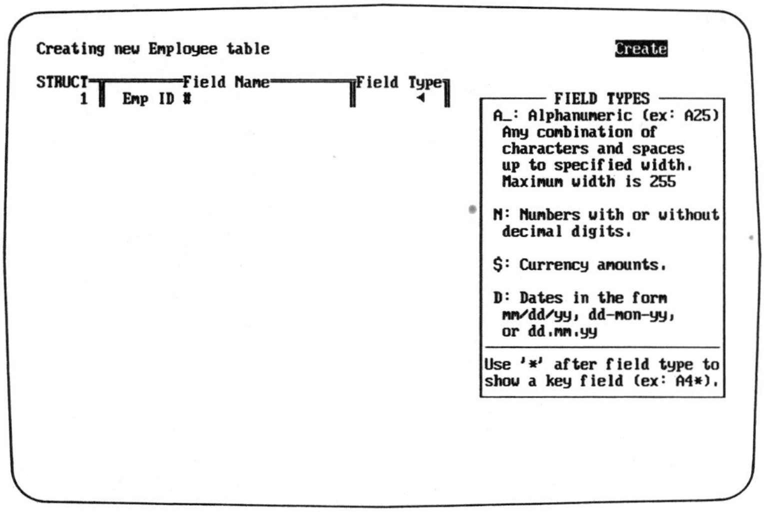
Creating new Employee table
Create
STRUCT Field Name Field Type
1 Emp ID #
FIELD TYPES
A_: Alphanumeric (ex: A25)
Any combination of
characters and spaces
up to specified width.
Maximum width is 255
N: Numbers with or without
decimal digits.
$: Currency amounts.
D: Dates in the form
mm/dd/yy, dd-mon-yy,
or dd.mm.yy
Use '*' after field type to
show a key field (ex: A4*).

Fig. 2.6.
Defining field type.

Assigning Field Type

Much like a spreadsheet, Paradox can do calculations with numeric data. But unlike a spreadsheet, the program cannot determine on its own whether you intend data to be numeric or text. The purpose of the Field Type column in the Struct table is to inform Paradox whether the data to be entered will be text, numeric, currency, or dates. For text (*alphanumeric*) fields, you must also specify the maximum length of the data.

If you are familiar with spreadsheets or other database programs, you may already be asking whether you can define field type even more specifically. For example, can you cause numbers to display only as integers (no decimal places)? Can you force dates to print in a particular format? The answer is yes, but not during the structure definition process. Refer to Chapters 8, 10, and 11 for discussions of customizing the way data is displayed or printed.

Paradox Field Types

Paradox makes defining field types a simple task. The field type choices include the following:

- ❑ *Alphanumeric:* To define a field as alphanumeric, press A followed by the number of spaces (from 1 to 255) you want to reserve for the longest data entry. For example, *A20* indicates an alphanumeric field with a maximum length of 20. Any combination of characters, numbers, and spaces is a valid alphanumeric entry. The following entries would all be valid in an alphanumeric field:

Every good boy
AB129878
#4&*00-123

- *Numeric:* Press N to define a field as numeric. Numeric data is any number with or without decimals. Paradox assigns the maximum length automatically. You can enter up to 15 significant digits (including decimal places). Numbers with more than 15 significant digits are rounded and stored in scientific notation. Numbers in numeric fields are normally displayed without commas and with only as many decimal places as are necessary to display the significant digits. Negative numbers are preceded by a negative sign. Refer to Chapters 3, 8, and 9 for information on changing the way numbers are displayed (formatted) on the screen in a table or form. The following are valid numeric entries:

  12345
  123.45
  .12345
  −12.345

- *Short number:* Press S to specify the short number field type. This field type, which is for use by advanced users who need to conserve disk storage, may contain only whole numbers (integers) in the range −32,767 to 32,767.

- *Currency:* Press $ to indicate a currency field. Paradox treats currency fields the same as numeric fields but displays currency data with commas and rounded to two decimal places. Negative numbers are displayed in parentheses. You do not type the dollar signs when entering currency data, but you can type the commas. All the following currency entries are valid:

  12345
  12,345
  12,345.67
  12345.678

  Paradox would display the last currency entry rounded to 12,345.68, but would still store and use in internal calculations the number 12345.678.

- *Date:* Press D to indicate a date field. Valid entries are any valid date between January 1, 100, and December 31, 9999, typed in the form mm/dd/yy, dd-mon-yy, or dd.mm.yy. If you ever enter dates that are not in the 20th century, be sure to include the full year. The following are valid date entries, all for the same date:

  3/09/78
  9-Mar-78
  9.03.78

  Eight other date formats are available for use in reports (see Chapters 10 and 11 for details on creating tabular and free-form reports).

As soon as you press Enter after indicating field type, Paradox drops the cursor to the next row in the Struct table so that you can define another field. Paradox can handle up to a maximum of 255 fields per table.

Field Type Guidelines

The following guidelines will help you decide how to assign field type:

1. Use the *date* type whenever each entry in the field will be a date. Don't be concerned at this point about how the date should be formatted for a report that you will need later. Paradox provides a total of 11 different date formats at the reporting stage.
2. Use the *currency* field type whenever you want commas displayed within numbers.
3. Always use *numeric* or *currency* field type when you may need to perform calculations with the data.
4. Assign the *alphanumeric* type for all fields that don't meet one of the previous guidelines.

These guidelines seem obvious, but falling into a trap is easy if you are not careful. For example, a five-digit ZIP code consists entirely of numbers, so you may be tempted to define a ZIP code field as numeric. This definition presents a problem, however, for ZIP codes that begin with a 0, because Paradox drops any leading 0 in numeric data. You should therefore define a ZIP code field as an alphanumeric field. This fact is more obvious with 9-digit ZIP codes because the hyphen, normally inserted between the fifth and sixth digits, cannot be entered in a numeric field.

Another trap laid at data entry time is the reverse of the problem just described. Alphanumeric fields containing numbers—such as ZIP codes—present a special problem if you intend to sort the records in the table by that field. Alphanumeric columns are sorted from left to right within the field, even if the data happens to be numbers. Therefore, the number 123 entered into an alphanumeric field is sorted before the number 21.

Avoid this problem by entering the same number of characters in this field in every record in the table. For example, you should enter *021* rather than *21*, because Paradox sorts 021 before 123.

Inserting and Deleting Fields

As you are building the table structure, you may decide that you don't like the order of the fields, or for some other reason decide that you need to delete a field definition or insert a new field between existing definitions.

To delete a field from the structure, simply press the Del key. Inserting a blank row for a field is just as easy: you press the Ins key.

Paradox normally displays a table's data in the order, from left to right, that the fields are listed in the structure. For your convenience then, you should define fields in the order you want them to appear on the screen. The only time field order matters to Paradox is when you are assigning *key fields*.

Assigning Key Fields

You may have noticed the last instruction on the Create mode screen shown in figures 2.5 and 2.6. That instruction states that you can use the asterisk (*) to indicate a *key field*.

What Is a Key Field?

Many database programs use the word *index* to describe the same concept, more or less, that Paradox calls a *key*. An index for a database table is analogous to the index of a book. For example, if you wanted to look up discussions about Query By Example in this book, you would turn to its index and look up "Query By Example" alphabetically. The book index would refer you to the appropriate pages. Much like a book's index, a Paradox table index keeps track of the data in the table, sorted in order alphabetically or numerically (according to field type). And just as a book index enables you to find information quickly on a particular subject, a database index speeds the computer's data search in a table.

Several aspects of Paradox key fields are unique. When you assign a single field as a key field, called a *single key*, it must be the first field in the definition (see fig. 2.7). In addition to creating an index on the values in the key field, Paradox does the following:

1. It prevents duplicate values in the key field.
2. It keeps the table sorted according to the values in the field.

In the sample table whose structure is being created in figure 2.7, Paradox will not allow the Emp ID # field to have duplicate values when you enter data. Paradox will also continually sort the records so that they are stored in order by the ID number. Finally, the program will create an index on the Emp ID # field that will speed up queries of the table.

One disadvantage of keying a table is that the maximum potential size of each record is reduced from 4000 bytes to 1350 bytes. Another problem is that data entry can be slowed somewhat while Paradox sorts the table and updates the index.

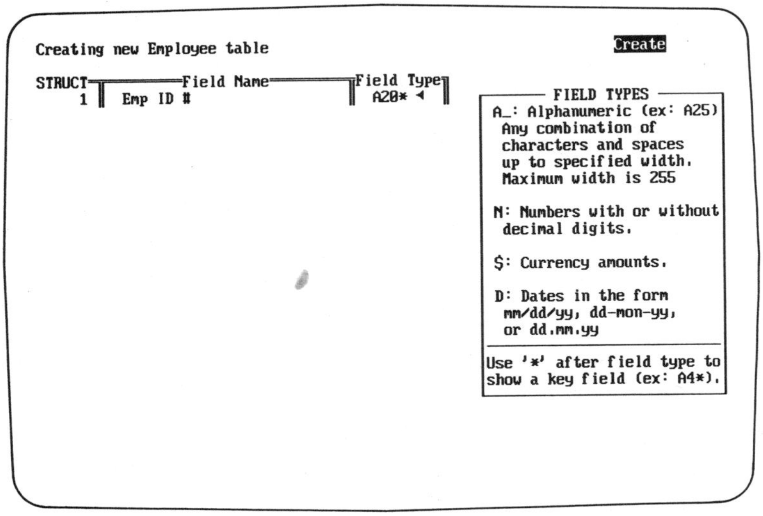
Creating new Employee table
Create
STRUCT
Field Name
Field Type
1
Emp ID #
A20*
FIELD TYPES
A_: Alphanumeric (ex: A25)
Any combination of
characters and spaces
up to specified width.
Maximum width is 255
N: Numbers with or without
decimal digits.
$: Currency amounts.
D: Dates in the form
mm/dd/yy, dd-mon-yy,
or dd.mm.yy
Use '*' after field type to
show a key field (ex: A4*).

Fig. 2.7.

Assigning a key field.

Using Multifield Keys

In some situations one field is not enough to prevent duplicate records. Figure 2.8 shows the Orders table and another table named Detail. The Detail table includes the model numbers and quantity of merchandise making up each of the orders in the master table, Orders. Because more than one model can be ordered under the same order number, the Detail table potentially contains multiple records with the same Order # entry. This field cannot be used as a *single key*. But, by adding (or concatenating) the Item # field to the key, you can create unique key values. For example, although three records in Detail have order numbers equal to 100, only one record has an order number of 100 *and* an item number of 1.

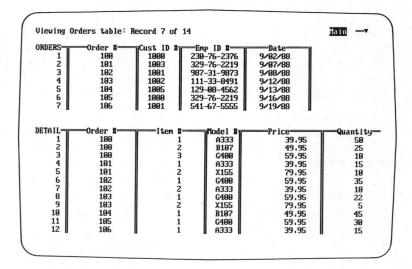

Fig. 2.8.

The Detail table requires a multifield key.

Viewing Orders table: Record 7 of 14 Main

ORDERS	Order #	Cust ID #	Emp ID #	Date
1	100	1000	230-76-2376	9/02/88
2	101	1003	329-76-2219	9/07/88
3	102	1001	987-31-9873	9/08/88
4	103	1002	111-33-8491	9/12/88
5	104	1005	129-08-4562	9/13/88
6	105	1000	329-76-2219	9/16/88
7	106	1001	541-67-5555	9/19/88

DETAIL	Order #	Item #	Model #	Price	Quantity
1	100	1	A333	39.95	50
2	100	2	B107	49.95	25
3	100	3	G400	59.95	10
4	101	1	A333	39.95	15
5	101	2	X155	79.95	10
6	102	1	G400	59.95	35
7	102	2	A333	39.95	10
8	103	1	G400	59.95	22
9	103	2	X155	79.95	5
10	104	1	B107	49.95	45
11	105	1	G400	59.95	30
12	106	1	A333	39.95	15

To create a *multifield* or *concatenated* key, place the asterisk (*) after the field type of each key field. All key fields must come before any non-key field in the definition. The first key field is called the *primary key*.

Once you create a multifield key, Paradox does the following:

1. It prevents the entry of records that duplicate the exact entry in all key fields of an existing record.

2. It keeps the table sorted first by the primary key field, then by the second key field in the definition, then by the third key field (if any), and so forth.

3. It creates a primary index on the concatenation of the key fields.

The definition of Detail is shown in figure 2.9. Notice that the Order # field and the Item # field are key and that they are the first two fields in the definition.

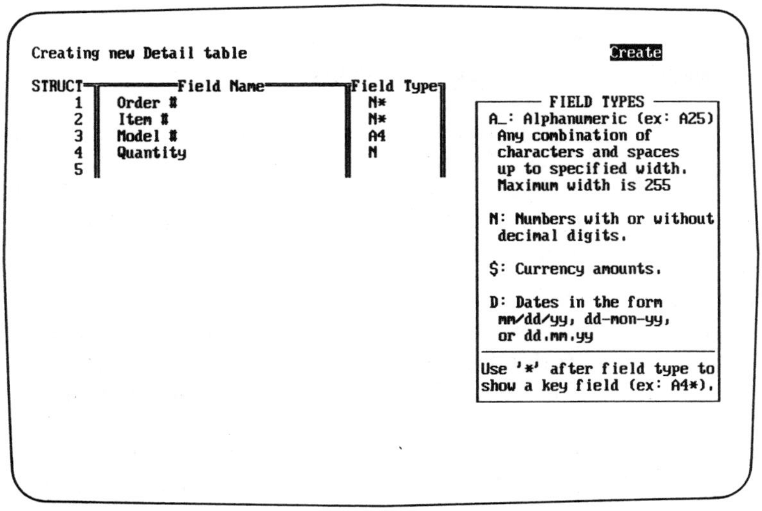
Creating new Detail table
Create
STRUCT Field Name Field Type
1 Order # N*
2 Item # N*
3 Model # A4
4 Quantity N
5
FIELD TYPES
A_: Alphanumeric (ex: A25)
Any combination of
characters and spaces
up to specified width.
Maximum width is 255
N: Numbers with or without
decimal digits.
$: Currency amounts.
D: Dates in the form
mm/dd/yy, dd-mon-yy,
or dd.mm.yy
Use '*' after field type to
show a key field (ex: A4*).

Fig. 2.9.

The definition of the Detail table.

When Should You Assign a Key?

Here are two closely related reasons for keying a field or fields:

- ❑ To prevent duplicate records
- ❑ To allow a field or fields to be used as a link between tables on the *one-side* of a *one-to-many* or *many-to-one* relationship

A cardinal rule of relational databases is that each record in every table should be unique. Whenever one field of a table is enough to determine the identity of a record, place that field first in the table definition and designate it the single key. As already discussed, some tables do not have a unique field. In those situations, you should use multifield keys to prevent duplicate records.

The second reason for keying a field is just a corollary of the first. It becomes important when you create multitable forms and reports. Because the *one-side* of a *one-to-many* or *many-to-one* relationship is by definition a table with unique records, you should key the linking field in the *one-side* table.

In the final analysis, every table should have at least one key field.

Borrowing Table Structure from Other Tables

This section describes how to *borrow* table structure (field definitions) from the definition of an existing table. The result is to give you fields in different tables with the same names and field types. Refer to the "Assigning Field Names" and "Assigning Field Type" discussions in this chapter to help you decide when you need to borrow table structure.

To borrow the table structure from another database, place the cursor in the Struct table at the position where the field definition(s) from the other table should start. Press F10 (Menu) to display the menu at the top of the screen and then select **B**orrow. Press Enter to see a list of available tables, and select the table from which you want to borrow. Paradox copies the field definitions from that table into Struct, beginning at the cursor position. For example, Figure 2.10 shows the result of using Borrow to copy the field definitions of the Orders table into the new structure of the Employee table.

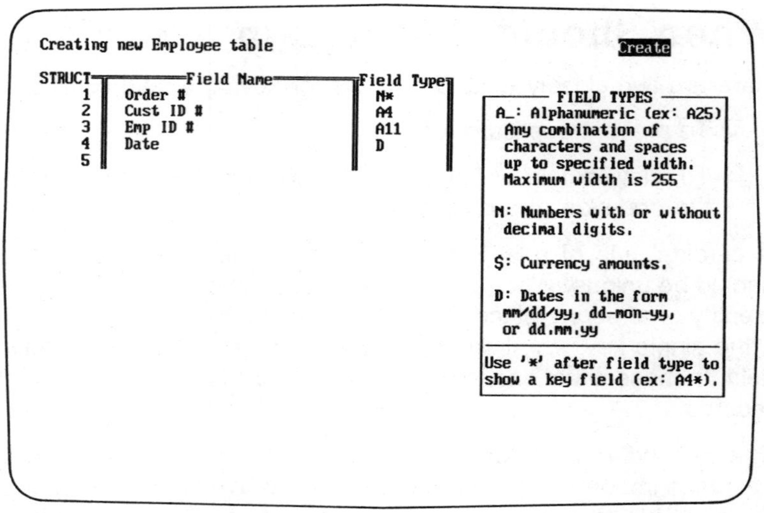
Creating new Employee table
Create
STRUCT
Field Name
Field Type
1 Order # N*
2 Cust ID # A4
3 Emp ID # A11
4 Date D
5
FIELD TYPES
A_: Alphanumeric (ex: A25)
Any combination of characters and spaces up to specified width. Maximum width is 255
N: Numbers with or without decimal digits.
$: Currency amounts.
D: Dates in the form mm/dd/yy, dd-mon-yy, or dd.mm.yy
Use '*' after field type to show a key field (ex: A4*).

Fig. 2.10.
Borrowing table structure.

Normally you do not need all the borrowed field definitions. The Employee table shown in figure 2.10 is going to be linked to the Orders table through the Emp ID # field. The definition of Orders was borrowed to ensure that this linking field is defined exactly the same way in both the Employee table and the Orders table. But the other fields from Orders (Cust ID # and Date) are irrelevant to Employee. Simply delete those unwanted field definitions. Place the cursor in the row to be deleted and press the Del key. The field definition vanishes.

Saving the Table Structure

As with most operations in Paradox, to complete the definition process and save the table structure, you press F2 (DO-IT!). Paradox returns to Main mode. The field definitions that had been listed in the Struct table are now stored as the definition of the new table. At this point, you are ready to begin entering data into the table. Whenever you define another table, Paradox clears the Struct table so that you can begin anew.

To abort the table definition process, without saving any of the table definition, press F10 (Menu) and then select **C**ancel.

Creating Tables on a Network

The major benefits of using Paradox on a network instead of most other PC-based database programs are summed up by two important properties: data integrity and data consistency.

Paradox automatically prevents potentially damaging conflicts between two or more users attempting to access the same data in the same table at the same time. Paradox also dynamically ensures that all users of a particular table are always provided the same correct version of the data, even if someone else is making changes to the table.

The program accomplishes these feats primarily through a system of progressively more restrictive locks automatically placed on shared Paradox objects. Here's a list of these locks, in order from most restrictive to least restrictive, and descriptions from the point of view of the user whose action caused the lock to be placed on a shared object:

Full lock	Totally prevents concurrent use by multiple users; the object can be used only by the current user.
Write lock	Other users have read-only access to the object; they can use the data but can neither change the data nor change the structure of the object.
Family lock	Same as write lock; it is automatically placed on an entire Paradox database family when it is being copied through the Tools menu.

Record lock	This write lock is placed on the individual record being edited.
Prevent write lock	Other users have complete access to the object but are prevented from placing either a full lock or a write lock on the object.
Prevent full lock	Other users have complete access to an object but are prevented from placing a full lock on the object.

Paradox automatically applies the lock or prevent lock that is least restrictive to concurrent use by multiple users that is consistent with the operation you are performing.

As you create a Paradox table on a multiuser network, Paradox places a full lock (the most restrictive lock available) on the table being created. No other user is allowed to create or rename a table with the same name until you are finished creating the table structure and have returned to the Main mode.

However, whenever you use the **B**orrow feature, Paradox places a prevent full lock on the table from which you are borrowing field definitions. This lock, the least restrictive type of lock or prevent lock, is effective only long enough to copy the definitions to the Struct table.

Modifying Table Structure

You will inevitably need to make some adjustment to the structure of one or more tables in your database. Programmers always say that a program is never truly finished, and you will find that your database is never exactly as you want it. You will always be able to think of improvements. This section of the chapter describes how to make changes to table structure by using the Restructure mode.

Enter the Restructure mode from the Main mode. From the Main menu select **M**odify **R**estructure and specify the name of the table whose structure needs to be changed. Paradox displays the existing definition with the word `Restructure` in the mode indicator (see fig. 2.11). The next several sections explain how to modify, insert, borrow, delete, and re-key field definitions as well as how to rearrange their order.

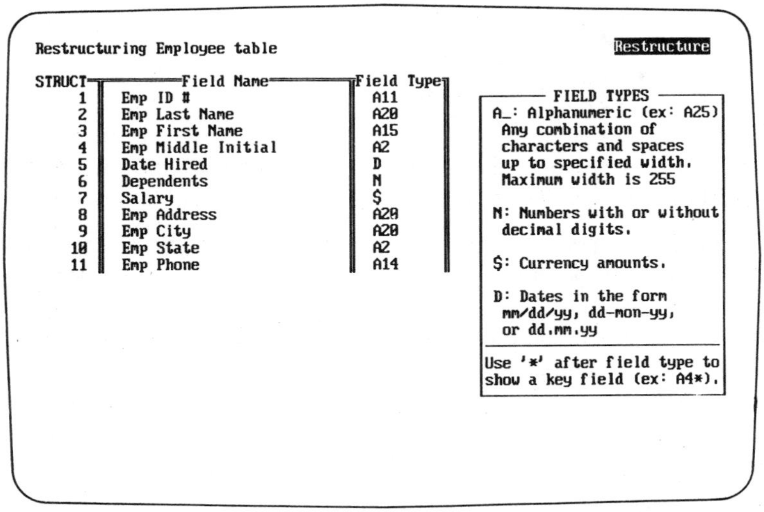

Fig. 2.11.

The Restructure mode.

Caution: As with any database program, restructuring a table is a potentially disastrous undertaking that can result in a loss of data. But Paradox does a good job of warning you when the program is about to discard previously entered information, and to a certain extent temporarily saves discarded information. Pay close attention to any messages displayed during the restructuring process.

You need to know that Paradox does not make a backup copy of your data before a restructure. For this reason, you should probably back up the data yourself. If the power fails, your data could be corrupted. Use the **C**opy command, discussed in Chapter 13, for this purpose.

Renaming a Field

Once the Struct table is displayed in the Restructure mode, the steps for modifying a field definition are the same as editing a definition during original creation. To change a field name, use the Backspace key to erase the current name, and type the correction. Alternatively, press Alt-F5 (Field View) and edit the name. Changing the name of a field has no effect on data already stored in the table.

Reassigning Field Type

Changing a field's type or length is just as easy as changing the field's name, but can drastically affect previously entered data. To change field type, use the Backspace key or the field view to edit the current entry in the Field Type column of the Struct table. Table 2.2 summarizes the effects of changes in field type on existing data.

Whenever existing data is not consistent with the new definition, Paradox does not transfer the data to the newly defined table. Unlike many lesser database programs, however, Paradox does not altogether abandon the problem data (with one significant exception explained in the "Changing Field Length" section). Instead, the program places offending records in a temporary table called Problems. You can later edit the data and add it back to the table, or rename the Problems table so that it is permanently saved.

Table 2.2
The Effects of Reassigning Field Type

Old Field Type	*New Field Type*	*Effect on Existing Data*
Any type	A	None, if the new length is sufficient to handle existing data
N, $, or S	N, $, or S	None, unless an N field is converted to an S field and the data is not an integer or is outside the range −32,767 to 32,767
A	N, $, or S	None for numeric entries; any entry containing non-numeric data is placed in Problems table
D	N, $, or S	All records placed in Problems table
A	D	None for records containing a properly entered date value (mm/dd/yy, dd-mon-yy, or dd.mm.yy); records containing non-date values placed in Problems
N, $, or S	D	All records placed in Problems table

Caution: All temporary tables in Paradox are just that—temporary. For example, the Problems table that is created when you redefine the Employee table is replaced if problems arise later in redefining some other table in the database. If you are going to edit and use the discarded data or want to rename the table to save it, you must do so before Paradox replaces it. (See this chapter's section on "Renaming Tables.")

Changing Field Length

Only alphanumeric field definitions explicitly include field length. When using the Restructure mode, you can freely increase the length of a field without being concerned about data loss. Shortening field length, however, can be hazardous to your data.

Paradox warns you about possible data loss when you attempt to save the new definition. As soon as you press F2 (DO-IT!), the program displays this message at the bottom of the screen:

```
Possible data loss for Xyz field
```

where `Xyz` is the field name. Paradox also displays at the top of the screen the menu shown in figure 2.12.

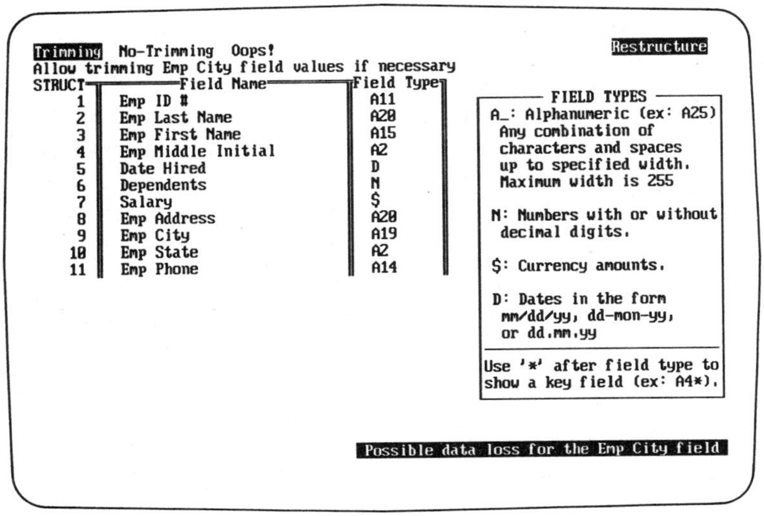

Fig. 2.12.

Confirming reduction of field length.

To truncate all information beyond the new length, choose **T**rimming from the menu.

Caution: In this situation, offending data is not placed in the Problems table but is *gone forever*. Choose this option only when you are *sure* that the data is shorter than the new length, or when you intend for the data to be erased.

If you are not sure whether the data in any record might be too long, or for some other reason you don't want any information trimmed away permanently, choose **N**o-Trimming. Paradox places any offending records in Problems.

The last menu choice, **O**ops!, places you back in Restructure mode so that you can increase the length of the field again.

These same messages and choices are displayed when you convert a numeric field or currency field to a small number field.

Inserting and Borrowing Field Definitions

When you need to add another field to a table, position the cursor at the row where you want to place the new field and press Ins. Paradox inserts a blank row in the Struct table, pushing the existing rows down one row. For example, suppose that you forgot to define a ZIP code field for the employee table shown in figures 2.11 and 2.12, and want to insert that field just after the Emp State field. You should first position the cursor in row 11, the Emp Phone field, because this spot is where you want the new field. Then press the Ins key. Paradox inserts a blank row 11 and pushes the Emp Phone field down to row 12, as shown in figure 2.13.

Now you can define the field as usual (see fig. 2.14). The **B**orrow feature works in the same manner in the Restructure mode as it does in the Create mode.

After you finish redefining the table, you can add data to the newly defined field(s) of existing records through the Edit mode. (For more information, refer to Chapter 3, "Using Paradox To Enter, Edit, and View Data.")

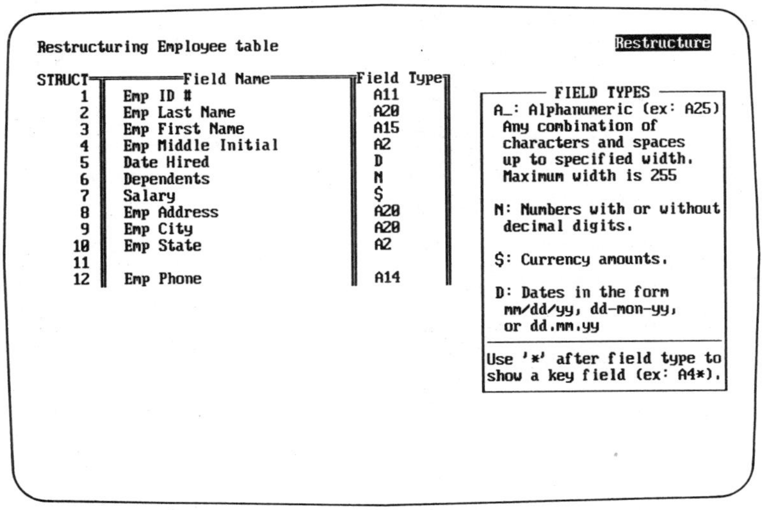

Fig. 2.13.

Inserting a field.

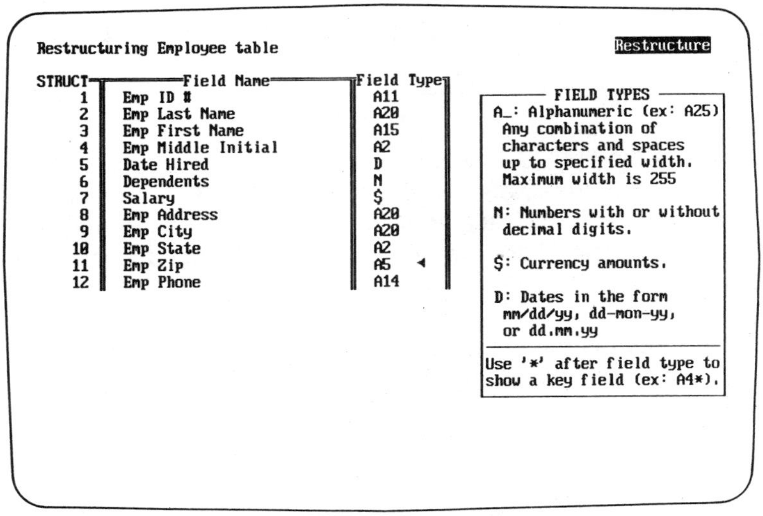

Fig. 2.14.

The newly inserted field.

Deleting a Field

Occasionally, you may decide that you don't need to collect the data for a particular field, or that you should have placed a certain field in another table. Once you are in Restructure mode, simply place the cursor in the offending row and press Del. The row containing the field's definitions is deleted from Struct. When you finish redefining the table, Paradox warns you that data is about to be lost. For example, figure 2.15 shows the message and menu Paradox displays if you attempt to delete the Dependents field from the Employee table.

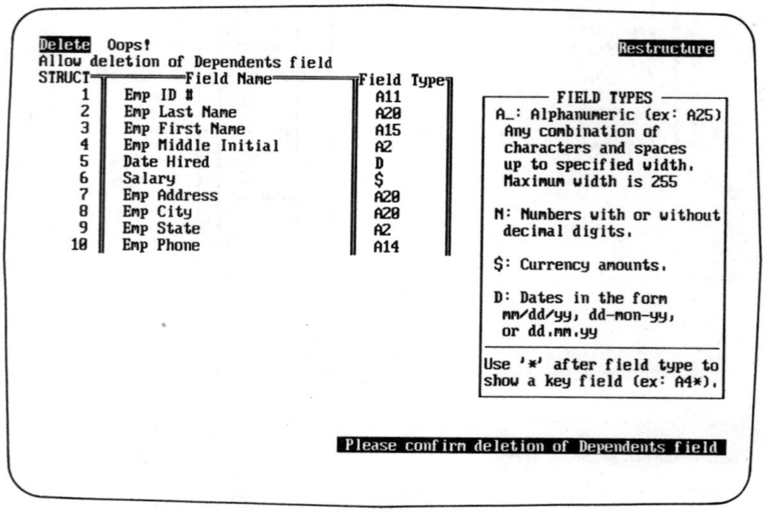

Fig. 2.15.

Confirming deletion of a field.

To confirm deletion of the field, select **D**elete. Otherwise, if you don't want to delete the field, select **O**ops!, and (to undo the potential for data loss) either reenter the definition of the deleted field, exactly as it was, or cancel Restructure mode by pressing F10 (Menu) and then selecting **C**ancel.

Caution: Deleted data is *not* placed in a temporary table. When you confirm field deletion, you irrevocably abandon the data of the deleted field.

Reassigning Keys

To change a non-key field to a key field, add an asterisk (*) to the field type. Conversely, removing the asterisk from the field type removes the key. In either case, you may have to rearrange the rows in Struct somewhat to ensure that the primary key is first and that all subordinate keys follow. Rearranging fields is discussed in the next section.

Changing keys can also create *key violations*, in which a record contains a value in the new key field that already occurs in the table—a duplicate.

Remember that key fields cannot contain duplicates. If this problem occurs, Paradox places the violating records into a temporary table called *Keyviol*. You can then either edit the records to eliminate the duplication, if appropriate, or rename Keyviol and thus save the offending data as another table.

Rearranging Fields

Normally, the order of the fields in table structure doesn't matter. But because of the way you define key fields in Paradox, you will probably have to rearrange field order when you change a table key. Paradox handles this situation in a simple but elegant way.

Assume that you have defined the Customer table as shown in figure 2.16, with Company Name as the single key. Later you decide that you should have assigned Cust ID # as the key.

You first remove the asterisk from the Field Type column of Company Name. Next you must rearrange the rows so that Cust ID # is first. With the cursor in the first row, press Ins to insert a blank row 1. Then type *Cust ID #* in the Field Name column of that row, and press Enter. Paradox recognizes that you already have a field by that name and thus moves the Cust ID # definition up to row 1 (see fig. 2.17). Your last step is to add the asterisk to the field type of Cust ID #, as the single key field. Follow this procedure any time you want to rearrange the order of the fields in a table structure.

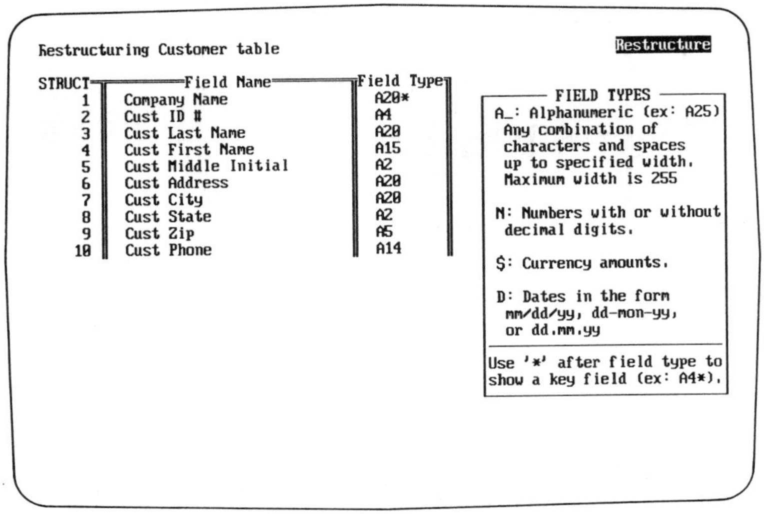

Fig. 2.16.

The original order.

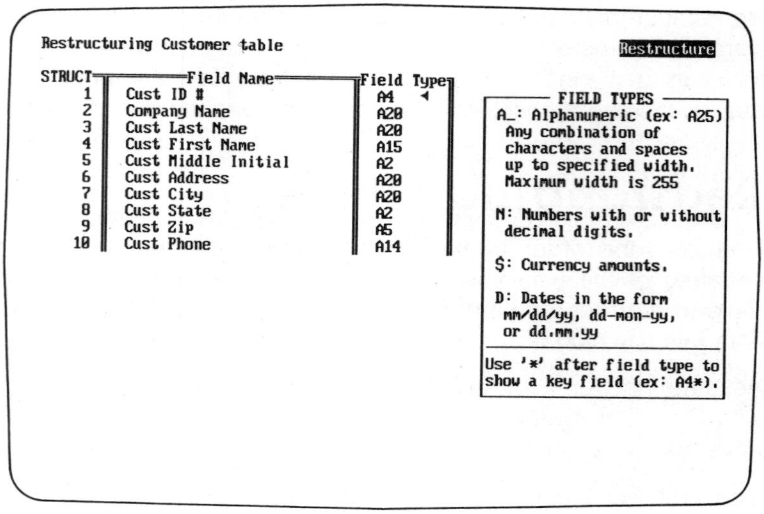

Fig. 2.17.

The new order.

Modifying Table Structure on a Network

While you modify the structure of a shared table on a multiuser network, Paradox automatically places a full lock on the table and all members of its family. Conversely, Paradox does not allow you to restructure a table while another network user is performing any operation with the shared table or any of its family members.

Saving Your Changes

When you have made all the necessary changes, press F2 (DO-IT!) to let Paradox know you are finished. Paradox then saves the new definition and rebuilds the table. Whenever you alter a table's structure, Paradox automatically makes corresponding adjustments to the entire family of objects associated with the table, including forms, reports, indexes, image settings, and validity check files.

Renaming Tables

For any number of reasons, you might want to change the name of a table. Because a table name cannot be used more than once in a DOS directory, for instance, you may want to change a table name so that you can use the original name for another table. Perhaps the nature of the data has changed, and the current name doesn't reflect the contents of the table. Or maybe for no particular reason you just don't like the current table name. Whatever the reason, you need a method of changing the table name, and Paradox provides one.

To change the name of a table, start at the Main menu and select **T**ools **R**ename **T**able. Type the table name you want to change, or press Enter to see the list of tables and then choose the appropriate table from the list. Remember that to choose from the list, you can either press the first letter of the table's name, or move the highlight to the table name and then press Enter. Paradox instructs you to enter a new name for the table. As usual, the table name must follow the rules listed in the section "Defining Table Structure." When you have finished typing the name, press Enter. Paradox renames the table and the other family members.

Understanding Temporary Tables

True to its relational origins, Paradox creates temporary tables in response to almost any situation. This chapter has already discussed the Struct table, the Problems table, and the Keyviol table, all of which are temporary. Paradox 3.0 creates a total of 12 different temporary tables:

Answer
Changed
Crosstab
Deleted
Entry
Family
Inserted
Keyviol
List
Password
Problems
Struct

(Paradox 2.0 creates only 11 temporary tables. Crosstab is new with Version 3.0.) As implied by their collective name, temporary tables are short-lived. Three events can cause a temporary table to be wiped clean:

1. The table is overwritten by a newer temporary table of the same type.
2. You use the Tools menu to change the working directory.
3. You end the current Paradox session (by selecting **E**xit).

Perhaps one of the most important uses for the renaming feature is to make permanent one of these temporary tables. To have Paradox permanently save the contents of a temporary table, just change its name to any valid table name (except one of the other 11 temporary table names, of course). For example, the Problems table may contain data that was discarded during table restructuring. To save the discarded data in Problems, you must give the table a new name before the program clears out the data. After you rename the table, Paradox treats the data in that table just as it does other nontemporary tables.

Adding Password Protection and Claiming Table Ownership on a Network

Paradox includes impressive password protection capability. When you create a table on a network it is particularly important that you protect your data against unauthorized access. The Paradox Protect option on the Tools/Move menu even enables you to permit some users full access to a table while limiting others to more restricted access. For example, you might want to allow all employees to view the table that includes their personal and salary information, but permit only the personnel department to make changes to the data. In a similar way Paradox also enables you to control access to reports and forms.

In order to guarantee that you will have control over granting of access to a table you have created, and to its family of objects, you should assign a password to a table as soon as you create it. This is important when the table is in a shared directory accessible by other users on a network. The first network user to place a password on a table effectively becomes the table's *owner*, and has the capability of locking all other users out, including *you*!

Refer to Chapter 13 for a complete description of how to use the Paradox protection features.

Chapter Summary

After completing this second chapter of the book, you are well on your way to becoming a Paradox pro, as promised. You are now armed with a fundamental understanding of database design in general, and detailed knowledge of Paradox table creation in particular. You are ready to move on to Chapter 3 and learn how to enter and edit Paradox data.

3

Using Paradox To Enter, Edit, and View Data

Data entry and retrieval are the primary missions of any database management system. This chapter shows you several methods of entering, editing, and viewing data with Paradox tables, and Chapter 4 introduces you to the fantastic Query By Example (QBE) data-retrieval method. Both chapters build on the foundation of Chapters 1 and 2, so you should be familiar with basic Paradox terminology and know how to create a database of Paradox tables before you begin this chapter.

Paradox is considered a "high-end" database program, despite its ease of learning and use, because of the program's abundance of powerful features. This chapter does not introduce you all at once to every data-entry and editing tool that Paradox has to offer, but gives you the basic tools necessary to get up and running. When you feel comfortable with the fundamentals presented here, turn to Chapter 8, "Designing and Using Paradox Forms," and Chapter 9, "Using Paradox Power Entry and Editing Features," to discover the most potent entry and editing capabilities of Paradox.

Enjoying the View

As explained in the "Understanding Paradox Views and Images" section of Chapter 1, Paradox presents data on the screen in one of two views. The *table view* is the familiar display of the data as a series of horizontal rows (see fig. 3.1). This view is the default view in which Paradox automatically starts. At any time, you can switch to the *form view* by pressing F7 (Form Toggle). Paradox then changes the screen to a vertical single record depiction of the same table.

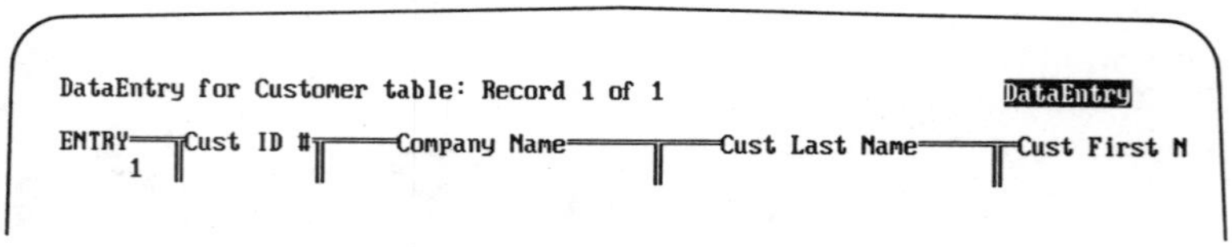

Fig. 3.1.

The table view.

Paradox automatically designs a *standard form* (form F) the first time you press F7 for a particular table. Figure 3.2 shows the standard form for a table named Customer. But you also have the option of custom designing as many as 14 additional forms per table. These custom forms are added to the table's family and are available for use any time you enter, edit, or view data from the table. Creating and using these custom forms is covered in detail in Chapter 8 of this book.

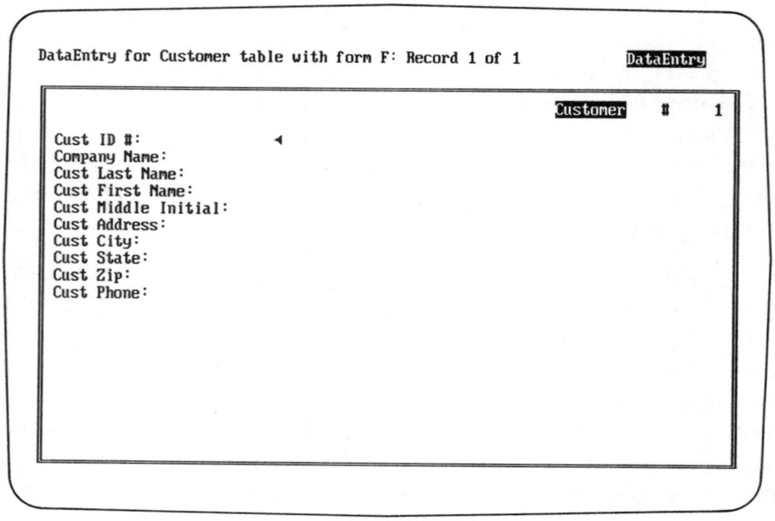

Fig. 3.2.

The standard form view.

Whichever view you use, Paradox also provides a wide variety of features that can help you ensure that data is entered or edited correctly in table fields. Some features even enter data for you, either as default data or data looked up from another table. These data entry/edit aids are collectively referred to as *validity checks* and can be created for use in all the dataentry and editing modes. Refer to Chapter 9 for a full discussion of these powerful features. For purposes of this chapter, assume that you are using either the standard table view or the standard form view with no validity checks, unless specifically stated otherwise.

Paradox is an amazingly flexible database program. In addition to providing two views, it enables you to enter data into database tables from three different modes—DataEntry, Edit, and CoEdit—and to edit data from the Edit and CoEdit modes. All these entry/edit options are introduced in this chapter.

Entering Data in DataEntry Mode

Of the three available modes for entering data, the DataEntry mode is the only one designed exclusively for that purpose. For this reason, Paradox does not display existing records in DataEntry mode. The data already stored on disk is thus protected from being accidentally changed.

To begin a DataEntry session, select **M**odify **D**ataEntry from the Main menu. Specify the table to which the data should be added (the *target* table). Paradox displays an empty temporary table named *Entry*, which has the same structure as the target table (see fig. 3.1). A status message at the top of the screen states that you are working on `Record 1 of 1`. A pointer (a left-pointing triangle) indicates the current field into which you are about to enter data. (If you want to switch to the form view, press F7.)

Entering data in either table view or form view is as simple as typing your entry on the screen. Use the cursor-movement keys to move between fields and records. If you need to refresh your memory about how these keys operate in the table and form views, refer to tables 1.3 and 1.4 in Chapter 1.

You can use the Backspace key to erase your mistakes, one character at a time. The Ctrl-Backspace key combination deletes an entire field entry. You can also use the *field view* (by pressing Alt-F5 or Ctrl-F) to edit errant entries while in DataEntry mode (see fig. 3.3).

To delete an entire record from the Entry table, place the cursor in the unwanted row and press the Del key.

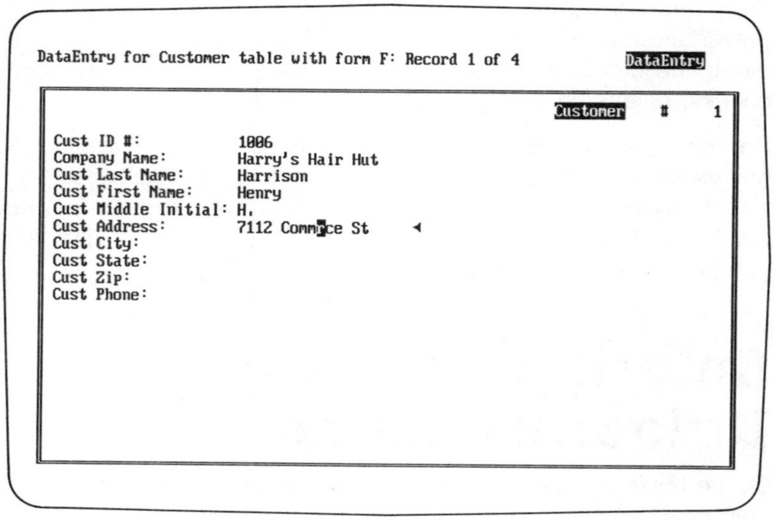

Fig. 3.3.

Using the field view.

As you enter data on the screen, Paradox is holding it in RAM (random-access memory), which is volatile—subject to loss if the power is interrupted before the data is saved to disk. Paradox by default activates an outstanding *autosave* feature that periodically saves your data to disk as you work. You may notice your disk drive light momentarily coming on during your data-entry session. If you ever lose power during data entry, the Entry table in which you were working will be safe in your working directory until you can restart your computer and return to Paradox. But be careful not to use the DataEntry mode again until you have copied the contents of Entry into the original target table. Use the **A**dd command on the Tools/More menu.

Saving or Abandoning the Entered Data

As you enter data, it is not going directly into the target table but is being added to the Entry table. The records in figure 3.4, for example, are displayed in the Entry table and have not yet been added to Customer. When you are satisfied that the record or records are correct, press F2 (DO-IT!). Paradox then saves the data to disk, adding the records to the target table. The program displays the message `Adding records from Entry to Cus-`

`tomer...` and returns you to Main mode with the Customer table as the current image, new records included.

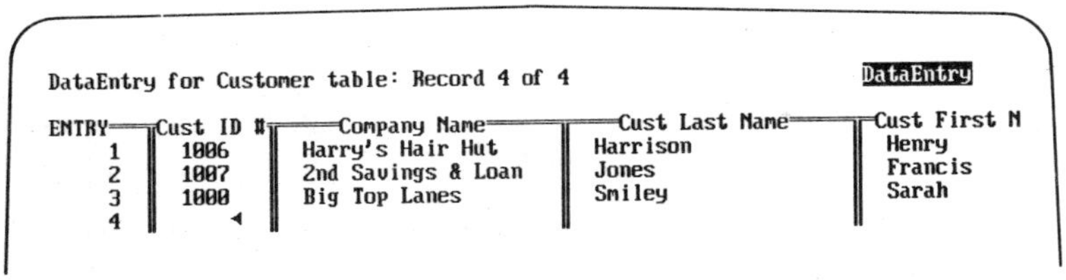

DataEntry for Customer table: Record 4 of 4
DataEntry
ENTRY Cust ID # Company Name Cust Last Name Cust First N
1 1006 Harry's Hair Hut Harrison Henry
2 1007 2nd Savings & Loan Jones Francis
3 1008 Big Top Lanes Smiley Sarah
4

Fig. 3.4.

Entering data in DataEntry mode.

On the other hand, you may decide that the data should not be added to the target table. In that case, press F10 (Menu) and then select **C**ancel **Y**es to cancel the data-entry session. Paradox abandons any information you entered into the Entry table, and returns to the Main mode and the work space, just as it was before you entered DataEntry mode.

Using Undo in DataEntry Mode

Paradox recognizes that nobody is perfect. The program has built in a life-saving *undo* feature. As you enter data, Paradox keeps track of your keystrokes in a *transaction log*. The Paradox undo feature enables you to undo one transaction at a time, starting with the most recent one, all the way back to the beginning of the current DataEntry session.

A transaction is defined by its beginning and end points in time. The *transaction beginning point* is the moment you move the cursor into a new or existing field. The *transaction end point* is the moment you leave the record or delete it. The transaction thus consists of any data entry or changes made to data in the Entry table that occurs between these two points in time.

Suppose that during data entry you realize that the first entry in the table shown in figure 3.4 is incorrect. The Company Name should be "Henry's Hair Hut" rather than "Harry's Hair Hut." But, in attempting to edit the Company Name field, you mistakenly press the Del key before accessing field view, and you erase the entire record (see fig. 3.5).

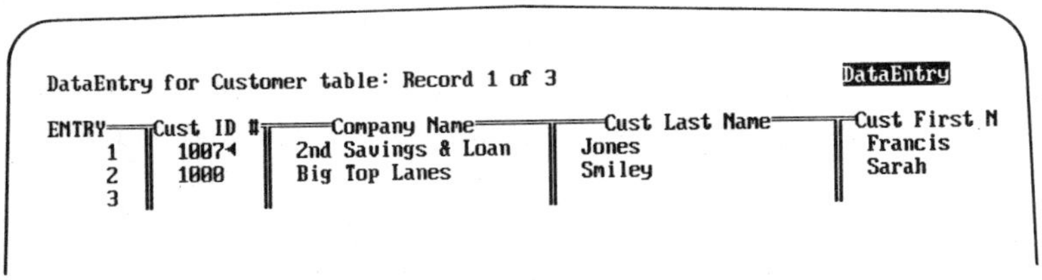

DataEntry for Customer table: Record 1 of 3
DataEntry
ENTRY Cust ID # Company Name Cust Last Name Cust First N
1 1007 2nd Savings & Loan Jones Francis
2 1008 Big Top Lanes Smiley Sarah
3

Fig. 3.5.

Accidentally deleting a record.

Of course, you could retype the entire record. To conserve your energy, however, simply press the Undo keystroke command: Ctrl-U. Paradox quickly reinstates the missing record to the Entry table and displays a message that the record was reinserted (see fig. 3.6).

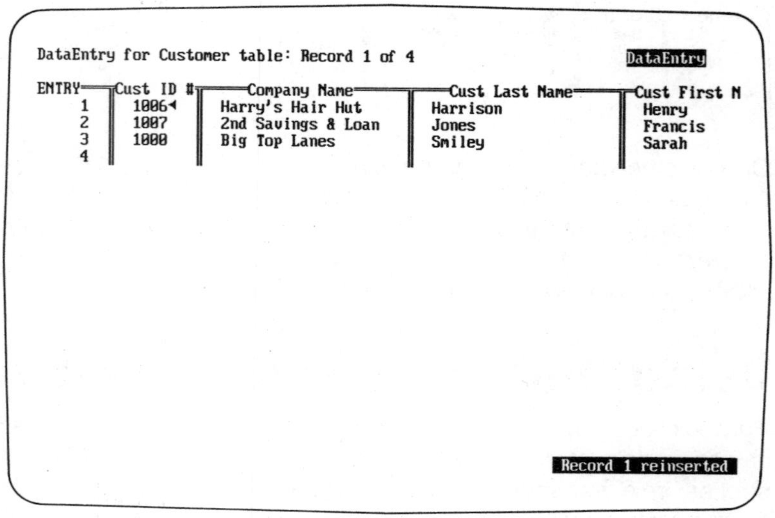

Fig. 3.6.
Using Undo to restore the deleted record.

Even though Paradox automatically saves your work to disk periodically (see the preceding tip), the program's documentation recommends that you also routinely clear the screen by pressing F2 (DO-IT!), explicitly instructing Paradox to save the new data. This step further ensures that you do not lose any data in a power failure. The drawback to following this advice is that F2 clears the undo transaction log and returns you to the work space. You cannot undo a mistake that occurred before you pressed F2.

Using Ditto in DataEntry Mode

Another labor-saving feature is Ctrl-D, the Ditto keystroke command. When you place the cursor in a blank field and press Ctrl-D, Paradox inserts into that field the entire contents of the same field from the preceding record. This feature works only for second and subsequent records in the Entry table.

Finding a Record with Zoom

When you are entering many records and want to take a look at a particular one in the Entry table, you can use the Zoom option to help you find the record. Refer to "Finding a Record with Zoom and Zoom Next" later in this chapter.

Working with the DataEntry Menu

Pressing F10 (Menu) in DataEntry mode displays the menu shown in figure 3.7.

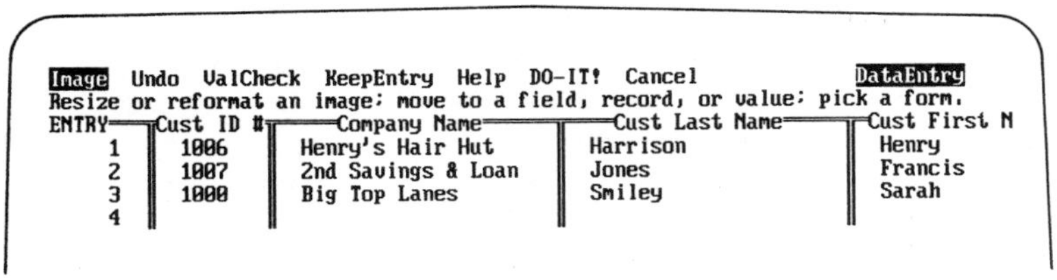

Image Undo ValCheck KeepEntry Help DO-IT! Cancel
DataEntry
Resize or reformat an image; move to a field, record, or value; pick a form.
ENTRY Cust ID # Company Name Cust Last Name Cust First N
1 1006 Henry's Hair Hut Harrison Henry
2 1007 2nd Savings & Loan Jones Francis
3 1008 Big Top Lanes Smiley Sarah
4

Fig. 3.7.

The DataEntry menu.

Here are brief summaries of the options that are included on the DataEntry menu:

Image — The first menu option, **I**mage, provides access to Paradox image-customization features. These features work in the same manner in any mode, so refer to this chapter's subsequent section on "Using the Image Options."

Undo — This menu choice has the same effect as Ctrl-U (Undo).

ValCheck — Validity checks are one of the most useful features of Paradox, both in preventing entry of invalid data and in helping you enter data by providing default values and automatic lookup from other tables. This option is one of the "power" features covered in Chapter 9, "Using Paradox Power Entry and Editing Features."

KeepEntry — This option temporarily saves the current Entry table to disk and ends the data-entry session. Refer to the "Using DataEntry Mode on a Network" section of this chapter for more discussion of the **K**eepEntry option.

Help — This menu selection has the same effect as the F1 (Help) key, discussed in Chapter 1.

DO-IT! — This option is equivalent to the F2 (DO-IT!) key.

Cancel — This option cancels data entry, discards all data entered during the session, and returns to the Main mode work space, as you left it before starting data entry.

Handling Keys and Key Violations in DataEntry Mode

Chapter 2 introduced you to the concept of *key fields*. The two primary effects of a key field or fields are to keep the records in a particular order and to prevent duplicates, often called key violations. During DataEntry mode, Paradox does not continuously monitor the key field(s) for either purpose. Instead, the program waits until you press F2 (DO-IT!) and then compares the new records with existing records.

Paradox stores the new records in their proper key order and looks for duplicates in the key field(s). Any duplicate records—records with a match in all key fields—are not added to the target table but are placed in the temporary table named Keyviol. Paradox displays the target table as an image in the Main mode work space and displays Keyviol, if duplicates were found, just below the target table. In the example shown in figure 3.8, the number *1000* was inadvertently reused in Cust ID #, a single key field. Paradox prevents this record from being added to Customer, placing the problem entry in the Keyviol table.

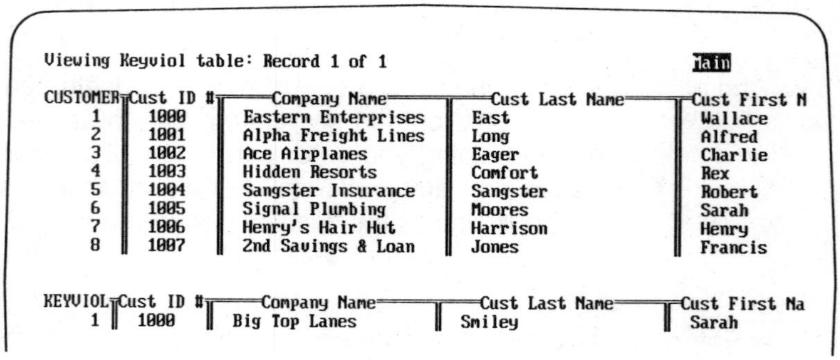

Viewing Keyviol table: Record 1 of 1 Main

CUSTOMER	Cust ID #	Company Name	Cust Last Name	Cust First N
1	1000	Eastern Enterprises	East	Wallace
2	1001	Alpha Freight Lines	Long	Alfred
3	1002	Ace Airplanes	Eager	Charlie
4	1003	Hidden Resorts	Comfort	Rex
5	1004	Sangster Insurance	Sangster	Robert
6	1005	Signal Plumbing	Moores	Sarah
7	1006	Henry's Hair Hut	Harrison	Henry
8	1007	2nd Savings & Loan	Jones	Francis

KEYVIOL	Cust ID #	Company Name	Cust Last Name	Cust First Na
1	1000	Big Top Lanes	Smiley	Sarah

Fig. 3.8.

Handling key violations in DataEntry mode.

To add records from Keyviol to the target table, first edit the offending entry and then add the corrected record to the target table. For example, to edit the violating record shown in figure 3.8, press F9 (Edit), change the

Cust ID # to *1008*, and press F2 (DO-IT!). To add the record to the Customer table, press F10 (Menu) and select **T**ools **M**ore **A**dd. Specify that Keyviol is the *source table* and that Customer is the *target table*. (The **A**dd command is discussed fully in Chapter 13.) For keyed target tables (target tables with one or more key fields), Paradox displays a submenu with the choices **N**ewEntries and **U**pdate. Select **N**ewEntries to instruct Paradox to insert the record into Customer. Paradox displays the message `Adding records from Keyviol to Customer` and then the screen shown in figure 3.9.

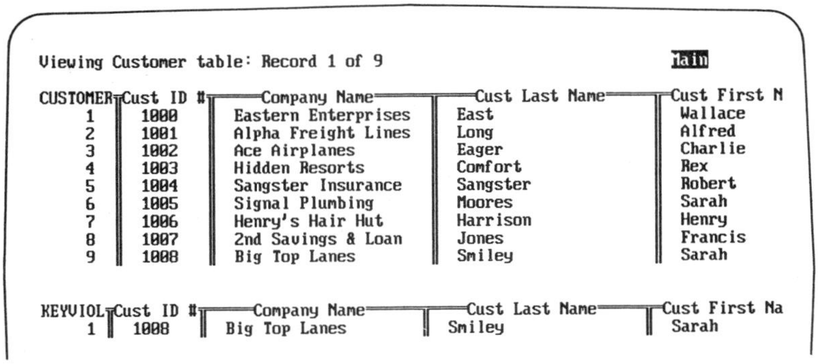

Fig. 3.9.

Adding the corrected entry to Customer.

The method Paradox uses to prevent key violations differs drastically among modes. Understanding the methods used in each of the three modes is essential.

Using DataEntry Mode on a Network

When you select the **D**ataEntry option on a network, Paradox places a *prevent full lock* on the table. In other words, no other network user can set a lock that requires exclusive use of the database. All other users have full access to the table. If a full lock is already in place on the shared table, Paradox does not let you begin a DataEntry session until the other user finishes the operation that required a full lock.

As soon as you attempt to complete your data-entry session by pressing F2 (DO-IT!), Paradox places a *prevent write lock* on the target table. No other user can write to the table until your Entry table records have been added. You may get a message, however, that the file is locked. This message indicates that another user is performing some operation with the shared table that placed a *write lock* on the file. You either have to wait until the other user is finished, or use the **K**eepEntry option on the DataEntry menu. KeepEntry temporarily saves the current Entry table to disk and ends the data-entry session, returning you to the Main mode work space. No changes are made to the target table. You can later use the **A**dd option to add the records from Entry to the shared target file.

To terminate a data-entry session with **K**eepEntry, first display the menu by pressing F10 (Menu) and then select **K**eepEntry. Paradox informs you that it is `Saving Entry table....` The Entry table remains as the current image, but in Main mode rather than DataEntry mode. Once the other user has unlocked the target table, you can add the records from Entry. To do so, select **T**ools **M**ore **A**dd from the Main menu. Specify *Entry* as the source table, and the shared table as the target. Paradox displays a message telling you that the program is adding records from Entry to the target table, and then displays the target table with new records added. If the target table is a keyed table, Paradox displays a submenu with the choices **N**ewEntries and **U**pdate. Select **N**ewEntries.

Caution: Make a practice of immediately renaming the Entry table whenever you use the **K**eepEntry command. The Entry table is one of several temporary tables created by Paradox, so this table is never a secure home for your data. Either a subsequent DataEntry session or the Paradox **E**xit command will wipe the Entry table clean. All data saved by **K**eepEntry will be gone. Changing the name of the table, however, completely protects the data from these disasters.

To rename the Entry table, start from the Main menu and select **T**ools **R**ename **T**able. Specify *Entry* as the current name of the table, type a new table name, and press Enter. When you later use the **A**dd command to place the data in the target table on the network, remember to use the new name as the source file.

Entering and Editing Data in Edit Mode

In *Edit* mode, Paradox displays existing data and permits you to change it. Making changes to your data is the primary purpose for the mode, but you can also use it to enter new data.

You have two ways to begin Edit mode: through the Main menu or with the F9 (Edit) key. The method you use depends on whether the table you want to edit is already in the work space. If the subject table is not currently displayed as an image in the work space, you must use the menu method. From the Paradox Main menu, select **M**odify **E**dit and indicate the table to be edited. Often, however, the table you want to edit is already an image in the Main mode work space. You could use the Modify menu to start Edit mode, but a much easier way is to press F9 (Edit). Paradox almost imperceptibly changes the mode from Main to Edit, and you are ready to make alterations or additions.

All tables with images in the work space are placed into Edit mode together, but you can make changes only to the current table. (Query forms, discussed in Chapter 4, cannot be edited during Edit mode.) You can press F3 (Up Image) or F4 (Down Image) before or after entering Edit mode until the status message at the top of the screen informs you that the table you want to edit is current, and then you can make changes (see figs. 3.10 and 3.11).

Paradox displays the existing records of the table in the current image in Edit mode, starting with record number 1. If the table is keyed, the records are in order by the key field(s). Paradox removes multiple images of any table from the screen to prevent inconsistent versions of the same table.

Viewing Employee table: Record 1 of 8 Main ▲

EMPLOYEE	Emp ID #	Emp Last Name	Emp First Name	Emp Middle In
1	111-33-8491	Jones	Harry	H
2	129-08-4562	Jones	Samantha	T.
3	230-76-2376	Bronson	Tim	C.
4	329-76-2219	Albertson	Sharon	B.
5	448-09-6721	Green	George	H.
6	541-67-5555	Kellogs	Emily	Q.
7	921-65-1234	English	Gertrude	M.
8	987-31-9873	Quick	Joseph	L

CUSTOMER	Cust ID #	Company Name	Cust Last Name	Cust First N
1	1000	Eastern Enterprises	East	Wallace
2	1001	Alpha Freight Lines	Long	Alfred
3	1002	Ace Airplanes	Eager	Charlie
4	1003	Hidden Resorts	Comfort	Rex
5	1004	Sangster Insurance	Sangster	Robert
6	1005	Signal Plumbing	Moores	Sarah
7	1006	Henry's Hair Hut	Harrison	Henry
8	1007	2nd Savings & Loan	Jones	Francis
9	1008	Big Top Lanes	Smiley	Sarah

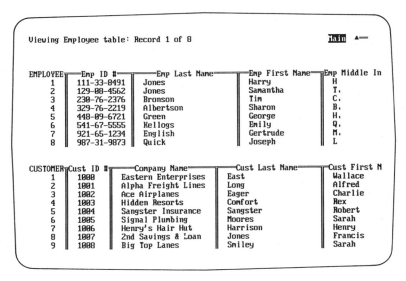

Fig. 3.10.

Making the Employee table current in Main mode.

Editing Employee table: Record 1 of 8 Edit ▲══

EMPLOYEE	Emp ID #	Emp Last Name	Emp First Name	Emp Middle In
1	111-33-8491	Jones	Harry	H
2	129-08-4562	Jones	Samantha	T.
3	230-76-2376	Bronson	Tim	C.
4	329-76-2219	Albertson	Sharon	B.
5	448-09-6721	Green	George	H.
6	541-67-5555	Kellogs	Emily	Q.
7	921-65-1234	English	Gertrude	M.
8	987-31-9873	Quick	Joseph	L

CUSTOMER	Cust ID #	Company Name	Cust Last Name	Cust First N
1	1000	Eastern Enterprises	East	Wallace
2	1001	Alpha Freight Lines	Long	Alfred
3	1002	Ace Airplanes	Eager	Charlie
4	1003	Hidden Resorts	Comfort	Rex
5	1004	Sangster Insurance	Sangster	Robert
6	1005	Signal Plumbing	Moores	Sarah
7	1006	Henry's Hair Hut	Harrison	Henry
8	1007	2nd Savings & Loan	Jones	Francis
9	1008	Big Top Lanes	Smiley	Sarah

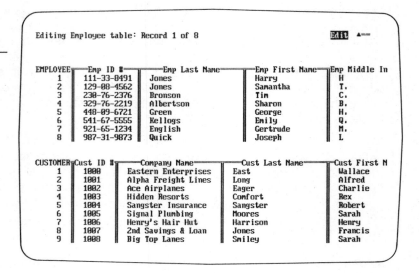

Fig. 3.11.

Editing the Employee table with multiple images in the work space.

Caution: The table you edit in Edit mode is not the temporary Entry table used by DataEntry mode. Additions and changes are made directly to the permanent table. Paradox does, however, maintain a transaction log during Edit mode so that the undo feature can return you to the original version of your table if you make a drastic mistake.

When entering data from Edit mode, you should be aware of the possibility of accidentally modifying existing records. A good way to reduce the risk is to always switch to form view (by pressing F7) if you are going to enter new records. While in table view, an errant keystroke may place you in the wrong record. And with multiple records on-screen, you may not immediately notice that you're in the wrong row. In form view you would be more apt to notice an accidental PgUp or PgDn because the entire screen would change, and the record number is conspicuous in the upper right corner of the form.

If your table is keyed, however, you have a compelling reason *not* to use Edit mode to enter new data. For more information, refer to the "Handling Keys and Key Violations in Edit Mode" section of this chapter.

Finding a Record with Zoom and Zoom Next

Often you will want to edit one particular record out of hundreds, or even thousands, in your database table. Paradox provides a number of ways to help you find the record quickly, but the easiest is the *zoom* feature. It works best if the table contains a single key field.

Suppose that you know the value of one of the fields in the record you want to edit. Place the cursor in that field in any record and press Ctrl-Z (Zoom). Paradox displays a prompt asking you to `Enter value or pattern to search for`. Type the value for the field and press Enter. Paradox scans the field from the top of the table to the bottom. When the program finds a match, it moves the cursor to that record so that you can edit it. If Paradox finds no match, you see the message `Match not found` in the bottom right corner of the screen, and Paradox does not move the cursor.

Sometimes the value in the field you are searching is not unique, and Paradox may not find the correct record on the first try. In that case, press Alt-Z (Zoom Next). Paradox continues scanning the field throughout the table until the program either finds a match or reaches the end of the table.

The zoom feature works well in tandem with a single key. The value in a single key field is by definition unique, so you always find the record you want on the first try.

You can also access the zoom feature through Paradox's menu. Refer to the "Using the Image Options" section of this chapter for a complete discussion of the Zoom menu options (called Goto in Paradox 2.0) and for a discussion of using *wild cards* to find particular items. Version 3

Ctrl-Z (Zoom) and Alt-Z (Zoom Next) work also in DataEntry and CoEdit modes.

Editing Fields

Cursor-movement and editing keys work the same way in Edit mode as in DataEntry mode. Review tables 1.3 and 1.4 in Chapter 1 for descriptions of how the cursor-movement keys operate in the table and form views. Recall that some of these keys have different effects in the two views. The PgUp key, for example, moves you to the previous screen of records in table view, but moves up no more than one record in form view.

Use the Backspace key to erase your mistakes, one character at a time, and the Ctrl-Backspace keystroke combination to delete an entire field entry. You can also use the field view (press Alt-F5 or Ctrl-F) to edit errant entries while in Edit mode. Accessing and using the field view is described in Chapter 1.

Deleting a Record

Almost any data in a Paradox table can eventually become obsolete. When you no longer have any reason to keep certain data in your database, you should delete that data. Deleting a record in Paradox is so easy that it is scary. Fortunately, the undo feature is just as simple.

To delete a record, place the cursor in the target record (in table or form view) and press the Del key. Zap, the record is gone! If you didn't mean to do it, use Ctrl-U (Undo) to recover the lost record.

Deleting records in Paradox discards the data but does not automatically recover the disk space that was used by the data. This feature may not seem to be a significant problem. For small tables it isn't. But it can be a real and serious problem if your Paradox table is large and you regularly delete many records. Ultimately, you may run out of disk space.

The easiest way to recover the lost space is to *restructure* the table, without changing the table definition at all. Just to be on the safe side, first make a copy of the table, using the **C**opy option on the Tools menu, and then follow the procedure outlined in Chapter 2 for restructuring a table. Be careful not to change the definition of any field. Just access the Restructure mode and press F2 (DO-IT!). Paradox makes a new copy of the table that takes up less room on the disk. Computers are notorious for losing data during this type of operation, so check the table when Paradox is done. Don't get rid of the backup copy you made until you are sure that no data was lost.

Saving and Canceling Changes

As with DataEntry mode, in Edit mode you have the option of either accepting all changes made during an edit session or discarding them. To save the changes and return to Main mode, press F2 (DO-IT!). To throw away the edits, press F10 (Menu) and select **C**ancel **Y**es.

Either approach returns you to the Main mode. The table you were editing will be the current image.

The autosave feature mentioned in a previous tip also operates during the Edit mode. Even though changes made during the edit session are not saved to disk until you press F2 (DO-IT!), the autosave feature still protects you from an unexpected power outage. You lose, at most, a few keystrokes if the power is interrupted while you are entering or editing data in the Edit mode. Because changes are being saved directly to the target table, you do not have to go through a copy procedure after the power loss.

Using Undo in Edit Mode

The undo feature in Edit mode is identical to that feature in DataEntry mode. Just keep in mind that the transaction log is cleared when you press F2 (DO-IT!). In other words, you have the opportunity to undo one transaction at a time, starting from the most recent transaction to the time you entered Edit mode. But once you confirm the changes by pressing F2, the edits are permanent and can be undone only manually through a subsequent editing session.

Using Ditto in Edit Mode

The Ditto command works practically the same way in Edit mode as it does in DataEntry mode. You first must clear any existing data from the field (with Ctrl-Backspace) and then press Ctrl-D (Ditto). Paradox reproduces the contents of the same field from the immediately preceding record.

Entering New Records

The Paradox Edit mode, although designed for making alterations to existing records, can be used to enter new data as well. You can either insert records within the table or add them to the end. For keyed fields, the location of the records doesn't matter, because Paradox inserts them in the proper order when you press F2 (DO-IT!).

Inserting Records within the Table

To insert a blank row in the table, position the cursor (in table or form view) anywhere in the record that should follow your new record. Then press the Ins key. Starting at the cursor, Paradox moves all rows down one row, incrementing the record numbers accordingly (see figs. 3.12 and 3.13). Use the blank row to enter a new record, as shown in figure 3.14.

Fig. 3.12.

Before inserting a blank row during Edit mode.

Editing Product table: Record 2 of 4 **Edit**

PRODUCT	Model #	Product Name	Price	Cost
1	A333	Standard Widget	39.95	19.75
2	B107	Enhanced Widget	49.95	23.60
3	G400	Deluxe Widget	59.95	25.15
4	X155	Imperial Widget	79.95	32.50

Fig. 3.13.

After inserting a blank row during Edit mode.

Editing Product table: Record 2 of 5 **Edit**

PRODUCT	Model #	Product Name	Price	Cost
1	A333	Standard Widget	39.95	19.75
2				
3	B107	Enhanced Widget	49.95	23.60
4	G400	Deluxe Widget	59.95	25.15
5	X155	Imperial Widget	79.95	32.50

Fig. 3.14.

The newly entered record in Main mode.

Viewing Product table: Record 3 of 5 **Main**

PRODUCT	Model #	Product Name	Price	Cost
1	A333	Standard Widget	39.95	19.75
2	A334	Standard Widget Plus	43.95	21.15
3	B107	Enhanced Widget	49.95	23.60
4	G400	Deluxe Widget	59.95	25.15
5	X155	Imperial Widget	79.95	32.50

Adding Records to the End of the Table

You probably will routinely add records to the end of the table rather than continually insert them within the table. To add a blank row at the end of the table during Edit mode, press the End key to move the cursor to the last record, and then press the down-arrow key. Paradox adds a new blank row, giving it the next record number in sequence (see fig. 3.15). You are now free to enter another record.

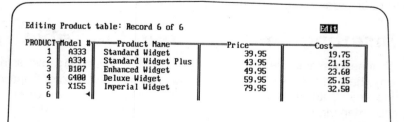

Fig. 3.15.

Adding a new row to the end of the table during Edit mode.

Editing Product table: Record 6 of 6 **Edit**

PRODUCT	Model #	Product Name	Price	Cost
1	A333	Standard Widget	39.95	19.75
2	A334	Standard Widget Plus	43.95	21.15
3	B107	Enhanced Widget	49.95	23.60
4	G400	Deluxe Widget	59.95	25.15
5	X155	Imperial Widget	79.95	32.50
6				

Handling Keys and Key Violations in Edit Mode

As in DataEntry mode, Paradox does not reorder the table or check for key violations in Edit mode until you press F2 (DO-IT!). But you may be surprised by the way Paradox handles key violations. The following example demonstrates the problem.

The Product table shown in figure 3.16 is keyed on the Model # field. Suppose that during the current editing session, you have added records 6 and 7. Notice that Paradox has neither put them in order by the key field nor prevented entry of a record with the same model number as an existing record. You don't have a problem at this point, because you haven't accepted the changes yet.

Editing Product table: Record 8 of 8 — Edit

PRODUCT	Model #	Product Name	Price	Cost
1	A333	Standard Widget	39.95	19.75
2	A334	Standard Widget Plus	43.95	21.15
3	B107	Enhanced Widget	49.95	23.60
4	G400	Deluxe Widget	59.95	25.15
5	X155	Imperial Widget	79.95	32.50
6	C777	Jumbo Widget	55.95	24.66
7	B107	Royal Widget	69.95	27.50
8				

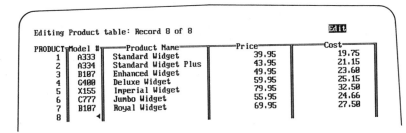

Fig. 3.16.

Entering a key violation in Edit mode.

Figure 3.17 shows the same table after you press F2. Two things have happened. First, Paradox moved Model # C777 to the fourth position, before G400 and after B107, which is what you would expect to happen. Second, the last entry shown in figure 3.17 has replaced the record that had the same model number—*without giving you any warning!*

Beware of key fields when using Edit mode. Better yet, read the discussion of the CoEdit mode—you may decide to use that mode instead.

Viewing Product table: Record 1 of 6 — Main

PRODUCT	Model #	Product Name	Price	Cost
1	A333	Standard Widget	39.95	19.75
2	A334	Standard Widget Plus	43.95	21.15
3	B107	Royal Widget	69.95	27.50
4	C777	Jumbo Widget	55.95	24.66
5	G400	Deluxe Widget	59.95	25.15
6	X155	Imperial Widget	79.95	32.50

Fig. 3.17.

How Paradox handles a key violation in Edit mode.

Using the Edit Menu

While in Edit mode, press F10 (Menu) to access the Edit menu, which includes the following options:

Image	This option provides access to Paradox image-customization features. These features work in the same manner in any mode, so refer to the "Using the Image Options" section later in this chapter.
Undo	This menu choice has the same effect as Ctrl-U (Undo).
ValCheck	Validity checks are one of the most useful features of Paradox, both in preventing entry of invalid data and in assisting you in data entry. They can provide default values and automatic lookup from other tables. Validity checks are covered in detail in Chapter 9, "Using Paradox Power Entry and Editing Features."
Help	This menu selection has the same effect as F1 (Help), discussed in Chapter 1.
DO-IT!	This option is equivalent to F2 (DO-IT!).
Cancel	Choosing this option cancels Edit mode, discards all changes made or data entered during the session, and returns to Main mode. The last table that you were editing remains the current image.

Using Edit Mode on a Network

Paradox automatically places a *full lock* on a shared table whenever you access it in Edit mode. No one else can use the table until you finish your edit session. Conversely, Paradox does not permit you to use Edit mode on a table that is already in use by any other individual on the network. For both of these reasons, you should use the CoEdit mode rather than Edit mode when editing shared network tables.

Entering and Editing Data in CoEdit Mode

This option's name derives from the fact that you can edit a shared table on a multiuser network at the same time that another network user is using the same table. The CoEdit mode is one of the jewels of the Paradox program. Not only can multiple users edit the same table at once, but everyone's screen is regularly updated to reflect changes made by other users.

You do not have to access a network, however, to make good use of this feature. On the contrary, CoEdit may be the best overall mode for entering and editing data with Paradox. As you can see from figure 3.18, CoEdit mode works in the actual target table, just as Edit does, rather than in an Entry table. In fact, the CoEdit mode is nearly identical in appearance to Edit mode.

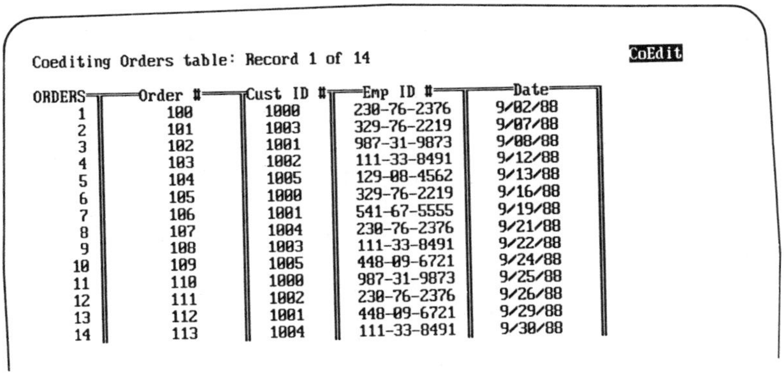
Coediting Orders table: Record 1 of 14 CoEdit

ORDERS	Order #	Cust ID #	Emp ID #	Date
1	100	1000	230-76-2376	9/02/88
2	101	1003	329-76-2219	9/07/88
3	102	1001	987-31-9873	9/08/88
4	103	1002	111-33-8491	9/12/88
5	104	1005	129-00-4562	9/13/88
6	105	1000	329-76-2219	9/16/88
7	106	1001	541-67-5555	9/19/88
8	107	1004	230-76-2376	9/21/88
9	108	1003	111-33-8491	9/22/88
10	109	1005	448-09-6721	9/24/88
11	110	1000	987-31-9873	9/25/88
12	111	1002	230-76-2376	9/26/88
13	112	1001	448-09-6721	9/29/88
14	113	1004	111-33-8491	9/30/88

Fig. 3.18.
Coediting the Orders table.

As with Edit mode, you can start CoEdit mode from the Main menu or through a function key command. To start CoEdit mode from the Main menu, select **M**odify **C**oEdit and specify the table to be edited. If the chosen table is already in the work space, Paradox enters CoEdit mode and makes the table current. Otherwise, the program adds the table to the work space as the last image and begins CoEdit mode (see fig. 3.19).

When the table to be edited is already in the work space, you can press Alt-F9 (CoEdit) to begin CoEdit mode. Like Edit mode, all tables in the work space are in CoEdit mode at once. You can use F3 (Up Image) or F4 (Down Image) before and after you enter CoEdit mode to move between images.

If you are using Paradox as a stand-alone system or using a nonshared database (directory) on a network, Paradox removes multiple images of any table from the work space when you begin CoEdit mode. But the program does not remove multiple images of shared network tables. Refer to this chapter's section on "Using CoEdit Mode on a Network" for an explanation of this apparent inconsistency.

All the fundamental operations for entering and editing data in Edit mode are done the same way in CoEdit: finding records to edit with Ctrl-Z

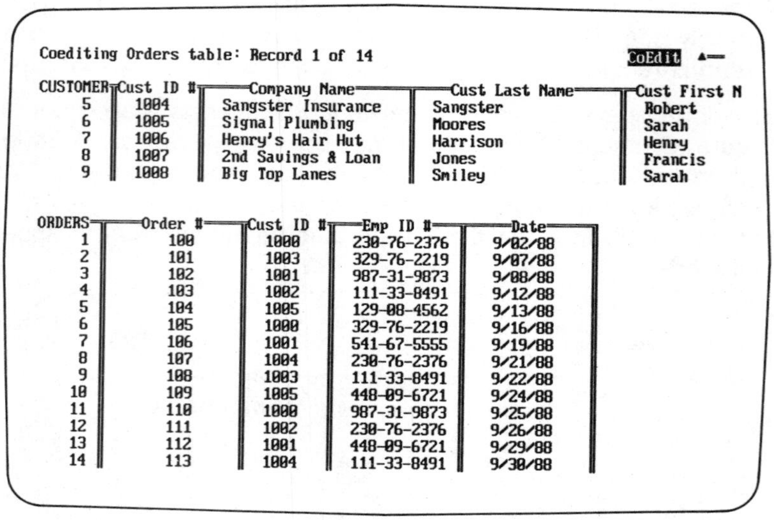

Coediting Orders table: Record 1 of 14 CoEdit

CUSTOMER	Cust ID #	Company Name	Cust Last Name	Cust First N
5	1004	Sangster Insurance	Sangster	Robert
6	1005	Signal Plumbing	Moores	Sarah
7	1006	Henry's Hair Hut	Harrison	Henry
8	1007	2nd Savings & Loan	Jones	Francis
9	1008	Big Top Lanes	Smiley	Sarah

ORDERS	Order #	Cust ID #	Emp ID #	Date
1	100	1000	230-76-2376	9/02/88
2	101	1003	329-76-2219	9/07/88
3	102	1001	987-31-9873	9/08/88
4	103	1002	111-33-8491	9/12/88
5	104	1005	129-08-4562	9/13/88
6	105	1000	329-76-2219	9/16/88
7	106	1001	541-67-5555	9/19/88
8	107	1004	230-76-2376	9/21/88
9	108	1003	111-33-8491	9/22/88
10	109	1005	448-09-6721	9/24/88
11	110	1000	987-31-9873	9/25/88
12	111	1002	230-76-2376	9/26/88
13	112	1001	448-09-6721	9/29/88
14	113	1004	111-33-8491	9/30/88

Fig. 3.19.

Coediting with multiple tables in the work space.

(Zoom), moving around fields and records with the cursor keys, entering and editing data in a field, using field view, inserting new records, deleting records, and using Ctrl-D (Ditto). A few operations, however, are a bit different in CoEdit mode.

Saving and Canceling Changes

You use F2 (DO-IT!) to complete CoEdit mode, just as you do in Edit mode. But unlike in Edit, using F2 is the *only* way to terminate a CoEdit session.

In CoEdit mode, Paradox posts data to disk after every record rather than at the end of the session. This difference is directly related to the goal of maximum concurrency for network users—allowing multiple users on a network to edit safely a shared table at the same time. Even for non-network users, this frequency of posting to disk is significant. It directly limits the number of transactions that can be undone. In CoEdit mode, changes are posted to disk after every record, so the CoEdit menu contains no **C**ancel option. In addition, the CoEdit mode's Undo command (Ctrl-U) backs out of one and only one transaction, the most recent one.

Using the CoEdit Menu

While in CoEdit mode, press F10 (Menu) to access the CoEdit menu. It contains the following options:

Image	The first menu option provides access to Paradox image-customization features. These features work in the same manner in any mode, so refer to the "Using the Image Options" section in this chapter.
Undo	This menu choice has the same effect as Ctrl-U (Undo). In CoEdit mode, this feature cancels the most previous transaction only. It cannot go back more than one transaction.
AutoRefresh	By default, Paradox refreshes your screen every three seconds with the most current content of the tables in the work space. Through this menu option, you can vary the autorefresh interval to as little as one second or as long as one hour.
Help	This menu selection has the same effect as F1 (Help), discussed in Chapter 1.
DO-IT!	Choosing this option is equivalent to pressing F2 (DO-IT!).

Adding New Records to Keyed and Non-Keyed Tables

For non-keyed tables, adding a record during CoEdit mode is the same as the equivalent procedure in Edit mode. You move to the last record, press the down-arrow key, and enter the new record. But in CoEdit mode Paradox monitors keys and key violations record-by-record rather than waiting for you to press F2 (DO-IT!).

As soon as you enter a new record into a keyed table during CoEdit mode and move to the next record, Paradox checks for key violations. If none are found, the new record is inserted in proper sorted order in the table. For example, figure 3.20 shows a new record being entered in the Product table from CoEdit mode. Notice the status message: `Entering new record - not yet posted to table`. Once the record is entered and you move to the next record, Paradox immediately posts the entry in the correct sorted order, in this case by the Model # field (see fig. 3.21).

For large keyed tables, the immediate posting that occurs in CoEdit mode can make new records seem to disappear as soon as you press Enter. But don't be concerned. They aren't gone but have merely been placed in the appropriate sorted order, which happens to be off the screen.

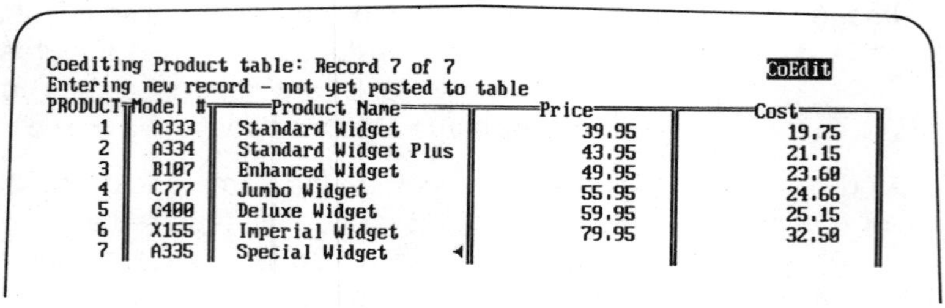

Fig. 3.20.

Entering a new record with CoEdit mode.

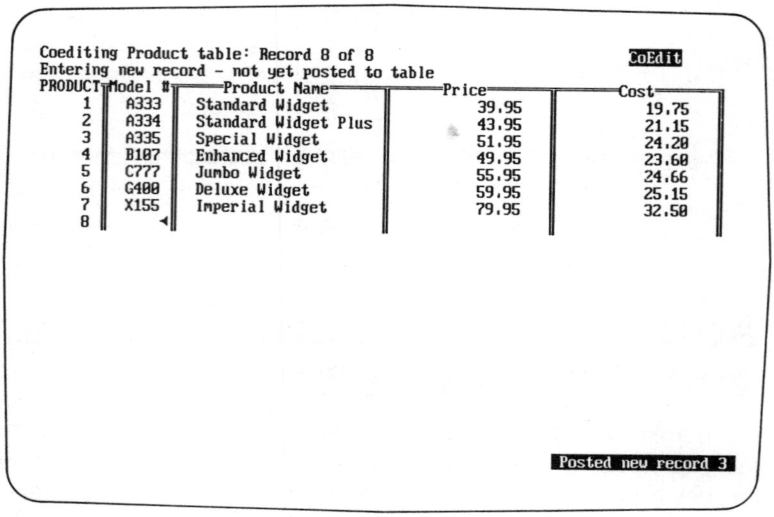

Fig. 3.21.

The new record posted in order by model number.

Handling Key Violations in CoEdit Mode

Figure 3.22 shows another record being entered in the same table, but this time a key violation has occurred. In sharp contrast to the way Paradox handles a key violation in Edit mode, in CoEdit mode the program gives you ample warning. Just as important, Paradox provides several alternatives to help you resolve the conflict:

- ❑ The keystroke combination Alt-L (Lock Toggle) has the effect in CoEdit mode of explicitly placing and removing a lock on an individual record. When you are making changes to a record, the record is already automatically locked, so pressing Alt-L removes the lock and causes the new record to be posted. At this point,

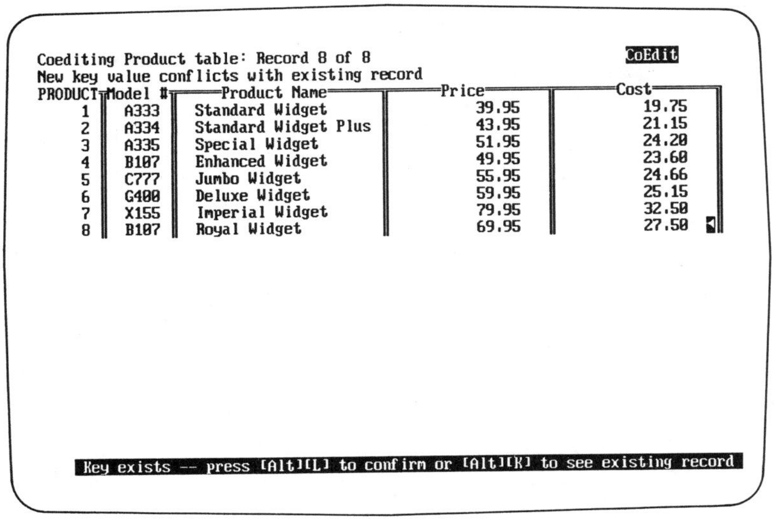
Coediting Product table: Record 8 of 8 CoEdit
New key value conflicts with existing record

PRODUCT	Model #	Product Name	Price	Cost
1	A333	Standard Widget	39.95	19.75
2	A334	Standard Widget Plus	43.95	21.15
3	A335	Special Widget	51.95	24.20
4	B107	Enhanced Widget	49.95	23.60
5	C777	Jumbo Widget	55.95	24.66
6	G400	Deluxe Widget	59.95	25.15
7	X155	Imperial Widget	79.95	32.50
8	B107	Royal Widget	69.95	27.50

Key exists -- press [Alt][L] to confirm or [Alt][K] to see existing record

Fig. 3.22.

Handling a key violation in CoEdit mode.

the new record replaces the one that has the same key value (Model # B107). This result is the normal effect of a key violation in the Edit mode.

❑ The keystroke combination Alt-K (Key Viol) is a toggle that alternately displays the new entry and the old entry so that you can decide which is correct. Press Alt-K once to see figure 3.23, showing the existing values in the last row of the table. Pressing Alt-K again switches back to the new value that is causing the conflict (see fig. 3.24).

In this example, suppose that you made a mistake in the Model # field. The number should be V107 rather than B107. The Model # field in the new record needs to be corrected. Once you fix the error, press Alt-L (Lock Toggle) to post the corrected record (see fig. 3.25).

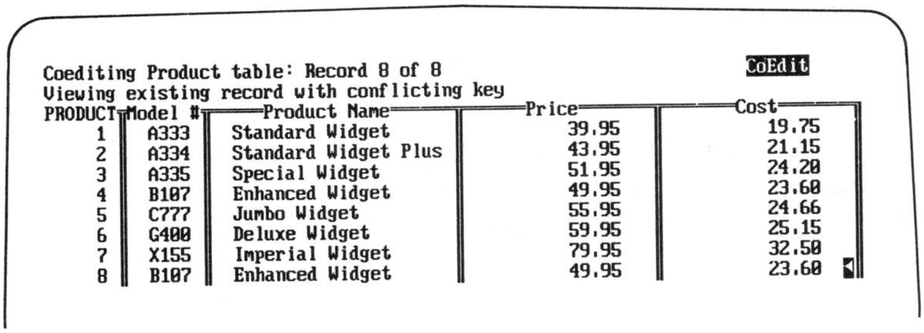
Coediting Product table: Record 8 of 8 CoEdit
Viewing existing record with conflicting key

PRODUCT	Model #	Product Name	Price	Cost
1	A333	Standard Widget	39.95	19.75
2	A334	Standard Widget Plus	43.95	21.15
3	A335	Special Widget	51.95	24.20
4	B107	Enhanced Widget	49.95	23.60
5	C777	Jumbo Widget	55.95	24.66
6	G400	Deluxe Widget	59.95	25.15
7	X155	Imperial Widget	79.95	32.50
8	B107	Enhanced Widget	49.95	23.60

Fig. 3.23.

Viewing the existing record with the conflicting key.

Fig. 3.24.

Viewing the new record with the conflicting key.

Coediting Product table: Record 8 of 8 CoEdit
New key value conflicts with existing record

PRODUCT	Model #	Product Name	Price	Cost
1	A333	Standard Widget	39.95	19.75
2	A334	Standard Widget Plus	43.95	21.15
3	A335	Special Widget	51.95	24.20
4	B107	Enhanced Widget	49.95	23.60
5	C777	Jumbo Widget	55.95	24.66
6	G400	Deluxe Widget	59.95	25.15
7	X155	Imperial Widget	79.95	32.50
8	B107	Royal Widget	69.95	27.50

Fig. 3.25.

After the key violation has been reconciled.

Coediting Product table: Record 8 of 8 CoEdit

PRODUCT	Model #	Product Name	Price	Cost
1	A333	Standard Widget	39.95	19.75
2	A334	Standard Widget Plus	43.95	21.15
3	A335	Special Widget	51.95	24.20
4	B107	Enhanced Widget	49.95	23.60
5	C777	Jumbo Widget	55.95	24.66
6	G400	Deluxe Widget	59.95	25.15
7	V107	Royal Widget	69.95	27.50
8	X155	Imperial Widget	79.95	32.50

Using CoEdit Mode on a Network

As previously stated, CoEdit is specifically suited for editing shared tables on a network. Although this mode is the preferred method for editing keyed tables on a stand-alone system, CoEdit shines in a network environment. Before further study of the specifics of using CoEdit mode, however, you need to be familiar with the concept of network privileges.

Understanding Network Privileges

The *owner* of a shared table on a network, usually the person who created the table, can place certain restrictions on the use of the table by other network users. The **P**rotect option on the Tools menu and the separate Protection Generator program provide several sophisticated tools for this purpose.

When you are the owner of a table, you should obviously have no problem accessing it in the CoEdit mode. You may run into certain restrictions, however, when you attempt to edit tables created by other network users. The owner of a Paradox table can grant or deny the following rights to the table itself (*table rights*):

- *ReadOnly:* The right to view but not edit a table

- *Update:* The right to change only non-key fields in existing records
- *Entry:* The right to enter new records and alter key fields using DataEntry mode or the **A**dd command; does not include the right to delete records
- *InsDel:* The right to change and delete existing records and to add new records
- *All:* Complete access to the table

The table owner can also assign the following levels of *field rights*:

- *ReadOnly:* The right to view the field values but make no changes
- *All:* The right to view and change values in the field

If the table owner has placed any restrictions on the table or fields, you may be asked for a password before you are granted access.

Refer to Chapter 2 and the discussion of the Protect option on the Tools/More menu for details on how to assign table and field rights.

Understanding the Locking System

The essential difference between using CoEdit mode and using Edit mode on a network is that CoEdit uses record-level locking while Edit locks the entire table. Paradox automatically places a *prevent full lock* on the table you are editing in CoEdit mode, which means that all other network users with appropriate table and field rights can have full access to the table but cannot place a full lock on the table. Until you begin to make a change to an existing record, or begin to add a new record, no further lock is placed.

As soon as you begin to edit or change a record, Paradox places a record-level lock that prevents any other user from having access to the record until you are finished with it. The record is unlocked either when you press F2 (DO-IT!) to leave CoEdit mode, or when you move the cursor to another record.

While an individual record is locked, other users have complete access to all the other records in the table. Contrast this flexibility with how network access is handled by the **E**dit command. With Edit mode, the entire table is completely locked (with a full lock) for the entire time you are using the table.

Using Explicit Record Locking

Occasionally, you may want to pre-empt another user from changing a record, but you aren't ready to change the table yourself, either. In that case, you can use Alt-L (Lock Toggle) to lock a record explicitly. Move the cursor to the record that you want locked against any changes, and press Alt-L. Paradox displays a message telling you that the `Record is locked`.

When you finally make your changes or are ready to unlock the record for another reason, you can remove the lock by doing one of the following:

- Press F2 (DO-IT!), indicating that you are finished with CoEdit mode. Paradox changes the message to `Record unlocked`, followed by the message `Ending CoEdit`.
- Press Alt-L to toggle the lock. Paradox displays the message `Record unlocked`.
- Move the cursor to a different record. Paradox displays the message `Record unlocked`.

Paradox posts the changes to the table and frees the record for access by other users.

Refreshing the Screen

Paradox was the first PC-based database program to provide real-time screen refresh for all users on a network. Other programs provided concurrent access to database tables, but a change made by one user was not immediately written to the screen of other users who were displaying the same record. dBASE IV™ has added this capability, but Paradox has boasted it since the program's inception.

For practical reasons, Paradox refreshes your screen at set intervals unless some other event causes the images on your Paradox work space to be brought up-to-date. You should therefore be aware of these events:

- Paradox automatically refreshes your screen every three seconds unless you change this interval through the **A**utorefresh choice on the CoEdit menu. You can adjust the refresh interval to as little as one second or to as long as one hour.
- Between automatic work space refreshes, you can press Alt-R (Refresh Image) to see all changes that have been made by other users to the tables visible on your screen.
- Each time you explicitly lock a record by pressing Alt-L (Lock Toggle), Paradox updates your work space. Because this

procedure locks out other users, the data in the record cannot change while you are working with the record.

- Any time you begin to change a record in a shared table, Paradox refreshes your screen so that you are sure to be working with the most current version of the record. The program also locks out other users until you are finished making your changes.

When you are using a shared keyed table in CoEdit mode, the record number is not a reliable identifier for particular records. Each time you (or any other users) enter a record, delete a record, or change a key value, many record numbers may immediately be altered as well. As Paradox refreshes your screen, don't be surprised to see record numbers continually changing as records are added to or deleted from the table.

Using the Paradox View Command

Once you have entered data into a Paradox table, you will often want to view the table's contents in the work space. Chapter 4 discusses how to use Query By Example (QBE) to ask for specific records and fields to be displayed. This section describes how to view an entire table.

Viewing a Paradox Table

To view a table, select **V**iew from the Main menu, and specify the table you want to see. Paradox adds the table to the work space as the current image. The work space remains in Main mode. The default view is table view, but once a table is in the work space, you can switch to the default form view by pressing F7 (Form Toggle). Each time you view another table, Paradox switches back to table view.

You can think of this look at your table as *home base*. Most other commands eventually return you here. When you are finished viewing the table, clear it from the screen by pressing either F8 (Clear Image) or Alt-F8 (Clear All). (Alt-F8 clears the entire screen.)

For those of you familiar with Lotus 1-2-3 spreadsheets, the **V**iew command is roughly equivalent to the 1-2-3 /**F**ile **R**etrieve command. The result—viewing a table in Main mode—is equivalent to 1-2-3's READY mode with a worksheet on-screen. The screen even looks much like a spreadsheet if you are using the table view.

Viewing Multiple Tables

With Paradox, you can have any number of tables in the work space, each as a separate image. Each time you use **V**iew, Paradox adds another image to the screen (unless you press F8 or Alt-F8 to clear the screen). If you are viewing a table in form view and add another table to the work space, Paradox automatically switches back to table view when the program displays the new image.

Move between images by using F3 (Up Image) and F4 (Down Image). You can use the cursor keys to move around in the table in either table view or form view.

Using the Image Options

The menu for each of the modes discussed in this chapter includes the option **I**mage. This option is used to give you some control over just how each image looks on the work space. The discussion here is generally applicable to the DataEntry, Edit, CoEdit, and Main modes, with a few variations that are mentioned.

To access the Image menu from any of these modes, press F10 (Menu) and select **I**mage. Paradox displays the following menu options in table view:

TableSize
ColumnSize
Format
Zoom
Move
PickForm
KeepSet

In form view a slightly different menu displays these options:

Format
Zoom
PickForm
KeepSet

Note: The **K**eepSet option (called **K**eepSettings in Paradox 2.0) is not available in either view from DataEntry mode. **Z**oom is available only in Paradox 3.0. Version 3.0 provides an additional choice, **G**raph, to the Main mode's Image menu. This new option is fully discussed in Chapter 12.

Modifying Table Size

Paradox automatically includes enough rows in the current image to display all the records of the current table, up to a maximum of 22 rows. When more than one table is in the work space, this automatic table size may be larger than necessary to see the records in which you are interested, and may not permit multiple images to be seen at once.

To change the number of records displayed in the current image, access the table view Image menu and select **T**ableSize. Paradox displays a screen similar to figure 3.26. Use the keys listed in table 3.1 to size the table.

Table 3.1
Paradox TableSize Keys

Key	*Effect*
Up arrow	Decrease the number of rows displayed (min. 2)
Down arrow	Increase the number of rows displayed (max. 22)
Home	Move to minimum number of rows (2)
End	Move to maximum number of rows (22)
Enter	Accept the new table size
Esc	Abort and return to previous table size

For example, the image of the Detail table shown in figure 3.26 completely fills the screen. Suppose that you also want to see a couple of other related tables, Product and Orders, on the same screen. Using the **T**ableSize option, you can reduce the size of each table until you can see portions of all three tables at once (see fig. 3.27). Use the **K**eepSet option from the Image menu if you want to make this setting permanent. Otherwise, Paradox uses the default length when displaying the table again.

Changing Column Size

Column widths in the table view are set automatically according to the field definitions. The **C**olumnSize option on the table view Image menu gives you the ability to increase or decrease this width. Several factors, however, limit how wide or narrow you can make a column.

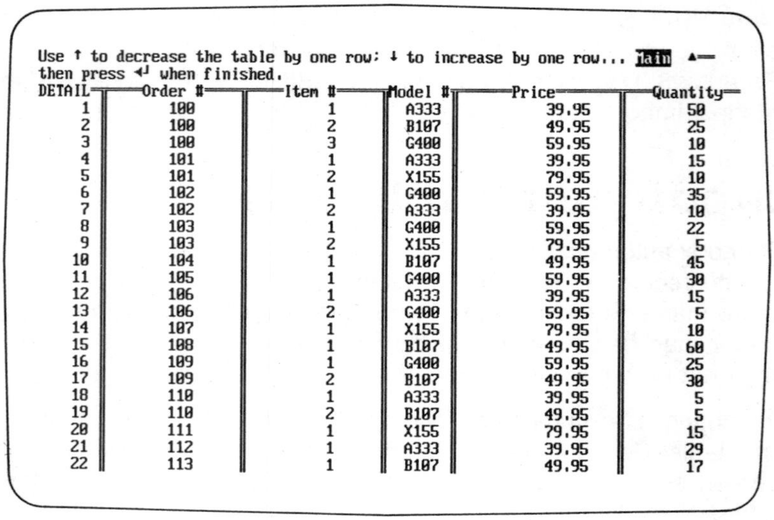

Use ↑ to decrease the table by one row; ↓ to increase by one row... Main ▲
then press ↵ when finished.

DETAIL	Order #	Item #	Model #	Price	Quantity
1	100	1	A333	39.95	50
2	100	2	B107	49.95	25
3	100	3	G400	59.95	10
4	101	1	A333	39.95	15
5	101	2	X155	79.95	10
6	102	1	G400	59.95	35
7	102	2	A333	39.95	10
8	103	1	G400	59.95	22
9	103	2	X155	79.95	5
10	104	1	B107	49.95	45
11	105	1	G400	59.95	30
12	106	1	A333	39.95	15
13	106	2	G400	59.95	5
14	107	1	X155	79.95	10
15	108	1	B107	49.95	60
16	109	1	G400	59.95	25
17	109	2	B107	49.95	30
18	110	1	A333	39.95	5
19	110	2	B107	49.95	5
20	111	1	X155	79.95	15
21	112	1	A333	39.95	29
22	113	1	B107	49.95	17

Fig. 3.26.

Modifying table size.

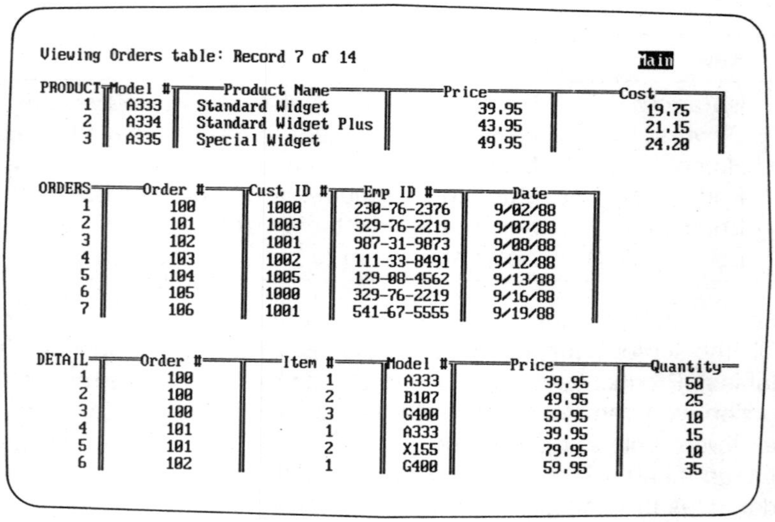

Viewing Orders table: Record 7 of 14 Main

PRODUCT	Model #	Product Name	Price	Cost
1	A333	Standard Widget	39.95	19.75
2	A334	Standard Widget Plus	43.95	21.15
3	A335	Special Widget	49.95	24.20

ORDERS	Order #	Cust ID #	Emp ID #	Date
1	100	1000	230-76-2376	9/02/88
2	101	1003	329-76-2219	9/07/88
3	102	1001	987-31-9873	9/08/88
4	103	1002	111-33-8491	9/12/88
5	104	1005	129-08-4562	9/13/88
6	105	1000	329-76-2219	9/16/88
7	106	1001	541-67-5555	9/19/88

DETAIL	Order #	Item #	Model #	Price	Quantity
1	100	1	A333	39.95	50
2	100	2	B107	49.95	25
3	100	3	G400	59.95	10
4	101	1	A333	39.95	15
5	101	2	X155	79.95	10
6	102	1	G400	59.95	35

Fig. 3.27.

Three tables displayed on the same screen after table size has been modified.

Paradox sets a maximum column width for each field type. The data itself places practical limits on how narrow a column can be, and Paradox permits no column to be less than one character in width. Table 3.2 lists the default widths and the maximum allowable widths for the various data types.

Table 3.2
Paradox Default and Maximum Column Widths

Type	*Default Width*	*Maximum Width*
A	The longer of defined field length or field name length, up to a maximum of 76 character-widths	The shorter of field length or screen width
N	The longer of field name or 12 character-widths	The longer of field name or 23 character-widths
$	The longer of field name or 15 character-widths	The longer of field name or 23 character-widths
S	The longer of field name or 6 character-widths	The longer of field name or 6 character-widths
D	The longer of field name or 10 character-widths	The longer of field name or 10 character-widths

If you reduce column width too severely, you affect the way data is displayed. Paradox truncates text fields (shortens them by dropping characters from right to left) on the screen and displays all other types of fields as asterisks (*) when you reduce field width too much. But in no case is the actual data stored on disk affected when you change a table's on-screen column width.

To modify column width, access the Image menu and select **C**olumnSize. Use the left- and right-arrow keys to move to the column you want to resize, and press Enter. Your screen will look similar to figure 3.28.

In this example, suppose that you want to make the Price column of the Detail table narrower so that the entire Quantity column can be seen. Use the keys listed in table 3.3 to size the column. Press Enter to accept the change, or Esc to return to the previous width. Figure 3.29 shows the results. Unless you use the **K**eepSet option on the Image menu, this new column width applies only to the current session. The next time you display the table, column widths return to the defaults.

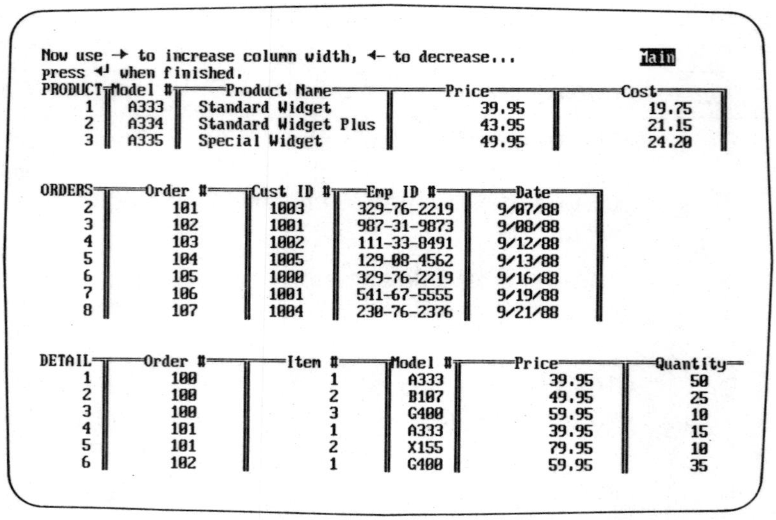

Fig. 3.28.

Modifying column width in the Detail table.

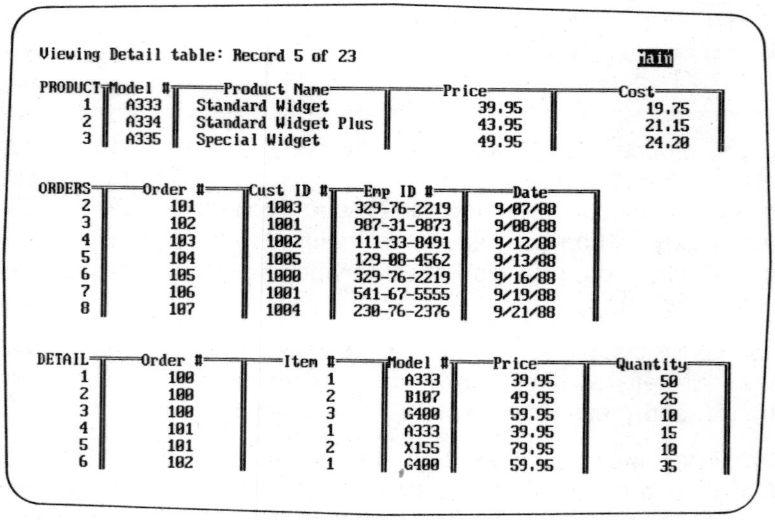

Fig. 3.29.

The result of reducing the width of the Price column in the Detail table.

Frequently you may have a text field on-screen that is not completely visible because of the column size. You can see the entire field by pressing Alt-F5 (Field View) and using the directional keys to pan right and left.

Table 3.3
Paradox ColumnSize Keys

Key	*Effect*
←	Decrease the column width
→	Increase the column width
Home	Move to minimum width
End	Move to maximum width
Enter	Accept the new column size
Esc	Abort and return to previous column size

Selecting Display Format

The concept of display *format* is a familiar one to seasoned spreadsheet users but may not be to others. Alphanumeric values are always displayed just as you entered them in the table, but Paradox permits you to choose between several display formats for number fields (N and $) and date fields. The data stored in your table is never affected when you change the on-screen format.

To change the format of a field in the current image, access the Image menu (in table view or form view) and select **F**ormat. Move the cursor to the column you want to format, and press Enter.

The available formats for number fields (N and $) include the following:

General — Numbers are displayed with as many decimal places as necessary to represent the number, up to a maximum set number of places. The default format for number fields is general format with two decimal places.

Fixed — Numbers are always displayed with a set number of decimal places.

Comma — This format separates whole numbers into three-digit groups with commas and a set number of decimal places. This format is the default for currency ($) fields.

Scientific — This format displays numbers in scientific notation.

Figure 3.30 shows examples of the four number formats. The same number was entered in all fields of each row to display the effects of the various formats. The column labeled `General 2 dec.` shows a number field in general format with two decimal places. The number 1234.567 has been *rounded* to 1234.57 when displayed. The `Fixed 3 dec.` column is formatted as fixed with three decimal places. The column labeled `Comma` is formatted in comma format with two decimal places, and the last column, `Scientific`, illustrates scientific format.

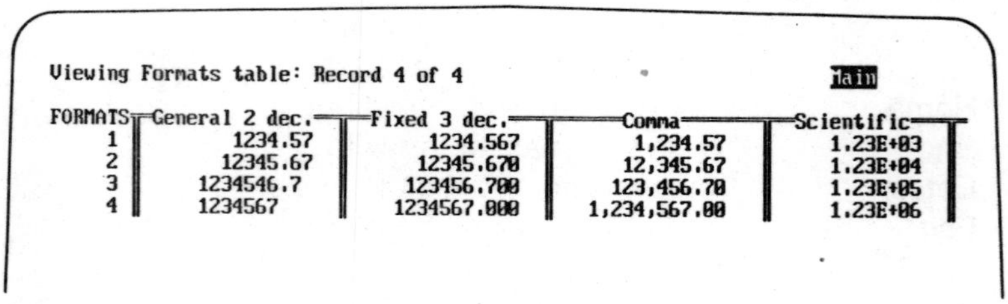
Viewing Formats table: Record 4 of 4 Main

FORMATS	General 2 dec.	Fixed 3 dec.	Comma	Scientific
1	1234.57	1234.567	1,234.57	1.23E+03
2	12345.67	12345.670	12,345.67	1.23E+04
3	1234546.7	123456.700	123,456.70	1.23E+05
4	1234567	1234567.000	1,234,567.00	1.23E+06

Fig. 3.30.
Number format options.

The available formats for dates are

MM/DD/YY	The default date format
DD-Mon-YY	Sometimes referred to as military format
DD.MM.YY	Often called European format

Samples of dates in these three formats are shown in figure 3.31.

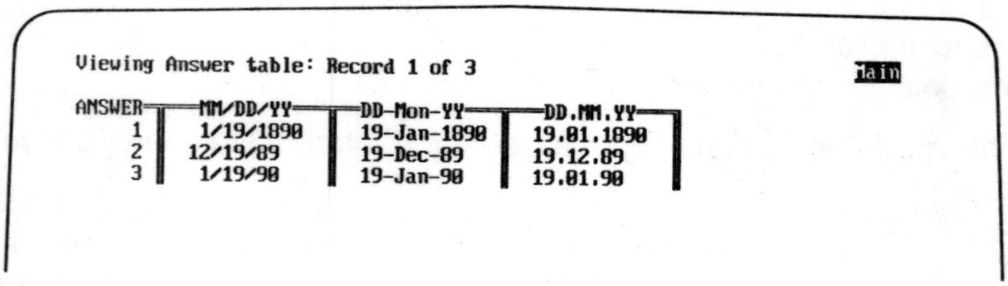
Viewing Answer table: Record 1 of 3 Main

ANSWER	MM/DD/YY	DD-Mon-YY	DD.MM.YY
1	1/19/1890	19-Jan-1890	19.01.1890
2	12/19/89	19-Dec-89	19.12.89
3	1/19/90	19-Jan-90	19.01.90

Fig. 3.31.
Date format options.

Using the Zoom Options

The **Z**oom option on the Image menu (called **G**oTo in Paradox 2.0) provides three shortcut methods to move around in a large table in either table view or form view. The Ctrl-Z (Zoom) feature described in this chapter's section on "Finding a Record with Zoom and Zoom Next" is equivalent to zooming to a value with the menu options.

Version 3

Zooming to a Field

Using this shortcut, you can quickly move to a particular field in a table. First display the Image menu and then select **Z**oom **F**ield. Paradox displays a list of available fields across the top of the screen (see fig. 3.32). Use the arrow keys to locate the name of the field to which you want to go, and press Enter. Paradox jumps the cursor to that field but remains in the same record.

```
Select a field to move to.                                            Main
Emp ID #  Emp Last Name  Emp First Name  Emp Middle Initial  Date Hired ▸
EMPLOYEE╤═Emp ID #═╤═══════Emp Last Name═══════╤══Emp First Name═══╤Emp Middle In
    1   ║ 111-33-8491 ║ Jones                   ║ Harry              ║ H
    2   ║ 129-88-4562 ║ Jones                   ║ Samantha           ║ T.
    3   ║ 230-76-2376 ║ Bronson                 ║ Tim                ║ C.
    4   ║ 329-76-2219 ║ Albertson               ║ Sharon             ║ B.
    5   ║ 448-09-6721 ║ Green                   ║ George             ║ H.
    6   ║ 541-67-5555 ║ Kellogs                 ║ Emily              ║ Q.
    7   ║ 921-65-1234 ║ English                 ║ Gertrude           ║ M.
    8   ║ 987-31-9873 ║ Quick                   ║ Joseph             ║ L
```

Fig. 3.32.

Selecting a field to zoom to.

Zooming to a Record

Sometimes you know the record number of a particular row and want to go directly to that record. Access the Image menu and select **Z**oom **R**ecord. Enter the target record number, and press Enter. Paradox jumps the cursor to that record without changing the current field.

Zooming to a Value

Of the **Z**oom options, this one is the most useful. You can use it to search quickly the entire table for a given field value. You can even use *wild-card* characters. This feature gives precisely the same result as the Zoom keystroke command, Ctrl-Z.

Display the Image menu, and select **Z**oom **V**alue. Move the cursor to the field you want Paradox to search, preferably a key field, and press Enter. Paradox shows a prompt at the top of the screen, instructing you to `Enter the value or pattern to search for.` Type the value that Paradox should try to match; then press Enter. Paradox starts at the top of the table and searches the specified field until finding the first match. The program then moves the cursor to the record that contains the match. If Paradox doesn't find a match, the cursor doesn't leave the record in which you started.

Sometimes you may be searching a field that is not unique, and Paradox may not find the correct record on the first try. The next time you use the **Z**oom **V**alue option, you don't have to retype the value. Or you can just press Alt-Z (Zoom Next) to repeat the search.

Whether you use the menu method or the Ctrl-Z keystroke command, you don't have to specify exactly how the target value is typed. You can use the following *wild-card* operators when building a search pattern:

- You can use two dots together (..) to represent any number of characters, including no characters and blank spaces. For example, the pattern

  Jo..

  tells Paradox to search for all words or phrases that begin with *Jo* and are of any length.

- The operator @ takes the place of any single character. The pattern

  M@

  tells Paradox to search for all values that begin with *M* and are two characters in length.

You can combine these wild-card operators in the same search pattern.

Zoom searches are a terrific way to find a record for viewing or editing. But keep in mind that when searching for exact alphanumeric values, Paradox is particular about whether data and search patterns are in the same case. In other words, the patterns *Jones* and *JONES* are not equivalent. The latter pattern is in all uppercase, but the former is not. Zoom searches using each of these patterns would find different results.

When you use a wild card anywhere in the pattern, however, Paradox is no longer quite so picky. The patterns *jones..*, *JONES..*, and *Jones..* all locate a record with the name *Jones* in the target field. When in doubt, add two dots to the end of your search pattern!

Moving Columns in Field View

One of the basic rules of a relational database is that the order of the fields in the table doesn't matter. You can rearrange field order at will without affecting the underlying data. This rule is true of Paradox tables. (***Note:*** The order in which fields are listed in table structure is significant if you have defined key fields, but the order of the fields in on-screen images is not.)

Paradox provides two ways to move columns on the screen to suit your preferences: through the Image menu and by using the Ctrl-R (Rotate) keystroke command.

Repositioning Columns with the Move Command

Paradox normally displays columns in the same order that they are listed in the table structure. For example, figure 3.33 shows the Employee table in the table definition order.

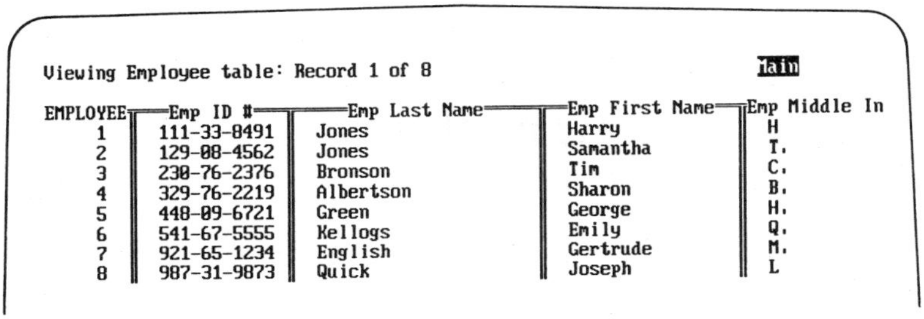

Viewing Employee table: Record 1 of 8
Main
EMPLOYEE Emp ID # Emp Last Name Emp First Name Emp Middle In
1 111-33-8491 Jones Harry H
2 129-08-4562 Jones Samantha T.
3 230-76-2376 Bronson Tim C.
4 329-76-2219 Albertson Sharon B.
5 448-09-6721 Green George H.
6 541-67-5555 Kellogs Emily Q.
7 921-65-1234 English Gertrude M.
8 987-31-9873 Quick Joseph L

Fig. 3.33. *The Employee table.*

Suppose that you want to see the Salary field listed to the right of the Emp Last Name field. To accomplish this task, access the table view Image menu and select **M**ove. Just as with the **Z**oom **F**ield command, Paradox displays a list of available fields. Select the field you want to move, and press Enter (see fig. 3.34).

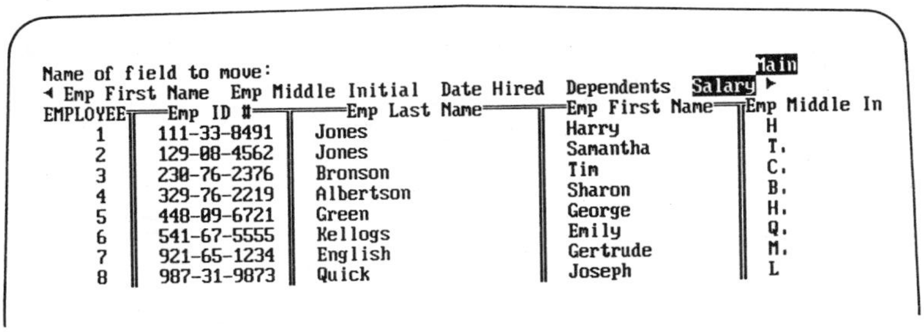

Fig. 3.34. *Selecting the Salary field to be moved.*

Paradox then instructs you to move the cursor to the new position and press Enter. In this example, place the cursor in the Emp First Name field (the new position for Salary) and press Enter. The result is shown in figure 3.35. Salary is now just to the right of Emp Last Name, and all other fields are pushed one column to the right.

Viewing Employee table: Record 1 of 8 Main

EMPLOYEE	Emp ID #	Emp Last Name	Salary	Emp First N
1	111-33-8491	Jones	32,250.00	Harry
2	129-88-4562	Jones	75,900.00	Samantha
3	230-76-2376	Bronson	41,400.00	Tim
4	329-76-2219	Albertson	21,870.00	Sharon
5	440-89-6721	Green	49,339.00	George
6	541-67-5555	Kellogs	23,875.00	Emily
7	921-65-1234	English	36,750.00	Gertrude
8	987-31-9873	Quick	53,000.00	Joseph

Fig. 3.35.

The relocated Salary field.

Repositioning Columns with the Rotate Command

An alternative to the **M**ove option on the Image menu is called the Rotate command (one of the keystroke commands listed in table 1.2). This command takes a little practice, but once you get the hang of it you will find the command tremendously helpful.

To accomplish the same result shown in figure 3.35 with the Rotate command, place the cursor anywhere in the Emp First Name field of the original Employee table, as shown in figure 3.33, and press Ctrl-R (Rotate). The effect of this command is to move the column at the cursor to the far right end of the table. Figure 3.36 shows the result of using this first Rotate command. Emp First Name is gone (moved to the end of the Employee image) and Emp Middle Initial has taken its place. To move Salary to the appropriate position, you have to use Ctrl-R repeatedly until Salary comes into view (three more times, in this particular case).

Viewing Employee table: Record 1 of 8 Main

EMPLOYEE	Emp ID #	Emp Last Name	Emp Middle Initial	Date Hired
1	111-33-8491	Jones	H	6/07/78
2	129-88-4562	Jones	T.	10/02/65
3	230-76-2376	Bronson	C.	11/23/69
4	329-76-2219	Albertson	B.	3/04/81
5	440-89-6721	Green	H.	8/15/79
6	541-67-5555	Kellogs	Q.	6/10/75
7	921-65-1234	English	M.	1/04/71
8	987-31-9873	Quick	L	5/21/83

Fig. 3.36.

The result of using Rotate.

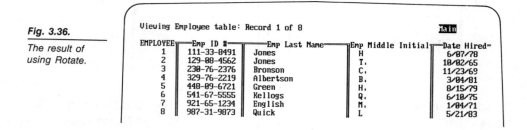

Using the PickForm Option

The third option on the Image menu in both field view and form view is **P**ickForm. This option is used to select a custom-designed form for the table in the current image. Chapter 8 is devoted entirely to the form-design process. Refer to that discussion for detailed information on the **P**ickForm menu command.

Saving Image Settings

The choices on the Image menu are relatively easy to use, and you probably will occasionally want to use them to customize a table or form view on the fly. But as you begin to use Paradox in your daily routine, you will not want to have to worry continually about sizing, moving, or formatting columns every time you use a table. Fortunately, Paradox provides the **K**eep-Set option to save image settings.

Whenever you have finished selecting your image settings, you can record them for future use by selecting **K**eepSet from the Image menu. Paradox records the settings in a file that becomes a member of the table's family. The program displays a message at the bottom of the screen that reads `Settings recorded....`

This option does not appear on the Image menu in DataEntry mode because you are always working in a temporary table. Saving image settings for a temporary table does not make sense.

Chapter Summary

This chapter has introduced you to the fundamentals of entering, editing, and viewing your database. Armed with these techniques and commands, you are ready to start pouring information into your computer. But putting data into your database and keeping it current is only half the story. The best part is still to come. Turn now to Chapter 4 to begin learning how to use Paradox's unique Query By Example (QBE) method. This simple method of asking questions gives you complete control over even the most complex Paradox database.

4

Getting Started with Query By Example

The first three chapters of this book have introduced you to many terms that may have been new to you. You have learned about tables, fields, records, objects, and views, among other things. You have also become familiar with the "look" of Paradox and the basics of moving around the program and the screen. In this chapter, you can have a little fun.

This chapter introduces you to the heart of Paradox, known as Query By Example (QBE). QBE is the Paradox method of retrieving information from your database. If you have never used a database program before Paradox, you will immediately take a liking to its *check-mark* and *example* methodology. If you are an experienced database user, you may have a little more trouble getting used to this unique procedure but will be amazed at just how easily you can retrieve the information you need.

Chapters 1, 2, and 3 have shown you how to put information into the computer. Now you are going to learn how to build Paradox queries so that you can retrieve precisely the data you want. As you read this chapter, put your fingers on the keyboard and try out what you learn. Play around with the tricks and techniques presented here, and you will certainly discover a few of your own. Above all, have a good time.

Understanding Query By Example

Before you get into the step-by-step details of building Paradox queries, you may have a couple of questions. What is a query? Why use Query By Example?

What Is a Query?

When your boss calls you on the phone and tells you he has to have your department's monthly sales figures for the last six months on his desk by 10:00 a.m., that is a *query*. In other words, your boss has made a specific request for information.

To do your job properly, your response or *answer* has to be as specific as the request. You have the information that your boss wants to see; but you shouldn't produce every number that you could possibly give him, just the sales figures. And you shouldn't give him every sales figure, just those for the last six months.

The same information retrieval principles apply when you are working with a computer database, but this time *you* are the boss. When you want to see certain information on your screen, you have to request the data specifically—that is, build a query. The computer then responds by displaying its answer. You have to learn how to query any computer database system before it can ever be useful to you.

Why Use Query By Example?

Database programs have always provided methods for retrieving data from storage. But learning how to understand fully and use those methods traditionally has been a task for programmers and "power users." Asking a question of a database often required knowledge of a cryptic computer database language with rigid syntax and dozens of commands. Of course, if you are a programmer or you regularly use either terms like *byte* or *nanosecond* in your daily conversation, these database systems may have given you no problem. For most of us, however, a new approach was needed that could allow us to ask complex queries of any database without resorting to programming. *Query By Example* attempts to fill that need. M. M. Zloof and others at IBM's Research Laboratory in Yorktown Heights, New York, developed the idea; and the designers of Paradox, Richard Schwartz and Robert Shostak, made QBE the hub of this powerful program.

Query By Example, in a nutshell, is a two-step process:

1. You request specific data from a database by constructing a *query statement* made up of one or more *query forms*.
2. Paradox responds to your query by producing the requested data in the form of a temporary table named Answer.

The entire QBE drama unfolds in query forms and answer tables. This chapter shows you how to build queries and retrieve information without writing a single line of program code.

Displaying a Query Form

To display a query form, select **A**sk from the Main Paradox menu. Specify the name of the Paradox table that contains the information you need. Paradox displays an empty table on-screen in Main mode that looks identical in structure to the table you are querying (see fig. 4.1).

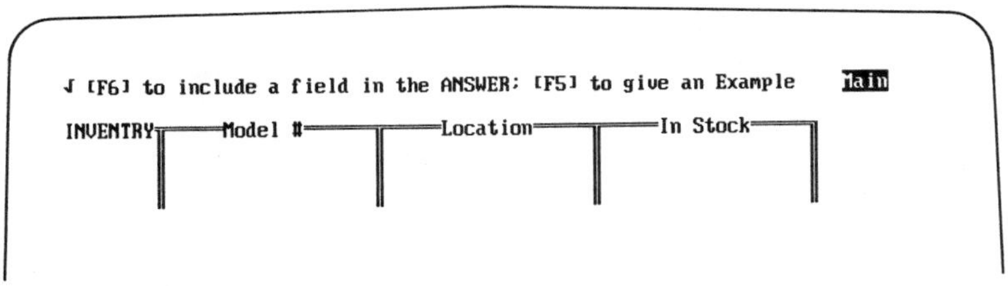

Fig. 4.1.

The query form.

Think of this image as an order form used to bring up records from your Paradox table. The image is not a table itself and is never stored to disk. Just check off the fields you want to see, and provide enough criteria for Paradox to be able to find specific records. For example, figure 4.2 asks Paradox to look in the Inventry (inventory) table to find how many of model number B107 are in stock. The details of building such a query form are presented in the next several sections.

You enter and edit information in a query form while in Main mode in almost the same manner you would enter and edit data in a normal table in Edit mode, including the use of field view (Alt-F5 or Ctrl-F). But because a query form is not a table, certain editing options are not supported, including Undo, form view, and most image-manipulation commands. You can rearrange the columns, if you want, with either the **M**ove command from the Image menu or the Ctrl-R (Rotate) keystroke command, but changing

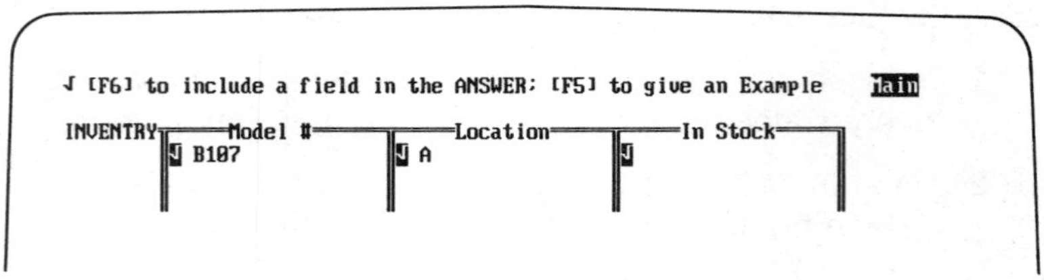

Fig. 4.2.

Querying the Inventry table.

the order of the columns in the query form normally has no effect on column order in the Answer table. Columns in Answer are initially in table definition (structure) order. Once Paradox produces the table, you can modify its image in all the normal ways described in Chapter 3.

Caution: Pressing F9 (Edit) or Alt-F9 (CoEdit) inadvertently in a query form puts you into an "edit" mode, just as if the form were a table. At that point, pressing F2 (DO-IT!) does *not* execute the query but instead ends the "edit" session. You then have to press F2 a second time to execute the query. Also, if you're in this mode, pressing F10 (Menu) gives you the Edit menu and not the Main menu. This situation can be confusing, so keep it in mind when you're working in a query form.

Version 3

Paradox normally displays fields in the Answer table in the same order as in the table definition. In Paradox 3.0 you can change this display through the Custom Configuration Program (CCP). Use the **Q**ueryOrder choice on the Defaults menu of the CCP to change the order of fields to **I**mageOrder rather than the default of **T**ableOrder. Be aware, however, that this selection may lead to problems. For example, you might perform two similar queries on a table, producing two Answer tables with exactly the same fields but in different field order. Paradox does not allow you to add these two tables with the **A**dd command, because the program considers them no longer to have compatible table structure. Refer to Appendix B for more details on the CCP, and to Chapter 13 for a discussion of the **A**dd command.

Queries can be composed of multiple query forms in the work space. Together, all query forms in the work space make up a *query statement*. This chapter discusses how to use single-form queries. Chapter 7 explains the more powerful and more complicated multiform query statements.

Caution: The fact that you can display more than one query form on the screen can be dangerous. Paradox tries to relate the query forms even if you want them separate. Therefore, when you query, always clear the screen first by pressing Alt-F8 (Clear All).

Displaying and Clearing the Answer Table

To tell Paradox to execute a query you have constructed, press F2 (DO-IT!). Paradox displays the message `Processing query..` and then presents the Answer table as the next image in the work space (see fig. 4.3).

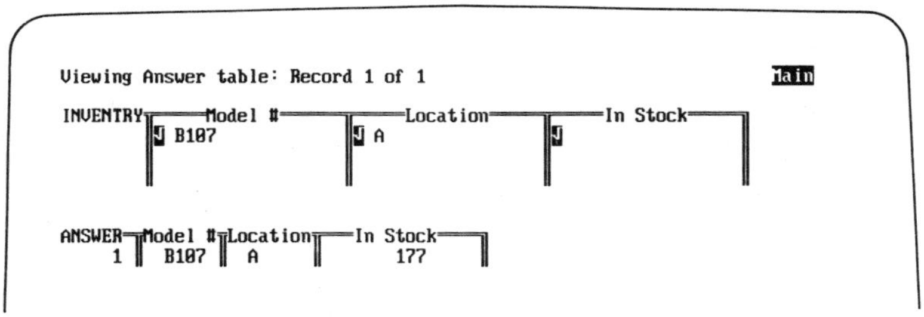

Fig. 4.3.

The Answer table.

The query form and the Answer table are each one image in the Paradox work space. At any time you can clear either one from the screen by making that image current and pressing F8 (Clear Image). To clear both query and answer from the screen, press Alt-F8 (Clear All).

Selecting Fields in Query By Example

When you build a query in Paradox, you have to specify which fields and which records from a table should be displayed. The basic method you use in Paradox for selecting fields is the *check mark*.

Using the Check Mark Key

The simplest way to include a field in the answer is to mark the field in the query form with F6, the Check Mark key. Move the cursor to each field you want included in the Answer table, and press F6 (Check Mark). Paradox places a check mark (the square root symbol in the IBM extended character set) at the left side of the column. Press F2 (DO-IT!), and Paradox produces a table that includes all the checked fields. Figure 4.4 shows a simple query form for the Employee table and the resulting Answer table. The fields Emp ID #, Emp Last Name, Emp First Name, and Emp Middle Initial in the query form are checked, so they are included in Answer. The Date Hired field contains no check mark and does not appear in the Answer table.

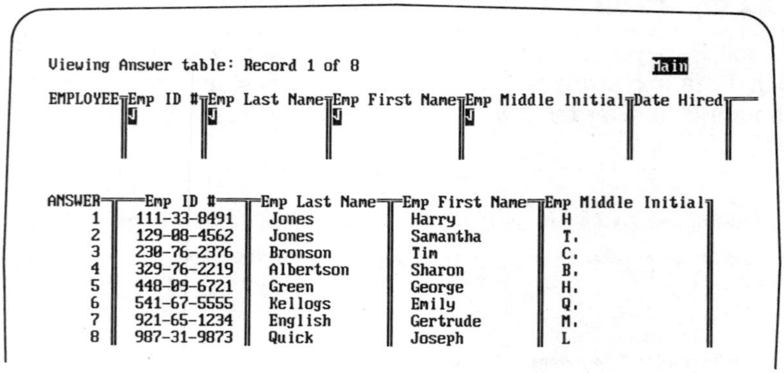

Viewing Answer table: Record 1 of 8 Main

EMPLOYEE	Emp ID #	Emp Last Name	Emp First Name	Emp Middle Initial	Date Hired
	√	√	√	√	

ANSWER	Emp ID #	Emp Last Name	Emp First Name	Emp Middle Initial
1	111-33-8491	Jones	Harry	H
2	129-08-4562	Jones	Samantha	T.
3	230-76-2376	Bronson	Tim	C.
4	329-76-2219	Albertson	Sharon	B.
5	448-09-6721	Green	George	H.
6	541-67-5555	Kellogs	Emily	Q.
7	921-65-1234	English	Gertrude	M.
8	987-31-9873	Quick	Joseph	L

Fig. 4.4.

Selecting fields with F6 (Check Mark).

F6 (Check Mark) is a toggle. Press it a second time in a query form field to remove the check mark.

If you want to include all fields of a table in a query, use this shortcut: Position the cursor in the first column of the query form, beneath the table name (the column that contains record numbers when the table is displayed), and press F6 (Check Mark). Paradox checks off all fields in the table. If any fields are already checked, they remain checked, and the rest of the fields are checked as well. A second press of F6 removes the check marks from all the fields.

Changing the Field Name

With Paradox 3.0, you can rename a field during a query so that the field name in the Answer table is different from the field name in the query form and underlying table. You simply type the word *as* followed by the new field name. For example, you can change the name of the Emp ID # column in the Answer table shown in figure 4.4 to Employee ID Number by typing *as Employee ID Number* in the Emp ID # column of the query form.

Displaying Duplicates

One of the rules of good relational database design is that no duplicate records should be allowed. As you already have learned, Paradox prevents you from entering duplicate records into any keyed table. For similar reasons, Paradox normally eliminates duplicate records (records that are identical to one or more previous records in the table) from Answer tables.

In figure 4.4, records 1 and 2 are both included because they are not *exactly* the same. Both employees have the same last name, but all the other field values are different. When only the Emp Last Name field is included, however, as in figure 4.5, Paradox automatically eliminates one of the Jones records.

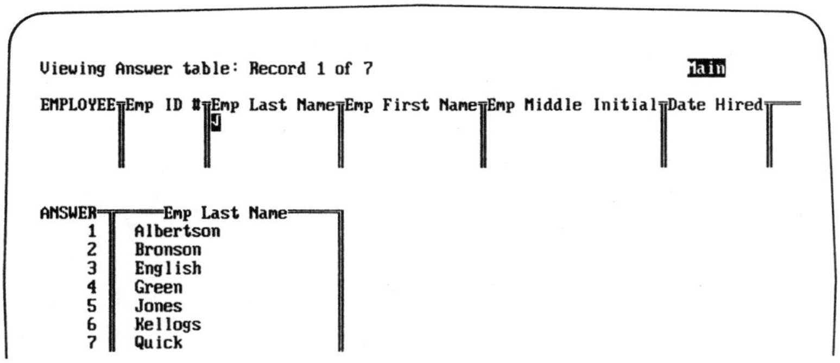

Fig. 4.5.

Using F6 (Check Mark) to avoid listing duplicate records.

Paradox provides a way for you to indicate that duplicates should be included in the Answer table. Use Alt-F6 (Check Plus) rather than F6 (Check Mark) in the first query form field (from left to right), and Paradox includes all records, whether or not they exactly duplicate other records in the table. The same query shown in figure 4.5 is redone in figure 4.6 with Alt-F6 (Check Plus). Both Jones employees are included in the Answer table.

For maximum speed, use Alt-F6 (Check Plus) in the first field that will be retrieved by the query. Because Paradox does not have to eliminate duplicates or sort the Answer table, the program displays the Answer table more quickly than it normally does.

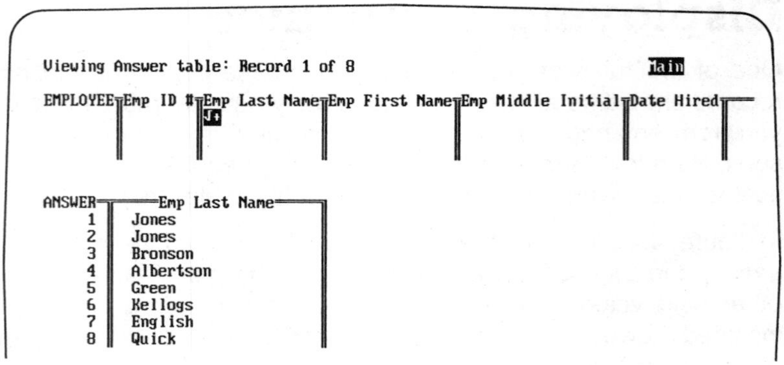

Fig. 4.6.

Using Alt-F6 (Check Plus) to return duplicate values.

Sorting the Answer Table in Ascending Order

Paradox stores table records in the order in which you entered them, unless you defined one or more key fields. Keyed records are stored in order by the key values in each record. When you perform a query, however, Paradox sorts the Answer table in ascending order by the left-most field also included in the query. Ties are broken by using the next field to the right in the table structure included in the query. Record sort order therefore is not affected by the order of the fields within the query.

The query form and Answer table in figure 4.7 show the same group of employees listed in figure 4.4, but this time the Emp ID # field has not been included. The order of the columns (fields) in the Answer table is determined by the order of the fields in the table structure, not in the query form (unless the CCP is used to switch to **Q**uery **O**rder). Even though Emp First Name is listed first in the Query form, it is second in the Answer table. Because Emp Last Name is the first field of the included fields in the Employee structure, Paradox lists the records in the Answer table in order by Emp Last Name. Because two employees are named Jones, the Emp First Name column is used to establish which record Paradox lists first.

Version 3

As mentioned previously, rearranging the order of the fields in the query form normally does not affect the Answer table. This statement is true for the sort order as well. If you use the Custom Configuration Program to change the **Q**ueryOrder option to **I**mageOrder, however, moving fields around in the query form with either Ctrl-R (Rotate) or the **M**ove command affects the order in which records appear in the Answer table. When Paradox sorts in **I**mageOrder, the program sorts the Answer table first by the values in the left-most column, regardless of the position of that field in the source table's structure. By default, Paradox normally sorts records by the values in the left-most column in the first source table's structure also included in the query. If you find that you often are using the **S**ort command to rearrange data in the Answer table, consider using the CCP to make this change to the **Q**ueryOrder option (possible in Paradox 3.0 only).

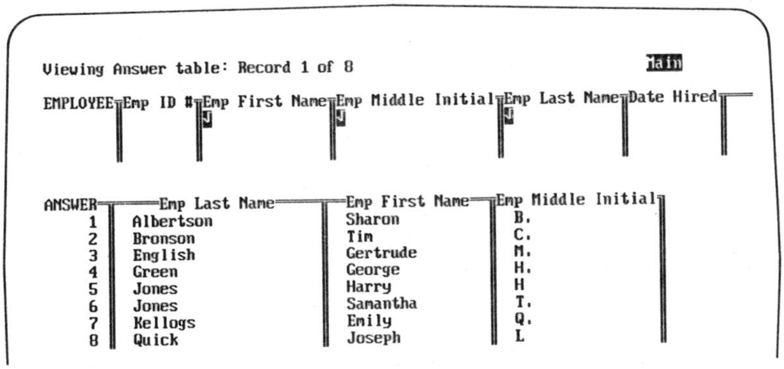
Viewing Answer table: Record 1 of 8 Main

EMPLOYEE	Emp ID #	Emp First Name	Emp Middle Initial	Emp Last Name	Date Hired
		✓	✓	✓	

ANSWER	Emp Last Name	Emp First Name	Emp Middle Initial
1	Albertson	Sharon	B.
2	Bronson	Tim	C.
3	English	Gertrude	M.
4	Green	George	H.
5	Jones	Harry	H
6	Jones	Samantha	T.
7	Kellogs	Emily	Q.
8	Quick	Joseph	L

Fig. 4.7.

Using F6 (Check Mark) to sort in ascending order.

Sorting the Answer Table in Descending Order

Version 3

Paradox 3.0 also provides a method for sorting the Answer table in reverse or *descending* order (as in Z to A, or 9 to 0). Rather than use F6 (Check Mark), use Ctrl-F6 (Check Descending) to mark the fields. Paradox places a downward-pointing triangle to the right of the normal check-mark symbol to indicate that the records will be sorted in descending order. Keep in mind, however, that Paradox still sorts the fields on the left first.

Figure 4.8 shows the Emp First Name field in descending order by itself. When the Emp Last Name field is added in figure 4.9 with a normal check mark, the records are ordered first by the Emp Last Name field, and then the ties are broken in descending order by the Emp First Name field. Samantha Jones comes before Harry Jones but only after following Albertson, Bronson, English, and Green.

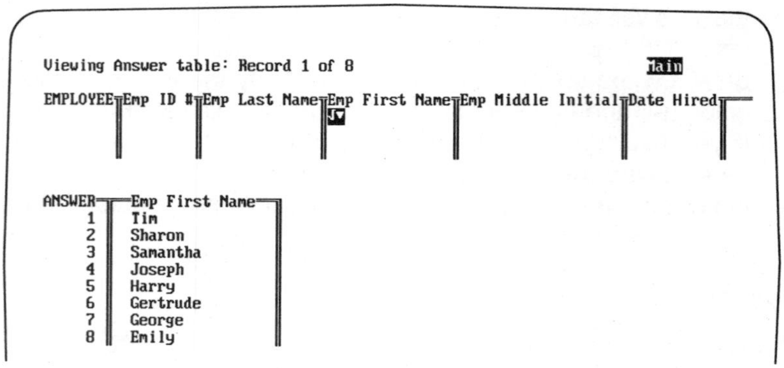

Fig. 4.8.

Using Ctrl-F6 (Check Descending) to sort in descending order.

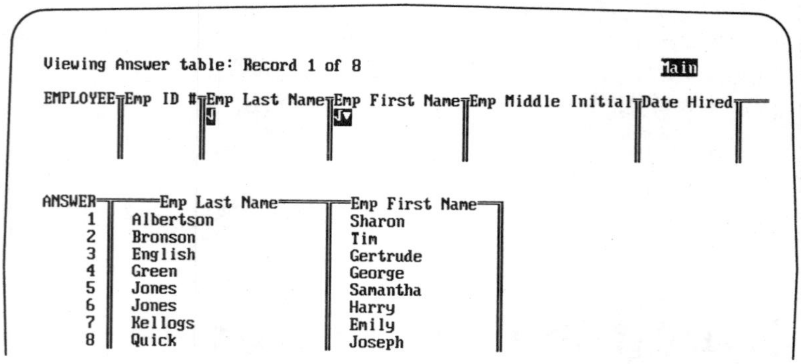

Fig. 4.9.

Sorting the second field in descending order.

Selecting Records in Query By Example

So far, you have learned how to select the fields that Paradox should include in the Answer table. You have seen that you can use F6 (Check Mark), Alt-F6 (Check Plus), and Ctrl-F6 (Check Descending) to pick fields in a query. When you press F2 (DO-IT!), Paradox displays the field(s) you indicated for *every* record in the table. This section of the chapter explains how to select particular records for Paradox to include in the Answer. You learn how to search for records that exactly match examples you give, that match a general pattern you provide, or that fall within a range of values you define.

Finding an Exact Match

In its simplest form, selecting records in Query By Example involves you filling in values in one or more of the query form fields and Paradox then looking for exact matches in the table. When you fill in the field values, you are providing the *example* part of Query By Example. When you tell Paradox to do it (with F2), the program takes your example and performs the query, trying to find any records that match the example exactly. In a properly designed database, you can use this simple method to find any record, because every record in every table is unique and can be precisely identified by the value in its key field(s). In this book, the value you can use to retrieve a record is referred to as the record's *identifying value*.

To find one of the employees in the Employee table, for instance, you can provide the employee's identifying value, which is the Emp ID #, as the example. This field is the single key field for Employee and is therefore a unique identifier for each record. Start with the empty query form, and type the employee's ID number in the appropriate field, as shown in the query form in figure 4.10. Select the fields you want to see by pressing F6 (Check Mark), and then press F2 (DO-IT!).

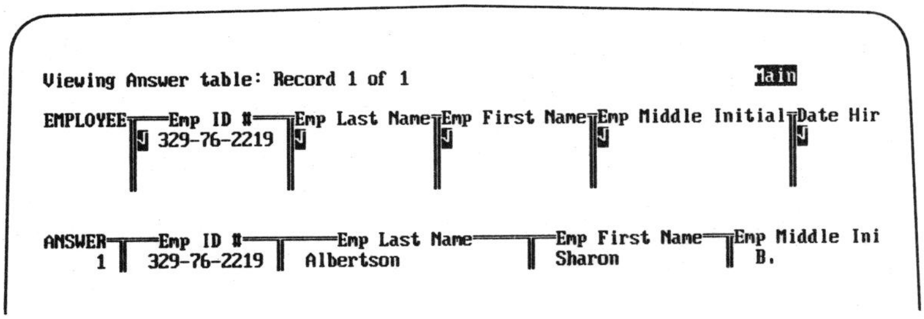

Fig. 4.10.

Finding an exact match.

When a table has a multi-field key, you have to provide an example in each of the key fields in order to retrieve just one record successfully. For example, suppose that you have a Detail table in which each record is identified by combining the Order # field with the Item # field. Together these fields constitute a unique identifier and have been defined as a multi-field key. The query in figure 4.11 indicates that you want to see the second item of order number 103.

Of course you often need to see more than just one record at a time, so you also can use Query By Example to retrieve multiple records that match a given set of identifying values or criteria. Suppose that you want to see a list of all order numbers credited to the employee listed in figure 4.10. To ask Paradox to produce that information, you type the employee's ID number in the Emp ID # field of the Orders table. Even though that field uniquely identifies the employee, each employee can handle more than one order, so the answer to this query includes more than one record (see fig. 4.12).

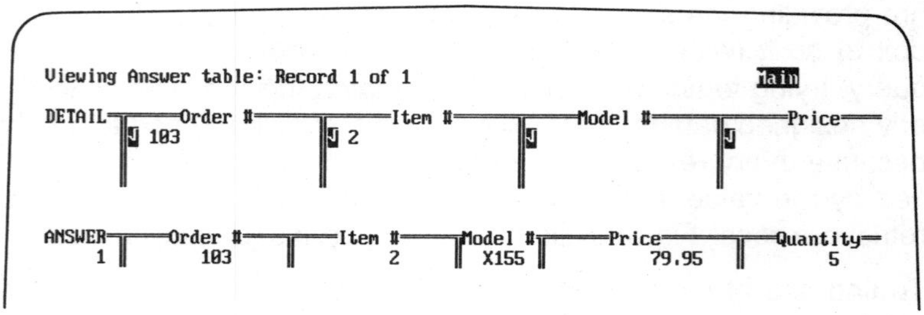

Fig. 4.11.

Using multiple fields to find a match.

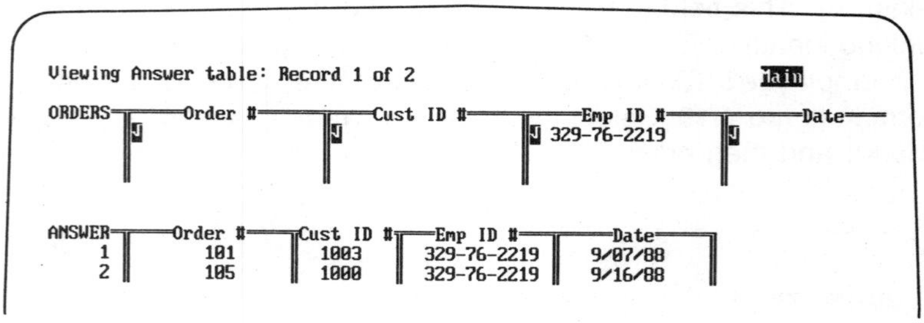

Fig. 4.12.

Matching multiple records.

Guidelines for Matching Values

You should keep several rules in mind when building queries that look for exact matches:

- ❑ Use precise spelling. (See also the discussion of the *like* operator in this chapter's section on "Making an Educated Guess with the Like Operator.")
- ❑ Remember that Paradox is case sensitive. If a value in the table was entered in all caps, search for the value in all caps; if it was entered in all lowercase, search in all lowercase; and so on. (Refer also to the discussion of *patterns* and *wild cards* in the "Matching a Pattern" section of this chapter.)
- ❑ When searching for a value that includes punctuation, enclose the entire field example in double quotation marks (as in "Clyde W. Davis, Jr."). When the value itself contains double quotation

marks, precede each pair of double quotation marks in the query example with a backslash character (\).

- If the identifying values contain any of Paradox's reserved words or operators, enclose those values in double quotation marks.
- When searching numeric fields, do not use whole number separators (the comma is the U.S. convention, and the period is the international convention) or the dollar sign. Always search for exactly two decimal places in currency fields. You can search for any number of decimal places in number fields, but two at most will display in the answer.
- Enter date values in any of the formats: MM/DD/YY, DD-Mon-YY, or DD.MM.YY. The format used in the example does not have to match the format that was used to enter the date originally.

Using Paradox Operators

Sometimes you may not be sure how the identifying value for a particular record or group of records is spelled. Maybe you can't remember whether data was typed in uppercase, lowercase, or some combination of both. Or perhaps you want to see a number of records that have nonidentical identifying values but fall into a certain pattern or occur within a certain range of values. Paradox provides tools that can help solve these problems: the *like* operator, *wild-card patterns*, and *range* operators. These tools all require that you have at least some idea of what the identifying values you are trying to match look like, but you do not have to ask for an exact match.

Making an Educated Guess with the Like Operator

One of the most amazing and useful features of Paradox is its *like* operator. The purpose of this operator is to locate information in your database based on your best guess as to spelling. Generally, you should use the like operator as a second resort, after failing at least once to find the data by using a more specific query.

To use the like operator, just type the work *like* in front of your best guess. For example, suppose that you want to see the entire record from the Customer table for a certain freight line, but the only name you can think of right now is "Alpo Freight Lines." You tried that name, but Paradox returned an empty table, meaning that no such record exists. Figure 4.13

shows the same query with the word *like* added before the original entry. This time Paradox returns a record. The correct company name was "Alpha Freight Lines." This operator does not work if you don't get at least the first letter correct.

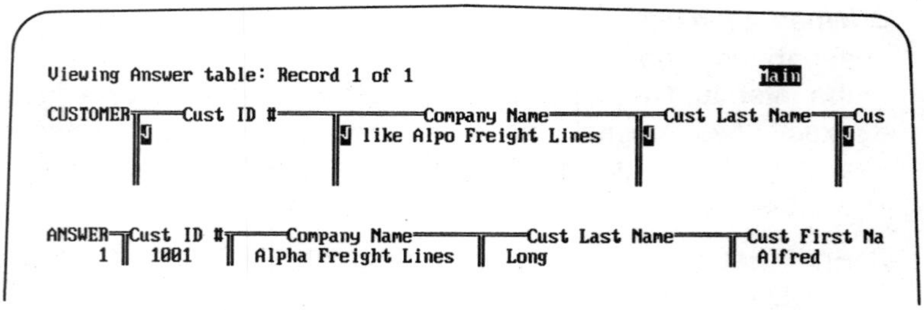

Fig. 4.13.

Making an educated guess with the like operator.

Matching a Pattern with Wild Cards

Paradox also permits you to specify *patterns* as search criteria. You can use *wild cards* in place of specific characters or numbers in your examples. Patterns provide another way to locate records without having to match identifying values exactly. Patterns have a broader usefulness than the like operator because you can more precisely control which records you locate. Paradox provides two wild cards you can use in building patterns: .. and @.

When you use two dots or periods side-by-side (..) in an example value, Paradox returns any alphanumeric character, number, or date of any length as a match, including no characters or blank spaces. Used by itself, the .. operator returns *every* record in the table. In fact, you could say that Paradox uses .. as the default entry in every field in Query By Example. The .. operator normally is not used alone but is used to represent a series of characters or numbers in an example value. Figure 4.14 shows a query that returns the Customer record of every company whose name begins with the letter *a*. When you use this operator, the case of any characters in the pattern no longer matters.

The other wild card, @, is used to represent any single character. Use @ when the position of specific characters in the example is important. For instance, to retrieve all names with the letter *r* as the second letter, use the pattern *@r..*, as shown in figure 4.15. By contrast, the pattern *@@r..* would find names with *r* in the third position.

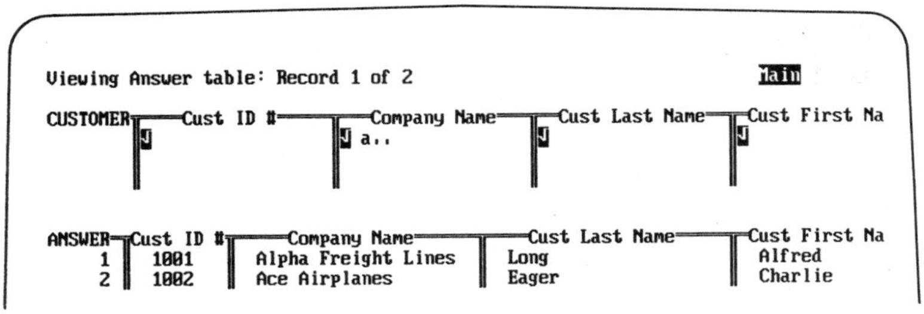

Fig. 4.14.

Using the .. wild card in a pattern.

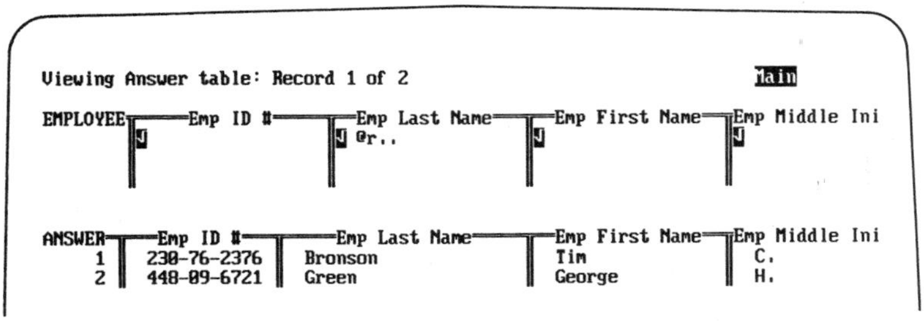

Fig. 4.15.

Using the @ wild card.

The following rules apply to using patterns in Query By Example:

- ❑ You cannot mix operators. In other words, you can't use the like operator with wild-card patterns in the same query example.
- ❑ Use double quotation marks around characters or words that have a special meaning to Paradox during query.
- ❑ Patterns in date fields must be in the current screen date format, even if you have used the **F**ormat option on the Image menu to change the way a particular date field is viewed. Refer to Appendix B for information on how to change the screen date format, using the **D**ateFormat option on the Custom Configuration Program's Int'l menu. The default format is MM/DD/YY.
- ❑ Don't use dollar signs or whole number separators with numbers. You should, of course, use the decimal point when appropriate. But because the period is also a part of the ... wild card, you should enclose the decimal point in double quotation marks to eliminate ambiguity. Always account for exactly two decimal places when building a pattern for currency fields. Patterns for number fields can search for any number of decimal places, but no more than two places are displayed in the Answer table.

Table 4.1 includes a few examples of valid query patterns, showing values that would be retrieved by a query and, in some cases, values that would not be retrieved.

Table 4.1
Examples of Valid Query Patterns

Pattern	*Matches*	*Does Not Match*
Jo..	Jones JOHNSON Jolliet Jo Jo	Mr. Jones
J@@n	Jean John	jeans Johnson
..q..	quick aquatic WMZQ FM	
@q..	aquatic	quick
..th..r	MOTHER path finder Fifth of October	Mothers Day
@@other	brother	mother
12/../88	Matches all dates in December 1988 if the current screen date format is set to MM/DD/YY (the default format unless you change it with the CCP)	
21..	21,000 210.45 21.3	.21 2.1
..21	13,018.21 456.021	130,182.1 321.00
3@@@.@@	3,000.00 3,000.01 3,724.15	3,000 3,000.1 3,724.156

Because the .. wild card renders Paradox insensitive to case, this operator provides an easy way to assure yourself that you will find the information you are looking for, even when you can't remember if the data was entered in uppercase, lowercase, or a combination of both. Just tack the .. wild card onto the end of the example. Be aware that you may get more than you bargained for, however, because with this method you are making the search pattern more general.

Finding a Range of Values

Another way to ask Paradox for a group of records is to specify a *range* of values, which can be a range of numbers, dates, or even alphanumeric characters. Use one or more of the five available range operators listed in table 4.2 to specify the limits of the range.

Table 4.2
Range Operators

Operator	*Meaning*
=	Equal to (optional)
>	Greater than
<	Less than
>=	Greater than or equal to
<=	Less than or equal to

Range operators most often are used with number, currency, and date fields. For example, you might want to see a list including every employee whose salary is less than $25,000. To display records in just that range, type <*25000* in the Salary column, as shown in figure 4.16. Because all salaries are necessarily greater than zero, you don't have to worry about the low end of this range. Paradox shows you the salaries less than $25,000 and greater than $0.

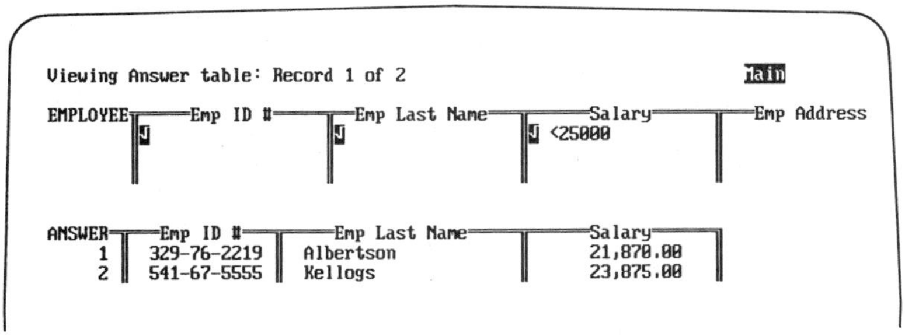

Fig. 4.16.
Finding a range of numbers.

A typical use of query ranges is to select records that occurred over a certain period of time. To see the orders placed from September 5 to September 20, 1988, you need to specify two conditions. The orders must have been placed on or after 9/5/88 AND on or before 9/20/88. Paradox enables you to include multiple conditions in the same query example; you must separate them with a comma. The complete selection criteria are shown in the query form in figure 4.17. When you include two conditions in the same field, Paradox assumes that both must be met before a particular record can be displayed. Using this type of criteria is sometimes referred to as combining the conditions with the logical operator *and*.

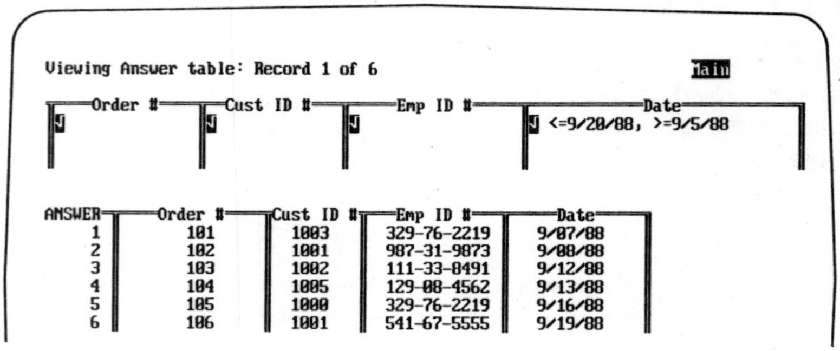

Fig. 4.17.

Finding a range of dates.

Using Special Query Operators

You could retrieve any record or group of records from your database tables by using one of the methods already covered in this chapter, but Paradox provides a number of other query functions that can help you select records more precisely with a minimum of effort. These operators are listed in table 4.3. The next several sections of this chapter explain the use of these special query operators.

Table 4.3
Special Query Operators

Operator	*Meaning*
today	System date
,	Logical "and" condition (when used between conditions in the same query row and field)
*or	Logical "or" condition
not	No match (not equal to)
blank	No data entered

*Paradox 3.0 only

Using the Today Operator and Date Arithmetic

All PCs have a built-in system clock. The correct date and time is either maintained by a battery, or you have to reset the date and time whenever you turn on your computer. Paradox gives you access to the current date through the special operator *today*. Keep in mind though that the today operator is always equal to the current *system* date, so your system clock must be properly set. You can use the today operator in a query the same way you would any date value.

Another feature often used in conjunction with the today operator is *date arithmetic*. This feature enables you to perform calculations on a date, usually addition (+) or subtraction (-). Paradox then arrives at a new date based on these calculations and the program's built-in calendar, which stretches from January 1, 100, through December 31, 9999.

Using ranges and date arithmetic together, the following query example would find records with dates spanning the last 180 days:

>today-180, <=today

All the standard arithmetic operators (+, −, *, /, and ()) are available for use in date arithmetic. See Chapter 7 for further discussion of performing calculations in Query forms.

Specifying Multiple Conditions—*And* versus *Or*

As mentioned in the previous section on "Finding a Range of Values," Paradox can handle multiple conditions in the same query example if you separate the conditions with a comma. To identify a record or records in your table precisely, you also may want to enter examples in more than one field. This situation is always true for multi-field keyed tables. As you probably have deduced by now, when you specify examples in multiple fields, Paradox assumes that you want all to be matched at once. This condition is the logical *and*. For example, because two employees in the Employee table are named Jones, you have to specify both first and last names to pick just one of those employees (see fig. 4.18).

The alternative to logical *and* is logical *or*. A more common way to express this idea is "either or." When two conditions are joined by logical *or*, the combined condition is met if *either* one *or* the other condition individually is met. If both are met, so much the better, but that match is not required.

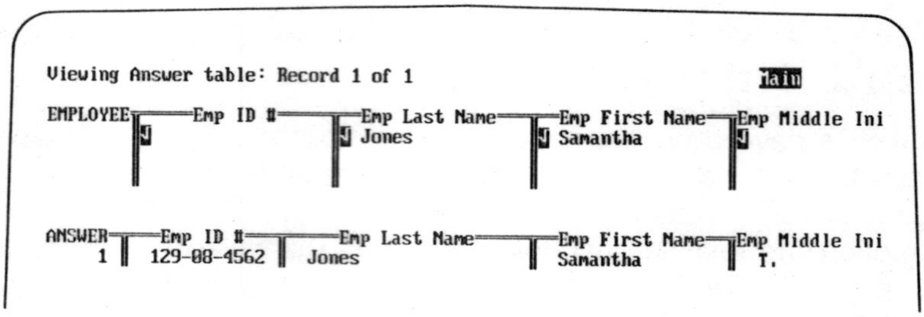

Fig. 4.18.

Using multiple fields to find a match (logical "and").

Paradox 3.0 provides two ways of joining conditions with logical *or*. With previous versions of Paradox, including Paradox 2.0, two rows in a query table are necessary to specify this condition. For example, to determine which orders include either of the two lowest price widgets, model A333 or model B107, you construct the two-row query shown in figure 4.19. You must check the same fields in both rows, and any other multi-field conditions must be repeated.

Version 3

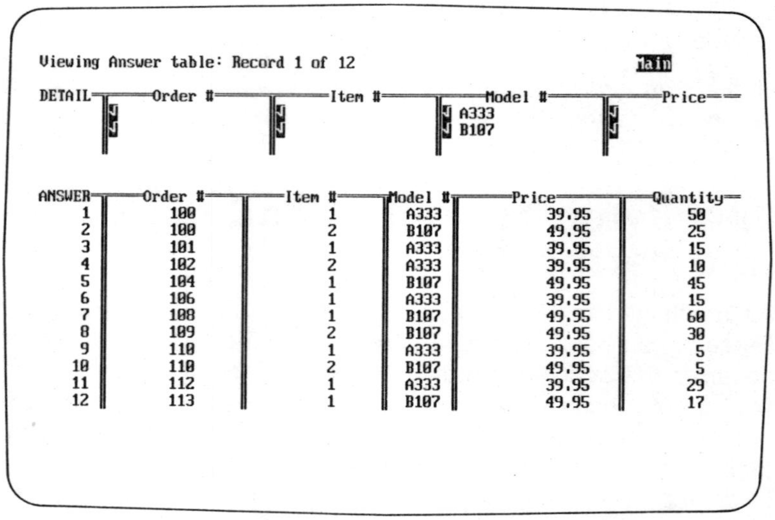

Fig. 4.19.

Using the multirow logical "or" method instead of the "or" operator.

Paradox 3.0 has added the *or* operator. With this feature you type both conditions in the query field side-by-side, separated only by the word *or*. The query in figure 4.20 duplicates the one in figure 4.19 but uses only one query form line.

The multiple-line method is sometimes still the appropriate way to specify a query criterion. Suppose that you are interested in all products in the Product table that are priced between $40 and $50 (inclusive), but you also

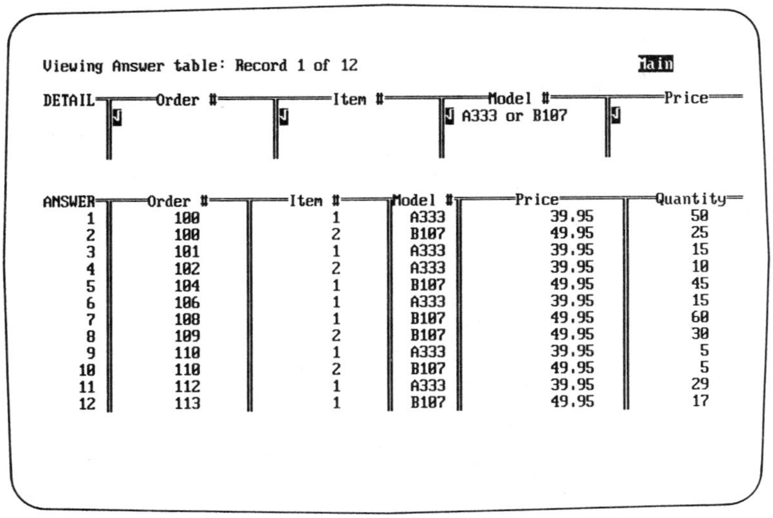

Viewing Answer table: Record 1 of 12 Main

DETAIL	Order #	Item #	Model #	Price
	✓	✓	✓ A333 or B107	✓

ANSWER	Order #	Item #	Model #	Price	Quantity
1	100	1	A333	39.95	50
2	100	2	B107	49.95	25
3	101	1	A333	39.95	15
4	102	2	A333	39.95	10
5	104	1	B107	49.95	45
6	106	1	A333	39.95	15
7	108	1	B107	49.95	60
8	109	2	B107	49.95	30
9	110	1	A333	39.95	5
10	110	2	B107	49.95	5
11	112	1	A333	39.95	29
12	113	1	B107	49.95	17

Fig. 4.20.

Using the single-row logical "or" method.

want to see any model whose cost is less than $20. The query to retrieve the records you want cannot be constructed all on one line of the query table, even with the *or* operator, because the *or* operator can be used only within a single field (see fig. 4.21).

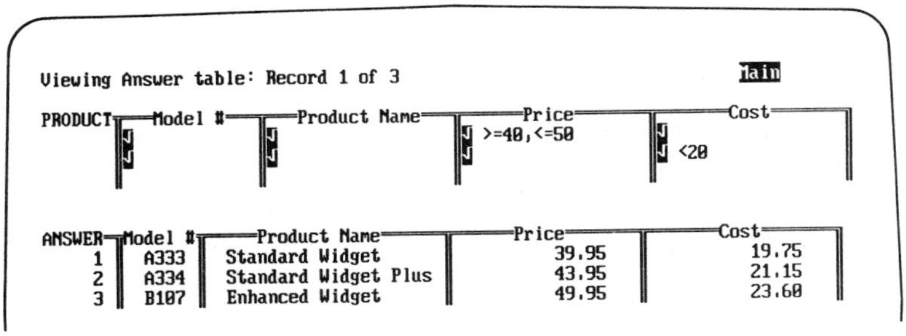

Viewing Answer table: Record 1 of 3 Main

PRODUCT	Model #	Product Name	Price	Cost
	✓	✓	✓ >=40,<=50	✓
	✓	✓	✓	✓ <20

ANSWER	Model #	Product Name	Price	Cost
1	A333	Standard Widget	39.95	19.75
2	A334	Standard Widget Plus	43.95	21.15
3	B107	Enhanced Widget	49.95	23.60

Fig. 4.21.

Using the multirow logical "or" method.

Finding Unmatching Records with the Not Operator

Occasionally you may not be looking for records that match a certain example; rather, you may be looking for those that don't. For example, you might want to see a list of all orders placed for products other than model G400. Paradox provides the operator *not*, which effectively finds all records that do not match a given value (see fig. 4.22). You can use this operator to reverse the effect of any of the other query operators, including like, arithmetic operators, range operators, and patterns. Used as a range operator, "not" means "not equal to."

Viewing Answer table: Record 1 of 16 Main

DETAIL	Order #	Item #	Model #	Price
	✓	✓	✓ not G400	✓

ANSWER	Order #	Item #	Model #	Price	Quantity
1	100	1	A333	39.95	50
2	100	2	B107	49.95	25
3	101	1	A333	39.95	15
4	101	2	X155	79.95	10
5	102	2	A333	39.95	10
6	103	2	X155	79.95	5
7	104	1	B107	49.95	45
8	106	1	A333	39.95	15
9	107	1	X155	79.95	10
10	108	1	B107	49.95	60
11	109	2	B107	49.95	30
12	110	1	A333	39.95	5
13	110	2	B107	49.95	5
14	111	1	X155	79.95	15
15	112	1	A333	39.95	29
16	113	1	B107	49.95	17

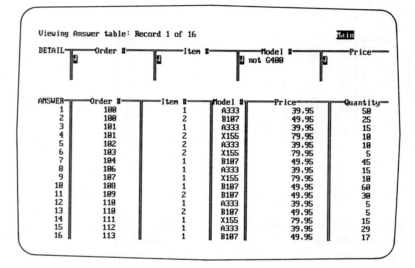

Fig. 4.22.
Using the "not" operator.

Finding Blank Values with the Blank Operator

The basic Query By Example methodology requires that you provide an example value in a particular field whenever you want Paradox to retrieve only records that contain that value in the field. Leaving a field blank in the query form means that you don't care what Paradox finds in that field. But what if you happen to need records that are identified by the lack of information in a certain field? You might, for example, want to see all Customer records that have no telephone number listed. If you perform a query and just leave all fields blank, Paradox returns all records from the table in the Answer. Instead, you should use the *blank* operator to indicate that you intend for Paradox to search for records that have no entry at all in the Cust Phone field (see fig. 4.23). If you type the word *blank* in the query form field, Paradox returns a match only if that field contains no data.

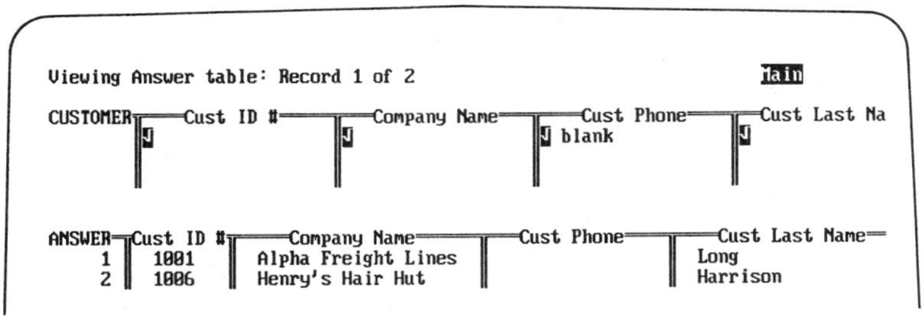

Fig. 4.23.

Using the "blank" operator.

Saving a Query

When you are first learning QBE, you should experiment freely with as many query approaches as you can think of. That method is the only way to learn the ropes. As you become more proficient, however, you will find yourself using the same queries with certain tables time and again. QBE may be fun, but eliminating repetition is what computers are all about, so Paradox provides a quick and easy way to save any query that you expect you may need to use again.

To save a query for later use, first construct it as usual and then press F10 (Menu) and select **S**cripts **Q**uerySave. Paradox prompts you to give the script a name. Type a unique script name and press Enter. (Refer to Chapter 6 for more information on scripts.)

The next time you need to retrieve information meeting these same criteria, select **S**cripts **P**lay from the Main menu. At the prompt, either type the script's name and press Enter, or press Enter at the blank line and select the name from a list of available scripts. Either way, Paradox reconstructs the query on the screen but does not execute it. All you need to do is press F2 (DO-IT!).

Chapter Summary

This chapter has introduced you to the feature of Paradox that seems to define its personality most: Query By Example. QBE is just one part of this sensational program, and you still have much to learn, but by now you should have a good idea of what Paradox is all about. Later, after you have had a quick look at the basics of creating reports in Chapter 5 and scripts in Chapter 6, you will return to QBE in Chapter 7 for an in-depth look at some of its most powerful features.

5

Paradox Reporting Fundamentals

Real-life database work is often one of those situations in which the tail wags the dog. All the data entry, editing, and querying you can muster is worth little if the output it produces doesn't please or inform your audience. Often the sensible approach is for you to look first at the overall design of the end product and then work backward to determine what data you need to collect and what queries you need to perform in order to produce that report. This chapter introduces you to the fundamentals of using Paradox report design features so that early in the database design process you can begin to think about how your printed output will look.

An underlying theme of Paradox is the philosophy that a computer program should do automatically as much of the work for you as possible—the ease-of-use side of the Paradox paradox. Faithful to this theme, Paradox provides you with instant reports literally at the touch of a keystroke command, Alt-F7. After a quick overview of the report design process, this chapter explains how to use the Instant Report feature.

True to the other side of the paradox as well, the program's reporting features provide all the capability you would expect from a full-featured database program, and then some. This chapter introduces you to the basics of creating customized tabular reports with Paradox and presents a number of tools you can put to use immediately. The discussion lays a foundation for Chapters 10 and 11, which cover more complicated tabular and free-form reports.

This chapter works with only one database table at a time in order to present Paradox report fundamentals most clearly. Keep in mind, however, that Paradox is meant to be used as a relational database, pulling information from many tables to build the output you need. Some of Paradox 3.0's most exciting new features involve the creation of multitable reports. But be patient. You will get to that level in due time. Study this chapter first to develop a clear understanding of basic terminology and a sound design approach.

An Overview of the Report Design Process

In previous chapters, you learned how to design database tables, enter and edit data, and retrieve particular fields and records from these tables into an Answer table. The Paradox Report Generator provides the means to produce and control the output of data from your database to a printer, to your screen, or to a file.

What Is a Paradox Report?

You may be an experienced database user, in which case you can skip this section. But if you're a new user, you may not have a clear idea yet of what is meant by a "report" in database jargon. Figure 5.1 shows the easiest type of report Paradox creates—the *instant report*. It is essentially just a version of your database table that can be printed, displayed to the screen, or saved to a file. Although reports are generally produced in hard copy, you usually preview the report to screen before printing and occasionally may want to create a text file that can be imported into a word processing program for inclusion in a longer document.

Figures 5.2 and 5.3 show two other reports, which use various fields from the Employee table shown in figure 5.1. The report in figure 5.2, similar to the instant report, arranges the data in rows and columns like the Paradox table that contains the data. This type of report is referred to as *tabular* style. Figure 5.3 shows a Paradox *free-form* report. When designing this type of report, you can place data in almost any position or order. In this chapter, you learn how to create Paradox reports like these.

With Paradox 3.0, you can also create reports that draw data from several tables at once, called *multitable* reports. Creation of multitable tabular reports is covered in Chapter 10, and multitable free-form reports in Chapter 11. Figure 5.4 is an example of an invoice produced by a multitable

```
Now Viewing Page 1 of Page Width 1
Press any key to continue...


 1/26/89                      Standard Report                     Page    1


Emp ID #     Emp Last Name           Date Hired   Salary
-----------  --------------------   ----------   ----------------
111-33-8491  Jones                     6/07/78          32,250.00
129-08-4562  Jones                    10/02/65          75,900.00
222-39-9999  Brown                    10/17/85          34,000.00
230-76-2376  Bronson                  11/23/69          41,400.00
311-99-5549  Harrison                 11/23/83          42,900.00
329-43-5855  Singer                    2/12/88          21,450.00
329-76-2219  Albertson                 3/04/81          21,870.00
349-04-9862  Harrell                   4/18/79          49,575.00
398-21-2198  Brown                    11/29/87          35,000.00
410-44-4232  Plum                      8/23/76          42,750.00
448-09-6721  Green                     8/15/79          49,339.00
541-67-5555  Kellogs                   6/10/75          23,875.00
553-09-3466  French                    9/01/88          28,550.00
```

Fig. 5.1.

The instant report.

```
End of Page
Press any key to continue...
         Employee Telephone Roster                       Page   1
         Current as of   January 25, 1989

                              Sales Department


                                          Phone Number
                                          ------------
          Albertson, Sharon B.            (703) 555-2361
          Bronson, Tim C.                 (703) 555-7630
          English, Gertrude M.            (703) 555-5575
          Green, George H.                (703) 555-9999
          Jones, Harry H.                 (703) 555-1234
          Jones, Samantha T.              (703) 555-8872
          Kellogs, Emily Q.               (703) 555-3378
          Quick, Joseph L.                (703) 555-1298
```

Fig. 5.2.

A tabular report.

report specification. Data for this report is drawn from the Detail, Customer, and Employee tables. It was produced by a tabular report specification but also could have been created as a free-form report.

```
Now Viewing Page 1 of Page Width 1
Press any key to continue...
  Sharon B. Albertson                       Tim C. Bronson
  770 Shaw Rd., Apt 23                      9828 Rocky Ridge
  Arlington, VA  22210                      Centreville, VA  22020


  Gertrude M. English                       George H. Green
  1601 School House Rd                      872B S. Hill St.
  Fairfax, VA  22030                        Mount Vernon, VA  22320


  Harry H. Jones                            Samantha T. Jones
  1711 Lakeview Dr.                         663 Yuppie Lane
  Burke, VA  22155                          McLean, VA  22101


  Emily Q. Kellogs                          Joseph L. Quick
  1000 Flake Way                            622 Sloth Street
  Alexandria, VA  22313                     Herndon, VA  22070
```

Fig. 5.3.

A free-form report (mailing labels).

```
End of Page
Press any key to continue...

                      INVOICE


Order #:  100
Customer: Eastern Enterprises
          1211 Commerce St.
          Springfield, VA  22150

Salesman: Tim C. Bronson


Item #  Model     Price        Quantity  Extended Price
------  -------  ----------   ---------  ---------------
     1  A333         39.95           50         1,997.50
     2  B107         49.95           25         1,248.75
     3  C400         59.95           10           599.50
                                          ==============
                                Total: $        3,845.75
```

Fig. 5.4.

A multitable report (an invoice).

What Is a Report Specification?

To provide maximum flexibility, Paradox gives you many report-writing options from which to choose. Using them can be fun at times, but you don't want to have to redraft the perfect report every time you need it. As you might expect, Paradox provides a way to save a report design. In Paradox, each report design is saved as a *report specification*. Each report specification is associated with a particular database table, called the *master table*. You can define up to 15 reports per table. A report is one of the objects in the table's family that is automatically reconciled whenever the table is restructured.

You may recall that a discussion in Chapter 2 about relationships between tables also used the term *master table*. The concept is the same here. In Chapters 10 and 11, the distinction between the master table and other related tables becomes more significant when you learn how to generate reports from more than one table. For now, the table you select for a report is simply the table whose data you want to print. This table might be one of the normal tables from your database, or it might be an Answer table generated by a query (when you use the **A**sk command).

Sometimes you may want to create a report from the data in an Answer table. For example, suppose that you want to create a telephone list for a single department of employees, but the table includes four departments. You can use **A**sk to create an Answer table that includes only the specific department.

If you want to use a report that you already designed for another table with the Answer table, you can use the **C**opy command from the Tools menu (see Chapter 13) to copy the report specification from one table to the other. For this procedure to work, however, you have to be careful when you perform the query that creates the Answer table. Make sure that in the query you include all the fields from the original table, even if some of them will not be included in the report. Otherwise, Paradox does not allow you to copy the report and informs you that the two tables (the table that owns the report and the new Answer table) have incompatible structures.

Design Considerations

The type of report you should choose, tabular or free-form, single-table or multitable, depends on the nature of your data and the message you want to convey. Your answers to the following questions can help you determine which style of table can best accommodate your data.

Can you visualize the way the report will look? Building a report is always easier if you sketch it on paper first. Better yet, if you are duplicating an existing form, work from that form. You might want to include some real data so that you get a better idea of how the final product will look.

Will your new report replace an existing report or form? When practical, design your report specification to look as much like the current form or report as possible. This consideration has little to do with computer software but a lot to do with human nature and resistance to change.

Will data be arranged in rows and columns or in groups? A telephone list of your department's employees, for example, should probably be a columnar table with each employee's name and phone number on a single row. But a report to print mailing labels to those employees should group the data about each employee vertically in several rows (compare fig. 5.2 and fig. 5.3).

Should the information be arranged in a particular order? Normally you do not just "dump" data on the page from your database. Instead, you organize the information in a manner that makes it easier to use or understand. Even a simple list of phone numbers is usually in alphabetical order by each person's last name.

Will records be grouped? A phone book for your entire company might also be grouped by department or division for convenience.

Will summary computations be necessary? When your data includes numeric information, you often need to perform summary calculations. Subtotals, subaverages, and so forth require that the data be appropriately grouped in the report.

Is all the necessary information in one table, or do you have to draw some data from other tables in the database? Paradox can combine data from related tables in two ways: multitable queries (Chapter 7) and multitable reports (Chapters 10 and 11—Paradox 3.0 only). You have to decide which method you are going to use before you begin to design your report. This factor is important even when choosing the master table for the report. To be able to create a report from multiple tables, the master table must be directly related or linked to each of the other tables, called *lookup* tables.

Version 3

As you are designing your report, you should also keep in mind the basic report-building capacities of Paradox, summarized in table 5.1.

If you can't decide which report style is best even after answering the questions listed in this section, try the tabular form first. It is more likely to present your data in a satisfactory format with a minimum of effort on your part. Or better yet, the instant report may be all that you need.

Table 5.1
Paradox Reporting Capacities

Feature	*Capacity*
Fields	255
Characters	2,000 per record
Tables	Any number of linked lookup tables in addition to the master table (Paradox 3.0)
Grouping (breaks)	16 levels
Width of page	10 to 2,000 characters
Length of page	2 to 2,000 lines
Width of report	2,000 characters
Length of report	Unlimited

Using the Instant Report Feature

Before you can try this feature, you of course must have already created a table and entered data. When you have proceeded at least that far, you are ready to display a report.

Select the **V**iew command from the Main menu to display the table you want to print. If you are editing the table, you must return to the Main mode before you can produce a report.

Next, use the **A**sk command to select the fields and records you want included in the report. You can skip this step if all the data in the table is to be printed.

Do not be concerned if your table includes too many columns to print on your printer. Paradox automatically breaks your report into page-size pieces, 80 characters by 66 lines. Before printing, set the left edge of the paper no more than two or three spaces to the left of the 0 mark on your printer's paper guide. Most printers print 10 characters per inch (often called *pica* style) by default, so with 8 1/2-inch paper you have only 1/2-inch total (5 spaces) to use for both left and right margins.

If you don't want your report to be split vertically, use a query to limit the fields included. A good rule of thumb is that the columns will fit on the paper if you can see them all on your screen at once.

Finally, make sure that your printer is turned on and properly connected to your computer. Then, while viewing the table you want to print (the Answer table, if you performed a query), press Alt-F7 (Instant Report).

Paradox prints a standard tabular report that looks similar to figure 5.1. The program prints the data in the same row and column order that is displayed, and prints a header of field names at the top of each page. It's not fancy, but this quick print of your data may often be just what you need. If this report is not quite good enough, read on!

Getting Started with the Report Generator

The next several sections describe how to create basic tabular reports, using the Paradox Report Generator and working with only one table at a time. You have already seen the Employee table in this book several times, beginning with Quick Start 1. For the purposes of this and later chapters, a Department field and a few more employees have been added so that the table now includes individuals from four departments: Sales, Administration, Accounting, and Production.

To start designing a report, you must first be in the Main mode. From the Main menu, select **R**eport **D**esign and choose a table. To use the Employee table, for example, you either type the name *Employee* and press Enter, or press Enter at the blank prompt and then select Employee from the list of available tables.

Naming the Report Specification

Once you have chosen the table for the report, Paradox prompts you to select a name from an unusual-looking menu (see fig. 5.5). This menu is a list of available report-specification names.

Paradox can store up to 15 report specifications (report specs) as a part of the table's family. Paradox automatically builds the spec named *R*, called the *preferred report*. When you press Alt-F7 (Instant Report), you get this report specification. You can modify report spec *R* if you prefer, and can create up to 14 additional specs.

Select a name (number) for the report. Paradox alerts you if the name has already been used and gives you a chance to either stop or replace the old specification with your new one.

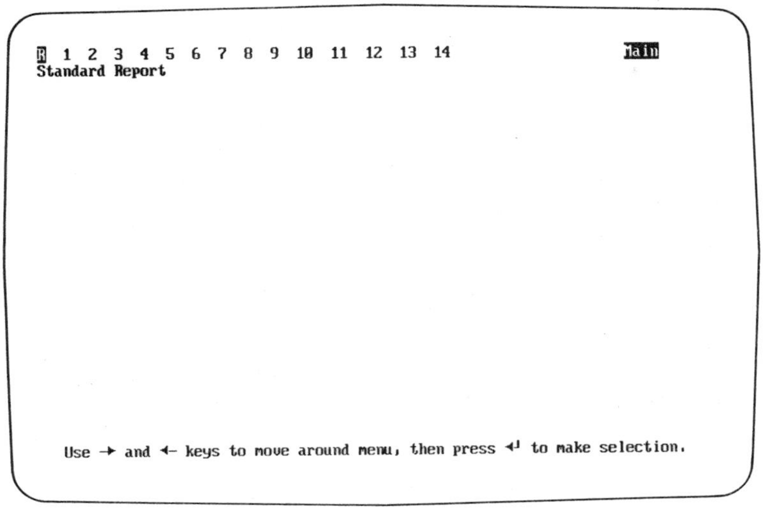

Fig. 5.5.

Selecting a name for the report specification.

The next prompt instructs you to enter a report description. This step is an optional but useful feature that serves two purposes:

- First, it gives you what amounts to a longer report name. Later, whenever the menu shown in figure 5.5 is displayed and you move the pointer to the report spec's name, the description displays in the line just below the menu (see fig. 5.6). You should enter a few words here that will help you remember what this report does. With 14 other specifications possible, you easily can get them confused if you don't take advantage of this memory aid.
- Second, the report description automatically becomes a report title that prints at the top of every page. You can modify the title or remove it from the report specification later if you decide not to use it.

Choosing Report Type

After you enter the report description, the next menu displayed requires that you choose between the two available report styles, **T**abular and **F**ree-form. The options and menus for each of the two report types are not the same from this point. The next several examples in this chapter assume that you are working with a tabular report.

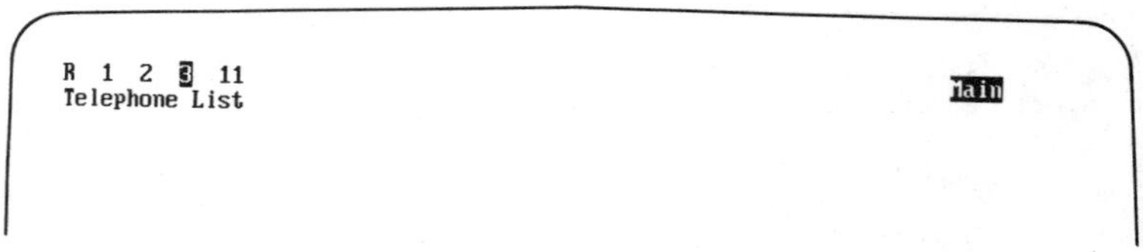

Fig. 5.6.

Using the report description to find the correct report specification.

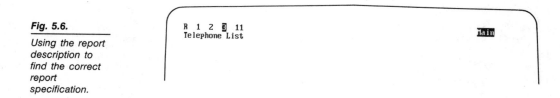

When you choose the **T**abular field type, Paradox displays a screen similar to figure 5.7, called the standard specification for a tabular report. The next portion of this chapter describes the various components that comprise the specification and then explains the fundamentals of customizing this "plain vanilla" report definition.

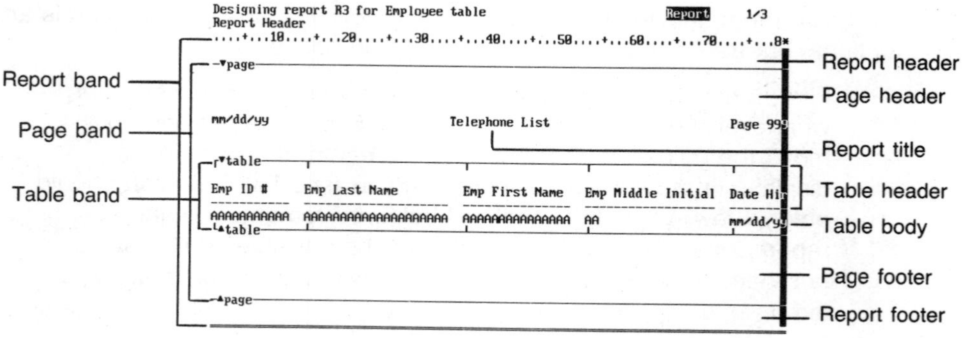

Fig. 5.7.

The standard tabular report specification.

Examining the Tabular Report Specification

The *tabular report specification* is a stylized version of how your report will look when it prints. When you begin designing the specification, Paradox displays the standard specification, which is almost identical to the preferred specification (report *R*) used when you press Alt-F7 (Instant Report). The only difference is that the instant report says `Standard Report` at the top (see fig. 5.1), and your report spec displays the report description you entered (see fig. 5.7).

The specification, as indicated in figure 5.7, is made up of three vertical *bands*. Each of these bands consists of two parts:

- *Report band*. A *report header* and *report footer* comprise the outside layer or band of the report. The header prints only once, at the beginning of the report. The report footer also prints only once, at the end of the report.
- *Page band*. The next layer is the *page band*, which also contains a *header* and a *footer*. These print at the top and bottom of each page, respectively.
- *Table band.* This area is where most of the action takes place. It includes two parts: the *table header* and the *body*. The table header, by default, prints at the top of every page, just above the fields and below the page header. Initially, the standard specification places the field names in this header, above the corresponding fields in the body. The body of the report prints once for every record in the table. The groups of As shown in figure 5.7 indicate that Paradox has placed each of the fields from the table into the table band. These letters are called *field masks* and show the field type and field size. (For more information on field masks, see this chapter's section on "Placing Regular Paradox Fields.") As you move the cursor into one of these masks, Paradox displays the field name in the top right corner of the screen, just below the mode indicator.

These report elements are shown in the specification in the same order they will print. In other words, the report header prints first, then the page header, the table header, and finally the records from your Paradox table. If you include a page footer, it prints at the bottom of each page. In multipage reports, both the page header and table header print at the top of every page. After all records have printed, the report footer prints, followed by the last page footer.

Figure 5.8 shows a simple report specification for a phone list with the various report elements labeled so that you can easily find them. The corresponding report, printed to screen, is shown in figure 5.9. Notice carefully the order in which each of these elements printed (don't be concerned about the order of the data at this point).

Paradox also permits you to add a fourth type of band: the *group band*. Some database programs call this type of band a *break*. Paradox permits up to 16 group bands in a single report. Inserting a group band causes two things to happen:

```
Changing report R5 for Employee table                              Report    1/1
Report Header
....+...10....+...20....+...30....+...40....+...50....+...60....*
Phone Roster       (This is a Report Header)
-▼page-----------------------------------------------------------
mm/dd/yy           (This is the Page Header)
┌▼table----------------------------------------------------------
 Employee          (This is the Table Header) Phone
 --------------------------------------------  -------------
 AAAAAAAAAAAAAAAAAAAAAAAAAAAAAA    (Body)      AAAAAAAAAAAAAA
└▲table----------------------------------------------------------
                   (This is the Page Footer)          Page 999
-▲page-----------------------------------------------------------
                   (This is the Report Footer)
```

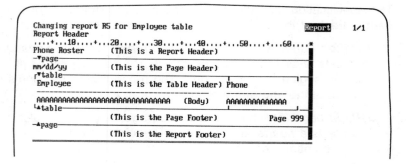

Fig. 5.8.

The report elements.

```
End of Report
Press any key to continue...
Phone Roster       (This is a Report Header)
 1/27/89           (This is the Page Header)
 Employee          (This is the Table Header) Phone
 --------------------------------------------  -------------
 Harry H. Jones                    (Body)     (703) 555-1234
 Samantha T. Jones                 (Body)     (703) 555-8872
 Bruce R. Brown                    (Body)     (703) 555-4421
 Tim C. Bronson                    (Body)     (703) 555-7630
 Steven M. Harrison                (Body)     (703) 555-4432
 Sarah S. Singer                   (Body)     (703) 555-8888
 Sharon B. Albertson               (Body)     (703) 555-2361
 Stanley Q. Harrell                (Body)     (703) 555-2351
 David E. Brown                    (Body)     (703) 555-9812
 Hercule P. Plum                   (Body)     (703) 555-2987
 George H. Green                   (Body)     (703) 555-9999
 Emily Q. Kellogs                  (Body)     (703) 555-3378
 Freda P. French                   (Body)     (703) 555-3322
 Angel L. Smith                    (Body)     (703) 555-2198
 Christopher P. Harvey             (Body)     (703) 555-3298
 Gertrude M. English               (Body)     (703) 555-5575
 Joseph L. Quick                   (Body)     (703) 555-1298
                   (This is the Report Footer)
                   (This is the Page Footer)          Page   1
```

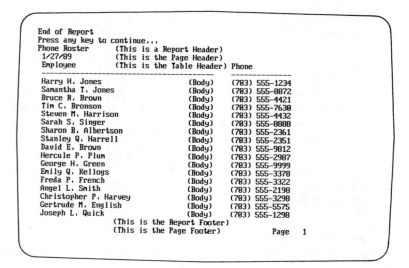

Fig. 5.9.

The report produced by the report specification in figure 5.8.

1. The data in the body is sorted and grouped according to a field that you specify.
2. You have the option of inserting blank lines, and summary calculations at the end of each group of records.

For example, suppose that you want to print a report of employee salaries, grouped by the four departments of your company. Within each department's grouping, you want to see the employee names in alphabetical order. This report would have two group bands: one for the Department field and one for the Emp Last Name field. The first group band causes the records to be grouped in the report by the employee's department. You then have the opportunity to subtotal the salaries by department. The second group band puts employee names in ascending order for the convenience of the reader, but no further subtotal is needed at this level. The specification shown in figure 5.10 produces just such a report. The report itself is depicted in figure 5.11. Creating this report is discussed in more detail in Chapter 10.

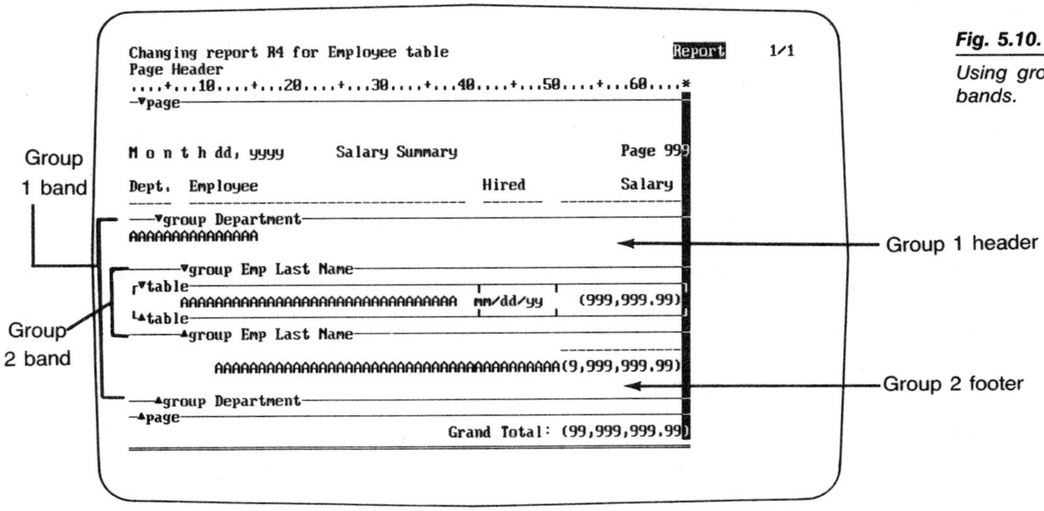

Fig. 5.10.

Using group bands.

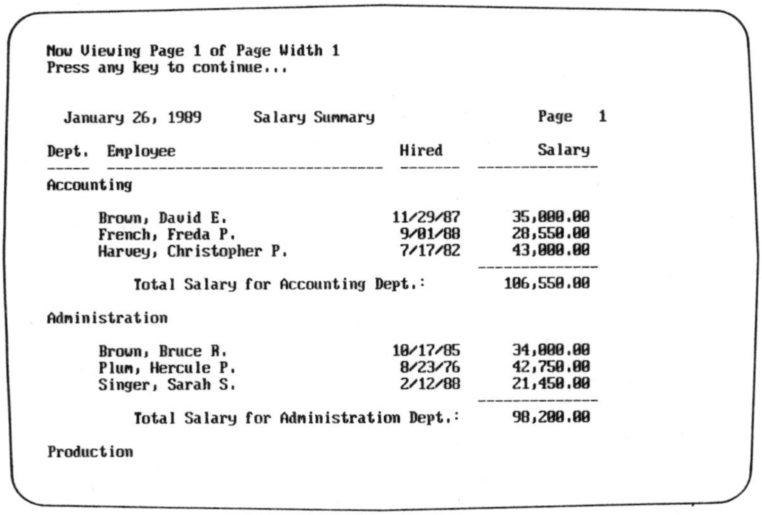

Fig. 5.11.

The grouped report.

Using the Keyboard When Designing Reports

Table 1.2 in Chapter 1 describes the special keys available in Paradox. In several situations, Paradox provides full screen-editing capabilities. Report design is one of these situations. The cursor keys assume slightly different meanings here than they do in other facets of the program. Take a look at table 5.2 for the specific effect of each cursor key on the report design screen. Several of the special keys and cursor-movement keys deserve special attention in this discussion.

Table 5.2
Using Cursor-Movement Keys on the Report Design Screen

Key	*Moves Cursor:*
Home	To first line
Ctrl-Home	To beginning of line
End	To last line
Ctrl-End	To last character of line
PgUp	Up one screen
PgDn	Down one screen
Left arrow	One character left
Ctrl-left arrow	Left one-half screen
Right arrow	One character right
Ctrl-right arrow	Right one-half screen
Up arrow	Up one line
Down arrow	Down one line
Enter	Down one line

Deleting Lines

As you edit a report specification, you sometimes may want to delete an entire line at once. To do so, press Ctrl-Y. Paradox deletes from the cursor position to the right side of your report spec. You occasionally may hear an irritating beep when you try this command. Paradox is telling you that nothing is there to delete. This situation occurs most often when you are attempting to delete a blank line. To delete a blank line, first place the cursor to the far left margin; then press Ctrl-Y.

Displaying a Vertical Ruler

You have probably already noticed that Paradox displays a ruler line along the top of the report spec, just below the status/message lines. This ruler helps you keep track of the size of your report horizontally. A related feature is the *vertical ruler*, which numbers the lines down the left side of the screen. The horizontal ruler is always displayed, but you have to turn on the vertical ruler to see it.

To display line numbers down the left side of the report spec, as shown in figure 5.12, press Ctrl-V. These numbers can be extremely helpful when you're designing a form to meet rigid space requirements, as when you are trying to print on a preprinted form.

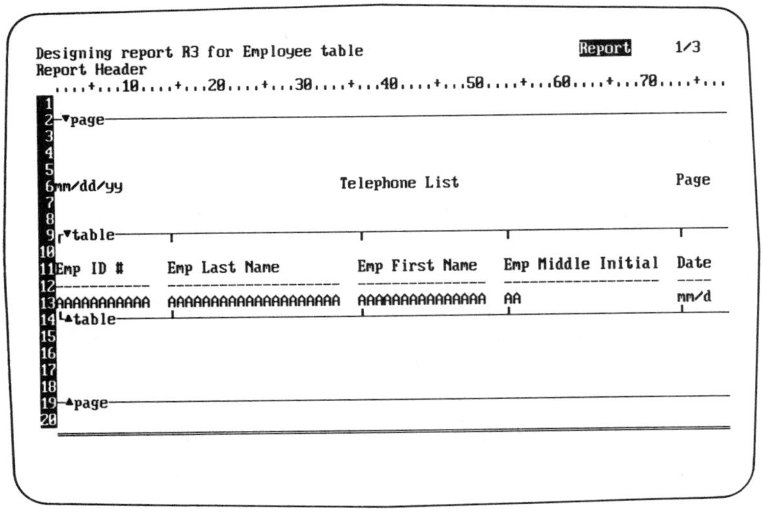

Fig. 5.12.
Displaying the vertical ruler.

Using Replace and Insert Modes

You already have learned that Paradox is normally in Insert mode when you are using the field view to edit existing data. But the report design screen is the opposite. It always begins in Replace mode, which means that existing text is replaced if you type new text on top of it. To switch to Insert mode, press the Ins key once. Paradox displays the message Ins at the right of the mode indicator. Press Ins again when you are ready to return to Replace mode.

You will note these two major differences between Insert and Replace modes:

1. Normally Paradox replaces existing text as you type. In Insert mode, however, the program pushes existing text and spaces to the right as you type.
2. While in Insert mode, Paradox adds a carriage return each time you press Enter. This feature is usually employed when you want to add new lines to a report.

Inserting Lines

If you already have typed text into any area of the report design screen before you decide to add more lines, follow these guidelines:

- To insert lines above an existing line of text, place the cursor at the beginning (left end) of the line, and press Enter.
- To insert a blank line below an existing line of text, place the cursor to the right of the last character on the line (the right end), and press Enter.

Adjusting the Page Layout

A tabular report, by definition, prints the data in columns and rows. Using this type of report is much like transferring the table directly from the disk to paper, with the same columns and rows. If all the columns do not fit horizontally within an 80-character width, Paradox splits the report and prints it on several *page widths* until all columns have been printed. With this method, Paradox can print tables up to 2,000 characters wide.

Printing the entire Employee table, for example, places fields up through the Date Hired column on the first page width. Then Paradox runs out of space, as shown in figure 5.13. In fact, the last two letters of the `Date Hired` heading do not fit on the page. The next page width is shown in figure 5.14, but even that page does not hold enough room for all the fields. Finally, after printing the third page width (see fig. 5.15), Paradox is finished. You have to bring out the tape or stapler and put the table back together. Obviously, you may not always want to follow this procedure to print a table.

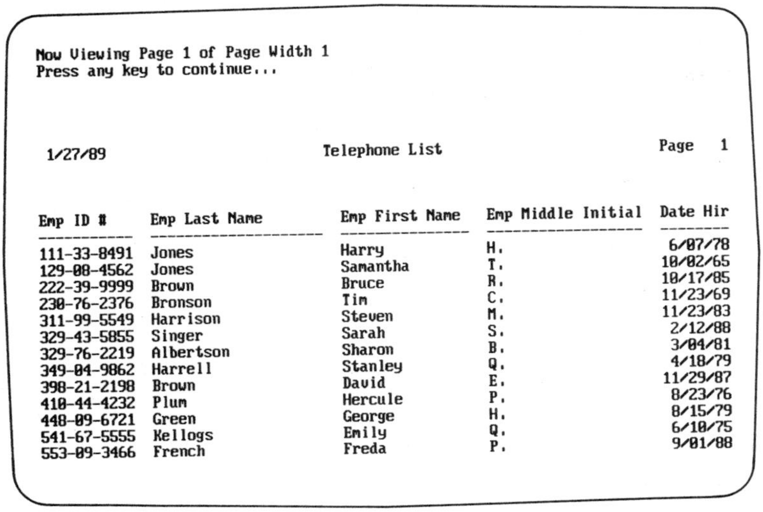

Now Viewing Page 1 of Page Width 1
Press any key to continue...

1/27/89 Telephone List Page 1

Emp ID #	Emp Last Name	Emp First Name	Emp Middle Initial	Date Hir
111-33-8491	Jones	Harry	H.	6/07/78
129-08-4562	Jones	Samantha	T.	10/02/65
222-39-9999	Brown	Bruce	R.	10/17/85
230-76-2376	Bronson	Tim	C.	11/23/69
311-99-5549	Harrison	Steven	M.	11/23/83
329-43-5855	Singer	Sarah	S.	2/12/88
329-76-2219	Albertson	Sharon	B.	3/04/81
349-04-9862	Harrell	Stanley	Q.	4/18/79
398-21-2198	Brown	David	E.	11/29/87
410-44-4232	Plum	Hercule	P.	8/23/76
448-09-6721	Green	George	H.	8/15/79
541-67-5555	Kellogs	Emily	Q.	6/10/75
553-09-3466	French	Freda	P.	9/01/88

Fig. 5.13.

The first page width.

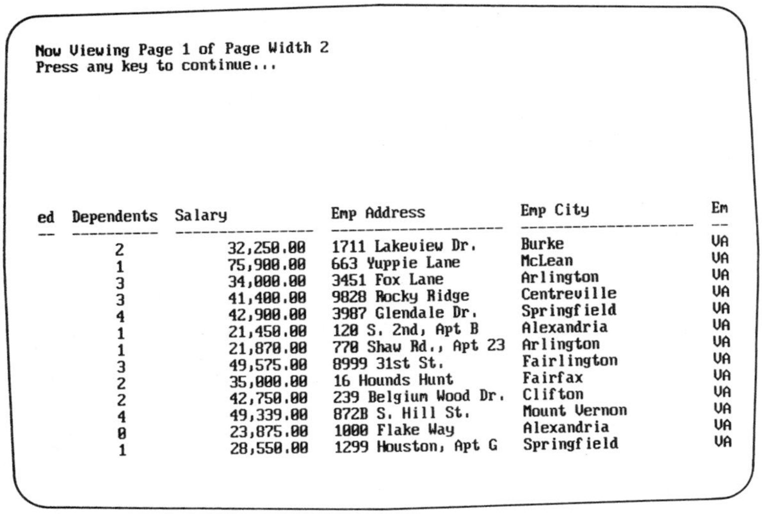

Now Viewing Page 1 of Page Width 2
Press any key to continue...

ed	Dependents	Salary	Emp Address	Emp City	Em
	2	32,250.00	1711 Lakeview Dr.	Burke	VA
	1	75,900.00	663 Yuppie Lane	McLean	VA
	3	34,000.00	3451 Fox Lane	Arlington	VA
	3	41,400.00	9828 Rocky Ridge	Centreville	VA
	4	42,900.00	3987 Glendale Dr.	Springfield	VA
	1	21,450.00	120 S. 2nd, Apt B	Alexandria	VA
	1	21,870.00	770 Shaw Rd., Apt 23	Arlington	VA
	3	49,575.00	8999 31st St.	Fairlington	VA
	2	35,000.00	16 Hounds Hunt	Fairfax	VA
	2	42,750.00	239 Belgium Wood Dr.	Clifton	VA
	4	49,339.00	872B S. Hill St.	Mount Vernon	VA
	0	23,875.00	1000 Flake Way	Alexandria	VA
	1	28,550.00	1299 Houston, Apt G	Springfield	VA

Fig. 5.14.

The second page width.

Fig. 5.15.

The third page width.

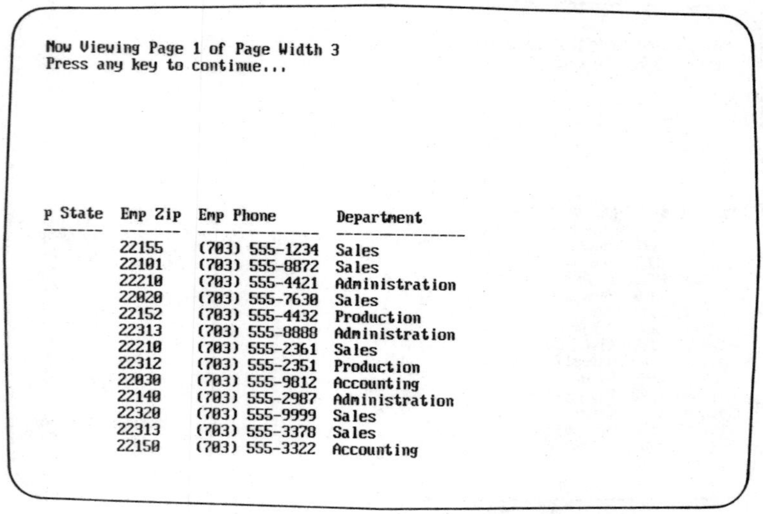

Changing the Page Width

The standard report specification starts with the page width set at 80 characters (unless you have changed the default through the Custom Configuration Program, discussed in Appendix B). On the report design screen, Paradox displays a vertical inverse video bar at the point at which the current page width ends (see fig. 5.16).

Fig. 5.16.

The report specification with a page width of 80 characters.

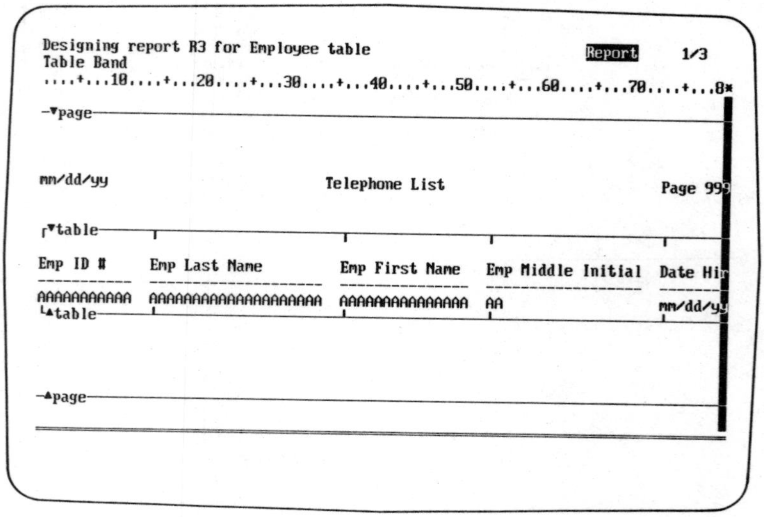

Notice also the message 1/3 in the upper right corner of the screen in figure 5.16. This message indicates that this screen is the first of 3 page widths. Paradox automatically figures how many 80-column page widths are required to print all the fields in the table, and establishes that figure as the *report width*. The report width for the report spec shown in figure 5.16 is 3 page widths, or 240 characters.

Assume that you want to create a telephone list from data in the Employee table. You need to include only each employee's name and phone number, so the information should fit easily within a normal page width. In order to leave an inch margin on the left and an inch on the right, you decide to print the report within a 65-character page width ([8.5 inches − 2 inches] × 10 characters per inch = 65 characters). To change the Paradox page width from the default of 80 to the new width of 65, display the Report menu by pressing F10 (Menu) and then select **S**etting **P**ageLayout **W**idth. Paradox displays the existing width, 80, and prompts you to enter a new one. Use the Backspace key to erase the current number; then type the new page width and press Enter.

Paradox responds to the page-width alteration by moving the vertical inverse video bar to the new margin, column 65 in the example (see fig. 5.17). The program also recalculates the number of page widths needed to display the report. The Employee table requires 4 page widths at 65 characters per page, as indicated by the 1/4 message in the upper right corner of figure 5.17.

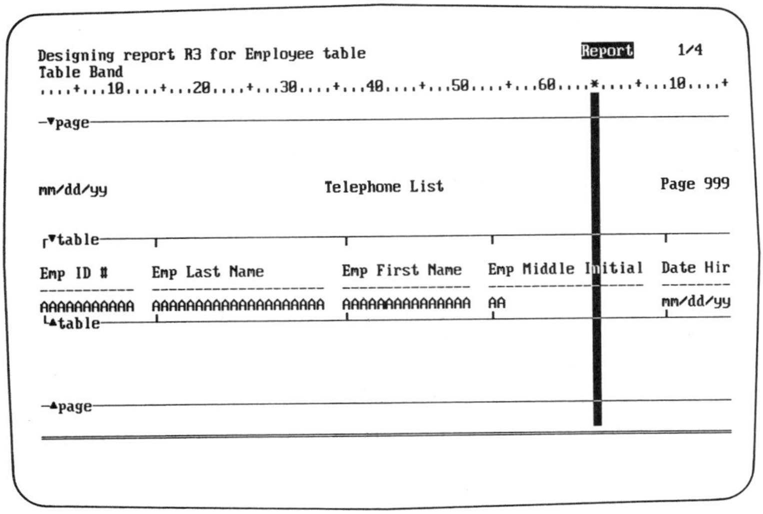

Fig. 5.17.

The report specification with a page width of 65 characters.

Changing the Page Length

You can alter page length in a manner similar to the way you modify page width. The default page length is 66 lines per page, which just barely fits your data on a page, printed 6 lines per inch—normal single spacing. To change the page length, access the Report menu and select **S**etting **P**ageLayout **L**ength. Backspace over the current setting, and enter the maximum number of lines per page you want to print. You might, for example, want to leave at least an inch margin at both the top and the bottom of the page. In that case you should make the page length 54 lines (66 lines − [2 inches × 6 lines]).

Another way to create a top margin is to leave blank lines at the top of the page header. If you use this method, deduct those lines from the formula used to calculate page length.

You can tell Paradox to print the report in one continuous page, with no breaks. Simply type the letter *c* rather than a number as the page length. Any page headers or page footers do not print.

Reducing and Increasing the Report Width

You seldom need to include all fields from a table in a report, so you may occasionally want to reduce the total report width. In the telephone list example, you could do that, but only after removing unneeded fields (refer to "Inserting and Deleting Fields" later in this chapter).

Paradox is "smart" enough not to print an empty page if your report width is wider than your report requires. You can thus leave the report width at the default size with no adverse effects.

Caution: Do not reduce the report width until you have removed the unwanted fields from the report spec, and the remaining fields fit within the new report dimensions. Otherwise, Paradox may remove fields from the screen that you intended to keep.

To reduce report width, first set the page width as you want it, and then access the Report menu by pressing F10 (Menu). Select **S**etting **P**age Layout **D**elete **O**K. Paradox deletes one page width from the total report width each time you repeat this procedure.

Conversely, you can increase report width one page width at a time by selecting **S**etting **P**ageLayout **I**nsert from the Report menu.

Changing the Left Margin

By default, Paradox starts printing reports at column 1 on your printer. In other words, the left margin is at 0. To change this setting, select **S**etting **M**argin from the Report menu. Backspace over the current margin setting, type the new one, and press Enter. Keep in mind that this margin setting is only for the left side of the page. The right margin is established by the page size. If you change the left margin, you may also have to adjust page size by the same amount. In the employee telephone list example, changing the left margin to 10 requires that the page size be increased to 75, the original 65 spaces plus 10 (see fig. 5.18).

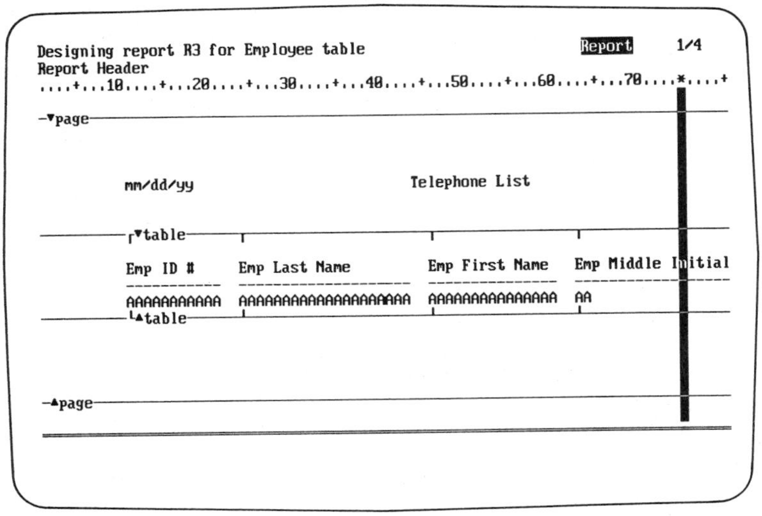

Fig. 5.18.

The report specification with a left margin of 10 and a page width of 75.

Modifying the Table Band

In Paradox tabular-style reports, all records print within the table band. Whenever you modify the standard specification, you almost are always making adjustments, additions, and deletions to this report component.

Because the standard spec always initially includes all the table's fields, you probably will have to delete a few fields right off the bat.

The table band is divided horizontally into columns, just as the underlying table is divided into fields. The boundaries of each column in the table are indicated by small *hash marks* (see fig. 5.18). As already discussed, the table band is also divided vertically into the *table header* and the *body*.

In the standard specification, Paradox places a field name in each column in the table header line, with the corresponding field value in the body below. But you can have an empty column and can even place more than one field value in a single column. To keep from confusing things, however, matching the number of columns to the number of fields is usually preferable.

Deleting Columns from the Table Band

To delete a column from the table, press F10 (Menu) and select **T**ableBand **E**rase. Position the cursor within the hash marks of the field you want removed, in either the table header or the body, and press Enter. Paradox removes the field—both field name and value—and fills the vacant space with any fields remaining on the right. Repeat these steps for each column you want to remove. In the telephone list, for instance, you can remove all columns except the four columns that contain Emp Last Name, Emp First Name, Emp Middle Initial, and Emp Phone. Compare figure 5.19 to figure 5.18.

Inserting Columns in the Table Band

Inserting a column is the reverse of deleting one, but Paradox does not automatically choose a field to go in the new column. When you insert a new column, it is blank. Placing a field in the column requires another step, described in "Inserting and Deleting Fields."

To insert a new column, press F10 (Menu) and select **T**ableBand **I**nsert. Move the cursor to the position in the table band where you want the new column to go, and press Enter. Paradox inserts a column that is 15 spaces wide.

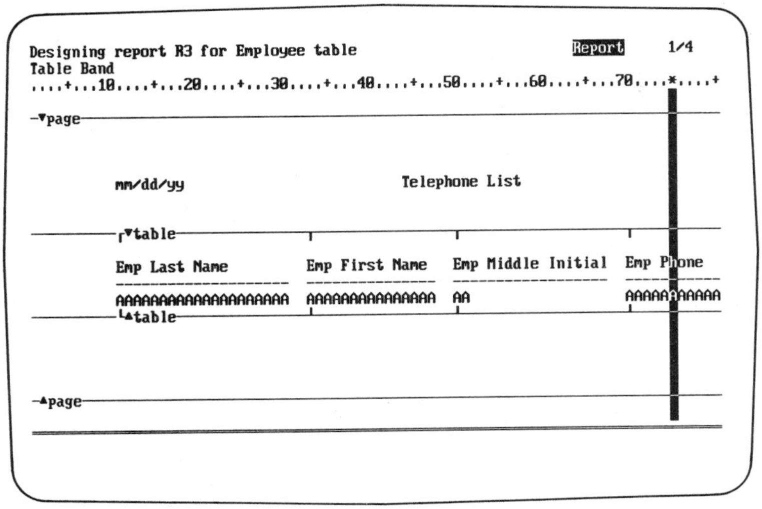

Fig. 5.19.

After deleting a column from the table band.

Resizing a Column in the Table Band

Often you need to change the size of a column to make your report fit within the available space. Figure 5.19, for example, shows that the Emp Phone field overlaps into the second page width. The obvious solution in this particular example is to reduce the width of the Emp Middle Initial column.

To reduce the width of a column, you first must reduce the size of any field or label that the column contains. Reducing the size of a field is called *reformatting* the field and is discussed in "Inserting and Deleting Fields" in this chapter. The Emp Middle Initial field already is small enough, but the heading is too big. You don't need this heading at all anyway, so you can use the Del key or the Backspace key to erase it. After deleting the heading, access the Report menu and select **T**ableBand **R**esize. Move the cursor to the far end of the column, away from the value (the AA in this example), and press Enter. Use the arrow keys to shrink the column, and press Enter when you are finished. The results are shown in figure 5.20.

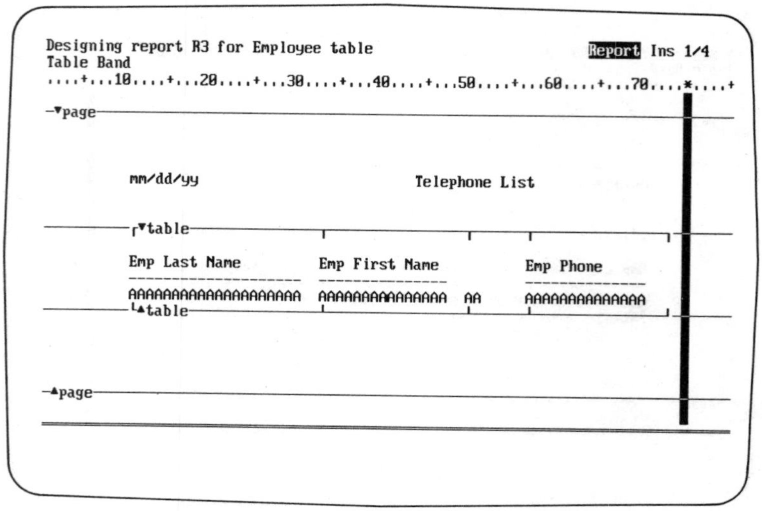

Fig. 5.20.

After resizing the Emp Middle Initial column.

Rearranging Columns in the Table Band

The **M**ove option on the TableBand menu works in a manner similar to the corresponding command on the Image menu. To move a column in the table band, access the Report menu and select **T**ableBand **M**ove. Use the arrow keys to position the cursor in the column that needs to be repositioned, and press Enter. Then move the cursor to the new position and press Enter again. Paradox moves the column. The **C**opy command works in the same way, but instead of moving the column, **C**opy makes a duplicate version. The Ctrl-R (Rotate) keystroke command, discussed in Chapter 3, is also available for rearranging columns quickly in the table band. Figure 5.21 shows the result of rearranging the employee name fields so that they are in the order of first, middle, and last.

Previewing the Report

A previous section of this chapter describes how you can produce a quick and easy report directly from the Main mode by pressing Alt-F7 (Instant Report). This keystroke combination has exactly the same effect during report design. You can use this feature to get a quick look at how your report looks.

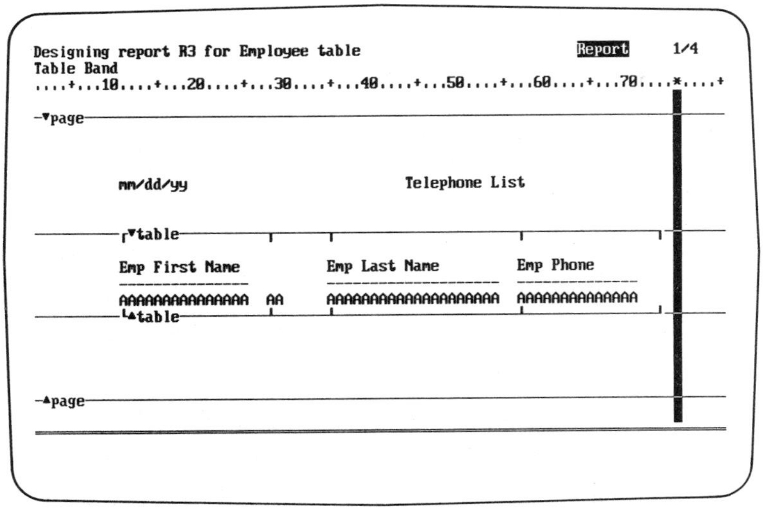

Fig. 5.21.

Rearranging columns in the table band.

Perhaps a better way to preview a report is on the screen. First access the Report menu by pressing F10. From that menu, use the commands **O**utput **S**creen. Paradox displays on-screen the report you are designing without you having to leave the report spec. Whenever you think that everything is how you want it, do a test run to the printer, using Alt-F7 (Instant Report). Figure 5.22 shows the current state of the employee telephone list that has been developed in this chapter.

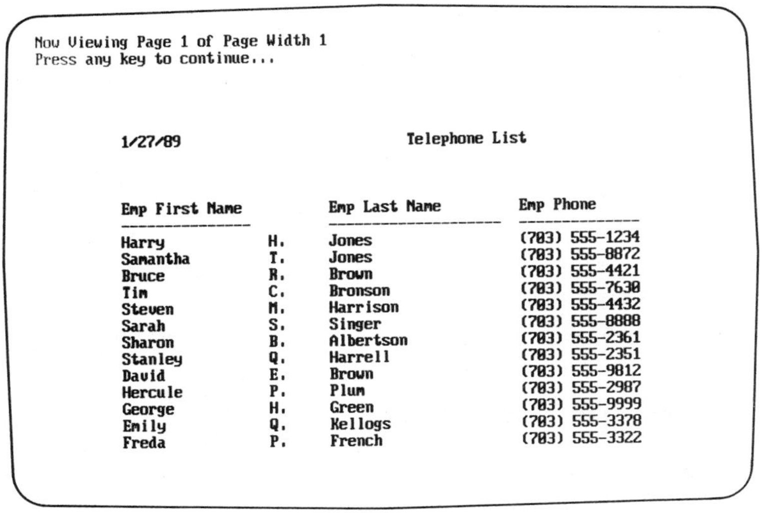

Fig. 5.22.

The telephone list report.

Inserting and Deleting Fields

Even though Paradox automatically places all of a table's fields on the specification for you, in many situations you need to add or delete fields. The telephone list you are creating, for example, would look better if the employee names were "squeezed" together. Accomplishing this task requires the use of one of the special field types, called a *calculated* field. The next several sections discuss how to insert regular Paradox fields as well as calculated fields, the *date* field, and the *page number* field.

Placing Regular Paradox Fields

To place a field from the table onto the report spec, access the Report menu and select **F**ield **P**lace **R**egular. Then pick the field name from a list provided by Paradox. Move the cursor to the position where you want the field to begin, and press Enter. Paradox places a *field mask* on the screen, beginning at the cursor location. The field mask shows you the field type and the field size. Table 5.3 lists the default field masks used to represent the various Paradox field types. Field length is represented by the length of the mask itself.

Table 5.3
Report Specification Default Field Masks

Field Type	*Field Mask*
A (alphanumeric)	AAAAAA
N (numeric)	9999999
$ (currency)	(999,999)
D (date)	mm/dd/yy

Erasing Fields

As you work in a report spec, you will probably make a number of false starts until the spec is designed exactly the way you want it. You therefore need some way to erase your mistakes, including fields that you may have placed in error.

To erase a field, access the Report menu and select **F**ield **E**rase. Move the cursor to the field to be removed, and press Enter. Note that Paradox does not remove any corresponding labels in the table header. To remove table header text, use either the Del key or the Backspace key.

Placing Calculated Fields

A *calculated field* in a report specification is a field whose value is derived from other fields in the table. This type of field can be numeric or alphanumeric. Each calculated field is defined by an *expression* consisting of field names, constant values, and operators.

When building an expression, you must enclose field names in brackets ([ ]) and enclose text constants in double quotation marks (" "). You can use the operators listed in table 5.4 when creating calculated fields. For example, to create a calculated field from Price and Quantity, you would use the expression

[Price]*[Quantity]

The * operator in this expression means to multiply the first field's value by the second field's value.

Table 5.4
Operators for Calculated Fields

Arithmetic Operator	*Meaning*
+	Add a numeric field or constant, or concatenate an alphanumeric field or constant
−	Subtract a numeric field or constant
*	Multiply a numeric field or constant
/	Divide by a numeric field or constant
( )	Perform operators within the innermost pair of parentheses first
Summary Operator	*Meaning*
Sum	Add the values of a field or expression over a specified group of records
Average	Average values of a field or expression over a specified group of records

Table 5.4—*Continued*

Summary Operator	*Meaning*
Count	Count the number of values in a specified group of records
High	The maximum value in a specified group of records
Low	The minimum value in a specified group of records

Note: The *summary* operators should be used only in a header or footer, usually in a footer. Summary operators are used with groups of records and are discussed more fully in Chapters 10 and 11.

Before you insert a calculated field, you must make sure that you have sufficient space in the report spec to contain the field. When placing fields in the table band, you may have to increase the size of a column (using the **R**esize command on the TableBand menu). In the employee telephone list example, for instance, you might decide to replace the name fields with one calculated field. But you must first remove the existing employee name fields. Figure 5.23 shows the report spec with only two columns remaining, the Emp Phone column, and one that will contain the new calculated field. The empty column has been resized to provide room for employee full names. The remaining label in the table header also has been shortened to `Phone`.

To insert a calculated field, position the cursor at the point at which you want the new field to start. Display the Report menu by pressing F10 (Menu) and select **F**ield **Pl**ace **C**alculated. Paradox then prompts for an `Expression`. Type the formula for the new field. Be sure to enclose field names in brackets, and text constants in double quotation marks. You can edit this expression in the same manner as you can any Paradox field, including use of the field view (Alt-F5). For example, the following expression creates a new employee name field that includes the three regular fields from the table:

[Emp First Name]+" "+[Emp Middle Initial]+" "+[Emp Last Name]

When the expression is as you want it, press Enter. Paradox prompts you to move the cursor to the starting position for the new field. If you have already moved the cursor to the proper starting point, just press Enter

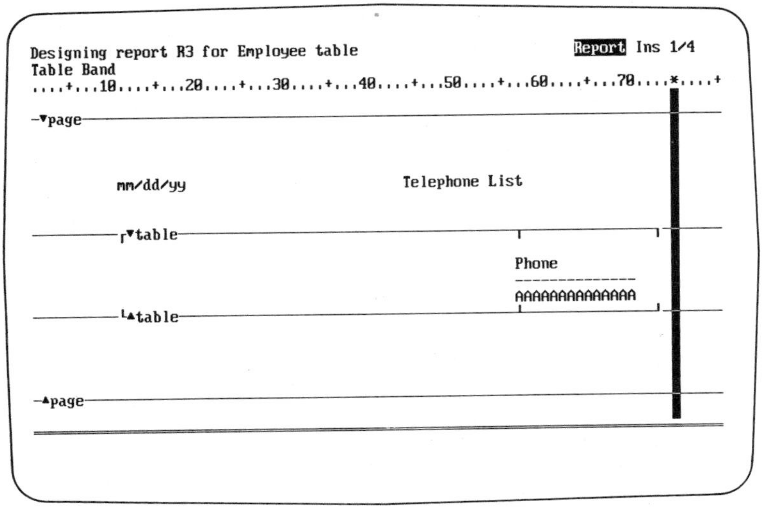

Fig. 5.23.

Making room for a calculated field.

again. Paradox places the field mask in the column in the indicated position. You can use the arrow keys to increase or decrease the size of the field mask. Accept the size by pressing Enter once more, and the field is defined (see fig. 5.24). Whenever the cursor is positioned within the field mask of a calculated field, Paradox displays the formula (the expression) in the second line at the top of the screen.

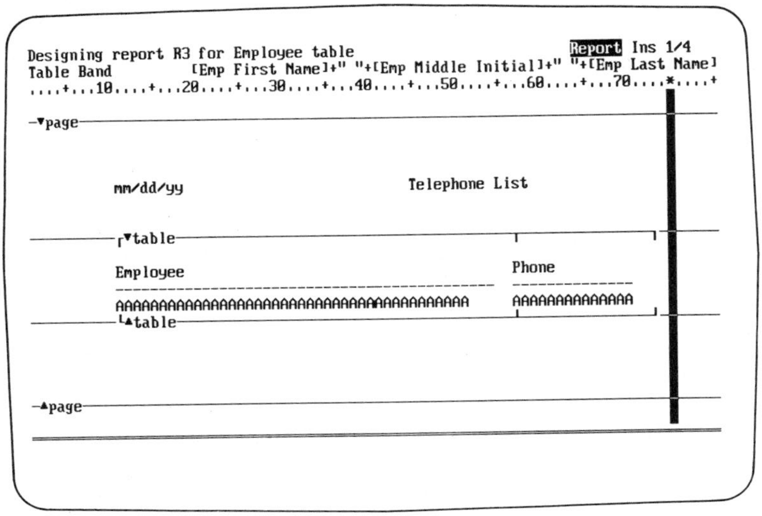

Fig. 5.24.

The calculated field.

Notice the use of the double quotation marks around each blank space in the expression for the new employee name field. This formula tells Paradox to leave one space between first name and middle initial, and one space between middle initial and last name, when printing the report. Figure 5.25 shows how the report looks when printed to screen.

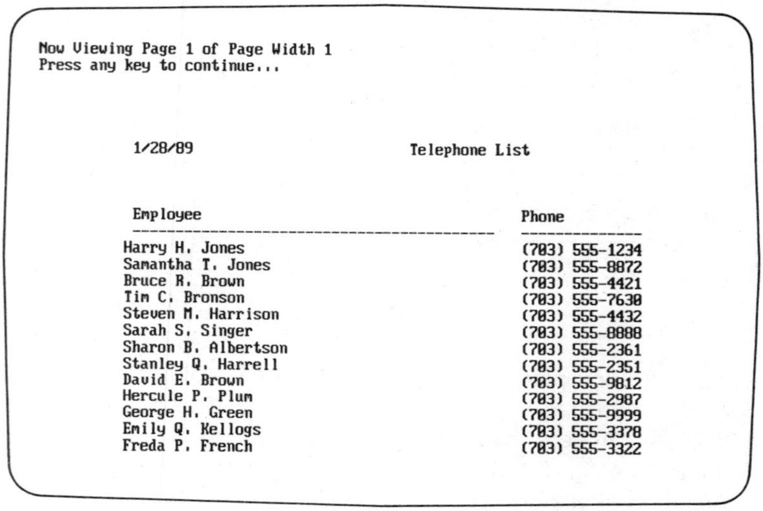

Now Viewing Page 1 of Page Width 1
Press any key to continue...

1/28/89 Telephone List

Employee	Phone
Harry H. Jones	(703) 555-1234
Samantha T. Jones	(703) 555-8872
Bruce R. Brown	(703) 555-4421
Tim C. Bronson	(703) 555-7630
Steven M. Harrison	(703) 555-4432
Sarah S. Singer	(703) 555-8888
Sharon B. Albertson	(703) 555-2361
Stanley Q. Harrell	(703) 555-2351
David E. Brown	(703) 555-9812
Hercule P. Plum	(703) 555-2987
George H. Green	(703) 555-9999
Emily Q. Kellogs	(703) 555-3378
Freda P. French	(703) 555-3322

Fig. 5.25.

The telephone list report with the calculated field.

Placing the Date and Page Fields

You may have noticed that Paradox automatically supplies both the system date and the page number at the top of each page when the program prints an instant report (see fig. 5.13). These two special fields are also included automatically in the standard specification, under the designations `mm/dd/yy` and `Page 999`, respectively (see fig. 5.7). With the cursor in the date field, a message at the top of the screen says `Current date`. Place the cursor in the page number field, and the message reads `Current page number`.

Note that the word `Page` is not part of the field but is a text label (or *literal*) often used in front of the page number field to label it clearly.

You can remove these fields if you prefer, by using the **F**ield **E**rase command from the Report menu, and place them anywhere in the report. Normally the page number is either in the page header or the page footer.

The date field is still visible in the employee telephone list spec, but the page number field seems to have disappeared (see fig. 5.24). The page number field is there, but was just pushed into the second page width when you changed the margin to 10. The page number field is now at column 13 of the second page width.

Suppose that you decide to erase the page number field and move it into the page footer instead. To place either a current page number field or a current date field in the report spec, press F10 (Menu) to access the Report menu. Then select **F**ield **P**lace, and choose **D**ate or **P**age. Position the cursor where the field should appear and press Enter. Finally, adjust the field size with the left- and right-arrow keys and press Enter again. For a page number field, you probably want to precede the field mask with the word *Page*, as shown in figure 5.26.

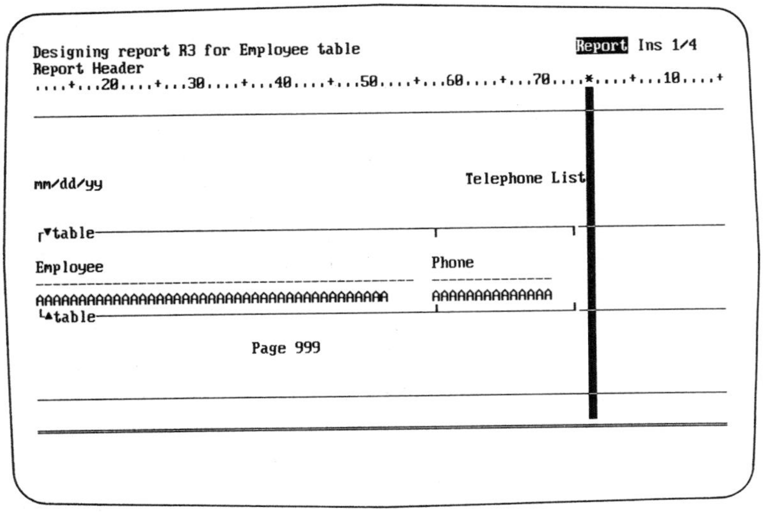

Fig. 5.26. *Placing the current page number field.*

Reformatting Fields

Paradox provides a way to change the size of alphanumeric and numeric fields (indicated on-screen by the size of the field mask) and the format of numeric and date fields.

To increase or reduce the field mask size, access the Report menu and select **F**ield **R**eformat. Move the cursor to the field to be modified, and press Enter. For alphanumeric fields, you then use the arrow keys to change field size, and press Enter to indicate when you are finished.

For numeric fields, Paradox presents the following menu choices:

- **D**igits. Choose this option to change the size of the mask. Use the arrows to adjust the size; then press Enter. The first time you press Enter, Paradox sets the size to the left of the decimal and then asks you to adjust the number of decimal places. Press Enter again when you're finished.
- **S**ign-Convention. After choosing this option, you must make another choice: between **N**egativeOnly, **P**arenNegative, and **A**lwaysSign. **N**egativeOnly, the default for number fields, shows a negative sign in front of negative numbers but no sign in front of positive numbers. The **P**arenNegative choice, the default for currency fields, places parentheses around negative dollar figures. The final option, **A**lwaysSign, shows either the plus (+) or minus (−) sign in front of each number, as appropriate.
- **C**ommas. Select this option if you want to add or delete the display of whole number separators.
- **I**nternational. You use this option to switch whole number separators from commas (**U**.S.Convention) to periods (**I**nternationalConvention).

To adjust the format of a date field, from the Report menu select **F**ield **R**eformat. Move the cursor to the date field and press Enter. Paradox displays a list of 11 formats:

1) mm/dd/yy
2) M o n t h dd, yyyy
3) mm/dd
4) mm/yy
5) dd-Mon-yy
6) Mon yy
7) dd-Mon-yyyy
8) mm/dd/yyyy
9) dd.mm.yy
10) dd/mm/yy
11) yy-mm-dd

Select the format you need. The first format, mm/dd/yy, is the default.

Using the Report Header

A *header* is that portion of the report that repeats at predetermined intervals, printing above the body. Headers can and often do include data from the table, but usually only for the purpose of labeling a grouping of data. A single Paradox report can have up to 19 different headers: the report header, the page header, the table header, and as many as 16 group headers. With this many choices, keeping them distinguished in your mind is sometimes difficult.

The *report header* is easy to distinguish from the other types of headers because the report header prints only once and always at the beginning. A fairly typical use of the report header is to create a title page. For example, you might want to use the following title page for the telephone list:

Wonder Widgets of America
Employee Telephone List

To begin creating this title page, position the cursor in the top line of the report spec screen by pressing the Home key. Your cursor is above the line labeled "page" and below the horizontal ruler line. A message on the second line of the screen lets you know that you are working in the report header (see fig. 5.27).

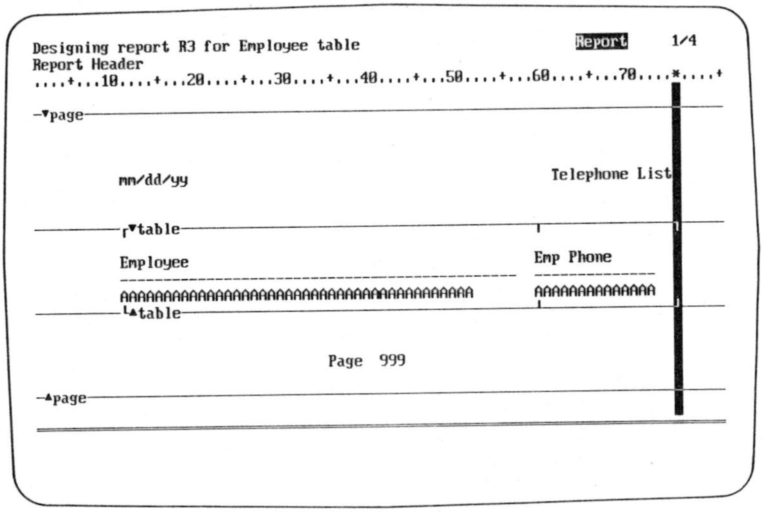

Fig. 5.27.

Working in the report header.

First, make some space in which to work by inserting several blank lines. Type the text that you want to appear on the title page. As you saw in figure 5.8, a report header does not normally get an entire page to itself. But you can insert anywhere in your report a *page break* that causes Paradox to skip to the next page whenever the program encounters the break. You simply type the word *PAGEBREAK* in all caps at the far left of the report specification. The finished report specification, with title page, is shown in figure 5.28. A screen print of the report is shown in figures 5.29 through 5.31.

```
Designing report R3 for Employee table                              Report Ins 1/4
Report Header
....+...10....+...20....+...30....+...40....+...50....+...60....+...70....*....+
                             Wonder Widgets of America
                              Employee Telephone List
          PAGEBREAK
-▼page--------------------------------------------------------------------------

          mm/dd/yy                                             Telephone List


---------┌▼table-------------------------------------------------┬--------------
          Employee                                            Emp Phone
          ---------------------------------------------      -------------
          AAAAAAAAAAAAAAAAAAAAAAAAAAAAAAAAAAAAAAAAAAAAAA      AAAAAAAAAAAAAA
---------└▲table-------------------------------------------------┴--------------

                                   Page  999

-▲page--------------------------------------------------------------------------
```

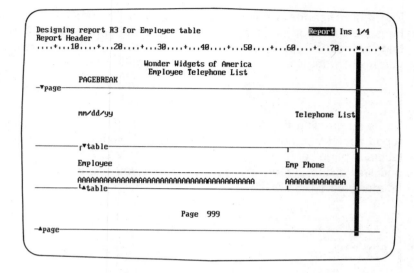

Fig. 5.28.

Creating a title page.

```
End of Page
Press any key to continue...
                             Wonder Widgets of America
                              Employee Telephone List
```

Fig. 5.29.

The title page of the telephone list report.

```
Now Viewing Page 1 of Page Width 1
Press any key to continue...
                             Wonder Widgets of America
                              Employee Telephone List

          1/28/89                                              Telephone List


          Employee                                            Emp Phone
          ---------------------------------------------      -------------
          Harry H. Jones                                      (703) 555-1234
          Samantha T. Jones                                   (703) 555-8872
          Bruce R. Brown                                      (703) 555-4421
          Tim C. Bronson                                      (703) 555-7630
          Steven M. Harrison                                  (703) 555-4432
          Sarah S. Singer                                     (703) 555-8888
          Sharon B. Albertson                                 (703) 555-2361
          Stanley Q. Harrell                                  (703) 555-2351
          David E. Brown                                      (703) 555-9812
          Hercule P. Plum                                     (703) 555-2987
          George H. Green                                     (703) 555-9999
```

Fig. 5.30.

The top half of Page 1 of the telephone list report.

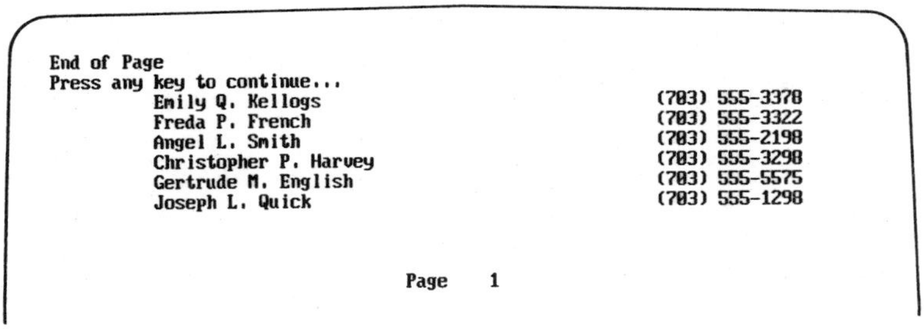

Fig. 5.31.
The bottom half of Page 1 of the telephone list report.

Saving the Report Specification

After all the work of designing your report, you certainly do not want to have to repeat the procedure all over again the next time you want to use the report design. Paradox makes saving the report specification an easy step. Just press F2 (DO-IT!). The report spec is saved to disk under the name you gave it. This report specification is a member of the family tied to the table for which you created the spec. If you later restructure the table, Paradox automatically reconciles the report, to the extent possible. For example, if you delete a field from the table structure, Paradox automatically deletes that field from the report.

Modifying the Report Specification

Nine times out of ten, you will decide that you want to change your report not long after you thought you had finished it. With Paradox, making alterations is simple. You essentially just pick up where you left off.

Access the Paradox Main menu and select **R**eport **C**hange. Choose the table's name and then select the name of the report you want to change. Press Enter at the `Report Description` prompt, and you are back in the report specification, just as you left it. The only visible difference in the screen is the status message that now says `Changing report R# for abc table`. (The report name/number appears in place of #, and your table name appears in place of `abc`.) All the features you have learned thus far about designing the report specification still apply. When you are finished making changes, press F2 (DO-IT!), and Paradox returns you to the Main mode.

Controlling Output

Once you design a report specification, you generally print the entire report on paper. Sometimes, however, you may want to print only a portion of the report, or perhaps send it to the screen rather than your printer. You may even want to create a file that contains an image of the report. Paradox provides the capability to do each of these things through the Report menus.

Using the Output Menu To Choose the Output Device

In addition to the Alt-F7 (Instant Report) keystroke option, Paradox has three ways to output your report through the Output menu: to printer, to screen, and to file. These choices are the same whether you are already in Report mode and in the middle of designing your report, or have saved the specification and are starting from the Main mode.

When starting from the Report mode, access the Report menu by pressing F10 (Menu) and select **O**utput. If you have finished designing your report and are back at the Main mode, access the Main menu and press **R**eport **O**utput. Your next step is to select a table and a report name. Paradox then displays the following choices:

- **P**rinter. This option sends the report to the printer. Choosing **P**rinter is the same as pressing Alt-F7 (Instant Report) while designing or changing the report specification.
- **S**creen. Use this choice to send the report to the screen. Paradox displays the report in screen-size chunks, but displays messages at the top of the screen to let you know the page and page width of the report currently being displayed.
- **F**ile. Make this selection to print the report to a file. When prompted, enter a unique file name (perhaps with the extension *.ASC* or *.TXT* to remind you that the file is in ASCII format) and press Enter. This file is an exact image of how the report will look when it is printed to paper. The file can be used by any other program that can handle plain ASCII files.

Changing the Output Range

Occasionally you may want to print only a few of the pages of your entire report. Paradox refers to the number of pages as the *output range*. When you need to change the output range, choose **R**eport **R**angeOutput from the Main menu. Select the proper table, report, and device (printer, screen, or file). Paradox then asks for the `Beginning page number` and suggests the number 1 as the default. Change this number to the number of the first page that should be printed; then press Enter. Next, enter the number of the last page to be printed. Leave this response blank if you want Paradox to print all the way to the end of the report. When you press Enter, Paradox sends the appropriate portion of the report to the chosen device.

Using Reports on a Network

Paradox takes special pains to make using reports on a network almost identical to using them on a stand-alone system. When you start to print a report based on a shared table, everything works the same as normal unless another user happens to be working with the table. In that case, Paradox takes a "snapshot" of the table during a period when no changes are being made to the table, and then runs your report from the snapshot. Using this method, you can print a report on a table even while it is being viewed or edited by another user on the network.

Chapter Summary

This chapter has been a Paradox report-writing primer, introducing you to the fundamentals of designing, building, and printing reports from your Paradox data. The chapter barely has begun, however, to show you all the program's reporting features. When you feel ready to delve a bit deeper into creating more powerful tabular tables, take a look at Chapter 10. And for details about creating custom free-form reports, check out Chapter 11. But before you move on to Part II of this book, "Tapping the Power of Paradox," read the next chapter to learn how you can use Paradox scripts to automate some of the commands and techniques you already have learned.

6

Recording Paradox Scripts and Keyboard Macros

One of the things computers do best is automate repetitive tasks. Paradox helps you automate your database-related tasks by enabling you to record your keystrokes for later use. The program stores the recorded keystrokes in *script* files. This chapter describes how to record and play back Paradox scripts, and introduces you to the Paradox Script Editor, which you use to modify and enhance your recorded scripts.

After discussing scripts in general, this chapter describes how to create *keyboard macros*, multiple keystrokes that you can execute by pressing a single key or key combination. In this chapter, you learn how to create keyboard macros to make your database usable by nearly anyone, with little or no training.

An Overview of Paradox Scripts

The first portion of this chapter gives you a brief overview of Paradox scripts. It answers several general questions you might have about scripts and their uses.

What Are Paradox Scripts?

Many of the most popular PC programs have some capability to record keystrokes. Recorded sets of keystrokes are often called *keyboard macros* because you usually run them by pressing a key or key combination. In Paradox, keyboard macros are just one special use of a more encompassing feature called *scripts*.

With Paradox, you can create a script to perform any task that you can do yourself. Normally you create scripts to automate those routines that you find yourself having to do over and over. The easiest way to create this type of script is to turn on a "keystroke recorder" and then press the proper keys for the operation. When the task is complete, turn off the recorder, and Paradox saves the script. The next time you want to perform the same operation, you *play* the script. Paradox executes every keystroke that you previously recorded.

If you prefer, you can assign a script to a particular key or key combination, which you then press to play the script. Scripts assigned to keys are called *keyboard macros*.

How Useful Are Paradox Scripts?

The most important use of Paradox scripts is to program entire turnkey menu-driven database applications. You can create these powerful scripts either through the applications generator, called the *Paradox Personal Programmer*, or by typing them yourself in the *Paradox Script Editor*. You can even incorporate already-recorded scripts into them. These types of sophisticated scripts use the commands of the *Paradox Application Language* (PAL). Because scripts that use PAL are essentially programs, Paradox users often use the terms "script" and "program" interchangeably.

This chapter, however, concentrates on creating simple scripts that are used to play back your keystrokes. Refer to Part III of this book for information on how to use Paradox, the Personal Programmer, and PAL for application development. Chapter 14 introduces you to creating scripts or programs through the Personal Programmer, and Chapter 15 briefly describes some of the additional enhancements and capabilities available through the Paradox Application Language.

Perhaps because of the fact that scripts can become a part of powerful, customized database applications, many users are reluctant to give scripts a try. But you have nothing to lose and much to gain by learning to create Paradox scripts. Even in their simplest form, these tools can increase both your speed and accuracy in performing nearly any database task. The computer can always press keys faster than you can, and never makes typos. As the complexity of your database tasks increases, the value of scripts to reduce repetition increases even faster. For example, playing a script that automates a multitable query saves you more keystrokes and effort than does using a script to perform a single-table query.

Scripts certainly save knowledgeable users time and effort. But, perhaps even more important, scripts can enable novice users to accomplish tasks they would otherwise not be capable of performing. Entering data in form view, for example, is something that most clerical personnel can handle. They may, however, be less comfortable having to execute the commands necessary to display the entry form in the first place. You can record a script to display the form, and let data-entry personnel stick to entering data.

What Kinds of Tasks Can Scripts Perform?

Almost any operation you can perform with Paradox can be assisted or completely automated by a script. For example, you could easily record as scripts the following tasks:

- ❏ Displaying the Customer table in form view and DataEntry mode
- ❏ Displaying data from the Orders and Detail tables together for a particular order number
- ❏ Printing a report showing employee salaries from the Employee table

You simply turn on the script recorder and go through the steps once. After that, you or anyone else can perform the operations by merely playing the script. You could probably even teach your boss how to do it.

Can You Edit Paradox Scripts?

Paradox has a built-in screen editor that you can use to modify and enhance your Paradox scripts. Through this *Script Editor*, you can delete or correct errant keystrokes, make changes necessitated by additions or deletions from your tables, and add the powerful features available through the Paradox Application Language.

How Are Scripts Stored?

Each script is a Paradox object and is saved to disk as a separate file. The *instant script* is always saved with the name *INSTANT.SC*. You must name other scripts according to the following rules. Paradox gives all scripts the file name extension SC.

1. The name can contain up to 8 characters (not including the file name extension).
2. You can use letters, numbers, and these special characters:

   $ # & @ ! ÷ ( ) – _ { } ‘ ^

3. You cannot include spaces.
4. You cannot create duplicate names.

Scripts are not a part of any one table's family of objects. If you modify the structure of a table in a way that causes a script no longer to work properly, Paradox does not automatically reconcile the error. You have to use the Script Editor to modify the script accordingly. (For more information, see the section on "Editing Scripts.")

Recording and Playing Scripts

You have three ways to record scripts:

1. You can use Alt-F3 (Instant Script Record) to create a temporary script to record keystrokes that you expect to use a number of times in the current session but don't want to save for later use.
2. You can use the **B**eginRecord command from the Scripts menu. Most scripts are recorded with this method.
3. You can use the Scripts menu's **Q**uerySave command, introduced in Chapter 4, to save a query for future use.

The first two of these methods are covered in the discussions that follow. Refer to Chapter 4 to review how to save a query with **Q**uerySave.

Recording and Playing an Instant Script

You can begin recording a script instantly by pressing Alt-F3 (Instant Script Record). Paradox places the letter R in the upper right corner of the screen to remind you that a script is being recorded. (If you are currently displaying the Main menu, the R symbol does not appear, because of lack of room on the screen.) You then execute the keystrokes and commands as usual. When you have finished the operation, stop the instant recorder by pressing Alt-F3 again.

Caution: Paradox treats the instant script much as the program treats temporary tables. Each time you create an instant script, any previous instant script is erased without warning. To save an instant script, use the **R**ename command on the Tools menu to rename the script named INSTANT to some other valid script name. You must rename the script *before* you start recording another instant script.

Playing an instant script is just as easy as recording it—just press Alt-F4 (Instant Script Play). Every keystroke you made while recording the instant script is played back in sequence, but you do not see the results of each key press. The screen remains unchanged until the script is finished. Then Paradox refreshes your screen.

Use instant scripts to perform tasks that you expect you will have to repeat a number of times within the same session. These tasks may be simple or complicated, but keep in mind that this type of script is temporary.

For example, suppose that you expect to view the Orders table a number of times during the current Paradox session, but you don't want to have to press continually the necessary keystrokes yourself, and you don't need a permanent script for this purpose. To record an instant script that displays Orders, start the recorder by pressing Alt-F3 (Instant Script Record). When you see the R message on-screen, execute the keystrokes to view Orders:

1. Press F10 (Menu) to display the Main menu.
2. Select **V**iew.
3. Press Enter and select the Orders table.

When the Orders table appears in the work space, turn off the recorder by again pressing Alt-F3. Paradox has recorded your keystrokes as the script named INSTANT. Press Alt-F4 (Instant Script Play), and Paradox immediately displays Orders. You don't even need to be at the Main menu, but you do need to be in Main mode.

A script can be successfully played only from the mode in which you recorded the script. If you try to run a script from a different mode, Paradox balks and displays a menu with two options: **C**ancel and **D**ebug.

For example, figure 6.1 shows the result of pressing Alt-F4 (Instant Script Play) to play the instant script for displaying Orders. Because Paradox is in Edit mode, and the script was recorded in Main mode, the script does not run. Instead, you see the **C**ancel and **D**ebug options.

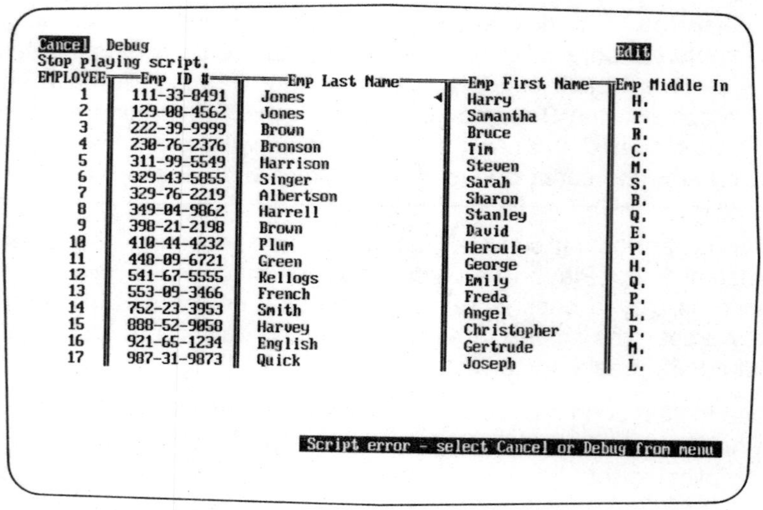

Cancel Debug
Edit
Stop playing script.
EMPLOYEE Emp ID # Emp Last Name Emp First Name Emp Middle In
1 111-33-8491 Jones Harry H.
2 129-08-4562 Jones Samantha T.
3 222-39-9999 Brown Bruce R.
4 230-76-2376 Bronson Tim C.
5 311-99-5549 Harrison Steven M.
6 329-43-5855 Singer Sarah S.
7 329-76-2219 Albertson Sharon B.
8 349-04-9862 Harrell Stanley Q.
9 398-21-2198 Brown David E.
10 410-44-4232 Plum Hercule P.
11 448-09-6721 Green George H.
12 541-67-5555 Kellogs Emily Q.
13 553-09-3466 French Freda P.
14 752-23-3953 Smith Angel L.
15 888-52-9058 Harvey Christopher P.
16 921-65-1234 English Gertrude M.
17 987-31-9873 Quick Joseph L.
Script error - select Cancel or Debug from menu

Fig. 6.1.

Playing a script from the wrong mode.

To discover why the script would not play, select **D**ebug. Paradox displays the message `Not a possible menu choice` near the lower right corner of the screen, and displays the offending line of the script in an inverse video line at the screen's bottom edge (see fig. 6.2).

In this case, the script contains only one line:

```
{View} {Orders}
```

This line means that you pressed the **V**iew and **O**rders selections on the menu in succession. Because the Edit menu does not include a **V**iew option, however, the script does not run. You have two easy ways to remedy this problem:

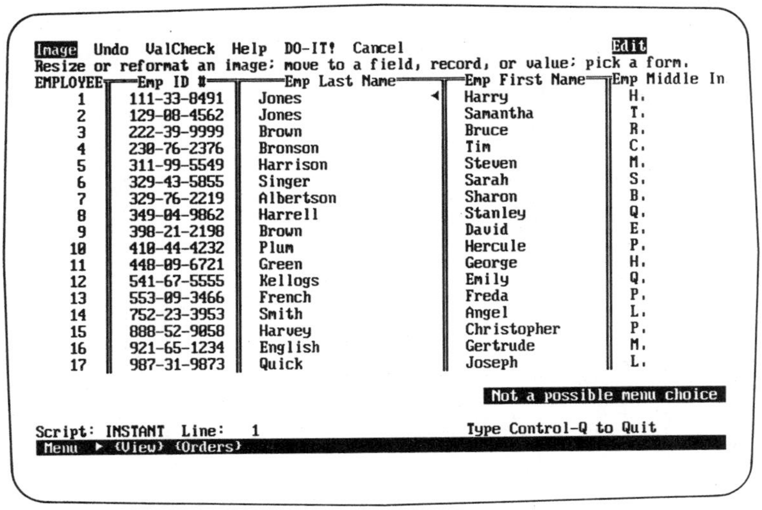
Image Undo ValCheck Help DO-IT! Cancel Edit
Resize or reformat an image; move to a field, record, or value; pick a form.
EMPLOYEE Emp ID # Emp Last Name Emp First Name Emp Middle In
1 111-33-8491 Jones Harry H.
2 129-08-4562 Jones Samantha T.
3 222-39-9999 Brown Bruce R.
4 230-76-2376 Bronson Tim C.
5 311-99-5549 Harrison Steven M.
6 329-43-5855 Singer Sarah S.
7 329-76-2219 Albertson Sharon B.
8 349-04-9862 Harrell Stanley Q.
9 398-21-2198 Brown David E.
10 410-44-4232 Plum Hercule P.
11 448-09-6721 Green George H.
12 541-67-5555 Kellogs Emily Q.
13 553-09-3466 French Freda P.
14 752-23-3953 Smith Angel L.
15 888-52-9058 Harvey Christopher P.
16 921-65-1234 English Gertrude M.
17 987-31-9873 Quick Joseph L.
Not a possible menu choice
Script: INSTANT Line: 1 Type Control-Q to Quit
Menu ► {View} {Orders}

Fig. 6.2.

Finding the error with Debug.

1. Cancel Debug by pressing Ctrl-Q. Return to the Main mode and rerun the instant script.
2. Return to the Main mode from Debug, in this case by selecting **C**ancel **Y**es, and continue the script by pressing Ctrl-G.
3. Return to the Main mode by pressing F2 (DO-IT!) and saving your work.

(A detailed discussion of the Paradox Debug program is beyond the scope of this book. See the *PAL User's Guide* volume of the Paradox documentation.)

Normally, if an error occurs while you're playing an instant script, you should just choose **C**ancel. Make sure that you are in the correct mode before trying to play the script again.

Using BeginRecord and End-Record To Record a Script

Paradox provides methods of recording a script from any Paradox mode. To start recording a script from the Main menu, select **S**cripts **B**eginRecord. Then type a valid script name and press Enter. If you enter a script name that you have already used, Paradox warns you and gives you a chance to either cancel the recorder or replace the existing script. As with instant scripts, once Paradox begins to record your keystrokes, it displays R in the upper right corner of the screen (see fig. 6.3). You can just execute keystrokes as usual, and Paradox shadows your every move.

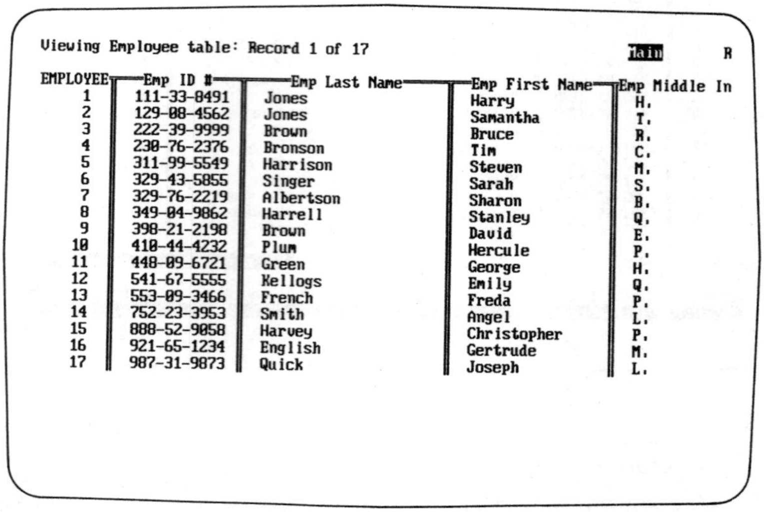
Viewing Employee table: Record 1 of 17 Main R

EMPLOYEE	Emp ID #	Emp Last Name	Emp First Name	Emp Middle In
1	111-33-8491	Jones	Harry	H.
2	129-88-4562	Jones	Samantha	T.
3	222-39-9999	Brown	Bruce	R.
4	230-76-2376	Bronson	Tim	C.
5	311-99-5549	Harrison	Steven	M.
6	329-43-5855	Singer	Sarah	S.
7	329-76-2219	Albertson	Sharon	B.
8	349-04-9862	Harrell	Stanley	Q.
9	398-21-2198	Brown	David	E.
10	410-44-4232	Plum	Hercule	P.
11	448-09-6721	Green	George	H.
12	541-67-5555	Kellogs	Emily	Q.
13	553-89-3466	French	Freda	P.
14	752-23-3953	Smith	Angel	L.
15	888-52-9858	Harvey	Christopher	P.
16	921-65-1234	English	Gertrude	M.
17	987-31-9873	Quick	Joseph	L.

Fig. 6.3.

The letter R, indicating that a script is being recorded.

If you need to begin recording in a mode other than the Main mode, use the PAL menu to access the Scripts menu. Press Alt-F10 (PAL Menu) and select **B**eginRecord.

To end the recording session from Main mode, press F10 (Menu) and select **S**cripts **E**nd-Record. Paradox saves the script as a file on your working directory and removes the R from the screen. The file has the same name as the script, with the file name extension SC.

As with the **B**eginRecord option, if you are not in Main mode when you need to end the recording, you have to use the PAL menu. In that case, press Alt-F10 (PAL Menu) and then select **E**nd-Record.

Suppose that you want to create a script named CENTRY (for Customer ENTRY) that displays the Customer table in DataEntry mode and form view. Start recording the script by pressing F10 (Menu) and selecting **S**cripts **B**eginRecord. Type *centry* and press Enter. Paradox begins recording and displays the message R. To access Customer in DataEntry mode, press F10 (Menu) and select **M**odify **D**ataEntry. Press Enter at the `Table:` prompt and choose the Customer table. Finally, switch to form view by pressing F7 (Form Toggle). Turn off the recorder by pressing Alt-F10 (PAL Menu) and selecting **E**nd-Record.

You now have a script named CENTRY that quickly will display the DataEntry form for the Customer table. The next section describes how to use the **P**lay option to run the script.

Sometimes you may decide that you have made a mistake while recording the script and just want to start over rather than try to fix the script later. To stop recording the script without saving it, press F10 (Menu) and select **S**cripts **C**ancel. Paradox erases the `R` from the screen and stops the recorder but does not write a script to disk.

Using the Play Option To Run a Script

Just as you can record a script from any Paradox mode, you can play a script from any mode. But you must play the script from the same mode in which you began recording it.

To play a script from the Main mode, press F10 (Menu) and select **S**cripts **P**lay. Press Enter at the `Script:` prompt to display a list of available scripts. If all your scripts begin with different letters, just press the first letter of the script you want. Otherwise, use the arrow keys to select your script and then press Enter. Paradox runs the script and displays the final screen.

For example, in the CENTRY example discussed in the preceding section, as soon as you press C (for CENTRY) at the list of scripts, Paradox displays the Customer DataEntry screen.

From any mode other than Main mode, use the PAL menu to start a script. Press Alt-F10 (PAL Menu), select **P**lay, and choose your script.

Caution: You can stop a script in midstream by pressing Ctrl-Break, but you should use this command carefully because it also is used to cancel other Paradox operations that you might be doing at the time. For example, suppose that while editing a table you run a script but then decide to stop it prematurely. You can press Ctrl-Break once to halt the script. If you accidentally press Ctrl-Break a second time, however, Paradox cancels your edit session without saving any changes or entries that you may have made.

Displaying a Script Step-by-Step

Occasionally you may not get the results you expected when you play a script. One way to discover the cause is to have Paradox display each step as the script is executed. This option is available only for scripts that begin in Main mode.

Normally Paradox just displays the final outcome of a script, but if you want the program to display the result of every step, press F10 (Menu) and select **S**cripts **S**howPlay. After you choose a script, Paradox displays another menu, which contains these options:

Fast. Choose this option to tell Paradox to play the script quickly. This speed is not particularly helpful when you're trying to discover an error, but the choice may be preferable if the script is long and you think the problem is near the end of the script.

Slow. This choice plays the script at a pace slow enough that you will be able to keep up easily.

The actual speed of either of these selections depends on the speed of your computer.

Running a Script Repeatedly

Version 3

One of the more interesting options available in Paradox 3.0 is the **R**epeat-Play choice on the Scripts menu and the PAL menu. To have the program run a script several times in rapid succession, press F10 (Menu) and select **S**cripts **R**epeatPlay, or press Alt-F10 (PAL Menu) and select **R**epeatPlay.

Select the script, and Paradox displays the prompt `Number of times to repeat:`. Type a positive whole number and press Enter. Paradox then executes the script the specified number of times. If you want Paradox to run the script continuously, enter the letter C rather than a number in response to the prompt.

This feature can be quite useful if you need to make the same change to a particular field in dozens of records. Rather than manually edit each record, you can record an instant script while correcting the first record, and use the **R**epeatPlay option to make the change to as many records as necessary.

You can also use this repeating feature to print multiple copies of a report. If you have a script that prints the report, use **R**epeatPlay to run the script once for each copy you want. Otherwise, just record an instant script to print one report and then use **R**epeatPlay.

Perhaps the flashiest use of **R**epeatPlay is to create a graphics show on a network. Refer to Chapter 12, "Creating Paradox Graphics," for a description of how to use this script feature to display a graph that is updated continuously as network users change the underlying data.

Starting the Custom Configuration Program

Paradox itself uses scripts to accomplish certain internal operations. For example, to customize the way Paradox looks and acts on your system, you can run the Custom Configuration Program (CCP), which is accessed through a Paradox script named CUSTOM. To run the CCP, however, you have to tell Paradox where (in which directory) to find it. Normally this directory is not your working directory but rather the directory that contains the Paradox files.

To run the CCP in Paradox 3.0, press F10 (Menu) and select **S**cripts **P**lay. At the `Script:` prompt, type the name of the directory that contains the Paradox program files, *c:\paradox3*, and press Enter. Paradox displays a list of scripts, including the CUSTOM script (it may be the only one listed). Press C to choose that script. Paradox then begins the Custom Configuration Program. Refer to Appendix B for details of when and how you should use this program.

Version 3

Editing Scripts

The Paradox Script Editor, as its name implies, provides a method for editing your scripts by hand. Without this feature, you would have to re-record any macro that required alterations, even if you needed to make only a minor change. This section only touches on the basic features of the Script Editor. Part III of this book introduces you to the use of the Script Editor as a tool for applications development and PAL programming.

Beginning the Script Editor

To begin the Script Editor and display a previously recorded script, press F10 (Menu) and select **S**cripts **E**ditor **E**dit. Select the script you want to change. Paradox displays your script in a screen similar to figure 6.4. Notice that Paradox is in Script mode.

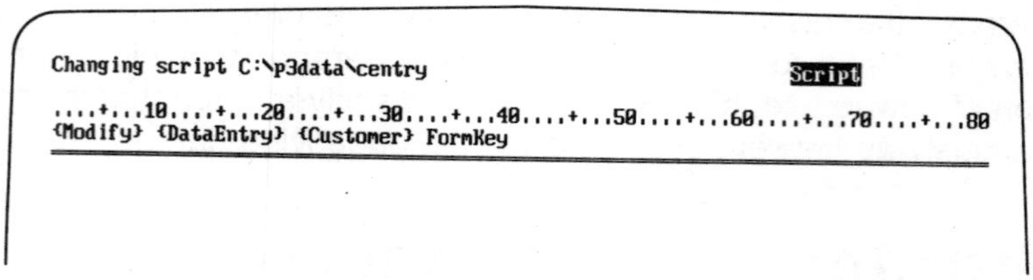

Fig. 6.4.

Using the Script Editor to edit the CENTRY script.

The Script Editor editing features are nearly identical to those found in the report design screen. Table 6.1 lists the cursor-movement keys you can use in the Script Editor. Refer to table 1.2 in Chapter 1 for a list of the special keystroke commands, which are also available in the Script Editor. In addition, you may want to look back at Chapter 5 for discussions of how to insert and delete lines and how to display a vertical ruler.

Table 6.1
Using Cursor-Movement Keys in the Script Editor

Key	*Moves Cursor*
Home	To first line
Ctrl-Home	To beginning of line
End	To last line
Ctrl-End	To last character of line
PgUp	Up one screen
PgDn	Down one screen
Left arrow	One character left
Ctrl-left arrow	Left one-half screen
Right arrow	One character right
Ctrl-right arrow	Right one-half screen
Up arrow	Up one line
Down arrow	Down one line
Enter	Down one line

A significant difference between the report design screen and the Script Editor's screen is their maximum widths. A report can be up to 2,000 characters wide, but the Script Editor width is limited to 132 characters.

Understanding Special Script Key Codes

When you display a recorded script, you probably will be able to recognize immediately most of the words the script has used to record the keys you pressed. Menu options are enclosed in braces ({ }), and keys and keystroke commands are represented by special code words that duplicate or closely resemble the key names or commands themselves. Table 6.2 lists these special codes.

Table 6.2
Script Codes for Special Keys and Keystroke Commands

Key or Keystroke Command	*Script Code*
Home	Home
End	End
PgUp	PgUp
PgDn	PgDn
Left arrow	Left
Right arrow	Right
Up arrow	Up
Down arrow	Down
Ins	Ins
Del	Del
Backspace	Backspace
Esc	Esc
Enter	Enter
Tab	Tab
Shift Tab	ReverseTab
Ctrl-Break	CtrlBreak
Ctrl-Home	CtrlHome
Ctrl-PgUp	CtrlPgUp
Ctrl-PgDn	CtrlPgDn
Alt-X	*CrossTab
Ctrl-D	Ditto
Ctrl-O	DOS
Alt-O	DOSBig
Ctrl-F	FieldView
Alt-K	KeyLookup
Alt-L	LockKey
Ctrl-R	Rotate
Alt-R	Refresh
Ctrl-V	VertRuler
Ctrl-Y	DeleteLine
Ctrl-Z	Zoom
Alt-Z	ZoomNext
F1	Help
F2	DO-IT!
F3	UpImage

*Paradox 3.0 only

Table 6.2—*Continued*

Key or Keystroke Command	*Script Code*
F4	DownImage
F5	Example
F6	Check
F7	FormKey
F8	ClearImage
F9	EditKey
F10	Menu
Alt-F3	InstantRecord
Alt-F4	InstantPlay
Alt-F5	FieldView
Alt-F6	CheckPlus
Alt-F7	InstantReport
Alt-F8	ClearAll
Alt-F9	CoeditKey
Ctrl-F6	*CheckDescending
Ctrl-F7	*Graph Key
Shift-F6	*GroupBy

*Paradox 3.0 only

For now, your only purpose for using the Script Editor should be to add, delete, or modify a command in a lengthy recorded macro so that you don't have to record the macro again. But you will certainly get more familiar with this Editor when you begin to use the Paradox Applications Language.

Assume that you want to modify the CENTRY script so that it uses CoEdit rather than DataEntry mode to enter new records into Customer. The {DataEntry} command in CENTRY should be changed to {CoEdit}, and the codes for the End and PgDn keystrokes should be added to the end of the script so that the cursor moves to a blank record at the end of the Customer table. Of course this script is so short that re-recording it would be just as easy as modifying it. But this example demonstrates the same methodology you would use to edit a longer script.

Whenever you are editing a script, you can make it easier to read and follow by moving each command to its own line. For example, in the CENTRY script, first turn on Insert mode by pressing the Ins key. Then place the cursor on the left brace portion ({) of the {DataEntry} command, and press Enter. {DataEntry} and the other commands to its right then move down to the second line (see fig. 6.5). After you repeat this procedure for the other two commands, Paradox displays the screen shown in figure 6.6.

```
Changing script C:\p3data\centry                                    Script Ins

....+...10....+...20....+...30....+...40....+...50....+...60....+...70....+...80
{Modify}
{DataEntry} {Customer} FormKey
```

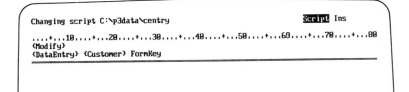

Fig. 6.5.

Pressing Enter before the {DataEntry} command.

```
Changing script C:\p3data\centry                                    Script Ins

....+...10....+...20....+...30....+...40....+...50....+...60....+...70....+...80
{Modify}
{DataEntry}
{Customer}
FormKey
```

Fig. 6.6.

Each command on its own line.

Then, using normal editing techniques, edit the CENTRY script and create the new version shown in figure 6.7.

```
Changing script C:\p3data\centry                                    Script

....+...10....+...20....+...30....+...40....+...50....+...60....+...70....+...80
{Modify}
{CoEdit}
{Customer}
FormKey
End
PgDn
```

Fig. 6.7.

The new version of CENTRY.

Saving a Script's Changes

As with many other Paradox commands, you can complete the script editing process and save your changes by pressing F2 (DO-IT!). Paradox replaces the original script with the newly modified version and then returns you to the Main mode.

Paradox also provides a way to save the script and immediately test it. Press F10 (Menu) and select **G**o. Paradox saves the new script and then plays it.

Refer to Chapter 15, "An Overview of the Paradox Application Language," for further ideas on using the Paradox Script Editor.

Using the INIT Script

Every time you turn on your computer, the operating system (DOS) searches the boot disk for a file named AUTOEXEC.BAT. If DOS can locate this special script-like file, the system executes it. If DOS cannot find the file, however, the system starts the computer by asking for the current date and time. Most PCs have an AUTOEXEC.BAT file on the root directory of the boot disk. This file is usually used to start a program or display a menu automatically when you turn on the computer. If you have a hard disk (which is a requirement for Paradox 3.0), your system undoubtedly has an AUTOEXEC.BAT file that is automatically executed at start-up.

Paradox does a similar thing every time it starts. Rather than look for an AUTOEXEC.BAT file, Paradox searches the start-up directory for a script file named INIT. The Paradox documentation suggests that you place this script file in the directory that contains the Paradox program files. This directory is the appropriate one only if you start Paradox from there. If you use the method suggested in both Quick Start 1 and Appendix A to start Paradox from your working directory, you can create and save the INIT script just as you would any other script. Paradox will save it to the proper start-up directory.

The INIT script is normally used to perform operations that you routinely do every time you start Paradox. The nature of these tasks depends entirely upon the type of work you do with the program. One powerful use of INIT is to assign keyboard macros for use throughout your Paradox session. The next section shows how you can use INIT in this manner.

Another way to run a script automatically is to use a command line argument when you load Paradox. For example, if you type

PARADOX3_CENTRY

Paradox 3.0 loads and runs the script called CENTRY. The main Paradox screen doesn't come up if you use this technique.

Creating Keyboard Macros

A *keyboard macro* is a script assigned to a particular key or key combination. This use of scripts is closest to the sort of macros found in most other popular programs.

You can create keyboard macros in a number of ways. The easiest method is to record the keystrokes for the macro as a normal script. Use whatever valid script name you want. Once the script is working properly, use the Script Editor to create another script that contains the following PAL command:

SETKEY x PLAY "script_name"

Replace *x* with one of the key codes listed in Appendix B of the Paradox *PAL User's Guide* (part of the documentation distributed with the program), and replace *script_name* with the name of the script that you recorded.

When assigning macro keys, you should follow several common-sense rules:

1. Do not assign a macro to any commonly used key, such as a single letter or a number.
2. Do not assign a macro to a key or key combination already used by Paradox for some special purpose.
3. Use mnemonics (memory aids) when assigning macro key names. For example, if your macro's purpose is to add data to the Customer table, use a name such as Ctrl-C for Customer.

Perhaps the best place for SETKEY commands, especially for assigning keyboard macros that you want to use routinely, is the INIT script, discussed in the preceding section. For example, you might want to assign the CENTRY script to the key combination Ctrl-C. Use the INIT script to set up this assignment so that the Ctrl-C key combination is redefined for the entire Paradox session. Then your data-entry person can press Ctrl-C from anywhere in Main mode to have Paradox immediately display a blank data-entry form. Use the Script Editor to place the following command in the INIT script:

SETKEY 3 PLAY "CENTRY"

The number 3 is the ASCII code for the Ctrl-C key combination. This code is found in Appendix B of the Paradox *PAL User's Guide*. Save the new INIT script by pressing F2 (DO-IT!). The next time you start Paradox, pressing Ctrl-C displays a CoEdit data-entry screen for Customer like the one shown in figure 6.8.

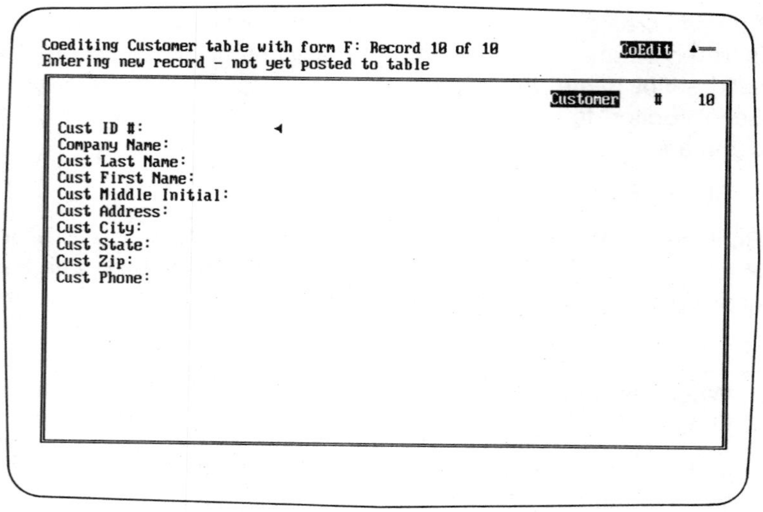

Fig. 6.8.

The Customer CoEdit mode data-entry screen.

Using Scripts on a Network

The following rules apply to the use of scripts from a shared network directory:

- Paradox imposes no limitation on how many users can play a particular script at once.
- No other user can play or edit a script that you already are editing.
- No other user can edit a script while you are playing it.

Chapter Summary

This chapter is the last one in Part I, "Paradox Fundamentals." Now that you have completed this portion of the book, take some time to practice all that you have learned. Create a database or two and play around with data entry, editing, queries, reports, scripts, and macros. Try each feature covered in these first six chapters until you clearly understand how it works and what it accomplishes. Learning any PC program, especially a database management system, is a building process. Once you feel confident in your understanding of Paradox fundamentals, move on to Part II, "Tapping the Power of Paradox."

II

Tapping the Power of Paradox

Includes

Quick Start **2**

Experimenting with More Advanced Paradox Features

This lesson is the second of two Quick Starts included in this book. Each Quick Start is designed to help you get a running start with Paradox. Quick Start 2 is based on the assumption that you have either finished Part I of this book or are generally familiar with the information covered there. Now that you have discovered the ease of working with the fundamental features of Paradox, you are ready to move on to the more powerful capabilities of the program.

In this lesson, you get a taste of the topics presented in Part II, from multitable queries to graphics. After building a few tables, you perform multitable queries to produce a list of orders showing customer names and to find the name of the customer who placed a particular order. Next, you design a data-entry form for the Orders table and add validity checking that prevents you from accidentally entering an invalid customer ID number or a nonexistent employee ID number. You then use your new form to enter several orders into the Orders table. To get a quick glimpse of custom report design, you next create a tabular report that calculates the totals for the orders entered in Orders and Detail. Then, in the last portion of this lesson, you create a graph that compares the numbers of each type of widget your company sold for the month.

You can use one of two approaches to studying this Quick Start. You can go straight through the Quick Start and then proceed to Chapter 7; or, if you prefer, you can step through this lesson one section at a time, stopping to study the applicable chapter before moving to the next part of the lesson. The various parts of this Quick Start are progressive, however, so you need to complete the earlier sections before you can do the latter ones.

Building the Database

Before you can begin this lesson, you need to have a few tables with which to work. If you haven't already done so, build the Employee table described in Quick Start 1. Then use the procedures you learned in Part I of this book to create the following tables. These tables are essentially the same ones that have been used to create the book's screen examples. Here are the table definitions:

Customer Field	*Type*	*Orders Field*	*Type*
Cust ID #	A4*	Order #	N*
Company Name	A20	Cust ID #	A4
Cust Address	A20	Emp ID #	A11
Cust City	A20	Date	D
Cust State	A2		
Cust Zip	A5		
Cust Phone	A14		

Product Field	*Type*	*Detail Field*	*Type*
Model #	A4*	Order #	N*
Product Name	A20	Item #	N*
Price	$	Model #	A4
Cost	$	Quantity	N

Use either table view or form view to enter the following data:

Customer Table

Cust ID #	*Customer Data*	*Cust ID #*	*Customer Data*
1000	Eastern Enterprises 1211 Commerce St. Springfield, VA 22150 (703) 555-2355	1001	Alpha Freight Lines 720 Port Royal Fairfax, VA 22030

1002	Ace Airplanes 777 Kittyhawk Dr. Gaithersburg, MD 20877 (301) 555-2777	1003	Hidden Resorts 6601 Wales Rd. Vienna, VA 22180 (703) 555-9662
1004	Sangster Insurance 1411 Reservation Dr. Springfield, VA 22152 (703) 555-9995	1005	Signal Plumbing 3333 Half Street Oxon Hill, MD 20745 (301) 555-8379

Orders Table

Order #	*Cust ID #*	*Emp ID #*	*Date*
100	1000	230-76-2376	9/02/88
101	1003	329-76-2219	9/07/88
102	1001	987-31-9873	9/08/88
103	1002	111-33-8491	9/12/88
104	1005	129-08-4562	9/13/88
105	1000	329-76-2219	9/16/88

Product Table

Model #	*Product Name*	*Price*	*Cost*
A333	Standard Widget	39.95	19.75
A334	Standard Widget Plus	43.95	21.15
B107	Enhanced Widget	49.95	23.60
C777	Jumbo Widget	55.95	24.66
G400	Deluxe Widget	59.95	25.15
X155	Imperial Widget	79.95	32.50

Detail Table

Order #	*Item #*	*Model #*	*Quantity*
100	1	A333	50
100	2	B107	25
100	3	G400	10
101	1	A333	15
101	2	X155	10
102	1	G400	35
102	2	A333	10
103	1	G400	22
103	2	X155	5
104	1	B107	45
105	1	G400	30

Notice the relationships between these files (including the Employee table from Quick Start 1). Using the notation technique described in Chapter 2, you can depict the relationships as shown in the following chart:

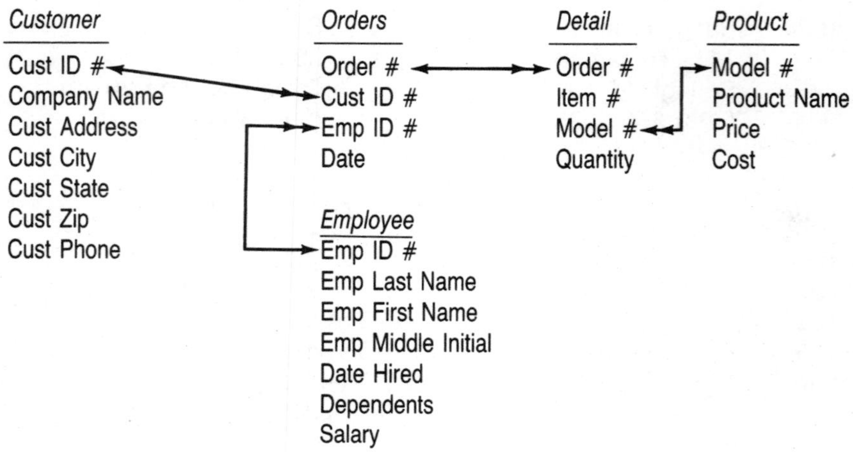

Performing a Multitable Query

Now that you have a database with several tables, you can perform a query to pull information from more than one table. (Chapter 7 covers the topic of multitable queries.) First, do a single-table query on the Orders table to look at the list of all orders. Then query both Orders and Customer to try to match the proper company name in the Customer table with each order in the Orders table. Finally, look up the data for Order #105 only. Here are the steps you need to follow:

1. To list all the orders, select **A**sk from the Main menu. Select the Orders table, and use F6 (Check Mark) in the query form to select the Order #, Cust ID #, and Date fields (see fig. QS2.1). Execute the query by pressing F2 (DO-IT!). Paradox displays the screen shown in figure QS2.2.

2. The Answer table does not yet show the name of the company that placed each order. To add that information, you need to query Customer along with Orders. Clear the Answer table from the work space by making that image current and pressing F8 (Clear Image). Press F10 (Menu) to display the Main menu,

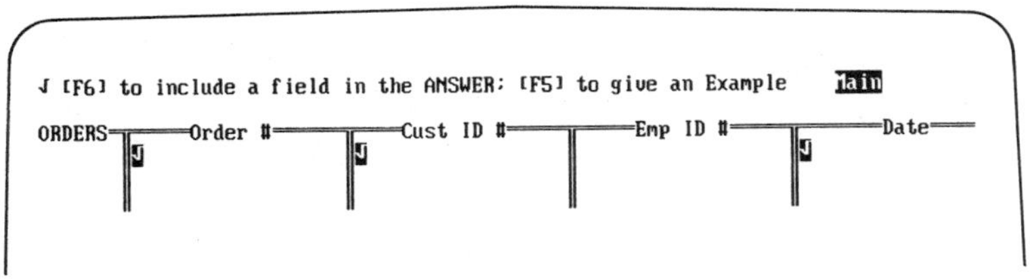

Fig. QS2.1.

Building a single-table query.

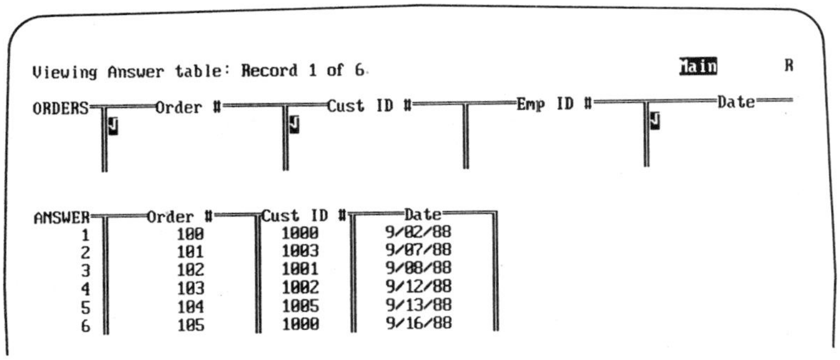

Fig. QS2.2.

The Answer table for a single-table query.

and select **A**sk. This time choose the Customer table. Paradox adds a second query form to the work space.

3. You need to tell Paradox to use the Cust ID # field as the link between the Customer and Orders tables. You send this message by using *example elements*. Move the cursor to the Cust ID # field of the Customer table, press F5 (Example), and type the letters *abc*. Paradox displays abc as the example element in the Cust ID # column of the query form. Also, place a check mark in the Company Name column so that it is included in the Answer table (see fig. QS2.3).

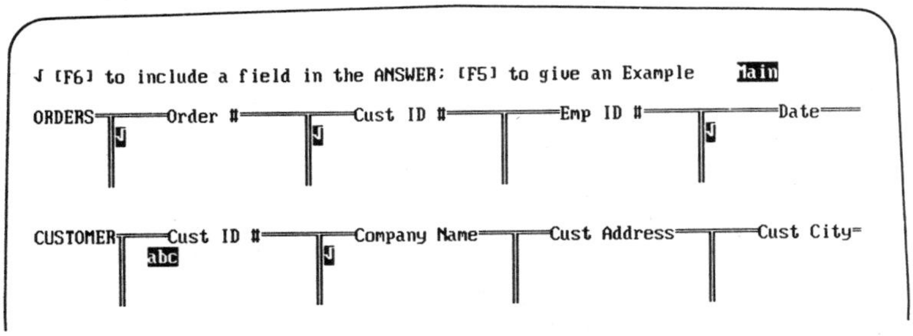

Fig. QS2.3.

Building a multitable query.

4. To complete the link between Orders and Customer, you must place a matching example element in the linking field of the Orders table. Press F3 (Up Image) and move to the Cust ID # field. Then press F5 (Example), type *abc*, and press Enter. Just as before, Paradox displays abc in the column in inverse video (see fig. QS2.4). Now press F2 (DO-IT!). The resulting Answer table shows the Order #, Cust ID #, Date, and Company Name fields (see fig. QS2.5).

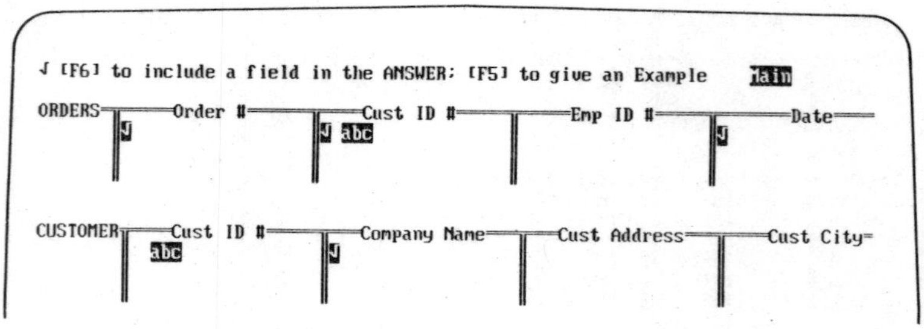

Fig. QS2.4.

Example elements linking Orders with Customer through Cust ID #.

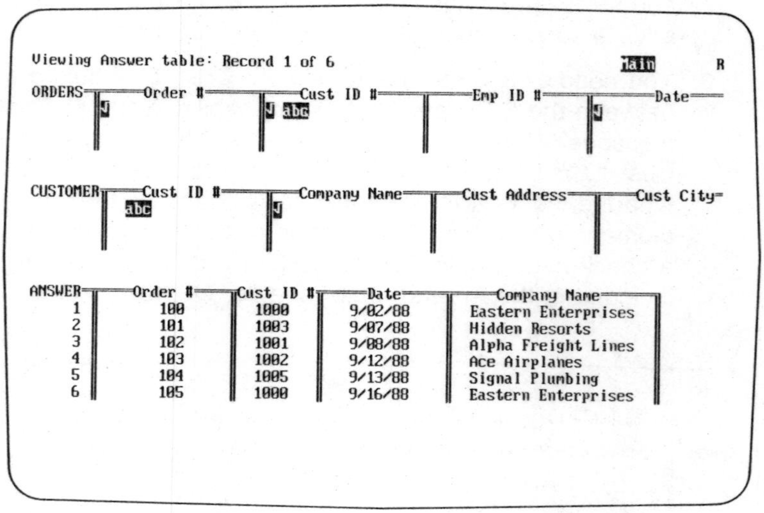

Fig. QS2.5.

The Answer table for a multitable query.

5. Next, you want to see the same information, but for Order #105 only. While displaying the screen shown in figure QS2.5, clear the Answer table by pressing F8 (Clear Image). It may at first appear that you have only one query form on the work space, but notice the *up pointer* in the upper right corner of the screen, which indicates a hidden image. Move to the top image,

the Orders query form, by pressing F3 (Up Image). To perform the query for Order #105 only, move the cursor to the Order # column, type *105* (do *not* press F5 this time), and press F2 (DO-IT!). This time, Paradox displays one row of data, for Order #105 only.

Designing an Entry Form

Paradox does a good job of automatically designing a form for each table, but you may sometimes want to design a form more to your liking. Certainly you will want to add many of the editing aids that Paradox makes available. In this portion of the lesson, you learn to custom design a form for the Orders table. Chapter 8 covers "Designing and Using Paradox Forms" in more detail.

1. To begin form design, first clear all images from the work space by pressing Alt-F8 (Clear All) and then select, from the Main menu, **F**orms **D**esign. Select the Orders table, press the number 1, and press Enter to select form number 1. At the `Form description:` prompt, type *Orders Entry Form* and press Enter. Paradox displays an almost blank screen with the message `Designing new F1 form for Orders` at the upper left of the screen, the mode indicator `Form` in inverse video and the message `1/1` in the upper right, and the cursor position indicator `‹1,1›` in the second line.

2. Notice that as you use the cursor-movement keys to move around the screen, the cursor position indicator changes. The first number tells you the screen row (1 to 23), and the second number tells you the screen column (1 to 80). Move the cursor to position <4,28> and type *Master Order Entry Form*. This phrase is a title for the form and does not affect data that goes into the Orders table. Also, type the following labels, starting at the positions indicated (see fig. QS2.6):

Order Number:	<7,10>
Date:	<7,45>
Customer Identification Number:	<10,10>
Salesperson's Identification Number:	<13,10>

3. Next, place the fields next to the labels. Move the cursor to the right of the Order Number label, to position <7,24>, leaving one blank space. Make sure that Paradox is not in Insert mode. To place the Order # field here, press F10 (Menu) and select

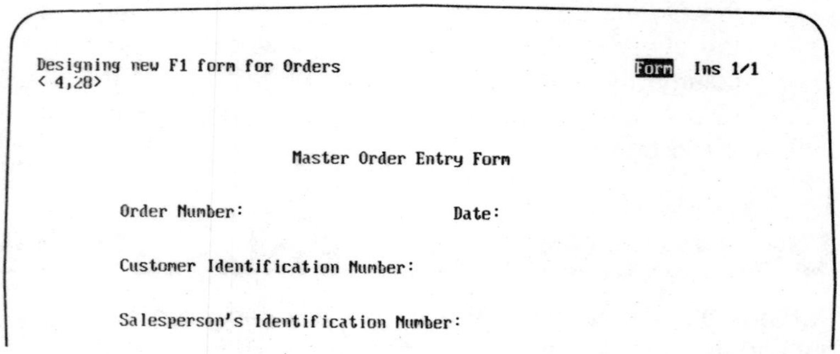

Fig. QS2.6.

The title and labels for the Orders table entry form.

Field **P**lace **R**egular **O**rder_#. Then press Enter. Paradox displays a dashed line 23 characters long. This line is too long, because the order numbers will never be that big, and the Date label is partially obliterated. Press the left arrow 16 times to shorten the line until exactly 7 dashes remain. Press Enter to accept this length for the field. Paradox responds by displaying a solid underscore, 7 characters in length, beginning at position <7,24>. Follow a similar procedure to place the remaining fields in the positions indicated:

Field	*Starting Position*	*Ending Position*
Date	<7,51>	<7,61>
Cust ID #	<10,42>	<10,45>
Emp ID #	<13,47>	<13,57>

4. Now draw a border around the form, putting the upper left corner at <2,5> and the lower right corner at <6,70>. Start by positioning the cursor at <2,5>. To draw the border, press F10 (Menu) and select **B**order **P**lace **S**ingle-line. Then press Enter. Use the arrow keys to move the cursor to position <16,70>, and press Enter.

   Note: You will be unable to see the position indicator, so you must move the cursor to the position on the screen that appears to be appropriate for the bottom right corner of the border and then press Enter.

5. When you are finished, your screen should look similar to figure QS2.7. To save the form, press F2 (DO-IT!).

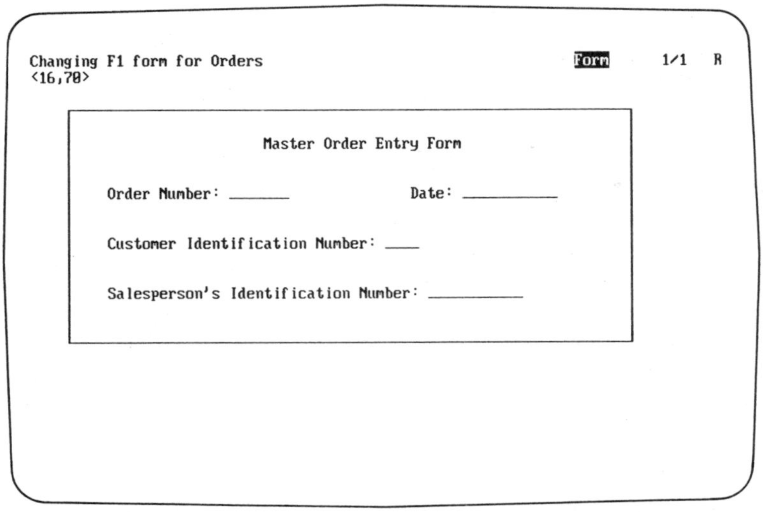

Fig. QS2.7.

The completed Orders table entry form, with fields and border.

Adding a Validity Check

In this part of Quick Start 2, you add a validity-checking feature to two fields of the form you designed for the Orders table. This feature prevents you from accidentally entering either a customer identification number (Cust ID #) or a salesperson's identification number (Emp ID #) that does not already exist in its respective table. The validity check also provides a way of "looking up" a correct value in the tables. This and many other power editing features are covered in Chapter 9.

1. First, you must get Paradox to display your new form. From the Main menu, select **M**odify **D**ataEntry and choose the Orders table. Paradox displays an empty record in normal table view. To display the new form, press F10 (Menu) and select **I**mage **P**ickform **1**. Paradox displays the form you designed in DataEntry mode.

2. Move the cursor to the Cust ID # field in the form (the label says `Customer Identification Number`) and press F10 (Menu). Then select **V**alCheck **D**efine. Press Enter to indicate that you want to check the Cust ID # field. From the next menu, choose **T**ableLookup and indicate the Customer table. From the third menu, select **J**ustCurrentField **H**elpAndFill. Paradox displays in the bottom line of the screen the message

Table lookup recorded. The second line from the top of the screen instructs you to Press [F1] for help with fill-in.

3. Now you can test your validity check. Use the form to enter a record. Type *106* as the order number, and *9/19/88* as the date of the order. Then try using *1110* as the customer's identification number. Figure QS2.8 shows the message that Paradox displays.

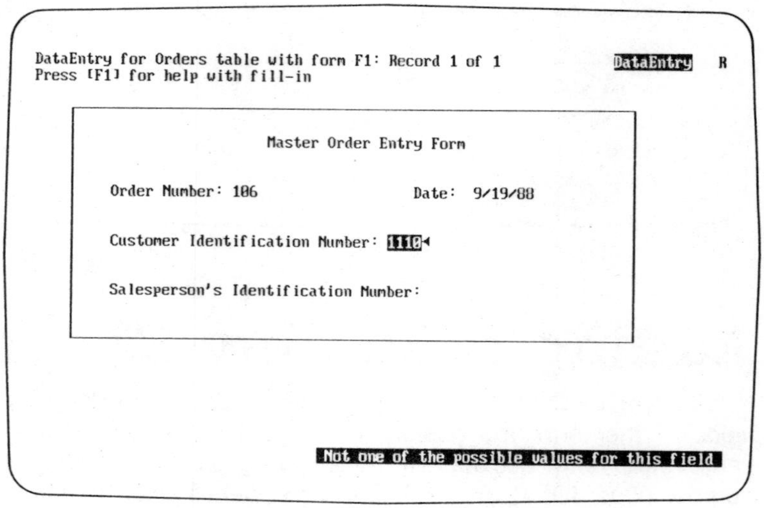

Fig. QS2.8.

The result of entering a nonexistent customer ID number.

4. To see a list of available customer identification numbers, press F1. Paradox shows you the Customer table. A message at the top of this screen tells you to use the F2 key to select the proper record. Use the down-arrow key to move down to Customer 1001, Alpha Freight Lines, and press F2. Paradox immediately returns to the Orders entry form and replaces the number you had entered in the Cust ID # field with 1001.

5. Move to the Emp ID # field (Salesperson's Identification Number) and add the same validity-checking feature. Press F10 (Menu), select **V**alCheck **D**efine, and press Enter. From the ValCheck menu, choose **T**ableLookup and select the Employee table. Again choose **J**ustCurrentField **H**elpAndFill.

6. Finish entering this record by using the lookup feature to choose the Emp ID # for Emily Kellogs (541-67-5555).

7. Use your form and the F1 and F2 keys (validity-checking options—explained in steps 4 and 5) to enter the following new data into Orders:

Order #	*Cust ID #*	*Emp ID #*	*Date*
107	1004	230-76-2376	9/21/88
108	1003	111-33-8491	9/22/88
109	1005	448-09-6721	9/24/88
110	1000	987-31-9873	9/25/88
111	1002	230-76-2376	9/26/88
112	1001	448-09-6721	9/29/88
113	1004	111-33-8491	9/30/88

8. To save the new records, press F2 (DO-IT!). Paradox returns to Main mode and displays the Orders table with the new records added.

9. Use any method with which you're familiar to enter the following records into the Detail table. They represent the detail information behind each of the orders you just entered into the Orders table.

Order #	*Item #*	*Model #*	*Quantity*
106	1	A333	15
106	2	G400	5
107	1	X155	10
108	1	B107	60
109	1	G400	25
109	2	B107	30
110	1	A333	5
110	2	B107	5
112	1	A333	29
113	1	B107	17
113	2	G400	8

Creating Custom Reports

This portion of Quick Start 2 demonstrates using lookup tables, grouping, and summary fields in a Paradox tabular report. This lesson gives you a chance to practice a few of the concepts you learned in Part I of the book, and also introduces some new ones. You build a tabular report that calculates the total bill for each of the orders by totaling the detail in the Detail table. Creating tabular reports with such features as grouping, multiple tables, and summary fields is discussed fully in Chapter 10. You can find similar coverage of free-form reports in Chapter 11.

Placing Lookup Fields and Grouping Records

One of the fields that you need in order to calculate the total bill for each order is the Price field, which contains the price of each model sold. This field has to be looked up from the Product table, based on the model number.

1. You are going to start with the standard tabular report specification for the Detail table. At the Main menu, select **R**eport **D**esign. Select the Detail table and form 1. Type the description *Summary Fields* and press Enter. Choose the field type **T**abular. Paradox displays the standard report specification.

2. Insert two new columns to the right of the Quantity field in the table band. To insert these columns, move the cursor into the table band, just to the right of the Quantity column. Press F10 (Menu), select **T**ableBand **I**nsert, and press Enter. Paradox inserts one column. Repeat this procedure for the second column.

3. Place the Price field, looked up from the Product table, in the first new column. To do so, place the cursor in the first new column, in the body of the table band, and press F10 (Menu). Then select **F**ield **L**ookup **L**ink and choose the Product table. Indicate that the Model # field is the link between Detail and Product so that the Price can be looked up. To define the Price field, press F10 (Menu) and select **F**ield **P**lace **R**egular. Use the arrow keys to move to the option that reads `[Product->]`, and press Enter. Paradox shows the available fields from the Product lookup table: Model #, Product Name, Price, and Cost. Choose Price. Press Enter to indicate where the field should begin, use the left-arrow key to shorten the field to `(9,999)`, and press Enter. Leave the number of decimal places at 2 by pressing Enter again. Add the word *Price* and an underline of hyphens to the table band header. Figure QS2.9 shows how the report specification should look at this juncture.

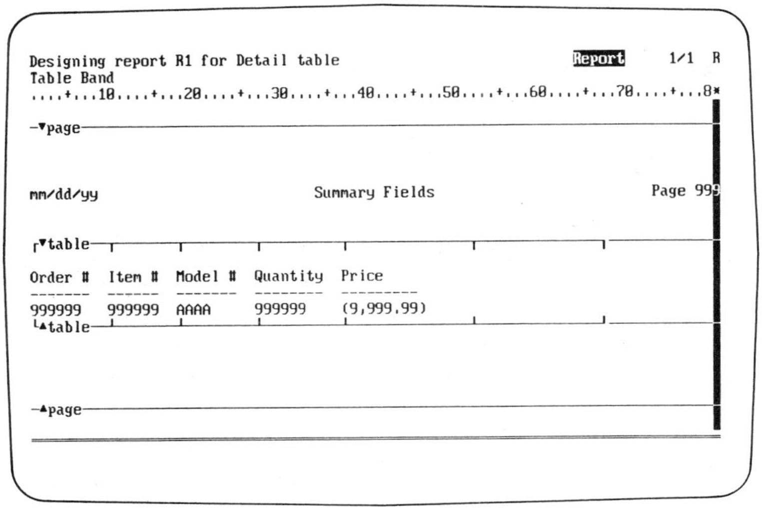

Fig. QS2.9.

Adding a lookup field to the report specification.

4. Next, place a calculated field in the second new column. This new field is the product of Quantity times Price. Because Price is a looked-up field, you have to use the special syntax *[lookup_table->fieldname]*, or in this case *[Product->Price]* in the expression for the calculated field. Position the cursor in the body of the second new column, press F10 (Menu), and select **F**ield **P**lace **C**alculated. Then type the expression

   [Quantity]*[Product->Price]

   and press Enter. Press Enter a second time to indicate where the field should begin in the column. Use the left arrow to adjust field length to `(99,999)`, and press Enter two more times. Place a heading above this calculated field that reads *Ext Price*, and type a line of hyphens beneath it.

5. Group the records in the report by order number. Place the cursor in the last line of the page header area, just above the table band, and press F10 (Menu). Then select **G**roup **I**nsert **F**ield **O**rder_# and press Enter. This step ensures that all records in the Detail table from each order are grouped together. To prevent the order number from being repeated every record, press F10 (Menu) and select **S**etting **G**roupRepeats **S**uppress.

Placing Summary Fields

Summary fields are often used to create totals and subtotals in reports. Place a summary field in the group footer of your report to get a total for each order, and a summary field in the report footer for a grand total at the end of the report. Both of these summary fields must sum up the calculated product of Quantity times Price.

1. First, to create the subtotal field, move the cursor into the group footer. Insert a blank line. Move the cursor just below the Ext Price column and create a line of hyphens that will indicate a total. Move the cursor to the second line of the group footer, press F10 (Menu), and select **F**ield **P**lace **S**ummary **C**alculated. Type the same expression you used for the Ext Price calculated field:

   [Quantity]*[Product->Price]

   Then select **S**um **P**erGroup to indicate that the results of calculations should be summed and subtotaled for each group (that is, for each Order # value). Press Enter to indicate the starting point of the field, and use the arrow keys to adjust its length to `(999,999)`. Press Enter twice.

2. Perform a similar operation in the report footer, just below the new subtotal field. Place a double line (using the equals sign [=]) in the first line of the report footer. Then move the cursor below the double line, press F10 (Menu), and select **F**ield **P**lace **S**ummary **C**alculated. Type the expression

   [Quantity]*[Product->Price]

   and press Enter. Then choose **S**um **O**verall. Press Enter to indicate position. Use the left arrow to reduce the size of the field to `(9,999,999)`, and press Enter twice. Your screen should appear similar to figure QS2.10.

3. Before saving the report specification, test it to the screen by pressing F10 (Menu) and selecting **O**utput **S**creen. Paradox sends the report to the screen. Your report should be similar to figure QS2.11. Once you have fixed any problems that you discover, save the report specification by pressing F2 (DO-IT!). The report is then ready to be sent to the printer.

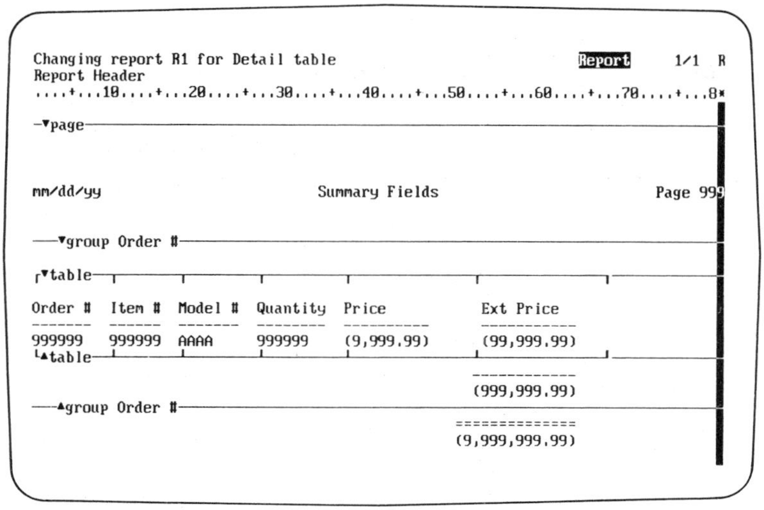

Fig. QS2.10.

The completed report specification with lookup field (Price), calculated field (Ext Price), and summary fields.

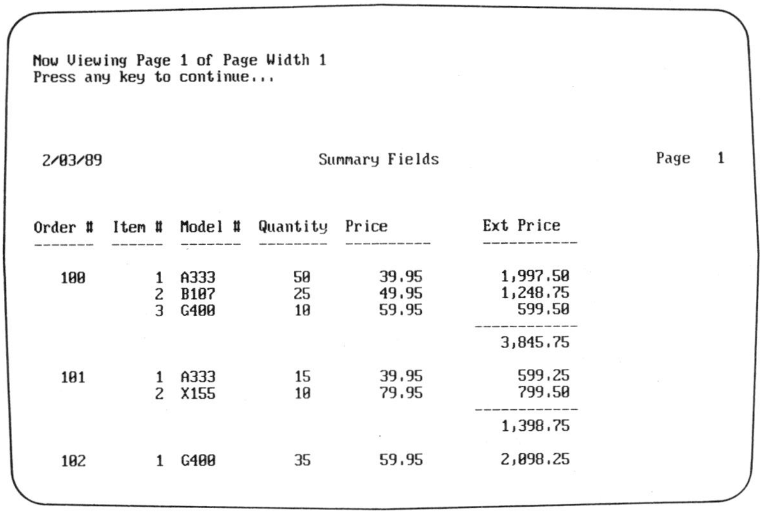

Fig. QS2.11.

The first page of the Summary Fields report.

Creating Graphs

Version 3

The graphics module of Paradox is brand new in Version 3.0. This section of Quick Start 2 gives you a good idea of how easy the graphics feature is to use, but keep in mind that Chapter 12 is completely devoted to Paradox graphics. In this part of the lesson, you use the Detail table and QBE to calculate the number of each model of widget sold, and compare the totals in a bar graph.

1. First, you need to use a query form to calculate the total number of each type of widget sold and at the same time to look up the name of each model from the Product table. Paradox makes this procedure easy. From the Main menu, choose **A**sk and select the Detail table. To place an example element in the Model # field, place the cursor in that field, press F5 (Example), type *123*, and press Enter. Paradox displays the example in inverse video. Move to the Quantity column and type *calc sum as Total*.

2. Add a second query form. Press F10 (Menu) and select **A**sk. Select the Product table. Move the cursor to the Model # column, press F5 (Example), type *123*, and press Enter. Move to the Product Name field and mark it with a check mark (press F6); then press Enter. The example elements in the Product and Detail tables correspond, which causes Paradox to match the proper product name with the model number listed in each Detail record. Because only one field is checked, the data is grouped by that field and the calc-sum field totals the quantities of each model sold. To execute the query, press F2 (DO-IT!). Figure QS2.12 shows the results.

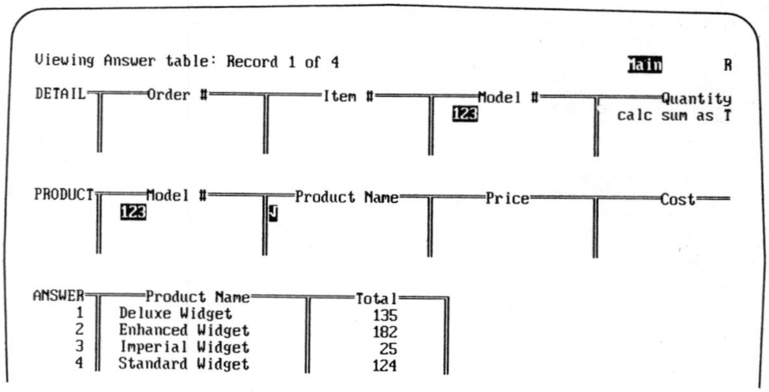

Fig. QS2.12.

Using a multitable query to calculate the total number of each model of widget sold.

3. Creating a graph is so easy that you can create one from the Answer table, but the graph will look a little better if you rename the table first. (Paradox by default uses the table name as the title of the graph.) To rename the table, access the Main menu with F10 (Menu) and select **T**ools **R**ename **T**able. Select

the Answer table. Type the new table name *Totals* and press Enter. Because Answer was the current image in the work space, Paradox automatically changes the name of the Answer table on the screen to Totals. Now you are ready to create the graph.

4. To display a bar graph that compares the total numbers of units sold, you must first place the cursor in the Total column of the Totals table. Then press F10 (Menu) and select **I**mage **G**raph **V**iewGraph **S**creen. Paradox displays the graph shown in figure QS2.13. Press Esc when you are finished viewing the graph.

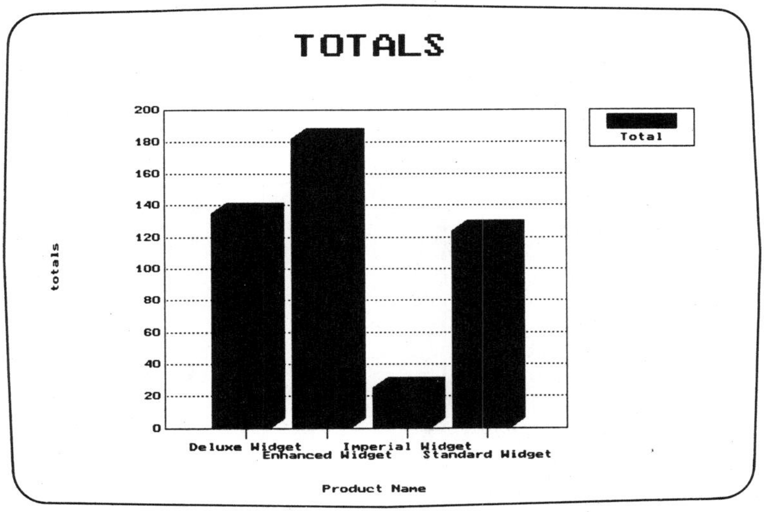

Fig. QS2.13.

The graph of the Totals table.

5. To print your graph, make sure that your printer is connected and on-line. Then press F10 (Menu) and select **I**mage **G**raph **V**iewGraph **P**rinter. Paradox prints the graph.

Quick Start Summary

You have now completed Quick Start 2. What you have seen here was just the appetizer. A feast of powerful Paradox features awaits you in Part II of *Using Paradox 3*. In the next chapter, Chapter 7, you learn how to use Query By Example to ask complex questions of your database.

7

Asking Complex Questions with Query By Example

This chapter is the first in Part II because developing a good understanding of how to use the full power of Paradox Query By Example (QBE) is important. The degree of your understanding of the Paradox QBE methodology will determine how satisfied you are with the program and how effective your use of it will be.

You were introduced to QBE fundamentals in Chapter 4, "Getting Started with Query By Example." By now, you should be able to use the techniques presented there to retrieve data from any Paradox table. But Chapter 4 covered queries of individual tables only. This chapter shows you how to use example elements to link multiple query forms so that you can retrieve information from any number of related Paradox tables. You learn how to create answers that combine records from related tables based on common data (called inner joins) and how to combine records even when no match exists (outer joins).

Version 3

In this chapter, you also discover how Paradox provides some of the number-crunching capability of spreadsheets, enabling you to refine raw data into information that shows you the "bigger picture." Another aspect of Paradox QBE, new in Version 3.0, is the capability to work with sets of data. This chapter teaches you how to use *set operators* in a query to answer a question like "Which customers have ordered every model of widget in the inventory?" The final portion of this chapter demonstrates how to use Query By Example operators to make changes to the contents of the tables.

As you go through this chapter, apply the concepts you learn to real-life examples. Use the tables you created in Quick Start 2, or, better yet, create some tables of your own. The key to understanding QBE lies in seeing it happen on your screen.

Building Multitable Queries

As a true relational database, Paradox allows you to work with many database tables at once. With Paradox QBE, you can combine data from multiple tables in a way that helps you focus on the information you want to find rather than have to worry about command syntax or programming. The QBE techniques used in multitable queries are natural extensions of the methods you have already learned in Chapter 4.

Normalizing a Database

A well-planned relational database is the model of efficiency. Every piece of information is in its place, and no data is duplicated. To accomplish this ideal, however, you usually have to divide (or *normalize*) the database into several relatively small tables. Unfortunately, this structure can sometimes make working with the data a little more confusing.

The sample database that has been used throughout this book has been normalized to eliminate any duplication of information. For each order that is placed for widgets, only one record exists in the Orders table. The Detail table contains one record for each line item in an order. Customer information is included only once, in the Customer table. The Employee table includes exactly one record for each employee. And the Product table includes one record for each model of widget.

As you work with this data, however, you routinely need to use or *link* information from two or more of these normalized tables. For example, you may want to get the name and address of the customer who placed order number 103. This information is split between two tables. The Orders table stores the customer ID number for each order, but the customer's name and address are in the Customer table. The tools that allow you to link these two tables in Paradox are called *example elements*.

Linking Tables with Example Elements

To combine or join data from two tables into one Answer table, you construct a *query statement*, made up of two or more query forms. You then place matching example elements in the fields that link the tables. In the Orders/Customer example, the linking field in each table is the Cust ID # field. By placing matching example elements in the Cust ID # field of each query form, you tell Paradox to look for a match in the data when performing the query. The basic techniques presented in Chapter 4 for selecting fields and records for inclusion in the answer still apply.

You place multiple query forms in the work space by using the **A**sk command several times in succession. The order of the forms in the work space does not affect which records Paradox includes in the Answer table, but the order does affect the order of the columns in the Answer table. Checked fields from the query form at the top of the work space become the leftmost fields in the Answer table. Fields from the second query form are added to the Answer table to the right of the first form's columns, and so forth. Because you can rearrange fields later by using the Image menu options and the Ctrl-R (Rotate) command, however, you don't need to be too concerned with the order of your query forms.

Paradox automatically uses sophisticated artificial intelligence (AI) procedures called Heuristic Query Optimization to ensure that every query is executed as quickly as possible. The order of the query forms in the work space has no effect on this optimization one way or the other. Users of competing PC-based QBE products may find that the order of the query forms in the work space is surprisingly significant in determining query speed. You don't have to worry about that problem with Paradox.

One of the options in the Custom Configuration Program of Paradox 3.0 allows you to specify that records be sorted during a query in **I**mageOrder rather than the default of **T**ableOrder. With this option set, rearranging column order in query forms does have an effect on the sorted order of the Answer table.

To place an example element in a query form field, you press F5 (Example), type a name for the example element, and press Enter. Paradox displays the entry in inverse video. When naming an example element, you can use any alphabetic characters (A through Z, upper- or lowercase) and the numbers 0 through 9. No spaces or other characters are permitted. Figure 7.1 shows an example element, abc, displayed in the Cust ID # field of each query form. The name does not have to match field type. Therefore, you could use the example element *123* in an alphanumeric field, and use *abc* in a numeric field; or, you could use a combination of letters and numbers. The example element you use is not determined by either the field name or field type.

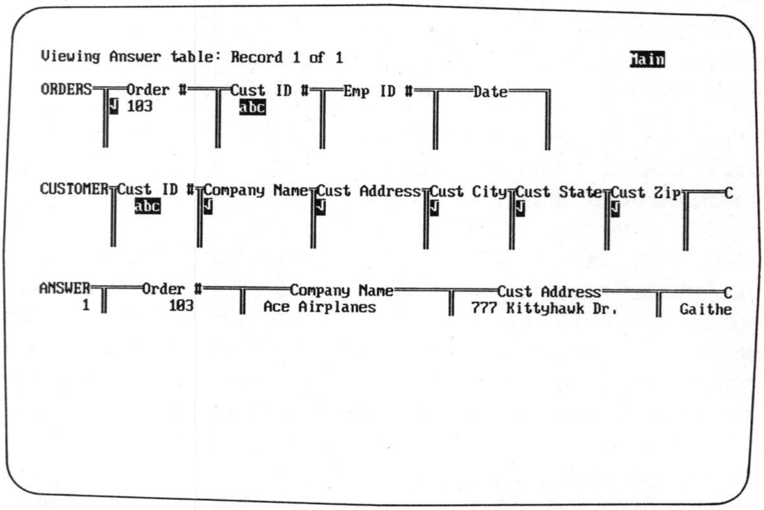

Fig. 7.1.
A multitable query showing example elements.

Placing identical example elements in two query forms defines the link between the two tables. In the example shown in figure 7.1, the example element *abc* asks Paradox to match records from the Customer table with records in Orders where the Cust ID # is a match. You place the number 103 in the Order # field to display the information about only that order. Notice that the customer's ID number is not checked and therefore does not display in the Answer table. Because the Company Name, Cust Address, Cust City, Cust State, and Cust ZIP fields contain check marks, those fields are included in the Answer table. (Note that the columns in both query forms in the figure were reduced in width through the Image menu so that they would all fit on one screen for purposes of illustration.)

You can link query forms with example elements whether or not you use F6 (Check Mark) to include the link field in the Answer table. But if you do want the link field in the Answer table, place a check mark in the link field of only one of the query forms. Otherwise, the Answer table includes the field more than once.

You are not limited in the number of tables you can join through a query (except by the RAM available in your PC). For example, you might want to build on the query shown in figure 7.1 and also show which salesperson was responsible for order number 103. To add a third query form to the work space, press F10 (Menu) and select **A**sk. Then choose another table, in this case Employee.

If there are other query forms on the work area that should not be related to your query, Paradox will attempt to link them. Make sure that you clear all unwanted query forms with F8.

To have the correct Employee record matched with each record in Orders, you use an example element in the Emp ID # field of each table. So that Paradox can distinguish this link from the link between Orders and Customer, you use a different example element name (something other than *abc*).

For instance, move the cursor to the Emp ID # field in the Employee query form and press F5 (Example). Then type *123* and press Enter. With F6 (Check Mark), mark the fields that you want included. In this example, mark the three fields that make up an employee's name: Emp Last Name, Emp First Name, and Emp Middle Name. Then move to the Orders query form by pressing F3 (Up Image) twice, and add the same example element, *123*, to the Emp ID # field of that form. Finally, perform the query by pressing F2 (DO-IT!). Paradox includes the Employee data in the Answer table, as shown in figure 7.2.

To build multitable queries successfully, you must clearly understand the relationships between the various tables in your database. Keep a diagram of your tables—the one with the lines and arrows that you created in Chapter 2—handy as you try the query techniques presented in this chapter. (See the tip included in the "Understanding How Tables Are Related" section of Chapter 2.) Such a diagram for the tables queried in figure 7.1 would quickly show you that Cust ID # is the link between Orders and Customer and therefore the field that should contain example elements.

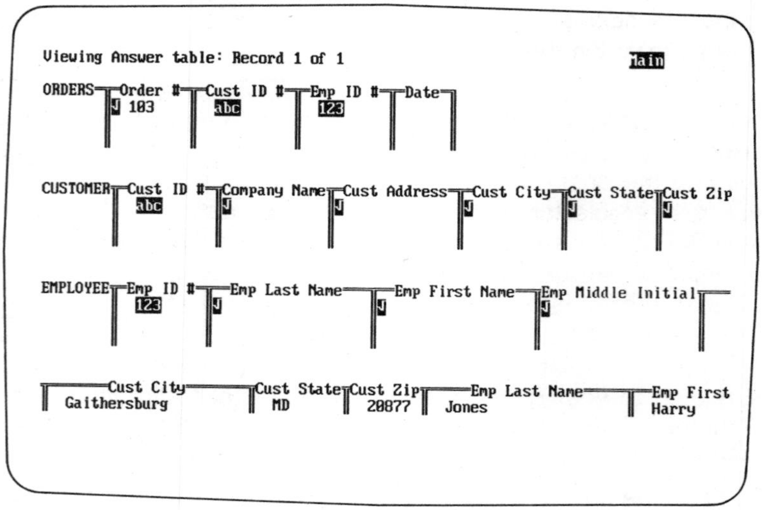

Fig. 7.2.

A three-table query.

Paradox does not erase the Answer table from the screen when you begin to construct another query. This design allows you to proceed step-by-step in a progression of more and more refined queries until you reach the Answer table for which you are looking.

Don't forget that you can save a query with the **Q**uerySave option on the Scripts menu. For more information, refer to Chapter 6.

Combining Selection Criteria

Chapter 4 introduced you to the concept of combining selection criteria in one query. You can construct single-table queries that find records meeting several criteria at once—the logical *and* condition. You can also create queries that select records meeting one or more of several criteria—the logical *or* condition. Multitable queries expand these ways of combining selection criteria.

Creating *And* Conditions

Three rules summarize how you can indicate that multiple query conditions should be met concurrently (the logical *and* condition):

1. Multiple conditions placed in the same field of a query form and separated by a comma (,) must be met at the same time for a record to be included in the Answer table.

2. Multiple conditions placed in the same row of a query form must be met concurrently.
3. When rows from different query forms are linked by example elements, Paradox treats the rows as if they are one row from one table, for the purposes of rule 2.

The first two rules were discussed in Chapter 4. The following example demonstrates the third rule. Suppose that you want to determine which customers have purchased more than 20 Deluxe Widgets. To produce the answer to this question, Paradox needs to look at information in four tables. The Detail table contains the model number and quantity of widgets sold in each order. The product name is found in the Product table, referenced by the model number. To know which customer made each purchase, you have to get the customer's ID number from the Orders table, and the customer company's name from the Customer table. Information from all these tables is necessary in order to produce an answer.

To perform this query, you first use **A**sk to display a query form for each of the four tables. The next step is to use example elements to specify linking fields between the related tables. You could, for example, use the words *red*, *blue*, and *green* as example elements. Figure 7.3 shows `red` as the example element linking the Order # fields in Orders and Detail. The word `blue` is used to link Cust ID # between Orders and Customer. The example element `green` in the Model # fields links the Product table to the Detail table.

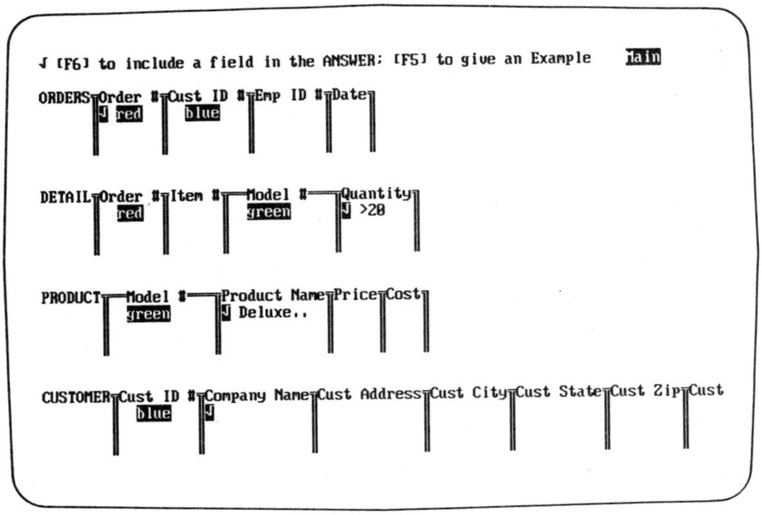

Fig. 7.3.

The logical and *condition.*

In this example, the Detail table is "controlling the action." If you do not specify any conditions before you execute the query, Paradox includes a record in the Answer table for every record in Detail. The reason is that Detail is on the *many-side* of *one-to-many* relationships with both the Orders table and the Product table. The fields that contain a check mark —Order #, Quantity, Product Name, and Company Name—will be the only fields in the Answer table.

To limit the records to just customers who bought Deluxe Widgets, you place the pattern *Deluxe...* (or you can spell out *Deluxe Widget* if you prefer) in the Product Name field of the Product query form. Then, to limit further the answer to customers who bought more than 20 widgets, you use the range *>20* in the Quantity field of the Detail query form, as shown in figure 7.3. When you execute the query with F2 (DO-IT!), Paradox retrieves only records that match both of these conditions, as shown in figure 7.4.

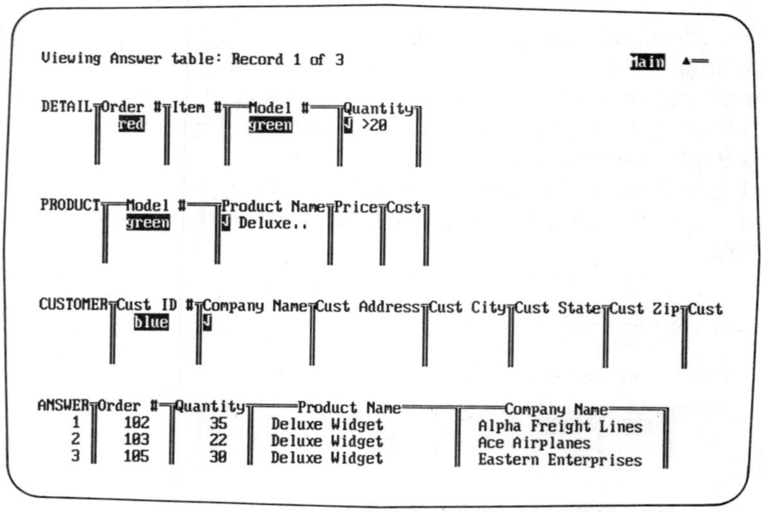

Fig. 7.4.
The Answer table.

Creating Or Conditions

You have two ways to create the *or* condition:

Version 3

1. Separate two or more criteria in the same field and same row with the operator *or* (Paradox 3.0 only).
2. Place criteria in separate rows of the same query form. This method is required when alternate conditions are not in the same field. In a single-table query, check marks and any

concurrent (*and*) conditions must be repeated in each row. In multiple-table queries, each new row has to be linked again to the other table(s) with different example element(s).

Building this type of query is like building two independent *and* conditions and then sticking the results together, especially when you are forced to use multiple rows.

You can build on the previous example by using the *or* operator. Assume that you want to know the names of customers who ordered more than 20 of either the Deluxe Widget or the Enhanced Widget. You can accomplish this query by using the *or* operator in the Product Name field. The new criterion becomes *Deluxe.. or Enhanced..* (see fig. 7.5), and the Answer table includes orders for Enhanced Widgets along with the orders for Deluxe Widgets.

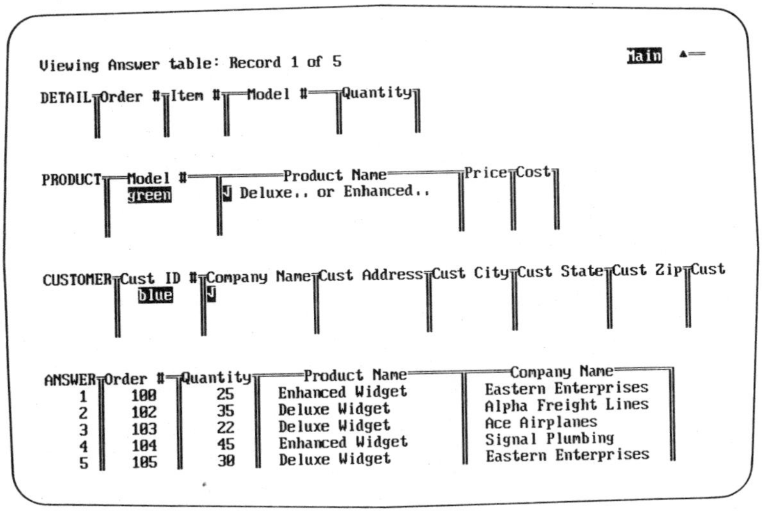

Fig. 7.5.
The logical or *condition in a single-row query.*

Often you cannot express search conditions all in one row. For instance, perhaps you want to know which customers ordered at least 25 Deluxe Widgets or at least 10 Imperial Widgets. You might attempt to construct this query by using the *or* operator in the Product Name field, as in figure 7.5, and the *or* operator in the Quantity field of the Detail table (*>=25 or >=10*). But this query may give you the wrong answer. It would erroneously select orders for Deluxe Widgets in the range 10 to 24. The proper query is shown in figure 7.6. As you can see, it requires another entire set of example elements—*cyan*, *gold*, and *orange*—and all check marks must be repeated in the second row. The Answer table, shown in figure 7.7, includes orders for 10 or more Imperial Widgets and 25 or more Deluxe Widgets.

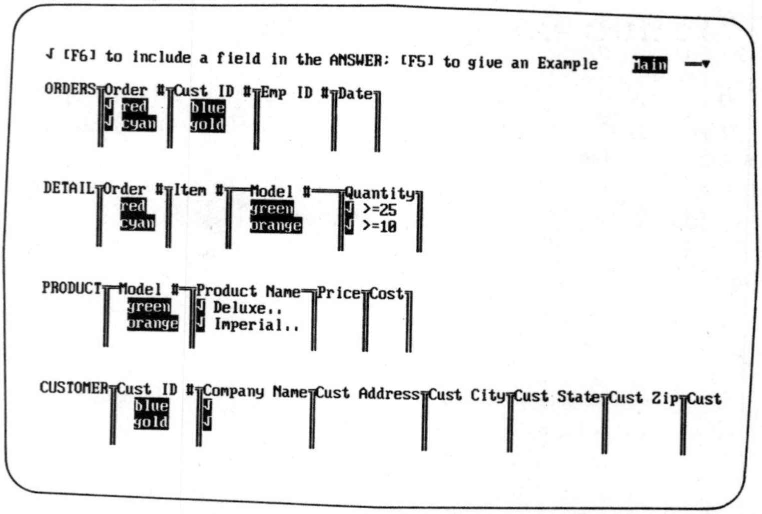

Fig. 7.6.

The logical or condition in multiple rows.

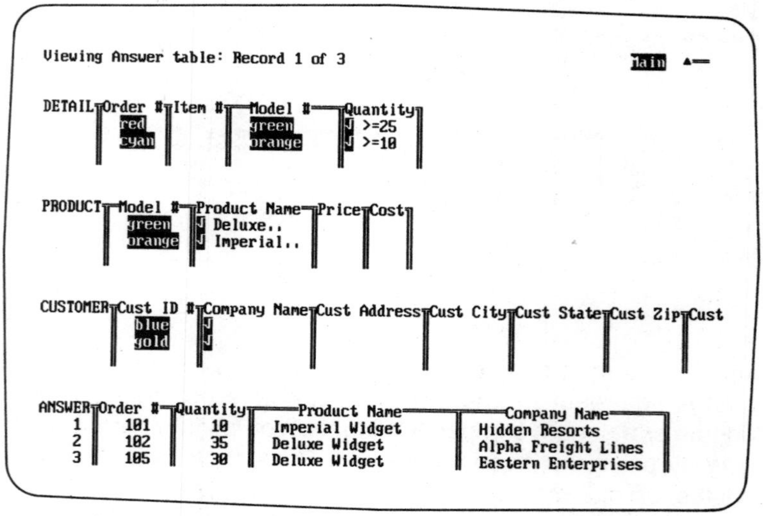

Fig. 7.7.

The Answer table for the query in figure 7.6.

Caution: You cannot use the *or* operator between example elements.

Creating *Both* Conditions

Using the same example element in more than one row of the query statement creates a special kind of *and* condition—what could be called a *both* condition. Suppose that you want to know whether any of your customers have ordered *both* Deluxe and Imperial widgets. If you try to use the normal *and* query and place the criteria *Deluxe..,Imperial..* in the Product Name field, you get an empty Answer table for the result. The reason is that no record in the Detail table contains *both* Deluxe and Imperial widgets.

You can accomplish the result you intended, however, by using the same example element in two rows of the Detail query form. Figure 7.8 shows the proper query. Two different example elements, *green* and *orange*, are used in the Model # field to link the two rows from the Product table. But the same example element, *red*, is used in the Order # field in both rows of the Detail query form. This setup causes Paradox to create a second Product Name column in the Answer table and returns the name of the customers who have ordered both Deluxe and Imperial widget models (see fig. 7.9). In this case, only one company, Ace Airplanes, has ordered both types of widgets.

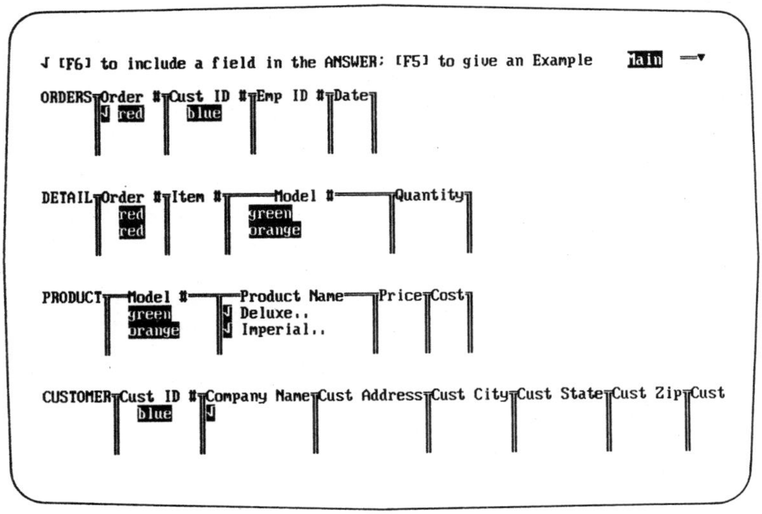

Fig. 7.8.

Creating the both *condition.*

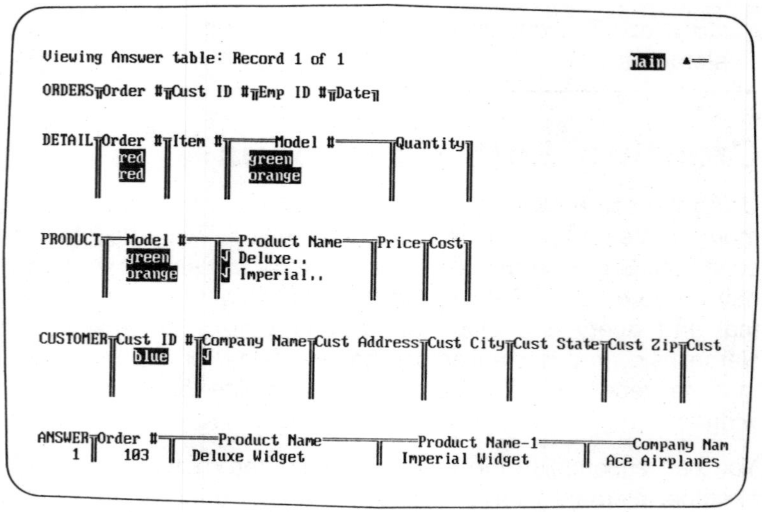

Fig. 7.9.
Who ordered both types of widgets?

Using Example Elements To Represent Values

One of the most interesting uses of example elements doesn't necessarily involve multiple tables at all. Sometimes you want to select records based on a match or comparison with another record in the same table. Suppose, for example, that you want to see a list of all employees whose salaries are greater than Tim Bronson's. You could, of course, do a query to determine Tim Bronson's salary. You would then manually type it as an example value in the Salary field and execute another query to find your answer. Using example elements, however, you can perform the operation in only one query.

The first line of this type of query finds the value that will be used for comparison. In figure 7.10, the example element *sal* is placed in the first row of the Salary column to represent the value of Tim Bronson's salary. No check marks are placed in this first row, but *Bronson* and *Tim* are entered in the Emp Last Name and Emp First Name fields, respectively. The second row then compares the salaries of all other employees to the example salary and builds the Answer table accordingly.

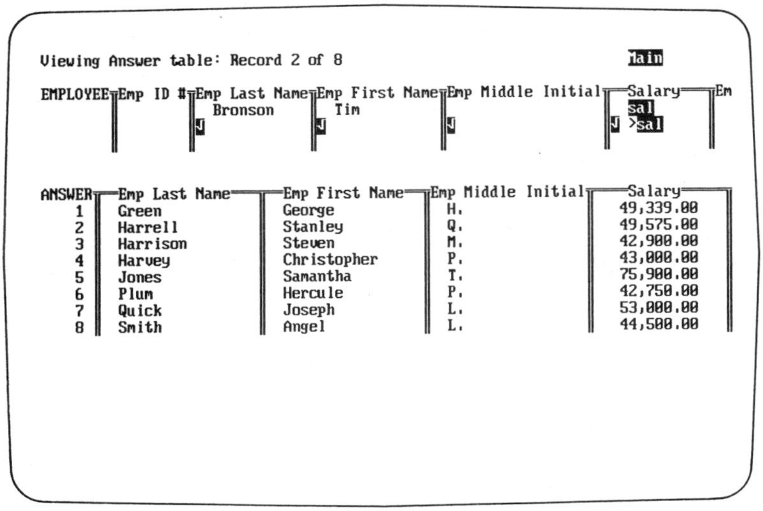

Fig. 7.10.

Using example elements to represent values.

Using the Inclusive Link

Version 3

So far, all the multiple queries you have studied in this chapter have created Answer tables that include only records in which a match occurs in all linked tables. This type of matching is sometimes referred to in database circles as an *inner join*, and it is usually the result you need.

In some situations, however, you may want to include even those records that don't produce a match. This type of matching is called an *outer join*. Paradox 3.0 has added an operator called the *inclusion* operator (it performs an inclusive link as opposed to an exclusive link). This operator is represented by the exclamation point (!) and is typed in the query column immediately after an example element.

For example, you might want to produce a list of all the recent orders sold by each of your company's salespeople. The normal inner join produces a complete list only if every salesperson has made a sale. An outer join, on the other hand, includes even nonproductive salespeople in the Answer table. Figure 7.11 shows just such a query. Notice that several salespeople have nothing listed in the Order # column.

Caution: The location of the inclusion operator is crucial to obtaining the result you intend. Make sure that you place the exclamation point (!) in the link field of the table containing the records that should be included, with or without a match. In the example in figure 7.11, had the inclusion operator been placed in the Orders query form, the Answer table would not have included salespersons who had made no sale. The reason is that their ID numbers do not appear in the Orders table.

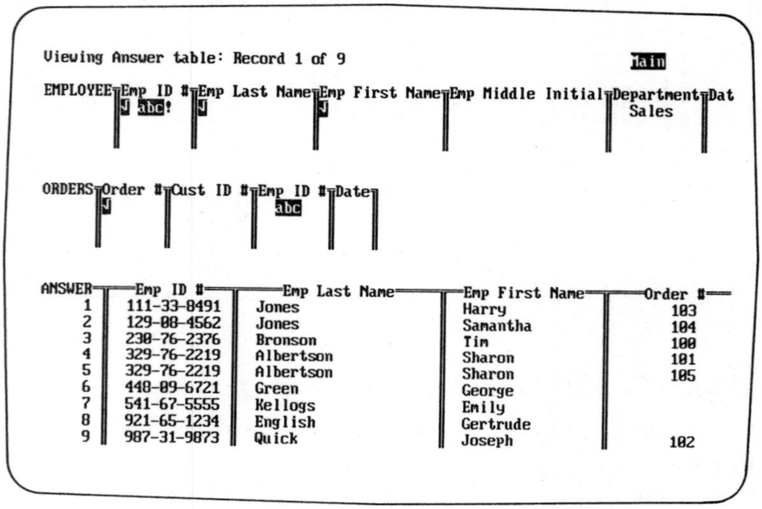

Fig. 7.11.

Creating an outer join.

The outer join shown in figure 7.11 has an inclusion operator in only one query form, the Employee form. This type of query statement is called an *asymmetrical outer join*. But another benefit of the inclusion operator is its capability to *union* several tables easily. You can place the inclusion operator on both ends of the query statement, creating a so-called *symmetrical outer join*.

Figure 7.12 shows an example of a query to create the union or *symmetrical outer join* of the Employee (Sales Department only), Orders, and Customer tables. Notice the exclamation points after every example element. The resulting Answer table is in figure 7.13. It shows customers who have not recently placed an order as well as employees who haven't made a sale. This information would not be displayed in a normal inner (exclusive) join, which is sometimes called an *intersection* of tables.

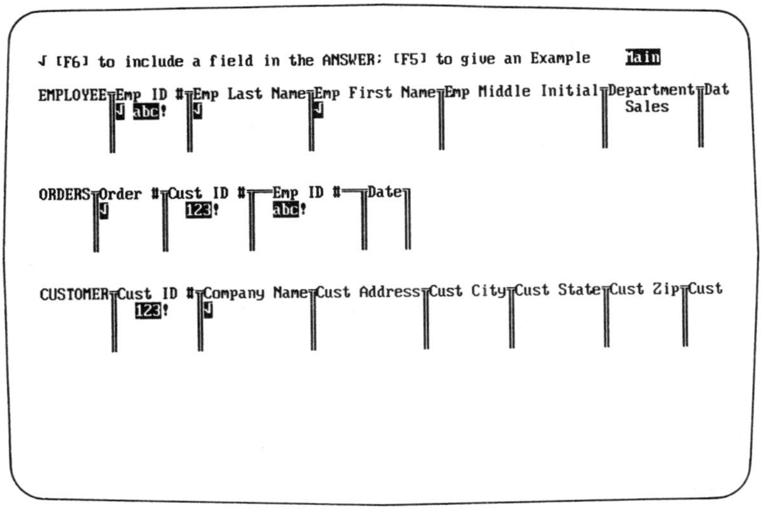

Fig. 7.12.

Creating a symmetrical outer join.

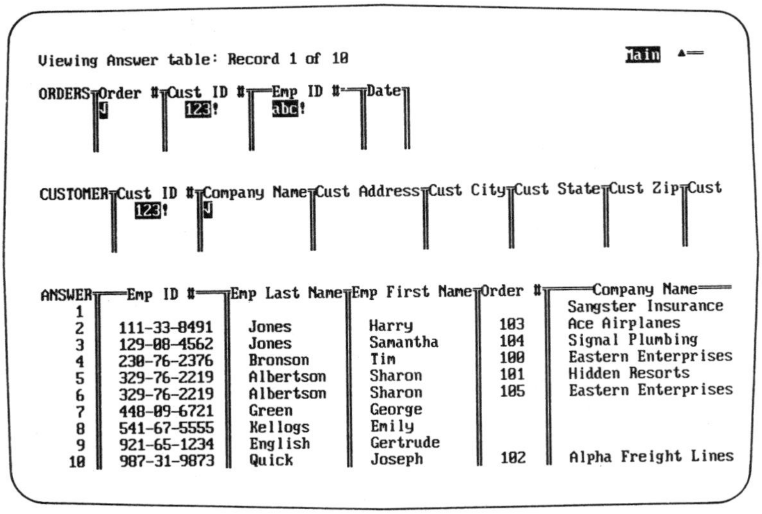

Fig. 7.13.

The result of the outer join.

When creating inclusive links in a query statement, you must follow three rules:

1. Do not mix inclusive and exclusive links in the same pairs of query statement rows (i.e., don't use an example element with an inclusion operator and an example element without an

inclusion operator in the same row—figure 7.12 shows an example of two inclusive links in the same row).

2. Subject to rule 1, you can use inclusive and exclusive links in the same query statement.

3. Use the inclusion operator on a particular example element no more than once per row and twice per query statement.

Keep in mind that Paradox processes links in the following order: exclusive links, asymmetrical inclusive links, and then symmetrical inclusive links.

Experiment with the inclusion operator. Creating inclusive links between the tables in your database can often reveal information that would otherwise go unnoticed.

Performing Calculations in Queries

Many PC users continue to force their database applications into spreadsheets—often because of the relative ease with which spreadsheet programs perform numeric calculations. But spreadsheets are marginal at best when working with real database tasks such as inputting, editing, retrieving, sorting, and reporting substantial amounts of data. Paradox combines high-powered database functionality with surprisingly flexible number-crunching capability to try to provide the best of both worlds.

Paradox can perform two general categories of calculations: operations that use numeric or text values from the fields in an individual record, and summary calculations that perform calculations over groups of records.

Performing Calculations within a Record

All calculations in Paradox query forms must be preceded with the *calc* operator. You can use this operator to combine a value in a Paradox table field with values from other fields in the record, with constant values, or with both. The formula you create is called a *calc expression*. The following basic rules apply when you're building calc expressions:

- Precede all calc expressions with the operator *calc*.
- Place calc expressions in any column of the query statement, separated from any other entry in the column with a comma.

- ❏ Combine numeric and date values with these arithmetic operators:

  + − * / ( )

- ❏ Combine (concatenate) alphanumeric values with the + operator.
- ❏ Represent each field value with its own example element.
- ❏ Enter constant numeric values and date values in the same way as in data entry (for example, 1234.7 and 12/31/89).
- ❏ Enclose alphanumeric constant values in double quotation marks (for example, "Current Resident").

The *calc* operator, like the check mark, causes Paradox to add a field to the Answer table. Paradox gives the new field a name based on the calc expression used, unless you use the *as* operator to rename the field. (The *as* operator is available in Paradox 3.0 only. For more information, see Chapter 4, "Getting Started with Query By Example.")

Version 3

Performing Numeric Calculations

The first step in performing numeric calculations is to construct the basic query statement, including any necessary links for multitable queries. Next, you must decide which fields in the query statement you need to use in the calculation. Place a unique example element in each of these fields, and place a check mark in the fields if you want them to be included in the Answer table. Once all necessary fields are named, you can construct the calc expression in any column of the query statement.

Figure 7.14 shows how you might build a calc expression to determine the total price for each row in the Detail table. (Note: The figure does not show the entire Answer table.) The *quant* example element represents the quantity ordered, and the *price* example element represents the price of the item. The *as* operator added to the end of the expression causes Paradox to name the calculated field *Total Price*. If you don't include this operator (available only in Paradox 3.0), Paradox names the new calculated field *Quantity * Price*.

If you use descriptive example element names, your calc expressions will be easier to build. For instance, the example element names shown in figure 7.14, *quant* and *price*, clearly describe the fields they represent, so the calc expression is easy to understand. You may also find the calc expression more readable if you construct it in an otherwise unused column.

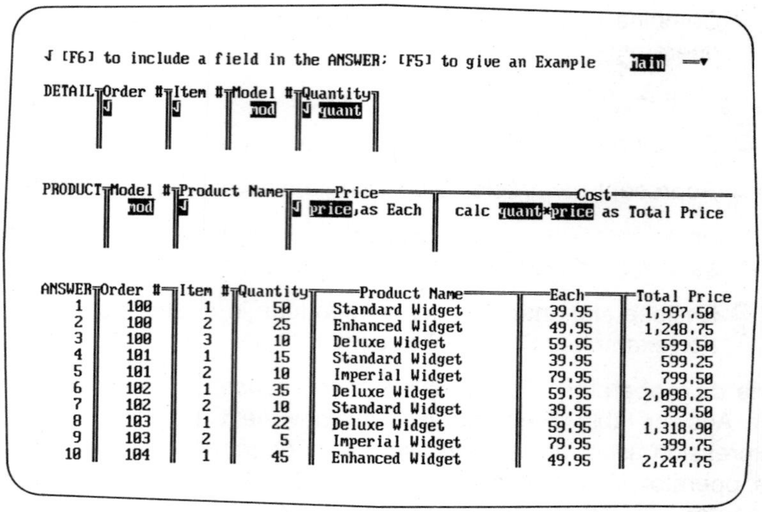

Fig. 7.14.
Figuring total prices.

Combining Alphanumeric Values

The *calc* operator also permits you to combine or concatenate alphanumeric values. This feature is most often used to construct names or phrases from available data. As with numeric calc expressions, you assign a separate example element to each field you want to include in the expression. You can add spaces and punctuation within the expression by enclosing them in double quotation marks. A typical example of alphanumeric concatenation is constructing a mailing list from your Customer table. You might, for example, assign the example elements *addr*, *city*, *st*, and *zip* to the Cust Address, Cust City, Cust State, and Cust ZIP fields, respectively. You then build the following calc expression:

calc addr+", "+city+", "+st+" "+zip

This expression causes Paradox to concatenate the values contained in the various fields into one field. Any trailing spaces at the end of the alphanumeric values are trimmed, so you have to add any necessary spaces or commas as alphanumeric constants within double quotation marks. Figure 7.15 shows the result of this query. The *as* operator at the end of the calc expression is used to give the calculated field the name *Address* in the Answer table.

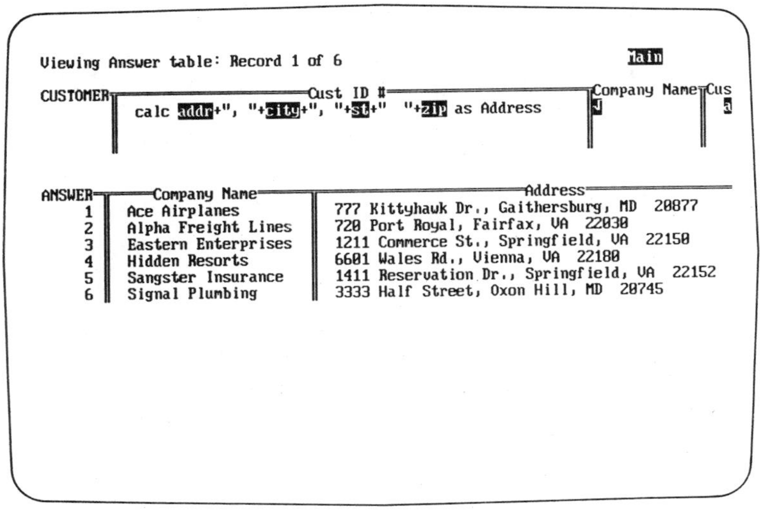

Fig. 7.15.

Concatenating alphanumeric values.

Using Summary Operators and Grouping Records

Paradox has a number of special operators that enable you to perform summary calculations during queries. Rather than operate on values from several fields within a single record, like the operators discussed in the preceding section, these summary operators calculate statistics over several records. Using query summary operators, you can find the sum, average, maximum, minimum, or number of values for groups of records. These summary operators are listed in table 7.1.

Table 7.1
Query Summary Operators

Operator	*Meaning*	*Applicable Field Types*	*Default Grouping*
average	Average of values in group	N,$,D,S	All
count	Number of values in group	All	Unique
max	Highest value in group	All	Unique
min	Lowest value in group	All	Unique
sum	Total of values in group	N,$,S	All

The *Default Grouping* column in table 7.1 refers to whether duplicate records are ignored by the operation. Generally, the sum and average operators calculate their statistics over all records in each group, while the count, max, and min operators ignore duplicates within each group. You can specify that the latter operators apply to all records by placing the word *all* in the query column, immediately after the operator.

You can also use these summary operators with range operators (see table 4.2 in Chapter 4) to select a group of records to be included in the Answer table.

Performing Calculations with Summary Operators

The following rules apply to the summary operators when you use them to perform calculations:

- Precede the summary operator with the *calc* operator.
- Place the summary operator in the column on which the computations should be performed.
- Do not place a check mark in the same field in which you place the summary operator.
- Place a check mark in the field or fields that you want to determine the grouping. Paradox performs the summary calculation on each group of records that have identical values in the checked fields.
- Leave blank all other fields in the query form in order to perform the summary calculation on all records.

The result for each grouping and calculation is a single record in the Answer table, containing all the checked fields as well as the newly calculated summary field.

For example, you may want to sum up the line item totals calculated in figure 7.14 so that you can have a grand total for each order. Suppose that you change the name of the Answer table in that figure to *Dtotals*. The Dtotals table then includes the fields Order #, Item #, Quantity, Product Name, Each, and Total Price. To sum the Total Price field for each order, you first place a check mark in the Order # column of the Dtotals query form. This step causes Paradox to group all records with the same Order #. Then you place the expression *calc sum as Order Total* in the Total Price column. When you perform the query by pressing F2 (DO-IT!), Paradox adds the values in the Total Price field for each group. The program creates an Answer table consisting of only two fields, Order # and Order Total, with a single record for each different order number (see fig. 7.16).

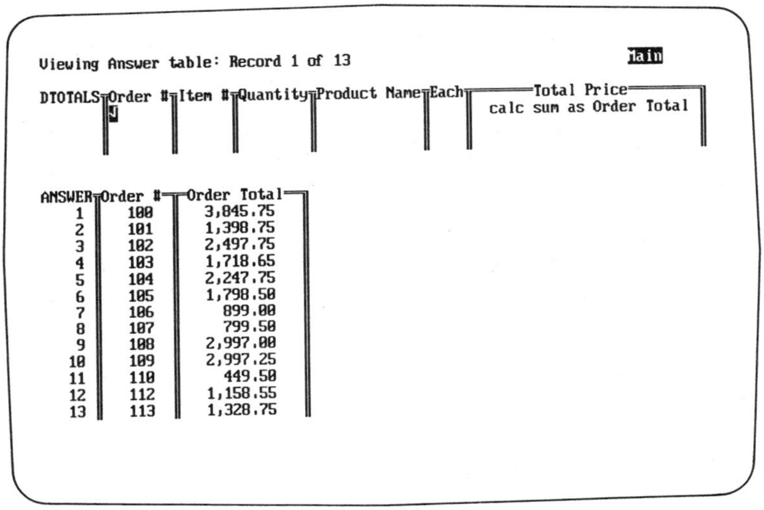

Fig. 7.16.
Performing a calculation with a summary operator.

Figure 7.17 shows an example that uses multiple tables and multiple checked fields. It determines the number of each model of widget sold by each sales representative. This query uses the *sum* operator to total the Quantity field for each group of records that have both identical employee ID numbers and identical model numbers. As usual, Paradox sorts records by the left-most field first, and then by other fields, from left to right.

Selecting Groups of Records with Summary Operators

Version 3

Chapter 4 discusses the concept of selecting groups of records with range operators (see table 4.2 for a list of range operators). And, as mentioned previously in this chapter, in Paradox 3.0 you can also use the summary operators with range operators to select a group of records. When used this way, the summary operator need not be preceded with *calc*.

Assume that you want to know which models of widgets have average orders of more than 15. The Detail table contains the information on how many of each model is ordered, so you need to construct a query on that table. Place a check mark in the Model # column to tell Paradox to sort

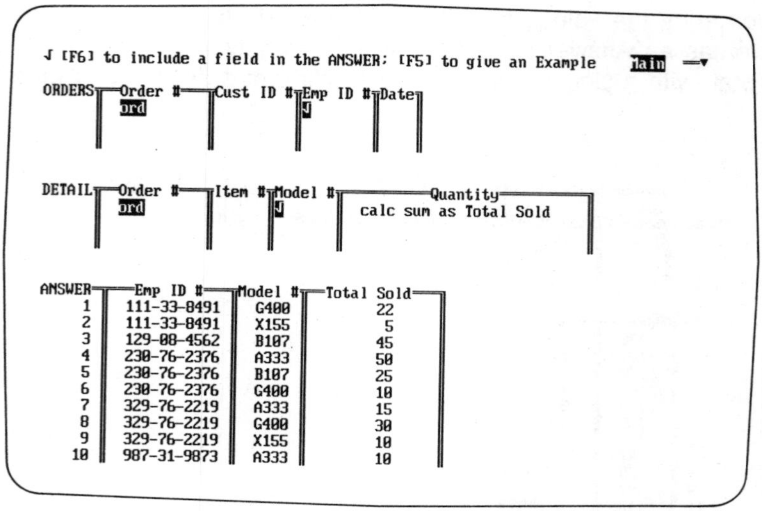

Fig. 7.17.

Using multiple tables and multiple checked fields.

and group the records by that field, and place the expression *average* > *15* in the Quantity column. Without the *calc* operator, the *average* operator is used for comparison. In this example, Paradox finds all models whose per-order quantity averaged more than 15. You can also include the *calc average* operator in the same query column if you want to see the actual average number sold in the selected range (see fig. 7.18).

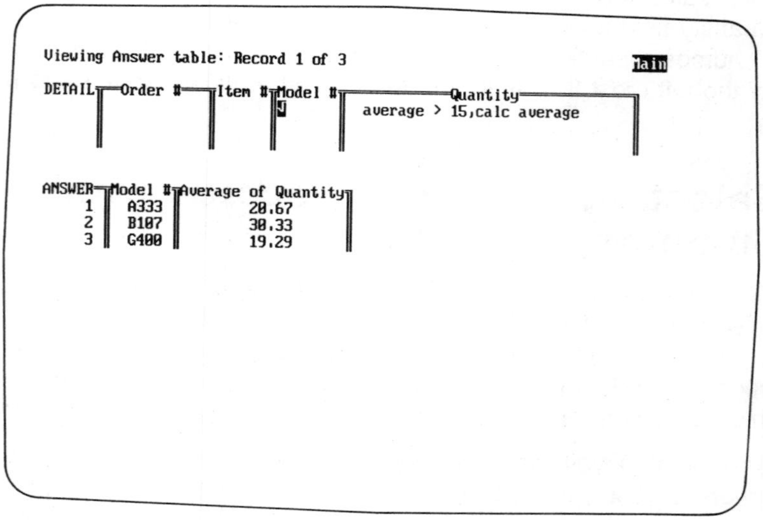

Fig. 7.18.

Selecting a group of records with a summary calculation.

Working with Sets of Records

A completely new category of queries is now available exclusively in Paradox 3.0. These queries enable you to establish an example group—a sort of "control" group—referred to as a *set*, and then to compare other groups of records to that set. Special operators, listed in table 7.2, permit you to ask questions such as these:

Which customers have ordered *only* widgets that have a price greater than $50?

Which customers have ordered *no* widget over $50 in price?

Which customers have ordered *every* type of widget that is more than $50 in price?

Which customers have ordered *every* widget over $50, *and only* widgets over $50 in price?

In all these examples, you are comparing the group of orders placed by each customer to the *set* of orders for widgets greater than $50. When a customer's group of orders passes the comparison test, the customer is added to the answer.

Table 7.2
Set Operators

Operator	*Meaning*
only	The values in the group contain only members of the set.
no	No value in the group contains a member of the set.
every	The group contains every member of the set.
exactly	The group contains every member of the set and only members of the set.

Constructing Set Queries

You must follow these rules when defining sets:

- Define a *set* with one or more linked query statement forms. Place the word *set* in the table name column of each row that is used to define the set.

- Do not use check marks or calc operators in rows that define a set.
- Use an example element to mark the field in the set that will be used for comparison—the *set comparison field*.

And consider the following guidelines as you define the records that you want to compare to the set:

- Define the records that are to be compared to the set by using one or more query forms. You can use multiple query forms or rows of the same query forms that define the set.
- Do *not* place the word *set* in the table name column of rows that define these records for comparison.
- Use an example element to indicate the *comparison field*, which is the field that you want to compare to the set comparison field. Precede this example element with one of the operators listed in table 7.2. Do not place a check mark or calc operator in this field.
- Place either a check mark (press F6) or a *groupby* operator (press Shift-F6) in the field that determines how the records should be grouped—the *grouping field*. This field *must* be in the same query form and row as the comparison field. (The *groupby* operator has the same effect as a check mark in grouping records but does not cause the field to be included in the Answer table.)

For instance, suppose that you want to determine which customers have ordered only widgets that have a price more than $50. The set, or control group, of records is in this case the list of all orders for products in that price range. An order number may appear more than once in this set if several different items priced greater than $50 were ordered at the same time.

You can define this list by constructing query forms from Product and Detail. Product contains the Price field, and Detail contains the orders placed for widgets of all prices. Link these two query forms with an example element (such as *mod*) in the Model # fields, and place the range expression *>50* in the Price field of the Product query form. To indicate that this query is a set definition, not a normal query, type the word *set* in the first column of each form.

The next step is to define the records that Paradox is to compare to the set you have defined. In this example you want Paradox to compare a list of all the orders of each customer to the comparison set of orders. That is, if any one order from a particular customer does not appear in the comparison set, then that customer should not be included in the Answer table. Also, customers with no orders in the comparison set should not be included in the answer. You can create a list of all orders and the corresponding customers by linking the Orders and Customer tables (by typing an example element in the Cust ID # field of each query form). Place a check mark in the Company Name field in the Customer query form, because you are looking for the customer's name.

To complete the process, you need to add matching example elements and a *set* operator to the comparison fields, and indicate the grouping field. Because you want Paradox to compare order numbers, add the example element *ord* to the Order # field in Detail, and then type the set operator *only* in front of the example element *ord* in the Order # field of the Orders table. Also, place the *groupby* (Shift-F6) operator in the Cust ID # column of Orders so that the answer is grouped by customer but without displaying the ID numbers. The completed query statement is shown in figure 7.19, and the answer in figure 7.20. Note that the *groupby* operator displays as a G on the screen.

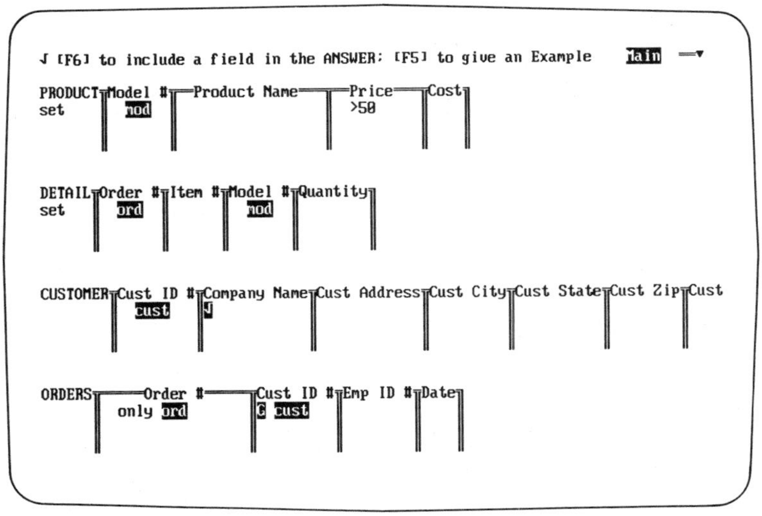

Fig. 7.19.
Which customers have ordered only widgets that have prices greater than $50?

Using Paradox set operators can be confusing. Following the rules presented in this section will help, but you may need to divide the process into manageable steps.

Start by building the set as a normal query. For example, you might build a query to display all orders for products more than $50 in price.

Then save this query and clear it from the work space. Next, build a query to define the records you want to compare to the set. In this chapter's example, this query should produce a list of all orders grouped by customer. Save this second query and clear it from the screen.

Now, use the Script Editor to view the first script. Use the **R**ead option on the Editor menu to add the second script at the end of the first, and delete the extra `Query` and `EndQuery` lines. Save the script and play it. Add the matching comparison field example element and set operator. When the query works as you intended, save it again.

The advantage of this method is that you can see each of the two groups of records separately before trying to compare them. If you do the procedure all in one step, you may not be able to get a clear picture of the data in either group and will consequently find yourself spinning your wheels and going nowhere.

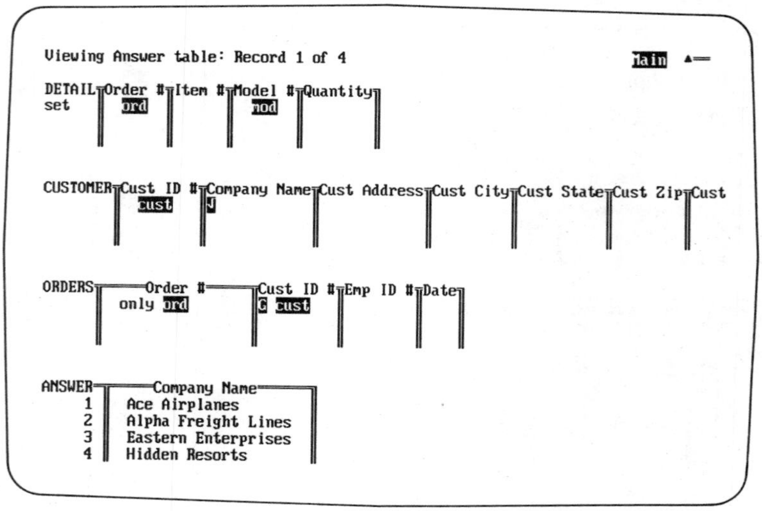

Fig. 7.20.

The answer to the query in figure 7.19.

Using Summary Operators in Set Queries

The summary operators discussed in the section on "Using Summary Operators and Grouping Records" work in set queries as well.

For instance, suppose that you want to know which orders for Enhanced Widgets exceed in number the average order for Standard Widgets. In this example, the comparison set and the records to be compared to the set both come from combining the Detail and Product tables. Figure 7.21 shows the two query rows used to create the set query statement.

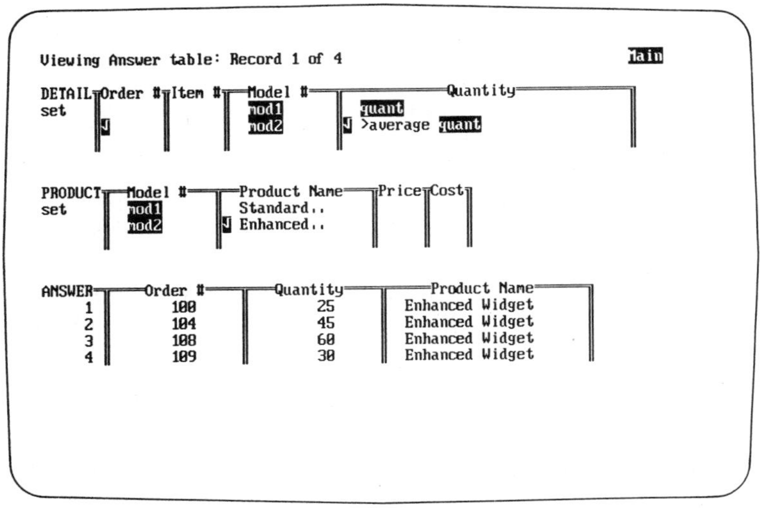

Fig. 7.21.

Using a summary operator in a set *query.*

Changing the Content of Tables with Query Operations

All the queries presented in the preceding sections of this chapter have no effect on existing tables. The queries simply produce a new table, the Answer table. Unless you choose to make the Answer table permanent, by changing its name, the results of all the queries discussed thus far are transitory. The query operations listed in table 7.3, however, with the exception of the *find* operation, act directly and permanently on a table in the database.

Table 7.3
Query Operations

Operation	*Meaning*
insert	Insert new records
delete	Delete selected records
changeto	Replace values in selected records
find	Locate selected records

Adding Records with the Insert Operation

Even though the **A**dd option on the Paradox Tools More menu (discussed in Chapter 13) enables you to add records from one table to another, that option is not always effective because it requires that the tables have identical structures. The *insert* query operation provides a more flexible alternative.

Suppose that a branch office of your company has been moved to the headquarters, and you want to consolidate customer lists. The branch office has been keeping track of its sales and other data on a spreadsheet, so the customer list is in that format. After using the Paradox **E**xportImport option on the Tools menu to import the data into the Cust table, it looks like figure 7.22. (A typical customer list would probably be much longer.) You need to add the table to the end of your headquarters' customer list.

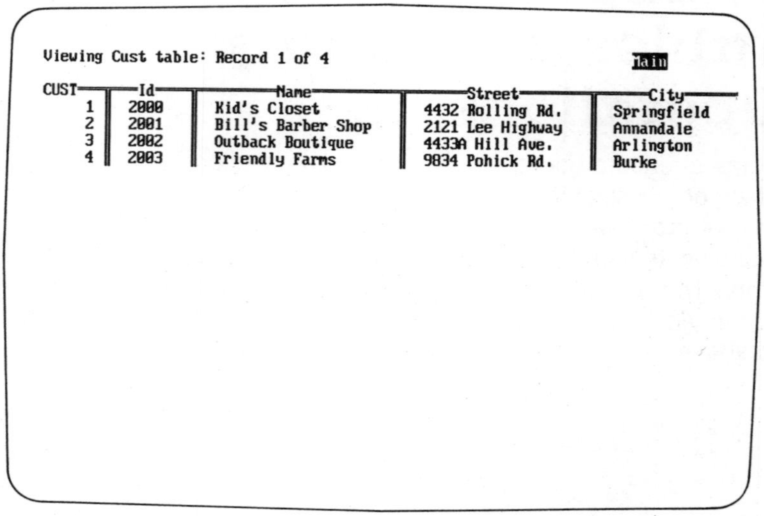

Fig. 7.22.

The imported table.

To use the *insert* operation to add records to a table, you display a query form for the *source* table and a query form for the *destination* table. In this example, the Cust table is the source, and the Customer table is the destination. Place unique example elements in each of the source fields. Type the word *insert* in the leftmost column of the destination query form and then place an example element in each field that has a corresponding field in the source table. You are "mapping" each field from the source table to a field in the destination table. Do not use any check marks.

When you have entered all the example elements, press F2 (DO-IT!). Paradox adds the new records from the source table to the destination table, and displays a table named *Inserted* (see fig. 7.23). This table is a temporary one that contains the newly inserted records. If you decide that you added the records in error, you can use the **S**ubtract option on the Tools More menu to subtract the Inserted table from the destination table. As with any temporary table, the Inserted table is overwritten the next time you use it, and is erased when you exit Paradox. The source table is not changed at all by the query operation.

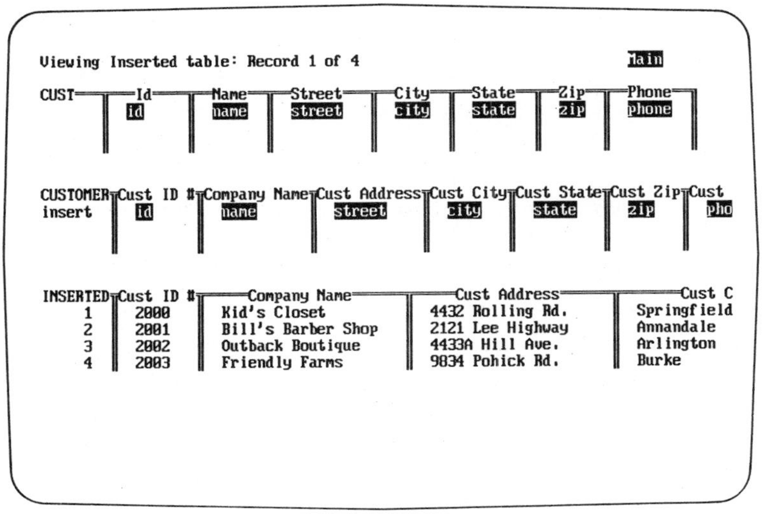

Fig. 7.23.

Using the insert *operation to add records.*

Observe the following guidelines when you perform an insert:

- ❑ Corresponding fields must be the same type.
- ❑ Place a constant value in a field to initialize all new records with this value.

- Empty fields in the destination query form result in blank fields in the new records.
- Use calc expressions when you want to alter the source data as it is being added to the destination table.
- When the definition of a destination alphanumeric field is shorter than the source data, the extra data is truncated (cut off).

Deleting Records with the Delete Operation

Sooner or later, nearly all data becomes obsolete. Paradox offers several methods for discarding unwanted data. You can use either Edit mode or CoEdit mode and delete records one at a time. This approach is probably the preferable method for removing just a few records. But when many records are involved, such as at the beginning of a new fiscal year, you will be glad that Paradox provides a method for deleting many records simultaneously. You can use the *delete* operation during a query to delete any number of records, so long as you provide appropriate selection criteria.

To delete a group of records, display a query form for the target table, and type the word *delete* in the left column (beneath the table name). Enter selection criteria in the other fields of the table, being specific enough to select only the records you want to delete, and press F2 (DO-IT!). Do not use check marks. Paradox deletes the records from the target table, places them in a temporary table named *Deleted*, and displays the Deleted table at the bottom of the work space.

You can undo this deletion operation by using the **A**dd option on the Tools More menu (see Chapter 13), if you do so before the temporary Deleted table is either overwritten or erased. Two convenient ways to archive these records is either to rename the Deleted table to a permanent name, or copy the records to another existing permanent table.

A good practice is to construct your query first *without* the word *delete* in the table name column. Check mark every column and execute this query, and Paradox displays the records that will be deleted. Once you confirm that Paradox will erase the correct records, you can remove the check marks, add the word *delete* to the table name column, and execute the delete operation with F2 (DO-IT!).

When Paradox deletes records, it does not automatically recover the file space that was used by the records. To tell Paradox to "pack" or recover this otherwise wasted space, use the **R**estructure option on the Modify menu. Don't change the structure. Just display the screen and press F2 (DO-IT!). You may also want to make a backup copy of your table and its family before running the restructure operation, especially when the table is large. This step protects you from data loss that could occur if the computer "hiccups" during the restructuring.

Making Global Changes with the *Changeto* Operation

The *changeto* operation is the Paradox equivalent of a search-and-replace option for a word processing program. You can make a change to every record in a table, or you can create a specific search criterion that applies the change to selected records.

To use the *changeto* operation, first use the normal query options to select the records that you want to change. For example, you might need to apply a 4 percent raise to all employees in the Production and Sales departments, a 4.5 percent raise to the Accounting department, and a 5 percent raise to Administration. Because the Production and Sales departments both get the same raise, you can process them on the same row of the query form for the Employee table. Type the criterion *Sales or Production* in the first line of the query form in the Department field. Because each of the other two departments get different percentage increases, however, you must select those departments in separate rows in the query form. As with *insert* and *delete*, do not use check marks.

Then, to apply a change to a field in a selected record, type the word *changeto* followed by the new value or expression. To create an expression that calculates a new value, you first type a unique example element in the field. Then type a comma and the word *changeto*, followed by the expression, as shown in figure 7.24.

Performing a query with the *changeto* operation does not create an Answer table but makes changes directly to the target table. To give you an escape hatch, in case you change your mind about the changes, Paradox temporarily saves the original version of the target table, without changes, in a temporary table named Changed. Paradox displays Changed at the com-

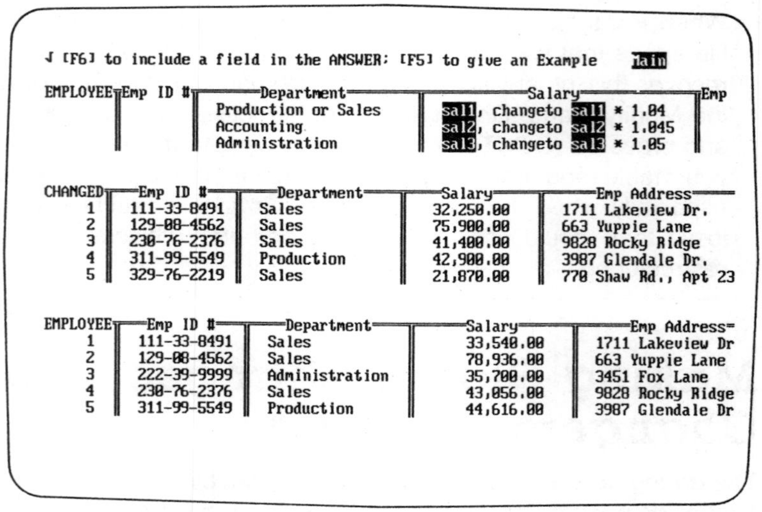

Fig. 7.24.

Using the changeto operation.

pletion of the query. You can then use the **A**dd option on the Tools More menu (see Chapter 13) to merge the records in Changed back into the table if you decide that you changed too much.

Finding Records with the Find Operation

The *find* operation in a query form serves a purpose similar to the **Z**oom option on the Image menu and the Ctrl-Z (Zoom) keystroke command, but provides the added flexibility of Query By Example. To use this operation, type the word *find* in the left column of the query form. You can then build a search criterion as normal, except that check marks and group operators are not permitted.

When performing a *find* query, Paradox places your cursor in the first record of the target table that meets the criterion. At the same time, the program creates (but does not display) an Answer table containing the selected records, arranged in the order displayed in the target table rather than in sorted order.

Use the *find* operation when you want to view or edit the target table. For example, you might want to check the date of the first order placed by customer Eastern Enterprises with salesman Harry Jones. A normal query would produce an answer table including this information, but you want to view the record for this order in the Orders table, in case you need to correct it. To find this record you can use the *find* operation. You first display a query form for Orders, then you type the word *find* in the first column (under *Orders*), type *1000* (the Cust ID # for Eastern Enterprises) in the Cust ID # column, and type *111-33-8491* (the Emp ID # for Harry Jones) in the Emp ID # column. When you press F2 (DO-IT!), Paradox moves the cursor to the proper order in Orders. It also creates an Answer table but does not display it on the work space.

Performing Queries on a Network

Using queries on a network is fairly worry-free. When you place a query form in the work space, Paradox checks to see whether anyone else has already placed a full lock on the table. If so, you have to wait until the other user is finished before you can do the query. Otherwise, Paradox places a prevent full lock on the table, allowing all other network users complete access to the table, short of locking it.

Except for the operations that change the original table (insert, delete, and changeto), Paradox takes a "snapshot" of the table during a period when no changes are being made, and then runs your query from the snapshot. Using this method, you can perform queries on a table even while it is being viewed or edited by another user on the network.

Chapter Summary

Now that you have a firm grasp of Paradox QBE, everything else will be easy. Interactive use of Paradox, as you have discovered, depends heavily on this methodology. In this chapter, you have learned how to use example elements, multiple query forms, and outer joins. You have also learned how to perform several types of calculations and comparisons on table data, including grouped summary calculations and set comparisons. And finally, you learned how to change Paradox tables directly and permanently by using special query operations.

Continue your tour through Paradox by turning to Chapter 8 on "Designing and Using Paradox Forms." Some of the multitable concepts discussed in this chapter come into play in that chapter also, as you explore how to create multitable and multirecord forms.

8

Designing and Using Paradox Forms

Up to this point, little has been said in this book about the form view of Paradox. After all, you can accomplish almost every Paradox task in a tabular format. The table view, however, is not always the best way to look at data. Because your screen is only 80 characters wide, data is almost always hidden off the screen. By contrast, with the form view you can use the entire screen and can often fit all the data from a record on one screen. This chapter explains how to design forms that present data exactly the way you want to see it on your screen.

This chapter describes how to create calculated fields, borders, multipage forms, and fields that provide automatic word wrap. You can even cause portions of the form to display in inverse video, intense video, blinking text, and, in Paradox 3.0, custom foreground and background colors.

Some of the most important enhancements provided in Paradox 3.0 involve forms. With Paradox 3.0, you can enter data into multiple tables from one form without creating a multientry map table (which is still available, and discussed in Chapter 9). You can also create multirecord forms that combine many of the advantages of both the table and form views. And, by combining these two new features—multitable and multirecord forms—you are able to design amazingly powerful forms. [3]

An Overview of Form Design

Building forms is similar to building reports. More is involved than just the raw data itself. In Paradox you can use forms for entering, editing, and viewing data in one or multiple tables. Whatever the use, someone is going to be looking at the form and trying to use the data it contains. You should therefore design Paradox forms with the typical user of your database in mind. When you are the only user, your main concern is probably speed and efficiency both in developing the form and in using it. But when you are building a form for someone else to use, you usually have to be a bit more concerned about clarity and on-screen prompts.

What Is a Paradox Form?

You can think of a Paradox form as an alternate front end for your database (the other front end being the table view). The form is a structure or positioning that Paradox applies to data while it is on-screen. Forms often include lines, labels, and prompts that surround your data as you enter it into a table but that have no effect on the data itself.

As you already know, Paradox displays your data in table view by default. Whenever you press F7 (Form Toggle), Paradox switches to form view, using the current *preferred form*. For any new table, Paradox automatically builds a standard form named *F* and assigns it as the preferred form. But because you know better than anyone else how you want the screen to look, Paradox enables you to customize forms to your heart's content. And you don't always have to use just one form for a particular table. With Paradox 2.0 and above, you can design up to 15 forms per table, which means you can create forms for special purposes as well as a customized form for the preferred form.

Paradox uses the standard form for form view unless you do one of the following:

- Alter the design of the standard form F.
- Use either the **R**ename option or the **C**opy option on the Tools menu to replace the standard form F with a form you have designed.
- Use the **P**ickForm option on the Image menu to select another form you prefer, and then save the settings with the Image menu's **K**eepSet option.

You can use the techniques described in this chapter to modify the standard form. The **R**ename and **C**opy options are discussed in Chapter 13, and the **P**ickform and **K**eepSet options in Chapter 3.

Design Considerations

Although many of the choices you make in form design involve personal preference, you should ask yourself the following important questions as you plan your form:

Who will be using the form? When you will be the only user, you can make your forms lean and mean. But you should design forms for novices and infrequent users to include plenty of clear on-screen help and instructions.

Can you visualize the way the form will look? Building the form is always easier if you sketch it on paper first. Better yet, if you are duplicating an existing paper form, work from that example.

Will your new form replace an existing form? When practicable, design your form to look as much like the current form as possible. This approach may go a long way toward quick acceptance of your form.

Will computations be necessary? When your data includes numeric information, you may want to create fields in the form that perform some calculation on-screen—price times quantity, for example.

Will you need to see multiple records in the form at one time? Often, being able to see previous entries in a table as you enter the next entry (as in table view) is convenient, but you don't want to give up the flexibility and additional features of form view. The Paradox multirecord forms capability gives you the best of both views. **[3]**

Is all the necessary information to go into one table, or will you have to place the data in several tables in the database? The Paradox 3.0 form generator can create multitable forms that allow this type of placement, but you have to make sure that your tables are properly defined and keyed. For one-to-many relationships, you can even combine multitable forms with multirecord forms. By combining several multirecord forms into a single multitable form, you can even create a "windowing" effect. **[3]**

As you are designing your form, you should also keep in mind the basic form capacities of Paradox, summarized in table 8.1.

Table 8.1
Form Capacities

Feature	*Capacity*
Fields	255
Tables	*1 master and 5 detail tables
Width	80 characters per line
Length	23 lines per page
Pages (screens)	15 per single record nonembedded form *1 per embedded form *1 per multirecord form
Records	*22 per multirecord form
Forms	15 per table

*Paradox 3.0 only

Examining the Standard Form

The standard form provides a good example of a completed form. Figure 8.1 shows the standard form for the Customer table. The following indicators help you keep track of the form screen:

- *Cursor position indicator*. On the second line of the screen for a new form, Paradox displays ‹1,1›. This set of coordinates represents the current cursor position. As you move the cursor around the screen, the coordinates change. The first number is the row position and the second number is the column position. The lower right corner of the screen is coordinate <23,80>. Note in figure 8.1 that the cursor is at position <4,17>.
- *Mode indicator*. In the upper right corner of the screen, you see that the work space is in Form mode.
- *Page indicator*. The page indicator, located to the right of the mode indicator, shows the page you are working on and the total number of pages in the form. For example, 1/1 means you are on the first page of a one-page form.

❑ *Field identifier.* Whenever you move the cursor into a field, Paradox displays the type and name of the field and indicates whether the field is a wrapped field. This information displays in the second line of the screen, just below the mode indicator. In figure 8.1, the cursor is in the Cust ID # field, a regular field.

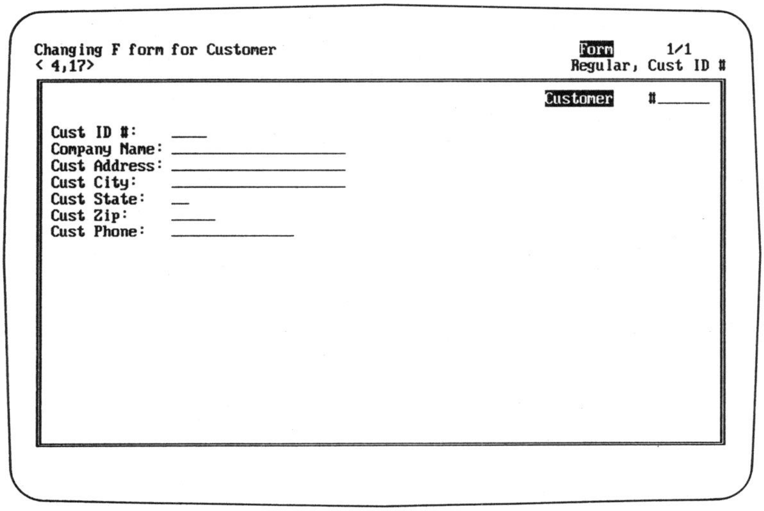

Fig. 8.1.

The standard form for the Customer table.

The standard form is reminiscent of the table structure screen (in Create mode). The field names are listed vertically on the left side of the screen rather than across the top as in standard table view. The standard form automatically displays up to 19 fields per screen and then adds another page. When you have more than 19 fields, Paradox continues to add pages to the form, 19 fields to each page. Paradox forms can have up to 15 pages (screens), which is more than enough room for the maximum number of 255 fields per table.

The field names that appear on the form are just text used for descriptive purposes, and they have no effect on the actual data you enter when you use the form. These labels are referred to as *literals*. The lines that appear to the right of the literals represent the fields into which you enter data.

The built-in standard form demonstrates only a few of the features of Paradox forms. The double lines drawn around the edge of the screen are called a *border*; the table name is displayed in inverse video in the upper right corner of the form; and the number symbol (#) followed by a field line is the record-number field. Otherwise, this form is a "plain vanilla" one.

The standard form is often adequate for small tables, especially if you are the only user who will be working with the data. But for most applications, you should design custom forms.

Starting the Form Generator

To begin creating a custom form, start from the Main menu and select **F**orms **D**esign. Then indicate the table for which you want to design a form.

Your next step is to name and describe your custom form. Paradox displays a list of 15 available form names: the letter *F* and the integers from 1 to 14. Remember that each form is a separate object and a member of the table's family of objects.

Choose one of the form names by using the arrow keys to point to your choice and then pressing Enter. Paradox alerts you if the name has already been used, giving you a chance either to stop or to replace the old form definition with a new one. The first form, F, is the standard form, and you normally should not use that name for a new form. You may want to use the standard form some other time.

Once you have selected a name for your form, Paradox instructs you to `Enter description for the new form`. You can enter any text up to 40 characters in length. (Paradox displays this description on the second line of the menu area whenever you highlight the form name on the form name list.) After you type your description and press Enter, Paradox displays an almost blank screen, as shown in figure 8.2. The top line reminds you that you are `Designing` a new form.

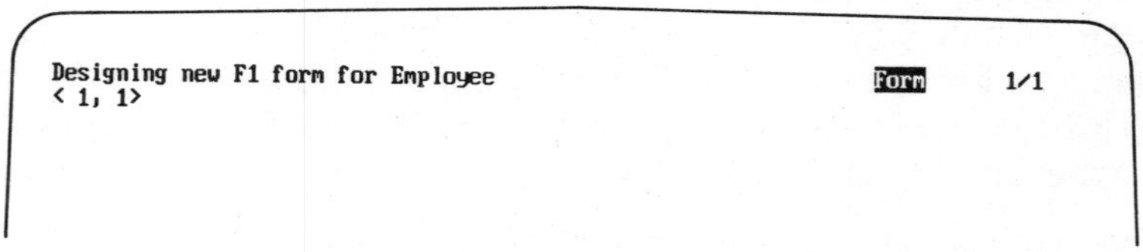

Fig. 8.2.

A new form design screen.

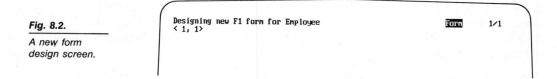

Later, after you have saved and tested your form, you may want to make changes. To alter the form, from the Main menu select **F**orms **C**hange. Indicate first the table and then the name of the form you want to change. The top line then reminds you that you are `changing` the form.

Adding Labels and Prompts to the Form

One of the major reasons for using a form rather than the table view is the ability to add text to the form. As mentioned previously, in Paradox the term *literal* is used to refer to words, numbers, or other characters that appear on a form. Literals are not data and have no effect on data entered or edited with the form. You will most often use literals to label fields, but you can also add literals as prompts, titles, and any text that you think would be helpful to users of the form.

Typing Literals

Typing literals on the form screen is similar to typing on the report design screen. Review table 1.4 in Chapter 1 for a summary of cursor key operation during form design. And remember that you can insert characters with the Ins key, and delete characters with the Del key.

Suppose that you are designing a form for the Employee table to include all fields from the table and a temporary calculated field to display the length of time an employee has been working for the company. Using simple typing techniques, the cursor-movement keys, and the Ins and Del keys, you can type field labels *anywhere* on-screen. But remember to leave enough space between labels for the fields themselves. Your screen might look like figure 8.3.

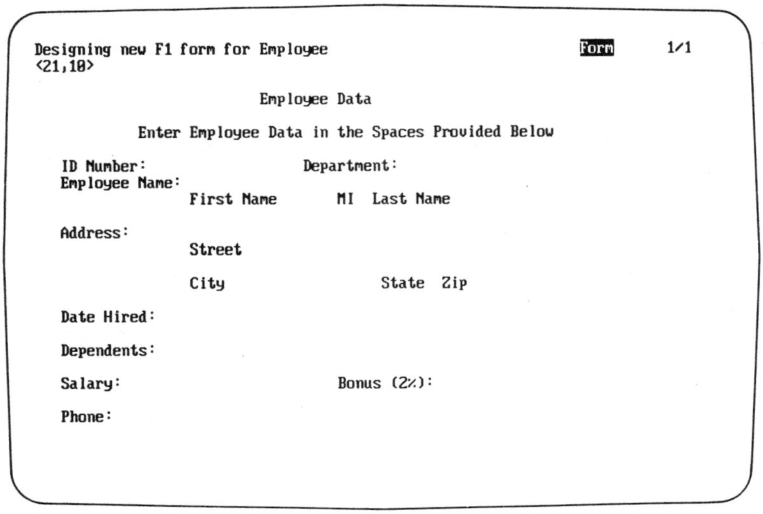

```
Designing new F1 form for Employee                          Form      1/1
<21,10>

                      Employee Data

           Enter Employee Data in the Spaces Provided Below

  ID Number:                  Department:
  Employee Name:
            First Name      MI  Last Name

  Address:
            Street

            City                State  Zip

  Date Hired:

  Dependents:

  Salary:                     Bonus (2%):

  Phone:
```

Fig. 8.3.

Literals for the employee data form.

Moving and Erasing Portions of a Form

The line-delete (Ctrl-Y) feature of the report design screen does not work during form design. Instead, Paradox uses an *area* or block erase method. To erase a portion of the form, press F10 (Menu) and select **A**rea **E**rase. Paradox prompts you to use the arrow keys to move to a corner of the area to be erased. Do so and press Enter. Next, follow the prompt to move the cursor to the opposite diagonal corner of the area to be erased. To delete a single line, you move the cursor to the opposite end of the line and press Enter. Paradox highlights the rectangular area between the starting position and the cursor. When all the area to be removed is highlighted, press Enter. Paradox erases everything in the highlighted block—literals and fields alike.

Inserting a blank line in a form is not quite as simple as doing so in a report, but you can *move* an area of the form as a block. Moving a block on the form is almost the same as erasing. Just choose the **M**ove option rather than **E**rase from the Area menu. When you press Enter at the second corner of the block, Paradox doesn't erase the block but prompts you to use the arrow keys to `...drag the area to its new location....` The text and fields in the highlighted area do not move, but the highlighting does. Press Enter when the highlighted rectangle is in the appropriate position. Paradox then moves the contents of the area to the new location.

Paradox automatically prevents you from accidentally overwriting a portion of your form. If you attempt to do so, the program displays the message `Area must be placed in a clear space.`

You will find yourself using both of these form-editing features often. For example, suppose that you are working on the form shown in figure 8.3 and decide that you want to put the Emp Phone field (labeled `Phone:`) just above the Date Hired field rather than at the bottom of the form. You decide to erase the literal `Phone:`, move down the labels `Date Hired:`, `Dependents:`, `Salary:`, and `Bonus (2%):`, and retype *Phone:* in the new position. When you are finished, the form looks like figure 8.4.

Placing and Erasing Fields on the Form

Ultimately, the purpose of a form is to enter, edit, and view data from one or more tables. Therefore, you must place fields on the form from the

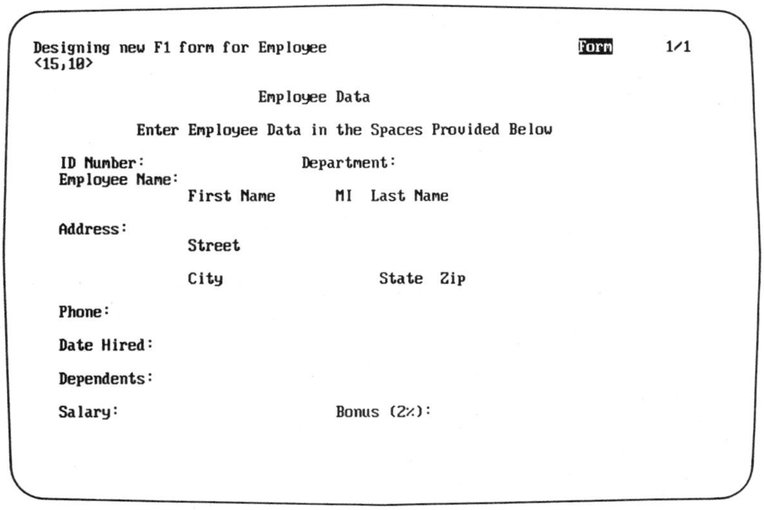

Fig. 8.4.

After rearranging the labels.

tables. These fields are equivalent to the blanks in a fill-in-the-blank form. During data entry, you enter information into these fields, and Paradox places it in the table. During form design, you do not have to place every field on the form, but for data-entry forms you usually will.

Not all fields on a form are necessarily even defined in the underlying table(s). All fields in the standard form are those that you defined during the table creation process. These fields are referred to as *regular* fields. But when you design your own forms, Paradox enables you also to place *display-only* fields, *calculated* fields, and *record-number* fields.

As you design your form, you may find yourself losing track of where you placed fields on-screen. Paradox has a handy feature to help you in this regard. To display field names where you place them, press F10 (Menu) and select **S**tyle **F**ieldnames **S**how. Then, as you follow the procedures described in the following sections for placing fields in the form, Paradox displays the field names rather than just a string of underscores. Of course, if the field name is longer than the field length, the name appears truncated on-screen.

Placing Regular Fields

Typically, you place each regular field next to some sort of label. Otherwise, when you use the form in form view, you will be unable to tell into which field you are entering data.

To place a regular field, press F10 (Menu) and select **F**ield **P**lace **R**egular. Paradox displays a list of available fields. Select the name of the appropriate field, position the cursor where the field should begin, and press Enter. (Paradox displays a line of hyphens, and prompts you to use the arrow keys to adjust the length of the field.) The line is normally at the maximum defined field length, so you can either leave it as is or use the left arrow to decrease the width and then press Enter. Paradox replaces the line of hyphens with a line of underscores. (***Note:*** With the **S**tyle **F**ieldnames **S**how option chosen, the field name also displays. In Paradox 2.0 the hyphens do not change to underscores but display as high intensity hyphens.) As you place more fields on the form, Paradox does not permit you to place the same field again.

Figure 8.5 shows the form for Employee data with all regular fields defined. Whenever the cursor is on one of the field lines of a regular field, the field identifier indicates the field type `Regular` followed by the field name.

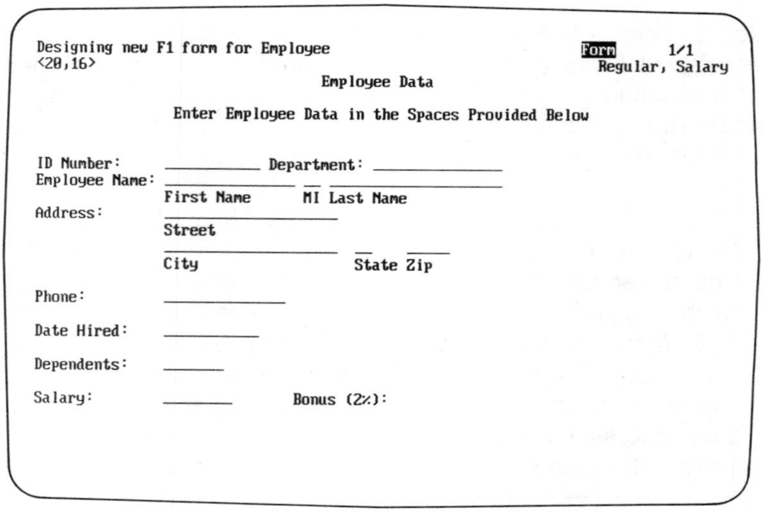

Fig. 8.5.

The employee data form with regular fields defined.

Sometimes the maximum field length defined in the table structure is wider than necessary for your data. This situation often occurs with numeric fields, because Paradox automatically allows a maximum of 23 spaces. Your form will look better and use space more efficiently if you shorten these fields to a size just wide enough for the data you intend to enter. Note, however, that you should not make the field length shorter than 5 spaces for a numeric field, even when the data needs no more than 1 space. Paradox needs a space each for a potential minus sign and decimal point, and two digits to the right of the decimal.

If you have already entered a literal to the right of where you are placing a field, the dashed line may seem to replace some or all of the literal. Don't despair. Just use the left arrow to shorten the field width, and the literal will reappear.

Placing Display-Only Fields

In some circumstances, you want to display data in a form but not permit a user to change the data. At other times, you may want to display on subsequent pages of a form data that was entered on a previous page. You can fill both of these needs by using *display-only* fields.

A display-only field is like an exhibit in a museum. You can see it but you can't touch it. That is, you can't change the data during data entry or edit. The cursor never even moves into a display-only field during data entry or edit.

To place a display-only field in a form, press F10 (Menu) and select **F**ield **P**lace **D**isplayOnly. Choose the appropriate field and then use the arrow keys to position it. Press Enter and adjust field length, just as you do with a regular field. When the field is the correct length, press Enter. When the cursor is resting on a display-only field during form design, the field identifier displays the field type `DisplayOnly`.

Suppose, for instance, that the form shown in figure 8.5 was intended for use by employees to keep their personal information up-to-date. You might want to make such sensitive fields as Salary and Date Hired display-only. Neither field should be modifiable by the employee.

Placing Calculated Fields

Because forms are often designed for simply looking at data, they are frequently good candidates for the inclusion of calculations based on record data. A calculated field in a Paradox form is defined by a formula that depends on the value of one or more regular fields. By changing the value of the regular field(s), you change the value of the calculated field.

To place a calculated field, press F10 (Menu) and select **F**ield **P**lace **C**alculated. Then type an expression (a formula) that will produce the result you need. Refer to the discussion in Chapter 5 on "Placing Calculated Fields" for details on how to type a formula for numeric and alphanumeric fields. The normal arithmetic operators (+, −, *, /, (, and)) are available for use in these formulas, but summary operators are not. After typing the formula, press Enter.

For example, the form in figure 8.5 includes the literal Bonus (2%) :. The value of this field for any particular record is determined by multiplying 0.02 (2 percent) by the employee's salary. Therefore the appropriate expression is

[Salary] * .02

When the cursor is in a calculated field, Paradox displays the formula in the field identifier (see fig. 8.6).

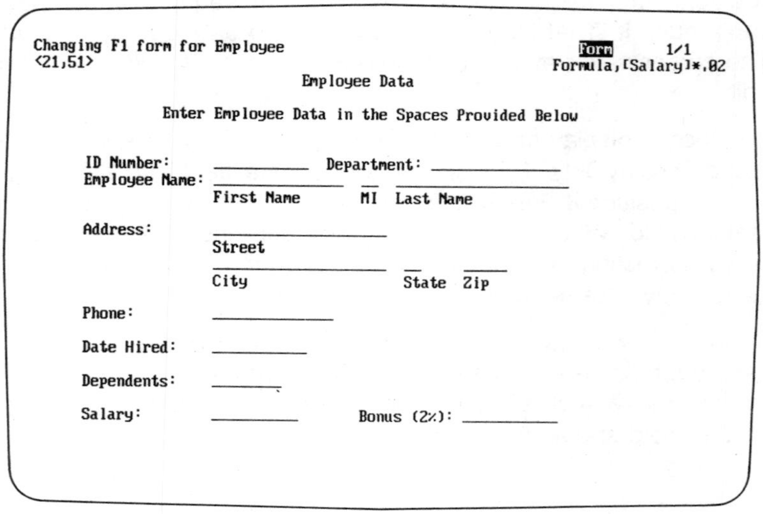

Fig. 8.6.

A calculated field.

To change a formula after you have placed a calculated field, use the **C**alcEdit option. Press F10 (Menu) and select **F**ield **C**alcEdit. Position the cursor on the calculated field whose formula you want to alter, and press Enter. Paradox displays the formula in the top line of the screen for editing. You can erase with the Backspace key, and retype or use the field view (press Alt-F5) to make changes. When the formula is correct, press Enter to accept it.

Placing the Record-Number Field

As you add records to a table, Paradox automatically assigns a record number. Having this number somewhere on your form is handy, although it is not crucial. To display the record number on the form, press F10 (Menu) and select **F**ield **P**lace **#**Record. Position the cursor where you want the field to begin, and press Enter again. Adjust the length if necessary and then press Enter, or just press Enter to accept the width.

Erasing Fields from the Form

To remove a field from a form, press F10 (Menu) and select **F**ield **E**rase. Move the cursor to the field to be removed and press Enter. Paradox erases the field from the form.

Reformatting a Field

If you decide that you initially placed a field with the wrong length, you can easily change it. Press F10 (Menu) and select **F**ield **R**eformat. Move the cursor to the field you need to lengthen or shorten, and press Enter. Paradox displays a dashed line. Use the arrow keys to increase or decrease the field length to suit your purposes. Press Enter to accept the new width.

Enhancing the Form

So far in this chapter, you have seen several of the advantages of custom forms over the standard form. You now know how to place any text you want on the form, how to position the fields where you need them, and how to use display-only and calculated fields. The next few sections describe how Paradox also enables you to create multiline fields with automatic word wrap, place borders around portions of the form, add pages to the form, and add special screen attributes.

Creating Multiline Fields with Word Wrap

A common problem with many database programs is how to allow for lengthy but workable alphanumeric fields. Paradox permits fields with a maximum width of 255 characters, but both table view and the standard form view allow you to see no more than a screen-width at a time. Using custom forms and Paradox's word-wrap feature, however, you can display long alphanumeric fields on multiple lines.

Placing a lengthy field on the form with word wrap is a two-step procedure. First, place the field on the form as usual. The left and right ends of this initial field define the left and right "margins" of the multiline field.

Then, to invoke the word-wrap feature, press F10 (Menu) and select **F**ield **W**ordWrap. Use the cursor keys to move to the target field, and press Enter. At the `Number of lines:` prompt, press the Backspace key to erase any existing entry, and type the number of lines that Paradox should reserve in the form for the field. The only way to tell whether a field is a wrapped field is to place the cursor in the field and look at the field identifier. When the cursor is resting in a word-wrap field, the message in the upper right corner is `wrap:n`, where `n` is the number you indicated as the maximum number of lines for the field.

Make sure that you leave enough empty space below a wrapped field for the maximum number of wrapped lines. Otherwise, when you attempt to save the form, Paradox informs you that the form contains insufficient space for the wrapped field, and the program refuses to save the field.

When you use this form for data entry and type text in the word-wrap field, Paradox knows when you type past the right margin of the field. The cursor automatically moves down to the next line. The program also detects spaces between words and does not split a word between two lines, unless the word is bigger than an entire line of the field.

Adding and Deleting Borders, Boxes, and Lines

Often, small things are what make a design look complete. When you are designing forms, you can use borders, boxes, or lines to make your forms look polished and professional.

Paradox refers to lines around portions of the screen as borders. To add a border, press F10 (Menu) and select **B**order **P**lace. Then choose among the following options:

- ❑ **S**ingle-line. Produces a single unbroken line
- ❑ **D**ouble-line. Produces a double unbroken line
- ❑ **O**ther. Forms a border from any repeating character you choose (e.g., *****)

After you choose the type of border, Paradox prompts you to use the arrow keys to move to a corner of the area that should be surrounded by the border. Then the program instructs you to use the arrow keys to move to the opposite diagonal corner of the form. As you move the cursor, Paradox draws the border on the screen. When the border is positioned the way you intended, press Enter.

Figure 8.7 shows a single-line border around the Employee data form. You are not limited to one border per form or even one per screen. Use the **B**order option to create as many boxes on the form as you want. This feature also is useful for creating straight vertical or horizontal single lines, double lines, or repeated characters on the form. You create straight lines by moving the cursor vertically or horizontally, but not both ways.

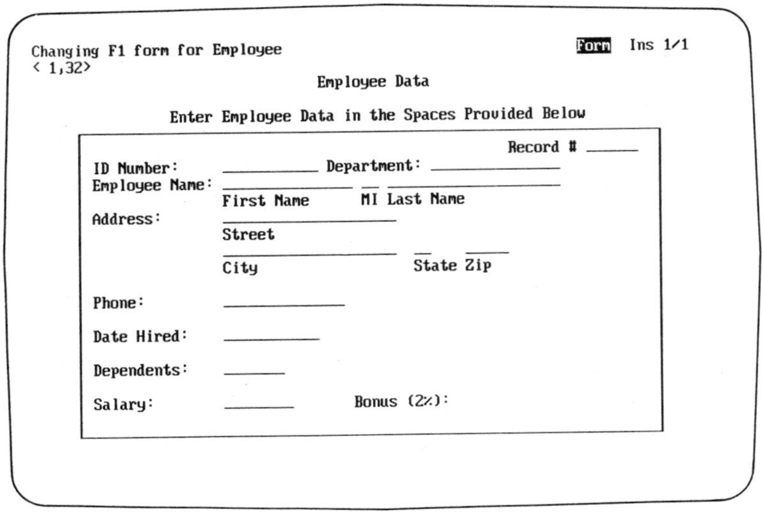

Fig. 8.7.

Enhancing the employee data form with a border.

A quick way to move to the other side of the screen is through the back door. To move from the left edge of the screen to the right edge, press the left arrow. The cursor wraps around to the right side of the screen. This process works left-to-right, right-to-left, top-to-bottom, and bottom-to-top. The technique is especially helpful when you are highlighting a large portion of the screen for a border or for a block move or erase.

Removing a border is almost the same as adding it. Press F10 (Menu) and select **B**order **E**rase. Position the cursor at a corner of the border, press Enter, move to the diagonally opposite corner, and press Enter again. Paradox erases the border.

Adding and Deleting Pages

Database tables can sometimes grow to encompass a large number of fields. Ideally, you should break up large tables into smaller tables, but that approach may not make sense in some cases. For extremely large tables, you may not be able to fit all the fields on one screen and leave any room for labels and prompts. Unlike in table view, Paradox does not permit you to scroll off the screen while in form view. But you can add pages. A page on a Paradox form is just another complete screen.

Paradox forms are by default only one page in size. To add a page, press F10 (Menu) and select **P**age **I**nsert. You then must choose to add the new page **A**fter or **B**efore the current page. As soon as you add the new page, Paradox places the cursor in that page at coordinate <1,1> so that you can begin designing it. Use the PgUp and PgDn keys to move between pages. You must place at least one regular field on each page. Paradox does not permit you to save the form until each page has at least one regular field.

If you decide that you don't need one of the pages after all, you can delete it just as easily as you added it. First, position the cursor in the page to be deleted. Then press F10 (Menu) and select **P**age **D**elete **OK**. Paradox removes the page and all its contents from the form.

Customizing Color [3]

Paradox 3.0 shows its "stuff" best on a color screen. Judicious use of color is an excellent way of accenting input forms and making them more interesting to use. With Paradox 3.0, you can apply as many as 128 color combinations to areas of the screen and to any borders you create with the **B**order option.

To add color, press F10 (Menu) and select **St**yle **C**olor. Choose to apply the new color combination to either an **A**rea of the form or to a **B**order. Then use the arrow keys to move to a corner of the area or border, press Enter, use the arrow keys to move to the diagonally opposite corner, and press Enter again. Paradox displays a color palette in the upper right corner of the screen. (***Note:*** The distributed Paradox 3.0 documentation indicates that you have to press Alt-C to toggle on this palette, but the reverse seems to be true; you use Alt-C to turn off the palette. You can change this default setting, so that the palette does not display automatically, by using the Custom Configuration Program described in Appendix B.) Use the arrow keys to move to the background/foreground color combination you prefer, then press Enter. You can use as many different colors on-screen as you want, but try not to get carried away with it. Use color to enhance the form, not overwhelm it.

Changing Screen Attributes

Both Paradox 2.0 and 3.0 provide methods for displaying literals and borders in high-intensity, blinking, or inverse video, but the two versions accomplish this task in different ways. In Paradox 3.0 these attributes also can be applied to fields. Only the *blink* attribute can be applied with a color. The other attributes discussed here are intended for use with monochrome monitors.

To add one of these screen attributes to your form when using Para- [3]
dox 3.0, press F10 (Menu) and select **St**yle **M**onochrome. Then choose between **A**rea and **B**order. Move to a corner of the area or border and press Enter; move to the opposite corner and press Enter again. Use the right- and left-arrow keys to switch between these attributes. Each press of the left or right arrow changes the screen attribute, in the following order:

Regular	Removes all monochrome and color settings
Blink	Literals or borders continuously blink; coexists with other settings
Nonblink	Removes blinking without changing other settings
Intense	Causes foreground to display in intense video; does not work properly on a color monitor, so use the **C**olor option in that situation
Inverse	Literals or borders display in inverse video; does not coexist with color settings
Intense-inverse	Displays in intense foreground and inverse video; does not coexist with color settings

(Note that applying the blink attribute with another screen attribute requires two separate steps. You have to go through the steps once to apply the blink attribute and go through all steps again to add the other desired attribute.)

When the area or border displays in the screen attribute you want to use, press Enter. Figure 8.8 shows the form title in inverse video.

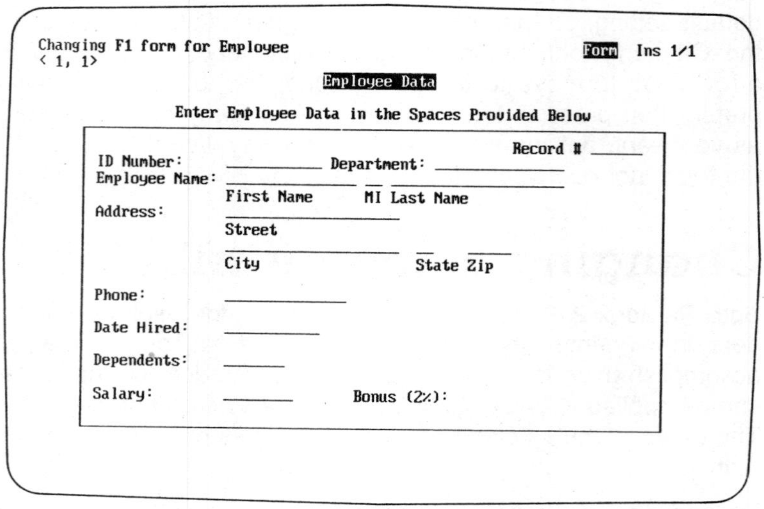

Fig. 8.8.

Adding inverse video to the form title.

By contrast, Paradox 2.0 has separate menu choices for **I**ntensity, **B**link, and **R**eversal on the Forms/Style menu. When you want to add a screen attribute in Paradox 2.0, choose the attribute immediately *before* you type the literal or draw the border. A *style indicator*, a triangular-shaped character between the mode indicator and the page indicator, displays in the currently chosen attribute. You cannot customize the form's color settings with Paradox 2.0.

You should routinely assign a color or screen attribute to literals in your forms so that you clearly distinguish them from fields. Otherwise, when you or someone else uses the form, distinguishing data from labels and prompts may be difficult. The easiest way is to assign the color combination you want for the entire form first, and then assign a different color to the data fields (Paradox 3.0 only). On a monochrome screen (monochrome or color screen if you're using Paradox 2.0), you might simply assign all literals the *intense* attribute.

Creating a Multirecord Form [3]

Forms offer many aesthetic advantages over table view, but until version 3.0, forms had one major disadvantage: you could see only one record on-screen at a time. Paradox 3.0 adds multirecord capability to forms without forcing you to give up the many positive aspects of using this alternate view.

For instance, in the table view of the Customer table, you can see the information from many customers at once but cannot see all the fields for one customer (see fig. 8.9). Conversely, the standard form for Customer shows all fields, but only one customer at a time (see fig. 8.10). A multirecord form can give you the best of both worlds.

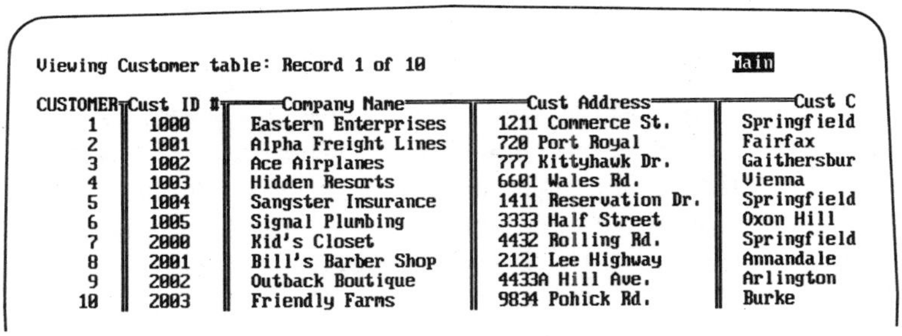
Viewing Customer table: Record 1 of 10 Main

CUSTOMER	Cust ID #	Company Name	Cust Address	Cust C
1	1000	Eastern Enterprises	1211 Commerce St.	Springfield
2	1001	Alpha Freight Lines	720 Port Royal	Fairfax
3	1002	Ace Airplanes	777 Kittyhawk Dr.	Gaithersbur
4	1003	Hidden Resorts	6601 Wales Rd.	Vienna
5	1004	Sangster Insurance	1411 Reservation Dr.	Springfield
6	1005	Signal Plumbing	3333 Half Street	Oxon Hill
7	2000	Kid's Closet	4432 Rolling Rd.	Springfield
8	2001	Bill's Barber Shop	2121 Lee Highway	Annandale
9	2002	Outback Boutique	4433A Hill Ave.	Arlington
10	2003	Friendly Farms	9834 Pohick Rd.	Burke

Fig. 8.9.

The table view of the Customer table.

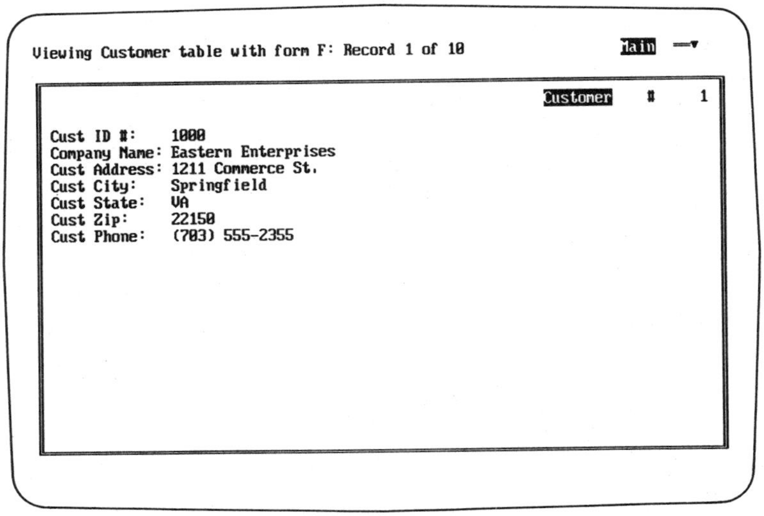

Viewing Customer table with form F: Record 1 of 10
Main
Customer # 1
Cust ID #: 1000
Company Name: Eastern Enterprises
Cust Address: 1211 Commerce St.
Cust City: Springfield
Cust State: VA
Cust Zip: 22150
Cust Phone: (703) 555-2355

Fig. 8.10.

The standard form view of the Customer table.

To create a multirecord form, you first place all the appropriate fields for one record. The fields do not have to be all on one line, but you should group them closely together so that you can fit more records on-screen at once. Figure 8.11 shows all the fields for the Customer table placed on a form. This first record is called the *original record*.

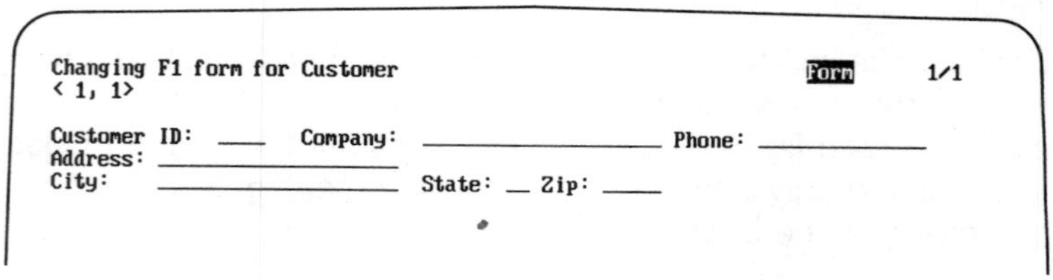

Fig. 8.11.

Beginning to build a multirecord form.

To multiply the original record, press F10 (Menu) and select **M**ulti **R**ecords **D**efine. Use the arrow keys to move to a corner of the area that contains the original record, and press Enter. Next, use the arrow keys to move to the other diagonal corner, and press Enter again. Paradox highlights the entire original record area. Then, each time you press the down arrow, Paradox adds another copy of the original record. Each time you press the up arrow, Paradox removes a copy of the original record. Paradox does not allow you to place more copies than will fit completely on the screen. Once you have added enough forms, press Enter.

Figure 8.12 shows the Customer form description multiplied four more times. Now you can see all fields for five customers at once. You can also scroll through the entire table, always viewing five records at a time.

Include at least one blank line at the beginning or end of the original record so that you have some space separating each record from the next.

As evident in figure 8.12, Paradox displays the multiple record area of the screen in inverse video (highlighting). To turn off this highlighting, press F10 (Menu) and select **S**tyle **S**howHighlight **H**ide. You can turn the highlighting back on by selecting **S**howHighlight **S**how.

If you decide to remove the multirecord feature from the form, press F10 (Menu) and select **M**ulti **R**ecords **R**emove. Paradox removes all copies of the original form, leaving only the first record.

The multirecord feature becomes extremely useful when coupled with the multitable capability, which is covered in the next section.

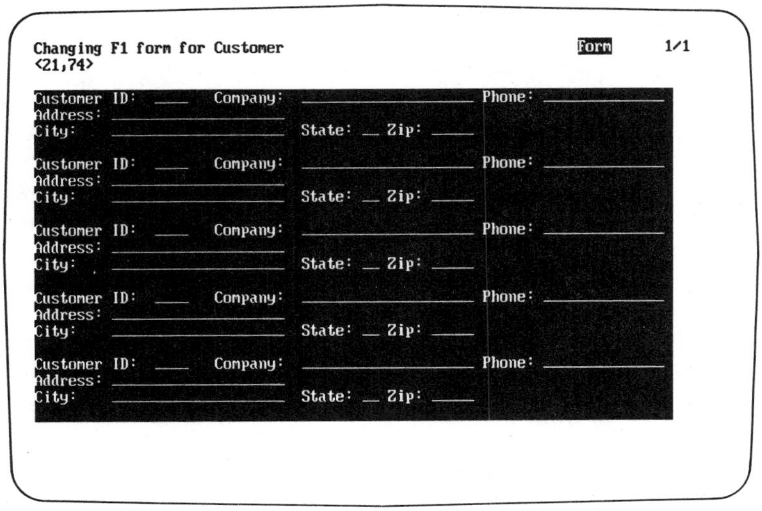

Fig. 8.12.

A multirecord form.

[3]

Creating a Multitable Form

Relational database theory and technology promise power, flexibility, and efficiency, but often at the cost of convenience to the typical user. A properly normalized order-entry database, such as the one used as an example in this book, uses at least five different tables to store information about any one order: Orders, Detail, Product, Customer, and Employee. If a new salesperson sells a new product to a new customer, entries must be made in all five tables to track one order. To help alleviate potential confusion and greatly speed data entry in such situations, Paradox 3.0 provides multitable forms that allow you to enter data into more than one table.

Understanding Relationships among Tables

Chapter 2 introduced you to the concept of relationships among tables. Because you need to have a good grasp of this concept before you can design multitable forms, you should review Chapter 2's discussion of table relationships. Paradox 3.0 enables you to create forms that not only service several tables but also, in certain instances, enforce the relationships among these tables.

When you build a multitable form, one table is designated as the *owner* of the form. That is, the form is a member of the table's family. The table that owns the form is also called the *master* table. Other tables serviced by the multitable form are called *detail* tables.

As you build multitable forms, Paradox automatically recognizes the relationships between pairs of tables, even if you don't. But you must have structured the tables properly for the necessary links to be established. The following two rules may help you:

1. The unique end of the link is the *one-side*.
2. The one-side link field must be keyed and therefore must be the first field in the table's structure.

Note: To keep this section from becoming too complex, multifield keys are not discussed. The basic concepts, however, are the same.

The tables used as examples in this book have the following relationships:

Tables	*Relationship*
Orders-to-Detail	One-to-many
Orders-to-Customer	Many-to-one
Orders-to-Employee	Many-to-one
Detail-to-Product	Many-to-one
Orders-to-Product	Many-to-many

In each case, the one-side table structure starts with the link field. The first field in Orders is the Order # field, which is the link to Detail; the first field in Customer is the Cust ID # field, which is the link to Orders; and so forth.

The most difficult relationship to understand is between Orders and Product. Because each order can potentially include more than one product, and each product can be found in more than one order, the tables meet the definition of a many-to-many relationship. To help you avoid having to deal directly with this relationship, you use the Detail table to buffer or link the two tables.

Caution: At times, you may want to see information from both Product and Orders on-screen at once, but Paradox does not allow a two-tier link in multitable forms. One solution to this problem would be to restructure Detail to include Product Name, Price, and Cost, but this approach would violate the basic rule of avoiding data duplication. Fortunately, you can use a special feature called *validity checks* to eliminate duplicate entry. Validity checks are discussed in the next chapter.

Multitable forms that use a one-to-one or one-to-many relationship get special editing support from Paradox. This support is called *referential integrity*.

Enforcing Referential Integrity

Referential integrity is much easier to understand than it is to say. Suppose that a customer places an order for three different kinds of widgets. To record this transaction, you have to add one record to Orders and three records to Detail. If, an hour later, you realize that you used the wrong order number and thus have to change the number in the Orders table, you must also change the number in each of the Detail records. Otherwise, the link is lost. Similarly, if the customer calls and cancels the order, you can't just delete the record from the Orders table. You also have to delete the three records from the Detail table. This example describes what is meant by referential integrity.

With respect to data entered in tables linked by either a one-to-one or one-to-many relationship, the concept of referential integrity can be summarized in the following two rules:

1. Any change to the link field in a master table record must be accompanied by a corresponding change to the link field of each referenced (linked) record in the detail table.

2. All referenced (linked) records in the detail table must be removed before a record in the master table can be removed.

When you use multitable forms to enter and edit data in tables with either one-to-one or one-to-many relationships, Paradox 3.0 helps you ensure that referential integrity is maintained. As soon as you alter the link field in the master table, Paradox automatically makes an identical change to the link field data in each corresponding detail record. This step enforces the first rule. And Paradox enforces the second rule by not allowing you to delete a master record until you remove all corresponding detail records. If you try to delete a master record, you see the message `Can't delete master record while detail records depend on it.`

Understanding the Structure of Multitable Forms

A multitable form is basically one or more detail forms *embedded* in a master form. You must follow these rules when building multitable forms:

- You can embed up to five detail forms in a master form.
- The master form can be multipage but cannot be multirecord.
- Each detail/embedded form can be multirecord but not multipage.
- One embedded form cannot contain another embedded form.

Building the Master Form

The first step in building a multitable form is deciding which table is the master table and thus the owner of the master form. Two sometimes competing considerations can help you determine which table should be the master:

- Paradox permits only direct links between master and detail tables. You should therefore try to choose as the master table the table with the most direct links to other tables. For example, the Orders table is linked directly to Customer, Employee, and Detail. Orders is not linked directly to Product, but that table is the only one that cannot be included if you use Orders as the master table.
- Paradox enforces referential integrity in one-to-one and one-to-many relationships. Master-detail tables should therefore fit into one of these categories. In this book's example, Orders and Detail are linked in a one-to-many relationship, but both Orders-to-Customer and Orders-to-Employee have the opposite relationship (many-to-one).

Assuming that the purpose of your form is primarily to enter order detail rather than customer or employee data, suppose that you decide to choose Orders as the master table and embed a form only from Detail.

If you want to show Customer and Employee data also, without risking referential integrity, you could embed forms from each of these tables and use only display-only fields in those embedded forms.

Once you have a master table, you then design the master form, using the procedures already covered in this chapter. Figure 8.13 shows a form containing the fields from the Orders table.

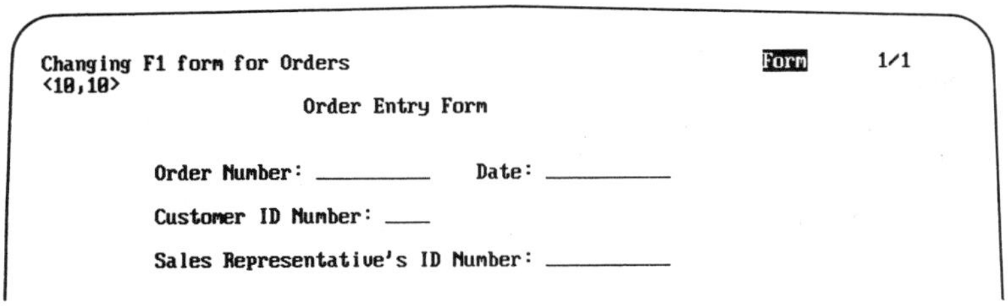

Fig. 8.13.
The master form for a linked multitable form.

Building the Embedded Forms

Next, you design the detail form(s). As you design and build each detail form, you should keep in mind that it will eventually become a part of the master form.

Consider the following rules when building forms that will be embedded:

- The link field(s) in the detail table must be keyed.
- The link field(s) cannot be placed as a regular field in the embedded form but can be placed as a display-only field.
- All fields that are not link fields must be placed in the form so that you can enter data in them. It is especially important that you place in the form all key fields that are not part of the link. These key fields are needed to "break ties" between detail records with identical link values.
- The size of an embedded form is determined by its *natural size*, the size from the top left corner of the form design screen to the diagonally opposite corner that includes all literals and fields. Therefore, the best place to build embedded forms is usually as near to the upper left corner of the screen as possible.

Because Detail can contain multiple records for the same order, you also should make this embedded form multirecord. Figure 8.14 shows a multi-record form for Detail. Notice that the form has no labels. The labels are provided in the master form. For single-record embedded forms, like this example, you don't want the labels to repeat over and over. You create a mini-table view of the embedded table by placing column headings in the master form and placing the multirecord embedded form beneath the headings. The table has only three fields. The Order # field is not included, because that field is the link between Orders and Detail.

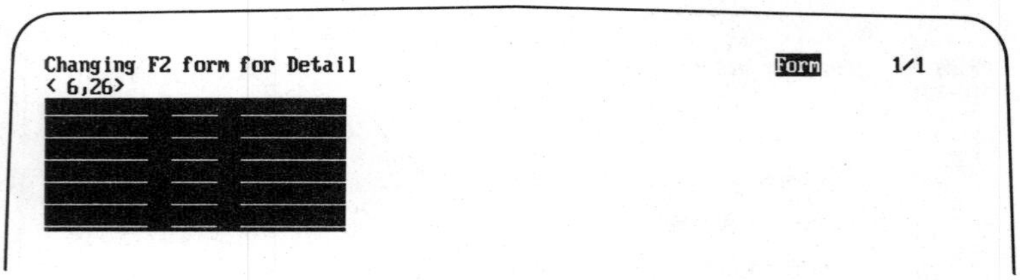

Fig. 8.14.
The Detail portion of the linked multitable form.

Embedding the Form

The final step is to embed the detail form into the master form. While in Form mode, and while either designing or changing the master form, press F10 (Menu) and select **M**ulti **T**ables **P**lace **L**inked. Indicate the Detail table and then the Detail form. Paradox determines the key field(s) that you have not placed on the detail form and asks which field(s) in the master table is (are) the corresponding link(s). In this example, the Order # field is the link.

Next, Paradox displays a highlighted block in the lower right corner of the screen that is the *natural size* of the detail form. Use the arrow keys to drag this block to the appropriate position, and press Enter. Paradox fills in the block with shading. Whenever you move the cursor into this area, Paradox displays a message near the upper right corner of the screen, indicating that this block is an `Embedded` table. Figure 8.15 shows the completed multitable form, after the form has been embedded and the labels added. When you use a multitable form for data entry, editing, or viewing data, you use F3 (Up Image) and F4 (Down Image) to move between the forms (see fig. 8.16).

Building and Using Unlinked Forms

Paradox enables you to create a "windowing" effect with form view by embedding forms without linking them. Unlinked forms are treated as completely unrelated. For this reason, you can use this procedure to combine almost any forms.

To embed an unlinked form, display one of the forms in the form screen and press F10 (Menu). Then select **M**ulti **T**ables **P**lace **U**nlinked. Indicate the appropriate table and form, use the arrow keys to position the highlighted block, and press Enter. Save the form by pressing F2 (DO-IT!). Figure 8.17 shows an example of an unlinked multitable form that includes

Employee data and Customer data on the same screen. You can switch between tables by pressing F3 (Up Image) or F4 (Down Image).

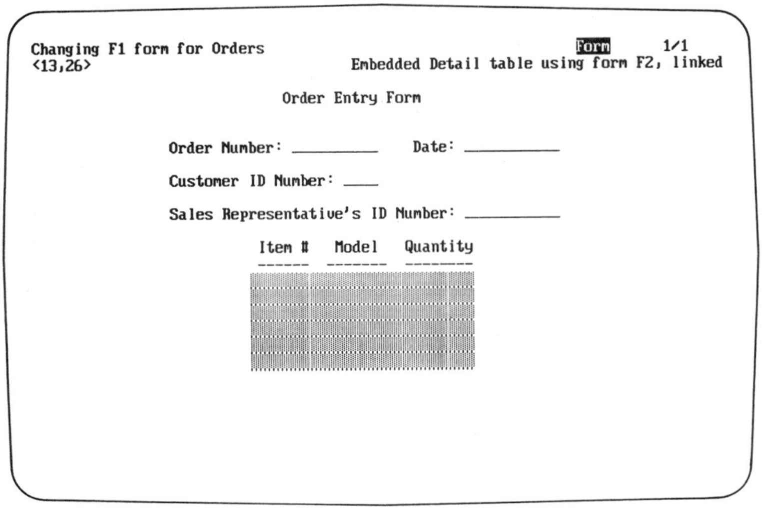

Fig. 8.15.

The completed linked multitable form.

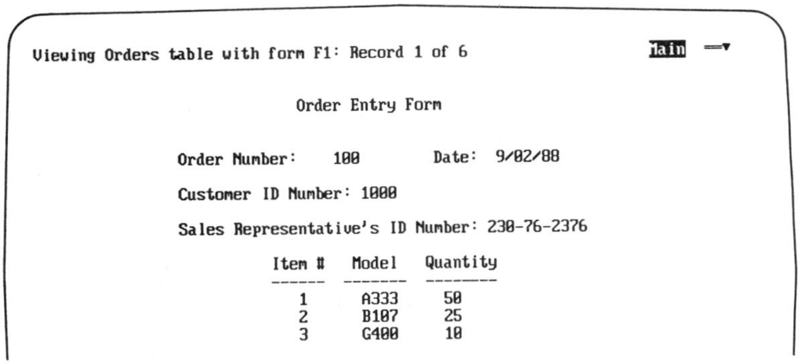

Viewing Orders table with form F1: Record 1 of 6
Main
Order Entry Form
Order Number: 100
Date: 9/02/88
Customer ID Number: 1000
Sales Representative's ID Number: 230-76-2376
Item # Model Quantity
1 A333 50
2 B107 25
3 C400 10

Fig. 8.16.

Using a linked multitable form.

Changing an Existing Form

After you have used a form, you may decide to make changes. To access the form again, you must press F10 (Menu), select **F**orms **C**hange, and specify the proper table.

Whenever you start the form generator with the **C**hange option, Paradox displays a list of only the previously defined forms. If you simply want to enhance the automatic standard form, you can choose F from the form name list.

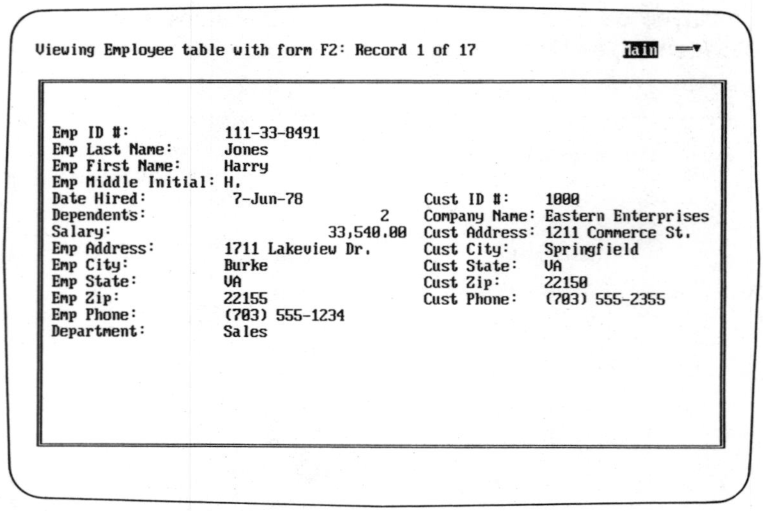

Fig. 8.17.

Using an unlinked multitable form.

When you want to enhance the standard form but keep an unaltered version as well, first copy the standard form definition to one of the other form names, using the **C**opy option from the Tools menu (see Chapter 13). You can then make the appropriate changes to the copy and leave form F intact.

Saving a Form

Once you have finished defining a form, you save it by pressing F2 (DO-IT!). Paradox saves the form as an object in the table's family of objects.

Using Forms on a Network

When you are designing or changing a form on a network, Paradox places a prevent full lock on the table on which the form is based but puts a full lock on the form itself. You cannot access a form while someone else on the network is using that form. Also, when one user is coediting with a multitable form, all users wanting to edit the table must use the same form.

Chapter Summary

This chapter has explained how to design forms that present data exactly the way you want to see it on your screen. But this chapter presents only half the story about entering and editing data. The form is the "canvas" that users see while adding to or changing data on your database, but Paradox provides a number of important behind-the-scenes edit and entry features that can help maintain valid data. These powerful features are discussed in Chapter 9.

9

Using Paradox Power Entry and Editing Features

This chapter introduces you to some of Paradox's most powerful data-entry and editing capabilities. The greatest database system in the world is no better than the data put in it. Paradox provides a number of special data-entry and editing tools (referred to as *validity checks*) to assist you in snagging errors before they are buried in your database. These error-prevention techniques amount to significant labor-saving devices as well. This chapter introduces you to these features and demonstrates how you might put them to good use.

Expanding on Chapter 8's discussion of forms, this chapter discusses how [3]
to use Paradox 3.0's multitable forms for DataEntry, Edit, and CoEdit modes, and explains how Paradox handles master records, linked fields, and key violations.

This chapter also covers the **M**ultiEntry option available in both Paradox 2.0 and 3.0. The **M**ultiEntry feature enables you to enter and edit data in multiple tables. Aspects of **M**ultiEntry are also important to **M**ultiAdd, covered in Chapter 13, and to the *multitable view* capability of the Paradox Personal Programmer and the Paradox Application Language. These last two topics are introduced in Part III, "Developing Menu-Driven Applications with Paradox."

Finally, you learn in this chapter how to use the Paradox **S**ort option to rearrange records into a particular sorted order.

Adding and Using Validity Checks

The term *validity check* in Paradox refers to a group of features that help you enter data more easily and more accurately. They are accessed from either the DataEntry menu or the Edit menu, but once established are also effective in CoEdit mode. Validity checks apply in both table view and form view and help you prevent the entry of invalid data. Paradox always provides a certain amount of validity checking based on the defined structure of a table. Text is never allowed in a numeric field, for example. The features discussed in this section go beyond this minimal screening.

Several of the validity checks do more than prevent the entry of invalid data. You can use the **T**ableLookup options, for example, to fill in data automatically. Once you see how well these features work, you will never want to edit a table without them.

All options discussed in this section are accessed through the **V**alCheck choice on either the DataEntry or the Edit menu and apply only to the current image. Whenever you add or clear validity checking, the change takes effect immediately. The validity settings current when you end an edit session are automatically saved as an object in the table's family for use in future sessions.

Controlling the Range of Acceptable Values

Normally Paradox permits the entry of any number in a numeric or currency field and any date in a date field. But in most database applications, field values usually occur within a fairly narrow range. For example, you might want to limit Salary values in the Employee table to the range $12,000 to $100,000. Paradox provides a group of validity-checking tools that allow you to place limits on acceptable data in numeric, currency, and date fields. (***Note:*** You can also apply these validity checks to alphanumeric fields, but such use is uncommon.)

To establish a minimum value for a field, press F10 (Menu) from either DataEntry or Edit mode, and select **V**alCheck **D**efine. Move the cursor to the target field and press Enter. Then select **L**owValue. For a numeric or currency field, you just type a number and press Enter. When you are placing a minimum on a date field, however, you can type either a specific date or the special keyword *today*, which represents the system-supplied date. Once you have made your entry, Paradox displays the message `Low value recorded`.

After you establish the minimum, Paradox prevents the entry of data below this value. For example, if you set a low value of 12000 for the Employee Salary field and then try to enter 11000, Paradox refuses to enter the data and displays the error message `Value no less than 12000.00 is expected`. Paradox does not allow the cursor to leave the field. You must either erase or correct the error before you can proceed. Refer to the section on "Using Lookup Tables" for a description of how to construct a list of acceptable values.

You establish a ceiling or maximum acceptable value in the same manner. From either DataEntry or Edit mode, press F10 (Menu) and select **V**alCheck **D**efine. Move the cursor to the target field and press Enter. Then select **H**ighValue. For a numeric or currency field, you just type a number and press Enter. Paradox displays the message `High value recorded`. For a date field, you may type either a specific date or the keyword *today*, and press Enter. As with the low value check, when you set a high value check, Paradox prevents the entry of data that falls beyond that upper limit.

Establishing a Default Value

Although in theory every record in your database is unique, in practice much of the information in many records is repetitive. The State field in the Employee table, for instance, contains `VA` in every record. To take advantage of this fact of life, you can establish a value for Paradox to enter automatically in a field whenever you leave the field blank during DataEntry, Edit, or CoEdit.

To assign a default value to a field, press F10 (Menu) from Edit or DataEntry mode, and select **V**alCheck **D**efine. Move the cursor to the target field and press Enter. Then select **D**efault. Type the value you want established as the default, and press Enter. Paradox displays a message at the bottom of the screen that reads `Default value recorded`.

For the State field in the Employee table, you might establish VA as the default. Then, each time you add a record, you can just leave the State field blank and let Paradox automatically fill in the correct value. If a new Employee lives in Maryland, you can override the default by just typing *MD* in the State field and pressing Enter.

Using Lookup Tables

Preventing the entry of data outside a given range is helpful but may still not be limiting enough to prevent errors. In many database applications, you should confine acceptable entries for a certain field to a finite set of values. In the Orders table, for example, the Cust ID # field should contain only values that occur in the Cust ID # field in the Customer table. Similarly, entries in the Orders table's Emp ID # field should each have a corresponding value in the Employee table. Paradox enables you to create a list of acceptable values for a given field. The program then compares new entries to the list, which is often referred to as a *lookup table*.

A lookup table is not a special kind of table, just a special way to use a table. In Paradox, you can use any table as a lookup table so long as it meets the following criteria:

- The field containing the validation data must be the first field in the table structure. This field is referred to as the *lookup field*.
- The lookup field must have the same data type, but not necessarily the same field name, as the field you want to validate.
- Normally you should key the lookup field, although this step is not a requirement.

The Customer table meets these criteria. Cust ID # can be used as the lookup field to validate entry of customer ID numbers in the Orders table.

Activating a Private Lookup

Sometimes you want to use a lookup table for a particular field but don't want to give users direct access to the list of acceptable values. In Paradox this type of lookup is referred to as a *private lookup*. To activate a private lookup, from either Edit or DataEntry mode, press F10 (Menu) and select **V**alCheck **D**efine. Move the cursor to the target field and press Enter. Then select **T**ableLookup. At the prompt for a table name, either type the name of the table containing the validation list, or press Enter and choose the table from the list of available tables. Then choose **J**ustCurrentField **P**rivateLookup. Notice that you don't specify the field to be matched in the other table.

Using Automatic Fill-In

The next logical step after simple data validation is for Paradox to permit you to select your entry from a list of valid data. This way you can't go wrong. Paradox calls this feature *HelpAndFill*.

To activate a HelpAndFill lookup, from either Edit or DataEntry mode, press F10 (Menu) and select **V**alCheck **D**efine. Move the cursor to the target field and press Enter. Then select **T**ableLookup. Indicate the lookup table and then choose **J**ustCurrentField **H**elpAndFill. Paradox displays this message at the bottom of the screen: `Table lookup recorded`. The program also adds a message on the second line of the screen, telling you that you can `Press [F1] for help with fill-in`.

When you press F1, Paradox temporarily displays the lookup table in the work space. A new message instructs you to `Press [F2] to select the record; Esc to cancel; [F1] for help`. Before pressing any of these keys, use the down- or up-arrow key to move to the record that contains the entry for which you are looking.

Suppose, for example, that you add a HelpAndFill lookup to the Cust ID # field in the Orders table to look up values from the Customer table (the lookup table). Then, when you are entering the next order in Orders and come to the Cust ID # field (see fig. 9.1), you don't need a list of valid numbers handy. Just press F1, and Paradox displays the Customer table (see fig. 9.2). Move the cursor down to the row for the customer, Sangster Insurance in this instance, and press F2. Paradox automatically enters the number 1004 into the Cust ID # field in Orders.

Keep in mind that you do not have to use this feature. You can type the valid data on your own if you prefer.

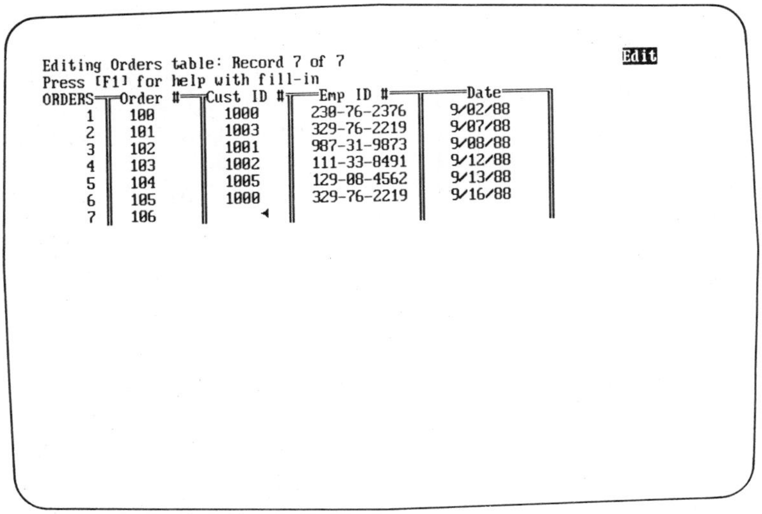

Fig. 9.1.

Using the TableLookup feature for automatic fill-in.

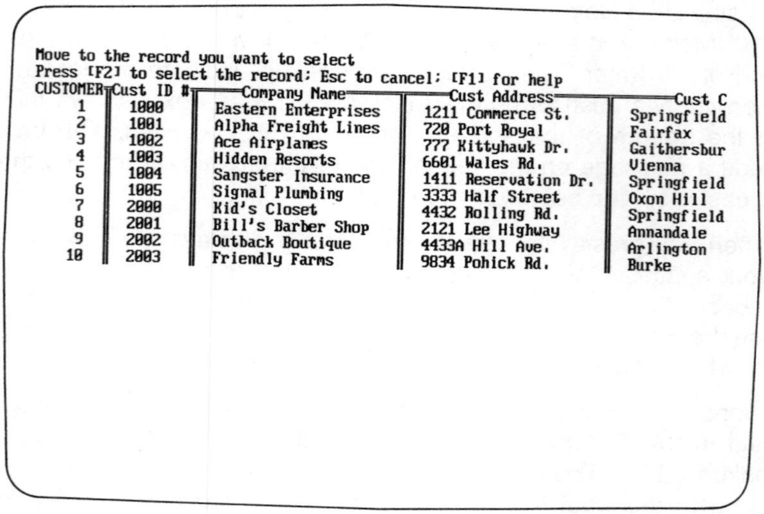
Move to the record you want to select
Press [F2] to select the record; Esc to cancel; [F1] for help
CUSTOMER Cust ID # Company Name Cust Address Cust C
1 1000 Eastern Enterprises 1211 Commerce St. Springfield
2 1001 Alpha Freight Lines 720 Port Royal Fairfax
3 1002 Ace Airplanes 777 Kittyhawk Dr. Gaithersbur
4 1003 Hidden Resorts 6601 Wales Rd. Vienna
5 1004 Sangster Insurance 1411 Reservation Dr. Springfield
6 1005 Signal Plumbing 3333 Half Street Oxon Hill
7 2000 Kid's Closet 4432 Rolling Rd. Springfield
8 2001 Bill's Barber Shop 2121 Lee Highway Annandale
9 2002 Outback Boutique 4433A Hill Ave. Arlington
10 2003 Friendly Farms 9834 Pohick Rd. Burke

Fig. 9.2.
Looking up the correct customer.

Using Multifield Automatic Fill-In

Paradox can even fill in multiple fields at once. You enter data into a field, and Paradox looks up and automatically fills in other fields with corresponding data from another table. For automatic fill-in to be successful, each field to be filled in must have the same name and data type as a field in the lookup table.

To activate a lookup with multifield automatic fill-in, from either Edit or DataEntry mode, press F10 (Menu) and select **V**alCheck **D**efine. Move the cursor to the target field and press Enter. Then select **T**ableLookup. Indicate the lookup table name, and choose **A**llCorrespondingFields. Finally, choose between **F**illNoHelp and **H**elpAndFill. The first option is equivalent to a private lookup. It checks the data entered for validity, fills in corresponding data when a match is found, but does not allow you to see the lookup table. The **H**elpAndFill option works the same as it does with single-field lookup. The next section describes an example that uses multifield lookup.

When you define a lookup with automatic fill-in, you should designate as display-only those fields that will receive the looked-up data. This approach helps you maintain data integrity by protecting the looked-up data from being altered.

Also consider the following guidelines when you add a multifield lookup:

- ❑ Paradox does not perform validity checks on the data being filled in.
- ❑ You cannot use one lookup/fill-in operation to trigger another, all in one step. That is, data that is filled in does not immediately cause Paradox to look up data from another lookup table. You need a second step. After the first lookup/fill-in, move the cursor to the second field for which you have defined a lookup. Press Alt-F5 (Field View) and Enter. Paradox performs the second lookup/fill-in.
- ❑ Changes to data in the lookup table are not retroactively posted to records in other tables where data was previously filled in.

Solving the Many-to-Many Problem

Chapter 8's section on building multitable forms included a brief discussion of many-to-many table relationships. The relationship between the Orders table and the Product table is of this type. Because of the difficulties of representing many-to-many relationships in forms and reports, the examples in this book have used the Detail table as a linkage between Orders and Product. Using the Detail table converts the relationship into reciprocal one-to-many (Orders-to-Detail) and many-to-one (Detail-to-Product) relationships. You might call this relationship *one-to-many-to-one*. [3]

Once the linkage table is added, you can more easily work with the database. For example, the multitable form developed as an example in Chapter 8 used Orders and Detail. As you work with database applications, you will find that many-to-many relationships are quite common. Conversion to a one-to-many-to-one relationship is the best way to handle them.

Sometimes, however, you want to see information from all three tables in one-to-many-to-one relationships on-screen at once. But the only way to handle this situation with properly normalized tables is to use the *middle* table—Detail in this example—as the master table for multitable forms, and use the other two tables as embedded detail tables. But this design defeats the protective features of Paradox's automatic enforcement of referential integrity. In such a form, the master-to-detail relationships are many-to-one, and Paradox maintains referential integrity only for one-to-many relationships.

You have one way to solve this problem. First, you decide which of the two *outside* tables in the relationship (Orders and Product in this example) you want to use as the master table in a form. The multitable form developed in

Chapter 8 used Orders as the master table. Next, you restructure the middle table to include all the fields from the other outside table that you want to see in the form. For example, you might want to see the Product Name and Product Price fields on the order-entry form constructed in Chapter 8. You thus need to restructure Detail to include these fields.

Restructuring the middle table in this way seems to violate the rule that says you should not enter the same data more than once. You might think that every time you sell model A333, for example, you also have to type in the model name—Standard Widget—and price—$39.95. Fortunately, you can use the **T**ableLookup feature to eliminate the need for this duplication of data entry.

Use the **T**ableLookup **A**llCorrespondingFields validity check on the field that links the middle table to the nonmaster outside table. In the example, the Model # field links Detail to Products, so you place a **T**ableLookup **A**llCorrespondingFields validity check on this field. Paradox then automatically fills in Product Price and Product Name when you provide the Model # field. To prevent any changes to the data after it is looked up, you might make the Product Name and Product Price fields display-only.

You can remake the order-entry form from Chapter 8 to include not only the model number of each product ordered but also its name, price, and even a calculated field showing price times quantity (see fig. 9.3).

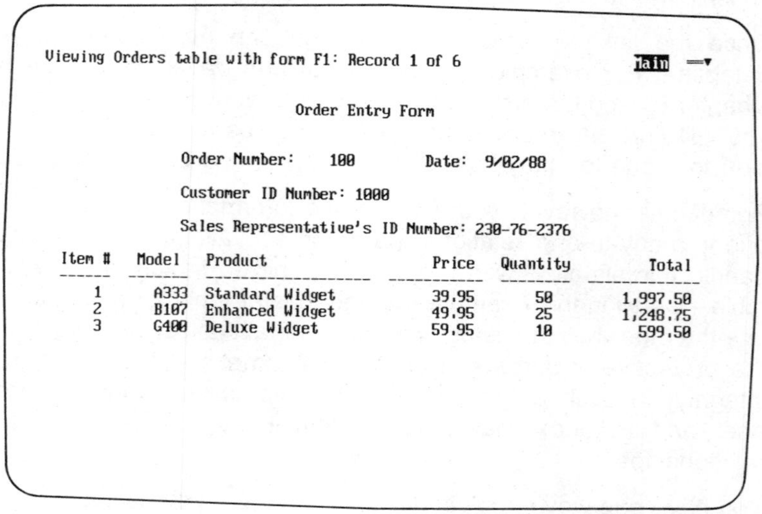

Fig. 9.3.
The order-entry form showing data from Orders, Detail, and Product.

Even though you may have defined validity checks for each table individually, if you plan to enter or edit data through a multitable form, you have to redefine these checks after you embed the table's form. In the form shown in figure 9.3, for example, you must add the **T**ableLookup **A**llCorrespondingFields validity check to the Model # field while using the multitable form for Edit or DataEntry mode.

While using the multitable form in Edit or DataEntry mode, place the cursor in the Model # column and press F10 (menu). Select **V**alCheck **D**efine and press Enter. Choose **T**ablelookup and indicate Products as the lookup table. Choose **A**llCorrespondingFields and either **F**illNoHelp or **H**elpAndFill.

Controlling Data Entry through Pictures

One of the most convenient ways to control data entry is referred to as a *picture*. This feature is especially convenient for entering rigidly formatted data. A picture gives you a way to create custom data types.

A picture is a template that defines character-by-character what Paradox should expect to be entered into a field. To add a picture to a field, from Edit or DataEntry mode, press F10 (Menu) and select **V**alCheck **D**efine. Move the cursor to the target field and press Enter. Then choose **P**icture. Paradox displays the prompt `Enter a PAL picture format` (e.g., ###-##-###). Use the codes listed in table 9.1 to type the format of the data for the field; then press Enter. Paradox displays the message `Picture specification recorded` at the bottom of the screen. The next time you enter data into this field, Paradox uses the picture to check the format of your entry.

Use one of the available codes to represent each of the characters or digits in the permissible entry. For example, you can ensure that a user types a letter in the first position of the Model # field by placing a ? in the first position of a picture for this field. If you want Paradox to convert the letter to uppercase, you can use an & in the first position instead. To force the user to type a number in the final three positions you can use ###. The complete picture for the Model # field is &###.

Table 9.1
Picture Codes

Code	*Meaning*
#	Character must be numeric digit
?	Character must be letter (upper- or lowercase)
&	Character must be letter; Paradox converts to uppercase
@	Can be any character
!	Can be any character; Paradox converts to uppercase
;	Take next character literally, where the next character would otherwise be interpreted as a picture code
*n	Repeat the next code *n* times, where *n* is a positive integer
[ ]	Any picture code inside the brackets is optional
{ }	Grouping operators to inhibit auto fill-in
,	Separator for a list of alternatives

Note: Any displayable character that you can type and that is not in this list can be used and will be taken literally.

The Emp ID # field in the Employee table provides a good illustration of using a picture. The company in this book's example uses an employee's social security number as an identification number. The picture for the Emp ID # field is therefore ###-##-#### (see fig. 9.4). This picture means that any number is acceptable in the first three positions, but the fourth position must be a hyphen. The fifth and sixth positions must be any number, and the seventh must be a hyphen. Finally, the last four positions must be numbers.

Contrast using a picture to specifying a default value, which was described in a previous section ("Establishing a Default Value"). Paradox uses a default value only if you leave the field blank. A picture value is always used.

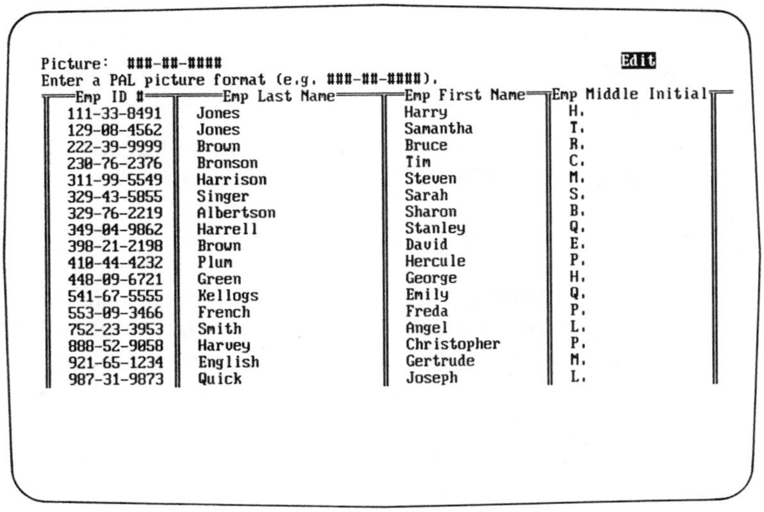
Picture: ###-##-####
Enter a PAL picture format (e.g. ###-##-####).
Edit

Emp ID #	Emp Last Name	Emp First Name	Emp Middle Initial
111-33-8491	Jones	Harry	H.
129-08-4562	Jones	Samantha	T.
222-39-9999	Brown	Bruce	R.
230-76-2376	Bronson	Tim	C.
311-99-5549	Harrison	Steven	M.
329-43-5855	Singer	Sarah	S.
329-76-2219	Albertson	Sharon	B.
349-04-9862	Harrell	Stanley	Q.
398-21-2198	Brown	David	E.
410-44-4232	Plum	Hercule	P.
448-09-6721	Green	George	H.
541-67-5555	Kellogs	Emily	Q.
553-09-3466	French	Freda	P.
752-23-3953	Smith	Angel	L.
888-52-9058	Harvey	Christopher	P.
921-65-1234	English	Gertrude	M.
987-31-9873	Quick	Joseph	L.

Fig. 9.4.
Using a picture to control data input into the Emp ID # field.

Using Automatic Fill-In

Paradox helps even more than may at first be apparent. In the Emp ID # example, as soon as you type the first three digits, Paradox automatically fills in the hyphen. And once you type the fifth digit, Paradox fills in the second hyphen. In other words, the program automatically fills in literal characters (characters that are not special picture codes). Paradox does not, however, fill in the first character or digit in a field.

Sometimes you may prefer that fill-in not be automatic, perhaps when the individuals entering data are touch typists and seldom look up at the screen. To inhibit auto fill-in, enclose the literal characters in braces ({ }). For example, you can prevent automatic fill-in of the hyphens in the Emp ID # field by using the picture ###{-}##{-}###. With this picture, Paradox fills in the hyphen when you press either the hyphen key itself or the space bar. Typing any character other than a hyphen at the fourth and seventh positions results in a beep, but no hyphen.

Using the Repeat Code

Some pictures may contain the same code many times in sequence. An alternate way of expressing such repeating codes is with the asterisk (*)

followed by a positive integer. The asterisk instructs Paradox to repeat the code that follows, and the integer tells Paradox how many times to repeat the code. You could therefore write the Emp ID # field picture as **3#-*2#-*4#*.

When you want Paradox to repeat a *series* of codes, enclose the codes in braces ({ }). The picture **2{##-}##* is equivalent to *##-##-##*.

Creating Optional Picture Codes

Pictures are excellent for maintaining data uniformity but occasionally may be too confining. Paradox provides a method for indicating that certain portions of the picture are optional. Just enclose the codes within brackets ([ ]). Paradox then uses the portion of the picture that is within the brackets only if you type a character that matches the portion's first character or you press the space bar.

For instance, you may want to provide a picture for a telephone number field that accounts for the possibility of an area code and a three-digit extension but doesn't force the entry of either in every case. The picture for such a field is *[(###)]###-####[/###]*. With this picture, the following phone numbers would all be acceptable:

(222) 333-3333
452-3449/123
989-7721
(703) 555-3321/876

Providing Alternatives

Another useful picture feature is the capability to limit the entry of data to a certain group of alternatives. This feature is similar in effect to the validation feature, but more flexible. To provide alternative pictures codes, separate them with commas. When each alternative includes more than one character, enclose all alternatives in braces ({ })

For example, the metropolitan Washington, D.C., area includes three area codes: 301, 703, and 202. You can limit phone numbers to numbers with these three area codes by using the picture *({301,703,202}) ###-####*. Then, whenever you enter *(3* in the field, Paradox automatically adds *01)* to complete the first alternative. If you type *(7*, Paradox adds *03)*; and if the first characters you type in the field are *(2*, Paradox finishes with *02)*. Paradox does not allow any other area code, and beeps if you try to enter one. But after the area code is entered, you can type any exchange and phone number. Paradox automatically fills in the hyphen.

If you want to use the picture statement, but two of the list choices start with the same letter, you can "embed" the braces. For example:

{J{an,uly},March,Apr}

Because January and July both start with J, Paradox waits for more characters to qualify it. Otherwise, the program takes the first occurrence of J.

Specifying a Required Field

In nearly every database table, at least one field contains essential information. Certainly data should be entered in every key field. Otherwise, you may not be able to identify reliably and retrieve the data in your table. Paradox provides a validation tool that you can use to force some type of entry in a given field.

To specify that a certain field must contain some type of entry, press F10 (Menu) from either Edit or DataEntry mode, and select **V**alCheck **D**efine. Move the cursor to the target field and press Enter. Then choose **R**equired **Y**es. Paradox displays the message `Required status recorded`. If you attempt to leave this field blank, Paradox informs you that `A value must be provided in this field`, and refuses to leave the field. You should always add this validity-check option to key fields.

Clearing Validity Checks

Paradox provides a number of ways to clear validity checks. You can undo or modify most of the options described in the previous sections by following essentially the same steps used to create them. For example, to remove the required status set on a field, press F10 (Menu) and select **V**alCheck **D**efine. Indicate the appropriate table, and choose **R**equired **N**o.

Another more generic method of removing validity checks is through the **C**lear option. From either Edit or DataEntry mode, press F10 (Menu) and select **V**alCheck **C**lear. You then have two choices: **F**ield and **A**ll.

To clear the validity checks from just one field, select **F**ield. Move the cursor to the field whose validity checks you want to remove, and press Enter. Paradox removes all validity checks from the field and displays the message `Validity checks removed from field`.

You can clear the validity checks for all fields at once by selecting **A**ll. Paradox then informs you that `All validity checks removed, deleting .VAL file...`.

Entering and Editing Data with Multitable Forms [3]

Chapter 8 described how to build multitable forms. It also introduced you to the concept of *referential integrity*. This chapter discusses how to use multitable forms for data entry and editing and explains how Paradox handles key violations with multitable forms. This discussion applies only to Paradox 3.0.

Using DataEntry Mode with Multitable Forms

Once you have built a multitable form, you can use it to enter data in DataEntry mode. From the Main menu, choose **M**odify **D**ataEntry and indicate the name of the master table. Paradox displays a blank record in table view and DataEntry mode. Then press F10 (Menu), select **I**mage **P**ickForm, and choose the appropriate multitable form. Paradox displays the empty form.

Don't forget that you can assign the multitable form as the preferred form. Either rename it to *F* or use **P**ickForm and then **K**eepSet from the Image menu while in Main, Edit, or CoEdit mode. After you do so, you can press F7 (Form Toggle) to display the multitable form. (The **P**ickForm and **K**eepSet options on the Image menu are discussed in Chapter 3.)

To make your system even easier to use, assign to a keyboard macro the keystrokes that display your multitable form in a data-entry mode. (For more information on keyboard macros, refer to Chapter 6.)

Entering Data

Enter data in the same manner you do in single-table forms, but move between master and detail forms with F3 (Up Image) and F4 (Down Image). When you have finished entering data in one transaction and want to move to the next, make sure that the cursor is back in the master table portion of the form, and press PgDn. If you press PgDn in another portion of the form, Paradox just beeps. Press F2 (DO-IT!) when you're finished.

Notice that when you are in a detail portion of the form, Paradox reminds you of the master-to-detail table relationship by placing a message in the top line of the screen. The message reads `(1-M Group)` for one-to-many relationships (see fig. 9.5), `(1-1 Group)` for one-to-one relationships, and `(Group)` for either many-to-one or many-to-many relationships.

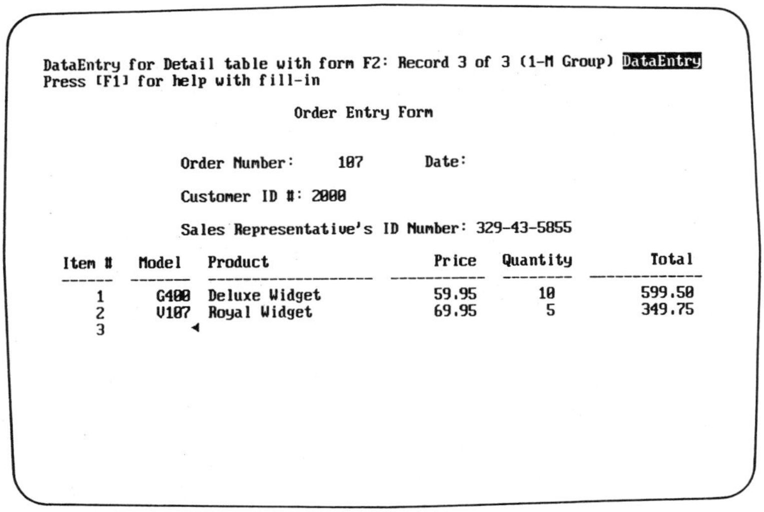

Fig. 9.5.
Entering data into a one-to-many multitable form.

Paradox places the following restrictions on data entry in *linked* multitable forms:

- Once you start entering data in a linked multitable form, Paradox *link locks* the tables, which simply prohibits you from entering data in table view during the current DataEntry session. Pressing F7 (Form Toggle) displays the master table in table view with the message `(Link Locked)` in the top line of the screen. Paradox requires that you return to the multientry form to continue data entry. Press F7 again, and continue. Note that you can start DataEntry mode in table view and switch to form view, but you can't switch back.

- For multitable forms in which the master-to-detail relationship is one-to-many or one-to-one, you must enter a value in the field that links the master table to a detail table before you can enter data in the detail table. This step automatically enters the value in the detail table's link field for each of the records you add to the detail table.

- For multitable forms in which the master-to-detail relationship is one-to-many or one-to-one, you cannot delete a master record while linked detail records exist. This restriction is to preserve referential integrity. If you decide to delete a transaction while in DataEntry mode, you must first delete the detail records and then the corresponding master record.

Handling Key Violations

In DataEntry mode, Paradox adds data to your tables only at the end of your DataEntry session when you press F2 (DO-IT!). If Paradox finds key violations in any of the records at this time, it places them in several temporary tables named Keyviol, Keyviol1, Keyviol2, and so forth. To inform you of these key violations, the program displays the Keyviol tables along with another temporary table named List. The List table shows which table in your form corresponds to each temporary Keyviol table (see fig. 9.6). You can then correct the offending records through Edit or CoEdit and use the **F**ormAdd option on the Tools More menu to add the records to their respective tables. (Chapter 13 discusses how to use the FormAdd operation.)

Using DataEntry on a Network

As described in Chapter 3, when you select **D**ataEntry on a network, Paradox places a *prevent full lock* on the table. In other words, no other network user can set a lock that requires exclusive use of the database. If a full lock is already in place on the shared table, Paradox does not let you begin a DataEntry session until the other user finishes the operation that required a full lock.

Using DataEntry with a multitable form on a network is essentially the same as on a stand-alone system. You must, however, have at least entry rights to the master table and each of the detail tables.

In addition, when you attempt to complete your data-entry session with F2 (DO-IT!), Paradox places a *prevent write lock* on the target table. No other user can write to the table until your new records have been added to the master table and detail table(s). If another network user has already placed a write lock on one of these tables, however, you either must wait until the other user is finished, or use the **K**eepEntry option on the DataEntry menu. KeepEntry temporarily saves the master and detail Entry tables to disk in a series of temporary tables named Entry, Entry1, Entry2, Entry3, and so forth. The program ends the DataEntry session and returns to the Main mode work space. No changes are made to the master table or detail table(s). You can later use the **F**ormAdd option from the Tools More menu (discussed in Chapter 13) to add the Entry records to the target tables.

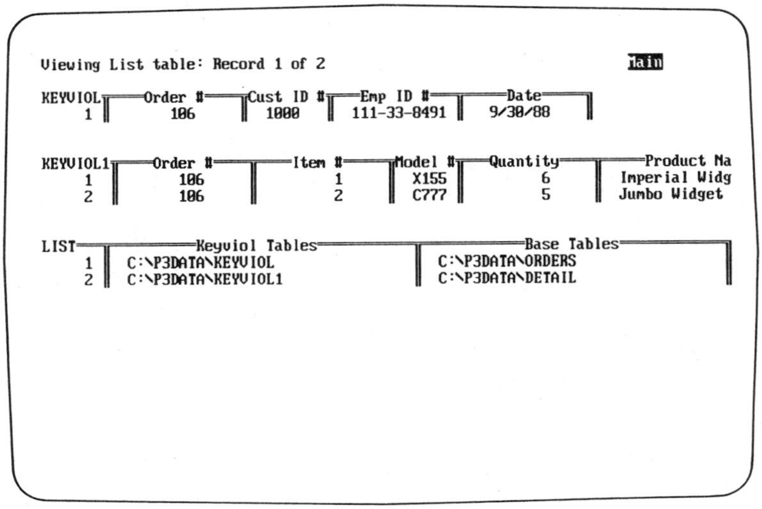

Fig. 9.6.

Handling key violations in a multitable form.

You can rename these Entry tables in the meantime to guard against their being accidentally overwritten or deleted before you can add them to their respective target tables. The **F**ormAdd command, however, is easiest to use if you do not rename the Entry tables because the command contains an option for adding data from Entry to target tables (see Chapter 13).

Using Edit Mode with Multitable Forms

You have three ways to begin Edit mode with a multitable form:

- *The menu method*. From the Main menu, select **M**odify **E**dit and specify the master table. Once the master table is displayed in Edit mode, use the **P**ickForm option from the Image menu to select the appropriate multitable form. Paradox then displays the multitable form in Edit mode.

- *Edit key method 1*. Use the **V**iew option on the main menu to view the master record. Then press F9 (Edit), and use the Image menu's **P**ickForm option to select the multitable form.
- *Edit key method 2*. Use the **V**iew option on the main menu to view the master record. Next, choose the **P**ickForm option from the Image menu to select the multitable form. Finally, press F9 (Edit).

Entering and Editing Data

When you are working with linked tables, the same basic restrictions listed in the preceding discussion of entering data with DataEntry mode apply to Edit mode as well.

Once you start entering or editing data in a linked multitable form, Paradox *link locks* the tables to prohibit you from entering or editing data in table view during the current Edit session. If you begin changing or adding to a table in table view, Paradox does not permit you to switch to a linked multitable form view to continue editing.

If the master-to-detail relationship in the form is one-to-many or one-to-one, you must enter a value in the field that links the master table to a detail table before you can enter data in the detail table. Paradox then automatically enters the value in the detail table's link field for each of the records you add to the detail table. Similarly, if you change a link field value in the master table, all corresponding values in the detail table(s) are automatically changed also.

If the master-to-detail relationship is one-to-many or one-to-one, you cannot delete a master record while linked detail records exist. You must first delete the detail records so that referential integrity is maintained.

Caution: Paradox automatically enforces referential integrity only when you use properly linked one-to-one or one-to-many multitable forms. In other words, you can intentionally or *unintentionally* delete a master record *without* first deleting detail records if you are not using one of these special multitable forms. You thus create "orphan" detail records.

Using Edit on a Network

Paradox automatically places a *full lock* on shared tables whenever you access them in Edit mode. No other user can use the table until you finish your Edit session. Conversely, Paradox does not permit you to use Edit mode on a table that is already in use by any other user on the network. For both of these reasons, you should use CoEdit rather than Edit when editing shared network tables.

Using CoEdit Mode with Multitable Forms

The same restrictions discussed in the preceding section on Edit mode apply to using CoEdit mode with multitable forms, with one distinction. Paradox does permit you to begin making changes or additions in table view and continue after switching to multitable form view. But if you switch back to table view while in the same CoEdit session, you can only "look" and aren't permitted to do any editing. This limitation protects the internal consistency of your data. Similarly, once you have started coediting with a multitable form, another network user wanting to coedit any of the tables included in the form can only do so by using the same multitable form. Other users can still view the data in table view but can make no changes.

Before allowing you to toggle to table view, Paradox may prompt you to post explicitly (by pressing Alt-L) any changes you have made. You receive this prompt when you are coediting a shared table and another network user is using the table. Your changes need to be posted to the shared table before you switch to table view. When you start making changes to the record, Paradox places a lock on this record. Pressing Alt-L (lock toggle) releases the automatic lock and posts any changes to the shared table. This step updates the records on which you were working, so that other network users view current records.

When using CoEdit mode with a multitable form on a network, if you place a lock (press Alt-L) on one of the tables (master or detail), Paradox also places a lock on all other tables in the form. You can place a lock only if none of the tables is already locked.

Adding Data with the MultiEntry Option

The Paradox **M**ultiEntry option gives you the capability to enter data into what appears to be one table and have the information inserted into multiple tables. This capability is not the same as using multitable forms, although for most purposes you can use a multitable form rather than **M**ultiEntry to accomplish the same result.

Using **M**ultiEntry requires that you first create a *source* table and a *map* table. The source table is equivalent to the Answer table created by a query, but used in reverse. Rather than join tables—the purpose of a query—a source table holds the data that is to be entered in other tables. You enter data into the source table, and then Paradox distributes the data among two or more tables. The purpose of the map table is to specify how the data is to be distributed.

In many ways the **M**ultiEntry feature has been superseded in Paradox 3.0 by the multitable form capability, particularly for one-to-many relationships. **M**ultiEntry is still useful, however, for breaking up large tables into smaller, more manageable tables without losing the convenience of single-form data entry. The Personal Programmer, introduced in Chapter 14, also makes special use of the source and map tables created by the **M**ultiEntry **S**etup operation. If you are a Paradox 2.0 user, you may find that the unique key-violation approach of **M**ultiEntry allows you to handle one-to-many relationships with a single data-entry form.

Creating Source and Map Tables

The first step in using **M**ultiEntry is to create the source table and the map table. A normal Paradox table, the source table is made up of fields from two or more target tables. Once you have constructed the source table, you can use it in table view or standard form view and can even design custom forms for it. But this table will never hold data. Instead, the source table is used to funnel data to the target tables.

The map table is also a Paradox table but has only three fields: Source Field, Target Field, and Target Table. Each record in the map table determines which target field and table is fed by a particular field in the source table.

To create the source and map tables to allow simultaneous data entry into a particular set of target tables, first create a query with the following properties:

- ❑ The query statement must include each of the target tables.
- ❑ Every field must contain an example element, a check mark, or both—and nothing else.
- ❑ One and only one field in each group of fields linked by a particular example element should have a check mark.
- ❑ Example elements can be used only once per query form.

Suppose, for example, that you have created a new table called Payroll, which includes the fields Emp ID #, Date Hired, Dependents, Salary, and Department. You have moved the last four fields and their data from the Employee table. Emp ID # provides a link between Payroll and Employee. The two tables have a one-to-one relationship. So that you can enter all the employee information from one form, you want to create multientry source and map tables. The appropriate query for this example is shown in figure 9.7.

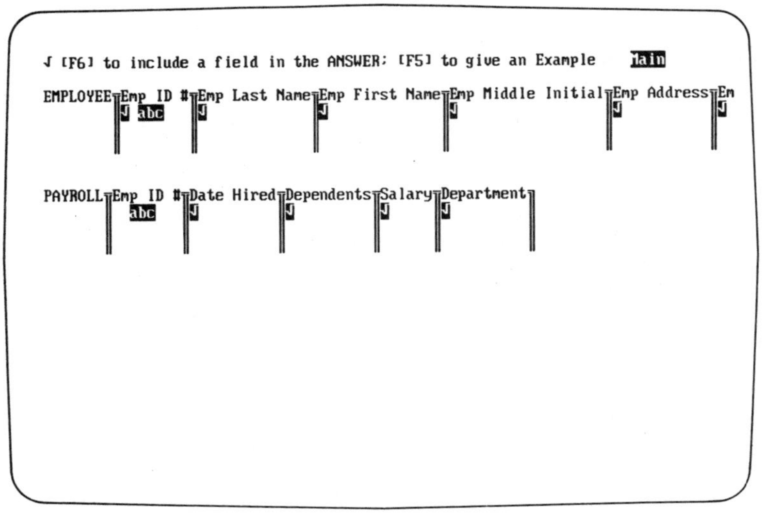

Fig. 9.7.

Building a query for use with MultiEntry.

Next, with the query statement in the work space, press F10 (Menu) and select **M**odify **M**ultiEntry **S**etUp. Paradox prompts you for the name of a source table. Type a unique name for the source table and press Enter. At the next prompt, type a name for the map table and press Enter again. Paradox then automatically builds both the source and map tables based on the query you created (see fig. 9.8). Epmap is the map table, and Emppay is the source.

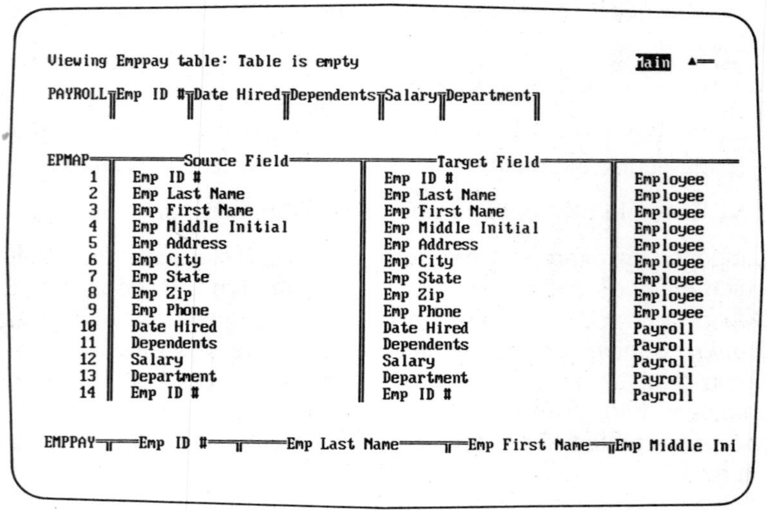

Viewing Emppay table: Table is empty
Main
PAYROLL Emp ID # Date Hired Dependents Salary Department
EPMAP Source Field Target Field
1 Emp ID # Emp ID # Employee
2 Emp Last Name Emp Last Name Employee
3 Emp First Name Emp First Name Employee
4 Emp Middle Initial Emp Middle Initial Employee
5 Emp Address Emp Address Employee
6 Emp City Emp City Employee
7 Emp State Emp State Employee
8 Emp Zip Emp Zip Employee
9 Emp Phone Emp Phone Employee
10 Date Hired Date Hired Payroll
11 Dependents Dependents Payroll
12 Salary Salary Payroll
13 Department Department Payroll
14 Emp ID # Emp ID # Payroll
EMPPAY Emp ID # Emp Last Name Emp First Name Emp Middle Ini

Fig. 9.8.

The source and map tables.

Entering Data

To use the source and map tables for entering data, select **M**odify **M**ultiEntry **E**ntry from the Main menu. Indicate the source table and the map table, and Paradox places you into what appears to be ordinary DataEntry mode (see fig. 9.9). At this point you enter data into the Entry table, as you normally do in DataEntry. But when you press F2 (DO-IT!) to end the session, Paradox uses the map table to determine how to split up the data you entered and place it in the correct target tables and fields. Figure 9.10 shows the record for Susan Carson entered in both target tables, Employee and Payroll. No records are added to the source table itself.

Caution: After you create the source and map tables, you can still use DataEntry, Edit, or CoEdit mode to add data to each target table separately. You may lose the logical one-to-one relationship with which you started, however, if you are not careful. In the Employee/Payroll example, you should be sure not to add a record to the Employee table without adding one to Payroll with the same Emp ID #.

You must also use caution when you edit the target tables, especially if you are making a change to the link field. Paradox does not provide a "**M**ultiEdit" option. If you change the link in one table, you must change the link in all the others, or the link is destroyed. And, just as important, you must not delete a record from one of the targets without deleting the corresponding record from all the other target tables. In essence, you have to maintain referential integrity on your own. If you use Paradox 3.0, using the multitable forms capability is a much better and safer choice.

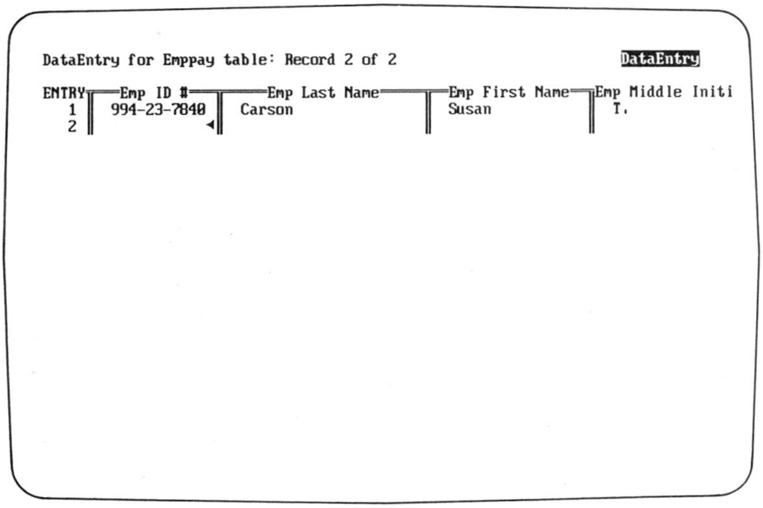
DataEntry for Emppay table: Record 2 of 2 DataEntry

ENTRY	Emp ID #	Emp Last Name	Emp First Name	Emp Middle Initi
1	994-23-7840	Carson	Susan	T.
2				

Fig. 9.9.

*Entering data into the source Entry table with **M**ultiEntry.*

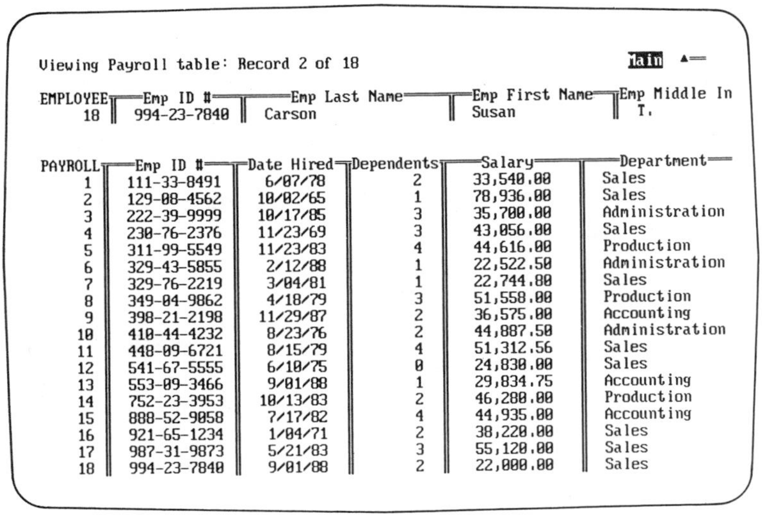
Viewing Payroll table: Record 2 of 18 Main

EMPLOYEE	Emp ID #	Emp Last Name	Emp First Name	Emp Middle In
18	994-23-7840	Carson	Susan	T.

PAYROLL	Emp ID #	Date Hired	Dependents	Salary	Department
1	111-33-8491	6/07/78	2	33,540.00	Sales
2	129-08-4562	10/02/65	1	78,936.00	Sales
3	222-39-9999	10/17/85	3	35,700.00	Administration
4	230-76-2376	11/23/69	3	43,056.00	Sales
5	311-99-5549	11/23/83	4	44,616.00	Production
6	329-43-5855	2/12/88	1	22,522.50	Administration
7	329-76-2219	3/04/81	1	22,744.00	Sales
8	349-04-9862	4/18/79	3	51,558.00	Production
9	398-21-2198	11/29/87	2	36,575.00	Accounting
10	410-44-4232	8/23/76	2	44,887.50	Administration
11	448-09-6721	8/15/79	4	51,312.56	Sales
12	541-67-5555	6/10/75	0	24,830.00	Sales
13	553-09-3466	9/01/88	1	29,834.75	Accounting
14	752-23-3953	10/13/83	2	46,200.00	Production
15	888-52-9058	7/17/82	4	44,935.00	Accounting
16	921-65-1234	1/04/71	2	38,220.00	Sales
17	987-31-9873	5/21/83	3	55,120.00	Sales
18	994-23-7840	9/01/88	2	22,000.00	Sales

Fig. 9.10.

The target tables.

Refer to Chapter 13 for a discussion of the **M**ultiAdd option on the Tools More menu. That option uses source and map tables created by **M**ultiEntry **S**etup to update records in multiple target tables. Also, take a look at Chapter 14, which introduces you to the Paradox Personal Programmer. The Personal Programmer uses source and map tables to produce a sort of "instant query" called a *multitable view*, which makes working with multiple tables easier in applications developed with the Programmer.

Handling Key Violations

The **M**ultiEntry feature of Paradox handles key violations a bit differently than does normal DataEntry mode. When you add records through DataEntry mode, and duplicate a key value, Paradox places the record containing the duplicate in the Keyviol table. The program follows this procedure without regard to the contents of the non-key fields in the offending record.

By contrast, when you enter a record with a duplicate key value during **M**ultiEntry, Paradox does not add the record to the Keyviol table if the record is an exact match of an existing record. That is, when every field in the new record matches every field in an existing record, the new record is not considered a key violation. But neither is the record added to the target table. Instead, the new record is "absorbed" into the existing record, enabling you to use **M**ultiEntry when a one-to-many relationship exists between target tables. But you would also have to do a lot of redundant typing. For example, if you used **M**ultiEntry to enter data into the target tables Orders and Detail, and then receive an order for five different widget models, you would have to enter the master order data five times.

When a key violation does occur—when non-key values do not exactly match—Paradox places the record in the temporary table Keyviol. You then need to correct the error, rename the Keyviol table with the **R**ename option from the Tools menu, and use **M**ultiAdd to insert the record into the target tables (see Chapter 13).

Using MultiEntry on a Network

When you select **M**ultiEntry on a network, Paradox places a *write lock* on the table. In other words, other network users can use the target tables but cannot change their structures or contents. If a full lock or prevent write lock is already in place on one of the shared target tables, Paradox does not let you begin the **M**ultiEntry session until the other user finishes the operation that required the lock.

As soon as you attempt to complete your data-entry session by pressing F2 (DO-IT!), Paradox places a *prevent write lock* on each of the target tables. No other user can write to the tables until your Entry table records have been added to the various target tables. You may get a message, however, that a file is locked. That message indicates that another user is performing some operation with a shared table and has placed a write lock on the file. You either have to wait until the other user is finished, or use the **K**eepEntry option on the DataEntry menu. **K**eepEntry temporarily saves the current Entry table to disk and ends the session, returning to the Main mode work space. No changes are made to the target tables. You can later use the **M**ultiAdd option from the Tools More menu to add the records from Entry to the shared target files.

Sorting Tables

Paradox provides several methods for sorting records in your database. For keyed tables, Paradox stores records sorted in ascending order by the key field(s). If you are satisfied with that sort order, you need do nothing but add data to the table. You may decide, however, that you want to see your data in a different order in your report. As mentioned in Chapter 5, Paradox automatically sorts data when you use the group band features. But perhaps your table is not keyed, or perhaps you want to work with a table that has data stored in a different sorted order. Paradox provides the **S**ort option on the Modify menu for these purposes.

To sort a table, access the Main menu and select **M**odify **S**ort. Then indicate the name of the table you want to sort. When the table is not keyed (has no key fields assigned), Paradox displays these choices:

Same. Paradox replaces the current contents of the table with the data sorted into the new order.

New. Paradox creates a new table to contain the sorted version of the table. Once you choose this option, Paradox prompts you for a table name.

For keyed tables, replacing the current table contents wouldn't make sense, because the key fields control record order. In that case, Paradox just asks you for a name for the new sorted table. If you supply a name that already exists, Paradox warns you and gives you a chance to back up and change the name (**C**ancel), or to go ahead and **R**eplace the existing table with the new one.

Next, Paradox displays a sort form that resembles the standard input form for the table. To indicate the order in which records should be sorted, you place numbers to the left of the appropriate field names. By adding the letter *D* after the sort number, you tell Paradox to sort in descending order by the indicated field.

For example, to sort the Customer table in order by Cust State, Cust City, Cust ZIP, and Company Name into a new table named Custsort, the sort form would look similar to figure 9.11. Once you have indicated the sort order you want, press F2 (DO-IT!). Paradox sorts the records, and places them in the table you indicated (see fig. 9.12). ***Note:*** For purposes of illustration, the fields in Custsort have been rotated to show all the sort fields on-screen. Paradox does not rearrange the fields during a sort, just the records.

Unless you specify descending order by adding the letter *D* after the sort number, Paradox sorts in ascending order. Ascending order for N, $, and S numeric fields is from lowest number to highest. For alphanumeric (A) fields, ascending order is in the default alphabetic sort order. (Refer to Chapter 14 of the *Paradox User's Guide* for instructions on changing the way Paradox sorts data.) Ascending order in date (D) fields is from earliest date to latest date.

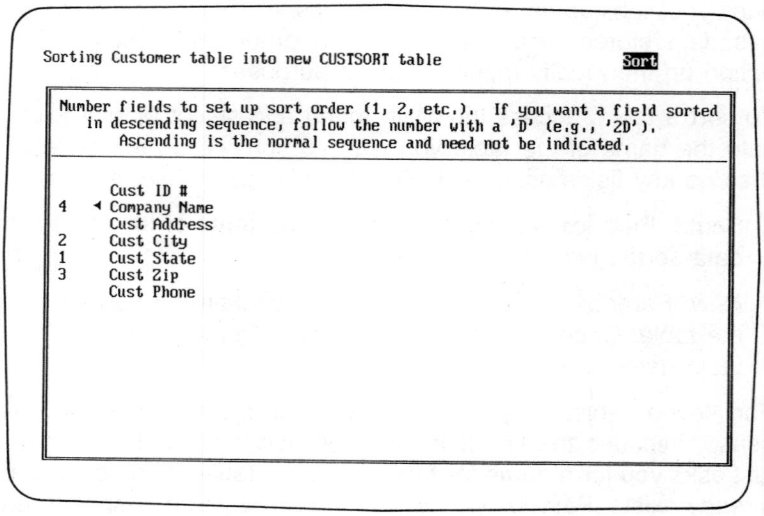
Sorting Customer table into new CUSTSORT table
Sort
Number fields to set up sort order (1, 2, etc.). If you want a field sorted
in descending sequence, follow the number with a 'D' (e.g., '2D').
Ascending is the normal sequence and need not be indicated.
Cust ID #
4 Company Name
Cust Address
2 Cust City
1 Cust State
3 Cust Zip
Cust Phone

Fig. 9.11.

The sort form.

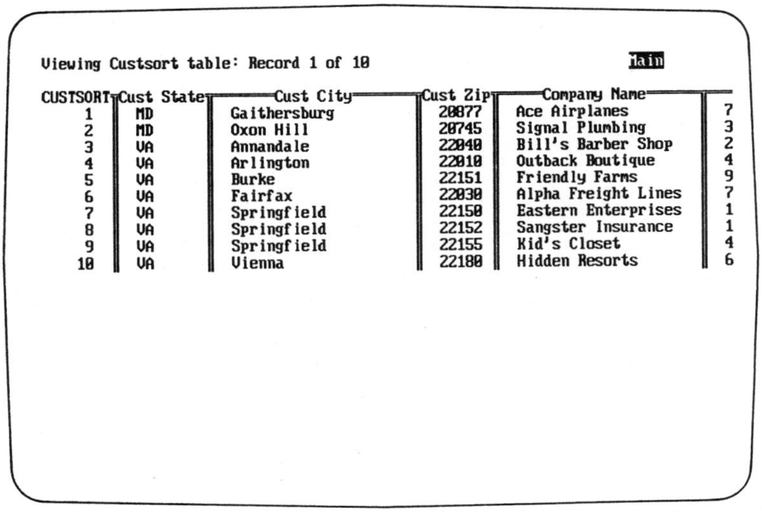
Viewing Custsort table: Record 1 of 10 Main

CUSTSORT	Cust State	Cust City	Cust Zip	Company Name	
1	MD	Gaithersburg	20877	Ace Airplanes	7
2	MD	Oxon Hill	20745	Signal Plumbing	3
3	VA	Annandale	22040	Bill's Barber Shop	2
4	VA	Arlington	22010	Outback Boutique	4
5	VA	Burke	22151	Friendly Farms	9
6	VA	Fairfax	22030	Alpha Freight Lines	7
7	VA	Springfield	22150	Eastern Enterprises	1
8	VA	Springfield	22152	Sangster Insurance	1
9	VA	Springfield	22155	Kid's Closet	4
10	VA	Vienna	22180	Hidden Resorts	6

Fig. 9.12.
The result of the sort.

Chapter Summary

This chapter has introduced you to some of Paradox's most powerful data-entry and editing capabilities, including validity checks; the use of multitable forms for DataEntry, Edit, and CoEdit modes; the **M**ultiEntry feature; and the Paradox **S**ort option. Through the use of these features and those you learned in previous chapters, you should be able to massage your database into perfect shape.

Once again, you are ready to turn to the topic of reports. The next chapter revisits tabular reports, discussed first in Chapter 5. Chapter 10 shows you everything you need to know to create beautiful printouts of your data in tabular format. Chapter 11 then turns to creation of the most flexible type of report, the free-form report.

10

Creating Tabular Reports

For most database applications, the primary purpose of collecting data in the first place is to be able to produce a document, schedule, invoice, list, or some other type of report. Multitable queries and forms are great, but you need to be able to control precisely how your data is printed out. Chapter 5 introduced you to the fundamentals of creating reports with Paradox. This chapter takes up where Chapter 5 left off, covering all the finer points of creating tabular reports. Chapter 11 finishes the report-design story with a discussion of free-form reports.

Grouping Records in Tabular Reports

In Chapter 5, you learned the basics of how to use group bands to group records in tabular reports and put records in sorted order. This part of Chapter 10 covers creating group bands, creating multiple levels of group bands, removing group bands, and regrouping bands.

Creating a Group Band

Data often sends a clearer message when the data is organized in some meaningful way. Paradox enables you to group records in several ways by creating group bands. And the program establishes the location of a header and a footer for each grouping that you define.

Often the primary purpose of grouping records with group bands is to compute summary statistics at the end of each group. Creating summary fields and calculations is discussed fully later in this chapter. Another reason for creating a group is to insert blank lines at appropriate places to enhance readability. Once you define a group, you can easily ensure that at least one blank line accompanies each group by placing a blank line in the group header or footer.

To place a group band in the report specification, press F10 (Menu) and select **G**roup **I**nsert. You then must choose among these three options: **F**ield, **R**ange, and **N**umberRecords.

Grouping by Field

Select the **F**ield grouping choice to group records that happen to have the same value in a particular field. When you make this selection from the Group Insert menu, Paradox presents the list of available fields, including fields from lookup tables.

For example, you might want to group salaries from the Employee table by the Department field. If you choose **D**epartment as the name of the field on which to group, Paradox prints all employees from the same department one after another in a group, before proceeding to the next department. The entire report is sorted by the Department field in ascending order so that the Accounting department and the Administration department print before Production and Sales. (***Note:*** You don't have to include in the report the field that establishes the group—in this case the Department field.)

Once you have chosen the field, position the cursor above the table band and below any page header that you may have established, and press Enter. Paradox marks the top edge of the group band header with a horizontal line, a downward-pointing triangle, the word `group`, and the name of the field (see fig. 10.1).

The bottom edge of the group header is determined by the top edge of the table band (or the next group header—see the section on "Creating Levels of Grouping"). The bottom edge of the group footer line begins with an upward-pointing triangle, the word `group`, and the field name. The top of the group footer is marked by the bottom of the table band (or the bottom of another group footer).

You may want to place the field that determines the group in the group header rather than in the table band. Then, the value that all the group records have in common prints only once. For example, figure 10.1 shows the Department field placed in the group header for that field.

You can accomplish the same purpose by using the GroupRepeats option. Press F10 (Menu) and select **S**ettings **G**roupRepeats **S**uppress. When you use this feature, you can leave the field in the table band, and Paradox prints only the first occurrence of each different value.

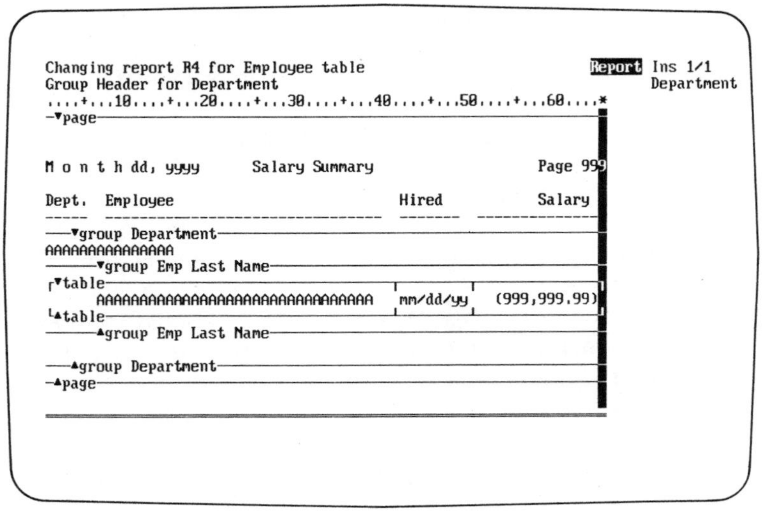

Fig. 10.1.

Inserting group bands to group by the Department and Emp Last Name fields.

Grouping by Range

Choose the **R**ange option to group records whose values in a particular field fall into a certain range. The sort order of the records is no different from when you group by field only. But the position of the header or footer, if any, does differ.

Paradox first asks the `Name of the field to group on`. Once you specify the field, you must indicate the range. Your response depends on the type of field you selected:

- ❏ When you select an alphanumeric field, Paradox asks for the `Number of initial characters in range`. You need to specify the number of initial characters in the field that must be the same in order for the field to be included in a grouping. For example, you might want all the products with model numbers beginning with a particular letter to be grouped. You would type *1* in response to the prompt.

- For numeric fields, Paradox asks for the `Size of range`. For example, to group employee records that fall within each $1,000 range ($0 to $999; $1,000 to $1,999; $2,000 to $2,999; and so on), you specify the number *1000*.
- If you select a date field, Paradox presents these choices: **D**ay, **W**eek, **M**onth, and **Y**ear. Select the increment of time you want Paradox to use for grouping records. For example, you may want to group employees by the year they were hired.

After selecting the field for grouping and specifying the range, position the cursor where the header should start, and press Enter. Paradox displays the header indicator and, below the table band, the footer indicator.

Grouping a Set Number of Records

Sometimes you just want to group a certain number of records, usually to make the report easier to read. For instance, you may find the data easier to read and comprehend if Paradox inserts a blank line every five records. Choose the **N**umberRecords option from the Group Insert menu, and Paradox prompts you to enter the number of records that it should include in each group. Then position the cursor where the group header should be placed, and press Enter. Paradox inserts the group header marker at the cursor, and inserts the footer marker below the table band. Paradox includes a blank line in the header and footer, leaving two blank lines between groups of records. If you want only one line, delete one with Ctrl-Y.

Creating Levels of Grouping

Chapter 5 mentioned that Paradox permits you to create up to 16 levels of grouping, sometimes called *breaks*, in a tabular report. Multiple group bands assume an order of priority determined by their positions in the report specification. The first group band listed in the report specification is given highest priority and is referred to as the *principal sort*. Paradox sorts the master table records in order first by the principal sort field, and then breaks any ties by looking to the other sort bands, in order.

The report specification shown in figure 10.1 has the Department field as the principal sort. If this field were the only group band, the records would be grouped by department, and the records for each department would be printed in the order in which they were entered into the Employee table (the master table). When you add the second group band (Emp Last Name), Paradox sorts the employee records within each department in ascending order by the employees' last names. Figure 10.2 shows the report generated by this specification.

```
Now Viewing Page 1 of Page Width 1
Press any key to continue...

 February 20, 1989      Salary Summary                    Page  1

Dept.  Employee                           Hired          Salary
-----  --------------------------------  -------   --------------
Accounting
       Brown, David E.                   11/29/87     36,575.00
       French, Freda P.                   9/01/88     29,834.75
       Harvey, Christopher P.             7/17/82     44,935.00

Administration
       Brown, Bruce R.                   10/17/85     35,700.00
       Plum, Hercule P.                   8/23/76     44,887.50
       Singer, Sarah S.                   2/12/88     22,522.50

Production
       Harrell, Stanley Q.                4/18/79     51,558.00
       Harrison, Steven M.               11/23/83     44,616.00
       Smith, Angel L.                   10/13/83     46,280.00

Sales
       Albertson, Sharon B.               3/04/81     22,744.00
```

Fig. 10.2.

The salary summary report.

You can combine the effects of the **F**ield, **R**ange, and **N**umber-Records grouping options. For example, even though you group records by department with the **F**ield option, you can also limit each grouping to five records by following the **F**ield group band immediately with a **N**umberRecords group band, indicating five as the number of records per group. The count starts over for each department. Just create no more than one header and footer for this pair of group bands.

Removing a Group Band

Sometimes you need to remove a group band from the report specification. Beware, however, that if you do, you also remove all fields that are placed in the group header or footer. To remove a group band, press F10 (Menu) and select **G**roup **D**elete. Move the cursor to the group band you want deleted (anywhere in the group band will do) and press Enter. Then confirm the deletion with **O**K. ***Warning:*** Paradox removes the group band and ***all its contents***.

Regrouping a Group Band

As you design your report, you may realize late in the game that you have used the wrong field for a group band. Or perhaps you decide that you want to create a range grouping rather than a grouping just by the field. In addition, suppose that you have already placed several fields and literals in the header and footer for this group, and you don't want to have to remove the group band and redefine it from scratch. Paradox provides the **R**egroup option for this very reason.

To select a different group field or grouping type, press F10 (Menu) and select **G**roup **R**egroup. Use the arrow keys to move the cursor to the group band that you want to regroup, and press Enter. Choose the correct grouping type and group field. Paradox redefines the group without deleting any existing literals or fields in the group header or footer.

Using Headers and Footers

As already explained in Chapter 5, a header in a Paradox report prints above the body (the fields in the table band), and a footer prints below the body. Paradox enables you to create many different headers and footers for your tabular report—as many as 19 distinct headers and 18 footers.

Using Report, Page, and Table Headers and Footers

Chapter 5 introduced you to the basic properties of report, page, and table headers and footers. The following paragraphs summarize that discussion:

- The report header prints once and only once at the beginning of the report. The report footer prints once and only once at the end of the report (before the last page footer).
- The page header prints at the top of each page, and a page footer prints at the bottom of each page.
- The table header prints at the top of each page, below the page header (but see the "Creating a Group of Tables or a Table of Groups" section later in this chapter).

Using Group Headers and Footers

You have certainly noticed that group bands also have their own headers and footers. A group header prints above each grouping of records, and the footer prints below the grouping. You typically locate summary computations in the footer. Group headers and footers print in the order listed in the report specification. The following rules define when group headers and footers print:

- All group headers print at the beginning of the report, in the order listed in the report specification.
- All group footers print at the end of the report, in the order listed in the report specification.
- Each group footer prints whenever its record-grouping condition is met and also when a higher-level footer prints.
- Each group header prints just after its corresponding group footer prints, except at the end of the report.
- Group headers print at the bottom of the page when a PAGEBREAK occurs in a lower-level footer (see the discussion of "Inserting a Page Break").
- Group headers print at the top of a page, below the page and table headers, if the group "spills over" to that page. You can suppress this spillover header by pressing F10 (Menu) and selecting **G**roup **H**eadings. Move the cursor to the group band, press Enter, and choose **G**roup. Paradox then prints the header only at the beginning of the group, not at the top of a spillover page.

Figures 10.3 and 10.4 should help you gain an understanding of the print order of headers and footers. Figure 10.3 shows a report specification with group headers and footers labeled, and figure 10.4 shows the resulting report.

Inserting a Page Break

The term *page break* is often used by word processing and other types of computer programs to mean "send a signal to the printer to eject the current page and start printing on a new page." Controlling the page breaks can be one of the simplest and yet sometimes most frustrating things about printing reports with multiple group bands.

Fig. 10.3.

A sample report specification with multilevel groups.

```
Changing report R5 for Employee table                                    Report Ins 1/1
Report Header
....+...10....+...20....+...30....+...40....+...50....+...60....*
Phone Roster                                                (Report Header)
-▼page-----------------------------------------------------------------
mm/dd/yy                                                      (Page Header)
--▼group Department----------------------------------------------------
 AAAAAAAAAAAAAAAA                               (1st Level Group Header)
------▼group Emp Last Name---------------------------------------------
                                                (2nd Level Group Header)
┌▼table----------------------------------------------------------------
 Employee                        (Table Header)  Phone
 --------------------------------------------    -------------
 AAAAAAAAAAAAAAAAAAAAAAAAAAAAAAAA(Body)          AAAAAAAAAAAAA
└▲table----------------------------------------------------------------
                                                (2nd Level Group Footer)
------▲group Emp Last Name---------------------------------------------
                                                (1st Level Group Footer)
--▲group Department----------------------------------------------------
                                               (Page Footer)   Page 999
-▲page-----------------------------------------------------------------
                                                          (Report Footer)
```

Fig. 10.4.

The report generated by the report specification in figure 10.3.

```
Now Viewing Page 1 of Page Width 1
Press any key to continue...
Phone Roster                                            (Report Header)
 2/21/89                                                  (Page Header)
 Employee                              (Table Header)  Phone
 ---------------------------------------------------   -------------
 (Accounting)                                  (1st Level Group Header)
                                               (2nd Level Group Header)
 David E. Brown                        (Body)      (703) 555-9812
                                               (2nd Level Group Footer)
                                               (2nd Level Group Header)
 Freda P. French                       (Body)      (703) 555-3322
                                               (2nd Level Group Footer)
                                               (2nd Level Group Header)
 Christopher P. Harvey                 (Body)      (703) 555-3298
                                               (2nd Level Group Footer)
                                               (1st Level Group Footer)

 (Administration)                              (1st Level Group Header)
                                               (2nd Level Group Header)
 Bruce R. Brown                        (Body)      (703) 555-4421
                                               (2nd Level Group Footer)
                                               (2nd Level Group Header)
 Hercule P. Plum                       (Body)      (703) 555-2987
                                               (2nd Level Group Footer)
```

As explained in Chapter 5, you can use the **L**ength option on the PageLayout menu to set the page length for your report. Paradox then uses this number to determine where page breaks should occur. Forcing a page break when a particular group changes, however, is a common practice. To cause Paradox to insert a page break whenever a group changes, type the word *PAGEBREAK* (in all uppercase letters) at the far left in the group's footer.

Caution: Typing *PAGEBREAK* in a footer causes the headers of higher-level groups to print at the end of the page before the page break. Therefore, either use PAGEBREAK only in the highest-level footer (see fig. 10.5); or, if you use PAGEBREAK in a lower-level footer, make sure that you leave higher-level headers blank.

For example, suppose that you want salary summaries for each department to be printed as separate pages. To accomplish this task, type the word *PAGEBREAK* in the footer for the Department group band, as shown in figure 10.5.

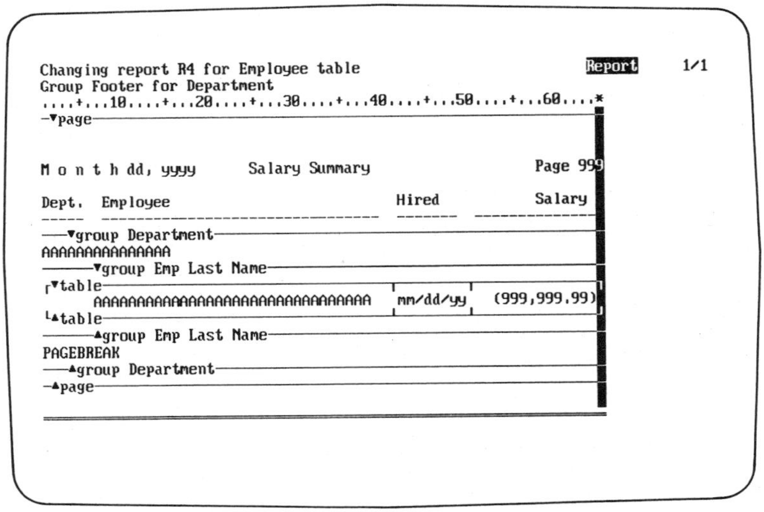

Fig. 10.5.
Using PAGEBREAK.

Creating Reports from Multiple Tables [3]

Just as you can create forms and queries from multiple tables, you can also create multitable reports. This Paradox 3.0 feature gives you a great deal of flexibility in how you design your database. Multitable reports enable you to divide your database into smaller, more manageable tables—so-called normalization—without losing the capability of creating reports that are based on any part of your data.

As you have seen in previous chapters, whenever you are working with several tables at once, a good understanding of table-to-table relationships helps. The terms *one-to-many*, *one-to-one*, *many-to-one*, and so on are defined in Chapter 2 and reviewed in Chapter 8. If they are not familiar to you, turn to these earlier discussions for a review before you proceed.

Choosing the Master Table

When you create multitable Paradox forms, you refer to the table that "owns" the form as the *master* table. The same is true with multitable reports. The first major step in designing a multitable report is to decide which table should be the master table. Your report becomes an object in the master table's family.

The tables that are linked into a multitable form are called detail tables. In report design, linked tables are called *lookup tables*.

Master and lookup tables must meet the following specifications before you can use them for multitable reports:

1. Each lookup table must be keyed. Every key field in a lookup table must have a corresponding field in the master table that has the same data type and will be used to link the tables logically. These linking fields in the master table do not have to be key fields.

2. All lookup tables must be linked *directly* to the master table. A field looked up from one lookup table cannot be used to generate another lookup.

3. The master-to-lookup relationship must be one-to-one, one-to-many, or many-to-one. Many-to-many relationships are not allowed.

4. You should select as the master table the table that has links to most other tables.

5. The master table records determine the contents of the report body. The body portion of the table band prints exactly one time for each record in the master table.

For instance, suppose that you want to print an invoice for each customer based on the data in the Orders and Detail tables. Assume that the structure of the tables in your database is as follows:

<u>Orders</u>		<u>Detail</u>
Order #	◄────────►	Order #
Cust ID #		Item #
Company Name		Model #

Cust Address
Cust City
Cust State
Cust Zip
Cust Phone
Emp ID #
Emp Last Name
Emp First Name
Emp Middle Initial
Date

Quantity
Product Name
Price
Cost

These tables are derived from the ones used as examples in previous chapters. During data entry, you look up the Product information you need for a report, and place that information in the Detail table by using the **T**ableLookup option on the ValCheck menu (see Chapter 9 for more information on **T**ableLookup). Similarly, customer and employee data are looked up from the Customer and Employee tables and stored in Orders. Orders and Detail are linked by the Order # field. Both tables meet the first four rules for creating multitable reports, but only the Detail table contains the information that should print as the body of the report. Detail is therefore the master table for a report to print an invoice.

Whenever you want to create a report from tables that have a one-to-many relationship, you nearly always use the many-side table as the master table. This approach is exactly the reverse of multitable forms in which the one-side table is usually the master table.

Beginning the Design of a Multitable Report

When you have determined the identity of the master table for the report, begin designing a report for this table. Follow the procedures outlined in Chapter 5 to start the Paradox Report Generator for tabular reports.

Once you have the standard specification on-screen, arrange the regular fields from the master table where you want them. For an invoice, you might delete the Order # field from the table band and place that field in a group band header that groups the records by the order number, as shown in figure 10.6.

Before you can place fields from a lookup table into the report, you must link the lookup table to the report specification.

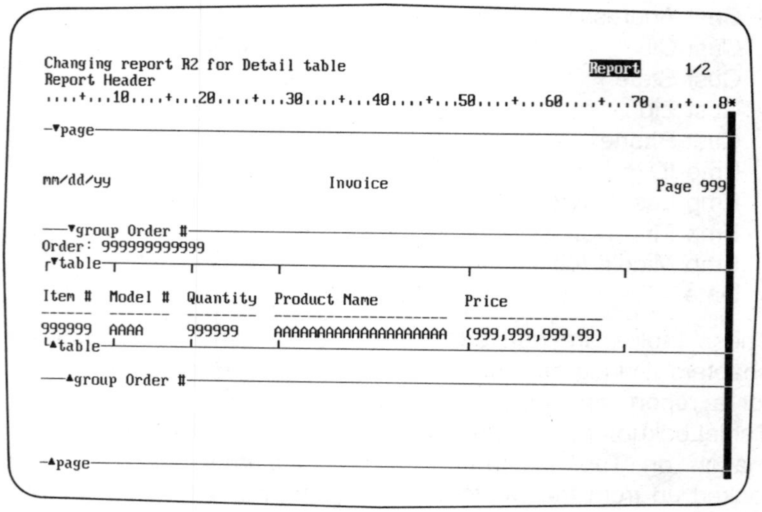

Fig. 10.6.

Grouping by order number in the invoice report.

Linking a Lookup Table

To link a lookup table to the report specification, press F10 (Menu) and select **F**ield **L**ookup **L**ink. Then indicate the name of the lookup table. Once you identify the lookup table, Paradox examines the lookup table structure and determines which field in the lookup table is the key field. The program then asks you which field from the master table is to be used to match the key field in the lookup table. (***Note:*** If the lookup table has a multifield key, Paradox asks for a matching master table field for each of the key fields.) In the invoice example, Order # is the name of the field in Detail that is used to match the key field in Orders.

Once you specify the link field(s), Paradox links the lookup table to the report specification, and the lookup table's fields are available for use.

Unlinking and Relinking a Lookup Table

As you design a report, you may change your mind about using a particular lookup table, or you may realize that you used the correct lookup table but the wrong link field. Paradox provides the **U**nlink and **R**elink options to help you correct either of these two errors.

To unlink a lookup table, press F10 (Menu) and select **F**ield **L**ookup **U**nlink. Then select the name of the lookup table from the displayed list. Paradox requires that you confirm the operation by selecting **O**K. Paradox then unlinks the lookup table from the report specification and removes any of the table's fields that you may have already placed.

When you discover that you made a mistake when specifying a link field but don't want to remove the link, use the **R**elink option. Press F10 (Menu) and select **F**ield **L**ookup **R**elink. Select the name of the lookup table whose link is mismatched. Then choose the correct link field from the list of master table fields. Assuming that you already placed looked-up fields on the report specification before discovering that the link field was wrong, this **R**elink option saves you the trouble of having to place these fields again.

Placing a Field from a Lookup Table

You will recall that the fields from the master table are normally referred to as *regular* fields. Once a lookup table is linked to the report specification for purposes of report design, the lookup table's fields are also considered regular fields. To place a linked field on the report specification, press F10 (Menu) and select **F**ield **P**lace **R**egular. Paradox displays the list of regular fields. In addition to the master table's fields, Paradox displays the name of the lookup table and the pointer symbol ->, enclosed in brackets (see fig. 10.7).

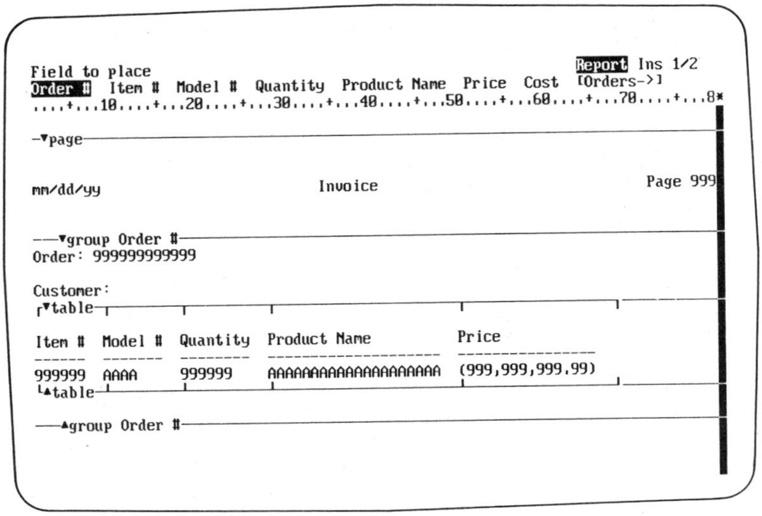

Fig. 10.7. *The list of regular fields, including the lookup table name.*

Move the highlight to the lookup table name, and press Enter. Paradox displays a new list of field names—this time the fields from the lookup table. The remaining steps are the same as with any regular field: select the field you want to place, indicate the proper position, and adjust field width.

Whenever the cursor is resting on a field from a lookup table, the field identifier in the upper right corner of the screen reminds you of the table name and field name. For example, the Company Name field from the Orders table is denoted by

```
[Orders->Company Name]
```

Creating Calculated Fields

Because they are treated as regular fields, you can use fields from lookup tables in calculated fields. When you type the field name, include both table name and field name in this format:

[table name->field name]

For instance, the formula to create a field that concatenates the Orders fields Cust City, Cust State, and Cust Zip is as follows:

[Orders->Cust City]+", "+[Orders->Cust State]+" "+[Orders->Cust Zip]

Remember that you must enclose alphanumeric constants in double quotation marks. Figure 10.8 shows the invoice report specification with regular fields and calculated fields from the Orders table placed in the group header area.

The calculated field containing the customer's name is the field to the right of `Customer:`. The formula for this field is shown at the top of the screen. The next field in the address block is the customer's street address. The third line is the calculated field whose formula was listed previously.

Creating a Group of Tables or a Table of Groups

Normally, Paradox prints the table header at the top of each page, just below the page header, even if multiple group headers print below the table header on a single page. Figure 10.9 shows this default format, which is called a *table of groups*.

```
Changing report R2 for Detail table                                    Report Ins 1/2
[Orders->Emp First Name]+" "+[Orders->Emp Middle Initial]+" "+[Orders->Emp Last
....+...10....+...20....+...30....+...40....+...50....+...60....+...70....+...8*
-▼page-----------------------------------------------------------------------------

mm/dd/yy                           Invoice                              Page 999

---▼group Order #------------------------------------------------------------------
Order: 999999999999

Customer: AAAAAAAAAAAAAAAAAAAA
          AAAAAAAAAAAAAAAAAAAA
          AAAAAAAAAAAAAAAAAAAAAAAAAAAAAAAAAA

Salesman: AAAAAAAAAAAAAAAAAAAAAAAAAAAAAAAAAAAAAAAAA

┌▼table─┬───────┬─────────┬──────────────────────┬────────────────┬──────────────
Item #  Model #  Quantity  Product Name           Price
------  -------  --------  --------------------   ----------------
999999  AAAA     999999    AAAAAAAAAAAAAAAAAAAA   (999,999,999.99)
└▲table─┴───────┴─────────┴──────────────────────┴────────────────┴──────────────
```

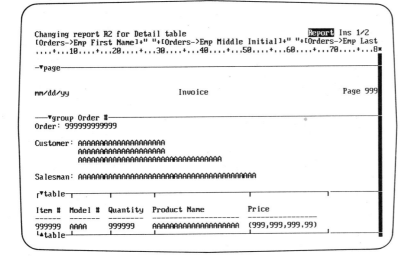

Fig. 10.8.

Placing a lookup calculated field.

```
Now Viewing Page 1 of Page Width 1
Press any key to continue...


 2/21/89                          Invoice                          Page    1


Item #  Model #  Quantity  Product Name           Price
------  -------  --------  --------------------   ----------------
Order:          100

Customer: Eastern Enterprises
          1211 Commerce St.
          Springfield, VA  22150

Salesman: Tim C. Bronson

     1  A333          50   Standard Widget                  39.95
     2  B107          25   Enhanced Widget                  49.95
     3  G400          10   Deluxe Widget                    59.95

Order:          101
```

Fig. 10.9.

Displaying the invoice report in the default format: a table of groups.

In either Paradox 2.0 or 3.0, you can cause the table header to print beneath the group headers, creating a *group of tables* rather than a *table of groups*. Press F10 (Menu) and select **S**etting **F**ormat **G**roupOfTables. Paradox displays the message `Settings changed` at the bottom of the screen. Figure 10.10 shows the result of this operation. Note that the table header prints beneath the group header.

Fig. 10.10.

After choosing ***S****etting* ***F****ormat* ***G****roupOfTables.*

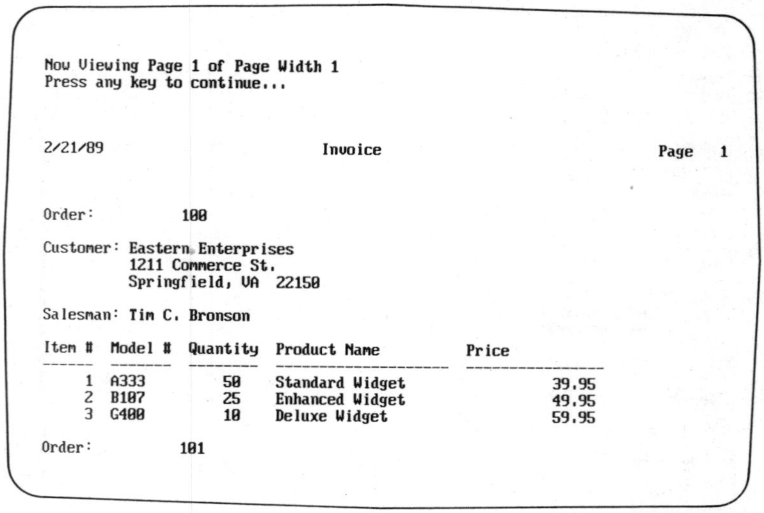

```
Now Viewing Page 1 of Page Width 1
Press any key to continue...


2/21/89                        Invoice                           Page   1


Order:          100

Customer: Eastern Enterprises
          1211 Commerce St.
          Springfield, VA  22150

Salesman: Tim C. Bronson

Item #  Model #  Quantity  Product Name          Price
------  -------  --------  --------------------  ---------------
     1  A333           50  Standard Widget                 39.95
     2  B107           25  Enhanced Widget                 49.95
     3  C400           10  Deluxe Widget                   59.95

Order:          101
```

Using Summary Operations

Frequently the purpose for grouping records with group bands is to perform summary computations on the groups. Paradox provides several ways to place summary fields on the report specification.

Placing Summary Fields

Whenever you have a numeric field (N, $, or S) in one of the tables of a report, you can create *summary fields* that compute certain statistics—using the sum, average, maximum, minimum, and count operators—on the values found in that field. For date fields you can compute average, count, maximum, and minimum. And for alphanumeric fields, you can choose between the count, high, and low operators. These computations are done across multiple records rather than on a single record. Calculated fields, by contrast, perform their computations on field values within the same record.

You can place a summary field anywhere in the report specification, but placing the field in a footer, below the field that is summarized, usually makes most sense. Note, however, that the summarized field does not have to appear in the report specification.

To place a summary field, press F10 (Menu) and select **F**ield **P**lace **S**ummary **R**egular. Select the field to summarize; then choose one of the available statistics. Paradox presents the choices **P**erGroup and **O**verAll.

When placing the summary field in a group footer, choose the first option —**P**erGroup. When you are placing the field in the report footer, select **O**verAll to summarize the field for every record in the body of the report. Then position the cursor where you want the summary field to be placed, press Enter, and adjust the field width. Paradox places the summary field in the report specification. Whenever the cursor rests on the field mask for the summary field, the field indicator displays a message that tells you the field name, the summary operation, and whether the field is per group or overall.

Returning again to the salary summary example, suppose that you want to see a total salary for each department. You therefore need to place in the footer for the Department group a summary field that computes the sum of the salary fields. Figures 10.11 and 10.12 show the report specification and the output.

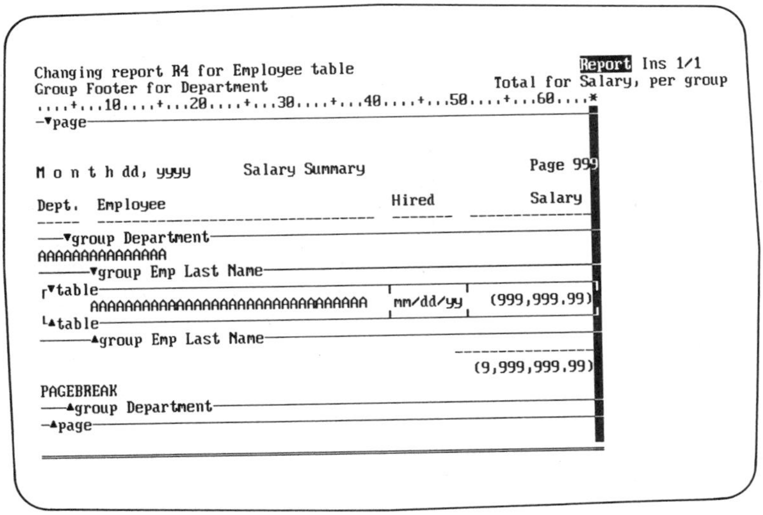

```
Changing report R4 for Employee table                          Report Ins 1/1
Group Footer for Department                              Total for Salary, per group
....+...10....+...20....+...30....+...40....+...50....+...60....*
-▼page
M o n t h dd, yyyy        Salary Summary                    Page 999
Dept.  Employee                              Hired         Salary
-----  ---------------------------------    -------  --------------
——▼group Department
AAAAAAAAAAAAAAA
————▼group Emp Last Name
▼table
    AAAAAAAAAAAAAAAAAAAAAAAAAAAAAAAAA   mm/dd/yy   (999,999.99)
▲table
————▲group Emp Last Name
                                                  ---------------
                                                  (9,999,999.99)
PAGEBREAK
——▲group Department
-▲page
```

Fig. 10.11.

Adding a summary field to total the salaries for each group.

Placing Summary/ Calculated Fields

In addition to summarizing regular fields, you can place *summary/calculated* fields to summarize calculations on fields. Again, you most often place these summary calculations in a footer below a corresponding calculated field. But the calculation being summarized does not have to appear in the report specification.

Fig. 10.12.

The report generated by figure 10.11.

```
End of Page
Press any key to continue...

 February 21, 1989      Salary Summary                Page  1

Dept.  Employee                            Hired          Salary
-----  ----------------------------------  -------  --------------
Accounting
       Brown, David E.                     11/29/87     36,575.00
       French, Freda P.                     9/01/88     29,834.75
       Harvey, Christopher P.               7/17/82     44,935.00
                                                    --------------
                                                       111,344.75
```

To place a summary/calculated field, press F10 (Menu) and select **F**ield **P**lace **S**ummary **C**alculated. Type the expression of the calculation to be summarized and then choose one of the available statistics. Choose between **P**erGroup and **O**verAll, and position and size the field.

For example, in the invoice report specification, you need to calculate Quantity times Price for each item, and then total the calculations for each order. Figure 10.13 shows the report specification after a calculated field that computes *[Quantity]*[Price]* is placed in the table band. A summary field is placed in the group footer to total this same calculation for all fields in each group. Figure 10.14 contains the resulting report.

Placing Calculated Summary Fields

A third type of summary field is the *calculated summary* field. It is basically just a more flexible alternative to the other two types.

To duplicate the effect of the regular summary field, you can create a calculated field that uses one of the following operators on a single regular field: sum, average, count, high, or low. (Calculated fields are discussed in Chapter 5.) You can apply these operators to a field or to any valid expression. Enclose the "argument" for the operation in parentheses. To apply the calculation to a group, add a comma and the word *group* within the

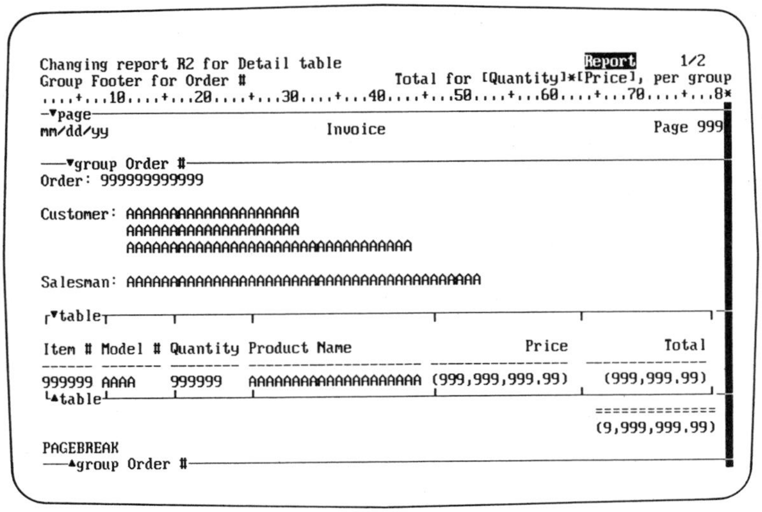

Fig. 10.13.

Creating a summary/ calculated field for totaling the orders.

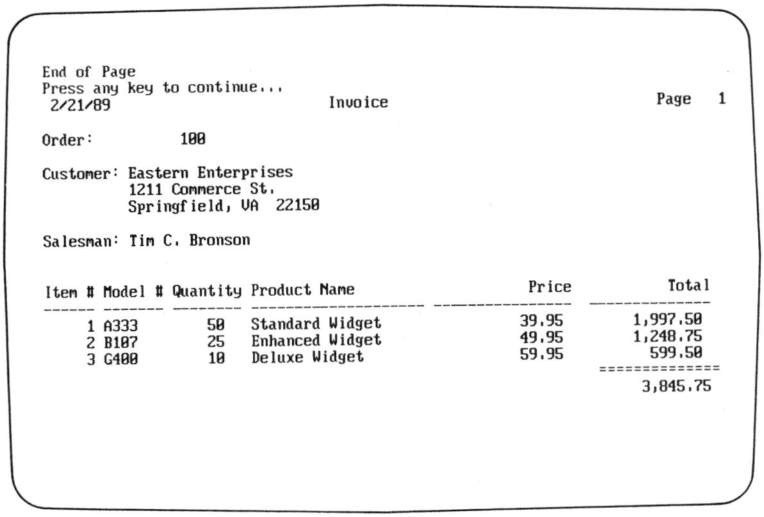

End of Page
Press any key to continue...
2/21/89
Invoice
Page 1
Order: 100
Customer: Eastern Enterprises
1211 Commerce St.
Springfield, VA 22150
Salesman: Tim C. Bronson
Item # Model # Quantity Product Name Price Total
1 A333 50 Standard Widget 39.95 1,997.50
2 B107 25 Enhanced Widget 49.95 1,248.75
3 C400 10 Deluxe Widget 59.95 599.50
==============
3,845.75

Fig. 10.14.

The report generated by figure 10.13.

parentheses. For example, in the salary summary example, you can total the Salary field with the expression

sum([Salary],group)

You can duplicate the summary/calculated field that computes the invoice total with the expression

sum([Quantity]*[Price],group)

This type of field is more flexible than the other two types of summary fields, because it permits you to combine several summary operations and to combine normal calculations with summary operations.

For example, you can add to the invoice a tax field that calculates a 4.5 percent tax, and a grand total that adds the tax to the total of quantity times price. The expression for the tax is

sum([Quantity]*[Price],group)*0.045

For the grand total, the expression is

sum([Quantity]*[Price],group)*1.045

Figure 10.15 shows the invoice report with these two calculated summary fields added.

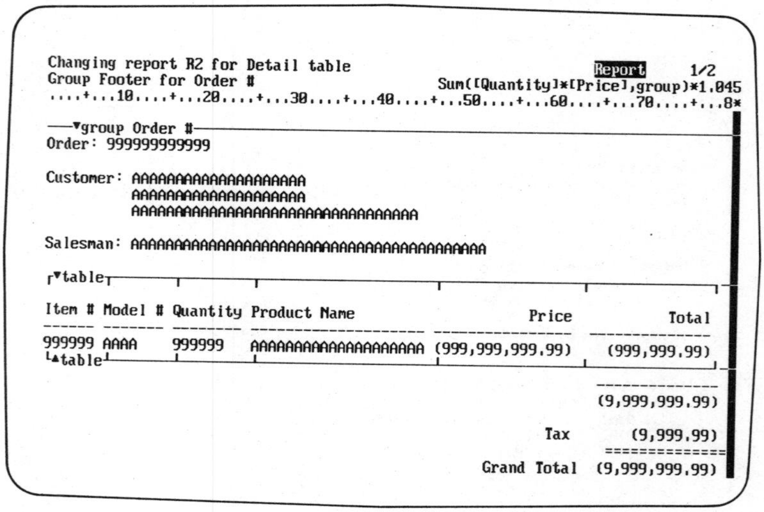

Fig. 10.15.

Creating a calculated summary field for figuring tax and a grand total.

Enhancing the Report

Paradox provides a number of features that help enhance the appearance of your report. You can automatically number the records in a report; place more than one field horizontally or vertically within a table band field; cause data within a report field to be left-justified, right-justified, or centered; and word-wrap text within a field.

Numbering Records in the Report

Occasionally you may decide that your report would be easier to understand if the records were numbered. To add record numbers to the report, press F10 (Menu) and select **F**ield **P**lace #Record. Then choose between **O**verall and **P**er-Group. Position the cursor where the field should be placed and press Enter. Select **O**verall to number records consecutively from the beginning to the end of the report. Choose **P**er-Group to number records consecutively, starting with 1 at the beginning of each group.

You might, for instance, want to number the employees in each department in the salary summary report. If you place the #Record field at the left end of the table band and choose the **P**er-Group option, Paradox automatically numbers the employees. You have to remove the Emp Last Name group band, however, or the count starts over whenever the Emp Last Name field changes (see fig. 10.16). (The #Record field is represented by `999` at the left end of the table band.) While the cursor is on this field, Paradox displays the message, `Current record number, per group` at the top of the screen.

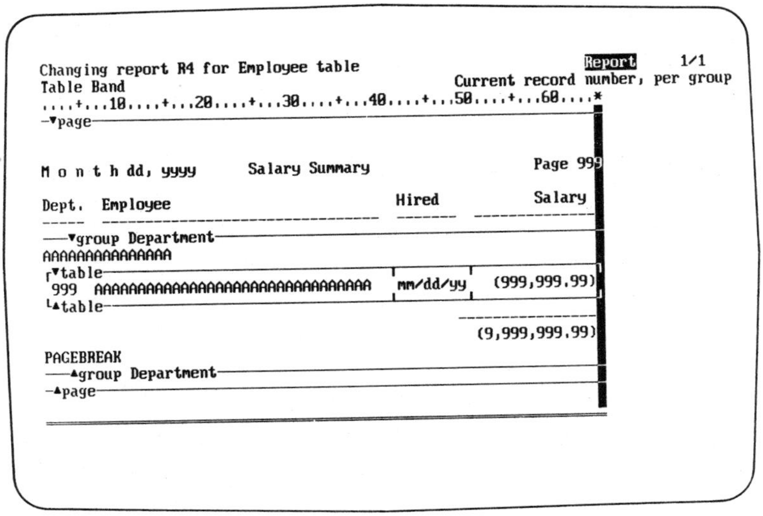

Fig. 10.16.
Numbering records.

Creating Multifield Columns

You have already seen that when you begin a new tabular report specification, Paradox creates a four-row table band. The first, second, and third rows make up the table header, and the fourth row is the report body. You are free to delete the table band's header rows, as in figure 10.16, and you can even delete the body row if all you need are summary computations that can be placed in group and report footers. (Chapter 5 explained how to insert and delete columns from the table band.)

In addition to deleting rows from the table band, you can insert new rows. This capability gives you the option of placing more than one field vertically in a table band column. (You can also place multiple fields horizontally in the same column, but you have no reason to insert multiple fields that way, because you can easily insert more columns.)

To insert a new row in the table band, turn on the Insert mode (press the Ins key), move the cursor to the bottom table band boundary line, and press Enter. Paradox inserts a blank line. Now you can place fields in this second body row. The two body rows together print once for each record in the master table.

Looking again at the employee phone list report, you might decide that you want to have each employee's address in the phone list, just below the employee's name. Figure 10.17 shows the phone list report specification with a second body row that contains a calculated field consisting of the Emp Address, Emp City, and Emp State fields. The resulting report is shown in figure 10.18.

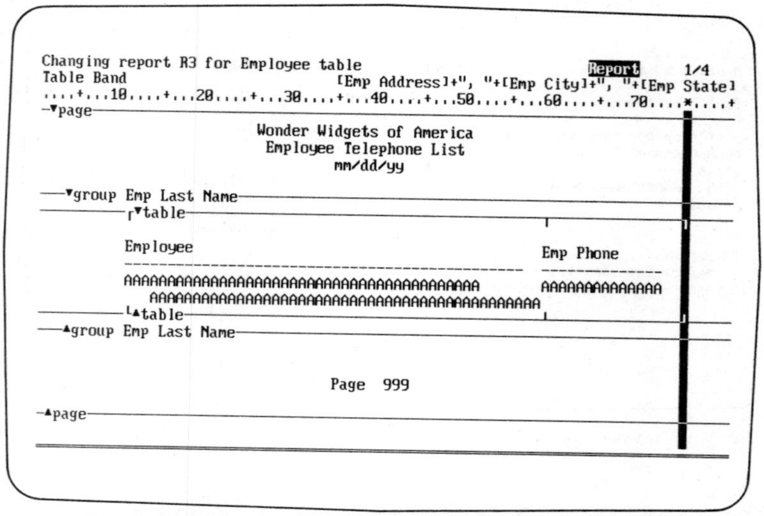

Fig. 10.17.

Adding another row to the table band.

```
Now Viewing Page 1 of Page Width 1
Press any key to continue...
                              Wonder Widgets of America
                               Employee Telephone List
                                       2/21/89


            Employee                                      Emp Phone
            ---------------------------------------------  --------------
            Sharon B. Albertson                           (703) 555-2361
               770 Shaw Rd., Apt 23, Arlington, VA
            Tim C. Bronson                                (703) 555-7630
               9828 Rocky Ridge, Centreville, VA
            Bruce R. Brown                                (703) 555-4421
               3451 Fox Lane, Arlington, VA
            David E. Brown                                (703) 555-9812
               16 Hounds Hunt, Fairfax, VA
            Susan T. Carson                               (703) 555-3434
               4252 Burbank St., Springfield, VA
            Gertrude M. English                           (703) 555-5575
               1681 School House Rd, Fairfax, VA
            Freda P. French                               (703) 555-3322
               1299 Houston, Apt G, Springfield, VA
            George H. Green                               (703) 555-9999
               872B S. Hill St., Mount Vernon, VA
```

Fig. 10.18.

The resulting report.

Altering Field Justification

Another fine-tuning adjustment you can perform on a report specification is *field justification.* When the value of a field in a Paradox tabular report is shorter than the field mask, Paradox has the choice of printing the value either *left-justified*, on the left side of the available space; *right-justified*, on the right side of the space; or *centered*. You don't normally have to assign justification explicitly. By default, fields are justified as follows:

- Numeric fields are right-justified.
- Alphanumeric fields are left-justified.
- Date fields in the format *M o n t h dd, yyyy* are left-justified. All other date formats always completely fill the field, so justification is not necessary.

To change the justification of a field, press F10 (Menu) and select **F**ield **J**ustify. Then move the cursor to the mask of the field to be affected, and press Enter. Finally, choose the alignment you want to use: **L**eft, **C**enter, **R**ight, or **D**efault.

Creating Word-Wrap Fields

When you're designing a report, one of the practical limitations that you should always be aware of is paper size. When you are limited to 8 1/2-inch-wide paper, you need to make sure that your report fits within that space. Paradox provides several options that affect the horizontal space used by your report. One of these options enables you to create alphanumeric fields that automatically continue onto subsequent lines when necessary. This feature is called *automatic word wrap* and is the counterpart to the word-wrap feature in Paradox forms, discussed in Chapter 8.

Normally you want to add the word-wrap feature to a field when one line of the report may not be enough space for all the data. To add the word-wrap feature to an alphanumeric field, press F10 (Menu) and select **F**ield **W**ord-Wrap. Position the cursor on the target field, and press Enter. Paradox prompts you to enter the `Number of Lines`. The number you enter here establishes the maximum number of lines per record Paradox will use to print data for this field. You can specify any positive whole number from 1 to 255. Type the number and press Enter. Paradox displays the message `Word wrap value recorded`.

Using this feature, you can reduce the horizontal space needed to display the Product Name field in the invoice report. The report that results after word wrap is added to the Product Name field is shown in figure 10.19.

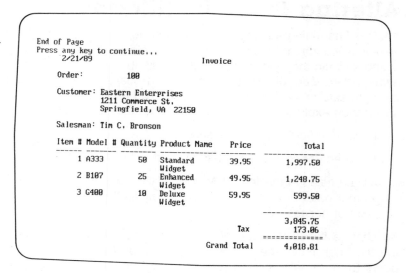

Fig. 10.19.

Using the word-wrap feature.

```
End of Page
Press any key to continue...
  2/21/89                          Invoice

    Order:         100

    Customer: Eastern Enterprises
              1211 Commerce St.
              Springfield, VA  22150

    Salesman: Tim C. Bronson

    Item # Model # Quantity Product Name    Price            Total
    ------ ------- -------- ------------- --------  --------------
         1 A333          50 Standard         39.95        1,997.50
                            Widget
         2 B107          25 Enhanced         49.95        1,248.75
                            Widget
         3 G400          10 Deluxe           59.95          599.50
                            Widget
                                                    --------------
                                                          3,845.75
                                             Tax            173.06
                                                    ==============
                                     Grand Total          4,018.81
```

Controlling the Printer

Ultimately, a report is useful to you only if you can create a permanent copy in the form of a printout. You therefore need to be able to use Paradox to set up your printer. Paradox enables you to control such things as the printer port to which the report is sent, a setup string to send to the printer before printing, and custom setup strings to be sent during the printout.

Choosing a Printer Port

By default, Paradox assumes that your report should print to the first parallel printer port, LPT1. If you never want to print to this port, you should use the Custom Configuration Program to change this default setting. To select another printer port for the current session only, press F10 (Menu) and select **S**etting **S**etup **C**ustom. Choose from among these ports: LPT1, LPT2, LPT3, COM1, COM2, and AUX. You may have to consult the user's manual for your computer to determine the appropriate port designation.

Once you choose the port, Paradox prompts you to supply a `Setup string`. The next section discusses the meaning of this message. To make no changes, just press Enter at the current setup string.

Controlling Printouts with the Setup String

In addition to making an assumption about the printer port, Paradox also assumes that you are printing on an IBM Graphics compatible printer in the normal character size and quality. In other words, by default Paradox sends ASCII text to the printer, preceded by no special printer setup string. Often this setup is adequate, but for special purposes or for wide reports you may want to add a setup string that causes your printer to switch to another type size and character spacing.

You have two ways to change the setup string. You can choose one of a number of predefined setup strings, or you can create your own string. To choose a predefined setup string, press F10 (Menu) and select **S**etting **S**etup **P**redefined. Then choose from among the predefined printer setup strings, which are listed in table 10.1. Choose the setup option that most closely matches your printer. In this list, the description `Small` means compressed print.

To specify the setup string on your own, or to edit an existing setup string, press F10 (Menu) and select **S**etting **S**etup **C**ustom. Select the proper port and then specify the setup string for your printer. You need to consult your printer manual for the appropriate setup code. These codes are often referred to as *escape codes* because they begin with the ASCII code for the Esc key. In constructing these codes, follow two rules:

1. Enter printable characters literally.
2. For nonprintable characters, use the ASCII equivalent code preceded by the backslash (\). For example, the ASCII code for the Esc key is 027. Any setup string using the Esc key must include the string *\027*. You can find the ASCII codes in Appendix C of the *PAL User's Guide*, included with your Paradox documentation.

Press Enter when you are finished typing the new setup string. Paradox saves the change with the settings for this table.

Table 10.1
Predefined Printer Setup Strings

Printer	*Predefined Setup String*
Standard Printer	(none)
Small-IBMgraphics	\027W \015
Reg-IBMgraphics	\027W \018
Small-Epson-MX/FX	\015
Small-Oki-92/93	\015
Small-Oki-192	\029
HPLaserJet	\027E
HP-Portrait-66lines	\027E\027&17.27C
HP-Landscape-Normal	\027E\027&l1O
*HP-Compressed	\027E\027(S16.66H
*HP-LandscpCompressed	\027E\027&l1O\027(s16.66H
Intl-IBMcompatible	\0276
Intl-IBMcondensed	\0276\015

*Paradox 3.0 only

Enhancing Specific Portions of Text

A third way to specify a setup string is to include it as a field in the report. Using this method, you can specify any number of setup codes in a report. For example, you can print headers in wide print but have the remainder of the report printed in normal text mode. To use this feature, place a setup string in a calculated field to the left of where the special print attribute should start. ***Note:*** These features do not cause text on-screen to show up in a different font or print size. Only the printout is affected.

Overriding the Print Settings

Normally Paradox uses the print settings stored with the report specification to print the report. Occasionally, you may want to print a report with a different setup string (e.g., to print in compressed type) or send the report to a different printer port, but not want to change permanently the print settings in the report specification. Paradox provides the **S**etPrinter option on the Report menu for that purpose.

To override the print settings stored with a report specification, before printing the report, from the Main menu select **R**eport **S**etPrinter **O**verride.

Paradox displays the following choices:

- **P**rinterPort. Use this option to choose a different printer port. The choices are LPT1, LPT2, LPT3, COM1, COM2, and AUX.
- **S**etup. Select this option in order to enter a new setup string.
- **E**ndOfPage. Choose this option to specify that the formfeed character should be used at the end of a page instead of a series of line feeds. This option may enhance the performance of certain laser printers.

To reset the printer settings so that Paradox uses the settings stored with report specifications, from the Main menu select **R**eport **S**etPrinter **R**egular. Reports printed after this command use the print settings stored with the report specification.

Chapter Summary

In this chapter, you have learned all the ins and outs of designing tabular reports, including grouping data; using group headers and footers; creating multitable reports; using summary operations to create summary, summary/calculated, and calculated summary fields; enhancing your reports by numbering records, adding rows, and wrapping fields; and controlling your printer so that you can produce your reports. Turn now to Chapter 11 to complete your report-writing knowledge by learning about free-form reports.

11

Creating Free-Form Reports

In Chapter 5, you learned report writing fundamentals, and in Chapter 10, you learned how to create more elaborate tabular reports. The third chapter about generating reports with Paradox, Chapter 11 shows you how to get the most out of the flexible Paradox *free-form* report generator.

Starting the Free-Form Report Generator

You begin a free-form report design session as you do a tabular report design session.

1. From the Paradox Main menu, select **R**eport **D**esign.
2. Specify the table for which you are designing the report, and choose a report name.
3. Fill in a description for the report. Paradox uses this description as a title in the page header of the free-form report. If you want, you can erase or change the description during report design.
4. Choose **F**ree-form.

Paradox displays the free-form standard report specification for the table with which you are working (see fig. 11.1).

Fig. 11.1.

A sample free-form report specification.

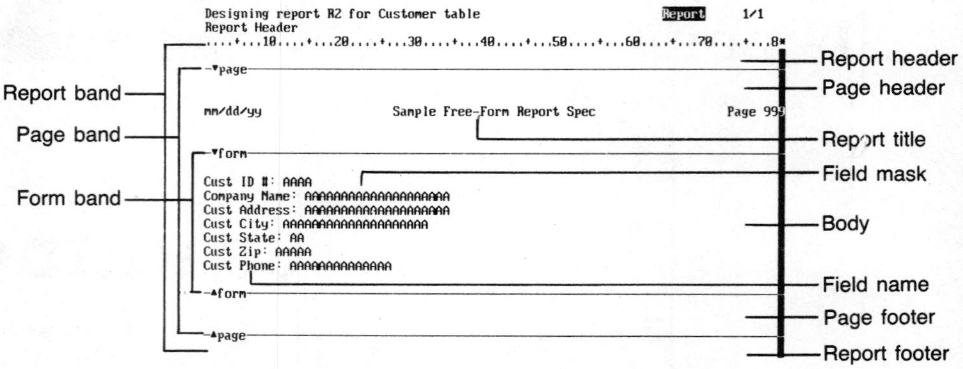

Examining the Standard Specification and the Form Band

The most obvious difference between a free-form report specification and a tabular report specification is the *form band* (see fig. 11.1). In free-form report specifications, the form band replaces the table band in tabular report specifications.

The form band looks like the standard input form f created by Paradox. The program places each field of the associated table in a separate line of the form band, preceded by the field's name as a literal. In operation, think of the form band as a column of a tabular report specification stretched out vertically.

When you finish designing the form, press F2 (DO-IT!) to save the form to disk. If you decide that you want to make changes to the specification, the steps are the same as described in Chapters 5 and 10.

Comparing Free-Form Reports to Tabular Reports

Most of what you have learned about report design also applies to designing free-form report specifications, including linking tables to create multi-table reports (Paradox 3.0 only). This chapter presents features unique to free-form design. The differences between free-form report specifications and tabular report specifications follow:

- *Field placement*. Fields placed in the form band are not limited to vertical columns as fields are in the table band of tabular reports. You can place regular, calculated, and looked-up fields anywhere in the form band.
- *Literal placement*. In free-form report specifications, you can type literals anywhere in the form band as if the band were a word processing screen. Each literal in the table band of a tabular report is associated with a particular field, must be placed above the field, and cannot straddle the boundary between table band columns.
- *Word and line squeeze*. In tabular report specifications, you create calculated fields to eliminate excess spaces between fields (e.g., [Cust First Name]+" "+[Cust Last Name]). When you use the Free-Form Report Generator, Paradox provides an easier way of *squeezing* unwanted spaces out of the form band. The program also enables you to squeeze excess blank lines out of the form band portion of the report.
- *Mailing labels*. The Paradox Free-Form Report Generator has a built-in mailing label feature. You design the layout for one label, and Paradox handles the behind-the-scenes work necessary to print multiple labels in one row. The tabular report specification format can handle only 1-across mailing labels.
- *Report Width*. The starting report width for a new free-form report specification is 80 spaces. Usually, the starting report width for a tabular report is larger because the report has to be wide enough to accommodate all fields horizontally. The maximum report width for both types of report specifications is 2000 spaces.

These differences make free-form reports ideal for generating mailing labels and short form letters.

Even with the special free-form design features, Paradox is not a match for most dedicated word processing and mail merge programs for creating lengthy mail-merge documents. Paradox's full-screen editing features are limited when compared to other programs. If your document is more than a page or two in length, consider using the **E**xport feature on the Tools/ExportImport menu to create a database file that can be used by your word processor or mail merge program (discussed in Chapter 13). Most of these programs can import or directly use one of the file formats that Paradox produces—1-2-3®, dBASE®, PFS®, or ASCII.

Squeezing Blank Spaces and Lines out of the Report

A common problem in report design is eliminating unwanted spaces between words. When you place field masks side by side and the data for the leftmost field does not fill the allocated space, unneeded blank spaces are left before the next field's value prints. Chapters 5 and 10 demonstrate how to solve the problem with calculated fields, but that method is cumbersome and requires you to type formulas to concatenate fields. You need a method to tell Paradox to delete excess spaces and to leave one space between fields. Paradox provides an option in free-form report design called *field squeeze*.

You also may want Paradox to delete blank lines from the form band. When you create mailing labels, for example, you do not want blank lines in the middle of a label. If some records have blank fields, however, blank lines can result.

Using Field Squeeze

To eliminate—*squeeze out*—extra spaces from between fields in the form band, press F10 (Menu) and make the following selections: **S**etting **R**emoveBlanks **F**ieldSqueeze **Y**es. Paradox displays the message `Settings changed`.

Figure 11.2 shows a free-form report specification for a letter to customers. (Note: This report is for the table Cust2, the Customer table with additional fields Title, Cust First Name, Cust Middle Initial, and Cust Last Name.) Compare the report output in figures 11.3 and 11.4. The first letter is the report output in the default condition. Paradox leaves blank spaces in the address block and in the body of the letter. Figure 11.4 is the same letter with the **F**ieldSqueeze option chosen. Notice that the extra spaces are gone.

```
Designing report R2 for Cust2 table                                Report     1/1
Page Header
....+...10....+...20....+...30....+...40....+...50....+...60....+...70....+...8*
-▼page
-▼form
                                    M o n t h dd, yyyy

AAAAAAAAAAAAAAA AA AAAAAAAAAAAAAAAAAAAA
AAAAAAAAAAAAAAAAAAAA
AAAAAAAAAAAAAAAAAAAA
AAAAAAAAAAAAAAAAAAAA
AAAAAAAAAAAAAAAAAAAA, AA  AAAAA

Dear AAAAAAAAAAAAAAA,

Wonder Widgets of America is proud to announce the Grand Opening of our second
showroom near your AAAAAAAAAAAAAAAAAAAA office:

     2121 Commerce St.
     Springfield, VA 22150

We invite you to attend our Grand Opening on March 1, 1989. Bring this letter
and receive an additional 10% off our already fantastic Grand Opening Sale
prices.
                                    Sincerely,
```

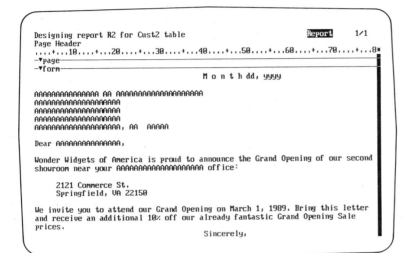

Fig. 11.2.

The free-form report specification for a form letter to customers.

Using Line Squeeze

Similar to the problem of excess spaces, you sometimes need to get rid of blank lines. Some of your customers may not have a title. Normally, the letter leaves a blank line in that position, as shown in figure 11.5. To delete excess lines, press F10 (Menu) and make the following selections: **S**etting **R**emoveBlanks **L**ineSqueeze **Y**es.

Paradox gives you two choices:

- **F**ixed. Choose this option when you are using continuous forms (page length C) and must account for every line. Paradox moves unneeded blank lines to the end of the form band, and total line count is not affected. Use this choice when building mailing labels.
- **V**ariable. Select this option when you want to use every available line and do not need all forms to be the same length. Paradox deletes unwanted blank lines but does not move them to the end of the form band.

Fig. 11.3.

The customer form letter before activating ***F****ieldSqueeze.*

```
Now Viewing Page 1 of Page Width 1
Press any key to continue...
                                        February 22, 1989

Wallace        M. East
President
Eastern Enterprises
1211 Commerce St.
Springfield      , VA  22150

Dear Wallace       ,

Wonder Widgets of America is proud to announce the Grand Opening of our second
showroom near your Springfield         office:

     2121 Commerce St.
     Springfield, VA 22150

We invite you to attend our Grand Opening on March 1, 1989. Bring this letter
and receive an additional 10% off our already fantastic Grand Opening Sale
prices.
                                        Sincerely,

                                        John Jones, President
```

Fig. 11.4.

The customer form letter after activating ***F****ieldSqueeze.*

```
Now Viewing Page 1 of Page Width 1
Press any key to continue...
                                        February 22, 1989

Wallace M. East
President
Eastern Enterprises
1211 Commerce St.
Springfield, VA  22150

Dear Wallace,

Wonder Widgets of America is proud to announce the Grand Opening of our second
showroom near your Springfield office:

     2121 Commerce St.
     Springfield, VA 22150

We invite you to attend our Grand Opening on March 1, 1989. Bring this letter
and receive an additional 10% off our already fantastic Grand Opening Sale
prices.
                                        Sincerely,

                                        John Jones, President
```

Figure 11.5 shows a blank line in the address block because the customer does not have a title. After selecting the **L**ineSqueeze option, the same letter prints without the extra line (see fig. 11.6).

```
Now Viewing Page 4 of Page Width 1
Press any key to continue...
                                        February 22, 1989

Henry H. Harrison

Henry's Hair Hut
7112 Commerce St
Springfield, VA  22150

Dear Henry,

Wonder Widgets of America is proud to announce the Grand Opening of our second
showroom near your Springfield office:

     2121 Commerce St.
     Springfield, VA 22150

We invite you to attend our Grand Opening on March 1, 1989. Bring this letter
and receive an additional 10% off our already fantastic Grand Opening Sale
prices.
                                        Sincerely,

                                        John Jones, President
```

Fig. 11.5.

The customer form letter without LineSqueeze.

```
Now Viewing Page 4 of Page Width 1
Press any key to continue...
                                        February 22, 1989

Henry H. Harrison
Henry's Hair Hut
7112 Commerce St
Springfield, VA  22150

Dear Henry,

Wonder Widgets of America is proud to announce the Grand Opening of our second
showroom near your Springfield office:

     2121 Commerce St.
     Springfield, VA 22150

We invite you to attend our Grand Opening on March 1, 1989. Bring this letter
and receive an additional 10% off our already fantastic Grand Opening Sale
prices.
                                        Sincerely,

                                        John Jones, President
```

Fig. 11.6.

The customer form letter with LineSqueeze.

Creating Mailing Labels

Virtually every business needs to generate mailing labels. For some companies, producing mailing labels is their business. With many programs, however, getting your data printed properly onto labels is not easy. True to its advertising campaign slogan, "Power Without Pain," Paradox makes swift work of mailing labels.

Designing a 1-Across Mailing Label Report

Designing a form to print mailing labels one to a row—1-across mailing labels—is simple.

1. Access the free-form design screen and delete all header and footer lines. You do all your work in the form band.
2. Toggle on the vertical ruler (Ctrl-V) to help you count lines.
3. Measure the size of a label in inches from the top edge of one label to the top edge of the next label. (Labels are usually 1 inch or 1 1/2 inches.)
4. Multiply the length by 6 to convert the measurement to printer lines. (Single spacing is 6 lines vertically per inch.)
5. Adjust the size of the form band on-screen, adding or deleting lines as necessary, until the same number of lines are available as on the label. Don't count the lines taken up by the page header and form header markers.
6. Measure a label horizontally, also in inches.
7. Multiply the label width by 10 if you are printing in a pica format (10 characters per inch) by 12 if you are printing in an elite format, or by 15 if you are printing in compressed type.
8. Set the page width to this number.
9. Set the page length to continuous (page length *C*).
10. When you line up the printer, make sure that the print head is where you want to begin printing. With all header lines removed, Paradox does not roll up a line before printing.
11. Place the fields in the form band as you want them to print, but do not use the last line of the form band. Leave this line blank to account for the vertical space between labels. Use only the first page-width.
12. Invoke the **F**ieldSqueeze and **L**ineSqueeze **F**ixed options to eliminate unneeded spaces and lines when Paradox prints the labels.

Figure 11.7 shows a report specification to print 1-inch, 1-across mailing labels. **F**ieldSqueeze and **L**ineSqueeze are activated. The report generated by this form is shown in figure 11.8.

```
Changing report R4 for Cust2 table                          Report      1/2
Page Header
....+...10....+...20....+...30....+...4*....+...10....+...20....+...30....+...4*
-▼page
-▼form
AAAAAAAAAAAAAAA AA AAAAAAAAAAAAAAAAAAAA
AAAAAAAAAAAAAAAAAAAA
AAAAAAAAAAAAAAAAAAAA
AAAAAAAAAAAAAAAAAAAA
AAAAAAAAAAAAAAAAAAAA, AA  AAAAA

-▲form
-▲page
```

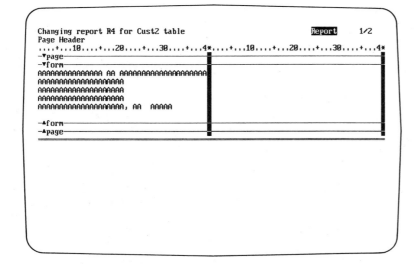

Fig. 11.7.

A free-form report specification to print mailing labels.

```
Now Viewing Page 1 of Page Width 1
Press any key to continue...
Wallace M. East
President
Eastern Enterprises
1211 Commerce St.
Springfield, VA  22150

Alfred H. Long
Chief Buyer
Alpha Freight Lines
720 Port Royal
Fairfax, VA  22030

Charlie Y. Eager
Ace Airplanes
777 Kittyhawk Dr.
Gaithersburg, MD  20877


Rex T. Comfort
Manager
Hidden Resorts
6601 Wales Rd.
Vienna, VA  22180
```

Fig. 11.8.

1-across mailing labels.

Designing a Report for N-Across Mailing Labels

Single column labels are great for use with a tractor-fed printer, but are not as useful with a friction-fed printer, and are practically useless with a laser printer. In the latter two situations, you use mailing labels with more than one label in a row. Fortunately, Paradox makes creation of labels for these forms as easy as for 1-across labels.

To create *n*-across labels, where *n* is the number of labels per row, follow the instructions found in the preceding section for 1-across labels. Set the page width by the distance from the left edge of one label to the left edge of the next label.

You also need to activate the **L**abels feature of Paradox. Press F10 (Menu) and select the following: **S**etting **L**abels **Y**es. Paradox responds by displaying the message `Label status has been recorded`.

Make sure that exactly *n* page widths are available. For example, if you have 3-across forms, make sure that you have a total of 3 page widths (refer to the Chapter 5 section on "Changing the Page Width"). Paradox uses the number of page widths to determine how many labels across should be printed.

For example, you can cause the report specification in figure 11.7 to print 2-across labels by activating the **L**abels feature. Notice that the report-width indicator in the top right corner of figure 11.7 already indicates two page widths. The resulting labels are shown in figure 11.9.

Fig. 11.9.

2-across mailing labels.

```
Now Viewing Page 1 of Page Width 1
Press any key to continue...
Wallace M. East                       Alfred H. Long
President                             Chief Buyer
Eastern Enterprises                   Alpha Freight Lines
1211 Commerce St.                     720 Port Royal
Springfield, VA  22150                Fairfax, VA  22030

Charlie Y. Eager                      Rex T. Comfort
Ace Airplanes                         Manager
777 Kittyhawk Dr.                     Hidden Resorts
Gaithersburg, MD  20877               6601 Wales Rd.
                                      Vienna, VA  22180

Robert M. Sangster                    Sarah G. Moores
Agent                                 Signal Plumbing
Sangster Insurance                    3333 Half Street
1411 Reservation Dr.                  Oxon Hill, MD  20745
Springfield, VA  22152

Henry H. Harrison                     Francis P. Jones
Henry's Hair Hut                      Chief Teller
7112 Commerce St                      2nd Savings & Loan
Springfield, VA  22150                2229 Hillcrest Dr.
                                      Arlington, VA  22210
```

Use group bands to sort labels. For example, if you want to sort the customer labels by ZIP code, add a group band that groups records on the field Cust Zip. After you add the group band, be sure to delete the blank lines in the group header and group footer, or these lines throw off the line count.

Chapter Summary

You have explored the many options provided by the Paradox Report Generator. Chapter 5 showed you report writing fundamentals. Chapter 10 explored the creation of reports from multiple tables, using grouping summary fields. This chapter presented the special features of free-form report design, including mailing labels. Continue to explore Paradox on your own, using this book as a reference and backup should you run into something you don't remember.

You have not heard the complete Paradox story. A major enhancement heralded by Paradox 3 is a business graphics facility. Presenting complex data in a picture is often the best way. Now that you have a good understanding of the standard reporting features of Paradox, creating graphs to bring your data to life is a snap. Turn to Chapter 12 to find out how easy graphics can be when an excellent program does most of the work for you. [3]

12

Creating Paradox Graphics

The Paradox graphics module is new in Version 3.0. Paradox is the only high-end PC database product to offer an integrated graphics capability. Like other portions of the program, the graphics function is faithful to the Paradox philosophy of providing powerful and easy-to-use features. Creating a graph is so easy that the process may become your favorite part of working with Paradox. [3]

An Overview of Paradox Graphics

Paradox makes creating an impressive graph simple. Two keystroke combinations can transform your mundane data into an impressive graph. Alt-X creates a cross-tabulated version of your data (see fig. 12.1). Ctrl-F7 (Graph) transforms the cross-tabulated table into a stacked bar graph with a title, labels, and legends (see fig. 12.2). Paradox also enables you to modify this standard graph, produced by Ctrl-F7, to create simple bar graphs, rotated bar graphs, 3-D bar graphs, line graphs, marker graphs, combined line and marker graphs, area graphs, X-Y graphs, and pie graphs. This section describes the graph types and the terminology you need to understand Paradox graphics.

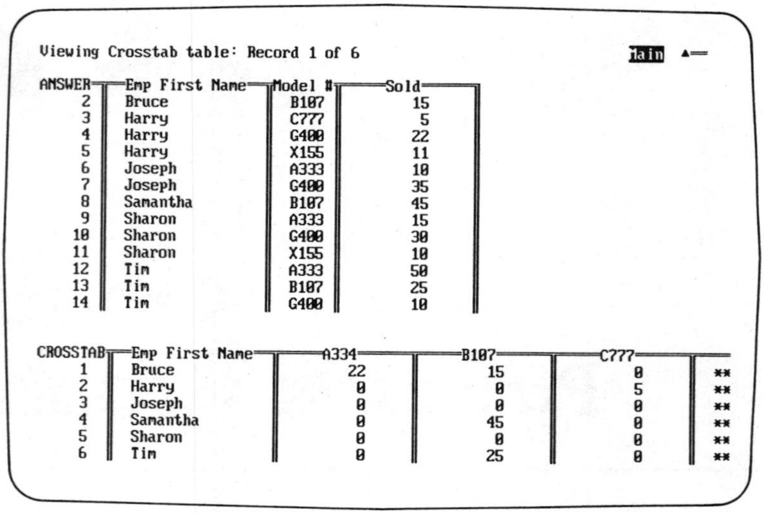

Viewing Crosstab table: Record 1 of 6 Main ▲

ANSWER	Emp First Name	Model #	Sold
2	Bruce	B107	15
3	Harry	C777	5
4	Harry	G400	22
5	Harry	X155	11
6	Joseph	A333	10
7	Joseph	G400	35
8	Samantha	B107	45
9	Sharon	A333	15
10	Sharon	G400	30
11	Sharon	X155	10
12	Tim	A333	50
13	Tim	B107	25
14	Tim	G400	10

CROSSTAB	Emp First Name	A334	B107	C777	
1	Bruce	22	15	0	**
2	Harry	0	0	5	**
3	Joseph	0	0	0	**
4	Samantha	0	45	0	**
5	Sharon	0	0	0	**
6	Tim	0	25	0	**

Fig. 12.1.

The Crosstab command.

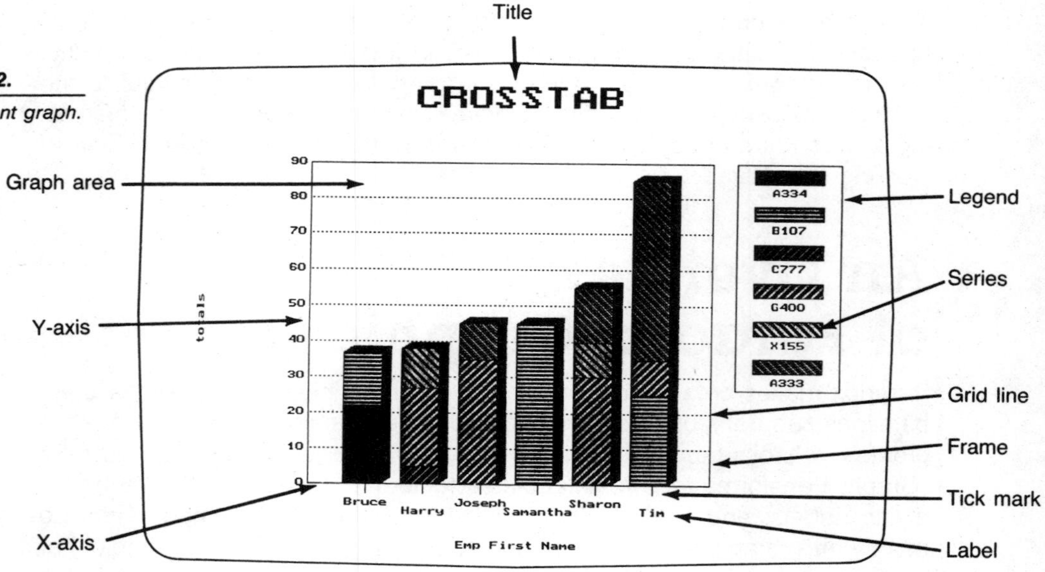

Fig. 12.2.

An instant graph.

Understanding Graph Elements

Business graphics programs have their own set of terminology. The various parts of a graph are referred to as *graph elements*. As you go through this chapter, you learn how to use and modify the following graph elements:

- *Graph area*. The large rectangular area containing bars, lines, markers, or a pie graph. All data is graphed in the graph area.
- *Axes*. All Paradox graphs except pie graphs have a horizontal line along the bottom edge called the *X-axis* and a vertical line along the left side called the *Y-axis*.
- *Frame*. The rectangle surrounding the graph area
- *Series*. Paradox enables you to show trends by indicating that several pieces of data belong in a set or category and should be graphed to show this relationship. Each of these groups of data is referred to as a *series*. Each of the six shadings in figure 12.2 depicts a data series. Paradox permits up to six data series per graph in all types except pie graphs. You can use up to nine series for a pie graph.
- *Tick marks; grid lines*. Each axis is divided into segments of equal length by *tick marks* or *grid lines*. Tick marks are short line segments, and grid lines extend across the entire width or height of the graph area.
- *Scale*. The distance, in units, between tick marks. The Y-axis in figure 12.2 is divided into 10 unit segments. The *scale*, therefore, is 10.
- *Labels*. Words or other characters along the X-axis. Labels are used to describe the data graphed at the corresponding tick mark. The names Bruce, Harry, Joseph and so on, are the labels in the graph shown in figure 12.2.
- *Titles*. Words or other characters above the graph area, below the X-axis labels, or along the Y-axis
- *Legends*. Paradox uses various *colored lines*, *shading*, and *marker shapes* to depict multiple data series in the same graph. The legend provides the key to identifying the proper series with each shading, line color, or marker. Figure 12.2 shows the legend as a rectangular box to the right of the graph area, and a model number is assigned to each shading used in the graph.

Examining the Graph Types

With Paradox, you can create ten types of graphs from your data. To decide which type can best present your message, you must be aware of the choices. The examples that follow illustrate the available graph types.

The actual steps you take to select one of the graph types for your data are explained later in the chapter.

Stacked Bar Graphs

Assuming that you have more than one series to graph, Paradox builds a *stacked bar graph* as the default graph. The graph in figure 12.2 is a stacked bar graph. Each series is represented as a different shading, and the height of each shaded portion of a bar represents one value in the series. The total height of the stacked bar shows the cumulative total of values from all series. This type of graph is good for comparing values that comprise a portion of a larger number you want to see. Figure 12.2 depicts the number of widgets of each type sold and the total widgets of all types sold by each of the five salespeople.

Simple Bar Graph, 3-D Bars

A *simple bar graph* shows multiple series in a different way. Instead of stacking the respective bars from each series as in figure 12.2, Paradox places the bars side by side. Figure 12.3 shows the same data as a simple bar graph. Because all the bars begin at zero, determining which salesperson has sold the most of a particular model is easier. With a simple bar graph, however, you can no longer easily compare the total sales of the salesperson. You can add the illusion of depth by creating a 3-D bar graph, like the one in figure 12.4.

Fig. 12.3.

A simple bar graph with multiple data series.

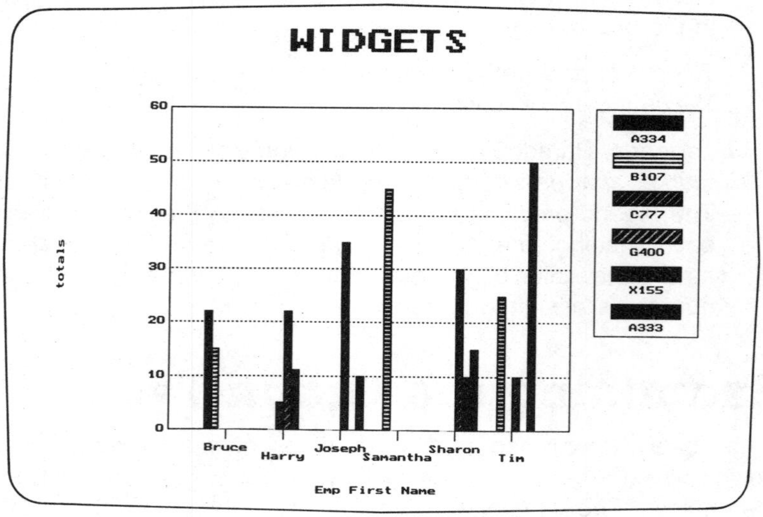

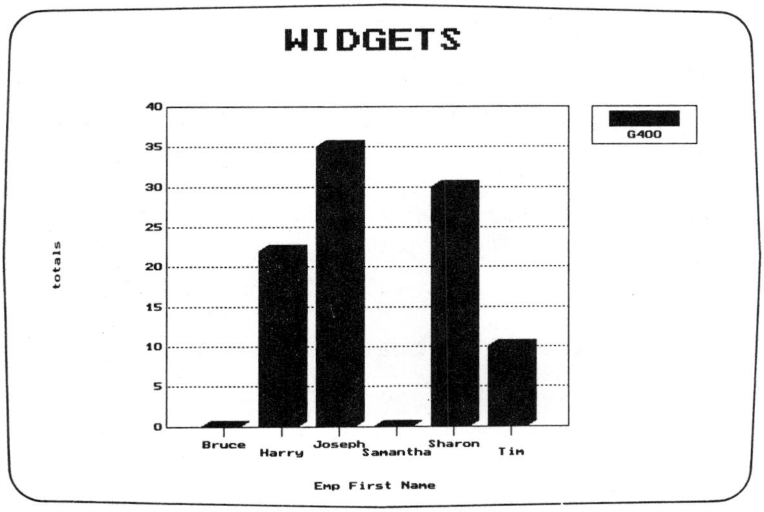

Fig. 12.4.

A 3-D bar graph with one data series.

Rotated Bar Graph

Another option is to create a *rotated bar graph* by turning the bars on their sides. Figure 12.5 shows the same data as figure 12.4, but the bars are turned.

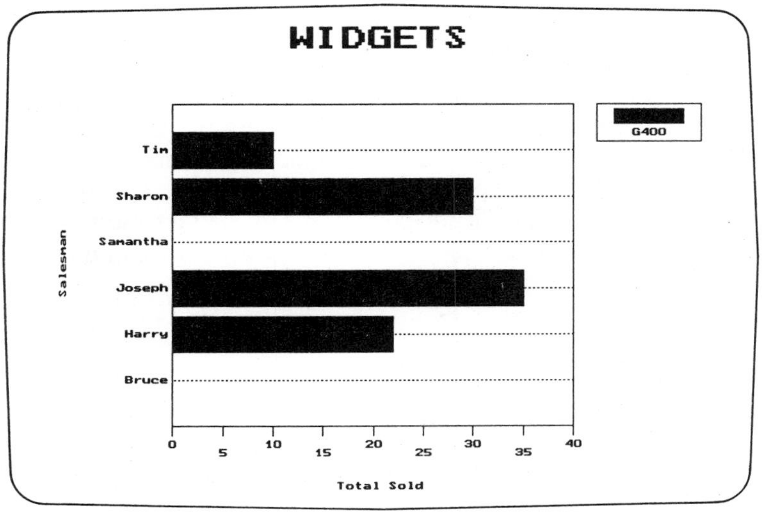

Fig. 12.5.

A rotated bar graph.

Line Graph, Marker Graph, Combined Lines, and Markers

A *line graph* is constructed with straight line segments connecting points. Each point represents one value in a series. All the points in the series are connected to form a continuous line. Figure 12.6 shows one series and therefore one line, but you can depict up to six series and have up to six lines per graph. Line graphs usually are used to show trends over time.

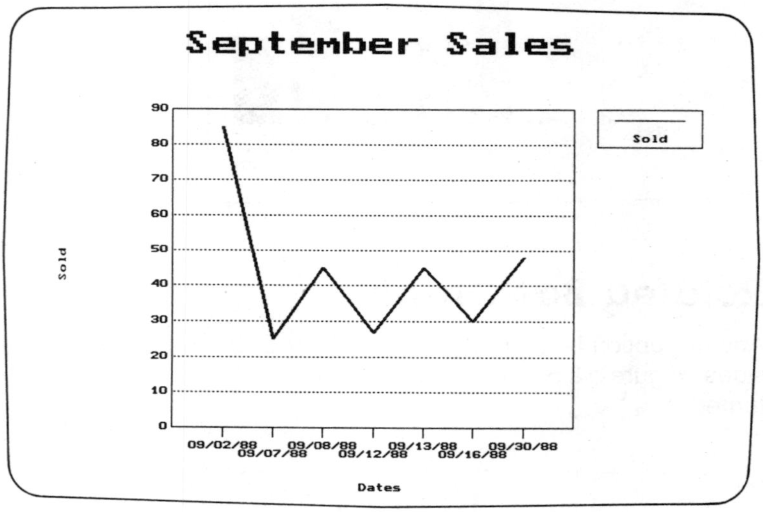

Fig. 12.6.
A line graph.

A marker graph is a line graph without the lines. The points representing series data values are denoted by markers and lines are not used to connect the points. You can, however, combine lines and markers, which sometimes makes distinguishing several lines in the same graph easier. Figure 12.7 shows a marker graph depicting sales of widget models on dates in September. The same data is graphed in figure 12.8 using a combined marker and line graph.

X-Y Graph

X-Y graphs are line graphs that compare one series of numeric data with another series. The classic example of this type of graph is used by economists to show that as prices go up, demand declines. Figure 12.9 shows an X-Y graph.

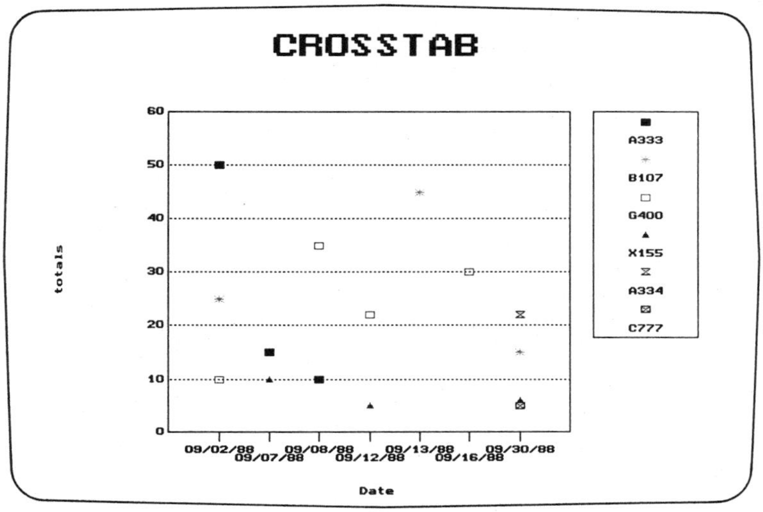

Fig. 12.7.

A marker graph.

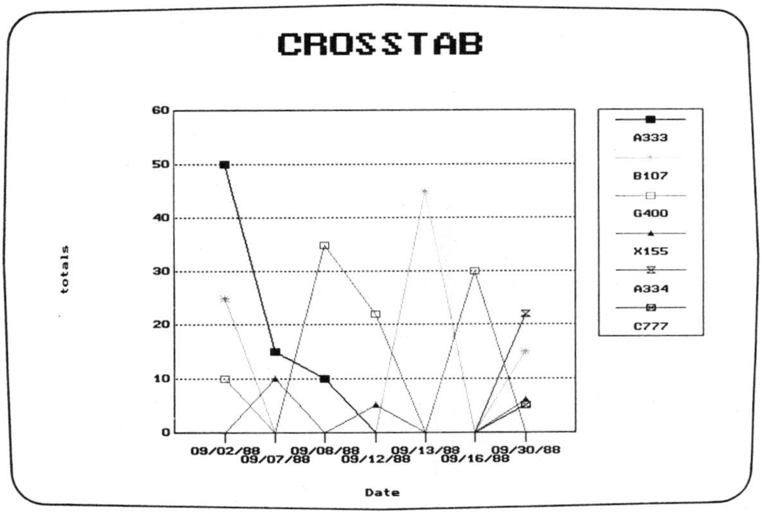

Fig. 12.8.

Combined lines and markers.

Pie Graph

Paradox also generates *pie graphs*. Each piece or slice of the pie represents a value series. Each series is shaded and colored (on a color monitor) differently. You can have up to nine series (slices) in a Paradox pie graph. One enhancement, shown in figure 12.10, can make one or more slices "explode" from the pie.

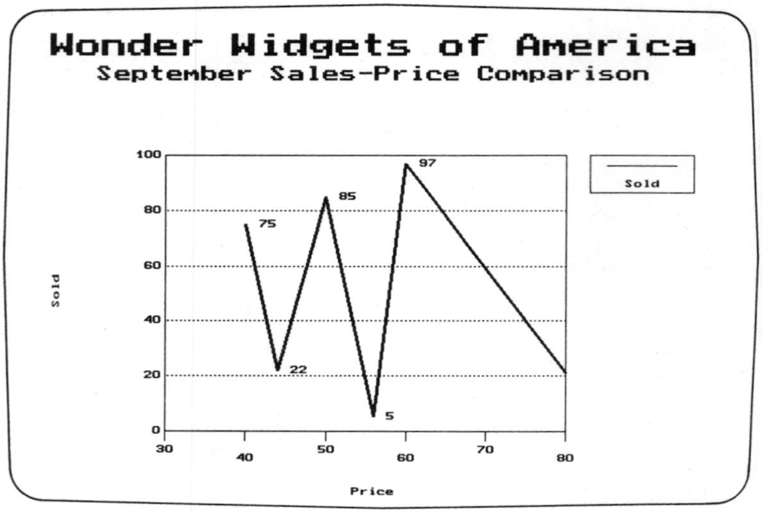

Fig. 12.9.

An X-Y graph.

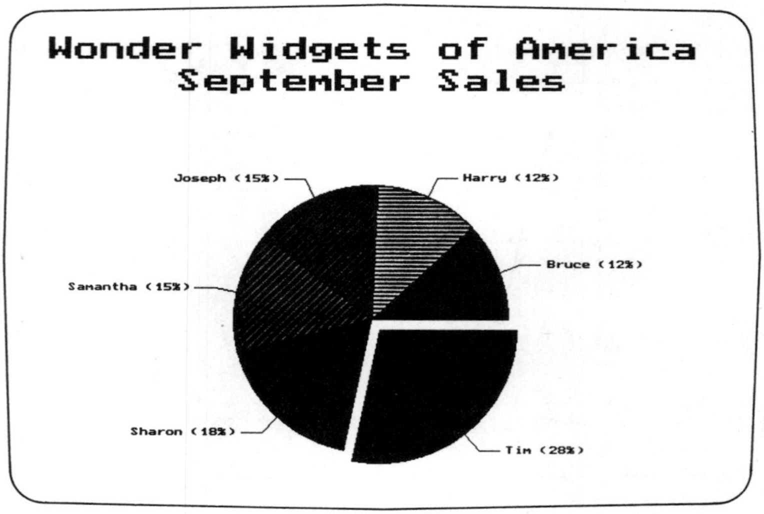

Fig. 12.10.

A pie graph.

Area Graphs

Another type of graph that can show cumulative totals, like stacked bar graphs, and trends, like line graphs, are called *area graphs*. This type of graph is a stacked line graph. Figure 12.11 shows the contribution of the various models of widgets to the total sales on various dates in September. The top line of the area graph shows the cumulative total of all the series' values for each date.

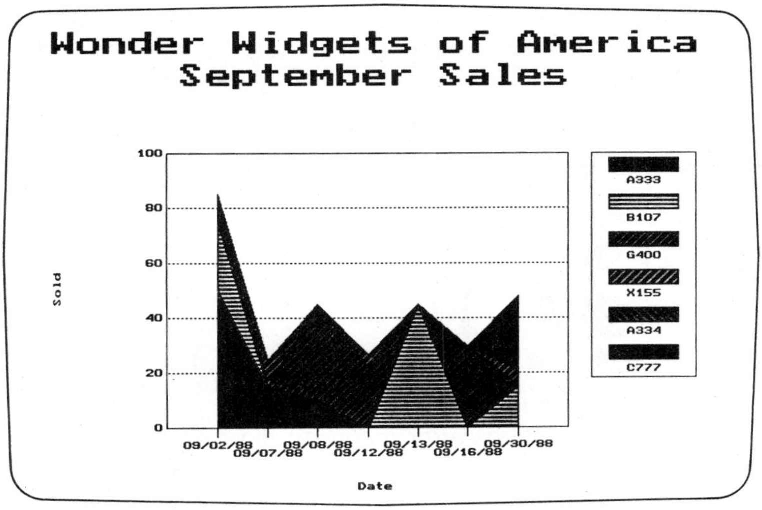

Fig. 12.11.
An area graph.

The Basics of Paradox Graphics

The terminology and graph types described in the preceding portion of this chapter are not unique to Paradox. Now that you have the necessary background, you are ready to learn the particulars of Paradox graphics.

The graphics-creating capability of Paradox builds on everything you have learned about using the program so far:

- ❑ *Table*. All graphs are generated based on data found in a Paradox table.
- ❑ *Paradox object*. A graph specification is a Paradox object that, like a form or report specification, can be saved and re-used.
- ❑ *Query by example*. You need a good understanding of query by example to successfully build the graph you want.
- ❑ *Instant graph*. Just as Paradox provides ready-made input forms and report specifications, the program also provides default graph settings that can be applied with a keystroke combination.
- ❑ *Full range of enhancements*. Paradox gives you instant graphs and provides a wide variety of enhancements.

To successfully tap the power of Paradox graphics, you have to understand how to set up a Paradox table for graphing. Paradox expects to find the data to be graphed in a certain position in the table. The program also uses data from the table to determine axis labels, legend labels, and graph titles. Paradox refers to the conversion from table to graph as *transformation*. The first step in learning Paradox graphics is learning *transformation rules*.

Understanding Transformation Rules

Paradox can create a graph only if you provide the following information in the table:

- *Series*. A series (group of data for graphing) must be a column in the table. A series also must be numeric. Paradox cannot produce a graph from alphanumeric or date fields. For a pie graph, one series column provides all the data and cannot be longer than nine rows. You can have a maximum of six series columns when generating other graph types.
- *X-axis data*. The data for the X-axis also must be a column in the table. X-axis data for X-Y graphs must be numeric. For all other graphs, X-axis data is used as labels and can be any data type.

You must provide each of these elements as separate columns in the current Paradox table. Because the maximum number of series columns is six, the minimum number of series is one. Because all graphs must have X-axis data, a table used for generating a graph should have from two to seven columns. Although you can create graphs from tables with more than seven columns, a maximum of seven columns is used for graphing. To make the discussion as clear as possible, this chapter shows how to create tables containing only essential columns.

Regarding the data you include in the table for graphing, Paradox makes the following assumptions about X-axis data:

- For keyed tables, the least significant (rightmost) key field becomes the X-axis data because the least significant key field always breaks the last "tie" to prevent duplicate records in the table. The value of this field in each record should be a good identifier for that record and is used to label the data for that record along the X-axis.
- In non-keyed tables, the first (leftmost) non-numeric column (field) in the table becomes the X-axis data. Paradox displays one tick

mark and one label along the X-axis for every row in the table. This column's field name becomes the *X-axis title*.

You usually build a graph from an unkeyed Answer table. You easily can *rotate* (Ctrl-R) the fields until the appropriate X-axis label field is the first one on the left.

Paradox also makes the following assumptions about series elements:

- ❏ The position of the cursor determines the first data series. Paradox assumes that the column containing your cursor is the first series of data. Each value in the column (field) becomes a value to be graphed.
- ❏ Series fields must be numeric. Paradox treats the next five numeric columns as additional series columns.
- ❏ Paradox uses the field names of these series columns in the legend to label the corresponding shading, line, or marker. Paradox automatically assigns the name `Totals` as the *Y-axis title*.

Paradox also assigns the table name as the graph's main title.

The other settings used by Paradox to create the standard graph are called the *default graph settings*. These settings are analogous to the standard Paradox report specification. The settings are used to produce the standard graph and can be fully modified, saved, and used again.

Examining the Default Graph Settings

Just as Paradox has a standard form and report specification, the program also has a standard graph specification. The first time you press Ctrl-F7 (Graph), Paradox uses the default graph settings to create a graph from the data in the current table on the workspace. Unlike the standard report specification and the standard form, the standard graph specification is not a format that you can view on-screen. This specification is a group of default settings Paradox applies to the data in the current table to generate a graph. The default graph settings are just the starting point. Making changes to these settings is the subject of "Enhancing the Graph" in this chapter. That section also explains how to save a modified specification to a file and how to load the settings later for application to the same or another table.

Table 12.1 lists the main default graph settings. Table 12.2 lists the settings that determine color and shading patterns applied to graphs, including the colors and patterns applied when you build pie graphs. You also can use the Custom Configuration Program (CCP), discussed in Appendix B, to make permanent changes to these settings.

Table 12.1
Default Graph Settings

Setting	*Default Value*
Graph Type	Stacked Bar
Override Types	None
Output Device	Screen
Scaling	Automatic
Main Title (1)	Current table name
Main Title (1) size	Autosize
Main Title (1) font	Default
Main Title (2)	Blank
Main Title (2) size	Autosize
Main Title (2) font	Default
X-axis Title	Field name of X-axis column
X-axis Title size	Autosize
Y-axis Title	`Totals`
Y-axis Title size	Autosize
Legend Labels	Series field names
Interior Labels	None
Axis scaling	Automatic
Low (X and Y)	0
High (X and Y)	0
Increment (X and Y)	0
Format (X and Y)	Fixed
Decimal Places (X and Y)	0
Minor Ticks (X and Y)	0
Alternate Ticks?	Yes
Display Axis Scaling?	Yes
Grid Line	1 (horizontal dotted line)
Grid Color	B (dark blue)
Frame Graph?	Yes
Frame Color	B (dark blue)

Table 12.2
Colors and Patterns—Default Graph Settings

Setting	*Color*	*Pattern*
Background	H (light gray)	
Main title (1)	B (dark blue)	
Main title (2)	B (dark blue)	
X-axis title	B (dark blue)	
Y-axis title	B (dark blue)	
1st Series/1st pie slice	B (dark blue)	B (filled)
2nd Series/2nd pie slice	C (green)	C (------)
3rd Series/3rd pie slice	D (cyan)	D (Lt ///)
4th Series/4th pie slice	E (red)	E (Hvy ///)
5th Series/5th pie slice	F (magenta)	F (Lt \\\)
6th Series/6th pie slice	G (brown)	G (Hvy \\\)
7th pie slice	H (light gray)	H (+ + + + + + +)
8th pie slice	I (dark gray)	I (crosshatch)
9th pie slice	J (light blue)	J (hatch)

The next two sections describe how to create a graph using these default settings.

Creating an Instant Graph

The trick to learning Paradox graphics quickly is to keep graphs simple, use a minimum of columns (fields), and develop a routine. The following two sections describe simple routines that work well and use the instant graph feature. This section describes how to create a simple bar graph in two steps; the next section demonstrates how to use a feature called *crosstab* to create a stacked bar graph in three steps. When you master these methods, you should be ready to learn how to create other types of Paradox graphs and to apply many other enhancements.

Step 1: Use Query By Example To Prepare a Table with Two Columns

To make learning and understanding the process easier, reduce the number of columns you are working with to two. You probably need to use query by example, and you may need to draw data from multiple tables. The first column is the X-axis data, and the second column is the data series that must be numeric. You can use Rotate (Ctrl-R) to place the columns in the right position, if necessary. After the two-column table is created and columns are in proper position, you are ready to create the graph.

Step 2: Position the Cursor in the Second Field and Press Ctrl-F7 (Graph)

To create a graph from a table, place the cursor in the data series column, the second column, and press Ctrl-F7 (Graph).

Suppose that you want to compare the widget sales of six salespeople. With the Orders and Detail tables, you use QBE to create a table containing each salesperson's name in the first column and the total quantity of widgets sold in the second column (see fig. 12.12). In the graph, you want to see the names displayed along the X-axis and the calculated field Sold displayed as bars in the graph area.

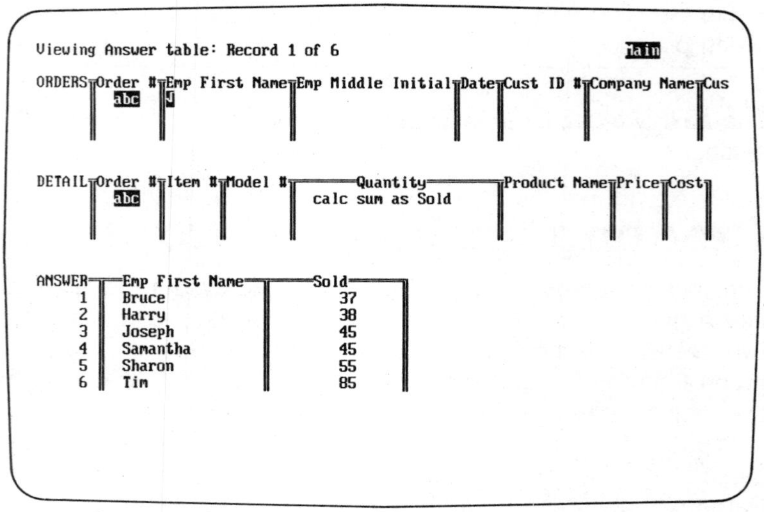

Fig. 12.12.
A query to determine the number of widgets sold by each salesperson.

To create a graph from this table, place the cursor in the Sold column and press Ctrl-F7 (Graph). Paradox displays the bar graph shown in figure 12.13. The names from the first column in Answer are now the labels along the X-axis. Values from the field Sold are depicted by the six bars.

This two-step method always works, but shows only one series of data at a time. The next section explains how to use the Crosstab function to create a stacked bar graph that shows up to six series of data.

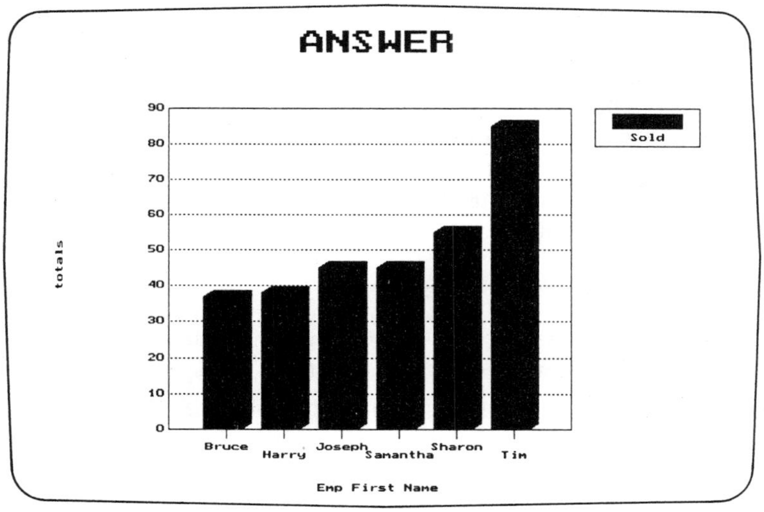

Fig. 12.13.

The default graph of the Answer table in figure 12.12.

Using Crosstab

You often want to compare several series of data with one another. For example, you may want to see the total widgets sold by each salesperson broken out by model—a separate data series for each model of widget that shows the number sold by each salesperson. You can compare these series in a bar graph. By default, Paradox graphs multiple series in a stacked bar graph.

To create an instant stacked bar graph, you need a table with the X-axis data in the first column and from two to six additional columns, each containing a numeric data series. In the widget example, you need the Emp First Name column, as in the Answer table, and you need a separate column for each of the six widget models.

Your database usually is not structured so that you easily can extract more than one series column. A normalized database has the data you want to compare in one column. (Designing a normalized database is discussed in the "Designing a Database" section of Chapter 2.) For example, you can use a query to generate an Answer table showing the number of each model of widget sold by each salesperson (see fig. 12.14). The data you want broken out into six columns—one for each model—is contained in the Sold column. To solve this problem, Paradox includes the *crosstab* feature. Crosstab automatically breaks the data series out for you.

Step 1: Use Query By Example To Prepare a Table with Three Columns

To use the crosstab feature, you need a table with at least three columns. For this discussion, assume that you have exactly three columns arranged so that the X-axis data column is first, the column with the series categories is second, and the numeric column is third. The Answer table in figure 12.14 shows this arrangement.

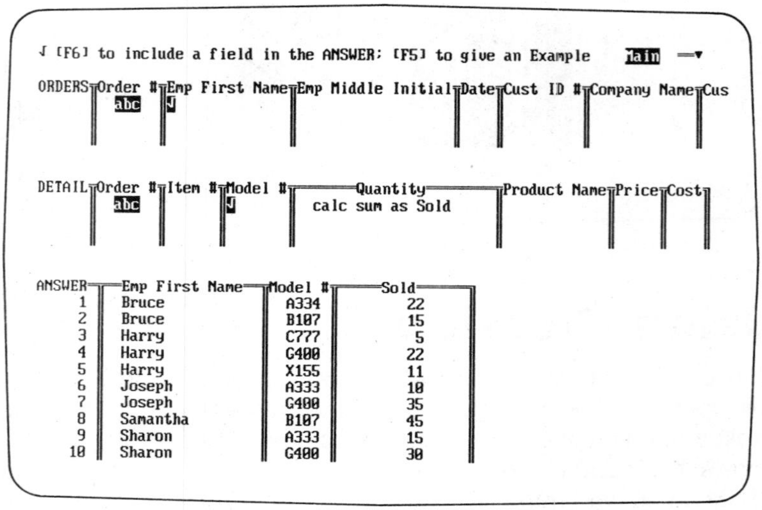

Fig. 12.14.

A query to determine the number of each model of widgets sold by each salesperson.

Step 2: Use Crosstab

After you have built the three-column table, move the cursor to the first column and press Alt-X (Crosstab). Paradox displays a new table called Crosstab. The first column of Crosstab contains the same values as the source table, except that the duplicates are removed. The values in the second column of the source column are now field names for the second and subsequent columns. These columns represent the data series to be graphed. The data from the original third column is broken out to the appropriate series column. The effect is to place the data from the third column into a matrix or spreadsheet structure.

Figure 12.15 shows the result of performing Crosstab on the Answer table from figure 12.14. Each of the widget models has its own column. The data from the Sold column in Answer is distributed among these six columns in Crosstab.

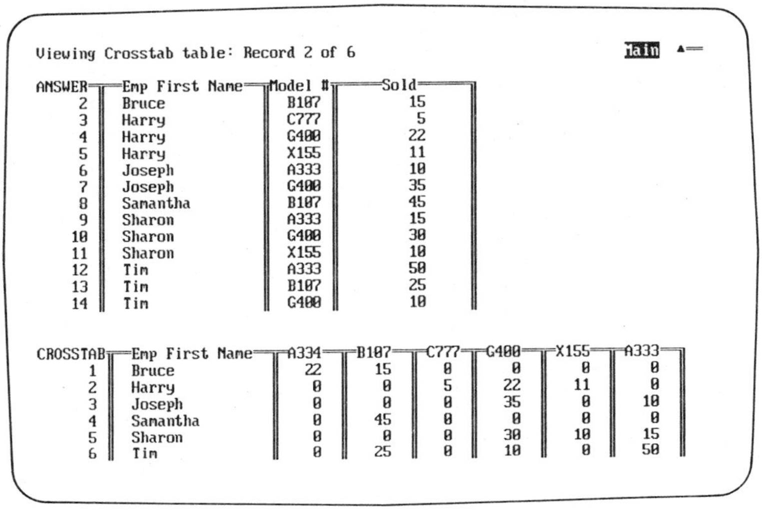

Viewing Crosstab table: Record 2 of 6 Main

ANSWER	Emp First Name	Model #	Sold
2	Bruce	B107	15
3	Harry	C777	5
4	Harry	G400	22
5	Harry	X155	11
6	Joseph	A333	10
7	Joseph	G400	35
8	Samantha	B107	45
9	Sharon	A333	15
10	Sharon	G400	30
11	Sharon	X155	10
12	Tim	A333	50
13	Tim	B107	25
14	Tim	G400	10

CROSSTAB	Emp First Name	A334	B107	C777	G400	X155	A333
1	Bruce	22	15	0	0	0	0
2	Harry	0	0	5	22	11	0
3	Joseph	0	0	0	35	0	10
4	Samantha	0	45	0	0	0	0
5	Sharon	0	0	0	30	10	15
6	Tim	0	25	0	10	0	50

Fig. 12.15.

Using the Crosstab command.

This explanation oversimplifies Crosstab, which actually performs a summation function while distributing data to the appropriate data series column. In the example, the summation is already performed in the query shown in figure 12.14 so that you don't notice that Crosstab also performs a summation. You obtain the same result even if the `calc` expression in the Quantity field (in the query in fig. 12.14) is replaced with a check mark.

Crosstab also is available on the Graph menu. Instead of pressing Alt-X, you can press F10 (Menu) and select **I**mage **G**raph **C**rosstab.

Paradox displays a menu containing the following statistical computations:

1) Sum **2**) Min **3**) Max **4**) Count

Select **1**) Sum from the menu to perform the same operation as Alt-X. Position the cursor in the X-axis data column and press Enter. Position the cursor in the series label column and press Enter again. Move the cursor to the data column and press Enter a third time. The other choices perform the respective computation as data is cross-tabulated.

Step 3: Display the Graph

When you perform the Crosstab, the table is ready to graph. To display a stacked bar graph, move the cursor to the first series column and press Ctrl-F7 (Graph). Figure 12.16 shows the graph based on the data in the Crosstab table shown in figure 12.15. Compare this graph to the graph in figure 12.13. The two graphs are the same, but the latter shows sales broken down by model as well as total sales.

Fig. 12.16.

The default graph of the Crosstab table in figure 12.15.

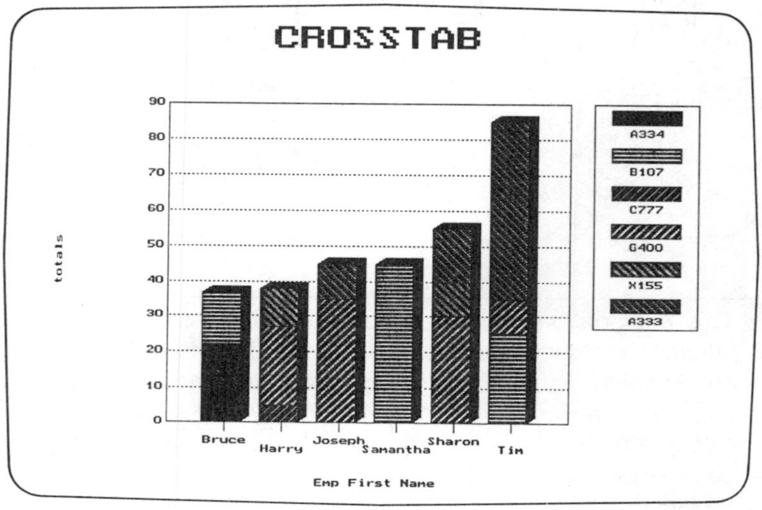

An easy way to obtain a presentable graph without doing much more work is to rename the Crosstab table (**R**ename is covered in Chapter 13). For example, you might rename the Crosstab table shown in figure 12.15 to Widgets. When you press Ctrl-F7 (Graph), Paradox uses the graph title `Widgets`, instead of `Crosstab`.

Enhancing the Graph

Paradox provides a significant number of enhancements that you can apply to your graph. In addition to the graph types already described, Paradox enables you to combine certain graph types, and you can customize all the settings listed in tables 12.1 and 12.2. These settings include the content, size, and font of all titles; labels; legends; scaling; tick marks; grid lines and color; frame color; markers; line color; area and bar color, and shading patterns.

Starting Graph Mode

All enhancements are chosen or modified from Graph mode. To access Graph mode, press F10 (Menu) and select **I**mage **G**raph **M**odify.

Paradox starts Graph Mode and displays the Graph Type form. To access the Main Graph menu, press F10 (Menu). Paradox displays the following menu:

Type **O**verall **S**eries **P**ies **V**iewGraph **H**elp **DO**-IT! **C**ancel

Altering the default settings with this menu is explained in the following discussions. After you make the desired change, press F2 (DO-IT!) to change the setting temporarily from the default value.

Saving the Graph Specification

Any changes you make to the default settings are effective only for the current Paradox session unless you save the changes to the file. To save an altered graph specification, from the Paradox Main menu, select **I**mage **G**raph **S**ave.

Type a name, following the same file naming rules in table 2.1 for tables and scripts, and press Enter. Paradox saves the graph specification to a disk file. For example, you can save the settings for your widget graph under the name Widget.

Loading a Graph Specification

Later, during the same or another Paradox session, you can load a saved graph specification. At the Paradox Main menu, select **I**mage **G**raph **L**oad.

Specify the name of the graph specification. Paradox replaces the default settings with the specifications loaded from disk.

Graph specifications are not necessarily identified with one table. After you modify the default settings or load a previously established specification, the new settings apply to any table you make current and graph with Ctrl-F7 (Graph).

Resetting the Graph Specification

After you make changes to the graph specification, you may decide that you need to return to the default settings. You need to reset the specification. Press F10 (Menu) and select **I**mage **G**raph **R**eset **O**K.

Paradox clears all modifications to the default sets and returns to the Main mode.

Selecting Graph Type

To change the graph type, press F10 (Menu), and select **I**mage **G**raph **M**odify.

Paradox displays Graph mode and the Graph Type form (see fig. 12.17). Choose from among the graph types listed on the right side of the form.

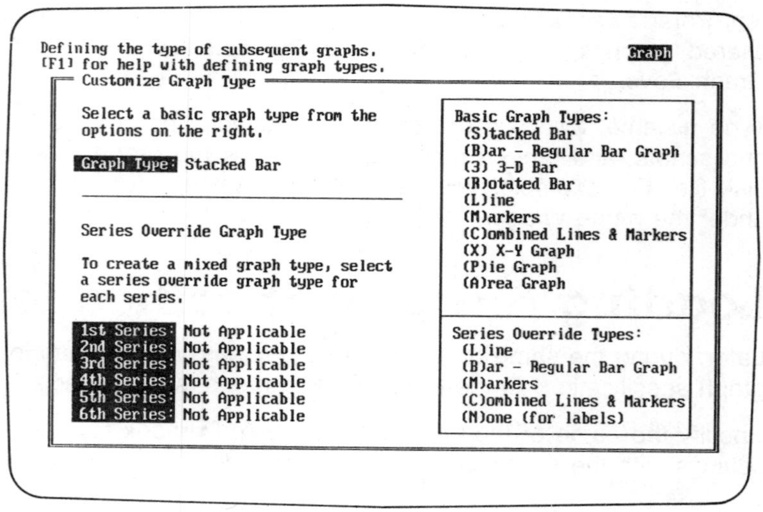

Fig. 12.17.

The graph type form.

The bottom portion of this form provides the *Series Override* option that enables you to mix any combination of the following graph types:

Line
Simple Bar
Marker
Combined Line and Marker

Move the cursor down to any one or more of the series lines and choose the desired override graph type. The chosen series is graphed with the override graph type, rather than the basic type chosen in the top half of the Graph Type form. Notice in figure 12.17 that because the graph type is `Stacked Bar`, series override is `Not Applicable`.

Customizing Graph Elements

Paradox Graph mode enables you to enhance the appearance of your graph by modifying the graph's titles, colors, fill patterns, scaling, label format, tick marks, grid lines, legends, and internal series labels. These modifications are made to the standard graph specification and do not affect the series data. To access Graph mode, press F10 (Menu) and select **I**mage **G**raph **M**odify.

When Paradox displays the Graph Type form, press F10 (Menu) again to access the Main Graph menu. You can look at the graph with the current settings at any time by pressing Ctrl-F7 (Graph). Press any key to return to the same Graph Mode screen.

When you finish making changes, press F2 (DO-IT!). Paradox returns to the Main mode.

Don't forget to save the graph specification to disk if you may want to use the specification in a later Paradox session. From the Main menu, press F10 (Menu) and select **I**mage **G**raph **S**ave.

Paradox does not save the specification to disk when you press F2 (DO-IT!). This feature is inconsistent with form and report design, but permits you to use one graph specification with more than one table.

Changing Overall Settings

Paradox divides graph elements into groups according to their scope. Because one group of graph elements applies generally to the entire graph, Paradox refers to the elements as *overall* settings. The overall settings include titles, color, scale, label format, and grids. To alter any of these settings, press **O**verall from the Main Graph menu.

Paradox lists the following options:

Titles **C**olors **A**xes **G**rids **P**rinterLayout **D**evice **W**ait

Each of these choices displays an options form on which you record the desired changes to the graph specifications. The discussions that follow introduce you to five of these options. **P**rinterLayout and **D**evice are discussed in "Creating Other Output" in this chapter.

When you complete your changes to an options form and want to go to another one, press F10 (Menu) to redisplay the Main Graph menu. When you finish making all changes, press F2 (DO-IT!). You also can cancel any changes made to the graph specification by pressing F10 (Menu) and selecting **C**ancel. Either way, Paradox returns to the Main mode.

While you are customizing the graph specification, you can view the graph by pressing Ctrl-F7 (Graph). Pressing any key returns you to the same Graph mode screen.

Customizing Titles

When you choose the **T**itles option on the Overall menu, Paradox displays the title options form. This form enables you to alter the main graph title or the axes titles.

Paradox graphs can have two main title lines centered above the graph area. The default setting uses the table name as the first line of the main title. Use the title options form to change, add, or delete either line of the main title.

You also can use this form to choose between eleven fonts for the main title: default, bold, triplex, sans serif, small, simplex, triplex script, euro style, complex, and gothic.

By default, Paradox assigns font size to titles. Use the title options form to choose small, medium or large font size.

The title options form also contains a section for modifying the content and size of the X-axis and Y-axis titles. By default, Paradox uses `Totals` for the Y-axis title, and the field name of the X-axis column as the X-axis title. Any entries made in this portion of the title options form override the default titles.

Customizing Colors

Select **C**olors to access the color options form. Use this form to alter the default color settings for screen display (with a color monitor) or color printing (with a color printer). You can choose from up to seven colors for the background and from 16 colors for the graph frame, grid, titles, and series data. Pie slice colors are not set on this menu. (Setting pie slice colors is discussed in "Customizing Pie Settings" later in this chapter.)

Customizing Axes

The **A**xes selection displays the axis scaling and tick options mark form. Use this form to adjust Y-axis and X-axis scaling.

By default, Paradox sets the low end of the scale to zero and the high end to the increment above the highest series value. Paradox also assigns the increment between tick marks. To override the default, fill in the `Increment` line on the form.

For the X-axis (except X-Y graphs), Paradox displays one tick mark and a label for each value in the X-axis data column. Fill in the `Minor Ticks` line to suppress some of the X-axis labels. The 1 in this line suppresses every other X-axis label; a 2 suppresses two out of every three labels, and so on. `Alternate Ticks` places X-axis labels on alternating levels, so that the labels are less likely to overlap.

Paradox abbreviates Y-axis tick mark values when the high end of the scale reaches 10,000. For example, the tick mark label 20,000 is abbreviated as 20 to keep from cluttering the image with zeros. The `Display Axis Scaling` line in this form determines whether Paradox displays the scaling factor beneath the Y-axis title (e.g., Paradox displays the word `thousands` to indicate that the Y-axis label 20 means 20 thousand). Don't get this option confused with the `Set axis scaling` option. These options are independent features. (The Paradox 3.0 documentation makes this mistake.)

Customizing Grids

Choosing the **G**rids option from the Overall menu displays the grid options form. Use this form to select one of six grid line choices and to change the grid display color. You also can turn off the grid by changing grid color to the same as the background color.

Also use this form to toggle the graph frame and set the graph frame color. The color option duplicates an option on the color options form.

Setting the Wait Duration

By default, Paradox displays your graph until you press a key. With the **W**ait option on the Overall menu, you can alter this setting so that the graph displays for a certain amount of time and then returns to the work space. Select **W**ait **D**uration.

Type a number that represents the number of seconds the graph should display and press Enter. The next time you display a graph, the new wait period takes effect. Paradox returns the screen to the work space.

To return the wait feature to the default conditions, select **W**ait **K**eystroke.

Customizing Series Settings

Another group of settings is the Series group. These graph settings affect the display of the numeric data portion of the graph—the series. Through the series settings you can customize the legends that describe each series on the graph, label the data inside the graph area, assign different marker shapes, assign different fill patterns, and access the color options form.

To modify one of the series settings, press F10 (Menu) from the Graph mode and select **S**eries.

Paradox displays the following menu:

LegendsAndLabels **M**arkersAndFills **C**olors

The next two sections discuss **L**egendsAndLabels and **M**arkersAndFills. **C**olors, however, takes you to the same color options form discussed in the preceding description of the Overall graph settings, and, therefore, is not covered again in this section.

Customizing Legends and Labels

The **L**egendsAndLabels option on the Series menu displays the series legends and labels options form. This form has spaces for up to six series legends. Paradox uses the field name of each series column as a label for the series in the graph's legend. Fill in the appropriate line to override the default.

Paradox also provides a method for labeling your graph. The default graph specification does not include any labels that show the exact value of a series. Having the underlying data printed on the graph, however, can be helpful. The series legends and labels options form provides the following label placement alternatives: center, above, below, right, left, none (to reset).

Customizing Markers and Fills

Choose **M**arkersAndFills to make changes to the fill pattern of a series element or the marker symbols used in marker graphs. You can assign any of the fill patterns or marker symbols listed in table 12.3.

Table 12.3
Fill Patterns and Marker Symbols

Code	*Fill Pattern*	*Marker Symbol*
A	Empty	Filled square
B	Filled	Plus sign
C	Dashed line	8-point star
D	Light ///	Empty square
E	Heavy ///	X
F	Light \\\	Dollar sign
G	Heavy \\\	Filled triangle
H	+ + + + + +	Hourglass
I	Crosshatch	6-point star
J	Hatch	Box with X inside
K	Light dots	Shadowed cross
L	Heavy dots	Vertical line
M	(None)	Horizontal line

Customizing Pie Settings

Pie graphs have their own graph elements options form. From the Main Graph menu choose **P**ies to display this form. You can set the format for pie slice labels, set colors and fill patterns, and explode pie slices.

The default label for each pie slice is the series value. For example, if a pie slice represents 65 widgets sold, 65 is the label. Paradox also enables you to label slices showing the percentage that each slice represents of the whole, to label slices as currency, or to suppress labels.

Paradox provides the same fill pattern choices shown in table 12.3, except fill pattern A (empty). All sixteen colors also are available for you to assign to any of the nine possible pie slices.

You also use this form to explode a pie slice. By default, no slices are exploded. To explode a slice, type *y* in the `Explode Slice` column to the right of the slice number.

Creating Other Output

So far this chapter has dealt with displaying your graph on-screen. Paradox also can print the graph on a graphics-capable printer or plotter and can save the graph to a file on disk.

Printing or Plotting a Graph

Before you can print or plot your graph, you have to use the Custom Configuration Program (see Appendix B) to define your printer or plotter driver as one of the four available printer setups. You also need to make this setup *current* and make sure that the printer layout is the way you want it.

Selecting a Printer or Plotter

By default, the printer or plotter you defined, using the CCP, as Printer 1 is the current printer, but you may have more than one printer or plotter attached to your system. To choose a different printer, make the following selections from the Main Graph menu:

Overall **D**evice **P**rinter

Choose one of the four printer/plotter setups. This setup becomes the current printer or plotter for the Paradox session until you select another one, **R**eset the graph specification settings, or quit Paradox.

Customizing the Printer Layout

The default settings for printer layout are listed in table 12.4. If these settings match the layout you intend to use to print your graph, you are ready to send the graph to the printer or plotter. To customize one or more of these settings, select **O**verall and **P**rinterLayout from the Main Graph menu. Paradox displays the printer layout options form.

Table 12.4
Printer Layout Settings

Setting	*Default Value*
Left Margin	0
Top Margin	0
Graph Height	0 (page size)
Graph Width	0 (page size)
Orientation	Landscape
Break Page	No
Plotter Speed	0

Use this form to change the left margin, top margin, graph height, and graph width. You also can choose whether the graph should print in landscape orientation (horizontal) or portrait orientation (vertical). Although the default width and height are set at 0, Paradox assumes that you are using an 8 1/2-by-11-inch page. To change the graph size, type appropriate numbers into these lines on the form.

Printing several graphs on one page is possible. For example, to print two graphs in portrait orientation on the same page, use `Graph Height` and `Graph Width` to reduce the graph size to a width of 8 inches and a height of 5 1/2 inches. Also make sure that the orientation is set to `Portrait` and the `Break Page` line contains an entry of `No`. After printing the first graph, Paradox does not eject the page, enabling you to print the second graph on the same page. The Plotter Speed option on this form enables you to choose plotter speed.

When you finish customizing these printer/plotter layout settings, press F2 (DO-IT!).

Sending the Graph to the Printer or Plotter

After making sure that the correct printer/plotter is current and adjusting the printer layout options, you are ready to print or plot your graph. Make sure that the printer or plotter is on, properly connected to your computer, and loaded with paper. When using a plotter, the pens must be mounted in their holders with the caps off. From the Main Graph menu, select **V**iewGraph **P**rinter.

Paradox sends your graph to the chosen printer or plotter.

Sending the Graph to a File

Instead of sending your graph to a printer or plotter, you may want to save the graph image (instead of the graph specification) to a disk file.

Before sending output to the file, select a file format. The default format matches the current printer (often called a *print image*). Paradox sends to the file the output needed to generate the graph on your printer/plotter. Paradox also enables you to save your graph in Encapsulated PostScript® (EPS) format or 1-2-3 (PIC) format. To choose one of these formats, select **O**verall **D**evice **F**ile from the Main Graph menu.

Choose **E**PS or **P**IC. EPS files can be used with other graphics programs and for desktop publishing.

When you are sure that you have chosen the correct file format, you are ready to send the graph to the disk. Select **V**iewGraph **F**ile from the Main Graph menu.

Type a unique file name and press Enter. Paradox generates the file in the format you have chosen. Files formatted for your printer or plotter have the extension GRF.

You can print a file formatted for your printer or plotter from DOS with the COPY command. You don't have to use the same computer, but you must be printing to the same type of printer or plotter. For example, if you name the file BARGRAPH, Paradox provides the extension GRF. To print the file, type *copy bargraph.grf prn*.

If the printer or plotter you want to use is not connected to the first parallel printer port, replace *PRN* with the appropriate port name (for example, LPT2). Do not use the DOS PRINT command.

You also should be aware that the default print image format creates very large files (often in excess of 500K). EPS and PIC formats are much more efficient.

Using Graphics on a Network

Generally, using Paradox graphics on a network with shared files is the same as with private files. To view a graph, you must have the data to be graphed in the current image. When you view a shared table or perform a query using a shared table, Paradox places a prevent full lock on the table. If another network user has already placed a full lock on a table that you need to use, you cannot generate the graph until that user is finished. After you generate the Answer or Crosstab table that is the actual basis of the graph, you are working with a private file.

Paradox takes some special steps to make network use of graphics efficient and enables you to create a continuously updating graph that reflects changes being made by multiple users of shared tables.

Using Crosstab on a Network

Similar to a query, the Crosstab function has to look at the data in a table, but doesn't make any changes to that data. When you perform Crosstab on a shared table, Paradox takes a "snapshot" of the shared table and processes the command. If another user is making a change to the table when you execute the Crosstab command, Paradox tries to take the snapshot until the other user releases the record. You see a message as this process takes place. You can press Ctrl-Break to abort the Crosstab if you don't want to wait.

Using AutoRegraph

One of the most impressive feats you can perform with Paradox graphics is referred to in the Paradox documentation as *autoregraph*. This operation uses the **R**epeatPlay option on the Scripts menu to continually redraw your graph. Autoregraph is effective only on a network where other network users are making changes to the data on which the graph is based.

The purpose of autoregraph is to see changes to shared data reflected in the graph as the changes are made. Autoregraph can be useful in sensitive business applications such as stock or commodities trading. Price or quantity updates of the underlying data, or both, are reflected in the graph, perhaps making trends easier to spot.

The first step is to design your graph. When you manually can produce the desired picture of your data, you are ready to make the graph automatic by following these steps:

1. Make sure that the proper graph specification is current. Load the specification from disk if necessary. Set the wait duration to the same number of seconds as the current Autorefresh setting. (The **A**utorefresh choice on the Tools/Net menu is discussed in Chapter 13.)

2. Clear all images from the workspace.

3. Start recording a script by selecting the following:

   Scripts **B**eginRecord

   Type a unique script name and press Enter.

4. Perform all the keystrokes necessary to display your graph, including any queries or crosstab.

5. Clear all images with Alt-F8 (Clear All).

6. Stop recording the script by selecting the following:

   Scripts **E**nd-Record

7. Play the script by selecting the following:

   Scripts **R**epeatPlay

8. Specify the script. When prompted for the number of times to repeat the script, type *c* and press Enter.

The graph is refreshed at approximately the same time that the data is refreshed and reflects the most current data.

Chapter Summary

The graphics facility of Paradox 3.0 is a significant new tool for quickly and easily analyzing your Paradox database. This chapter introduced the tools available in the Paradox graphics module and demonstrated the easiest way to get started at building informative graphs from tables. You can learn to enhance your graphs to their fullest potential. Graphics products are designed to be experimented with. If your graph doesn't look right at first, play around with the graph options until you are satisfied.

13

Using Paradox Tools

Throughout this book you have noticed references to the Tools menu. Probably, you have turned to this chapter before finishing all the chapters that precede it. Like any good tool box, the Paradox Tools menu contains tools for many purposes. You never know when it may come in handy. Just the same, some of the tools are so specialized that you may never need to use them. At least you should be aware that they exist.

This chapter is near the end of the book because it covers a broad range of topics. The Paradox Tools menu includes tools that supply information about your database; exchange files with other programs; rename, copy, and delete Paradox objects; add and subtract tables; speed up queries; provide password protection; provide access to the operating system; and allow you to lock, unlock, and prevent locking of shared tables on a network. Some of these features were mentioned briefly in other chapters, in the context in which they may be used, but each is explained again here for your convenience.

The Tools menu has so many options that the top line of the menu continues on a second screen. To access the Paradox Tools menu, select **T**ools from the Paradox Main menu. Paradox displays the following menu:

Rename **Q**uerySpeedup **E**xportImport **C**opy **D**elete **I**nfo **N**et **M**ore

The last choice, **M**ore, serves only to display the second page of this menu:

Add **M**ultiAdd **F**ormAdd **S**ubtract **E**mpty **P**rotect **D**irectory **T**oDOS

For clarity, this chapter refers to the first page as the Tools menu, and to the second page as the Tools/More menu.

Obtaining Information about Your Database

Working with Paradox, you may encounter many situations in which you need an answer to questions like the following:

- How did I define the Cust ID # field: as a numeric field or an alphanumeric field?
- What was the name of the table I created the day before yesterday: Detail or Details?
- How many reports have I defined for the Employee table?
- Who else on the network is working in Paradox right now?
- What are the current locks on the Orders table?

You can obtain the answers to each of these questions using the **I**nfo option on the Tools menu. Consistent with virtually all other procedures in Paradox, all answers are provided in the form of a temporary table that can be queried, renamed, and printed. From the Tools menu, select **I**nfo; Paradox displays the following choices:

- **S**tructure. Choose this option and specify the table name to list quickly the structure of a table in the temporary table Struct.
- **I**nventory. Choose this option to show another menu:

  Tables **S**cripts **F**iles

Choose **T**ables to build a list of all tables in the current directory or another specified directory (see fig. 13.1). Paradox displays the temporary table List. This list shows table names and the date on which they were last modified. Temporary tables always have today's date because they are deleted at the end of each session. Choose **S**cripts to produce a List table of scripts in the current or specified directory. When you choose **F**iles, Paradox asks for a DOS pattern. Press Enter to list all the files in the current directory, or specify a valid DOS search pattern (including path) to produce a List table of files from a different directory. The **F**iles option provides a convenient way to produce a catalog of all the files on your disk.

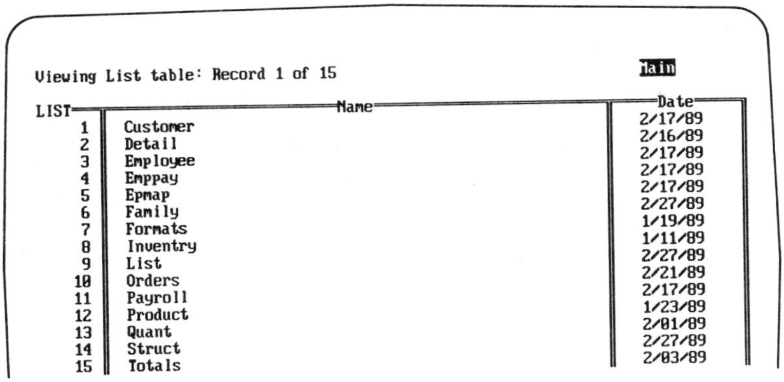

Viewing List table: Record 1 of 15 Main

LIST	Name	Date
1	Customer	2/17/89
2	Detail	2/16/89
3	Employee	2/17/89
4	Emppay	2/17/89
5	Epmap	2/17/89
6	Family	2/27/89
7	Formats	1/19/89
8	Inventry	1/11/89
9	List	2/27/89
10	Orders	2/21/89
11	Payroll	2/17/89
12	Product	1/23/89
13	Quant	2/01/89
14	Struct	2/27/89
15	Totals	2/03/89

Fig. 13.1.

An inventory of all tables in the current directory.

- ❑ **F**amily. Choose this option and specify a table, and Paradox displays a list of all the members of the table's family of objects as a temporary table named Family (see fig. 13.2).

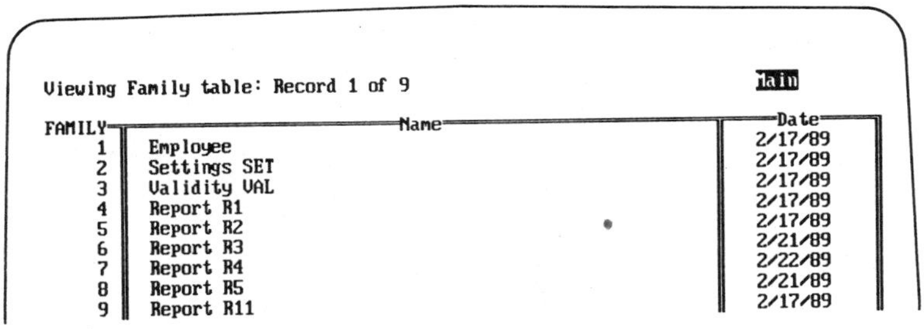

Viewing Family table: Record 1 of 9 Main

FAMILY	Name	Date
1	Employee	2/17/89
2	Settings SET	2/17/89
3	Validity VAL	2/17/89
4	Report R1	2/17/89
5	Report R2	2/17/89
6	Report R3	2/21/89
7	Report R4	2/22/89
8	Report R5	2/21/89
9	Report R11	2/17/89

Fig. 13.2.

The Family table.

The last two options on the Tools Info menu, **W**ho and **L**ock, are discussed in "Using Tools on a Network" later in this chapter.

Renaming Paradox Objects

As you have discovered, Paradox makes liberal use of temporary tables. Queries create the Answer table, DataEntry creates the Entry table, key violations create the Keyviol table, and the **I**nfo option discussed in the preceding section creates several different temporary tables. The potential problem with temporary tables is that their contents are not safe until you either copy the data to another table or give the temporary table a new name. Changing the names of temporary tables is the most common use of the **R**ename option on the Tools menu, although you also can rename scripts, graphs, forms, and reports.

Renaming a Table

To rename a table, temporary or otherwise, select **T**ools **R**ename **T**able from the Main menu. At the first prompt, specify the name of the table whose name is to be changed. At the next prompt, type a new table name, and press Enter. Make sure that you do not use one of the following temporary table names:

Answer	Changed [3]
Crosstab	Deleted
Entry	Family
Inserted	Keyviol
List	Password
Problems	Struct

Paradox renames the table and all family members with the new name.

Renaming Forms and Reports

In Paradox, the names of forms and reports are not really significant, with two major exceptions: the standard form F is the default preferred form, invoked by pressing F7 (Form Toggle); the standard report specification R is selected by default by pressing Alt-F7 (Instant Report). As suggested in previous chapters, you may want to create your own customized form and report specification to replace the default choices. One method of accomplishing the replacement is through the **R**ename command.

To rename a form, select **T**ools **R**ename **F**orm from the Main menu. Specify the table that contains the form. To help you, Paradox displays a list of defined forms. Select the one to be renamed, and then select the new name. Paradox warns you if the new name you type is already in use. Then you must decide whether to **C**ancel the operation or **R**eplace the existing form.

Changing the name of a report is accomplished in a similar way.

Renaming Scripts and Graphs

Paradox scripts and graphs (graphs are available only in Paradox 3.0) are [3]
stored as files outside of a table's family of objects. Because scripts and graph specifications can be used with more than one table, they have their own name, and are not automatically renamed when you rename the table.

The Instant script, recorded when you press Alt-F3 (Instant Script Record), is similar to a temporary table in that it is temporary also. If you think that you may want to use the Instant script again, you must rename it to preserve it.

Paradox does not create temporary graph specifications, but it is possible that you may want to change the name of a graph specification to more clearly reflect its content, or perhaps so that you can use the name for a different graph.

To change the name of a script file, select **T**ools **R**ename **S**cript from the Main menu. Specify the name of the script, type the new name, and press Enter. If you select a name that already exists, Paradox gives you a choice of canceling the **R**ename operation or replacing the existing script.

Follow a similar procedure to rename a graph specification.

Copying Paradox Objects

The **C**opy option on the Tools menu enables you to make copies of Para- [3]
dox tables, forms, reports, scripts, graphs (Version 3.0 only), and a family of objects with the parent table.

Copying Tables

When you copy a table, you copy the table and its entire family. For this reason, you should always use the **C**opy option whenever you want to make a backup of a table. In one step you copy the table and its forms, reports, indexes, validity checks, and settings. As long as you copy to a different disk or directory, you can even use the same name for the copy.

To copy a table, select **T**ools **C**opy **T**able from the Main menu. At the prompt for the table name, indicate the name of the table to be copied, and at the prompt for the new name, type the name of the new table. Paradox informs you if a table by the same name already exists and gives you a chance to cancel or proceed with the copying process.

Copying Forms and Reports

The procedures for copying forms and reports are nearly identical. To copy a Paradox form, select **T**ools **C**opy **F**orm from the Main menu. Then choose between the following menu options:

- **S**ameTable. Select this choice when you want to copy the form in the same family of objects. When prompted, specify the table containing the form, the form to be copied, and a name for the copy.

- **D**ifferentTable. Choose this option to copy the form to a different table. For this to work, both tables must have identical structures. If they do not, Paradox displays a message stating that the tables do not have the same field names or field types. When prompted, supply the name of the source table, the destination table, and the name of the form.

Follow similar steps to copy a report specification. The most likely situation for copying a report occurs when you want to use an existing report specification to print an Answer table. The Answer table must have a structure identical to the source table.

Copying Just a Table's Family

Although separate options exist for copying forms and reports, it may be convenient to copy an entire family of objects from one table to another. This is particularly true if you have chosen validity checks for use with forms, or have several forms or reports to copy. The **J**ustFamily option copies all objects, including validity checks and image settings. The **J**ustFamily option copies a table's family of objects, without copying the table itself. The target table must already exist, however, and must have a structure identical to the source table.

To copy a family of objects without copying the table to which the family belongs, select **T**ools **C**opy **J**ustFamily from the Main menu. Specify the source table and the target table. Then choose **R**eplace to indicate that any existing family objects should be replaced.

You are most likely to use the **J**ustFamily option to add forms, reports, validity checks, and settings to a table just extracted from another table through a query operation. You may decide to create a separate telephone list for the Sales department, for example. To do this, you first use QBE to create an Answer table containing only employees from the Sales department. Next, you use the **R**ename **T**able option to change Answer to Sales. Finally, you use the **J**ustFamily option to copy all forms, reports, and so forth, to the Sales table. Not only do you have the telephone list report available, you also have any other reports and all forms, validity checks, and other settings.

Copying Scripts and Graphs

The steps for copying scripts and graphs are nearly identical to the steps for renaming these objects, except that you select **C**opy instead of **R**ename from the **T**ools menu. Refer to "Renaming Scripts and Graphs" for detailed instructions.

Deleting Objects and Emptying a Table

The **D**elete choice on the Tools menu provides options to delete tables, forms, reports, scripts, query speedups, image settings, validity checks, and graphs (Version 3.0 only). These operations are self-explanatory, but because they are irreversible, they should be used with caution.

Caution: Use all of the **D**elete options with caution, but be particularly sure that you really want to delete a table before selecting that option. Deleting a table also deletes its family of objects.

The **E**mpty option on the Tools/More menu provides a method of deleting all records from a table without deleting the table's structure or family. To use this option, select **T**ools **M**ore **E**mpty from the Main menu and specify the table to be emptied. Paradox requires that you confirm the deletion with **O**K.

Empty provides an alternative to using the **C**opy option to copy **J**ustFamily to a new table. Instead, you can use **E**mpty to delete the existing records and **A**dd (see "Adding and Subtracting Tables" in this chapter) to add the records from the new table to the emptied table. One advantage of the **E**mpty-**A**dd method is that key-field assignments are maintained; they are lost in the **C**opy-**J**ustFamily method.

For example, you may use query by example on the Employee table to create an Answer table containing only employees from the Sales department. Answer tables do not have key fields, and using the **C**opy/**J**ustFamily tool does not create the key fields. To use the **E**mpty method, you first make a copy of the Employee table (using the **C**opy/**T**able options from the Tools menu) perhaps with the name Sales. Then use **E**mpty to remove all records from Sales. Finally use

Add from the Tools/More menu to add the Sales department employees to the Sales table. The Emp ID # field in Sales is still the key field, and Paradox stores records in order by that field.

Adding and Subtracting Tables

Several options on the Tools/More menu enable you to add and update data from table to table. One option permits you to use one table to specify deletions in another table, and another option adds or updates data from one table to two or more tables at once.

Adding and Updating Records from One Table to Another

Unlike the **C**opy and **R**ename operations, the **A**dd option can handle tables without identical structures. To add one table to another using **A**dd, however, the two tables must have the same number of fields, in the same order, and with compatible field types (numeric matched to numeric, alphanumeric matched to alphanumeric, and date matched to date).

To add one table to another, select **T**ools **M**ore **A**dd from the Main menu. Specify the source table and the target table. If the target table is not keyed, Paradox adds the new records to the end of the table. If the table is keyed, you must choose between the following menu options:

- **N**ewEntries. Choose this option if the records being added do not yet exist in the target table. When Paradox performs the **A**dd operation, any key violations are placed in the Keyviol table. This choice essentially is a mass DataEntry session.

- **U**pdate. When some or all of the records you are adding may already exist in the target table, use the **U**pdate option. This selection acts much like an Edit session. Old field values where key values match new records are replaced by new field values. Where no matching record already exists, the new record is merged into the target table in key-field order. The original values of any existing records that have been updated are placed in a temporary table named Changed so that you can easily determine what changes have been made.

Database users commonly distribute to satellite offices portions of a master database. A problem that is just as common is how to later reconcile the master database with any changes made by the various satellite offices to their portion of the database. The **A**dd **U**pdate option provides a possible solution.

Adding and Updating from One Table to Two or More Tables

The **M**ultiAdd option on the Tools/More menu is the counterpart to the MultiEntry feature. Indeed, to use **M**ultiAdd, you must first have created a source table and a map table using the **M**ultiEntry **S**etup option from the Modify menu (refer to Chapter 9).

To add data from one table to two or more tables, select **T**ools **M**ore **M**ulti-Add from the Main menu. Specify the source table (created by **M**ultiEntry **S**etup) and the map table. Paradox displays the following options from which you must select:

- **N**ewEntries. Choose this option when you want to add the new records to the tables, rather than update records that already exist in the target tables. As with MultiEntry, Paradox places in Keyviol tables key violations that occur during the **M**ultiAdd operation. A new record that *exactly duplicates*, in every field, an existing record is not considered a key violation, but is also not added to the table. Such an exact duplicate is "absorbed" into the existing record, or, in other words, ignored. When a key violation does occur, correct the error and use **M**ultiAdd to insert the record into the target tables.

You must rename the Keyviol table using the **R**ename option before Paradox allows you to add the corrected records with **M**ultiAdd.

- **U**pdate. Select this option to use the source table to update the target tables. For non-keyed target tables, records are added to the end of the table. For keyed target tables, records with no match are merged in key order; records matching the key fields are used to update values in the matching records in the target tables. A Changed table is not created, as opposed to using a "change to" query, which creates a temporarily changed table—see Chapter 7.

Using a Multitable Form To Add or Update Multiple Tables

Sometimes it is necessary to consolidate data from several sources into one set of tables. When several of the target tables are logically related—one-to-one, one-to-many—it is best to use all available tools to ensure referential integrity. The **F**ormAdd option on the Tools/More menu is the batch-processing equivalent of using a multitable form during DataEntry. **F**ormAdd is analogous to **M**ultiAdd but needs no map table because the multitable form *is* the map. [3]

In order to use **F**ormAdd to add to or update one set of related tables from a corresponding set of related tables, the following must be true:

- Each of the source tables has a structure compatible with its corresponding target table: fields in the same order, same number of key fields, compatible field types (numeric fields match numeric fields, alphanumeric fields match alphanumeric fields, and date fields match date fields).
- A multitable form exists that contains all the fields of the target tables.

The next sections describe several scenarios for using **F**ormAdd.

Adding Multiple Entry Tables

Whenever you use DataEntry to add records to your database through a multitable form, Paradox builds a series of Entry tables with the names Entry, Entry1, Entry2, and so on, depending on the number of tables linked in the multitable form. When you press F2 (DO-IT!) to complete DataEntry, Paradox attempts to add the data from these Entry tables to the target tables, using the multitable form as a map. If it is successful, you can forget about the Entry tables.

Two eventualities can prevent successful addition of all the new records to the target tables:

- **K**eepEntry. On a network, another user may have locked one of your target tables. In this case, Paradox informs you that the table is locked. You may choose to wait for the other user to finish, or choose the **K**eepEntry option from the DataEntry menu. (See Chapter 9 for a discussion of entering records from multitable forms.) **K**eepEntry makes sure that all the new records are in the Entry tables, clears the form from the screen, and returns to Main mode.

- Key violations. A key violation in adding records to one or more of the target tables causes Paradox to build a set of Keyviol tables: Keyviol, Keyviol1, Keyviol2, and so forth. These tables contain the offending records. Paradox also does not immediately erase the Entry tables. (Keep in mind that Keyviol tables and Entry tables are *temporary*.) When such a key violation occurs, Paradox builds the Keyviol tables, adds nonoffending records to these tables, adds nonoffending records to the target tables, and returns you to Main mode.

In either of these two cases, you must add records to the target tables in a batch, instead of one at a time. In the first situation, you add the Entry tables; in the second situation, you add the corrected records that caused key violations. As suggested in a tip in Chapter 9, you probably want to use the Entry tables in both cases as source tables for a **F**ormAdd operation.

As mentioned in Chapter 9, Paradox balks at adding Keyviol tables using **F**ormAdd because it doesn't maintain key fields in the Keyviol tables. Instead of using these tables, correct the key violations in the Entry tables and then use **F**ormAdd. Ignore the second set of Keyviol tables, if applicable (unless you made a mistake correcting the first violations—the second set of tables appears when some of the new records are successfully added during the first try with DataEntry).

To add Entry tables to existing compatible target tables, select **T**ools **M**ore **F**ormAdd from the Main menu. Specify the name of the master target table at the first prompt and choose the multientry form from the next prompt. Then select **E**ntryTables from the menu that Paradox displays. Paradox locates the Entry tables and adds the new records to the target tables.

Adding to or Updating Multiple Tables Using AnyTables

When you are not adding Entry tables, you must take a few more steps to use **F**ormAdd. From the Main menu, select **T**ools **M**ore **F**ormAdd. Specify the target master table at the first prompt and multitable form at the next prompt. Then select **A**nyTables from the menu. Paradox provides the following menu options from which you can choose:

- **N**ewEntries. When all the source records are either completely new or exact duplicates of existing records, choose this option. Paradox places key violations in the Keyviol tables. (Contrary to the Paradox documentation, exact duplicates are not ignored. See also the tip below.)

- **U**pdate. Select this option to use the source tables to update the target tables. Because you should always use keyed tables, records with no match are merged in key order, and records that match the key fields are used to update values in the matching records in the target tables. Changed tables *are* created for detail tables (contrary to a statement in the Paradox documentation). Paradox names these tables Changed1, Changed2, and so forth, and displays a List table that maps each Changed table to its corresponding detail table (see fig. 13.3). If you are adding records to target tables that are not keyed, the records are added to the end of the table.

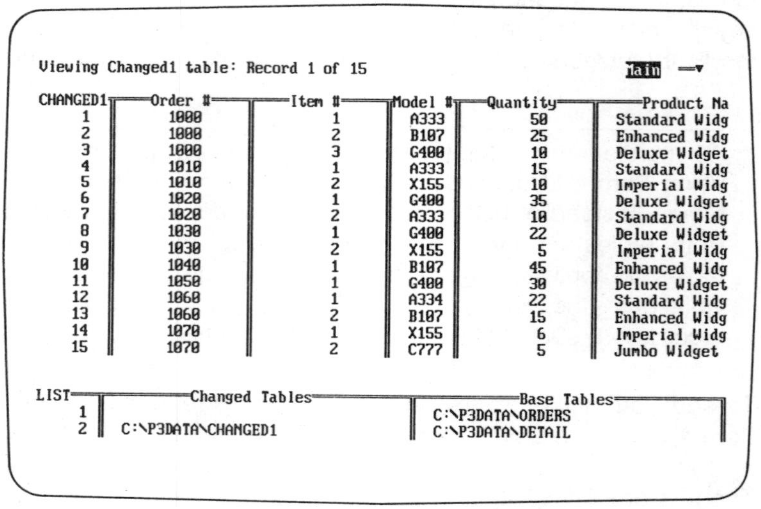

Viewing Changed1 table: Record 1 of 15 Main

CHANGED1	Order #	Item #	Model #	Quantity	Product Na
1	1000	1	A333	50	Standard Widg
2	1000	2	B107	25	Enhanced Widg
3	1000	3	G400	10	Deluxe Widget
4	1010	1	A333	15	Standard Widg
5	1010	2	X155	10	Imperial Widg
6	1020	1	G400	35	Deluxe Widget
7	1020	2	A333	10	Standard Widg
8	1030	1	G400	22	Deluxe Widget
9	1030	2	X155	5	Imperial Widg
10	1040	1	B107	45	Enhanced Widg
11	1050	1	G400	30	Deluxe Widget
12	1060	1	A334	22	Standard Widg
13	1060	2	B107	15	Enhanced Widg
14	1070	1	X155	6	Imperial Widg
15	1070	2	C777	5	Jumbo Widget

LIST	Changed Tables	Base Tables
1		C:\P3DATA\ORDERS
2	C:\P3DATA\CHANGED1	C:\P3DATA\DETAIL

Fig. 13.3.
The Changed1 table created during FormAdd.

Regardless of whether you choose **N**ewEntries or **U**pdate, you must choose source tables that match the target tables included in the multitable form, starting with the master table. Paradox prompts you for the correct number of tables based on the number of tables used in the multitable form. As soon as you select the last source table, Paradox performs the **F**ormAdd operation.

Key violations are not handled particularly well in the FormAdd Any-Tables situation. As already stated, key violations are placed in a series of Keyviol tables (Keyviol, Keyviol1, Keyviol2, and so on). Paradox does not index these tables and does not allow you to use them with **F**ormAdd, despite what the Paradox documentation says. The easiest way to add corrected records is as follows:

1. Correct, in the source tables, the errors that caused the violations *not* in the Keyviol tables.
2. Use **F**ormAdd to add the source tables again to the target tables. Ignore any *new* key violations. Check to make sure that you did not make a mistake correcting the first errors; otherwise any new violations are caused by records successfully added the first time.

Subtracting Tables

Occasionally you will compile a table that contains a list of records that should be deleted from another table. You may have just updated your product line, for example, adding new models and deleting slow sellers. You could, of course, manually go through the Products table and delete each obsolete model, but an easier method is to compile a list of the model numbers and use the **S**ubtract option on the Tools/More menu to delete all the obsolete models at once.

To use this option, select **T**ools **M**ore **S**ubtract from the Main menu. Specify the name of the table that includes the records to be deleted. Then specify the target table. The structures of the source and target tables must be compatible, not necessarily identical. The way Paradox handles the deletions depends on whether or not the tables are keyed, as described below:

- ❑ When the tables are keyed, Paradox deletes any records in the target table that match the key field or fields of the source table. That means you can leave blank all source fields except key fields and still delete the obsolete records.
- ❑ If tables are not keyed, Paradox deletes only the target-table records that are exact matches of source-table records.

Exporting and Importing Tables

If life were perfect, everyone in the world would use Paradox for database applications and you would not have to worry about other file formats. Because life is never perfect, Paradox provides a number of tools that enable you both to export to and to import from file formats used by other programs.

Exporting Paradox Tables

Occasionally you must use data contained in a Paradox table with another program. Translating the data from the file format used by Paradox to that of the other program is referred to as *exporting* the file. To export a Paradox table, select **T**ools **E**xportImport **E**xport from the Main menu. Paradox presents a list of the formats to which you can export the Paradox table. Choose the appropriate format:

- **Q**uattro. Use this option to create a Quattro spreadsheet file. [3]
- **1**-2-3. Select this option to create a Lotus 1-2-3 spreadsheet. Then choose **1**)_1-2-3_Release_1A or **2**)_1-2-3_Release_2, depending on the version of 1-2-3 to be used.
- **S**ymphony. Choose this format to create a Symphony spreadsheet. Then select **1**)_Symphony_Release_1.0 or **2**)_Symphony_Release_1.1, depending on the version of Symphony to be used.
- **D**base. To create a dBASE file, choose this option. Then select **1**)_dBase_II or **2**)_dBase_III, depending on the version of dBASE to be used.
- **P**fs. This selection creates a file in a format compatible with PFS:File or IBM Filing Assistant.
- **R**eflex. Select this format to export the table as a Reflex database file. Then select **1**)_Reflex_Release_1.0 or **2**)_Reflex_Release_1.1, depending on the version of Reflex to be used. [3]
- **V**isicalc. Select this option to create a file for use by any program that can use a DIF file.
- **A**scii. Use this option to convert the table into an ASCII file. Then choose **D**elimited (fields are separated by commas; records are on separate lines) or **T**ext (use only with a table containing exactly one field where the field is an alphanumeric field).

After selecting the export format, specify the name of the Paradox table to export and the name of the target table. You can use the same name for the target table because Paradox adds a different extension, depending on the export format chosen. Paradox converts the source data to the selected format. Table 13.1 lists how Paradox converts data types during **E**xport.

Table 13.1
Paradox 2.0/3.0 Export/Import Data Type Conversion

Format	*Export Target Data Type*	*Paradox Data Type*	*Import Source Data Type*
Quattro, 1-2-3, or Symphony	Labels	Alphanumeric (A)	Labels
	Numbers	Numeric (N)	Numbers
	Numbers (2 decimals in currency format)	Currency ($)	Numbers (2 decimals in currency format)
	Numbers (formatted as dates)	Date (D)	Numbers (formatted as dates)
dBase	Character	Alphanumeric (A)	Character
	Number	Numeric (N)	Number (19 digits, 14 whole, 4 decimal)
	Number (2 decimals)	Currency ($)	Number (2 decimals)
	Date (dBASE III) or Character (dBASE II)	Date	Date (dBASE III)
	Number (5 digits)	Short (S)	
	Character	Alphanumeric (A) (length 255)	Memo (dBASE III)
	Character	Alphanumeric (A) (length 1)	Logical
Pfs	Character string	Alphanumeric (A)	Contains any nonnumeric character
	Character string	Numeric (N)	All numeric characters
	Character string	Currency ($)	All numeric and 2 decimals
	Character string	Date (D)	All values in yy/mm/dd or mm/dd/yy format
	Character string	Alphanumeric (A) (length 255)	Attachment pages

Table 13.1—*Continued*

Format	*Export Target Data Type*	*Paradox Data Type*	*Import Source Data Type*
Reflex	Text	Alphanumeric (A)	Text
		Alphanumeric (A)	Repeating text
	Numeric	Numeric (N)	Numeric
	Numeric (formatted as currency)	Currency ($)	Numeric (formatted as currency or financial)
	Integer	Short (S)	Integer
	Date (formatted as mm/dd/yy)	Date (D)	Date
Visicalc	Text	Alphanumeric (A)	Text
	Numbers	Numeric (N)	Numbers
	Numbers (2 decimals)	Currency	Numbers (2 decimals)
	Text (formatted as mm/dd/yy)	Date	Text (formatted as mm/dd/yy)

Importing Data from Other Formats

One of the rules of thumb stated early in this book is never to enter data more than once. An even better rule, when you can get away with it, is never to enter data at all—let someone else do it for you. If anyone ever offers you data created in the format of another program, take it. More likely than not, Paradox can *import* (bring in) the file.

To import data from another file format, select **T**ools **E**xportImport **I**mport from the Main menu. Choose the appropriate file format (the same choices listed in the "Exporting Paradox Tables" section are presented, except for ASCII files, which are described in the next paragraph). Then specify the file to be imported, including the DOS path if the file is not in your working directory. Finally, type a name for the new Paradox table. Paradox converts the data to a Paradox table, following the conversion rules listed in table 13.1.

You can import ASCII files into a new table automatically created by Paradox, or you can add the ASCII data to an existing Paradox table. To Import an ASCII file into a Paradox table, select **T**ools **E**xportImport **I**mport **A**scii from the Main menu. Then choose from the following options:

- **D**elimited. Choose this option when the ASCII file is stored as comma delimited (the CCP program discussed in Appendix B enables you to configure Paradox so that it will use some other delimiting character, if necessary) and you want Paradox to create a new file automatically.
- **A**ppendDelimited. Make this choice to add an ASCII file to an existing Paradox file. This option works in the same fashion as the **A**dd choice on the Tools/More menu. Refer to the "Adding and Updating Records from One Table to Another" section of this chapter for details. Contrary to the Paradox documentation, this feature does not create a Changed table.

Once you have selected the **D**elimited or **A**ppendDelimited option, specify, at the first prompt, the source file name (including the path if the file is not in the current directory) and the name of the target table at the second prompt.

Speeding Up Queries with QuerySpeedup

A consistent complaint that daily users of database products have is that data retrieval is too slow. One of the hallmarks of Paradox is the use of artificial intelligence (AI) routines that find the fastest possible route to your data. For this reason, with Paradox you seldom have to worry about query speed.

This book encourages creation of at least one key field (*primary index*, see the "Assigning Key Fields" section in Chapter 2) per table. Several reasons for the use of key fields in Paradox exist, and one of them is to help speed up queries. Because Paradox always stores tables in order by key fields, and because queries are often done by key field, you get the fastest query response possible.

Situations arise when you routinely use a query that may benefit in terms of speed by maintenance of an index on a field other than key fields. Such an index is called a *secondary index*.

To try to speed up a query, first construct the query statement on the work space, and then select **T**ools **Q**uerySpeedup from the Main menu. Paradox displays the message `Processing query speedup`. Often, however, Paradox is using the fastest search method already, and displays the message `No speedup possible`. Paradox does not build a secondary index, which increases program overhead, unless the secondary index can increase the speed of the search.

Protecting Your Files

One of the inherent weaknesses of the PC DOS/MS-DOS operating system is a lack of system-level file protection. DOS provides no utility for securing your programs or data against tampering by other users. The only protection you can place on a file with DOS is the read-only attribute (DOS 3.2 and later), and that only prevents accidental modifications or deletions. Anyone with access to the disk that contains the file can remove the attribute and delete the file.

The Paradox **P**rotect tool on the Tools/More menu significantly improves your ability to protect data from unauthorized access. With this feature you can add sophisticated password protection to tables and scripts, and Paradox-specific, read-only protection to tables.

Adding Password Protection to a Paradox Table

Paradox enables you to claim *ownership* of a Paradox table by adding a password. The original password placed on a table is called the *owner* password (also called the *master* password). Placing an owner password on a file does the following:

- *Encryption*. Adding a password encrypts the table and all its family members so that they can no longer be used without the password.

- *Ownership*. Knowledge of the owner password enables you to assign multiple *auxiliary passwords* that grant limited access to the table or its family of objects.

Assign the same password to all related tables for the following reasons:

- *Convenience*. Entering the password once during a Paradox session grants you access to all tables with the same password.

- *MultiTable Forms*. Paradox does not prompt you for a password for detail tables embedded in a multitable form. Unless one password accesses the master table and all detail tables, Paradox displays the message `Insufficient rights for Detail table` when you try to use a multitable form.
- *Memory* (yours, not the computer's). Remembering one password is easier than remembering several for a single database.

To assign an owner password, select **T**ools **M**ore **P**rotect **P**assword **T**able from the Main menu. At the first prompt, specify the table you want to protect. At the Password prompt, enter a password of up to 15 characters, including numbers and spaces, and press Enter. Paradox prompts you to enter the password again, to confirm the original entry. Use a word that you can remember, or write it down where you can find it. If you forget the password, you cannot use the table or any of its objects.

As an added precaution against forgetting your password, assign yourself an *auxiliary password* with **A**ll rights. Refer to "Assigning Table Rights, Family Rights, and Field Rights" in this chapter for more information. You then have to forget both passwords to be completely locked out of the table.

After confirming that the password was entered properly the second time, Paradox enters Password mode and displays the *auxiliary password form* (see fig. 13.4). Using this form, you can assign table rights or family rights to other users as discussed in the following section. This form is actually a special data-input form for a table named Password. You can press F7 (Form Toggle) to see the Password table in table view, if you want.

When you have finished adding auxiliary passwords, press F2 (DO-IT!) to complete definition of the passwords. Paradox displays the message `Encrypting...` and converts the target table and all family members into an encrypted format. After a table and its family of objects is encrypted, you can access them only with the proper password.

Assigning Table Rights, Family Rights, and Field Rights

When you are the only user of your database, you already have all rights to use, modify, and delete the table and all its family members, whether or not you add personal protection. When others need to use some or all of the

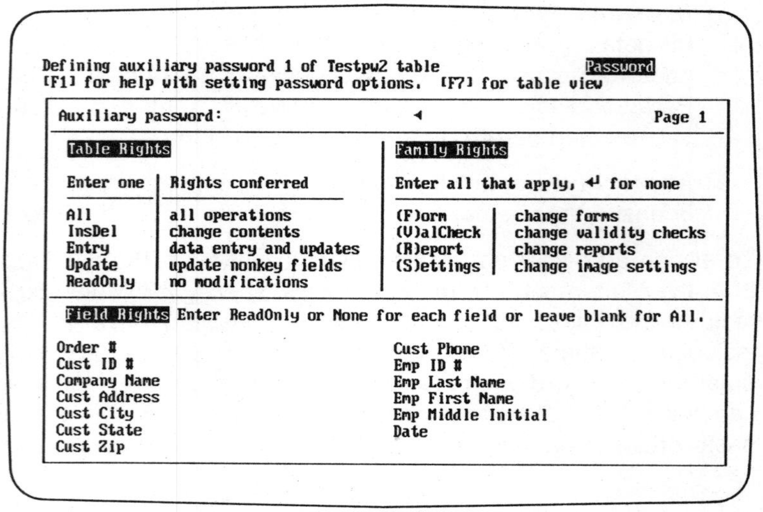

Defining auxiliary password 1 of Testpw2 table
Password
[F1] for help with setting password options. [F7] for table view
Auxiliary password:
Page 1
Table Rights
Enter one
Rights conferred
All — all operations
InsDel — change contents
Entry — data entry and updates
Update — update nonkey fields
ReadOnly — no modifications
Family Rights
Enter all that apply, ↵ for none
(F)orm — change forms
(V)alCheck — change validity checks
(R)eport — change reports
(S)ettings — change image settings
Field Rights
Enter ReadOnly or None for each field or leave blank for All.
Order #
Cust ID #
Company Name
Cust Address
Cust City
Cust State
Cust Zip
Cust Phone
Emp ID #
Emp Last Name
Emp First Name
Emp Middle Initial
Date

Fig. 13.4.
The auxiliary password form.

tables in your database, however, such as in an office environment or on a network, you may want to grant each of the users a level of access consistent with their needs. You assign certain access rights to auxiliary passwords and provide the password only to those users who need the corresponding level of access.

For each auxiliary password, you can grant any one of the following table rights by making a choice in the Table Rights section of the auxiliary password form:

- **R**eadOnly. The user who knows (and uses) the auxiliary password can view the table but cannot make changes or deletions.
- **U**pdate. The user can view the table and make changes to nonkey fields, but cannot insert or delete records or make any changes to key fields.
- **E**ntry. The user has Update rights, and can enter records into the table using DataEntry or Add.
- **I**nsDel. The user has Entry rights, and can change the content of all fields, insert and delete records, and change key fields.
- **A**ll. This right is equivalent to ownership, but because the user obtains access with an auxiliary password, not the owner (master) password, he or she doesn't have access to other tables unlocked by the owner password.

Grant each auxiliary password any combination of the following rights, with respect to the family of objects belonging to the protected table, through the Family Rights section of the auxiliary password form. Type the first letter of each choice, and Paradox displays the letters you type to the right of the label `Family Rights` on the auxiliary password form:

- (F)orm. The user who knows (and uses) the auxiliary password can design, change, and delete forms in the protected table's family.
- (V)alCheck. The user can assign, change, or delete validity checks for members of the protected family.
- (R)eport. The user can design, change, and delete report specifications in the protected family.
- (S)ettings. The user can add, change, and delete image settings.

You can even control access to specific fields with the Field Rights section of the auxiliary password form (choose only one):

- **R**eadOnly. The user can view but not change the protected field values.
- **N**one. The user can neither see nor alter the values in the field.
- (blank). All field rights, including the right to view and change any value in the field, are granted.

Once you have assigned all the desired access rights to the auxiliary password, press PgDn to display new forms for additional auxiliary passwords or press F2 (DO-IT!) to indicate that you are finished.

Whenever you are working on the auxiliary password form and press F10 (Menu), Paradox presents the following Password Mode menu:

Undo **H**elp **D**O-IT! **C**ancel

These options work exactly like their namesakes in the Edit mode. You also can press Ctrl-U (Undo) to back out of changes made to the Password table, one transaction at a time.

Assigning Passwords to Scripts

The purpose and effect of assigning a password to a Paradox script is different from that of password-protecting a table. Tables can contain sensitive or valuable information that needs to be protected from unauthorized access, but a script is just a program. The reason for protecting a script is not to prevent the use of it, but to prevent anyone from changing it.

To add a password to a script, select **T**ools **M**ore **P**rotect **P**assword **S**cript from the Main menu. Specify the name of the target script. Type the desired password and press Enter, and type the password again and press Enter for confirmation. Paradox displays the message `Encrypting....` You do not have to supply the password to play the script, just to edit or debug it.

Changing and Removing Passwords

Occasions almost certainly will arise when you need to remove or change a password. To delete or make changes to a password, select **T**ools **M**ore **P**rotect **P**assword from the Main menu, and then choose either **T**able or **S**cript, depending on the entity for which you want to change the password.

For a table password, specify the name of the protected table. If you have not already accessed this table during the current session, you must enter the current password. Then choose **M**aster or **A**uxiliary. Choosing **M**aster enables you to enter a new password. To delete the current password, just press Enter. Whenever you delete the owner (master) password, Paradox displays the message `Decrypting...` as it unprotects the indicated table. Choosing **A**uxiliary, on the other hand, displays the Password table in the auxiliary password form, and enables you to make changes.

For a script password, specify the script name and enter the current password. To change the password, type the new one and press Enter. To remove the password without replacing it, press Enter at the prompt for the new password.

Clearing Passwords

For your convenience, Paradox does not require you to enter your password every time you redisplay a protected table in a given session. If you walk away from your computer for a short time without exiting Paradox, however, someone else may access the protected files you opened.

To prevent this from occurring, before you leave the computer, select **T**ools **M**ore **P**rotect **C**learPasswords from the Main menu. Paradox clears everything from the work space and displays the message `All passwords cleared`. This does not remove the passwords, but simply resets the protection feature so that anyone trying to access the table must know the proper passwords. When you return to the computer and start to use the protected table again, you must enter the password again.

Using the Write-Protect Option

The Paradox write-protect feature (for tables only) is similar in concept to the DOS read-only attribute or the write-protect notch on a floppy disk (or the write-protect slide on a 3 1/2-inch disk). This feature is only effective in Paradox, however; it does not prevent access, alterations, or deletions from DOS.

To add the Paradox write-protect feature to a table, select **T**ools **M**ore **P**rotect **W**rite-protect from the Main menu. Specify the name of the table to be protected. Then choose **S**et. This feature provides protection against accidental changes and deletions from within Paradox, but does not prevent unauthorized access to your data. Although a table is write-protected, Paradox does not permit you to edit or delete records in the table.

To remove Paradox write-protection, select **T**ools **M**ore **P**rotect **W**rite-protect from the Main menu. Specify the name of the protected table. Then choose **C**lear.

Changing the Working Directory

The DOS directory that contains your database is called the *working directory*. Appendix A, "Paradox 3.0 Installation and Start-Up," explains how to start Paradox from the working directory. When you use that procedure, Paradox automatically reads and saves tables to the working directory. The **D**irectory option on the Tools/More menu provides a method of changing the working directory after you begin Paradox.

To change the working directory, select **T**ools **M**ore **D**irectory from the Main menu. Backspace over the current working directory name and type a new directory name. Press Enter and then select **O**K.

Caution: This operation not only changes the directory, but also clears any images on the work space and deletes all temporary tables. Make sure that you rename any temporary tables that you want to save before executing this option.

Accessing the Operating System

Paradox provides three methods of accessing DOS without exiting Paradox. Two are equivalent. From the Main menu you can press **T**ools **M**ore **T**oDOS. Paradox displays the following warning:

```
WARNING! Do not delete or edit Paradox objects, or load RAM-
resident programs. To return to Paradox, type exit.
```

Paradox saves the current Paradox state, loads a DOS shell, and displays the DOS prompt. Paradox still occupies about 420K of memory, so keep this memory restriction in mind when you perform any DOS operations.

The keystroke command Ctrl-O (DOS) is equivalent to the **T**oDOS menu option.

At times, the preceding options do not leave you enough DOS memory to execute the desired operation. In such cases, use the keystroke Alt-O (DOS Big). With this option, Paradox uses only about 100K of memory, but because it saves the Paradox environment temporarily to disk, it is slower than the other options.

Whenever you access DOS using any of these methods, observe the following precautions:

- Do not delete, rename, or change any Paradox system files or objects. If you do, Paradox may not be able to resume when you try to exit DOS.
- Do not load additional RAM-resident programs. Paradox needs all the memory it released to DOS.
- Do not use the DOS Print or Mode commands.
- If you change disks or directions while accessing DOS, return to the original directory before exiting the DOS session.
- Terminate the DOS session by typing *exit* on a DOS command line.

These guidelines help ensure that you don't corrupt your database when performing a DOS operation.

Using Tools on a Network

All the tools discussed thus far in this chapter also can be used on a network. The password and access rights features in particular are even better suited for use on a network than on a single-user system. A few special considerations apply when some of the tools are used on a network, and Paradox has several tools of interest only to network users.

Special Considerations

Whenever you use Paradox tools on shared objects on a network, you have to keep in mind the locks that Paradox places on these objects. Locks are described in "Creating Tables on a Network" in Chapter 2. Table 13.2 lists the locks placed on source and target objects as you work with the various tools discussed in this chapter.

Table 13.2
Locks Placed When Using Tools on a Network

Tool	*Type of Lock*
Add	Write lock on source, prevent write lock on target
Copy	
Table	Write lock on source, full lock on target
JustFamily	Write lock on source, prevent full lock on target
Form, Report	Write lock on source, full lock on target, prevent full lock on table
Script, Graph	Write lock on source, full lock on target
Delete	
Table	Full lock on table and its family
Form Report	Full lock on target object and prevent full lock on table
Script, Graph	Full lock on target object
QuerySpeedup	Full lock on target object and table
KeepSet	Full lock on target object and table
Empty	Full lock on table
Export	Write lock on source table
FormAdd	Write lock on all source tables, prevent write lock on all target tables
Import	Full lock on target table

Table 13.2—*Continued*

Tool	*Type of Lock*
Info	
Structure	Prevent full lock on table
Family	Write lock on table and family
MultiAdd	Write lock on source and map tables, prevent write lock on all target tables
Protect	Full lock on table or script
Subtract	Full lock on both tables

Assigning a User Name

Many networks enable you to establish a *user name* that identifies you to other network users for such things as electronic mail. Paradox automatically uses this name, if it exists. Paradox also has its own facility for assigning user names. The Paradox user name overrides any other name you may be assigned on the network, but only during the Paradox session. You can use this feature even if your network does not directly support user names.

You should encourage all network users of Paradox to establish user names because the names help you determine who is using and locking shared resources. Whenever you attempt to use a table but are prevented because the table is locked, Paradox can give you the name of the user who locked it only if a user name is assigned.

To assign a user name, select **T**ools **N**et **U**serName from the Main menu. Type your new user name (up to 15 characters, no spaces) and press Enter. Confirm the new name by selecting **O**K. Paradox displays a message indicating your new user name. This new name is in effect for the current Paradox session only.

A more permanent way to assign a user name is available through the Custom Configuration Program. Refer to Appendix B for details.

When using Paradox on a large network, include each user's telephone number (or extension) as a part of the user's name. Although most networks provide a method of communicating through the network itself, it may be more convenient just to pick up the phone and call the user who has locked you out of a table you need.

Assigning a Private Directory

Whenever you use Paradox on a network, you must have both a *working directory* and a *private directory*. Because the purpose of using Paradox on a network is to share files, your working directory obviously cannot be accessible only to you; but you should have a place for all temporary objects created by Paradox that is not accessible to other network users. You also can place permanent objects you don't want to share with other users into the private directory.

To assign or reassign a private directory during a Paradox session, select **T**ools **N**et **S**etPrivate from the Main menu. Type the complete path for the private directory and press Enter. Then confirm the change by selecting **O**K.

Caution: Changing the private directory during a Paradox session clears the work space and deletes all temporary objects. Be sure that you have renamed any temporary objects that you want to save for future use.

If your workstation has its own hard disk, assign the private directory to this hard disk. This gives Paradox the quickest access, and by definition, there is no need for other users to access this disk.

On a workstation with no local storage, check with your network administrator for assistance in creating a directory on the network that is accessible only by you. Use that directory as your Paradox private directory.

As with your user name, it is probably easiest to assign your Paradox private directory permanently through the CCP (refer to Appendix B).

Because it is imperative that you have a private directory whenever you use Paradox in a network environment, Paradox attempts to assign one automatically if you don't have one. By default, Paradox looks first to the directory from which you started Paradox on your local hard disk. For workstations without a C drive, Paradox tries to use the network directory from which you started Paradox. If this network directory is shared, Paradox displays the message `Can't start Paradox: can't get private directory.`

Placing Explicit Locks and Prevent Locks on Paradox Objects

As explained throughout this book, Paradox automatically places locks and prevent locks on Paradox objects as you use them. The specific type of lock or prevent lock is based on the type of operation you perform. Paradox tries to provide all users the maximum level of concurrent access to shared tables and objects consistent with the current needs of individual users.

Situations may arise when the automatic locks and prevent locks that Paradox applies are not sufficient protection. In such cases, Paradox enables you to place explicit locks and prevent locks on objects as well.

To place an explicit lock on a Paradox object, select **T**ools **N**et **L**ock from the Main menu. Then choose one of the following options:

- **F**ullLock. Choose this option to gain exclusive access to a table and its family of objects.
- **W**riteLock. Select this option to prevent other users from changing the structure or content of a table and its family of objects while still permitting users to manipulate the table and other objects in other ways.

After choosing the type of lock you want to impose on the table, specify the name of the table to be affected and choose **S**et. Paradox displays the message `Full lock set` or `Write lock set`. When you have finished using the table, don't forget to clear immediately the lock, using the same keystrokes, **T**ools **N**et **L**ock **F**ullLock/**W**riteLock, and choosing **C**lear at the end. Paradox then displays the message `Full lock cleared` or `Write lock cleared`.

To place an explicit prevent lock, select **T**ools **N**et **P**reventLock from the Main menu. Then choose one of the following options:

- Select **F**ullLock to prevent other network users from placing a full lock on the table and its family of objects.
- The **W**riteLock choice prevents other network users from placing either a write lock or a full lock on the table and its family.

After choosing the type of prevent lock, specify the target table, and choose **S**et. As with explicit locks, don't forget to explicitly **C**lear each prevent lock you assign.

Table 13.3 shows which locks and prevent locks can be applied to a table at the same time by several network users.

Table 13.3
Locks and Prevent Locks That May Coexist on a Table

	Full Lock	*Write Lock*	*Prevent Write Lock*	*Prevent Full Lock*
Full Lock				
Write Lock		X		X
Prevent Write Lock			X	X
Prevent Full Lock		X	X	X

Regulating AutoRefresh

As explained earlier in this book, Paradox keeps all current network users of a shared table up-to-date by continually refreshing the screens with changes being made by other users. The default interval for screen refreshes is 3 seconds. If this interval is not appropriate for your current needs, you can change it. To do so, select **T**ools **N**et **A**utoRefresh from the Main menu. Backspace over any existing number, and type a new number between 1 and 3600. The number you type represents a particular number of seconds. Leave the interval blank to disable autorefresh.

Gathering Network Information: Who Is Using Paradox? What Locks Are Placed?

When you intend to use a feature of Paradox that needs to place a lock on a shared table, you may want to determine first what locks are already in place on the table. Even if the table is not currently locked, you may want to see who else is using Paradox on the network. This may tell you whether to expect another user to compete with you for use of the table. The **I**nfo choice on the Tools menu gives you all of this information.

To see a list of locks in place on a table, and who placed them, select **T**ools **I**nfo **L**ock from the Main menu. Specify the target table. If any locks are currently in place on the table, Paradox displays a temporary List table containing the locks placed and the user name (if available) of the individual who placed each lock.

To see a list of network users currently using Paradox, select **T**ools **I**nfo **W**ho from the Main menu. Paradox displays the list of users in a temporary List table.

Chapter Summary

Now you have finished the last chapter in the second part of this book, "Tapping the Power of Paradox." This chapter has helped you examine the tools Paradox provides for accomplishing such tasks as exchanging files with other programs; renaming, copying, and deleting Paradox objects; adding and subtracting tables; speeding up queries; adding password protection; accessing the operating system; and locking and preventing locking of shared tables on a network. With this chapter, you have completed your tour of the interactive features of Paradox. As you may guess, you can still learn more about this seemingly boundless program. Turn now to the last part of the book, "Developing Menu-Driven Applications with Paradox," for an introduction to the use of the Paradox applications generator called the Personal Programmer and an overview of the Paradox Application Language (PAL).

III

Developing Menu-Driven Applications with Paradox

Includes

Using the Personal Programmer

An Overview of the Paradox Application Language

14

Using the Personal Programmer

Chapter 6 introduced you to simple Paradox Application Language (PAL) scripts that you can create by recording keystrokes. This chapter introduces you to the Paradox Personal Programmer, a powerful package used to generate scripts. You can use the Personal Programmer to generate an entire application simply by making menu selections and supplying the *parameters* (answers to questions) for which the Personal Programmer asks.

After you develop a menu structure, or hierarchy, and attach an action to each menu selection, the Personal Programmer generates a series of scripts necessary to run your application. The PAL scripts control your application by doing the following actions:

- ❑ Displaying a splash screen
- ❑ Performing password and table rights checking
- ❑ Displaying menu selections
- ❑ Prompting for user input
- ❑ Executing queries
- ❑ Displaying forms
- ❑ Performing edits
- ❑ Updating tables
- ❑ Printing reports

This chapter discusses the use of the Personal Programmer as a tool to develop Paradox applications. It covers most of the menu selections available to the user, but because the Personal Programmer is so big and powerful, this chapter focuses on the options offered only by the Personal Programmer and not offered by Paradox. To get the most out of this chapter, you should have a good understanding of the topics covered in the previous chapters.

The beauty of the Personal Programmer is its ease of use coupled with its power. Paradox's Personal Programmer is a menu-driven system. If you learn the menu structure of the Personal Programmer, therefore, you are on your way to writing complex PAL programs without learning the Paradox Application Language. For those who want to learn something about PAL, Chapter 15 of this book presents an overview to get you started.

Recommendations for Using the Personal Programmer

Before describing the technical aspects of the Personal Programmer, this section provides some recommendations on how to use it. The recommendations in the following sections may save you valuable time and allow you to manage your system better.

Design the Application on Paper First

Before using Paradox or the Personal Programmer, design your application thoroughly on paper. Make sure that the following design elements have been adequately thought out:

- ❑ Tables
- ❑ Forms
- ❑ Multitable forms
- ❑ Multirecord forms
- ❑ Multitable views (source and map tables)
- ❑ Queries
- ❑ Settings and validity checks
- ❑ Reports

- ❑ Multitable reports
- ❑ Menu structure (hierarchy)

Paradox and the Personal Programmer are flexible and can accommodate change nicely, but they are not as flexible as an eraser. The benefits of designing on paper first become more apparent when you have to change a large application. You may have a long wait as the Personal Programmer regenerates the application.

Use Paradox To Create Objects

Use Paradox to create the following objects:

- ❑ Tables
- ❑ Forms
- ❑ Multitable forms
- ❑ Multirecord forms
- ❑ Source and map tables (using MultiEntry multitable views)
- ❑ Queries
- ❑ Settings and validity checks
- ❑ Reports
- ❑ Multitable reports

Paradox handles these objects better than the Personal Programmer. The Personal Programmer's strength is in pulling them together into an application.

For example, you can use Paradox to create source and map tables for multitable views (using **M**ultiEntry/**S**etup from the Modify menu—discussed in Chapter 9; multitable views are discussed later in this chapter). You can assign names consistent with your naming conventions. Meaningful names improve the value of the Personal Programmer's self-documentation function (**S**tructure) and can aid in the design, development, and maintenance of your application.

Pull It All Together with the Personal Programmer

Use the Personal Programmer to pull all the parts of your application together. The strength of the Personal Programmer is in generating PAL scripts that provide a menu, create queries, display forms and tables, and perform table updates.

Starting the Personal Programmer

The Paradox Personal Programmer is a program separate from Paradox, so it must be started independently. Just as you should place a normal Paradox database in its own directory, you should create a separate directory for each application you want to generate with the Personal Programmer. If you do, you also need to add the directory that contains the Personal Programmer to the path. Once you have done these two things, you easily can create an application in that directory. Just use the change directory command (CD) to change to the proper directory for the application, type *pprog*, and press Enter.

Using the Personal Programmer

The first step to using the Personal Programmer is understanding the menu selections available. Like Paradox, the Personal Programmer contains a series of menus and submenus.

To use the Personal Programmer, you select a series of menu options and supply short answers to questions that the Personal Programmer asks. When you complete all the menu selections required by an application, the Personal Programmer generates the necessary scripts for that application.

The Personal Programmer provides much on-screen information. The screens are designed so that the menu selections appear horizontally across the top. When you place the cursor on a screen selection, the selection is highlighted, and a description explaining that selection appears. In addition, the Personal Programmer provides information in the double-lined box that occupies the lower half of the screen. With these two sources of on-screen information, you should be able to determine the most appropriate screen selection for your application.

Creating an Application

As the Personal Programmer is loading, the greeting or Personal Programmer splash screen is displayed. When the Personal Programmer is loaded into your system, the greeting screen is replaced by the Main menu screen (see fig. 14.1).

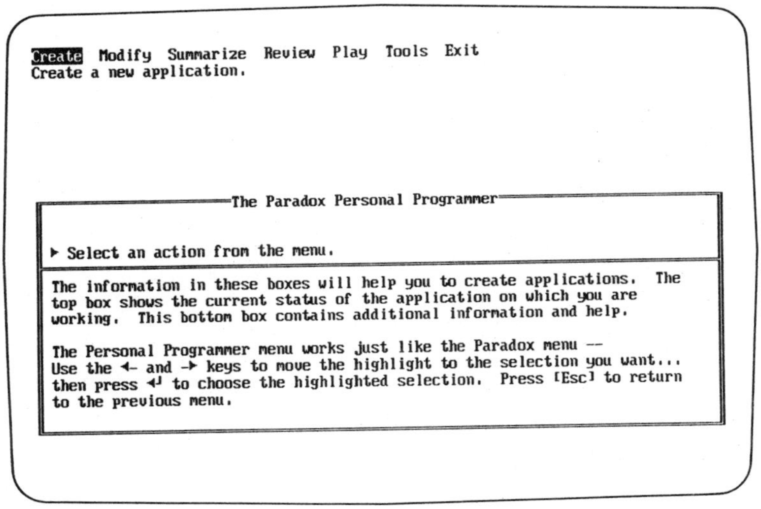
Create Modify Summarize Review Play Tools Exit
Create a new application.
The Paradox Personal Programmer
▸ Select an action from the menu.
The information in these boxes will help you to create applications. The top box shows the current status of the application on which you are working. This bottom box contains additional information and help.
The Personal Programmer menu works just like the Paradox menu --
Use the ← and → keys to move the highlight to the selection you want...
then press ↵ to choose the highlighted selection. Press [Esc] to return to the previous menu.

Fig. 14.1.

The Personal Programmer Main menu.

The following sections explain the various steps you take to create an application in the Personal Programmer.

Getting Started

Select **C**reate from the Personal Programmer Main menu to generate a new application. The Personal Programmer asks you to supply a name for the application. The application name can be from one to five characters long, with no blanks. The name must start with a letter, but the other characters in the name can be letters, numbers, the dollar sign ($), underscore (_), or exclamation point (!). The name should be meaningful. The example used in this chapter has the name IWLP, which stands for "I Wanna Learn Paradox." Type the name of your application and press Enter.

Selecting Tables for the Application

When you press Enter after typing the name of your application, the Personal Programmer displays the Table Selection screen (see fig. 14.2). This screen is used to create or modify the list of tables accessed by your application. The Personal Programmer does not allow your application to access tables not on the list.

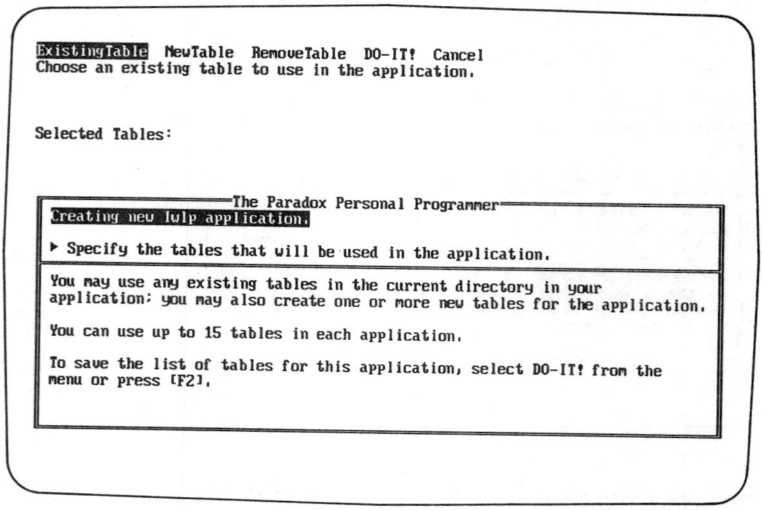

ExistingTable NewTable RemoveTable DO-IT! Cancel
Choose an existing table to use in the application.
Selected Tables:
The Paradox Personal Programmer
Creating new Iulp application.
▸ Specify the tables that will be used in the application.
You may use any existing tables in the current directory in your application; you may also create one or more new tables for the application.
You can use up to 15 tables in each application.
To save the list of tables for this application, select DO-IT! from the menu or press [F2].

Fig. 14.2.
The Personal Programmer Table Selection screen for an application.

Note: At this level, you select tables to be used by the application. Only tables actually stored on the disk should be placed on the list.

Tables created as a result of queries (discussed fully in Chapters 4 and 7) are called Answer tables. Answer tables are not retained when you leave the application and should not be placed in the list. The maximum number of tables allowed on this list by the Personal Programmer is 15.

Select **E**xistingTable from the Table Selection screen to add tables to your application that have been created previously and reside in the current directory.

At the prompt to enter a table name, press Enter; the Personal Programmer displays a list of available tables. This list includes all the tables in the current directory. Select a table to be used by your application by placing the cursor on the name of the table wanted and pressing Enter. Repeat this process (i.e., choose **E**xistingTable, press Enter, and select a table) until all the tables to be included in the application appear on the list.

Select **N**ewTable from the Table Selection screen to create a new table that is to become part of your application. The Personal Programmer prompts you for a table name. Type the name of the table and press Enter. The Personal Programmer displays the table Structure screen in Create mode. Refer to Chapter 2 for a complete discussion of how to define a table in Create mode. Press F2 (DO-IT!) when you finish defining the table, and return to the Personal Programmer.

Select **R**emoveTable from the Table Selection screen to remove from the list a table no longer used by the application. When you select **R**emove Table, the Personal Programmer displays the tables currently on the list. Move the cursor to the table you want to remove and press Enter. The Personal Programmer removes the table from the list. It is good practice to retain only the tables used by the application. Extraneous tables needlessly add to overhead and should be removed.

Once you have added all the necessary tables to the list, press F2 (DO-IT!) to save the list of tables. The Personal Programmer prompts you for a description for each table. Type a meaningful description for each and press Enter. After the last table has been described, the Personal Programmer displays a screen used to define the application's Main menu.

Defining the Applications Main Menu

Figure 14.3 shows the screen used to define the application's Main menu. The Personal Programmer displays a *menu creation box* at the top of the screen with the word `Main` highlighted at the top right.

The Personal Programmer displays a blank, highlighted line 120 characters long in the top line of the menu creation box. Type the name of the first Main menu selection of your application and press Enter. This name is called the *selection name*. The Personal Programmer then provides a long blank highlighted area (60 characters) on the second line of the menu creation box in which you type *an explanation* for that menu selection. Type a meaningful description and press Enter. The Personal Programmer displays another blank highlighted area in which you can type another Main menu selection name. The process of adding menu selection names and explanations continues until you have entered the last selection. You can enter as many menu choices as you want, but if they will not fit across the screen side-by-side (leaving two spaces between the selection names), those that don't fit will be hidden. The Programmer will indicate that one or more menu selections are hidden by placing a pointer at the end of the menu. You usually should define no more selections on each menu than can fit across the screen at once. The longer the selection names, the fewer will fit.

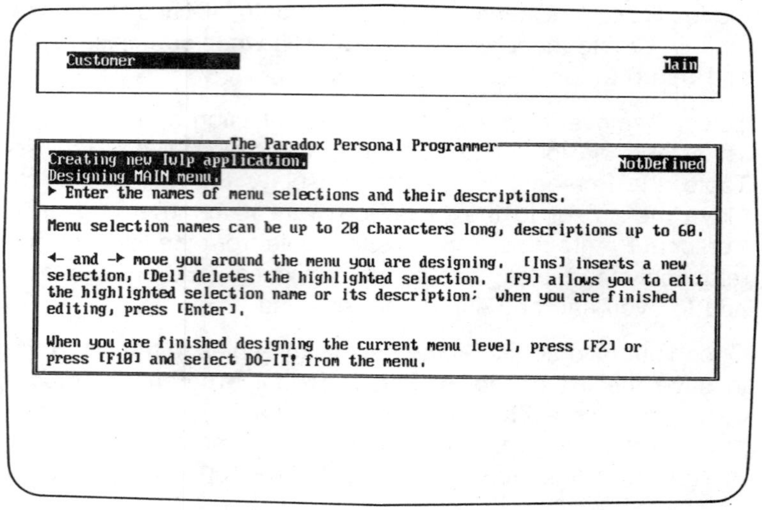

Fig. 14.3.

Defining the Main menu.

The Personal Programmer automatically adds a menu selection (**L**eave) to the Main menu of your application. This selection will be used during the application to return to Paradox. Leave room for this selection name as well when deciding what your Main menu selections will be. To tell the Programmer that you are finished defining menu selections, press F2 (DO-IT!).

The explanations you enter are displayed when your application is played, just like the descriptions provided when the cursor is placed on the Personal Programmer menu selections.

After you have defined the Main menu selections and descriptions, the Personal Programmer displays the Definition menu. This screen contains the following three menu selections:

SpecifyAction **D**o-It! **C**ancel

Specifying the Action

To specify an action for the current (blinking) menu option, select **S**pecify-Action from the Definition menu and the Action menu appears (see fig. 14.4). The Action menu is used to attach an action required by your application to the current menu selection. The *current menu selection* is the

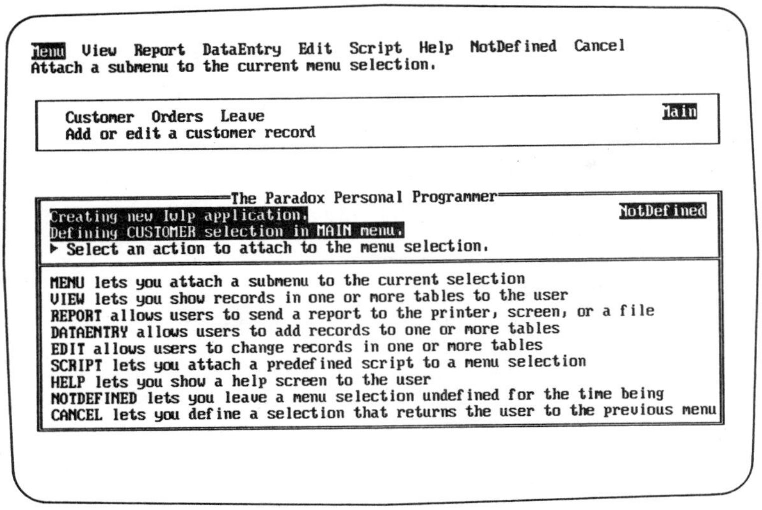
Menu View Report DataEntry Edit Script Help NotDefined Cancel
Attach a submenu to the current menu selection.
Customer Orders Leave
Main
Add or edit a customer record
The Paradox Personal Programmer
Creating new lwlp application.
NotDefined
Defining CUSTOMER selection in MAIN menu.
▸ Select an action to attach to the menu selection.
MENU lets you attach a submenu to the current selection
VIEW lets you show records in one or more tables to the user
REPORT allows users to send a report to the printer, screen, or a file
DATAENTRY allows users to add records to one or more tables
EDIT allows users to change records in one or more tables
SCRIPT lets you attach a predefined script to a menu selection
HELP lets you show a help screen to the user
NOTDEFINED lets you leave a menu selection undefined for the time being
CANCEL lets you define a selection that returns the user to the previous menu

Fig. 14.4.

The Personal Programmer Action menu.

blinking selection on the Main menu screen. You must define one action for each menu selection in order, from left to right. You can skip selections, if you want, by assigning the action **N**otDefined to them, and then come back later (using the **M**odify feature discussed later in this chapter) and assign the desired action.

The following sections explain the various Action menu selections and how to use them.

Defining a Submenu

Select **M**enu from the Action menu to attach a submenu to your current menu selection. By placing submenus under current menu selections, you can develop a hierarchy within your application, similar to the hierarchical menu structure used by Paradox and the Personal Programmer. The Personal Programmer allows 10 levels of menus.

Creating a submenu is almost the same as creating a Main menu selection. For submenus, however, the Personal Programmer does not automatically create a **L**eave selection. After creating a submenu, complete the submenu definitions by attaching the actions required. If you cannot complete the submenu definition now, attach **N**otDefined action to the selection and return to complete it later (using **M**odify).

When naming the menu selections for your application, try to use a unique first letter for each menu selection in a menu or submenu level. This allows the user of your application to make menu selections by pressing the first letter of the selection. If you develop an application with the following Main menu, the users of your application must use the arrow keys to move the cursor to the option and then press Enter to select **A**djustCredit or **A**djustDebit because the two menu selections both begin with *A*:

AdjustCredit **A**djustDebit **B**ackOutBill **M**aintenance **P**rint

Displaying your menu selections alphabetically makes it easier to spot the selections you want. It also makes it easier to see whether there are multiple selections that start with the same first letter.

Do not create a Main menu or submenu that requires left and right scrolling to reveal all the selections (i.e., too many selection names to fit on the menu line at once). Paradox avoids such an inconvenience by using the **M**ore selection on the Tools menu to display menu selections that do not fit on the original Tools menu. You should follow this example in your own menus to make the selection spillover more obvious. Menu selections not displayed immediately may not be noticed by a novice or occasional user of your application.

Selecting View, Report, DataEntry, or Edit

Select **V**iew from the Action menu (see fig. 14.4) to display a table or multitable view in Form, Table, or FormToggle mode, or to display a multitable or multirecord form. The View action does not allow updating of the table. Select **R**eport from the Action menu to cause the menu selection to print, display, or file a report. Choose **D**ataEntry when the action should allow the user to enter data in DataEntry mode (see Chapter 3). Choose **E**dit from the Action menu when you want to allow the user to edit a table or tables through the current menu selection. The sections that follow describe the next selections you must make in defining your application.

Selecting Tables for the Action

Several options available on the Action menu require that you specify a table or tables on which they will act (**V**iew, **R**eport, **D**ataEntry, and **E**dit). Once you select one of these actions, the Personal Programmer displays the menu shown in figure 14.5.

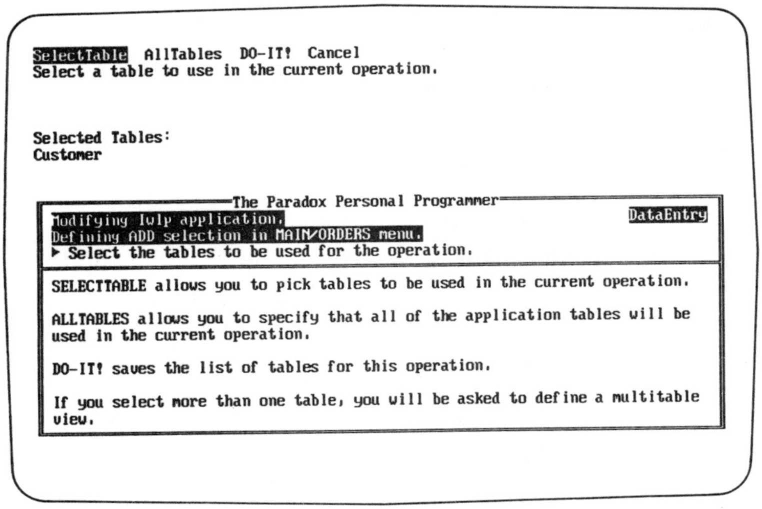
SelectTable AllTables DO-IT! Cancel
Select a table to use in the current operation.
Selected Tables:
Customer
The Paradox Personal Programmer
Modifying Iwlp application.
DataEntry
Defining ADD selection in MAIN/ORDERS menu.
▸ Select the tables to be used for the operation.
SELECTTABLE allows you to pick tables to be used in the current operation.
ALLTABLES allows you to specify that all of the application tables will be used in the current operation.
DO-IT! saves the list of tables for this operation.
If you select more than one table, you will be asked to define a multitable view.

Fig. 14.5.

Selecting a table for an action.

The following list describes the various selections possible from this screen.

- ❑ **S**electTable. Choose this option to specify a table to be used by the current action. (The Personal Programmer displays the list of available tables.) Specify the desired table by typing the first letter of its name, or move the cursor to the name and press Enter. You can specify multiple tables by using this option several times in sequence. When using a multitable form or multitable report, select only the master table. The Personal Programmer automatically recognizes the detail tables associated with the form.

- ❑ **A**llTables. Select this option to choose all the tables available in the application for the current action. The Personal Programmer displays the list of tables selected.

- ❑ **D**O-IT!. Choose this option when you are ready to save the table list for this action and proceed to the next step. Alternatively, you can press F2 (DO-IT!).

- ❑ **C**ancel. Do not select this choice unless you want to stop selecting tables and return to the Action menu. None of the table selections made are retained.

Specifying Fields for the Action

Once you press F2 (DO-IT!), or select **D**O-IT! from the table selection menu, the Personal Programmer sometimes asks you to specify fields for the action. When you specify only one table to be acted on by the chosen action, and when you are defining a View action (i.e., not for **R**eport, **D**ataEntry, or **E**dit), the Personal Programmer displays two choices. You must tell the Programmer to use all the fields from the table selected or to use only specific fields by selecting one of the following two menu choices:

- **S**electFields. Choose this option to specify the fields to be displayed from the table. The Personal Programmer displays a query form for the table. Select the fields you want displayed by placing a check mark in the field locations on the form. Use the arrow keys to select the desired fields and press F6 to place a check mark next to the field. When you are finished selecting fields for display, press F2 (DO-IT!).

- **A**llFields. Make this selection when you want to specify that all the fields in the table are to be displayed.

When the action is **R**eport or **E**dit, and you specified only one table for the action, the Personal Programmer assumes you want to use all fields and skips to the record selection menu described in the next section. When the action is DataEntry, the Personal Programmer skips to the View menu.

If you selected multiple tables in the preceding step, a different menu appears, listing these choices:

- **C**reate. Choose this option to build a multitable view consisting of a map table and a source table. Use the same procedure described in the "Entering Data with MultiEntry" section of Chapter 9.

- **B**orrow. Select this choice to use a multitable view that you have previously defined. You have to specify the source table and map table.

Paradox 3.0 enables you to create multitable forms, as described in Chapter 8. For use with **V**iew, **E**dit, and **D**ataEntry, the multitable form all but supersedes multitable views. To use a multitable form with the Personal Programmer, select only the master table in the table selection step, and then choose the multitable form using the **F**orm view/**B**orrow selection described in the "Selecting a View" section later in this chapter. [3]

Selecting the Records for the Action

Next, except for use with DataEntry, you must specify the records in the table that are to be affected by the action. The Programmer displays the following choices:

- ❑ **A**llRecords. Choose this option to use all the records in the table or multitable view.
- ❑ **S**electRecord. Make this selection if only a specific record or records from the table, or multitable view, are to be used. The Personal Programmer displays a query form for the table or multitable view defined for the action. If you want to allow the user to provide selection criteria, indicate the selection criteria by placing a variable name preceded by a tilde character (~) in the required field area(s). Such a variable is called a *tilde variable*. When you are finished indicating the selection criteria, press F2 (DO-IT!).

If you want to display a specific customer from the Customer table, for example, type ~*cust* in the Customer Number field location in the query form as shown in figure 14.6. Then press F2 (DO-IT!).

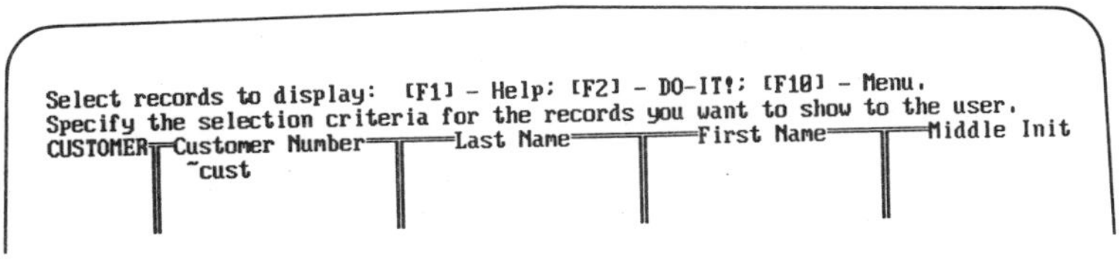

Fig. 14.6.

Setting up a tilde variable in the IWLP application.

After you press F2 (DO-IT!), if you defined a tilde variable, the Personal Programmer asks you to enter a prompt to be displayed when the application is run. This prompt should instruct the user to enter the appropriate data to take the place of the tilde variable.

Using the example from the Customer table, you might type the following prompt:

Enter the customer number:

After typing the prompt, press Enter.

The Programmer then asks you to approve the data type assigned to the tilde variable. The Personal Programmer defaults to the data type assigned when the field was defined in the table. You can change the default data type and length; normally, however, you keep the default type. Press F2 (DO-IT!) to continue. (Refer to Chapter 2 for more information on data types and length.)

To indicate multiple selection criteria, place a different tilde variable in each of the fields required for selection. The Personal Programmer asks you to supply a prompt and approve the data type for each tilde variable entered.

Selecting a View

Once you have specified the tables(s), field(s), and record(s) to be used by the action, for **V**iew, **E**dit, and **D**ataEntry, you must specify the view that you want the user to see. The Personal Programmer displays the following menu choices:

- **F**ormView. Select this option to display the information in form view.
- **T**ableView. Make this choice to display the information in table view.
- **F**ormToggle. Choose this option to display the information in form or table view. The user of the application can use the F7 key to switch between form and table views as the information is displayed.

If you select **F**ormView or **F**ormToggle, you also must make a selection from the following menu choices:

- **D**esign. Choose this selection to create a new form, using the form design procedure described in Chapter 8.
- **B**orrow. Select this option to use a form already designed. The Personal Programmer lists the forms and corresponding form descriptions that can be borrowed for this action based on the table or multitable view assigned to the action. Use the arrow keys to move the cursor to the desired form name and press Enter.
- **S**tandardForm. Make this choice to display the form created by Paradox or the Personal Programmer when the table was created.

For **V**iew actions, selecting a view returns you to the Action menu either to define the action for the next menu selection, or to complete the application design with F2 (DO-IT!)

Selecting a Report Specification

When you are defining a Report action, after you have specified the table and records for the report, you also must specify a report specification. The Personal Programmer displays the following menu choices:

- ❑ **D**esign. Select this option to create a new report for this menu selection by using the Paradox Report Generator described in Chapters 5, 10, and 11.
- ❑ **B**orrow. Choose this option to use a report specification already designed. The Personal Programmer displays a list of form names. Move the cursor to the desired form name and press Enter.
- ❑ **S**tandardReport. Choose this option to pull in the report created by Paradox or the Personal Programmer when the table was created.

After defining the parts of the table to be used in the report and the report form to be used, you must select the destination of the report. The Personal Programmer displays the following menu selections:

- ❑ **P**rinter. Select this option to have the report sent to a printer.
- ❑ **S**creen. Make this choice to have the report displayed on-screen.
- ❑ **F**ile. Choose this option to have the report written to a file. Indicate the file name.

Once you select the report form and specify the destination, the Personal Programmer returns to the Action menu with the next undefined menu selection blinking (if any). You can continue defining more actions, or press F2 (DO-IT!) to complete the application.

Indicating Settings and Validity Checks

For **D**ataEntry and **E**dit actions only, the Personal Programmer provides you with a chance to modify display formats and define *validity checks*. The following selections are displayed (***Note:*** The second selection on this menu is for **E**dit only):

Settings **I**nsertDelete **D**O-IT! **C**ancel

Select **S**ettings to display the following Settings menu choices, which allow you to modify formats and define the validity checks:

- ❑ **F**ormat. Make this choice to change the format of the data being displayed. For an explanation of the Format capability, see "Using the Image Options" section of Chapter 3.
- ❑ **V**alCheck. Use this option to define validity checks. For a detailed explanation of validity checking, see Chapter 9, "Using Paradox Power Entry and Editing Features."

- **D**O-IT!. Select this option to save the format definitions and validity checks and return to the previous menu.
- **C**ancel. Choose this option to return to the Settings menu without saving any format definitions or validity checks.

For **E**dit actions, you can choose the **I**nsertDelete option to enable the application user both to insert new records and to delete existing records during an edit session. Press F2 (DO-IT!) to save the settings made and to return to the Action menu. You can continue to define any remaining menu selections, or press F2 (DO-IT!) again to complete the application.

Attaching a Script

Select **S**cript from the Action menu to have your menu selection play a PAL script. The Personal Programmer asks you for the name of the script to play with the following prompt:

```
Script:
```

Enter the name of the script to play, or press Enter for a list of scripts from which you can choose. The script must be in the current directory for the Personal Programmer to use it.

Generating certain functions as separate applications and having the applications called (or played) by the main application is sometimes better than creating one very large application. This practice can help break large applications into smaller, more manageable subapplications. If you were developing an accounting system, for example, it may be better to create a Main menu structure with each selection being a subapplication. When a Main menu selection is made, the subapplication is played as a script. When you use this method, however, you must use the PAL Script Editor and make some minor modifications to the subapplication's scripts. When the Personal Programmer generates an application, it does not know whether it is to be used as a subapplication and therefore attaches code to return the user to the Personal Programmer's Main menu when you exit the application. When you use an application as a subapplication, you should modify this code to return the user to the Main menu of your application.

Defining Help

Select **H**elp from the Action menu to provide on-screen assistance to the users of your application. Quite often users must make decisions about selections, and a little bit of on-screen coaching can make a big difference. A help screen can provide enough information for the user to complete a task without pulling out a manual, making a phone call, or postponing the task. One of the strengths of the Personal Programmer is the amount of assistance displayed on each screen for every menu selection. You can follow this example by including help screens in your application. Help screens can make the difference between a good product and a great product.

The creation of a help screen is similar to the creation of a form, except that no data fields are displayed. Only textual information is displayed on a help screen. Refer to Chapter 8 for information of form design.

Leaving Menu Selections NotDefined

Select **N**otDefined from the Action menu to attach a dummy (or do-nothing) definition to the current menu selection. The **N**otDefined option allows you to skip the definition of a specific action for the present. Initially, you can set up all menu selections with the **N**otDefined action so that you can study your menu structure before attaching actions.

Attaching Cancel

Select **C**ancel from the Action menu to return the user to the preceding menu. This option has no effect on other actions performed by other menu selections in your application. Each menu level of your application can contain a **P**revious or **R**eturn menu selection that performs the **C**ancel action to give the user an explicit way of returning to the next higher menu. If you do not define a **P**revious or **R**eturn selection, the user can always press the Esc key to return to the preceding menu. This type of action, therefore, is really redundant. The Personal Programmer automatically attaches a **L**eave selection to your application's Main menu. When the user selects **L**eave, your application is exited and the Main menu of Paradox appears.

Creating a Splash Screen

After you have finished defining the action for the last menu selection of your application, or when you press F2 (DO-IT!), the Personal Programmer displays the following SplashScreen menu options:

- **S**plashScreen. Choose this option if you want to create a system greeting screen. Developing a splash screen is similar to developing a form, except that no data is displayed. Normal keyboard symbols can be used, and, if you want to get fancy, you also can use ASCII characters. ASCII characters are listed in Appendix C of your *PAL User's Guide*.
- **N**oSplashScreen. Make this choice if you want to bypass the creation of a system greeting screen at this time. You can define one later using the Modify mode; of course, it may be that you do not want a splash screen at all.

Once you choose one of these two options, the Personal Programmer presents the final menu containing two options: **D**O-IT! and **C**ancel. Select **D**O-IT! (or press F2) to save the application. The Personal Programmer generates the PAL script to create an application that will perform all the menu selections you have defined. Don't use **C**ancel! **C**ancel discards all your work!

Modifying an Application

The **M**odify selection allows you to make changes to an application. You can add or remove tables, change the menu structure, change the actions assigned to existing menu selections, define actions to selections previously assigned the **N**otDefined option, and add or modify a splash screen. The procedures for modifying an application are similar to those performed when creating the application. To begin modifying an application, select **M**odify from the Personal Programmer Main menu.

The Personal Programmer asks for the name of the application to be modified. Type the name of the application and press Enter. The Personal Programmer displays the screen shown in figure 14.7.

The following sections explain the various selections available on the Modify menu and how to use them.

Changing the List of Tables Used by the Application

Select **T**ables from the Modify menu to modify your application's list of tables. The Personal Programmer lists the tables currently defined for your application. You can add tables that are in the current directory, create a new table, or remove a table currently in the list of tables. The Personal

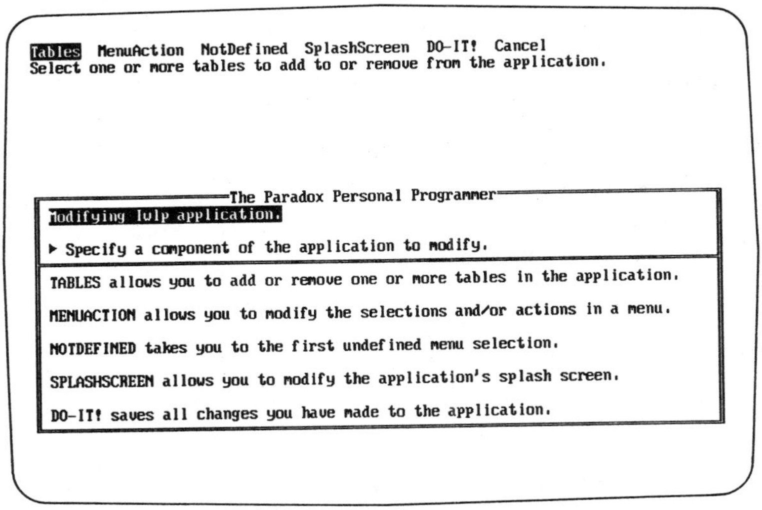
Tables MenuAction NotDefined SplashScreen DO-IT! Cancel
Select one or more tables to add to or remove from the application.
The Paradox Personal Programmer
Modifying Iulp application.
Specify a component of the application to modify.
TABLES allows you to add or remove one or more tables in the application.
MENUACTION allows you to modify the selections and/or actions in a menu.
NOTDEFINED takes you to the first undefined menu selection.
SPLASHSCREEN allows you to modify the application's splash screen.
DO-IT! saves all changes you have made to the application.

Fig. 14.7.

The Personal Programmer Modify menu.

Programmer displays the following menu options when **T**able is selected from the Modify menu:

ExistingTable **N**ewTable **R**emoveTable **D**O-IT! **C**ancel

The procedure used to modify the application's table list is the same as the procedure used to create the table list, with one exception. The **R**emoveTable selection does not allow you to remove a table if a menu selection has been defined that uses this table.

Modifying the Menu Action

Select **M**enuAction from the Modify menu to modify the menu structure and the actions associated with the menu selections. The **M**enuAction option allows you to add or remove menu selections, change the hierarchy of the menu, and change the actions assigned to a menu selection.

When you select **M**enuAction, the Personal Programmer displays the Main menu of your application. Make menu selections on your application menu as if you were using the application itself, until you arrive at the menu selection you want to change. Press F10 (Menu). The following menu options appear:

Menu **A**ction **D**O-IT! **C**ancel

Select **M**enu to add a menu selection, change a menu selection, or delete the current menu selection. Use the keys in table 14.1 to modify the menu.

Table 14.1
Keys To Modify the Menus

Key	*Use*
← and →	Move left and right over the current selections
Ins	Insert a new menu selection to the left of the selection currently highlighted
Del	Remove the current selection
F9 (Edit)	Edit the current selection and its description (press Enter when finished editing)
F2 (DO-IT!)	Save the changes made to the menu

Caution: The Del key removes the current menu selection and any submenus attached to it. Re-creating a series of submenus and related actions entails much additional work. Be sure of what you are deleting. You may want to relocate the menu selection using the **M**oveDown or **B**orrow commands described in the following paragraphs instead of deleting the selection.

Select **A**ction from the MenuAction menu to modify the action assigned to the current menu selection. The Personal Programmer displays the following menu options when you select **A**ction:

- **D**efine. Use this choice to make major changes to the action currently assigned to the menu selection or to define a menu selection currently assigned the NotDefined action. The Personal Programmer asks you to confirm this selection by selecting **C**ancel or **R**eplace. **C**ancel returns you to the preceding menu without redefining the current menu selection; **R**eplace allows you to proceed with the redefinition of the current menu selection. At this point, the procedure to define the action attached to the current menu selection is the same as the procedure used when creating the application.

- **R**evise. Select this option to make minor changes to the current menu selection. The Personal Programmer walks you through the current definition and displays the selections made when you created or last modified the definition. The Personal Programmer asks if you want to **K**eep or **C**hange the current selection at each step of the definition. When **K**eep is selected, the Programmer retains the original selection and continues with the next selection until the all the selections for that definition are covered. When **C**hange is selected, the Programmer allows you to modify the original selection and then continues with the next selection until all the selections are covered for that definition.

- **B**orrow. Use this choice to copy a menu selection action already defined. After selecting **B**orrow, make menu selections on your application as if you were actually running it, in order to select the menu whose action you want to borrow. Then press F10 (Menu) to display the following menu options:

  BorrowAction **C**ancel

  Select **B**orrowAction to copy to the current menu selection the action that you want to borrow.

  The **B**orrow command can save time when similar menu definitions are needed. Use **B**orrow to copy similar definitions, and then use the **R**evise function to modify the definition.

- **M**oveDown. Use this choice from the Action menu to move the current menu selection and all its submenus to a lower level in the menu structure. The Personal Programmer lowers the existing menu selection and its submenus and actions, and places a blank menu selection in the original selection's place, which you must then name (see fig. 14.8). No definitions are lost. The **M**oveDown function allows you to add more levels of detail to your menu structure without redefining current menu definitions.

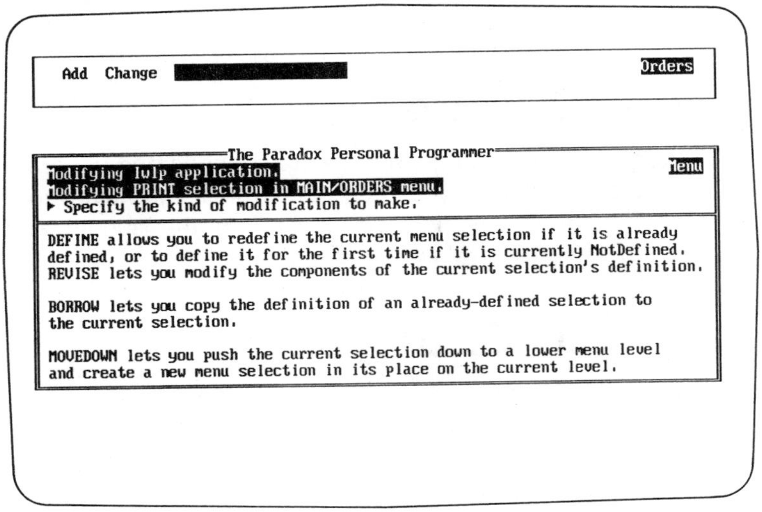

Add Change
Orders
The Paradox Personal Programmer
Modifying Iwlp application.
Menu
Modifying PRINT selection in MAIN/ORDERS menu.
▸ Specify the kind of modification to make.
DEFINE allows you to redefine the current menu selection if it is already defined, or to define it for the first time if it is currently NotDefined.
REVISE lets you modify the components of the current selection's definition.
BORROW lets you copy the definition of an already-defined selection to the current selection.
MOVEDOWN lets you push the current selection down to a lower menu level and create a new menu selection in its place on the current level.

Fig. 14.8.

The Personal Programmer **M**odify **M**oveDown example.

Once you finish with any one of the options on the MenuAction/Action menu, the Personal Programmer returns you to the main menu of your application for further modification. Press F2 (DO-IT!) to save the changes and to return to the Modify menu.

Finding the NotDefined Menu Selections

The Personal Programmer provides a function to locate the menu selections assigned the action NotDefined. By selecting **N**otDefined from the Modify menu, the Programmer places you at the first (highest and leftmost) undefined action in the menu structure. This feature allows you to go directly to the **N**otDefined actions so that you can define them.

Changing or Adding a Splash Screen

Select **S**plashScreen from the Modify menu to create a splash screen or to modify the application's existing splash screen. The Programmer displays the following submenu options when you select **S**plashScreen:

- **D**esign. Select this option to create a new splash screen.
- **M**odify. Use this choice to change the application's splash screen.
- **N**oSplashScreen. Make this choice to indicate that the application is not to have a splash screen.

Saving the Changes

Press F2 (DO-IT!) from the Modify menu to save the changes and generate the modified scripts and libraries for your application after you have modified it. When the Programmer is finished generating the scripts and libraries, the Personal Programmer Main menu appears.

Canceling the Changes

Select **C**ancel from the Modify menu to cancel the changes made to the application. The Personal Programmer does not regenerate the application's scripts and libraries and the Personal Programmer Main menu appears.

Playing Your Application

The **P**lay option is the function that actually plays (or executes) your application or script.

Select **P**lay from the Personal Programmer Main menu. The Personal Programmer prompts you for the name of the application you want to play. Type the name of the desired application and press Enter. The Personal Programmer loads the application into the computer's memory and displays the splash screen, if you designed one.

The Personal Programmer has passed control of your computer to your application. You navigate your application in the same way you navigate the Personal Programmer: by making menu selections and answering the prompts in your application. When you are finished playing your application, select **L**eave from the Main menu (remember that the Personal Programmer added the **L**eave selection for you). The Main menu of the Personal Programmer appears. Now you can select any of the options available in the Personal Programmer, or you can exit the Personal Programmer and return to the operating system.

Once your application works the way you intend, you can also run (play) it from within Paradox or directly from DOS. To play an application from within Paradox, first make the application's directory the working directory by using Tools/More/Directory, or by starting Paradox from that directory (explained in Appendix A). Then, from the Main menu choose **S**cripts, **P**lay, type the script name, and press Enter.

To play the application from DOS, refer to Appendix A for instructions on setting the DOS path. Change to the directory that contains the application. Finally, type *paradox3* (*paradox2* for Version 2.0), followed by a space and then the name of the application. Press Enter. When the program starts, it goes directly to your application rather than to the Paradox Main menu.

Tools

The Personal Programmer's tool box includes utilities necessary to manage Paradox applications. These utilities provide the capacity to change the current directory and to copy, delete, and rename applications. In addition, the tool box provides the capacity to modify the help level provided on the Personal Programmer screens, to change printer options, and to suppress the writing of scripts when generating an application.

To access the tool box, select **T**ools from the Personal Programmer Main menu. The submenu shown in figure 14.9 appears.

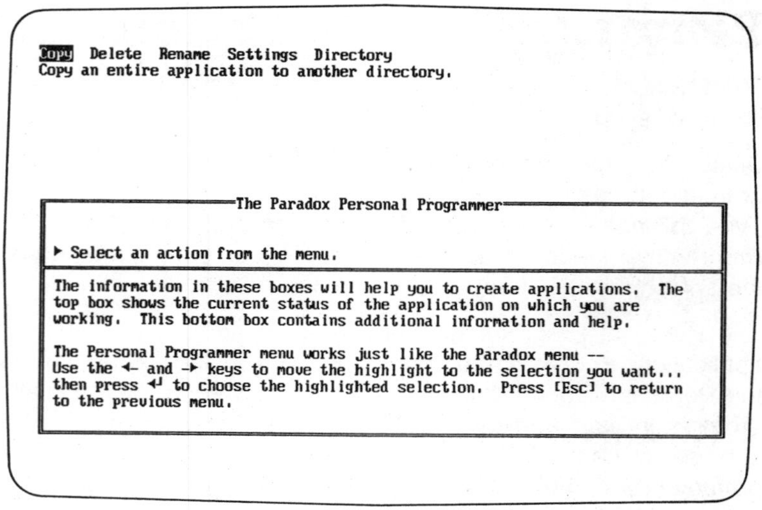
Copy Delete Rename Settings Directory
Copy an entire application to another directory.
The Paradox Personal Programmer
▸ Select an action from the menu.
The information in these boxes will help you to create applications. The top box shows the current status of the application on which you are working. This bottom box contains additional information and help.
The Personal Programmer menu works just like the Paradox menu -- Use the ← and → keys to move the highlight to the selection you want... then press ↵ to choose the highlighted selection. Press [Esc] to return to the previous menu.

Fig. 14.9.

The Personal Programmer Tools menu.

The following sections explain each of the options on the Tools menu.

Copying an Application

Select **C**opy from the Tools menu to copy to another directory an application created by the Personal Programmer. The Personal Programmer asks you for the name of the application to copy. The application you are copying must reside in the current directory. Type the name of the application you want to copy and press Enter.

The Personal Programmer asks you for the name of the directory to which you want to copy the application. Type the name of the directory and press Enter.

Deleting an Application

Select **D**elete from the Tools menu to remove an application from your system. The application to be deleted must be in the current directory. The Personal Programmer asks you for the name of the application to delete. Type the name of the application you want to delete and press Enter.

The Personal Programmer deletes the files (tables, scripts, and libraries) associated with that application and created by the Personal Programmer. Any tables and scripts defined by the user outside the Personal Programmer are not deleted automatically.

Renaming an Application

Select **R**ename from the Tools menu to change the name of an application. The Personal Programmer asks you for the name of the application that you want to rename. Type the name and press Enter. The application must be in the current directory.

The Personal Programmer asks for the application's new name. Type the new name and press Enter. The Personal Programmer regenerates the application using the new name provided. This option changes the name of all objects created by the Personal Programmer, as well as all references to those objects in the code.

Changing Settings

The **S**ettings option on the Tools menu provides the capability to modify printer information, help levels provided by the Personal Programmer, and library and script settings.

Select **S**ettings from the Tools menu; the following Settings submenu options appear:

- **P**rinterSetup. Make this choice to change the printer port assigned to the Personal Programmer, enter a printer setup string, or change the width of printed reports. The Personal Programmer displays the following submenu options:

  PrinterPort **S**etUp **W**idth

  Select **P**rinterPort to change the port to which the summary reports are sent. Select **S**etUp to define a printer setup string (refer to Chapter 10 for more details on using setup strings). Once defined, the Personal Programmer sends the setup string to the printer when any reports are printed. Select **W**idth to change the print width. The Personal Programmer accepts print widths from 80 to 132 characters.

- **H**elpMode. Use this option to modify the level of help provided by the Personal Programmer to you during application development. The Programmer displays the following submenu options:

  Verbose **T**erse

  Select **V**erbose for the most on-screen help. Select **T**erse to remove on-screen help and leave only the status displayed. You may want to do this once you become a Personal Programmer "expert."

Beginning users should use the **V**erbose option, which is the default for the Personal Programmer. The help area of the screens provides good coaching when you need to make a choice and are not sure of the options.

- **L**ibrariesOnly. Make this choice when you want to suppress the writing of scripts. The Personal Programmer displays the following submenu options:

  No **Y**es

  Select **N**o if you want scripts and libraries written when you generate your application. Select **Y**es if you want only the libraries to be written.

  Both versions of the application run the same. The difference is that libraries without scripts take less space on the disk. Unfortunately, they also cannot be modified. Make sure that you keep at least one copy of your application saved with both libraries and scripts together so that you will be able to make changes later, if necessary.

Changing the Current Directory

Select **D**irectory from the Tools menu to change the current directory. Because the Tools menu contains the Delete and Directory commands (both beginning with *D*), you must move the cursor to the Directory option and press Enter. The Personal Programmer asks for the name of the directory to which you want to change.

Type the complete DOS path (for example, *c:\paradox3\pprog\papp*) and press Enter.

The Personal Programmer clears the current work space and changes to the requested directory. The name of the selected directory displays on the bottom right corner of the screen.

Exiting from the Personal Programmer

To leave the Personal Programmer and return to DOS, from the Main menu select **E**xit **Y**es.

Version Compatibility

The Personal Programmer Version 3.0 automatically converts applications generated by Versions 1.1 or 2.0 of the Personal Programmer to Version 3.0 applications. Applications generated by Personal Programmer 3.0 do not work with Versions 1.1 or 2.0.

Chapter Summary

After completing this chapter, you should be familiar with the Personal Programmer as a tool to generate the Paradox Application Language (PAL) scripts needed to control an application. You are familiar with the menu selections and the capabilities of the Personal Programmer. The hints and suggestions provided should assist you with the various aspects of the Personal Programmer. You now have at your command the fundamentals necessary to develop complex applications. To really sharpen your Personal Programmer skills, however, you need to use it.

The next chapter presents an overview of the Paradox Application Language (PAL). It discusses the commands available and offers some suggestions on how to develop applications with the Personal Programmer and how to use the PAL editor to change the application's scripts to fine-tune your application.

15

An Overview of the Paradox Application Language

This chapter provides an overview of the capabilities of the Paradox Application Language (PAL), a complete database application development environment. In this chapter you learn the major features of this programming language and how to use some of the built-in programming facilities, such as the Paradox Script Editor and the PAL Debugger.

Programming with PAL is much like programming with any high-level programming language. Thus, as you might expect, PAL's full capabilities and complexities cannot be covered in just one chapter. Because this book is focused primarily at helping you use Paradox interactively to its full potential, extensive coverage of the programmable side of Paradox is beyond the book's scope. This chapter is intended to help you get started with PAL but will not make you a PAL expert. Use this chapter to learn the basic ways you can create, run, modify, and debug (correct errors in) PAL programs and to discover the wide array of PAL commands and expressions that are available to you.

Even if you're an experienced programmer, you may want at least to skim the chapter to get a quick idea of PAL's features and to learn the fundamentals of using the built-in editor and the debugging facility. You should also refer to the *PAL User's Guide*, distributed with Paradox, for more details on all features discussed in this chapter.

What Is PAL?

PAL is a high-level database programming language that allows you to create structured programs. It is the language used by the Personal Programmer to create menu-driven applications, as discussed in Chapter 14. By modifying programs created by the Personal Programmer or by writing programs completely on your own, you can develop database applications of almost unlimited power and complexity.

The Paradox Application Language is not a beginning programmer's tool. If you are a seasoned programmer, the structure and commands should be easy for you to understand. If you are a novice at programming, you should take time to learn some basic programming concepts before trying to develop an application with PAL. Either of the following books is a good resource for programming fundamentals:

- *Using QuickBASIC 4* by Tom Rugg and Phil Feldman
- *Using Turbo Pascal* by Michael Yester

After you have gained expertise, you might want to advance your knowledge by reading *Turbo Pascal Tips, Tricks, and Traps* by Tom Rugg and Phil Feldman. All three books are published by Que Corporation.

Understanding PAL Scripts

PAL programs are called *scripts*. Chapter 6 first introduced you to scripts and demonstrated how to record keystrokes into a script that you can play again later. In that chapter, you also learned how to use the SETKEY command to create keyboard macros from PAL scripts. Applications generated by the Personal Programmer, discussed in Chapter 14, are also PAL scripts. These menu-driven applications should give you an idea of the capability of the PAL programming language. PAL commands not only enable you to perform any task that you can perform yourself interactively in Paradox, but they also allow you to create database applications completely customized to your exact specifications.

PAL scripts are stored on disk as ASCII (American Standard Code for Information Interchange) files. Each script consists of a series of PAL commands used to manipulate Paradox tables, forms, and reports. Paradox reads and executes these commands from top to bottom and from left to right, just as you read a book. You do not need special commands to start or end a PAL script. Paradox begins executing commands at the top and quits when it runs out of commands to execute. Several commands are available for altering this top-to-bottom program flow, which allows you to create more powerful and more structured programs. (These commands are listed in this chapter's section on "Program Control Commands.")

Comparing PAL to Other Languages

The PAL programming language is similar in many ways to traditional programming languages like C or Pascal. Some examples are the following:

- *Placement of commands*. PAL is a free-form programming language. Lines can be up to 132 characters long. You can start a command anywhere on a line, which means that you can indent commands to enhance code readability. You also can place multiple PAL commands on one line or split one command onto several lines (so long as you do not split a keyword, name, or data value onto more than one line). You can use either upper- or lowercase letters when you type PAL commands. Internally documenting or explaining the operation of the script is easy, because Paradox ignores any text typed to the right of a semicolon (;), unless the semicolon is contained in text that is enclosed in double quotation marks (e.g., "ice cream; cake; cookies"). Also, blank lines do not affect how a script operates, so you can use them as often as you want in order to make the script easier to read.
- *Modularization*. PAL enables you to *modularize* your programs—break a program into more manageable pieces—by using one script to play (execute) any number of other scripts. Scripts played from another script are often referred to as *subroutines*.
- *Structure*. You can create *structured* programs, scripts that are internally modularized, by using PAL program control commands.
- *Procedures*. You can make your programming more efficient by converting an often-used script operation into a *procedure*. Using a procedure is similar to playing another script as a subroutine. The difference is that a script resides on disk as an ASCII file, but a procedure resides in RAM in an interpreted format. If a subroutine script is to be used more than once in a program, Paradox has to read the subroutine script from the disk and interpret each command whenever the subroutine is played. But a procedure is read from the disk only once, usually at the

beginning of the script, and stored in RAM in interpreted format. Then whenever a procedure is used, Paradox doesn't need to read the commands from the disk or reinterpret the commands.

Procedures can even be stored in *procedure libraries* and read into RAM as a group. You can then use the procedures as if they were built-in PAL commands or functions, giving you in effect unlimited ability to create custom commands that perform nearly any database-related operation you can think of.

- *Functions*. PAL has an extensive list of built-in formulas referred to collectively as *functions*. They allow you to perform both simple and complex computations and manipulations with any type of data that can be entered in Paradox, including text, numbers, dates, and time. Functions are also available for returning information about the current status of various aspects of Paradox.

In spite of all these similarities, PAL is not exactly like every other programming language. For instance, PAL variables—temporary fields enabling a script to manipulate information in RAM—are handled in a manner that may be different from what you expect. To learn to use PAL successfully and efficiently, you need to become familiar with PAL's features and capabilities. But after all is said and done, the only way to learn to program is to roll up your sleeves and write programs. This chapter helps you get started. Use it as a springboard into the *PAL User's Guide*, and you will be on your way to creating powerful database applications with PAL.

Creating a PAL Script

You can create PAL scripts in several ways:

- You can use the **B**eginRecord command on either the Scripts menu or the PAL menu to record your menu selections and other keystrokes. This method is the subject of Chapter 6, "Recording Paradox Scripts and Keyboard Macros."
- As described in Chapter 14, you also can use the Personal Programmer to generate scripts that make up an entire menu-driven application. You can then use the Script Editor or a suitable ASCII editor to modify these scripts. (See this chapter's section on "Editing a Script.")

- Another way to create a PAL script, as discussed in Chapter 4's section on "Saving a Query," is to use the **Q**uerySave option on the Scripts menu to create a special type of script that builds a query statement. Like scripts generated by the Personal Programmer, a query saved as a script can be modified with the Script Editor.

  It is not a good idea to try to edit a query saved with the **Q**uerySave option. The syntax of scripts created by the **Q**uerySave option is much different from that of other PAL commands. And Paradox doesn't "help" you with the construction of the query, as the program does when you build a query interactively in Main mode. Instead of using the Script Editor to correct a script saved with the **Q**uerySave option, you should first play the existing script and then modify the query, using the techniques described in Chapters 4 and 7. Once the query produces the results you want, you should save it again by using **Q**uerySave with the same script name, thus replacing the old version. You can then use the **R**ead option in the Script Editor to add the corrected query to your program.

  You also can use PAL *keypress interaction* commands, such as {ASK}, and PAL *work space* manipulation commands, such as CHECK and MOVETO, to build a query in a script. These commands use more common PAL command syntax, and are easier to modify with an editor. Keypress interaction commands and work space manipulation commands are listed later in this chapter. Refer to the *PAL User's Guide* for a description of how to use each command.

- You can write a script from scratch by using Paradox's Script Editor or any suitable ASCII editor. (See this chapter's sections on "Using the Script Editor" and "Attaching an Alternate Editor.") The available PAL commands are introduced in this chapter and explained in detail in the *PAL User's Guide* that accompanies the Paradox program. If you are not already an "ace" programmer, however, and if your application will be complex, you may want to let the Personal Programmer have first crack at creating the script. You can then make modifications to meet your application's needs. If you are an experienced programmer, take a look at the code generated by the Personal Programmer and then decide for yourself whether you prefer to start from there and add enhancements, or write your script from scratch.

Playing a Script

Once you have created a script, executing or running it is referred to as *playing* the script. You can play a script either within Paradox or at the DOS prompt.

Playing a Script within Paradox

You have several ways to play a script within Paradox. First make the script's directory the working directory by using the **D**irectory option on the Tools/More menu or by starting Paradox from that DOS directory (see Appendix A). Then use one of the following methods to play the script:

- From the Paradox Main menu, choose **S**cripts **P**lay. At the prompt for the script name, type the script name and press Enter. Paradox plays the script.
- From any Paradox mode, press Alt-F10 (PAL Menu) and choose **P**lay. At the prompt for the script name, type the script name and press Enter. Paradox plays the script.
- To play a script more than once, choose **R**epeatPlay from either the Scripts menu or the PAL menu. At the first prompt, indicate the script that you want to play. At the next prompt, type a number to specify how many times you want Paradox to run the script, or press C to indicate that the program should run the script continuously. Press Enter, and Paradox runs the script the number of times you specified. If you requested continuous play, you must stop the script manually by pressing Ctrl-Break and choosing **C**ancel from the resulting Error menu.

Playing a Script from DOS

To play a script from DOS, refer to Appendix A for instructions on setting the DOS path so that it includes the directory containing the Paradox system files. Change to the directory that contains the script, and type *paradox3* (or *paradox2* for Version 2.0) followed by a space and the script name. Then press Enter. Paradox starts and immediately plays the script. For example, to play a script named MYSCRIPT from DOS, type *paradox3 myscript*, and press Enter.

Playing a Script from Another Script

You can play a script from another script—sometimes called *nesting scripts* or *calling subroutines*. PAL scripts can be nested in as many levels as you want. The first script can call a second script, the second script can call a third, and so on. The PAL command for playing a script is PLAY. Typing *play "myscript"* plays the script named MYSCRIPT.

Creating programs in small manageable scripts is sometimes referred to as *modularization*—creating the program in self-contained modules.

Editing a Script

Paradox provides a built-in editor, the Paradox Script Editor, that you can use to create and edit PAL scripts. The program also permits you to use another editor that may be your favorite. Obviously, the Script Editor is more tightly integrated with Paradox than other editors are, but Paradox does make attaching another editor fairly convenient.

Using the Script Editor

The Script Editor creates PAL scripts in straight ASCII text, without any special formatting characters. Each line can contain up to 132 characters. You can start the Script Editor in one of two ways: from the Main menu, or while you're in the PAL Debugger.

To start the Script Editor from the Paradox Main menu, choose **S**cripts **E**ditor. Then select **W**rite to begin a new script, or **E**dit to edit an existing script. Finally, specify the script name. When naming a script, you can use as many as eight characters (with no file name extensions). You can use letters, numbers, and these special characters:

$ # & @ ! % ( ) - _ { } ` ^

Note that you cannot use spaces or duplicate names.

To start the Script Editor while you're in the PAL Debugger, press Alt-F10 (PAL Menu) and select **E**ditor to edit the script you're debugging. Pressing Ctrl-E also starts the Script Editor while you're in the Debugger. (For more information on the Debugger, see this chapter's section on "Using the PAL Debugger.")

The editing features of the Script Editor are nearly identical to those found on the report design screen. Table 15.1 lists the available cursor-movement keys, and table 15.2 includes the special key-combination commands.

Table 15.1
Cursor-Movement Keys in the Script Editor

Key	*Moves Cursor*
Home	To first line of script
End	To last line of script
PgUp	Up one screen
PgDn	Down one screen
Left arrow	One character left
Right arrow	One character right
Up arrow	Up one line
Down arrow	Down one line
Ctrl-Home	To beginning of line
Ctrl-End	To last character of line
Ctrl-left arrow	Left one-half screen
Ctrl-right arrow	Right one-half screen

Table 15.2
Special Keystroke Commands in the Script Editor

Command	*Effect*
Ctrl-O	Suspend Paradox, go to DOS
Alt-O	Suspend Paradox, go to DOS with maximum available RAM
Ctrl-V	Show vertical ruler
Ctrl-Y	Delete line

Refer to Chapter 5, "Paradox Reporting Fundamentals," for discussions of how to insert and delete lines and how to display a vertical ruler. A significant difference between the report design screen and the Script Editor screen is the maximum width. A report can be up to 2,000 characters wide, but the Script Editor width is limited to 132 characters.

When you press F10 (Menu) in the Script Editor, Paradox displays these choices:

- **R**ead. Select this option to load another script from the disk. Paradox inserts the previously created script at the cursor position.

- **G**o. Choose this option to save the script to disk, end the Script Editor session, and play the script. This option has the same net effect as pressing F2 (DO-IT!) and then playing the script through the **S**cripts **P**lay option on the Main menu. The **G**o method saves you several keystrokes.
- **P**rint. Select this option to send a copy of the script to your printer. You can obtain the same result by pressing Alt-F7 (Instant Report). To adjust the length of the pages that print, you can use the Custom Configuration Program (CCP) and change the Report Page Length setting. Appendix B discusses how to use the CCP.
- **H**elp. This selection accesses the Paradox help facility. Choosing this option has the same effect as pressing F1 (Help).
- **D**O-IT!. Choose this option to save the script to disk, end the Script Editor session, and return to Main mode. You can achieve the same result by pressing F2 (DO-IT!).
- **C**ancel. Select this option only if you want to end the Script Editor session without saving any entries or changes you have made since starting the session. Paradox returns to the Main mode.

Attaching an Alternate Editor

If you don't care for the built-in Script Editor, you can use an alternate editor to develop or modify your scripts. As long as your ASCII editor does not attach special non-ASCII formatting codes to the files it edits, you can use the editor of your choice.

In fact, you can attach your editor to Paradox by using the Custom Configuration Program so that you can call the editor within Paradox. Attaching your editor to Paradox is a good idea. That way, you do not need to exit Paradox whenever you want to edit a script. And you can still edit encrypted scripts with the proper password, just as you can with the Script Editor. You have no way to edit directly an encrypted script with an editor that is started outside Paradox.

Using the PAL Debugger

Paradox provides an excellent interactive tool for finding errors in your PAL scripts. The *PAL Debugger* is used to test scripts while in the development process or to locate errors in a problem application. This tool helps you locate two types of errors in your program: *syntax errors* and *run errors*.

Syntax errors occur when PAL commands are not properly constructed. Examples include misspelled commands or missing punctuation. Run errors occur when the commands are properly constructed but the logic of the program is faulty, resulting in a condition that PAL is unable to handle. An example of a run error is when a variable is used in a command before the variable has been assigned a value.

Accessing the Debugger

You have four ways to access the Debugger:

- If Paradox encounters an error while playing a script, the program presents the Script Error menu containing the choices **C**ancel and **D**ebug. Choose **D**ebug. The Debugger starts debugging the script at the line that caused the error.
- Insert a DEBUG command in the script. The Debugger begins debugging the script at the line that follows the DEBUG command.
- Press Ctrl-Break during script execution, and choose **D**ebug from the PAL menu that displays. The Debugger starts debugging the script at the next line that was to be executed when you pressed Ctrl-Break.
- Press Alt-F10 (PAL Menu) and choose **D**ebug from the PAL menu. Specify the script to debug. Paradox starts debugging the script at line 1 of the script.

Whenever you invoke it, the Debugger does not completely take over the screen but merely uses the next to last screen line to display the script's name and the current line number. This line is called the *status line*. On the last line of the screen, the Debugger displays the current line of code. This line is the Debugger *script line*. A single script line can contain several commands, so the Debugger indicates the next command to be executed by displaying a triangular-shaped pointer. If invoked by an error, the Debugger also displays an error message describing the apparent error condition so that you can try to determine what the problem is.

Using Special Keys in the Debugger

If the Debugger detects a syntax error, you have to fix the mistake (using the Script Editor or another ASCII editor) before you can try to play the script again. But when the error is a run error, you can skip the erroneous line of code and try to continue the script by pressing Ctrl-G (Go). Several other special keystroke commands available in the Debugger are listed in table 15.3.

Table 15.3
Special Keystroke Commands in the Debugger

Key	*Effect*
Ctrl-E (Edit)	Start Script Editor
Ctrl-G (Go)	Resume script play
Ctrl-N (Next)	Skip current command; move to next command
Ctrl-O	Suspend Paradox, go to DOS
Alt-O	Suspend Paradox, go to DOS with maximum available RAM
Ctrl-P	"Pop" up to the calling script (if any), or quit (if script was not called by another script)
Ctrl-Q (Quit)	Exit Debugger
Ctrl-S (Step)	Execute the current command
Ctrl-W (Where)	Show current level of nesting

Using the Debugger Menu

While using the Debugger, you can access several options through the Debugger menu. Press Alt-F10 (PAL Menu) and choose one of the following selections:

Value **S**tep **N**ext **G**o **M**iniScript **W**here? **Q**uit **P**op **E**ditor

Choose **V**alue to calculate the value of an expression or variable. You use this command most often to determine whether a particular variable has the proper value whenever a run error is causing a script to stop. After you choose **V**alue, the Debugger asks you for an expression. To find the value of a variable, type the variable name and press Enter. The Debugger displays the value in the message window at the lower right corner of the screen.

Choose **S**tep to execute the current command (at the pointer) and move to the next command. This option enables you to go through the script, examining the effect of each command, one step at a time. This option is the same as Ctrl-S (Step) and cannot be used after a syntax error.

The **N**ext option skips the current command (at the pointer) and advances the pointer to the next command in the script being debugged. This option is the same as Ctrl-N (Next) and cannot be used after a syntax error.

Choose **G**o to continue playing the script, starting with the current command. This option is the same as Ctrl-G (Go) and cannot be used after a syntax error.

Use the **M**iniScript option to create a one-line script, up to 175 characters in length. When you have finished typing the *miniscript*, press Enter. The miniscript becomes the current script line, and the first command in the miniscript becomes the current command. To play the miniscript, press Ctrl-G (Go) to start continuous play, or press Ctrl-S (Step) to step through the miniscript one command at a time.

Miniscripts are often used to perform temporary "patches" so that you can continue to work on the original script you are debugging without having to start over whenever you find an error. Just remember to make appropriate permanent fixes to the script itself later. Of course, an error in the miniscript causes processing to halt and displays the Script Error menu. Choose **D**ebug to debug the miniscript.

Select the **W**here? option to see the current level of script (or procedure). This option is the same as Ctrl-W (Where). When you are debugging a multilevel, nested script, use **W**here to determine which script contains the current command. When you choose this option, the Debugger displays an image on-screen that appears to be several stacked pages. The page on top of the stack is the Debugger itself. The second page in the stack is the script that contains the current command.

Choose the **Q**uit option when you want to quit the Debugger and cancel the playing of the script (at all levels). This option is the same as Ctrl-Q (Quit).

Use the **P**op option to cancel only the current level of the script and return to the script that called the current script. This option is the same as Ctrl-P. When you are debugging a script that was not played by another script, choosing **P**op has the same effect as choosing **Q**uit.

Select **E**ditor when you want to fix the script now rather than skip the erroneous command or try a quick patch with a miniscript. This command leaves the Debugger and takes you to the Script Editor (or your alternate editor) with the current script loaded for editing. When you have made the necessary corrections and want to replay the script, select **G**o from the Editor menu. (When using an alternate editor, press Ctrl-G when you return from the editor to Paradox.)

An Overview of PAL Commands

Paradox provides more than 150 PAL commands. These commands, used to develop scripts, fall into four groups: *programming* commands, *keypress interaction* commands, *abbreviated menu* commands, and *procedure/procedure library* commands. The next sections of this chapter briefly introduce you to these commands and can help you gain a general understanding of the types of PAL commands available. Refer to Part IV, Chapter 20, of the *PAL User's Guide* for a complete command reference that shows you proper syntax and provides an explanation of how to use all these powerful commands.

Programming Commands

Paradox provides more than 85 PAL *programming* commands. This wide selection of commands extends the power of Paradox by performing tasks in ways not available interactively in Paradox. The programming commands can be further divided into six general categories according to their effects: work space manipulation, input/output, variable/array manipulation, program control, system control, and multiuser.

Work Space Manipulation Commands

The commands in this category enable you to control what is happening in the Paradox work space. Many of the commands duplicate the effects of the function key commands and other special keystroke commands available interactively in Paradox. The following commands fall in this category:

CHECK
*CHECKDESCENDING
CHECKPLUS
CLEARALL
CLEARIMAGE
DITTO
DOWNIMAGE
FIRSTSHOW
*GROUPBY
LOCATE
MOVETO
PASSWORD
REQUIREDCHECK
ROTATE
SELECT
*SETNEGCOLOR
*SETQUERYORDER
*SETRECORDPOSITION
SKIP
SYNCCURSOR
TYPEIN
UNPASSWORD
UPIMAGE

(The * in this and subsequent lists in this chapter indicates that the command or function is available only in Paradox 3.0.)

Input/Output Commands

The commands in this category enable you to take charge of what information Paradox displays on-screen, sends to the printer, and accepts from the keyboard. These types of operations are normally referred to as *input* and *output* operations. The following commands are in the input/output group:

?	*PAINTCANVAS
??	PRINT
@	PROMPT
ACCEPT	*SETMARGIN
BEEP	SETPRINTER
*CANVAS	SHOWARRAY
CLEAR	SHOWFILES
CLOSE PRINTER	SHOWMENU
CURSOR	SHOWTABLES
ECHO	STYLE
KEYPRESS	TEXT
MESSAGE	TYPEIN
OPEN PRINTER	WAIT

Variable/Array Manipulation Commands

These commands enable you to create and use temporary fields referred to as *variables*, and groups of fields called *arrays*. (See the discussions of variables and arrays in this chapter's section on "An Overview of PAL Expressions.") Paradox tables are always saved to disk, but variables and arrays exist only in RAM. (You can save them to disk, however, with the SAVEVARS command.) Variables and arrays are used in PAL scripts to hold information temporarily so that the script can use the data in some way. The following PAL commands are used to manipulate variables and arrays in PAL scripts:

=	*FORMTABLES
ARRAY	RELEASE
COPYFROMARRAY	*REPORTTABLES
COPYTOARRAY	SAVEVARS

Program Control Commands

These PAL programming commands enable you to control the sequence in which script commands are executed. Without program control commands, scripts execute from left to right and top to bottom. You can use the PAL commands in this category to cause program execution to branch to a particular portion of the script, based on the occurrence of a given condition;

repeat the execution of part of the script until a certain test is met; or return from or leave a section of the script when a certain condition is met. This group includes the following commands:

FOR	QUITLOOP
IF	RETURN
LOOP	SCAN
PROC	SWITCH
QUIT	WHILE

System Control Commands

This group is a miscellaneous category of commands that are used to perform such tasks as start the Debugger, pause the script for a set number of seconds, and execute a DOS command or program from a script. Several of these commands are used to control the Paradox environment, such as returning Paradox to Main mode, setting maximum table size, and manipulating the transaction log. The following commands fall into this category:

DEBUG	RUN
*EDITLOG	SETKEY
EXECUTE	SETMAXSIZE
RESET	SLEEP

Multiuser Commands

You use the commands in this category to perform network-related tasks. If your script is executed on a network, you can use these commands to control multiuser access to shared images, tables, and records. You also can perform a number of other network-related operations, such as refreshing the screen and setting a new private directory. The following commands are in this group:

IMAGERIGHTS	SETPRIVDIR
LOCK	*SETRESTARTCOUNT
LOCKKEY	SETRETRYPERIOD
LOCKRECORD	SETUSERNAME
PRIVTABLES	UNLOCK
REFRESH	UNLOCKRECORD

Some Examples of Programming Commands

Many of the commands listed in this section are used with one or more supporting *keywords*. For example, the program control command IF is always used with the ENDIF and THEN keywords, and often with the ELSE keyword. The following discussion gives you a brief glimpse of how PAL uses commands and keywords together in PAL scripts. Refer to the *PAL User's Guide* for more information about these supporting keywords.

Together, the IF command and the supporting keywords form what is referred to as a *control structure*. The IF-THEN-ELSE control structure gives a script the capability to "decide" between two options, based on the occurrence of a given condition. This type of control structure is called a *branching* command:

```
IF myval > 10
   THEN
      ; PAL commands here are executed when myval > 10
   ELSE
      ; PAL commands here are executed when myval <= 10
ENDIF
```

In this example, any PAL commands inserted between THEN and ELSE are executed if and only if the value of the variable *myval* is greater than 10. (See this chapter's section on "Variables" for a discussion of how PAL uses them.)

For more complex decision-making requirements, you can nest IF-THEN-ELSE control structures (often called *IF statements*):

```
IF myval1 > 10
   THEN
      IF myval2 > 10
         THEN
            ; PAL commands here execute when
            ; myval1 > 10 and myval2 > 10
         ELSE
            ; PAL commands here execute when
            ; myval1 > 10 and myval2 <= 10
      ENDIF
   ELSE
      ; PAL commands here execute when myval1 <= 10
ENDIF
```

Another PAL branching command is the SWITCH command, which operates much as multiple independent IF statements do, but is a bit easier to follow. You use the SWITCH command with multiple CASE statements, where each CASE statement tests for the occurrence of a different condition. You can use an OTHERWISE statement to specify what command(s) should be executed if none of the CASE conditions are met:

```
SWITCH
   CASE myval = 1 :
      ; PAL commands here execute when myval = 1
   CASE myval = 2 :
      ; PAL commands here execute when myval = 2
   CASE myval = 3 :
      ; PAL commands here execute when myval = 3
   OTHERWISE :
      ; PAL commands here execute when none of the
      ; preceding CASE conditions were met
ENDSWITCH
```

SWITCH is often combined with the SHOWMENU command to enable the user to control the sequence of script execution interactively. The SHOWMENU command is used to display Paradox-like menus. In the following example, each menu selection name is enclosed in double quotation marks and followed by a colon. Then an explanation or description of the menu selection is placed after the colon, also enclosed in double quotation marks. When the script executes, a menu with the choices **B**enefits, **E**mployee, **S**alary, and **L**eave displays at the top of the screen in the same manner as a normal Paradox menu. The final line of the SHOWMENU command is the TO statement. When the user selects one of the menu options, the TO statement causes the name of the user's selection to be placed in a temporary field or variable that can then be tested by a SWITCH control structure:

```
SHOWMENU
   "Benefits": "Add, change, display, print benefit info,"
   "Employee": "Add, change, display, print employee info,"
   "Salary": "Add, change, display, print salary info,"
   "Leave": "Leave the application"
TO response
SWITCH
   CASE response = "Benefits":
      PLAY "Exben"
   CASE response = "Employee":
      PLAY "Exemp"
```

```
   CASE response = "Salary":
      PLAY "Exsal"
   CASE response = "Leave":
      QUIT
ENDSWITCH
```

If the user selects **B**enefits, Paradox plays the Exben script. If the user selects **E**mployee, Paradox plays the Exemp script, and so on. The last menu option, **L**eave, causes the script to QUIT, which stops execution of the script and returns the user to Paradox.

Refer to Chapter 4 of the *PAL User's Guide* for more information and discussion on the use of PAL control structures and the other available PAL programming commands.

Keypress Interaction Commands

PAL *keypress interaction* commands enable you to replicate the effects of pressing keys during an interactive Paradox session. Paradox uses this type of command to record your keystrokes when you create a script with the **B**eginRecord option, as described in Chapter 6.

Menu selections are placed in curly braces, as in {Modify} and {Edit}. Cursor-movement selections are represented by commands such as DOWN and LEFT. Function keys are represented by PAL commands such as CHECK (F6), EXAMPLE (F5), and DO_IT! (F2). Table 6.2 in Chapter 6 provides a complete list of keypress interaction commands that correspond to Paradox function key commands and to Paradox special keystroke commands.

You can use this type of PAL command to reproduce any command you can enter at the keyboard, including query operations. Scripts created by the **Q**uerySave option, referred to as *query images* (described in Chapter 4), fall into this category of PAL commands.

Keystrokes that will result in characters being typed onto the work space must be enclosed in double quotation marks. For example, if you create a script for entering data in a table, you must enclose the entry in double quotation marks.

Abbreviated Menu Commands

PAL commands in the *abbreviated menu* category represent menu options and can often replace several keypress interaction commands. For example, a script that renames the Employee table to Emptemp by using keypress interaction commands includes the following commands:

MENU {Tools} {Rename} {Table} "Employee" ENTER "Emptemp" ENTER

The following single abbreviated menu command accomplishes the same result:

RENAME "Employee" "Emptemp"

Table 15.4 lists the available PAL abbreviated menu commands and the corresponding menu options in Paradox. Refer to the *PAL User's Guide* for the proper syntax of these commands.

Table 15.4
PAL Abbreviated Menu Commands

Abbreviated Menu Command	*Mode*	*Menu Options*
ADD	Main	Tools/More/Add
CANCELEDIT	Edit, Report, Form	Cancel/Yes
COEDIT	Main	Modify/CoEdit
COPY	Main	Tools/Copy/Table/Replace
*COPYFORM	Main	Tools/Copy/Form/Replace
*COPYREPORT	Main	Tools/Copy/Report/Replace
CREATE	Main	Create
DELETE	Main	Tools/Delete/Table/OK
EDIT	Main	Modify/Edit
EMPTY	Main	Tools/More/Empty/OK
EXIT	Main	Exit/Yes
INDEX	Main	Tools/QuerySpeedup
LOCK	Main	Tools/Net/Lock
	Main	Tools/Net/PreventLock
PICKFORM	Main, Edit, CoEdit	Image/PickForm
PLAY	All	Scripts/Play
PROTECT	Main	Tools/More/Protect/ Password/Table
QUERY	Main	Ask
RENAME	Main	Tools/Rename/Table/Replace
REPORT	Main	Report/Output/Printer
SETDIR	Main	Tools/More/Directory/OK
SETPRIVDIR	Main	Tools/Net/SetPrivate
SETUSERNAME	Main	Tools/Net/UserName
SORT	Main	Modify/Sort
SUBTRACT	Main	Tools/More/Subtract

Table 15.4—*Continued*

Abbreviated Menu Command	*Mode*	*Menu Options*
UNLOCK	Main	Tools/Net/Lock
	Main	Tools/Net/PreventLock
UNPASSWORD	Main	Tools/More/Protect/ ClearPassword
VIEW	Main	View

*Paradox 3.0 only

Procedure and Procedure Library Commands

As you learn to program with PAL, you will notice that many of your scripts include similar series of PAL commands. And sometimes a single PAL script performs identical or nearly identical steps in more than one portion of the script. You already have learned that the PLAY command provides a method for one script to run another script. You can thus create a second script that includes the commands that you noticed were common to several portions of your original script, and use the PLAY command at the appropriate places to run this new *subroutine* script. This process is called *modularizing* your program and makes for programs that are efficient and easy to follow and debug.

The extensive use of scripts as subroutines, however, can result in an unmanageable directory full of script files that just make your programming efforts more confusing. Also, each time Paradox plays a subroutine script, the program must reread the script from the disk and interpret each command from ASCII into the form that Paradox can execute—referred to as *parsed* format.

A PAL *procedure* is used much like a subroutine script in that it enables you to modularize your program, writing code in manageable blocks and avoiding repetition. Procedures, however, do not clutter your disk with additional files and are quicker in operation than subroutine scripts. You type a procedure in a script, just as you do a normal subroutine, but when you play the script that contains the procedure, Paradox loads it into RAM in interpreted (parsed) format. Loading the procedure into RAM is called *defining* the procedure. You then can use the procedure anywhere in any script during the Paradox session (or until you clear the procedure from memory), and Paradox does not have to read or parse it again.

To convert a script into a procedure, add the PROC command, followed by the procedure name, before the first command of your script. Add the END-PROC command after the last command of the original script. For example, the following script, when executed, defines the procedure *Eris1Menu*. You then can have other scripts use this procedure by simply including in the script the command *Eris1Menu*. This particular procedure displays a menu of options, each of which will play another script when selected by the user:

```
PROC Eris1Menu
   SHOWMENU
     "Benefits": "Add, change, display, print benefit info,"
     "Employee": "Add, change, display, print employee info,"
     "Salary": "Add, change, display, print salary info,"
     "Leave": "Leave the application"
   TO response
   SWITCH
     CASE response = "Benefits":
        PLAY "Exben"
     CASE response = "Employee":
        PLAY "Exemp"
     CASE response = "Salary":
        PLAY "Exsal"
     CASE response = "Leave"
        QUIT
   ENDSWITCH
ENDPROC
```

PAL *procedure libraries* give you even more flexibility. Procedure libraries contain one or more procedures that Paradox already has interpreted into parsed format. Obviously, Paradox can load and use *preparsed* procedures more quickly than procedures stored as ASCII files that must still be interpreted, but other advantages exist as well, including the following:

- *Memory management*. Even parsed commands consume space in RAM. Therefore, when you are running a large application that uses most of the RAM available in your computer, the loading of a procedure may require that you first release from memory one or more other unneeded procedures to make room. Paradox takes care of this swap for you automatically when the procedures are called from a library. But if the procedures are not called from a library, you have to use PAL commands to remove unneeded procedures from memory.

- *Consolidation of procedures*. Even if you develop an application in small modules, you can use procedure libraries to put all the modules together as a library of procedures (up to a maximum of 300 procedures). Then you can use a single script, often called a *driver* script, to load and orchestrate the various modules. A program that would otherwise consist of many scripts and therefore many files can be reduced to a library file and a driver script file.
- *Keyboard macros*. Procedure libraries are ideal for holding keyboard macros (discussed in Chapter 6). At the beginning of each Paradox session, you load the procedure library that contains all the macros you have developed. Then you can operate the macros as quickly as if they were a part of the Paradox program itself.

To enhance efficiency further, Paradox Version 3.0 gives you the ability to [3]
create *closed procedures*. Closed procedures are completely self-contained procedures that can take special advantage of PAL's automatic memory-management features. To use closed procedures, you must observe a number of special restrictions. For example, closed procedures can be called only from a procedure library. Refer to Chapter 6 of the *PAL User's Guide* for more information on when and how to use this powerful type of procedure.

The following PAL commands are used to create and use procedures and procedure libraries:

CREATELIB	READLIB
*EXECPROC	RELEASE
INFOLIB	SETSWAP
PROC	WRITELIB

An Overview of PAL Expressions

Many PAL commands require that you provide certain information before the program can perform its intended operation. For example, the VIEW command by itself is incomplete. You have to provide the name of a table that is to be viewed in the Paradox work space before this command can have an effect. Each piece of information that you must provide to a command is called an *argument* of the command. Many PAL commands require you to provide more than one argument.

In PAL, command arguments are supplied in the form of *expressions*. Expressions are made up of any one or more of the following building blocks: constants, blank values, variables, arrays, operators, field specifiers, and functions. These elements of expressions are discussed in the sections that follow.

Constants and Blank Values

A *constant* is simply a data value, such as the number *3* or the word *zebra*. It is called "constant" because its value does not change during the script's operation. A *blank value* is simply the absence of a value. Each constant must be one of the following types: alphanumeric, numeric, date, or logical. For example, if your script contains the command

```
VIEW "Employee"
```

the argument is the alphanumeric constant *Employee*.

Alphanumeric constants can be from 1 to 255 characters long and must be enclosed in double quotation marks. You can use any of the 256 characters in the IBM extended ASCII character set. To include characters that cannot be displayed by simply pressing a key, hold down the Alt key and type on the numeric keypad the ASCII code for the character. These codes are listed in Appendix C of the *PAL User's Guide*.

Alternatively, you can type the ASCII code itself into the constant, but you must precede the code with a backslash (\). For example, the IBM ASCII code for the Greek letter *alpha* (α) is 224. The constant *"\224"* therefore displays an alpha.

PAL provides a special set of *backslash sequences* that provide shortcuts for several ASCII characters that have special uses in controlling your printer. Table 15.5 lists these codes. The last two codes in table 15.5 are included because both the quotation mark and the backslash have special uses in constructing alphanumeric constants. (The double quotation marks [" "] are used to enclose alphanumeric constants, and the backslash [\] precedes an ASCII code.) A blank alphanumeric value is represented by two double quotation marks (" "), not a space (ASCII code 32).

You enter a *numeric* constant in a script as a series of digits with or without a minus sign or decimal point. You also can use scientific notation. The following examples are all valid numeric constants:

```
656
656.44
-656.44
6.6E+2
```

The last example, which is in scientific notation, means 6.6×10^2, or 660.

Table 15.5
Backslash Sequences for Alphanumeric Constants

Backslash Sequence	*Function*	*ASCII Code*
\t	Tab	9
\n	Newline	10
\f	Formfeed	6
\r	Carriage return	12
\"	Quotation mark	34
\\	Backslash	92

Do not use dollar signs or whole-number separators. The values $656 and 6,560 are not valid PAL numeric constants. The built-in function BLANKNUM is used to represent a blank numeric value.

Date constants must be entered in one of the following formats:

mm/dd/yyyy
dd-Mon-yyyy
dd.mm.yyyy

When the date is in this century, only the last two digits of the year portion are necessary. The built-in function BLANKDATE is used to represent a blank date value.

You must enter *logical* constants as either *true* or *false*. You can, however, use the built-in FORMAT function to change these constants to *On/Off* or *Yes/No* for purposes of creating screen or printer output.

Variables

Because the value of a command argument may not be known when you create the script, you need a way to supply the necessary value during the operation of the script. *Variables* serve this purpose. You can think of a PAL variable as a temporary field of any data type that enables the script to store information in RAM for later use. During the execution of the script, the user or some other part of the script supplies data that is stored in a variable. Then a PAL command uses this variable as its argument.

You do not need to predefine the PAL variables or preset the data type of PAL variables. You simply set a variable as equal to a particular expression, using the equal sign (=). For example, the PAL command

```
table1 = "Employee"
```

creates the alphanumeric variable *table1* and sets it equal to the constant value *"Employee"*. Then, your script might contain the command

```
VIEW table1
```

The variable *table1* is the argument for the VIEW command. Because *table1* has the value *"Employee"*, this command displays the Employee table.

Variable names can be up to 132 characters long, must begin with a letter, and cannot contain spaces. Do not use the name of a PAL command, function (discussed later in this chapter), or keyword (listed in Part IV of the *PAL User's Guide*) as the name of a variable. A variable's data type is determined by the data type of the expression to which the variable is equal.

This type of variable, which you create by simply setting it equal to an expression, is called a *global variable*. This name is appropriate because, once defined, the variable remains active during the current Paradox session and can be accessed and modified by any script or procedure. You can use the RELEASE command at the end of a PAL script if you don't want the global variables and their current values to carry over to the next script executed during the Paradox session.

You can limit the use of a particular variable to a specific procedure by defining the variable as *private*. You simply use the PRIVATE keyword in the script that defines the procedure. The following commands, when used in a script that defines a procedure, create the private variable *table1* and then assign it the value *"Customer"*:

```
PRIVATE table1
table1 = "Customer"
```

Unlike the global variable *table1* created in the preceding example, this *table1* variable is available only to the procedure that creates it.

Arrays

An *array* is a number of temporary fields that you can reference as a group. Because a record in a Paradox table is also a group of fields, arrays are often used to store and manipulate entire records at once.

You define arrays with the ARRAY command. Array names can be up to 132 characters long, must start with a letter, and cannot contain spaces. Do not use the name of a PAL command, function (discussed later in this chapter), or keyword (listed in Part IV of the *PAL User's Guide*) as the name of an array. For example, the command

```
ARRAY emp[13]
```

creates an array named *emp* with 13 elements. In other words, the *emp* array can contain 13 separate values. You could then use the COPYTOARRAY command to copy a record from the Employee table into this array. Refer to Chapter 14 of the *PAL User's Guide* for more information on when and how to use arrays.

Operators

Just as you can use operators in Paradox to combine data and perform calculations in queries, forms, and reports, you can use operators to combine data and perform calculations in PAL expressions. Table 15.6 lists each available operator and its meaning.

Table 15.6
PAL Operators

Type	*Operator*	*Meaning*
Alphanumeric (A)	+	Concatenation
Numeric (N,S,$)	+	Addition
	−	Subtraction
	*	Multiplication
	/	Division
Date (D)	+	Addition of integers to dates
	−	Subtraction of integers from dates; days between
Comparison	=	Equal to
	<>	Not equal to
	<	Less than
	<=	Less than or equal to
	>	Greater than
	>=	Greater than or equal to
Logical	AND	Logical AND
	OR	Logical OR
	NOT	Logical NOT

Whenever you include more than one operator in an expression, Paradox evaluates operations in the order of precedence listed in table 15.7. You can use parentheses, however, to control explicitly the order of operation. Operations in the innermost parentheses are calculated first. Operations of the same level of precedence and same level of parentheses are evaluated from left to right.

Table 15.7
Order of Precedence of PAL Operators

Precedence	*Operators*
1	( )
2	* /
3	+
4	= <> < <= > >=
5	NOT
6	AND
7	OR

Field Specifiers

As you know, all Paradox data is stored in fields. Because your scripts are intended to work with Paradox data, PAL must provide a way to refer to data fields in PAL expressions. The various ways to specify Paradox fields are collectively called *field specifiers*. Table 15.8 lists the field specifier formats that are available for use in PAL commands. These specifiers are used to refer to a field displayed in a table or query form on the Paradox work space. For example, [Employee->Emp City] represents the Emp City field in the current record of the Employee table on the Paradox work space. [Employee(Q)->Emp City] refers to the same field, but in a query form for the Employee table on the work space.

Table 15.8
Field Specifiers

Format	*Meaning*
[ ]	Current field in current image
[#]	Current record number in current image
[fieldname]	Field *fieldname* in current image

Table 15.8—*Continued*

Format	*Meaning*
[tablename->fieldname]	Field *fieldname* in current record of table *tablename*
[tablename(n)->]	Current field in the *n*th image of table *tablename*
[tablename(n)->fieldname]	Field *fieldname* in the *n*th image of table *tablename*
[tablename(Q)->]	Current field in query image of table *tablename*
[tablename(Q)->fieldname]	Field *fieldname* in query image of table *tablename*

Whenever Paradox evaluates an expression that contains a reference to a field from a particular table, the value for that field is taken from the current record in that table. The current record of the current image is the record that contains the current field, and the current field is the field that contains the cursor. For other images on the work space, the current field and record are the last field and record that contained the cursor.

Functions

PAL functions are built-in formulas that operate on expressions and generate values. PAL functions look much like PAL commands but have a distinctly different purpose. In a PAL script, a PAL command controls the actions of Paradox, but a PAL function produces a value that can be used in a PAL expression. Just as several categories of PAL commands exist, PAL functions fall into several groups according to the type of operation or calculation they perform.

String Manipulation Functions

The following functions are used to perform such operations as convert text strings (alphanumeric values) to other data types, convert other data types to text strings, return information about text strings, and format text strings:

ASC	DATEVAL
CHR	FILL

FORMAT	SPACES
LEN	STRVAL
MATCH	SUBSTR
MENUCHOICE	UPPER
SEARCH	WINDOW

Date Manipulation Functions

You can use the following functions to work with and generate date values:

BLANKDATE	MOY
DATEVAL	STRVAL
DAY	TIME
DOW	TODAY
FORMAT	YEAR
MONTH	

Mathematical Functions

The following functions perform trigonometric, logarithmic, and other mathematical calculations:

ABS	LN
ACOS	LOG
ASIN	MOD
ATAN	PI
ATAN2	POW
BLANKNUM	RAND
COS	ROUND
EXP	SIN
FORMAT	SQRT
INT	TAN

Statistical Functions

The following functions generate statistics:

CAVERAGE	*IMAGECAVERAGE
CCOUNT	*IMAGECCOUNT
CMIN	*IMAGECMIN
CSTD	*IMAGECSUM
CSUM	MAX
CVAR	MIN

Financial Functions

A number of PAL functions perform calculations of interest in financial analyses:

CNPV	PMT
FV	PV

Information Functions

These functions gather information that is needed by various PAL commands. For example, before attempting to display the Employee table, you might include an IF statement that uses the ISTABLE function to determine whether the table even exists. If it does not exist, script execution branches around the VIEW command:

```
IF ISTABLE ("Employee")
   THEN
      VIEW "Employee"
ENDIF
```

The following functions fall into this category:

ARRAYSIZE	HELPMODE
BOT	ISASSIGNED
CHECKMARKSTATUS	ISBLANK
DIREXISTS	ISEMPTY
EOT	ISENCRYPTED
ERRORCODE	ISFILE
ERRORMESSAGE	ISSHARED
ERRORUSER	ISTABLE
FAMILYRIGHTS	ISVALID
FIELDRIGHTS	TABLERIGHTS
FILESIZE	TYPE

System Status Functions

These functions are similar in purpose to the information functions but provide information about the system or system defaults. For instance, you may want to use the SYSMODE function to check the current Paradox mode at the start of a script. Then, if the program is not in the proper mode to run the script, you can execute commands to change the mode rather than have the script fail. The following functions are in the system status group:

DIRECTORY
DRIVESPACE
DRIVESTATUS
*GRAPHTYPE
*ISBLANKZERO
ISRUNTIME
MEMLEFT
MONITOR
NETTYPE
PRINTERSTATUS
PRIVDIR
*QUERYORDER
RETRYPERIOD
SDIR
SORTORDER
*SYSCOLOR
SYSMODE
USERNAME
VERSION

Work Space and Canvas Status Functions

These functions check various conditions on the work space itself and on the PAL canvas (the screen):

ATFIRST
ATLAST
BANDINFO
BOT
CHECKMARKSTATUS
COL
COLNO
CURSORCHAR
CURSORLINE
EOT
FIELD
FIELDINFO
FIELDNO
FIELDSTR
FIELDTYPE
*FORM
IMAGENO
IMAGETYPE
ISFIELDVIEW
ISFORMVIEW
ISINSERTMODE
*ISLINKLOCKED
*ISMULTIFORM
*ISMULTIREPORT
*LINKTYPE
LOCKSTATUS
MENUCHOICE
NFIELDS
*NIMAGERECORDS
NIMAGES
NKEYFIELDS
NPAGES
NRECORDS
NROWS
PAGENO
PAGEWIDTH
RECNO
ROW
ROWNO
SYSMODE
TABLE
WINDOW

Using the Value Option To Calculate an Expression

The PAL menu contains an option that enables you to calculate interactively the value of any PAL expression. From any mode in Paradox, press Alt-F10 (PAL Menu) and choose **V**alue. Paradox prompts you to `Enter expression to calculate`. Type any valid PAL expression, and press Enter. The expression can be as simple as a numeric formula, such as 3*225, or as complex an expression as you can type in the available 175 characters, using any of the expression elements discussed in the previous sections. Once you press Enter, Paradox evaluates the expression and displays its value in the message window at the lower right corner of the screen.

Chapter Summary

This chapter, the last of the book, has presented an overview of the major features of PAL that enable you to create sophisticated relational database applications. Use what you have learned here to get started at writing your own PAL scripts. Paradox is already an incredibly powerful database program even without programming. But only after you learn to use the Paradox Application Language will you realize its true, practically unlimited potential.

A

Paradox 3.0 Installation and Start-Up

This appendix explains how to install Paradox 3.0 and begin using the program. Installation of Paradox on a local area network server is not discussed in this appendix. Network administrators should see the *Network Administrator's Guide* included in the Paradox documentation for help.

Understanding System Requirements

Before installing Paradox 3.0, ensure that your system meets the minimum requirements to run Paradox 3.0 as a single-user program. You must have a hard disk with at least 2M of free memory space (more than 4M if you include all optional programs and files), at least 512K RAM, and DOS 2.0 or higher. Performance and capacity are improved if your system includes expanded memory (LIM/EMS, or EEMS).

To take advantage of all Paradox's capabilities, you also need a graphics capable monitor and graphics printer or plotter, or both.

Installing the Main Program

Paradox 3.0 is distributed on fifteen 5 1/4-inch 360K disks and eight 3 1/2-inch 720K disks. The installation process is similar for either disk size, but the 3 1/2-inch disks require less disk swapping.

To begin installing Paradox, you must be at the DOS prompt. The current drive should be the hard disk on which you want to install Paradox 3.0. To install Paradox on your hard drive (usually drive C), you should be at the DOS prompt, `C>`. (`C>` is the default prompt, but many systems are set up to display `C:\>`.)

Place the distributed Paradox disk marked Installation/Sample Tables Disk into drive A (the first floppy drive). Type *a:install* and press Enter. Paradox displays the initial installation screen. Read this screen and press Enter to continue.

The second screen asks for the installation type. Type *1* for `Hard Disk Installation` and press Enter. Confirm the source drive, `A`, as the drive containing the Installation/Sample Tables Disk and press Enter. Confirm the destination drive, `C`, and press Enter.

The next screen displays the default directory for the installation of Paradox 3.0 files, `C:\PARADOX3`. If you prefer that Paradox be installed in a different directory, backspace over this directory name, type the new path specification, and press Enter. Otherwise, just press Enter.

The installation program examines the CONFIG.SYS file on your hard disk and modifies the file by adding a FILES command if necessary. If Paradox makes some change to the file, the program saves a copy of the original version first as CONFIG.PDX.

DOS reads CONFIG.SYS each time you restart the computer. For Paradox 3.0 to work properly, the following lines need to appear in this file:

```
FILES = 20
BUFFERS = 20
```

Paradox ensures that these lines exist as part of the installation process, but you may accidentally change or delete this file sometime later. If you have trouble getting Paradox to start, look at this file by using the DOS type command:

```
TYPE CONFIG.SYS
```

If necessary, add the FILES and BUFFERS lines listed above using any text editor that produces pure ASCII text files.

On the next screen, choose the appropriate country group. This choice affects date formats, whole number separators, and alphabetic sort order. Assuming that you are using Paradox in the United States, type the number *1* and press Enter. Paradox displays the message `Copying files...` and instructs you to insert System Disk 1 into the source drive.

Insert the distributed System Disk 1 (System Disk 1/2 if installing 3 1/2-inch disks) and press Enter. Paradox displays the Paradox Personal Signature form (see fig. A.1). Be careful about how you fill in this screen. Each time you start Paradox, this information is displayed at the bottom of Paradox's greeting screen. You must fill in all fields in the form. The Paradox serial number is the number appearing on the label of the 5 1/4-inch Installation/ Sample Tables Disk.

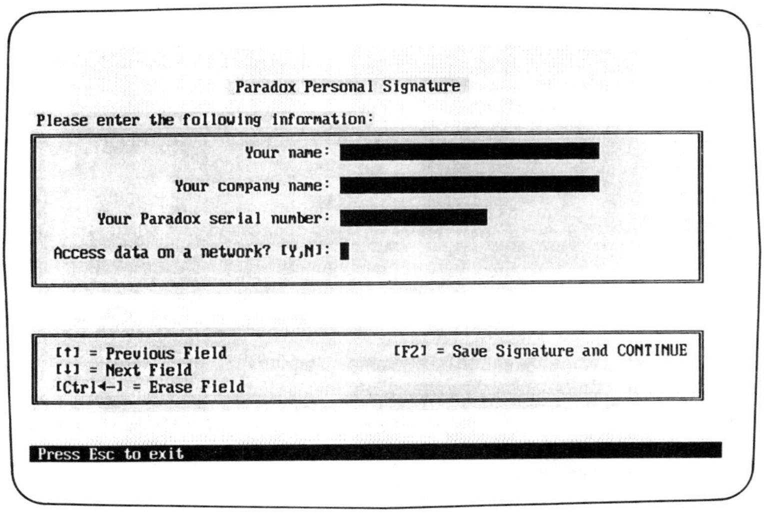

Fig. A.1.

The Paradox Personal Signature form.

If you may be accessing data on a network from your stand-alone copy of Paradox, answer *Y* to the last question, `Access data on a network?` Paradox asks you for the network type and directory containing the file PARADOX.NET. (Obtain this network related information from your network administrator.) When you finish entering your signature information, press F2 to save the information and continue with the installation process. Because Paradox saves the signature information to the Installation/ Sample Tables Disk, you don't have to enter the information again if you reinstall Paradox on your system.

Paradox begins copying files to your hard disk. Follow the instructions on-screen. Insert a new disk when instructed to do so. When installing

5 1/4-inch floppies, you insert System Disk 2, System Disk 3, System Disk 4, Custom Configuration Disk 1, and Custom Configuration Disk 2. With 3 1/2-inch disks, you have two disks—System Disk 3/4 and Custom Configuration Disk 1/2.

Paradox finishes copying files and instructs you to place the Installation Disk back into the floppy disk drive. Paradox uses your previous country code selection to configure the sample tables contained on the Installation/ Sample Tables Disk. The tables, however, are not copied to the disk. Installation of the sample tables is a separate and optional step when installing Paradox. (See the next section, "Installing the Optional Software.")

Insert Data Entry Toolkit Disk 1 (or Data Entry Toolkit Disk 1/2 for 3 1/2-inch disk installation) into the floppy drive so that Paradox also can configure the tables on this disk using the proper country code.

Paradox displays the Optional Software Installation form shown in figure A.2. To exit the installation program at this point, type *6*, press Enter, and skip the following section of this appendix. Go to the section entitled "Starting Paradox 3.0." If you later decide to install any of the optional software, see the instructions in the next section. To install any optional software, proceed to the next section.

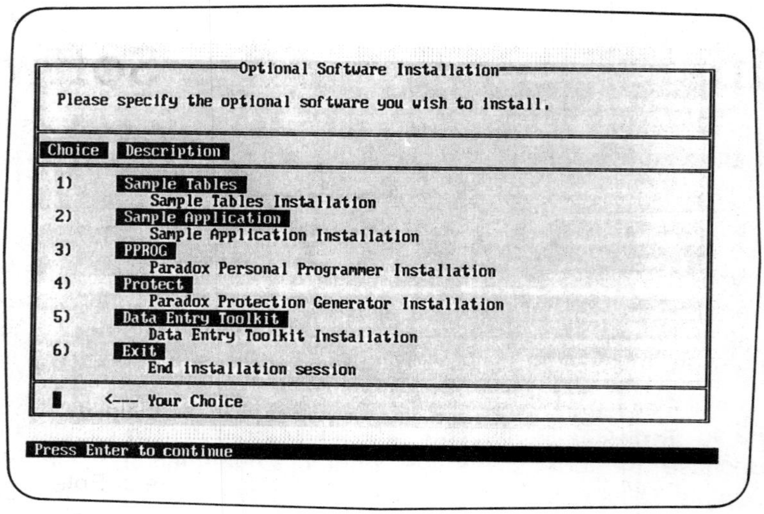

Fig. A.2.

The Optional Software Installation form.

When you complete the installation process, Paradox displays the screen shown in figure A.3. As this screen indicates, you should reboot your system before using Paradox to ensure that DOS reads the modified CONFIG.SYS file. Otherwise, Paradox may not work properly.

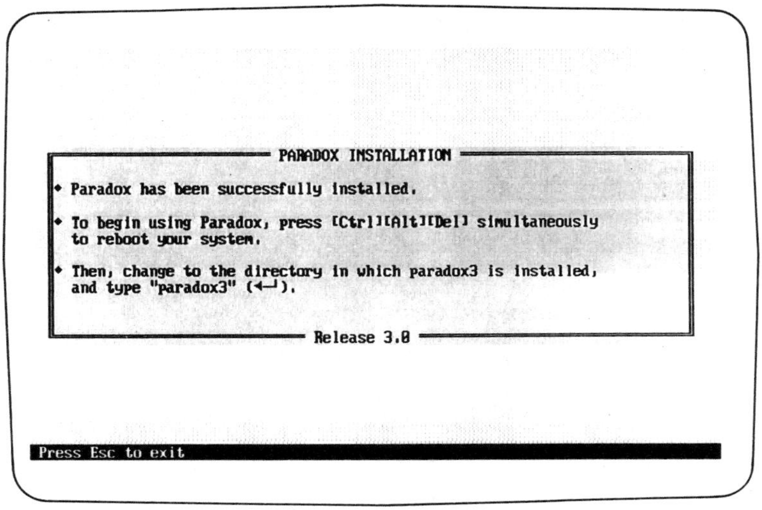

Fig. A.3.

Paradox 3.0 successfully installed.

Installing Optional Software

The Paradox 3.0 disks include a number of optional programs and files. If you do not install these programs and files, you still can use the Paradox program.

To install the optional software, display the Optional Software Installation screen (see fig. A.2). If you are installing Paradox and that screen is displayed, you are ready to take the next step. If you previously installed Paradox and chose not to install the optional files, you can display the Optional Software Installation screen by completing the following steps:

1. Place the distributed Paradox disk marked Installation/Sample Tables Disk into drive A (the first floppy drive).
2. From the DOS prompt, type *a:install* and press Enter.
3. When Paradox displays the initial installation screen, press Enter to continue.

4. At the next screen, type *3* and press Enter. Paradox displays the Optional Software Installation screen.

Installing Sample Tables

The introduction to the Paradox documentation includes a tutorial demonstrating many of the program's features. Before you can follow along with this tutorial, you have to install the sample tables. The other books in the Paradox documentation also develop examples that refer to these sample tables.

To install the sample tables, complete the following steps:

1. Type *1* at the Optional Software Installation screen and press Enter.
2. At the next screen, accept the default directory, C:\PARADOX\SAMPLE, or type an alternative directory, and press Enter.
3. When Paradox prompts you to insert the Installation Disk, insert the Installation/Sample Tables Disk and press Enter.

   Paradox creates the directory for the sample files, if the directory doesn't already exist, and copies the files to your disk. When finished, Paradox displays the message `Sample Tables installation completed`.
4. Press Enter to return to the Optional Software Installation screen. You can exit the installation program or continue to install other optional files.

Installing the Personal Programmer

All features described in the first two parts of this book, "Paradox Fundamentals" and "Tapping the Power of Paradox," are included in the Paradox 3.0 main program. To use the Paradox Personal Programmer discussed in Chapter 14, you need to install the Personal Programmer.

To install the Paradox Personal Programmer, complete the following steps:

1. At the Optional Software Installation screen type *3* and press Enter.

2. At the next screen, accept the default directory, C:\PARADOX\PPROG, or type an alternative directory, and press Enter.

3. When Paradox prompts you to insert Personal Programmer Disk 1 into the floppy drive, place the disk (Personal Programmer Disk 1/2 for 3 1/2-inch installation) into drive A and press Enter.

   Paradox creates the directory for the Personal Programmer, if the directory doesn't exist, and copies the files to that directory on your disk.

4. Insert the disks holding the rest of the Personal Programmer when prompted to do so. When finished, Paradox displays the message `Paradox Personal Programmer installation completed`.

5. Press Enter to return to the Optional Software Installation screen. You can exit the installation program or continue to install other optional files.

Installing the Sample Application, Protection Generator, or Data Entry Toolkit

Paradox 3.0 provides a complete high-level database programming language and applications development environment. Part III of this book introduces you to the Personal Programmer and provides a brief overview of the Paradox Application Language. This book is not intended as a guide to developing sophisticated Paradox programs. Because the optional *Sample Application* and *Data Entry Toolkit* files are of interest only to Paradox programmers, installation of these files is not discussed in this appendix. See Part V of the *PAL User's Guide* for help installing these files.

The *Paradox Protection Generator* enables Paradox programmers and network administrators to have enhanced file protection capabilities. See Chapter 11 of the Paradox *Network Administrator's Guide* for help installing this program.

Getting Started

Now that your program is installed, you are ready to start Paradox. This section explains how to access Paradox and start the Paradox Personal Programmer.

Starting Paradox 3.0

The screen shown in figure A.3 instructs you to change to the directory in which Paradox 3.0 is installed, type *paradox3*, and press Enter. This method works every time, but is not usually the best method.

When you create database files with Paradox, the program normally places them in the directory from which you start the program. If you start Paradox from the directory containing the Paradox program, you mix data files with program files. This poor file management leads to problems as you create more and more database tables.

A better way to use Paradox is to create a separate directory on your hard disk for each database application and to start Paradox from that directory. This method, however, requires a little preparation. The following discussion explains how to enter the necessary DOS commands and shows you how to use a *batch* file to consolidate the commands.

To create a directory on your hard disk for a Paradox database, start at the DOS prompt with the root directory of your hard disk current. For example, if your hard disk is designated drive C, the prompt is `C>` or `C:\>`. Create a new directory with the MD command (for Make Directory). To create a directory with the name PDATA, type *md \pdata* at the DOS prompt and press Enter. Change to the new directory by typing *cd \pdata* and pressing Enter. Starting Paradox from this directory stores new database files in this directory.

So that DOS can find the Paradox program files, draw a map by defining the *path* to the Paradox directory. For example, assuming that your DOS files are in the DOS directory, type *path c:\paradox3;c:\;c:\dos* and press Enter. Insert the appropriate directory name into the PATH statement for your system.

To start Paradox 3.0, type *paradox3* and press Enter. As Paradox loads you see a title screen similar to figure A.4 showing the *signature* information you supplied during the installation process. This screen is followed by the Paradox Main menu. Paradox is ready to use.

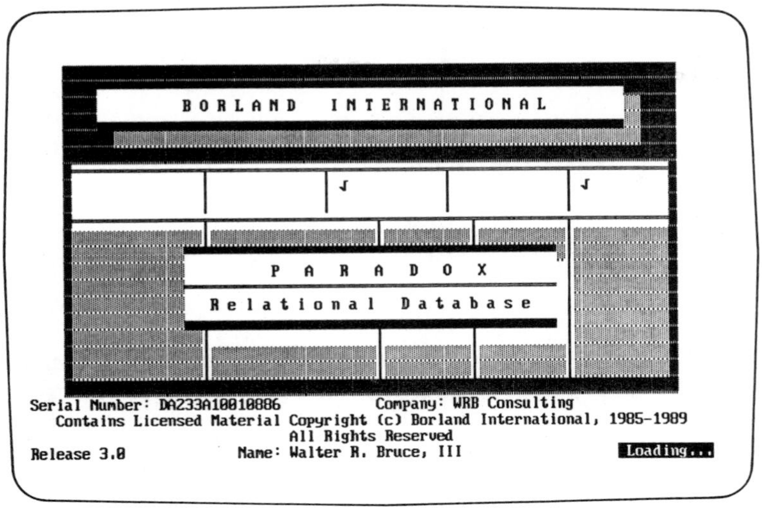

Fig. A.4.

The Paradox 3.0 title screen.

Using a Batch File To Start Paradox 3.0

Consolidate the commands that start Paradox into one command by creating a batch file. Access DOS at the root directory of your hard disk and type the following commands, pressing Enter at the end of each line:

```
copy con p3.bat
echo off
cls
path c:\paradox3;c:\;c:\dos
cd \pdata
paradox3
cd \
```

After the last line, press F6. DOS displays `^Z`. Press Enter. You should see the message `1 File(s) copied`, and your screen should look similar to figure A.5. This process creates a batch file named *P3.BAT*.

To start Paradox, type *p3* at the DOS prompt and press Enter.

Create several batch files to start Paradox, each of which makes a different directory the working directory, to ensure that unrelated data is not mixed in the same directory. For example, if you build a database to process orders for your company's merchandise, you might place the database in a directory named C:\ORDERS. You can create a batch file named

Fig. A.5.

Creating a batch file to start Paradox 3.0.

```
C>copy con p3.bat
echo off
path c:\paradox3;c:\;c:\dos
cd \pdata
paradox3
cd \
^Z
        1 File(s) copied

C>
```

ORDERS.BAT that starts Paradox from this directory—ensuring that all data for this database is placed in the C:\ORDERS directory. To create this batch file, type the following at the DOS prompt, pressing Enter at the end of each line:

```
copy con orders.bat
echo off
cls
path c:\paradox3;c:\;c:\dos
cd \orders
paradox3
cd \
```

Press F6 and Enter. Place this file in the root directory, so that you can use it from any directory. When you type *orders* and press Enter, Paradox starts, and the working directory is C:\ORDERS.

Starting the Personal Programmer

The Paradox Personal Programmer is a program separate from Paradox and must be started independently. You should create a separate directory for each application you want to generate with the Personal Programmer. You also need to add the directory containing the Personal Programmer to the path. After you complete these two steps, you can create an application in that directory. Use the *cd* command to change to the proper directory for the application, type *pprog*, and press Enter.

B

Configuring Paradox

This appendix describes how to use the Custom Configuration Program (CCP), a utility for customizing many Paradox features. The program modifies the file PARADOX3.CFG (PARADOX2.CFG for Paradox 2.0) located in the directory containing Paradox (usually C:\PARADOX3 or C:\PARADOX2).

Starting, Leaving, and Canceling the CCP

The Custom Configuration Program is accessed through a Paradox script named Custom.

To run the CCP in Paradox 3.0, press F10 (Menu) and select **S**cripts **P**lay. **[3]**

At the `Script:` prompt, type the name of the directory containing the Paradox program files, *c:\paradox3*, and press Enter. (For Paradox 2.0, type *c:\paradox2*.) Paradox displays a list of scripts. Select **C**ustom.

Paradox displays a greeting screen and asks whether you are using a `B&W` monitor because the highlighted text on-screen usually is not readable on a black-and-white monitor with a CGA, EGA, or VGA adapter. Paradox changes the default settings to ensure readability. Supply an answer corresponding to your system by pressing **Y**es or **N**o.

Paradox displays the Main CCP menu:

Video **R**eports **G**raphs **D**efaults **I**nt'l **N**et **P**AL **A**scii **H**elp **D**O-IT! **C**ancel

Make all selections from this menu to configure Paradox with the CCP. When you finish customizing Paradox, select **D**O-IT! to save the new configuration. You also can press F2 (DO-IT!) from any CCP screen to save all changes made up to that point.

Paradox gives you a choice of saving the new configuration to one of the following:

- **H**ardDisk. Choose this option when using Paradox on a standalone computer. Paradox saves the new configuration file to the directory containing the Paradox system files (C:\PARADOX3 or C:\PARADOX2).
- **N**etwork. Select this option if you are using Paradox on a network. Paradox prompts you to enter a directory. Type the name of your *private directory* and press Enter. See "Assigning a Private Directory" in Chapter 13 for information on how to determine which directory is your private directory.

After you indicate where the new configuration file should be stored, Paradox returns you to the operating system. The next time you start Paradox, the system uses the new settings you established with the CCP.

To cancel the Custom Control Program session without saving changes, select **C**ancel on the Main CCP menu.

The remaining sections of this appendix discuss changes you can make to the Paradox default settings with the Custom Configuration Program.

Setting Video Defaults

Select **V**ideo on the Main CCP menu to alter the default video settings. Paradox displays the following options:

- **M**onitor. Paradox knows the type of video adapter installed in your computer, but the program cannot determine which type of monitor you are using. If highlighted text on your screen is normally readable when you use Paradox, don't change this option. If highlighted text on your screen is normally difficult to read, select **M**onitor and choose **M**ono, **B**&W, or **C**olor. For example, if you are using a B&W monitor with a CGA adapter, then you need to choose **B**&W.
- **S**now. Choose this option to eliminate snow-like interference on color/graphics cards.

- **C**olors. Select this option to access the Paradox 3.0 color customization system, discussed in "Customizing Screen Color" of this appendix. (In Paradox 2.0, a similar but less capable option is **D**isplayColor. **D**isplayColor does not give you the flexibility of this **C**olors option, but does allow you to select from seven preset color combinations.) [3]
- **N**egativeColors. Choose this option when you want to change how Paradox uses color with negative numbers. On the resulting submenu, choose **B**othDifferent to color negative numbers and negative currency different from positive numbers, **N**umbers to color only negative numbers differently, **C**urrency to color only negative currency values differently, or **S**ame to color negative and positive numbers and currency the same. [3]
- **F**ormPalette. Use this option to specify whether the color palette should be displayed during form design. [3]
- **R**eturn. Select this option to return to the Main CCP menu.

Another way to identify your monitor type is by using *command line configuration*. For example, to use the black-and-white setting without running the CCP and changing default video settings, type the following command to start Paradox 3.0: *paradox3 -b&w*.

The following options also can be uses in the same way:

- *-color*. Add this command to the start-up command to indicate that a color monitor is attached to a compatible adapter.
- *-snow*. Use this command to eliminate snow-like interference on color/graphics cards.
- *-mono*. Use this command line option to indicate that you are using a monochrome monitor and adapter.

Customizing Screen Color

You can use the CCP to customize screen color in Paradox 2.0 and 3.0, but the options available in Version 3.0 are more extensive. To customize screen colors in Paradox 3.0, choose **C**olors from the Video menu. Paradox begins the color customization system with its own set of menus. First, Paradox displays the following menu:

ExistingSettings **M**odify **H**elp **R**eturn

The CCP enables you to create several color settings and to give each setting a name. The setting that Paradox is using is called the *active setting*. The setting that you are changing with the CCP is called the *current setting*. When you first start the CCP, the active setting is also the current setting. When you start Paradox for the first time, the program uses a set of default color settings for the active setting.

To make changes to the current color setting, choose **M**odify. Paradox displays the color customization screen. Use this screen to select a foreground/background color combination for the work space, the top two lines and menu choices, the current menu selection, and the annotation line describing the current menu selection. As you make adjustments, Paradox displays a miniature version of the screen that demonstrates the effect. When you finish, do the following:

1. Press F10 (Menu) and select **S**ave.
2. Type a new name and press Enter.
3. Provide a description for the new setting that helps you remember which setting it is.
4. Press Enter, and Paradox saves the current color setting under the name you provided.

When you want to make a named setting current, choose **E**xistingSettings, **S**elect, and the desired color setting. Also use the **E**xistingSettings option to rename or delete existing color settings.

Choose **R**eturn to continue customizing the Video settings. Paradox makes the current setting active when you press F2 (DO-IT!) to end the CCP session. In other words, the setting that was the current setting when you pressed F2 (DO-IT!) will determine the screen colors the next time you start Paradox.

Paradox 2.0 enables you to choose among seven background colors: dark blue, white, green, yellow, light gray, cyan, magenta, and brown. When you choose background color, Paradox 2.0 selects compatible colors for foreground, high intensity, and inverse video.

Customizing the Report Generator

Choose **R**eport from the Main CCP menu to alter the default Report Generator settings and the predefined setup strings used to control your printer. Paradox displays the following options:

- **P**ageWidth. Select this option to set the default page width for report specifications. The original setting is 80.
- **L**engthOfPage. Choose this option to set the default number of lines per page for report specifications. The original setting is 66.
- **M**argin. Select this option to set the default left margin. The original setting is 0.
- **W**ait. Select this option to determine whether the printer should pause between pages. The original setting is **N**o.
- **G**roupRepeats. Choose the default setting for **G**roupRepeats. The original setting is **R**etain.
- **S**etups. Use this option to select a default setup. Also use **S**etups to add, alter, or remove a printer setup, including setup name, printer port, and setup string. The available setup strings are included in table 10.1. Choose the setup that matches your normal printer configuration. The Standard Printer is the original setting with printer port LPT1 and no setup string.
- **F**ormFeed. Select this option to determine whether form feeds should be used at the end of pages, instead of line feeds. The original setting is **N**o.
- **R**eturn. Use this option to return to the Main CCP menu.

Customizing Graph Settings

Choose **G**raph from the Main CCP menu to change the default graph settings. The original settings are listed in table 12.1. Paradox displays the following options: [3]

- **G**raphSettings. Select this option to modify the main graph settings listed in table 12.1. See Chapter 12 for information about these settings. Make changes to default graph settings only if you manually change a setting frequently from within Graph mode.
- **P**rinters. Choose this option to establish your default graphics printer. You can define up to four printers or plotters. Choose the manufacturer, model, mode (resolution—for example, 120 x 72 [medium resolution]), device (printer port—parallel port, serial port, or EPT), and decide whether to pause between pages.

- **S**creen. Select this option to set the screen display for graphics. This option is independent of **M**onitor on the Video menu. Unless Paradox fails to recognize your screen type, leave the setting on **A**uto.

- **R**eturn. Use this option to return to the Main CCP menu.

Customizing Other Default Settings

The CCP groups several default settings under the menu choice **D**efaults. To change these settings, select **D**efaults from the Main CCP menu. Paradox presents the following options:

- **S**etDirectory. This option gives you an alternative to using the batch file described in Appendix A to select a working directory. The next time you start Paradox, a directory set with this option is used as the working directory, overriding the start-up directory. If you have several unrelated databases, however, don't use this option because you do not want to put unrelated tables in the same directory. The original setting uses the start-up directory as the working directory. (***Note:*** In Paradox 2.0, this option is on the Main CCP menu.)

- **Q**ueryOrder. Select this option to determine whether Paradox constructs answer tables with fields in table order or in image order. See Chapters 4 and 7 for details on query by example (QBE) and the significance of field order. The original setting is **T**ableOrder. [3]

- **B**lank=Zero. Choose this option to indicate whether Paradox should treat blanks in numeric fields as zeros in arithmetic operations. The original setting ignores blanks.

- **E**MS. Select this option to allocate a percentage of expanded memory to the disk cache. This topic is for advanced users only. See Chapter 14 of the Paradox *User's Guide* and the *PAL User's Guide* for more information about customizing Paradox memory management.

- **A**utoSave. Use this option to enable or disable the AutoSave feature. When this feature is on, Paradox uses idle time between keystrokes to save data to disk, reducing the potential for data loss through a power failure. The original default setting is **Y**es.

- **D**isableBreak. Choose this option to enable or disable the Ctrl-Break keystroke combination. When it is enabled, Ctrl-Break interrupts the current operation and returns to the previous one, and can result in data loss. The original default setting is **E**nable.
- **R**eturn. Use this option to return to the Main CCP menu.

Customizing International Settings

Select **I**nt'l from the Main CCP menu to alter the default date format and number format used to display data on-screen and in reports. Paradox displays the following options:

- **D**ateFormat. Select this option to set the default date format. Choose one of the following options: *mm/dd/yy*; *dd-Mon-yy*, or *dd.mm.yy*. The original setting is *mm/dd/yy*.
- **N**umberFormat. Choose this option to set the format used to display separators in currency values and decimal numbers. The available choices are **U**SFormat, which separates whole numbers with commas and uses dots (.) to divide whole numbers from decimal digits, or **I**nternationalFormat, which separates whole numbers with dots and uses commas to separate whole numbers from decimal digits.
- **R**eturn. Use this option to return to the Main CCP menu.

Customizing Network Settings

Choose **N**et from the Main CCP menu to alter the network-related default settings. Paradox displays the following options:

- **U**serName. Select this option to specify a default user name. Paradox identifies your workstation by this name when other users need shared resources that you have locked. You do not have to manually set the user name for each Paradox session. During a Paradox session, this option also overrides the user name established by your network administrator.

- **S**etPrivate. Use this option to establish your Paradox private directory. This directory is used for files that cannot be shared, such as temporary tables.
- **A**utoRefresh. Choose this selection to modify the interval at which Paradox refreshes your screen with changes made to a shared table. The original default time is 3 seconds. Specify a new time in seconds—0 disables the feature.
- **R**eturn. Use this option to return to the Main CCP menu.

Customizing PAL Settings

Choose **P**AL from the Main CCP menu to modify the default PAL settings. Paradox displays the following options:

- **M**aintainIndexes. This option is for advanced users. See Chapter 14 of the Paradox *User's Guide* and the *PAL User's Guide* for more information on how Paradox maintains indexes. The original default setting is **Y**es.
- **E**ditor. Use this option to link an ASCII text editor to Paradox. See chapter 10 of the *PAL User's Guide* for information on attaching your favorite text editor to Paradox.
- **R**eturn. Use this option to return to the Main CCP menu.

Customizing ASCII ExportImport Settings

Select **A**scii from the Main CCP menu to modify the settings for exporting and importing ASCII database files. Paradox displays the following settings:

- **D**elimiters. Select this option to modify the default characters used to enclose or *delimit* fields in ASCII files. The original setting is a double quotation mark. Paradox also recognizes single quotation marks as delimiters by default. You also can specify which type of field should be delimited.
- **S**eparator. Use this option to change the character used to separate fields when importing and exporting ASCII files. The original setting is a comma.

- **Z**eroFill. Use this choice to determine whether Paradox places zeros in blank numeric fields during ASCII export. The original default setting is **N**othing.
- **C**hooseDecimal. Choose this option to indicate whether to export or import ASCII files in International format. The original setting is **P**eriod.
- **R**eturn. Use this option to return to the Main CCP menu.

INDEX

A

B

C

D

E

F

G

H

I

K

L

M

Q

R

S

T

U

V

W

Z

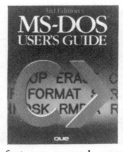

ORDER FROM QUE TODAY

Item	Title	Price	Quantity	Extension
874	Using Sprint	$21.95		
834	Using Quattro	21.95		
838	MS-DOS User's Guide, 3rd Edition	22.95		
882	Upgrading and Repairing PCs	24.95		

Book Subtotal	
Shipping & Handling ($2.50 per item)	
Indiana Residents Add 5% Sales Tax	
GRAND TOTAL	

Method of Payment

☐ Check ☐ VISA ☐ MasterCard ☐ American Express

Card Number ______________________ Exp. Date ______________________

Cardholder's Name ____

Ship to ____

Address ____

City ______________________ State ____________ ZIP ____________

FOLD HERE

Place
Stamp
Here

Que Corporation
P.O. Box 90
Carmel, IN 46032

R859—Using Paradox 3

REGISTRATION CARD

Register your copy of *Using Paradox 3* and receive information about Que's newest products. Complete this registration card and return it to Que Corporation, P.O. Box 90, Carmel, IN 46032.

Name ____________________ Phone __________

Company ____________________ Title __________

Address ______________________________

City ______________ State _______ ZIP _______

Please check the appropriate answers:

Where did you buy *Using Paradox 3*?

- ☐ Bookstore (name: ____________________)
- ☐ Computer store (name: ________________)
- ☐ Catalog (name: ______________________)
- ☐ Direct from Que ______________________
- ☐ Other: _____________________________

How many computer books do you buy a year?

- ☐ 1 or less
- ☐ 2–5
- ☐ 6–10
- ☐ More than 10

How many Que books do you own?

- ☐ 1
- ☐ 2–5
- ☐ 6–10
- ☐ More than 10

How long have you been using Paradox?

- ☐ Less than 6 months
- ☐ 6 months to 1 year
- ☐ 1–3 years
- ☐ More than 3 years

What influenced your purchase of *Using Paradox 3*?

- ☐ Personal recommendation
- ☐ Advertisement
- ☐ In-store display
- ☐ Price
- ☐ Que catalog
- ☐ Que mailing
- ☐ Que's reputation
- ☐ Other: _____________________________

How would you rate the overall content of *Using Paradox 3*?

- ☐ Very good
- ☐ Good
- ☐ Satisfactory
- ☐ Poor

How would you rate *Chapter 4: Getting Started with Query by Example*?

- ☐ Very good
- ☐ Good
- ☐ Satisfactory
- ☐ Poor

How would you rate *Chapter 15: An Overview of the Paradox Application Language*?

- ☐ Very good
- ☐ Good
- ☐ Satisfactory
- ☐ Poor

How would you rate the *tear-out menu map*?

- ☐ Very good
- ☐ Good
- ☐ Satisfactory
- ☐ Poor

What do you like *best* about *Using Paradox 3*?

What do you like *least* about *Using Paradox 3*?

How do you use *Using Paradox 3*?

What other Que products do you own?

For what other programs would a Que book be helpful?

Please feel free to list any other comments you may have about *Using Paradox 3*.

____

____

____

____

____

____

FOLD HERE

Place Stamp Here

Que Corporation
P.O. Box 90
Carmel, IN 46032